AUSTRALIAN POLITICS IN THE TWENTY-FIRST CENTURY
OLD INSTITUTIONS, NEW CHALLENGES

The global political environment in the twenty-first century is proving dynamic and challenging for Australian policymakers and political institutions. Locally, the rise of small political parties and independents has disrupted the idea of a stable two-party system, and environmental, civil rights and national identity challenges could reshape political institutions.

Australian Politics in the Twenty-first Century is a comprehensive and thoughtful account of Australian politics that contextualises the political landscape through an institutional lens. It examines the legislative and judicial bodies, minor parties, lobby groups, the media and the citizenry, providing historical and contemporary facts, explaining political issues and examining new challenges. The second edition has been thoroughly updated to reflect the application of political theories in today's civic environment. New spotlight boxes highlight issues including marriage equality, COVID-19 and federalism, the inclusion of First Nations peoples in the political system, and gender equality in public policy. Short-answer, reflection, research and discussion questions encourage students to test and extend their knowledge of each topic and to clearly link theory to practice.

Written in an accessible and engaging style, *Australian Politics in the Twenty-first Century* is an invaluable introduction to the Australian political system.

Stewart Jackson is a Senior Lecturer in the Department of Government and International Relations at the University of Sydney, Australia.

Joff Lelliott is a political scientist at Queensland University of Technology (QUT) in Brisbane.

Shannon Brincat is a Senior Lecturer in Politics and International Relations at the University of the Sunshine Coast.

Josephine Bourne is a Lecturer in the Department of Political Science and International Studies at the University of Queensland.

Nick Economou is an Australian political scientist and regular commentator on Australian politics.

Cambridge University Press acknowledges the Australian Aboriginal and Torres Strait Islander peoples of this nation. We acknowledge the traditional custodians of the lands on which our company is located and where we conduct our business. We pay our respects to ancestors and Elders, past and present. Cambridge University Press is committed to honouring Australian Aboriginal and Torres Strait Islander peoples' unique cultural and spiritual relationships to the land, waters and seas and their rich contribution to society.

SECOND EDITION

AUSTRALIAN POLITICS IN THE TWENTY-FIRST CENTURY
OLD INSTITUTIONS, NEW CHALLENGES

STEWART JACKSON
JOFF LELLIOTT
SHANNON BRINCAT
JOSEPHINE BOURNE
NICK ECONOMOU

CAMBRIDGE
UNIVERSITY PRESS

Shaftesbury Road, Cambridge CB2 8EA, United Kingdom

One Liberty Plaza, 20th Floor, New York, NY 10006, USA

477 Williamstown Road, Port Melbourne, VIC 3207, Australia

314–321, 3rd Floor, Plot 3, Splendor Forum, Jasola District Centre, New Delhi – 110025, India

103 Penang Road, #05–06/07, Visioncrest Commercial, Singapore 238467

Cambridge University Press is part of Cambridge University Press & Assessment, a department of the University of Cambridge.

We share the University's mission to contribute to society through the pursuit of
education, learning and research at the highest international levels of excellence.

www.cambridge.org
Information on this title: www.cambridge.org/highereducation/isbn/9781009108232

© Cambridge University Press & Assessment 2018, 2022

This publication is copyright. Subject to statutory exception
and to the provisions of relevant collective licensing agreements,
no reproduction of any part may take place without the written
permission of Cambridge University Press & Assessment.

First published 2018
Second edition 2022

Cover designed by Marianna Berek-Lewis
Typeset by Integra Software Services Pvt. Ltd.
Printed in China by C & C Offset Printing Co., Ltd., July 2022

A catalogue record for this publication is available from the British Library

A catalogue record for this book is available from the National Library of Australia

ISBN 978-1-009-10823-2 Paperback

Additional resources for this publication at www.cambridge.org/highereducation/isbn/9781009108232/resources

Reproduction and communication for educational purposes
The Australian *Copyright Act 1968* (the Act) allows a maximum of
one chapter or 10% of the pages of this work, whichever is the greater,
to be reproduced and/or communicated by any educational institution
for its educational purposes provided that the educational institution
(or the body that administers it) has given a remuneration notice to
Copyright Agency Limited (CAL) under the Act.

For details of the CAL licence for educational institutions contact:

Copyright Agency Limited
Level 12, 66 Goulburn Street
Sydney NSW 2000
Telephone: (02) 9394 7600
Facsimile: (02) 9394 7601
E-mail: memberservices@copyright.com.au

Cambridge University Press & Assessment has no responsibility for the persistence or accuracy of
URLs for external or third-party internet websites referred to in this publication
and does not guarantee that any content on such websites is, or will remain,
accurate or appropriate.

*Please be aware that this publication may contain several variations of Aboriginal
and Torres Strait Islander terms and spellings; no disrespect is intended. Please note
that the terms 'Indigenous Australians' and 'Aboriginal and Torres Strait Islander
peoples' may be used interchangeably in this publication.*

CONTENTS

Guide to online resources	x
About the authors	xi
Acknowledgements	xii

CHAPTER 1
INTRODUCTION TO 21ST-CENTURY AUSTRALIAN POLITICS — 1

Introduction	2
What is politics?	2
Key features of Australian politics	7
Why and how do we study Australian politics?	11
Contemporary challenges in Australian politics	13
Overview of the book	18
Summary	19
Discussion questions	20
Further reading	20
References	20

CHAPTER 2
THE AUSTRALIAN FEDERATION: FROM COLONY TO COMMONWEALTH — 23

Introduction	24
What is federalism?	24
The Australian variation, its history and evolution	27
Fiscal federalism	34
From COAG to National Cabinet: Coordinating policy	39
Reforming the Federation and the future of states	44
Summary	47
Discussion questions	48
Further reading	49
References	49

CHAPTER 3
THE LEGISLATURE: REPRESENTATIVE DEMOCRACY 52

Introduction 53
The early colonial legislature 54
The legislature as an institution 59
The functions of parliament 62
Legislation 67
New challenges to an old practice 70
Summary 75
Discussion questions 76
Further reading 76
References 77

CHAPTER 4
THE EXECUTIVE: FUNCTIONS, POWER AND ACCOUNTABILITY 79

Introduction 80
Political executive vs administrative executive 80
Executive power and its functions 84
Prime minister and Cabinet government 88
Executive power and accountability 98
Summary 102
Discussion questions 103
Further reading 103
References 103

CHAPTER 5
THE 'RULEBOOK': NATIONAL GOVERNANCE AND THE AUSTRALIAN CONSTITUTION 107

Introduction 108
What is a constitution? 108
The Australian Constitution 113
The 1975 constitutional crisis 118
The High Court 122
Constitutional reform 124
Summary 126
Discussion questions 127
Further reading 128
References 128

CHAPTER 6
BUREAUCRACY: THE APS AND PUBLIC POLICY — 131

Introduction	132
What is bureaucracy?	132
The Australian Public Service	135
Public policy and the policy process	142
From government to governance	144
The APS today and tomorrow	147
Summary	151
Discussion questions	152
Further reading	153
References	153

CHAPTER 7
ELECTIONS, THE ELECTORAL SYSTEM AND THE AUSTRALIAN VOTER — 158

Introduction	159
Australian electoral systems	160
Australian elections	168
The development and role of political parties	170
The impact of parties on parliament	174
Theorising the Australian voter	176
Summary	180
Discussion questions	180
Further reading	181
References	181

CHAPTER 8
THE ORIGINS AND EVOLUTION OF THE MAJOR PARTIES — 184

Introduction	185
Australia's major parties: History and evolution	185
Australia's major parties and voters	199
Theorising Australia's major parties	201
Understanding Australia's parties from a comparative perspective	204
Summary	206
Discussion questions	207
Further reading	208
References	208

CHAPTER 9
THE MINOR PARTIES AND INDEPENDENTS — 211
- Introduction — 212
- The point and purpose of minor parties — 213
- The key minor party players — 215
- Independents — 227
- Summary — 229
- Discussion questions — 230
- Further reading — 231
- References — 231

CHAPTER 10
FOLLOW THE LEADER: POLITICAL LEADERSHIP IN AUSTRALIA — 235
- Introduction — 236
- Leadership and democracy — 236
- Theorising political leadership — 240
- Political leadership in Australia — 245
- Does Australia have a leadership problem? — 248
- Gender and leadership — 252
- Summary — 255
- Discussion questions — 256
- Further reading — 257
- References — 257

CHAPTER 11
THE FOURTH ESTATE: NEWS MEDIA IN THE DIGITAL AGE — 261
- Introduction — 262
- The 'Media Sphere' — 264
- The public sphere — 265
- Theories of media — 269
- The changing Australian media landscape — 278
- Opportunities and challenges of digital media technologies — 284
- Summary — 290
- Discussion questions — 291
- Further reading — 292
- References — 292

CHAPTER 12
HAVING A VOICE: CITIZEN PARTICIPATION AND ENGAGEMENT — 298

- Introduction — 299
- The organisational landscape of citizen participation — 299
- Beyond the electoral cycle: Government mechanisms for engaging citizens — 311
- Key challenges for citizen participation and engagement — 316
- Summary — 320
- Discussion questions — 321
- Further reading — 321
- References — 322

CHAPTER 13
CONCLUSION — 326

- Introduction — 327
- Six key challenges for Australian democracy in the 21st century — 327
- Does domestic politics matter? Has globalisation constrained governments? — 336
- Summary — 337
- References — 338

Glossary — 341

Index — 347

GUIDE TO ONLINE RESOURCES

Additional online resources for *Australian Politics in the Twenty-first Century* for students are freely available at www.cambridge.org/highereducation/isbn/9781009108232/resources. Visit the site to explore suggested responses to short-answer questions and response prompts for reflection questions for each chapter, and a glossary of key terms.

 This icon is used throughout the book to indicate that a resource is available online.

AUSTRALIAN POLITICS IN THE TWENTY-FIRST CENTURY

Chapter 1

Introduction to 21st-century Australian politics

Reflection questions 1.1

1. Can you think of an aspect of your daily life that is not political?

   To what degree is your personal life free from politics? To what extent are all family relationships, even friendships, political? Are activities and practices such as exercising, vegetarianism, enjoying music, popular culture and art free from politics?

2. List all the ways in which you regularly interact with governments.

   What public services do you regularly use and how do governments shape access to these? For example, how do you travel to and from university and in what ways do governments regulate the transport sector? Are you employed? How do governments regulate aspects of working life?

Short-answer questions 1.1

1. Which of Kelly's five characteristics do you think continues to play the most significant role in Australian politics?

   The White Australia policy legacy remains to this day. Debates about race and immigration are framed to privilege the views of white Australians in such a way so that white Australia is seen as the norm.

2. Which of Kelly's five characteristics do you think is least relevant in contemporary Australia?

   Imperial benevolence has no significant role in shaping Australian responses to international events anymore. Australia now relies on the United States more than the United Kingdom for military and security support and assurances.

ABOUT THE AUTHORS

DR STEWART JACKSON is a Senior Lecturer in the Department of Government and International Relations at the University of Sydney, Australia. He researches green and environmental parties in the Asia–Pacific region. He also has research interests in the structure and composition of social movement mobilisations in Australia. His previous book, *The Australian Greens: From Activism to Australia's Third Party*, was published in 2016, and he is currently working on a new monograph on the life and times of Australian antinuclear activist and former Greens Senator, Jo Vallentine.

DR JOFF LELLIOTT is a political scientist at Queensland University of Technology in Brisbane, specialising in Australian politics. He previously spent ten years teaching public policy and political science at the University of Queensland, again specialising in Australian politics. He has extensive experience teaching Australian and overseas public servants about political institutions and their interaction with the public service and public policy. He has also written widely in the mainstream media on political and social issues. Before academia, he worked as a public servant and then as a Public Policy Advisor in financial services.

DR SHANNON BRINCAT is a Senior Lecturer in Politics and International Relations at the University of the Sunshine Coast, Australia. His research focuses on international relations theory; recognition and cosmopolitanism; dialectics; and climate change. He has been the editor of a number of collections and has articles published in the *European Journal of International Relations*, *Review of International Studies*, *Constellations* and *Antipode*, among others. He is the co-founder and co-editor of the journal *Global Discourse*.

DR JOSEPHINE BOURNE is a Lecturer in the Department of Political Science and International Studies at the University of Queensland. Her research explores the nature of Indigenous leadership in the Indigenous-State political interface through the design and use of contemporary governance mechanisms. Josephine has a background in working with State and Commonwealth governments and civil society organisations to explore constitutional reform options and treaty-making with First Nations peoples in the 21st Century.

DR NICK ECONOMOU is an Australian political scientist and former Senior Lecturer in the School of Political and Social Inquiry at Monash University, where he taught Australian politics and governance from 1992 to 2021. He was the Sir Robert Menzies lecturer in Australian Studies at the Institute of Commonwealth Studies (London University) between 1995 and 1996. Nick is a habitual commentator on Australian politics and a pundit on behalf of a number of media outlets that have included the ABC, the BBC and various newspapers. Nick's research interests include Australian national and state governance; federal, state and local elections and electoral systems; and the role and behaviour of Australia's political parties.

ACKNOWLEDGEMENTS

Cambridge University Press would like to thank the following for permission to reproduce material in this book.

Figure 2.1: © Getty Images/Illustrious. **Figure 3.2**: © Commonwealth of Australia (Australian Electoral Commission) 2018. **Figure 7.2**: Watson, J. & Reynolds, J. (1770). *Edmund Burke, head-and-shoulders portrait, facing left, in medallion/Sr. Joshua Reynolds pinxt.; James Watson fecit.*, 1770. [London: Printed for J. Watson ..., June] [Photograph]. Retrieved from the Library of Congress, https://www.loc.gov/item/2001696982/.

Table 2.1: © Commonwealth Grants Commission. Reproduced under Creative Commons CC BY 4.0 (https://creativecommons.org/licenses/by/4.0/).

Extract from the Constitution of Australia: sourced from the Federal Register of Legislation. Reproduced under Creative Commons Attribution 4.0 International (https://creativecommons.org/licenses/by/4.0/). For the latest information on Australian Government law please go to https://www.legislation.gov.au.

Every effort has been made to trace and acknowledge copyright. The publisher apologises for any accidental infringement and welcomes information that would redress this situation.

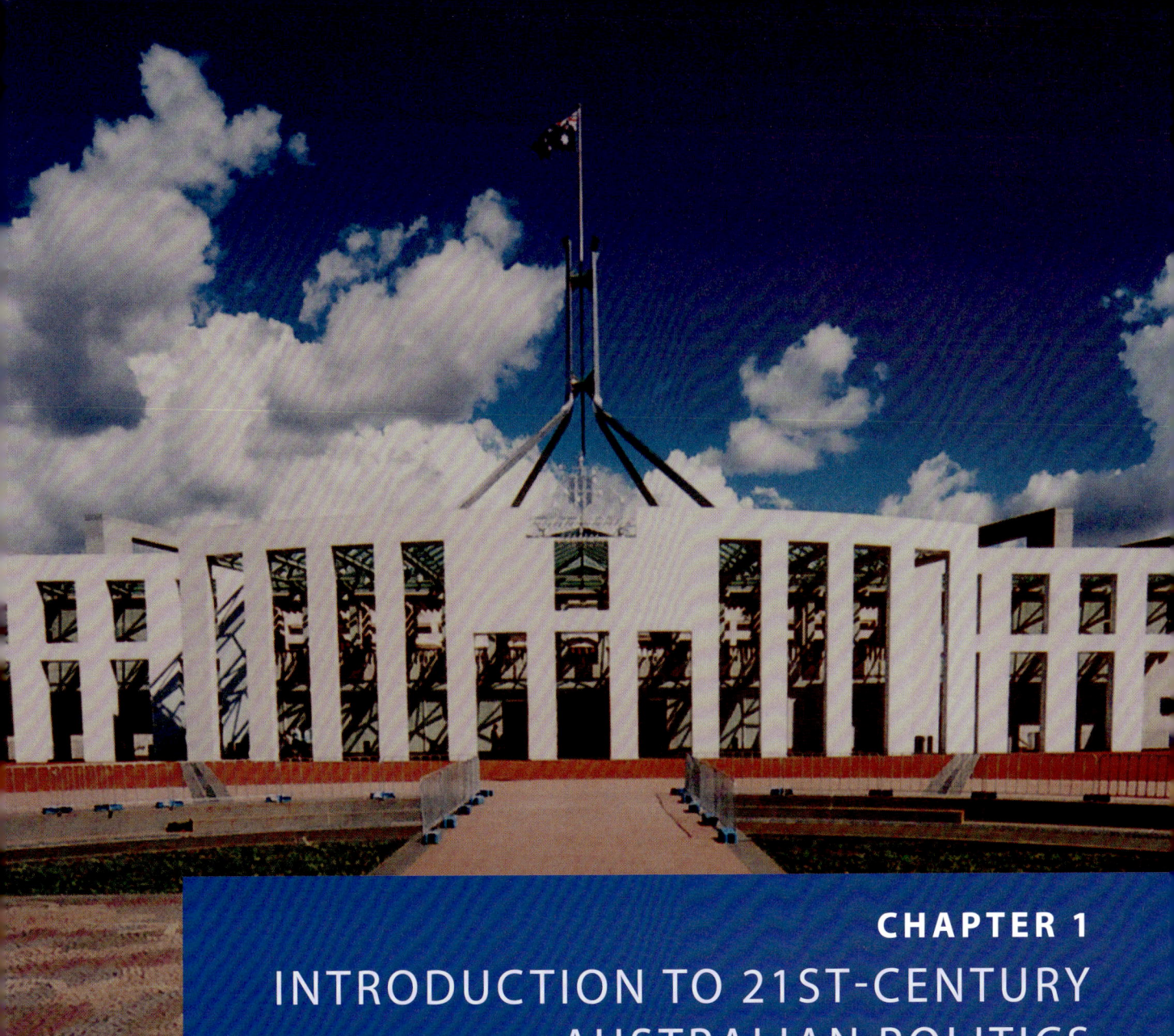

CHAPTER 1
INTRODUCTION TO 21ST-CENTURY AUSTRALIAN POLITICS

LEARNING OBJECTIVES

After reading this chapter, you should be able to:

1. Describe some of the approaches to understanding politics
2. Explain some key features of Australian federal politics
3. Understand how and why we study Australian politics
4. Identify some of the recent domestic and international challenges to Australian federal politics

INTRODUCTION

You might expect a textbook on Australian politics to begin with a discussion of contemporary Australian politics taking place in a strangely shaped building in Canberra, or with a somewhat esoteric discussion of colonial parliaments (don't worry, that comes later in Chapter 3). What we will explore in this first chapter are two connected ideas: what is politics and why do we study it. There will, of course, be an overview of the **POLITICAL INSTITUTIONS**, as well as discussion of some important terms, and a peek at what challenges might lie ahead for Australian political structures.

Firstly, however, we need to acknowledge that politics in Australia did not start on 1 January 1901, the date of Federation. Nor did it start on 9 July 1900, the date the Constitution Act was signed into law by Queen Victoria. Equally, it was not during the period 18 January–26 January, when Captain Phillip and the First Fleet arrived in Botany Bay before transferring to Port Jackson and Sydney Cove. It was not even during the period leading up to the Fleet leaving England, including the decision about the Fleet itself or the social conditions that gave rise to the need for the Fleet.

The real politics and history of Australia starts somewhere between 50 000 and 65 000 years prior to white settlement – although how far back is not clear. Perhaps between 300 000 and a million people lived in Australia when Phillip arrived to establish the colony of New South Wales, and the interactions between different clans, groups and peoples were governed by complex rules based in a primarily oral tradition. While 'politics' as the study of human interactions within institutions and political structures might have been unknown, that 'politics' happened as interactions between extended groups and families is undoubted.

So how should we think about an examination of contemporary politics in Australia? We should begin with acknowledging that the politics we study now is the product, one way or another, of a series of activities, actions and interactions that stretch far back in time. How, you might ask, does that help us understand what is happening now? If we acknowledge the past, we can understand how it has shaped our contemporary society and armed with that knowledge can begin to pick through the reasons why particular events happen in the way they do, why particular institutions operate in the manner they do, and why we use particular cultures and societies as reference points.

> **POLITICAL INSTITUTIONS:** Bodies that influence the distribution of power, and can be formal, informal, bureaucratic or cultural such as parliament, federalism, political parties, churches and the state.

WHAT IS POLITICS?

The first question that you might ask is: 'what is politics?' There are many ideas about what constitutes politics, from Harold Lasswell's classic description as 'who gets what, when, how' through to Michel Foucault's notion that 'there are no relations of power without resistances'. Indeed, the study of politics can be defined as the study of power relations, and that power is the distribution of resources within society. In the context of Australian politics, we could say this amounts to the institutions of government (parliaments, Cabinets, courts and the public sector), institutions of information (media, internet), and the institutions of business (industry, commerce, and attendant representational bodies). To these centres of power, we can also add institutions of labour (unions and industrial tribunals) and non-governmental institutions (think tanks, universities, and civil society organisations), which while less controlling of the actual levers of legislative power, have significant informal power within society.

But aside from this view of politics as being a set of 'institutions' or 'power relations', we need also consider the set of relationships and interactions that exist between the various **POLITICAL ACTORS** and with the broader society. We can therefore think about politics in terms of a set of arenas and processes – and that conflict arising from the exercising of power is as inevitable as the politics of that exercise.

POLITICS AS AN ARENA

We should firstly note that the previously mentioned institutions or centres of power are not monolithic nor all-encompassing, and that the relations between them are necessarily complex. That said, the important distinction between politics as an arena and politics as a social process is how we define them. An arena would be the place in which something happens, *sans* people, as opposed to how and why things get done. When we talk of the **NATION-STATE**, we are discussing a bounded area, with the idea of the nation itself a product of decisions taken nearly five centuries ago. When you hear people talk about the Peace of Westphalia (also described as the Treaty of Westphalia), we are describing the outcome of 30 destructive years of European war. The Peace established the notion that one state could not interfere in the affairs of another, and that a nation's sovereignty extended from border to border. This established the notion of the nation-state.

The key here is that while the nation is the bounded geographical space, **THE STATE** is the mechanisms by which the citizens within that boundary are governed. Politics then becomes the study of the state. Bob Jessop neatly described the state as encompassing the territory, an administrative apparatus, and a population upon who decisions are binding (Jessop 2012). The study of the state as politics therefore narrows further to the examination of the actions and activities of those apparatus and entities of the state, to the formal exercise of authority, and the mechanisms by which sovereignty is exercised.

When Robert Dahl described his concept of power as 'A has power over B to the extent that he can get B to do something that B would not otherwise do' he was referring to the very literal and observable exercise of power (Dahl 1957). We might argue that power is not as simple as this (and we'll come back to what else it might be shortly), but we also have to understand the mechanisms of how power is exercised. Dahl went on to describe how a police officer has certain power to direct traffic – the recognition that the police officer can legitimately tell others what to do, in a specified context, and so it is with the various institutions described previously. We can then begin to observe power/politics in action within a particular arena – a space where it is legitimate for particular actions to occur. Thus, we expect and legitimise a democratically elected parliament to set generalisable laws and a properly constituted court to interpret those laws in an individual context.

The question that naturally arises is the scope of that arena and how all-encompassing it might be. If we venture further into Dahl, we find he went on to describe formal power settings within the highly circumscribed confines of parliamentary or legislative practice. His observable frame was the processes of firstly the US Senate and then later the city council chamber. Within this constituted framework, it was possible to understand who had power over who in directly observable terms – including who was able to persuade others of the rightness of their arguments, or who was able to muster their colleagues to vote with them. This remains a core defining principle of who has power within society.

POLITICAL ACTORS: Individuals who seek to influence the distribution of power either directly or indirectly, whether by standing for election, lobbying politicians or campaigning on issues.

NATION-STATE: A geographically defined area in which sovereignty is claimed over the area and its citizens.

THE STATE: A political entity that exercises sovereign jurisdiction over a defined area and the population residing within it, via institutions that structure and organise public life.

POLITICS AS A SOCIAL PROCESS

However, others, such as Stephen Lukes (2005), and Peter Bachrach and Morton Baratz (1963), started to unravel this concept of power by asking the question how we define the arena of decision-making and when is an observed action an effect of authority and not power (Bachrach and Baratz 1963; Lukes 2005). In beginning to unravel the more simplistic – although nonetheless foundational – notion of power defined by Dahl, these and other scholars began to chart how the arena can be expanded from the easily observed, for instance, to who controls the agenda of the observed meeting or relationship. Further to that, Lukes and others demonstrated that if there is a pervading idea of those in power (the 'A' in Dahl's equation) controlling the established ideas of what is correct in society, they have the potential of controlling what others (the 'B' in Dahl's equation) have of thinking is reasonable and unreasonable. The Italian Marxist Antonio Gramsci coined the phrase 'cultural hegemony' to describe this (Bates 1975). While necessarily contested, the concept of political and cultural hegemony allows us to look past observable examples of power to uncover the power within particular social and class relations.

When we study politics as a social process, we need to look further than who regulates the states (all the while accepting the legitimacy of the state to make such laws and take a generally juridical approach to determining outcomes) to understand who obtains resources and why. This question should spur us to consider the structure of not just the state, but the society it is based upon – whether there are classes of people within society; are there ethnic, linguistic or cultural differences between people; and who has the majority share of wealth and power within the nation. Consider Australia: we could argue that white Australia has the monopoly on both power and wealth and that there is now a hierarchy of power, from European colonisers and their descendants, past historical migrants first from Europe and then from Asia, through to Australian First Peoples at the bottom. A strictly legal approach would suggest this is not the case, as we are equal before the law, and all laws apply equally to all people. The difference between these two versions of power and resource distribution in Australia is then a debate about how we understand social processes and the politics of those processes.

REFLECTION QUESTIONS 1.1

1. Can you think of an aspect of your daily life that is not political?
2. List all the ways in which you regularly interact with governments.

Response prompts are available at www.cambridge.org/highereducation/isbn/9781009108232/resources

---

THE INEVITABILITY OF POLITICS

Thinking again about Lasswell's aphorism regarding distribution, we can see that at its core it is concerned with who decides how that distribution occurs and who reaps the benefits. If we now try to think of many examples or definitions of 'politics', we may come up with a long (and continuingly lengthening) list of points, from the formal arena of parliaments and laws right through to who does the dishes in your household. It may be that a set of rules has been established and this governs how household chores are to be rostered, but who set up the roster? Who decided who would be on the roster, and what would count as a chore? This might seem fairly mundane – and it is – but it serves as a useful set of questions when examining who has power in any given arena and how that power is exercised.

If we then consider that idea extrapolating to the world outside: who decides the nature and structure of the places we live in, who makes the rules that generally keep us safe on roads and public transport, and how do we make decisions about these things? This seems to be the realm of mechanistic engineering, but when we realise that the first motorcars were heavily regulated because citizens, particularly in rural areas, felt that motorised transport disturbed their peace and interfered with their going about their business. They made a claim on the state (the body that establishes and enforces the rules) and the state reacted with regulation. From this we begin to see the necessity of sets of rules, a body that can make and enforce rules, and a mechanism to make claims against that body to deal with grievances – thus we approach the inevitability of politics, as the decisions being made are being made by other citizens, and so are bound by the same rules.

THE PRIMACY OF POLITICS

Sherri Berman, in her book *The primacy of politics*, explains the 20th century as a series of political arguments between competing political ideologies, with one, social democracy, arguing for 'the primacy of politics, and cross class collaboration' (Berman 2006). This at once challenges the notion of both orthodox Marxist class struggle between workers and the ruling class, and the liberal homo-economicus, bent on the self-interested accumulation of wealth. Politics, as the navigation between competing ideas towards various forms of cooperation and collaboration, would therefore appear to offer a way to adjudicate demands without resorting to violence and war. The 20th century, with its revolutions and multiple multi-state conflagrations, would appear to be a textbook example of the Clausewitz aphorism that 'war is a mere continuation of policy by other means' – except in reality it is the *failure* of politics that has resulted in war (Clausewitz 1918). Clausewitz does go on to argue that war is also a political instrument (i.e. a tool of the state) – as an 'act of violence intended to compel our opponent to fulfil our will'. This would be a straightforward example of power as described by Dahl, except it is now stripped of the political possibilities of compromise or cooperation – it is now just a means to an end, which is the subjugation of the other.

Is politics a simple case of subjugating the 'other'? If we consider that our formal political structures in Australia allow a variety of people to represent quite different ideas within parliaments, whether they be Gough Whitlam, John Howard, Pauline Hanson or Bob Brown – and we could continue on to consider the many different characters and parties in Australian political life. The defined arena of parliament, as a place to debate and discuss what should be done in respect of regulating Australian life – and how far that should go – uses the mechanisms of political action to reach conclusions that produce laws. Sometimes this is by brute force, where parties push through laws when they have control of parliament, at other times by compromise or cooperation, where the structures of parliament mean laws need to be discussed by a variety of political actors.

SPOTLIGHT 1.1 DESCRIBING POLITICS

Colin Hay, in his book *Why we hate politics*, compiled a non-exhaustive list of 12 definitions of 'political' in trying to describe the different ways we understand 'political participation' (Hay 2007, 61–2):

1. Politics as any and all social interactions occurring within the sphere of government.
2. Politics as government, where government is understood as a formal decision-making process the outcomes of which are binding upon the members of the community in question.
3. Politics as a public and formal set of processes and rituals through which the citizens of a state may participate, often at arm's length, in the process of government.
4. Politics as the noble art of preserving a community of citizens (the 'republic') through the construction, pursuit and defence of the common or public interest.
5. Politics as the art of stabilizing and insulating the power and authority of those with access to and control over public institutions through the use of resources that they thereby possess.
6. Politics as a process of public deliberation and scrutiny of matters of collective concern or interest to a community.
7. Politics as a process for holding to account those charged with responsibility for collective decision making within the community.
8. Politics as a perverse set of influences upon society, associated with the deception, duplicity and the promotion in the name of collective good of singular or sectional interests.
9. Politics as a descriptive noun for a range of collective and public, yet informal and extra-governmental/parliamentary, activities designed to draw attention to issues of contention.
10. Politics as concerned with the distribution, exercise and consequences of power.
11. 'Political' as an adjective to describe the motivations of participants and non-participants in a range of both formal and informal, public and private, processes – where such motivations are political to the extent to which they reflect or express a view as to the legitimacy of the process.
12. 'Political' as an adjective to describe the motivations of participants in matters of public governance or social interaction – where such motivations are political to the extent to which they reflect or express the narrow self-interest of the participant.

Source: Hay (2007, 61–2).

QUESTION

While the first three descriptions are straightforward in describing institutionalised processes, to what extent are the others more inclusive or exclusive of what happens in society?

RESEARCH QUESTIONS 1.1

With reference to the definitions cited in Spotlight 1.1 'Describing politics', why is morality so closely associated with politics? To what degree is it possible to separate the two concepts?

KEY FEATURES OF AUSTRALIAN POLITICS

It is often argued that Australia is unique, and that the political system has an institutional and social framework to match. While the level of exceptionalism is debatable (Dowding 2017), the Australian nation-state combines features inherited from the United Kingdom and borrowed from the United States to produce one of the most stable liberal democracies in the world. The elements incorporated into Australia's institutional architecture are very much a product of Australia's colonial origins, in respect of the coloniser and their beliefs and attitudes, as well as sensibilities of those who debated the form of **FEDERATION** and were central to the creation of the Australian nation-state. Understanding the way these features have been combined and the impact they have on shaping Australian politics is key in deciphering how the Australian political system functions, yet we also need to be mindful of the context of Australia's founding to understand the claims made upon it.

INDIGENOUS POLITICAL STRUCTURES, PRE- AND POST-INVASION

The land and waters that are within the nation-state of Australia include two distinct First Nations peoples, referred to today as Aboriginal people and Torres Strait Islander people. Within these two distinct groups are hundreds of diverse language groups, Indigenous nation groups with tribe and clan groupings, and broader kinship systems. These lateral systems of governance connected First Nations across the continent and beyond the relatively new nation-state borders (Brigg, Graham and Murphy 2019). Possession of the continent was based on the claim that the land was *terra nullius* (land belonging to no-one). Systems were so different from the hierarchical order and compartmentalised structures from European concepts of governance. The establishment of the Australian nation-state permanently disrupted the lives of Aboriginal and Torres Strait Islander peoples. Aboriginal and Torres Strait Islander peoples were not considered to have their own social and political ordering despite having their own systems and concepts of governance and various knowledges and knowledge practices, for example, in land management, land and sea navigation, and astronomy.

The establishment of the colonies and formation of the states from 1788 to 1901 was a process of overlaying new boundaries and a new political order over the existing systems that existed for thousands of years prior to British arrival. As the nation-state of Australia asserted its claim to sovereignty over the continent, the use of force and might, with a growing majority of non-Indigenous population, sealed the fate of Australia's first peoples to become a marginalised and structurally disadvantaged population on their own lands and waters. Historians and anthropologists provide accounts of the colonial violence on Aboriginal peoples (Evans, Saunders and Cronin 1993; Reynolds 2013) and Torres Strait Islanders (Beckett 1990; Sharp 1993) in the pre-Commonwealth period.

COLONIAL POLITICS

An important origin of the current federal arrangements of Commonwealth, states and territories derives from the colonial period between 1788 and 1900 (see Figure 1.1). The early part of this period, when Australia was under military government as a penal colony, is the part we hear about when we talk of the first settlement at Camp Cove, followed by the 'Second Settlement' at

FEDERATION: One of three common systems of government used in organising modern nation-states (unitary and confederal being the others). It involves a division of power between a central government and subnational governments. There are generally three layers of government: federal, state/provincial and local. Unitary systems, in contrast, have no division between central and subnational units, while confederal systems imply states that have come together under an overarching body which has limited power.

Parramatta. Hobart was established in 1803, Brisbane in 1824, and the other main population centres – today's state capitals – over the next 20 years. The earliest politics were of establishing law and order, first military and penal, but then increasingly civilian as the increasing numbers of settlers and former convicts demanded a say in the administration of the colonies. The original colony was New South Wales, with the others being named as they were formerly established, beginning with Western Australia in 1825. It is important to note here, that the settling of Victoria and Western Australia was as much out of fear of French claims over the continent as of a need for new land for settlers and convicts.

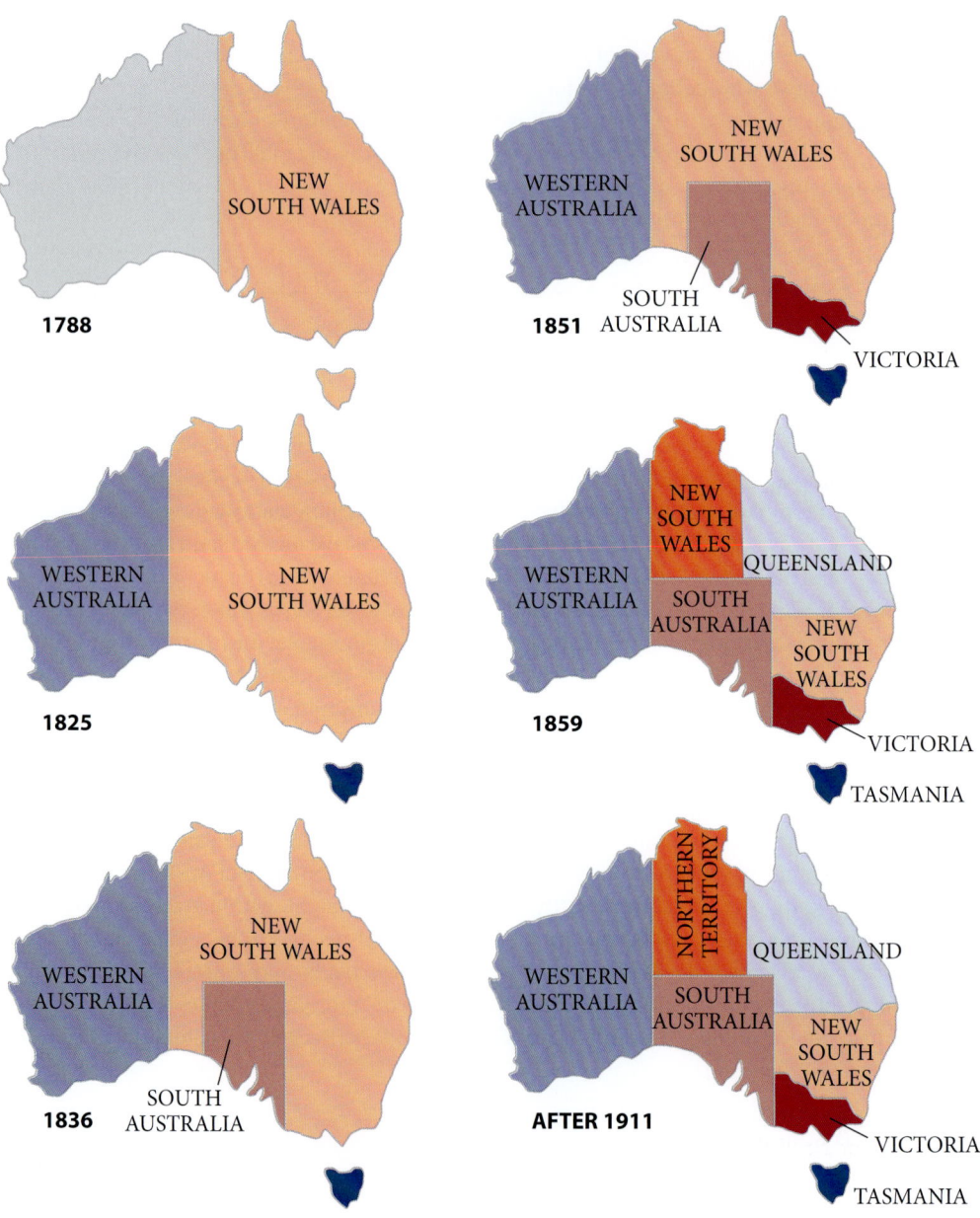

Figure 1.1 History of Australia's colonies from 1788 to Federation.
Source: Adapted from Hughes (1986) (see also Australian Electoral Commission (n.d.)).

As the colonies grew, they developed their own relationships with each other and the United Kingdom, though finding they had more in common with each other, as well as with New Zealand and Fiji. Through the second half of the 19th century, from 1850 onwards, each colony established their own system of self-government, with their own parliaments. As each colony was a separate entity, and often enjoyed better relations with the United Kingdom than each other, inter-colonial negotiations required regular conferences to deal with coordination issues arising from separate tariff regimes, railways gauges and penal codes. Indeed, the need to do away with barriers to trade between the colonies was a major motivator for federation negotiations (De Garis 2001). The original discussions regarding creating a new federation began in the 1870s, as the British began reducing their military presence in the colonies, and regional security became an issue of concern. By the 1880s and early 1890, the six original colonies were earnestly discussing at several constitutional conventions the very real prospect of creating a single unified entity. By July 1900, after much discussion and several votes taken in each colony, a draft of the proposed Constitution was produced and sent to the UK parliament in Westminster, to be finally passed as the *Commonwealth of Australia Constitution Act 1900*. The structure of the Constitution was heavily influenced by two things – Tasmanian delegate Andrew Inglis Clark's plan for the House of Representatives and Senate, and the need for the colonies to reserve considerable power for themselves. The structure of the Constitution, including the powers given to the Commonwealth and states, reflects this bargaining.

THE NEWLY FEDERATED NATION

On 1 January 1901, the Commonwealth of Australia was declared in Centennial Park in Sydney. The first Prime Minister, Edmund Barton, was a former New South Wales politician, Attorney-General and opposition leader who had campaigned vigorously for federation. However, prior to his appointment as the first leader of a federated Australia, there exists a moment when that honour might have gone to a different colonial-era politician. The first Governor-General of Australia, appointed by the Imperial Parliament to oversee the transition from colonies to federation, was John Hope, the Earl of Hopetoun. Lord Hopetoun, following precedent, appointed Sir William Lyne to lead the interim government, which would be in office between Federation Day on the 1st of January and when the results of the first election in March were known. However, due to Lyne having been against federation no other colonial politician would serve under him. This caused Lyne to return his commission, and Barton was duly appointed on 24 December 1900 to lead the first Australian Government. This episode became known as the 'Hopetoun Blunder'.

Following his appointment, Barton then won the first election in March 1901, and remained prime minister, with the support of the Australian Labour Party, until his retirement to become one of the founding justices of Australia's newly created High Court. Lyne too had a role in the new government, serving as the Home Affairs minister for the next two years. The rest of the Cabinet positions were filled by either former premiers or by strong supporters of federation. Following the election, Barton was able to put together a minority government, made up of his Protectionist bloc and the Labour Party under Chris Watson. Watson would himself go on to be Australia's third prime minister – and Labour's first for a brief 113 days in 1904. Free Traders under former NSW Premier George Reid, although the larger bloc in parliament, would have to wait until later in 1904 to take the ministerial benches. Alfred Deakin – the architect of the 'Australia settlement' and close friend of Barton – was to be the second prime minister in 1903, and in 1909 brought his liberal Protectionists into alliance with Reid's Protectionists to create 'the Fusion' – the forerunner to today's Liberal Party.

SPOTLIGHT 1.2 THE AUSTRALIAN SETTLEMENT

Kelly's 1992 book *The End of Certainty* has become one of the most influential analyses of the rise of the Australian Federation. In it, Kelly (1992, 2–11) argued that five policies were central to the growth of the nation.

1. White Australia: One of Australia's most controversial sets of policies in its history, the White Australia policy and its predecessors, aspired to a nation of racially white people primarily through immigration protections.

2. Industry protection: Rejecting free trade, this policy setting moved to provide industry protection ('protectionism') through government intervention, primarily via the imposition of tariffs on imports.

3. Wage arbitration: This recognised the principle of the 'fair go' and sought to end the deeply divisive union–employer battles of the late-colonial period.

4. State paternalism: This described the principle of promoting 'individual happiness through government intervention'. So, in other words, it allowed for governments to intervene in markets to maintain employment.

5. Imperial benevolence: This described 'the belief that Australian prosperity and security was underwritten by the [British] Empire'.

In contrast, Stokes (2004) contends that the Australian settlement comprises nine elements. In addition to the elements identified by Kelly, such as the White Australia policy, and arbitration and conciliation, Stokes argues for the inclusion of, for example, *terra nullius*, masculinism and state secularism.

QUESTION

What are the defining characteristics or policies of Australian politics in the 21st century?

SHORT-ANSWER QUESTIONS 1.1

1. Which of Kelly's five characteristics do you think continues to play the most significant role in Australian politics?

2. Which of Kelly's five characteristics do you think is least relevant in contemporary Australia?

 Suggested responses are available at www.cambridge.org/highereducation/isbn/9781009108232/resources

LIBERAL DEMOCRACY: Representative democracy, rather than direct democracy, that includes free and fair elections with individual rights enshrined in a constitution and an active civil society.

With the establishment of responsible government in the Westminster tradition, creation of a High Court, and now the development of the extra-parliamentary phenomena of political parties, the newly federated nation now had all the key elements of a functioning western **LIBERAL DEMOCRACY**.

The politics of the newly created nation at first mirrored what had occurred in the decade prior to Federation. Governments might last a few months or years, but could turn over quickly, even as elections were held at fairly regular intervals. Most members of parliament (MPs) initially saw themselves as independents, not allied to formalised parties, but collected broadly into groups either for or against free trade. The presence, however, of the Australian Labor Party (the 'u' in Labour was dropped in 1918) as an effective voting and policy bloc meant that by 1909 consistent parties began to be a regular feature of the Commonwealth Parliament. Although both Labor and the various conservative parties would continue to split and reformulate for the next 30 years, the basic formula of Labor versus a conservative **COALITION** was set. By end of the Second World War the three major parties, Labor, Liberal and Country Party (now Nationals), were set.

COALITION: A group of two or more parties who agree to a common leader and platform for government. Coalitions may be formed prior to or after elections, but when in government all MPs of the parties agree to be bound by decisions of the Cabinet.

SIX KEY FEATURES OF THE AUSTRALIAN POLITICAL SYSTEM

The Australian political system has not changed much since the Federation, with only minor changes to the Constitution. The functioning of the system itself can be summed up in six key features, which will be discussed further as we move through the rest of this book.

1. Parliamentary system – this means that citizens elect a local representative to parliament, who then, as part of a party or with others forming a majority, determine who will form the executive and govern. This includes who will be the prime minister.
2. Federalism – in the Australian context this means the division of responsibility for different administrative tasks between the three tiers of government: Commonwealth, state and local.
3. Constitutional government – the system of government used in Australia is somewhat of an amalgam of both UK and US traditions, with Australia relying on a founding constitution as the basis of state authority (as in the United States) but relying on conventions to manage that operation (as in the United Kingdom).
4. Constitutional monarchy – while Australia is a representative democracy, it still retains the British crown as Head of State, who is represented by the Governor-General at the federal level and Governors at the subnational level.
5. Strong bicameralism – Australia retains, with exception of Queensland and the territories, a history of strong bicameralism, with the two chambers of parliament – upper and lower houses – generally having relatively equal powers. At the federal level this means the Senate retains significant powers to block legislation.
6. Majoritarianism – with most of the electoral systems in use in Australia having lower house MPs elected in single-member districts, and with the addition of strong party discipline, Australia has exhibited strong majoritarianism, consistent with the Westminster system.

SHORT-ANSWER QUESTION 1.2

Why has the Australian Constitution seen so few changes to it?

 Suggested response is available at www.cambridge.org/highereducation/isbn/9781009108232/resources

WHY AND HOW DO WE STUDY AUSTRALIAN POLITICS?

The Australian political system, as we have seen in the overview so far, is as complex as any other nation. Bringing together ideas, traditions and institutional structures from across the liberal democratic world, Australia has been, from Federation to the present day, one of the world's safest and most prosperous places to live. Australia has successfully navigated a series of wars, economic instabilities and environmental disasters in a way that many of our trading partners and regional neighbours in the Asia–Pacific have struggled with. A good example of this is Australia's good fortune in being able to avoid the worst effects of the 2008 **GLOBAL FINANCIAL CRISIS**, which saw unemployment rise considerably and economic growth slow dramatically across North America and Western Europe. While globalisation meant that Australia could not avoid all impacts, our economy slowed far less and recovered more quickly than that of almost any other country (McDonald and Morling 2011). How do we explain this durability? Without understanding the Australian political system – including its history, actors and institutions – it is impossible to answer this question.

GLOBAL FINANCIAL CRISIS: Also known as 'the great recession', emerging in 2007–08 to refer to the global downturn in economic growth resulting from the collapse of several US and European financial institutions.

THE 'LUCKY COUNTRY' OR THE LUCKY FEW?

You may have heard people refer to Australia as the 'lucky country'. But what is it that makes us lucky? And just how widely dispersed is this supposed luck? The person who is considered to have coined the phrase, Donald Horne, had actually meant the description to be an acerbic condemnation of a country he considered to have wandered into democracy without war or struggle, and gained prosperity without significant input from its social, cultural and political leaders (Horne 1964). Horne's critique of the lack of innovation, intellectual life and the colonial hangover still resonates for many Australians today. For others, contemporary Australia remains a shining beacon of the best parts of the British Empire that landed here in the 18th century. There are, of course, a further wide variety of perspectives on this topic, but the characterisation of Australia as 'lucky' is one that stuck.

We equally need to consider that the 'luck' the nation has experienced was also based on another group within the country suffering dispossession and subjugation. Any discussion of Australia must then contend with the relationship and history between Indigenous and non-Indigenous populations. Very few debates in Australia generate as much heat as those about the history of this relationship. Much of the controversy relates to competing ideas about who Australians are and what our role and place is on this landmass we call home. While the plight of Indigenous people waxes and wanes in importance for many Australians, the evidence clearly shows that governments of both major parties have failed to meaningfully 'close the gap' between Indigenous and non-Indigenous Australians in ways that lead to lasting improvements in Indigenous people's lives (Brennan 2016).

The reality is that while many of our citizens are wealthy, healthy and happy compared to citizens of other countries, considerable numbers of Australians still live in poverty and are socio-economically disadvantaged (Whiteford 2018). The variation in living standards among Australian citizens also extends beyond race. Australia is not just a nation-state; it is a continent. With a landmass as large as almost the whole of Western Europe, Australia is a federation with distinct regional variation. The lived experiences for those who live in Northern Tasmania compared to those who live in inner-city Sydney is very different. Considering the different employment prospects and services available to them, for example, it is unsurprising that voters in these two regions, or any others you wish to compare, have different political and policy preferences.

SHORT-ANSWER QUESTIONS 1.3

1. What exactly is it about Australia that makes its citizens 'lucky'?

2. Thinking about your responses above, re-examine them and consider was this really 'luck' or was it the product of the hard work and foresight of many Australians that led us to this point?

 Suggested responses are available at www.cambridge.org/highereducation/isbn/9781009108232/resources

CONTEMPORARY CHALLENGES IN AUSTRALIAN POLITICS

Australian politics has long been viewed through the lens of firstly British but more recently US politics. Sometimes said to be 'riding on the sheep's back' due to the importance of the wool trade for Australia, and particularly Australian wool exports to the United Kingdom, Australia might also be said to be riding on the Haulpak's back, given the nation's reliance on mineral exports – the Haulpak being a type of truck used to haul materials out of open-cut mines. Fiscal challenges such as the 2008 global financial crisis caused instability for a short period within Australian markets, including a downturn in mining exploration. The change from a Trump-led White House in 2020 has meant a renewed focus on climate change mitigation – with the potential of a fall in sales of thermal coal (the type of coal used in electricity production).

Looking further afield from just the immediate post-pandemic struggles – and re-establishing baseline growth for Australia – the refocusing of the United States on the Pacific as an arena of contest will bring into question the Australia–United States alliance, and potentially disrupt Australia–China relations and trading partnerships. These broader geopolitical elements, which have undermined the Trans–Pacific Partnership, a 12-nation regional trade agreement, also bring into sharp focus Australia's relations with near-neighbours such as Indonesia and South Pacific Island nations. At the same time, security issues remain critical, as Australia deals with various forms of domestic and international terrorism. While the devastating Bali bombing in 2002, which killed 88 Australian tourists, proved Australians were potentially in danger abroad, the increasing focus on domestic terrorism, whether religious-based or from white supremacists, has continued to be a concern.

FISCAL CHALLENGES

Australian fiscal arrangements, based originally on the existing arrangements between colonies in 1901, have undergone substantial changes in the past 120 years. The original Commonwealth Government began life with limited income and a tiny bureaucracy, whereas today the Commonwealth draws the bulk of total public income when compared to states (ABS 2021). The total taxation revenue in Australia in 2019–20 was $552 billion, of which $447 billion was collected by the Commonwealth – meaning that 81 per cent of revenue was collected by the Commonwealth, with just a quarter ($109 billion) redistributed back to states from the collection of the goods and services tax. The effect of this on states is that the Commonwealth has the capacity to make large grants to states and tie those grants to particular projects. The problem for states is that while they still hold some payroll and stamp duty taxes (taxes on the payment of wages and the transfer of property, respectively), they are reliant on the Commonwealth for income.

Into this financial imbalance we need to consider what it is we expect from government. We might start asking who pays for the basic services we have come to expect – the states or the Commonwealth? Who actually pays to build the roads, schools and hospitals? Who makes the welfare payments when we are sick, disabled or elderly? And can we expect the same level of service (think telephones, health and education services) no matter where we live? Australia has in the past divided up the payment of these items between states and the Commonwealth, and tried to make clear demarcations between them, even while recognising that there is a continued financial imbalance between who collects the money and who spends it (and what on).

On top of issues of fiscal imbalances – even as we have expectations of services being available – Australia has undergone significant changes to its workforce structure – who is employed in what jobs in which industries. This means that while certain skilled jobs in finance and IT have become well paid, other skilled jobs – say in vehicle or household white goods manufacturing – have all but disappeared. The various mining booms Australia has seen over the past 200 years have required fewer and fewer workers as the industry has become increasingly mechanised – and the same can be said of agricultural businesses. The shift from small and particularly medium-sized Australian businesses involved in these industries has shifted to them being owned by multinational corporations who repatriate profits to their home countries.

Taking all this into consideration we can begin to see that the changes wrought on the Australian economy in the last 30 years from the lowering of tariffs and the major shifts in workforce structures have left Australia somewhat vulnerable to shifts in global economic fortunes – and of shifts in global alliances and trade disputes. While Australia was well placed during the 2007–08 global financial crisis, with few ramifications from the finance sector's pain, this was principally due to robust trading links with China and a buoyant domestic property market. However, changing alliances and friendships (particularly as the United States looks to curtail China's ambitious Belt and Road initiative) may expose Australia to sharper shocks than we have seen for a very long time. The onset of COVID-19 as a global pandemic destabilised Australia but did not fundamentally upset the financial arrangements. However, global movements to climate change may see unfortunate consequences for Australia. Who then pays the bills for the services we have come to see as key to our way of life?

ELECTORAL CHALLENGES

Australia has long been seen as a nation that has engaged in electoral experimentation. While this may seem odd in a period of seeming stability of proportional upper houses and single-member electorates for lower house, it is worth remembering that with the nine Commonwealth, state and territory jurisdictions there remains considerable variance in how MPs are elected at the federal, state or local levels of government. The search for a 'fairer' method of election has bedevilled different politicians over the years, whether it be Andrew Inglis Clark and his 19th century search for the fairest method of electing MPs into multi-member electorates or the current 'fairness' clause in South Australian electoral legislation. How and why we elect people to parliaments remains, therefore, a real and live issue for those parliaments to tackle.

Some of these challenges are fairly apparent – what do the different houses of parliament seek to represent? Why do we have upper and lower houses of parliament in the first place, and who or what do they seek to represent? Aside from the obvious challenges, there are new issues such as how to represent people who may live in far-flung places – if the purpose of representation is to provide access to MPs for everyone. How can you provide that access in electorates that may be the size of the Northern Territory (the seat of Solomon covers all but Darwin and Palmerston in the Northern Territory)? Further still, significant debates have occurred over whether to provide designated seats (Legislative Council 2002) or a distinct voice to the federal parliament that 'would sit alongside Parliament to provide non-binding advice on legal and policy matters affecting Aboriginal and Torres Strait Islander peoples' (McKay 2017).

Lastly, in an emerging age of global pandemic, the issue of how we conduct our elections has also come into sharp focus. While the provision of a paper ballot, to be marked in pen or pencil, has been seen as somewhat anachronistic at times, it still remains the surest way of counting formal votes. However, calls for electronic voting have increased as both the ubiquity and security of the internet has meant many Australians lead an increasingly online life. COVID-19 and its variants sweeping globally with a series of lockdowns, government ill-preparedness, and a general hesitancy on how to conduct elections when a highly contagious disease is abroad have meant reconsidering what an election 'event' might entail. The pandemic of 2020–21 has meant that elections must now be conducted with these further constraints on not just who but also how we vote.

RESEARCH QUESTION 1.2

What are some of the parties, actors or movements that are challenging this traditional dominance of the major parties and how are they changing politics as we know it?

ENVIRONMENTAL CHALLENGES

Climate change is one of the most obvious challenges that Australia and the rest of the world faces, yet environmental challenges to development existed in Australia prior to any recognition of it. Droughts and flooding rains were conjured up in Dorothea Mackellar's famous poem *My Country* in 1908 (Mackellar 1988), and wildfires have been a constant partner of plains and forests alike. Australia was already a land that had been changed by both climate and people by the time white colonisers arrived and begun clearing land for cattle and grain. If put aside the almost existential threat of climate change and simply focus on the changes wrought on Australia in the past two centuries, we can begin to understand the pre-existing problems that climate change is now exacerbating.

Firstly, we need to consider water resources. Australia started as a dry country, with few permanent free-standing water sources across much of the land. The Murray–Darling River system (or Basin) carries enormous amounts of water from the western sides of the Great Dividing Range in Queensland, New South Wales, and Victoria through to the mouth of the Murray River in South Australia. Yet continual drawing of water for farming, irrigation and mining – all allowed under state-issued licences – has caused the flow to be so restricted that various authorities, agreements and Acts of Parliament have been established and passed to try to regulate the usage of water. The Constitution of Australia gives states control of water resources, and it is in each state's interest to maximise the usage for their own citizens' benefit. However, the water licences themselves are tradeable – that is, can be bought and sold – in a 'water market'. That market, which theoretically might lead to better allocation of water resources, in fact allows for high-value crops at the expense of other crops – and that may not be good for local communities. It also allows for and encourages a pattern of over-use in some areas and, as a consequence, lack of availability in others. So how this is resolved is of critical importance to the environment, and local communities and economies (Hasselman and Stoker 2017). And this is before we discuss the impact of climate variation that will change rainfall patterns.

We might also consider the problem of fire. During a hot summer, wildfires occur on a semi-regular basis. Again, the responsibility for fire control and management is a state responsibility, but fire management is a vexed conservation issue, as periodic burning of forests and grasslands reduces habitat for many already endangered native species. We need to remember that much of the habitat of native animals has been cleared in the last 200 years. Recognising this, national and state governments have created parks and conservation areas to preserve that habitat. Unfortunately, this has disrupted previous patterns of land management undertaken for millennia by Aboriginal people, leading to an increasing prevalence of serious fires. The impact of climate change exacerbates the potential for hotter fires, which become extremely dangerous wildfires (Ehsani et al. 2020). The impact of climate on a country prone to fire is not something that state and Commonwealth governments have yet to come to terms with.

Australia therefore faces some very serious environmental challenges going forward, but at the same time many peoples' livelihoods are tied up in extractive industries such as mining and forestry, with many more engaged in farming. How compatible will these industries be with future governments trying to provide a climate-safe environment for both native flora and fauna and for citizens?

NATIONAL IDENTITY AND CIVIL RIGHTS CHALLENGES

When, in 2006, Prime Minister John Howard announced that there would be a citizenship test, the question of what it meant to be 'Australian' became a somewhat vexed question. Bromfield has spent some time examining the use of prime ministerial speeches to put forward notions of what being Australian means (Bromfield 2018). The perhaps unsurprising finding is that prime ministers use opportunities such as Australia Day and ANZAC Day speeches to put forward their vision of Australian-ness, even while navigating party sensitivities, utilising nationalistic rhetoric to this effect. When John Howard visited Gallipoli in 2000, he was following what two previous Australian prime ministers, Hawke and Keating, had done in travelling to Gallipoli to honour war dead. However, the importance of Gallipoli – itself a disastrous campaign defeat for the western allies but a momentous victory for Kemal Atatürk and Turkey – in Australian minds was now fixed: Gallipoli was glorious rather than an example of the incompetence of the British High Command, and thus should be considered some form of Australian birthright. At its heart, symbolised by Hawke's 1990 speech at Lone Pine in the Dardanelles, was an idea that it is 'mateship' and a commitment to Australia that was embodied in Gallipoli.

Yet this does not settle the question of the Australian identity. Who Australians are is still deeply contested, certainly prefigured on your relationship with the state. The cases of people who have lived in Australia their whole lives but were deported because they never became citizens and had now failed the 'character test' by being jailed raises the question of whether being Australia is simply about obeying the law (even when we eulogise the bushranger Ned Kelly in song and story). We could consider that Australian-ness is exhibited by giving everyone a fair go, but this never considers what that fair go might be nor how it is affected by your circumstances, health, education or background – nor even if you are a model citizen.

Tied to identity are the claims on rights that many Australians would make for themselves. Perhaps not surprisingly, Herbert Evatt, the third President of the United Nation's General Assembly and only Australian to hold the position, was a great champion of human and civil rights and oversaw the passing of the Universal Declaration on Human Rights. However, the Australian Constitution contains very few 'rights' *per se*, with what we take for civil rights derived from legislation passed by parliament. Just who has access to those rights has at times been a vexed question. For instance, do asylum seekers have access to the rights we take for granted or is it only for citizens? Asylum seekers arriving in Australia are subject to mandatory detention and have been since 1992. This might seem reasonable for reasons of health or security controls. But what happens if a decision is made to deport the asylum seeker, but their home country does not want them or they would potentially be executed if sent home? This has been the situation for a number of asylum seekers detained on a number of offshore islands, whereby they are effectively held in detention indefinitely. Are civil rights being breached at this point? Or is it as much a case of determining who will be considered Australian and who will not?

A further right claimed by many Australians is that of 'free speech'. The role of free speech in society is often held up as critically important for an open democratic society like Australia's, but does that include vilification of people based on their aboriginality (Gelber 2013)? The question of what free speech entails, and who has access to it, was brought to prominence in 2011 in a case before the High Court which found that columnist Andrew Bolt had contravened the *Racial Discrimination Act 1975* by questioning the aboriginality of high-profile Aboriginal people that he claimed looked 'non-Aboriginal' and were only claiming to be Aboriginal to gain monetary benefits. The case became a discussion point around what 'freedom of expression' means, and whether this allows people to make claims about or insult others. A very real question, though, is whether it is appropriate for someone in a position of some power (a commentator with a major daily newspaper) to use that position to potentially denigrate others. The question remains unresolved about whether we should be relying on a juridical solution or perhaps should be seeking a greater tolerance within society.

REFLECTION QUESTIONS 1.2

1. Do you consider the weakening of Australia's major political parties a threat to stability or an opportunity for renewal in the Australian political system?
2. To what extent is Australia a master of its own destiny in addressing the challenges faced in the 21st century?

Response prompts are available at www.cambridge.org/highereducation/isbn/9781009108232/resources

FIRST NATIONS POLITIES: SOVEREIGNTY AND REPRESENTATION CHALLENGES

First Nations peoples are a minority in Australia's liberal democracy, comprising 3.3 per cent of the national population (ABS 2016). Being a minority, coupled with having different cultural values and political principles creates barriers to participating in the political parties that rely on majority rules elections. In the 20th century, policies promoting forced removal, state control, assimilation and integration provoked resistance and protest. Advocacy focused on designated seats in parliament, civil rights, recognition of Indigenous people's sovereignty, reconciliation, and ongoing calls for treaty.

The marginalisation of First Nations peoples is further compounded by ongoing racial violence through institutions (Cunneen 2011), inter-generational and trans-generational trauma from colonisation (Zubrick et al. 2010), and a lack of truth-telling about the nation's history in school curriculums (Appleby and Davis 2018). In the 21st century, Aboriginal and Torres Strait Islander people are focused on recognition of Indigenous rights through structural reform and treaty-making. They continue to advocate for a say in legislation, resource allocation and programs that directly affect their lives. In 2017, a federal government Referendum Council of Indigenous and non-Indigenous representatives presented 'The Uluru Statement from the Heart' calling for voice, truth and treaty. The then Liberal Government, led by Prime Minister Malcolm Turnbull, did not support the statement's model for a referendum. Since then, jurisdictions, such as Western Australia, have negotiated large settlement agreements. Victoria, Queensland and Northern Territory governments have allocated resources to begin the process of preparing for treaty-making with First Nations peoples in their jurisdictions. The absence of treaty-making and recognition of First Nations peoples' sovereignty is considered 'unfinished business' and continues to inform resistance and guide protest and advocacy.

OVERVIEW OF THE BOOK

Twelve chapters follow this introduction, each of which introduces and contextualises the traditional and more recent institutions of Australian politics. Through the lens of these institutions, each chapter will present the contemporary challenges that affect them. Chapter 2, *The Australian Federation: From colony to Commonwealth*, considers the way federalism has significantly shaped Australian democracy since Federation and demonstrates how federalism is a key defining feature of Australian political life. Chapter 3, *The legislature: Representative democracy*, discusses how the legislature makes laws, how it can provide a check on executive power, and potential changes in the function and functioning of parliament in Australia. Chapter 4, *The executive: Functions, power and accountability*, investigates the tensions between executive power and accountability, where the relationship between prime ministers, their Cabinets and the Governor-General is explored. Chapter 5, *The 'rulebook': National governance and the Australian Constitution*, discusses the role that the Constitution plays in setting the 'rules of the game' and how this impacts the operation of the Federation, as well as examining the institutions that support a 'national' approach.

The role that the public service plays in Australian political life is reflected upon in Chapter 6, *Bureaucracy: The APS and public policy*. This chapter also considers the shift from 'government to governance' and what this means in terms of the delivery of policy outcomes. Chapter 7, *Elections, the electoral system and the Australian voter*, outlines the systems and rules used to govern elections in Australia. It includes a discussion of the role that parties play during the election process and how voters, as a collective group, can be understood in terms of the choices they make at the ballot box. This leads into the discussions in Chapters 8 and 9. The historical relationship between the major parties and different sections of the Australian community are discussed in Chapter 8, *The origins and evolution of the major parties*. The chapter considers how this has changed over time and analyses whether Australia's major parties are different to those in other comparable democracies. Chapter 9, *The minor parties and independents*, reflects upon the growing importance of minor parties and independents in Australia and evaluates the effect the growing role these party and non-party actors will have on Australian democracy. Chapter 10, *Follow the leader: Political leadership in Australia*, argues that leadership is not simply about the leaders of the major political parties and examines the tension between leaders and the liberal democratic framework they work in. In Chapter 11, *The Fourth Estate: News media in the digital age*, the public sphere is introduced, and the competing theories of the media are analysed in the context of contemporary Australian politics. Key units of civil society who do not directly contest elections are evaluated in Chapter 12, *Having a voice: Citizen participation and engagement*. Changing modes of participation and engagement with Australian democracy are also considered. Finally, Chapter 13, *Conclusion*, describes and evaluates the current state of contemporary Australian politics in light of the chapters that precede it, with particular focus on the key challenges that confront the Australian political system.

SUMMARY

Learning objective 1: Describe some of the approaches to understanding politics

In this chapter, two broad approaches to understanding the scope of politics as a field of study were introduced: the 'politics as an arena' and 'politics as a social process' views. The arena view is generally limited to formal decision-making and focuses on governments and public life, while the social process view is much broader, encompassing the public and private spheres of life, formal and informal institutions, and power relationships among people in society at large.

Learning objective 2: Explain some key features of Australian federal politics

While there will always be some debate about what the key features of Australian politics are, there is little doubt that the parliamentary system of government is one of these. This clearly signals a difference between Australia and, for example, the United States, based on the separation of powers. Equally important is federalism and the role of the Constitution. These two features ensure that sovereignty is divided between different layers of government and set the stage for a key source of political conflict within Australia: intergovernmental relations. Moreover, while in practice the role of the monarchy in Australian federal political life may be largely limited and ceremonial, in theory Queen Elizabeth II remains Australia's Monarch, and her representatives, the Governor-General and the Governors, remain within the executive.

Learning objective 3: Understand how and why we study Australian politics

The Australian political system is complex. Combining a myriad of different electoral systems, with parliamentary government and within a federal structure, means the process and practice of politics in Australia can be confusing. Only through deepening our knowledge of the key actors, institutions and ideas that shape Australian politics can one hope to really appreciate power in Australia. In this chapter, students were introduced to some of these debates, and these will be expanded upon further throughout the course of this text. Nonetheless, it is important to recognise that there is no one-size-fits-all approach to studying Australian politics. Not only are there different theoretical lenses that can be used but there are also a variety of methods.

Learning objective 4: Identify some of the recent domestic and international challenges to Australian federal politics

The 21st century global political environment is proving dynamic and challenging for Australian policymakers and political institutions, particularly in regard to new security threats, such as Islamic fundamentalism, and economic uncertainty in the aftermath of the global financial crisis. Within Australia, the ongoing contention about how best to return the federal budget to surplus has hit several hurdles in recent years, with prominent debates centring on welfare and entitlements relating to superannuation savings and housing investors. Further, the rise of small political parties and independent representatives in the Commonwealth and state parliaments has made the passage of legislation increasingly difficult, thereby disrupting the idea that Australia has a relatively stable two-party dominated system. In managing the natural environment, Australian policymakers have a number of significant issues to tackle including learning to live with consequences of climate change, the governance of water resources, and working towards a lower carbon-emitting energy sector. Finally, a number of simmering civil rights and national identity challenges have frequently dominated Australia's political discourse in recent years, and these are likely to reverberate through, and potentially reshape, Australian political institutions into the 21st century.

DISCUSSION QUESTIONS

1. Which view of politics do you find most persuasive: the arena or process view? Justify your view.
2. Develop a list of the major external challenges for Australian politics. Can you rank these challenges according to their severity? What factors underpin your views in this regard?
3. Commentator Paul Kelly has described Australia's politics as 'broken'. What does he mean by this, and do you agree with his assessment?
4. Do you think Australia is lucky or is our economic and political stability down to good management?
5. Of the six key features of the Australian political system listed, which of these would you most like to change and why?

FURTHER READING

Behrendt, L. (2003). *Achieving Social Justice: Indigenous Rights and Australia's Future*, Alexandria: Federation Press.

Horne, D. (2009/1964). *The Lucky Country*, Ringwood VIC: Penguin.

Hughes, R. (1987). *The Fatal Shore: A History of the Transportation of Convicts to Australia 1787–1868*, London: Collins.

O'Sullivan, D. (2021). Treaties and re-setting the colonial relationship: Lessons for Australia from the Treaty of Waitangi. *Ethnicities*, **21**(6), 1070–92. https://doi.org/10.1177/1468796821999863

REFERENCES

Appleby, G. & Davis, M. (2018). The Uluru statement and the promises of truth. *Australian Historical Studies*, **49**(4), 501–9. https://doi.org/10.1080/1031461X.2018.1523838

Australian Bureau of Statistics (ABS). (2016). *Estimates of Aboriginal and Torres Strait Islander Australians*. (Release date 28 August 2018). Canberra: Australian Bureau of Statistics. Retrieved from https://www.abs.gov.au/statistics/people/aboriginal-and-torres-strait-islander-peoples/estimates-aboriginal-and-torres-strait-islander-australians/latest-release

—— (2021). *Taxation Revenue, Australia*. (Release date 27 April 2021). Canberra: Australian Bureau of Statistics. Retrieved from https://www.abs.gov.au/statistics/economy/government/taxation-revenue-australia/latest-release#taxation-revenue-by-level-of-government

Australian Electoral Commission. (n.d.). *The Development of the Colonies*. Retrieved from https://education.aec.gov.au/making-a-nation/module2/pdf/AEC-Mod-2-Activity-1.pdf

Bachrach, P. & Baratz, M.S. (1963). Decisions and nondecisions: An analytical framework. *American Political Science Review*, **57**(3), 632–42. https://doi.org/10.2307/1952568

Bates, T.R. (1975). Gramsci and the Theory of Hegemony. *Journal of the History of Ideas*, **36**(2), 351–66.

Beckett, J. (1990). *Torres Strait Islanders: Custom and Colonialism*, Cambridge: Cambridge University Press.

Berman, S. (2006). *The Primacy of Politics: Social Democracy and the Making of Europe's Twentieth Century*, Cambridge: Cambridge University Press.

Brennan, B. (2016). Malcolm Turnbull hands down Closing the Gap report showing Indigenous life expectancy has not improved, *ABC News*, 10 February. Retrieved from http://www.abc.net.au/news/2016-02-10/indigenous-life-expectancy-has-not-improved-closing-the-gap/7154566

Brigg, M., Graham, M. & Murphy, L. (2019). Toward the dialogical study of politics: Hunting at the fringes of Australian political science. *Australian Journal of Political Science*, **54**(3), 423–37. https://doi.org/10.1080/10361146.2019.1625863

Bromfield, N. (2018). The genre of prime ministerial Anzac Day addresses, 1973–2016. *Australian Journal of Politics & History*, **64**(1), 81–97. https://doi.org/10.1111/ajph.12426

Clausewitz, C.v. (1918). *On War* (J.J. Graham, trans., F.N. Maude ed.), London: Kegan Paul, Trench, Trubner & Co.

Cunneen, C. (2011). Indigenous incarceration: The violence of colonial law and justice. In P. Scranton and J. McCulloch (eds), *The Violence of Incarceration*, Abingdon: Routledge, pp. 209–24.

Dahl, R.A. (1957). The concept of power. *Behavioral Science*, **2**(3), 201–15. https://doi.org/10.1002/bs.3830020303

De Garis, B. (2001). Federation. In R.M. Manne (ed.), *The Australian Century: Political Struggle in the Building of a Nation*, Melbourne: Text Publishing, pp. 11–47.

Dowding, K. (2017). Australian exceptionalism reconsidered. *Australian Journal of Political Science*, **52**(2), 165–82. https://doi.org/10.1080/10361146.2016.1267111

Ehsani, M.R., Arevalo, J., Risanto, C.B., Javadian, M., Devine, C.J., Arabzadeh, A. & Behrangi, A. (2020). 2019–2020 Australia fire and its relationship to hydroclimatological and vegetation variabilities. *Water*, **12**(11), 18. https://doi.org/10.3390/w12113067

Evans, R., Saunders, K. & Cronin, K. (1993). *Race Relations in Colonial Queensland: A History of Exclusion, Exploitation, and Extermination*, St Lucia: University of Queensland Press.

Gelber, K. (2013). Secrecy provisions in Australian counter-terrorism policy: Violating international human rights standards? *Australian Journal of Human Rights*, **19**(2), 25–46. https://doi.org/10.1080/1323-238X.2013.11882125

Hasselman, L. & Stoker, G. (2017). Market-based governance and water management: The limits to economic rationalism in public policy. *Policy Studies*, **38**(5), 502–17. https://doi.org/10.1080/01442872.2017.1360437

Hay, C. (2007). *Why We Hate Politics*, Cambridge: Polity.

Horne, D. (1964). *The Lucky Country: Australia in the Sixties*, Ringwood: Penguin.

Hughes, R. (1986). *The Fatal Shore*, New York: Vintage Books.

Jessop, B. (2012). The state. In B. Fine, A. Saad-Filho and M. Boffo (eds), *The Elgar Companion to Marxist Economics*, Cheltenham: Edward Elgar Publishing, pp. 333–40.

Kelly, P. (1992). *The End of Certainty: Power, Politics and Business in Australia*, Sydney: Allen & Unwin.

Lukes, S. (2005). *Power: A Radical View*, London: Red Globe Press.

Mackellar, D. (1988). *My Country' (1908)*, Frenchs Forest: Child & Associates.

McDonald, T. & Morling, S. (2011). The Australian economy and the global downturn, Part 1: Reasons for resilience. *Economic Roundup Issue 2*. Retrieved from http://www.treasury.gov.au/publicationsandmedia/publications/2011/economic-roundup-issue-2/report/part-1-reasons-for-resilience

McKay, D. (2017). *Uluru Statement: A Quick Guide*. Canberra: Australian Parliament. Retrieved from https://www.aph.gov.au/About_Parliament/Parliamentary_Departments/Parliamentary_Library/pubs/rp/rp1617/Quick_Guides/UluruStatement

Reynolds, H. (2013). *Forgotten War*, Sydney: NewSouth Publishing.

Sharp, N. (1993). *Stars of Tagai: The Torres Strait Islanders*, Canberra: Aboriginal Studies Press.

Stokes, G. (2004). The 'Australian settlement' and Australian political thought. *Australian Journal of Political Science*, **39**(1), 5–22.

Whiteford, P. (2018). Don't believe what they say about inequality: Some of us are worse off. *Australian Options*, (89), 7–8.

Zubrick, S.R., Dudgeon, P., Gee, G., Glaskin, B., Kelly, K., Paradies, Y. & Walker, R. (2010). Social determinants of Aboriginal and Torres Strait Islander social and emotional wellbeing. In N. Purdie, P. Dudgeon and R. Walker (eds), *Working Together: Aboriginal and Torres Strait Islander Mental Health and Wellbeing Principles and Practice*, Canberra: Commonwealth of Australia.

CHAPTER 2
THE AUSTRALIAN FEDERATION
From colony to Commonwealth

LEARNING OBJECTIVES

After reading this chapter, you should be able to:

1. Explain how and why federalism divides powers
2. Analyse the Australian variant of federalism and explain how it has evolved
3. Explain how the way states are funded enlarges the role of the Commonwealth
4. Analyse bodies like the National Cabinet (and COAG before it) and explain their importance to contemporary politics and policymaking
5. Make an informed judgement about the need for, and prospects of, reforming the Federation

INTRODUCTION

If you search for 'federation' on the internet, you will find accounts of systems of government in which sovereignty is divided between a central, national government and a series of regional, partially self-governing states. You may well find a webpage of the Parliamentary Education Office recording that, 'in a process known as Federation' Australia 'became a nation on 1 January 1901 when six British colonies – New South Wales, Victoria, Queensland, South Australia, Western Australia and Tasmania – united to form the Commonwealth of Australia' (PEO 2020). You may also see links to various peak associations such as the National Farmers Federation, the Australian Federation of Air Pilots or the Australian Judo Federation. These search results suggest some key takeaway points for students of Australian politics.

First, a federation is a particular form of political system where two tiers, or levels, of government (national and regional) share power and neither has authority over the other. Second, when capitalised 'Federation' describes the process which resulted in the creation of Australia at the dawn of the last century. The final point to note is that Australia's federal system shapes its politics and other activities. Federalism is a good example of how 21st century Australian politics remains in the grip of institutions established in the distant past for often forgotten reasons. In this chapter we will explore these points, beginning with an examination of the theory of federalism.

WHAT IS FEDERALISM?

FEDERALISM:
'The principle of sharing sovereignty between central and state (or provincial) governments' (Hague and Harrop 2013, 255), each with a defined set of powers and neither with authority over the other. The alternative is a unitary system, where sovereignty is held by one central government which devolves power to others as it sees fit.

DIVISION OF POWERS:
Found in federal systems, where the responsibility for some policy areas is allocated to a national government and other policy areas are reserved for subnational governments.

FEDERALISM allows diversity within a single, unified political system. The American political scientist W.H. Riker defined a federal system as 'a political organisation in which the activities of government are divided between regional governments and a central government in such a way that each kind of government has some activities on which it makes final decisions' (Riker 1975, 101). According to Cook, Walsh and Harwood (2009, 114), '[f]ederalism is a mechanism for sharing powers and responsibilities between members of political executives at a central and regional level. It is characterised by a division of powers, shared sovereignty and financial independence.' Hollander (2014, 316) writes that '[f]ederalism is defined by divided sovereignty, an arrangement whereby government authority is divided between different levels of government, with neither having the legal authority to intervene in areas of the others' sphere of competence'.

Instead of providing for the constitutional separation of powers, federalism prescribes shared sovereignty and the **DIVISION OF POWERS** between constitutionally separate national and subnational (i.e. regional) tiers of government. In short, federations are political systems that seek to prevent any single group from monopolising power by requiring that the legislative and executive responsibilities of government be divided between a national-level government and a set of subnational governments (whether called states, provinces or something else).

AUSTRALIA'S VERSION OF FEDERALISM

In Australia's federation, the national-level government is known as the Commonwealth Government (or federal government or simply the Australian Government). Meanwhile the subnational tier of government comprises six states (New South Wales, Victoria, Queensland,

Western Australia, South Australia and Tasmania) plus the Australian Capital Territory and Northern Territory (see Figure 2.1). Beyond this, there are over 500 local (municipal and shire) governments (ALGA 2021). While the existence of the federal and state governments is enshrined in the Constitution, which also sets out their respective powers, local government is not constitutionally enshrined. Local governments only exist at the whim of state governments who can arrange them as they decide and give them as much or as little power as they wish.

Figure 2.1 Australia's states and territories

The various subnational governments within Australia's federal system do not all enjoy the same constitutional status. The Constitution establishes an identical range of policy areas that fall within the jurisdiction of each of the states and which cannot be overruled by the Commonwealth. But the Australian Capital Territory and the Northern Territory are self-governing territories exercising an authority extended to them by the Commonwealth Parliament. Legislation enacted by territory parliaments can be overridden by the Commonwealth Parliament, something which has happened several times.

REFLECTION QUESTIONS 2.1

In 1995, the Northern Territory Parliament passed the controversial *Rights of the Terminally Ill Act* allowing euthanasia for dying Territorians. The Commonwealth Parliament shortly after legislated the *Euthanasia Laws Act 1997*, which nullified the Northern Territory legislation. Is it desirable that the Commonwealth should be able to override laws properly approved by the elected Northern Territory legislature? If a state parliament were to pass a similar Act could the Commonwealth override it?

Response prompt is available at www.cambridge.org/highereducation/isbn/9781009108232/resources

---

FEDERALISM IN INTERNATIONAL CONTEXT

Some 85 per cent of United Nation member states have unitary rather than federal systems. New Zealand, Indonesia, China, France and Japan are all examples. In unitary systems, all executive and legislative powers that a government is entitled to exercise are constitutionally located in a single, national-level government, but even here political power is generally devolved to regional or municipal subnational governments. Although only a small minority of countries have federal structures, federal systems can be found across all continents, including in the United States, Canada, Argentina, Mexico, Switzerland, Germany, Austria, Malaysia, India and Nigeria.

It is sometimes said 'there are likely as many different federalisms as there are federations' (Anderson 2010, 130). Although the Australian version of federalism draws heavily on the US version, the scale of the Australian Federation is a distinctive feature. The United States has 50 states and Nigeria 36. India's federation encompasses 29 states (plus seven union territories). Switzerland has 26 cantons. Brazil also has 26 estados plus a federal district. In contrast, Australia, with six states and two self-governing territories, has relatively few subnational governments. The small scale of Australia's federation has, literally, made it possible for state, territory and Commonwealth representatives to 'sit around the table'. It has allowed collaboration between governments not so easily achieved in larger federal systems.

Taken as a group, however, federal countries do tend to have some common features in their institutional arrangements (although these are not exclusive to federal systems):

1. A written constitution that is difficult to amend
2. A bicameral legislature with a strong federal chamber to represent the constituent regions
3. A supreme or constitutional court to protect the constitution through the power of judicial review
4. Intergovernmental institutions and processes to facilitate collaboration in areas of shared or overlapping jurisdiction. (Galligan 2008, 267)

In practice, the increasingly complex business of governing a country cannot be effectively managed from national capitals, such as Beijing, Tokyo or Wellington, nor by a single government. Indeed, around the globe, and in political systems having very different institutional forms, we have seen the emergence of de facto federations and 'a revolution' involving the extensive devolution of decision-making to subnational governments (Martinez-Vazquez 2011, 1), for example, with the creation of devolved governments for Scotland, Wales and Northern Ireland within the United Kingdom. Some scholars go so far as to say that federalism is particularly well suited to the circumstances of the globalised world of the 21st century (see e.g. Galligan 2008, 262–3).

In short, both unitary and federal systems have 'some vertical hierarchy among different levels of government' (Beramendi 2009, 753). However, in unitary systems the devolution of decision-making to subnational governments can be reversed by national governments: 'regional or provincial officials do not have constitutional status as effective actors in a bargaining process with the center' (Beramendi 2009, 754). This contrasts with federal systems where constitutions entrench the authority and autonomy of subnational governments. Constitutions of countries with federal systems tend to be significantly more difficult to amend than those of unitary systems, further entrenching federalism and the specific division of powers (see Chapter 5 for more on the difficulty of amending the Australian Constitution).

There are several rationales for adopting a federal system, some more theoretical or philosophical and some simply practical. Federalism can seek to divide power to prevent its growth and its abuse, as well as to bring government 'close to the people'. In seeking to limit the power that governments can accumulate, it falls within a centuries-old liberal tradition. Classical liberalism accepts governments are necessary to preserve social order and a political community that can secure citizens their rights and freedoms. But liberals also fear governments will grow to make and enforce unnecessary or illiberal laws, and thus come to threaten these prized individual rights and freedoms. Federalism offers one way of preventing the abuse of power by government, proposing its fragmentation and distribution in a system of multiple subnational governments. A further rationale for adopting a federal system, seen in many federal systems, is to accommodate the ethnic, linguistic and cultural diversity of different regions. As we will see later, in Australia's case federalism resulted less from any theoretical considerations and more from practical realities, firstly of creating one country out of six existing colonies and, secondly, of trying to govern such a huge country.

THE AUSTRALIAN VARIATION, ITS HISTORY AND EVOLUTION

'Federation' has several meanings. While it describes a political arrangement in which power is constitutionally divided between central and subnational governments, in an Australian setting, federation also refers to the process that gave birth to Australia as a nation (what in many other countries is referred to as 'independence'). Prior to 1901, Australia was a continent, not a country. New South Wales, Victoria, Queensland, Western Australia, South Australia and Tasmania were all separate entities, much as Australia and New Zealand are today. In the 19th century, each was a self-governing British colony, and border control measures restricted trade and travel between what are now neighbouring Australian states. Federation describes the process whereby the six colonies agreed to form a single country and share the task of governing with a new Commonwealth government with jurisdiction over the entire country. This agreement was cemented in a constitution drafted by a series of Conventions, meeting between 1891 and 1897; approved by voters in the various colonies at referendums held between 1898 and 1900; legislated as the *Commonwealth of Australia Constitution Act 1900* by the British parliament; and assented to by Queen Victoria on 9 July 1900. It took effect on 1 January 1901. Despite the profundity of federation, and the huge impacts it would have on everybody in Australia, the process and decision-making were almost exclusively carried out by white Anglo-Celtic men. Indigenous people and other non-white people were excluded, while women and the working classes were kept at the margins.

The 'federal compact' struck by the colonial politicians who negotiated the 1901 Constitution founding Australia has since shaped its politics. Australia's Federation, with its roots in an agreement struck in the 1890s, is creaking at the seams and has plenty of critics. John Howard, Liberal prime minister from 1996 to 2007, believed Australia would likely opt for a centralised, not a federal, system of government 'if we had our time again' (Howard 2005). Australian federalism is often seen as a source of duplication, inefficiency and bureaucracy which slows the country down. According to the influential Business Council of Australia, the 'poor performance of the current system of federal–state relations' explains many of the 'policy failings and reform limitations holding Australia back' (BCA 2007, 21). States depend heavily upon the Commonwealth: they are only able to fund the roads, police, hospitals and schools for which the Constitution gives them responsibility with the assistance of the Commonwealth. Another frequent cry is that Australians are 'over governed'. However, demanding reform is one thing, achieving it is quite another. Within the legacy Australia has inherited from the politics of the 1890s is a difficult-to-change Constitution that entrenches a federal system.

'THE ONLY WAY TO MAKE A NATION'

From time to time, Australia's federal system has been portrayed as an essential safeguard of individual freedom. For example, in the midst of the Second World War with national survival at stake, a Labor government proposed altering the Constitution to give the Commonwealth additional powers to facilitate Australia's defence. But the then opposition leader (and, later, Liberal Party founder) Robert Menzies refused support, pointing to the 'necessity of divided power for liberty' and the 'unsound doctrine' holding that 'central governments should always be presumed to be wiser and more efficient than local government' (Tiver 1978, 130). In this vein, Smith (2013, 362) writes that '[t]he evolution of the Australian federation is rooted in a deep understanding of the need to limit government, while ensuring it is used to preserve a free society'. Former Prime Minister Tony Abbott (2008, 3) has a more prosaic view: the Constitution's authors did not set out to safeguard against government tyranny; rather federalism 'was the only way to make a nation out of six colonies'.

Like Menzies before him, Abbott served as Liberal leader and prime minister. Yet his view of federalism is very different and points to a more recent shift in Liberal Party thinking. Abbott's account of Australia's Federation as a pragmatic solution to the challenge of nation building in the 1890s rather than a product of a liberal concern to entrench freedom has merit. Those involved in designing the Australian Constitution (such as Queensland premier Sir Samuel Griffith) were often colonial political leaders. Most saw their role in the same way as the New South Wales premier Henry Parkes who told the 1891 Australasian Federation Conference 'it will be our duty to see that our respective colonies are not injured' in their joining together (Official Report 1891, 910–11). The records of the various Conventions which gathered during the 1890s contain no fine speeches on the 'necessity of divided power for liberty' nor a spirited advocacy of federalism as a way of securing individual freedom for Australia's citizens. Even the liberal participants like Alfred Deakin had more practical concerns with how the Federation might be best organised – for example, with questions of how taxation powers might be shared between the Commonwealth and states in ways that would secure free trade between colonies.

The smaller states had a further concern with the six colonies joining together: being dominated by the much larger populations of Sydney and Melbourne. Adopting a federal structure not only offered protection by leaving some policy areas in the hands of the new state governments, it also facilitated other safeguards for smaller states such as equal representation of states in the Senate and the double majority requirement for amending the Constitution.

While the adoption of a federal structure was overwhelmingly a practical decision rather than one borne out of any philosophical tradition, there was one issue of political theory which did concern delegates in the 1890s, including Griffith, Deakin and others. That was the inherent tension between federalism and the Westminster system. The two systems point in different directions: while federalism seeks to disperse power, Westminster concentrates it. Unsurprisingly, the outcome was a system which included both, allowing the colonies to continue as state governments without undue loss of power and influence. The compromise led one delegate to predict that one system would ultimately kill the other, the only question was which one would win that struggle.

REFLECTION QUESTION 2.2

In the 1890s, federation was a politically expedient way of uniting the various Australian colonies. But is Australia today well-served by the federal system that was conceived more than a century ago?

Response prompt is available at www.cambridge.org/highereducation/isbn/9781009108232/resources

COORDINATE FEDERALISM

When Deakin told the 1897 Convention that '[w]e should make the spheres of state and federal finance as distinct as they can be made' (Official Records 1897, 56), he was advancing a particular understanding of federalism. **COORDINATE FEDERALISM** holds that no level of government ought to be subordinate to another. It stresses 'the importance of national and state governments each occupying a discrete sphere of activity' in which they are 'independent, distinct and separate from each other' (Windholz 2011, 4). The theory of coordinate (or dual) federalism appears to have held sway during the drafting of the 1901 Constitution, which carefully enumerated the powers that were to be available to the Commonwealth.

The Constitution gives the Commonwealth a limited range of *exclusive* powers including the right to make laws regulating currency (Section 115), the raising of military forces (Section 114), Commonwealth public service departments, and the collection of customs and excise duties (Section 90). Section 51 lists many other areas in which the Commonwealth Parliament may legislate. These *specific* powers range from the right to make laws about trade and commerce with other countries to the regulation of lighthouses and marriage. Mostly these specified powers are *concurrent* and thus are also available to states. A constitution which hands states and the Commonwealth concurrent powers to legislate may initially appear incompatible with the theory of coordinate federalism, but this principle is ensured by Section 109. It establishes that Commonwealth legislation must prevail where laws passed by the Commonwealth and a state parliament clash. It is noteworthy that the right to pass laws pertaining to taxation was specified as a *concurrent* power, available to both the Commonwealth and the states so that neither would financially depend on the other.

COORDINATE FEDERALISM: A theory which holds that regional and national governments within a federation should be substantially independent of one another and free to exercise their allocated powers without interference from each other.

While the Constitution handed the Commonwealth Parliament a range of specific powers, it made no mention of many policy responsibilities including transport, policing, education, hospitals and public health. Section 108 defined these as *residual* powers and established them as policy areas in which only the states might make laws. Many residual powers – for example, those pertaining to health – involve policy areas that directly impact the lives of citizens. In dividing legislative responsibilities between the two levels of government as they did, the Constitution's authors intended states to continue alongside the Commonwealth as separate and important political actors. As Wanna et al. (2009, 11) suggest, '[t]he Australian federation was designed on the assumption that the levels of government would operate with a high degree of independence'. But coordinate federalism is more a legalistic concept than a practical formula for government. In embracing it, the 1901 Constitution 'made little provision for integration of policymaking and implementation between the Commonwealth and the states' (Wanna et al. 2009, 11).

SHORT-ANSWER QUESTIONS 2.1

1. Explain the way that the Constitution divides powers between the Commonwealth and the states.
2. There is a Commonwealth Education Minister, but does the Constitution actually give responsibility for education to the Commonwealth Government?

Suggested responses are available at www.cambridge.org/highereducation/isbn/9781009108232/resources

SPOTLIGHT 2.1 MARRIAGE EQUALITY

The late-2010s saw a high-profile campaign and public debate over marriage equality. Until 2004, the Commonwealth *Marriage Act* did not fully define marriage, but the Howard Government added a definition stating marriage was between a man and a woman, which clearly precluded same-sex marriages. Through the 2000s, campaigns to allow same-sex marriage gained momentum and public opinion moved decisively in favour of it. The Australian Labor Party (ALP) and the Greens were both supportive, while the Liberal Party was divided on the issue. Section 51(xxi) of the Constitution includes marriage as a concurrent power, so while many state and territory governments wanted to legislate for marriage equality, Section 109 prevented this because it states 'when a law of a State is inconsistent with a law of the Commonwealth, the latter shall prevail'. When the Coalition regained power federally in 2013, pressure built on the Liberal Party, both internally and externally, deepening existing divisions. As a remedy, the government proposed a plebiscite on the issue but in the end asked the Australian Electoral Commission to run a voluntary postal survey. The result from the public was a resounding 'yes' to marriage equality and in late 2017 the *Marriage Act* was amended again to remove the stipulation that marriage was between a man and a woman. At that point, the states and territories could finally legislate to allow same-sex couples to marry.

QUESTION

Can you find other policy areas with concurrent powers where there have been frictions between federal and state governments?

INVENTING COOPERATIVE FEDERALISM

The practical business of governing confounds the notion that governments might operate with a high degree of independence. To take a very simple example, interstate road and rail networks cannot be built without neighbouring states first reaching an agreement. Similarly, management of the Murray–Darling River system cannot be achieved by governments acting independently of one another: it requires their interaction and agreement. Reaching agreements of this kind 'requires an architecture of cooperation' (Wanna et al. 2009, 3). The problem with the original design of the Australian Federation is that it provided few mechanisms to allow **COOPERATIVE FEDERALISM**. These had to be invented, often in an ad hoc fashion to deal with challenges as they arose.

Section 101 of Australia's Constitution provides for an Inter-State Commission to administer free trade between the states, but it has largely been ignored. Although an Inter-State Commission was established, it failed and eventually disappeared. Because the Constitution did not provide a viable architecture to enable intergovernmental cooperation, it proved necessary to build new structures outside of its provisions. For example, prior to Federation the premiers of the various colonies had periodically met to discuss matters of common concern. The Constitution did not provide for such a meeting but as early as 1901, state premiers found it necessary to revive this practice. Thereafter, Special Premiers' Conferences were expanded to include the prime minister and met annually for much of the last century.

The resurrection of Premiers' Conferences signalled the beginning of a 'cooperative federalism' characterised by formal agreements establishing 'joint schemes of policy and legislation' and a **PRAGMATIC** approach to the creation of 'new national intergovernmental bodies' (Painter 1996, 101). The River Murray Commission was another institution created as part of Australia's improvisation of cooperative federalism. It was established to give expression to the 1915 River Murray Waters Agreement and to integrate the actions of the Commonwealth, New South Wales, Victoria and South Australia, all with a stake in the river system. Like the Premiers' Conference, which ultimately morphed into the expanded and formalised Council of Australian Governments (COAG) in 1992, the River Murray Commission was replaced (in 1988) by the Murray–Darling Basin Commission and then the Murray–Darling Basin Authority (MDBA) (in 2008).

Following the path pioneered by Premiers' Conferences (and extending the emerging architecture of cooperation), state and Commonwealth ministers with similar portfolios began to meet regularly with the goal of avoiding duplication and developing uniform policy. The first such ministerial council originated in 1923 with the creation of the Loan Council as part of an informal agreement between the Commonwealth and states to act collectively to secure more favourable terms in borrowing from banks. In 1934 the Australian Agriculture Council was established to harmonise the regulation of primary industries spanning state borders. In 1936 state education ministers agreed to meet regularly as the Australian Education Council. Meetings of ministerial councils were often preceded by meetings of state and Commonwealth public servants to hammer out the details of complementary policies. During the last century, ministerial councils grew in number (peaking at over 40) and progressively became an important vehicle for intergovernmental relations and thus for cooperative federalism.

The development of the Loan Council took an unusual course. It evolved into a statutory body in 1927 when the Commonwealth imposed a *Financial Agreement* as a condition for taking over state debts, and its work was subsequently given a constitutional basis (by a 1928 referendum approving Section 105A). It continues today, although with a diminished brief, no longer setting borrowing limits, but instead shining light upon the extent of public sector borrowing. There

COOPERATIVE FEDERALISM: A type of federalism where the different levels of government consult and collaborate in developing policy solutions to their common problems.

PRAGMATIC FEDERALISM: A willingness to unsentimentally adapt or replace institutions to suit particular needs is a hallmark of Australian federalism (Hollander and Patapan 2007). In the absence of clear direction from the Constitution, Australia has relied on ad hoc arrangements, such as the National Cabinet, the Council of Australian Governments and the Murray–Darling Basin Authority.

is one further noteworthy part of the architecture of cooperation devised in the decades after Federation that survives today with an important role. The Commonwealth Grants Commission was established in 1933 following a series of ad hoc Royal Commissions that had advised upon federal–state financial relations. Its role was to advise the Commonwealth on how special financial assistance grants provided for in **SECTION 96** should be distributed between claimant states with different populations, needs and economic circumstances. The Grants Commission is a quasi-judicial statutory authority, not a ministerial council. (This is an area where federal Cabinets are keen to insulate themselves from political acrimony that inevitably attaches to decisions to support or reject pleas for assistance from claimant states.) Today the role of the Grants Commission is primarily to advise how goods and services tax (GST) revenue collected by the Commonwealth on behalf of the states should be distributed.

> **SECTION 96:** The section of the Constitution that empowers the Commonwealth to set conditions on how states must spend any grants that it provides them.

SHORT-ANSWER QUESTIONS 2.2

1. What is the difference between 'coordinate' and 'cooperative' federalism'?
2. How has Australia evolved into a form of cooperative federalism not provided for in the Constitution?

Suggested responses are available at www.cambridge.org/highereducation/isbn/9781009108232/resources

COOPERATIVE FEDERALISM IS A MISLEADING TERM

Since 1901 Australia has devised various 'pragmatic arrangements enabling governments to work together horizontally and vertically. These arrangements, sometimes called the "gossamer strands" that tie the federation together, have broadened and deepened over the years' (Wanna et al. 2009, 13). This institutional architecture includes the Premiers' Conference, COAG, and more recently the **NATIONAL CABINET**, as well as more specialised bodies such as the MDBA and Commonwealth Grants Commission. None were originally described in the Constitution but were invented as practical ways to help Commonwealth and state governments to act collaboratively. Without the protection of the Constitution such arrangements are always vulnerable to political pressures.

> **NATIONAL CABINET:** A forum for intergovernmental collaboration, established in mid-2020, which brings together the leaders of state, territory and Commonwealth governments. It is a significantly overhauled version of the Council of Australian Governments, which it replaced.

Clearly Australian federalism has departed from the coordinate vision of the Constitution's authors. It is now better seen as a form of cooperative federalism. But cooperative federalism is a rather misleading term. It refers to an institutional architecture that allows the national and subnational units within a federal system to interact where effective policymaking requires consultation and joint action. It does *not* imply that governments within a federation will work harmoniously together (and even less that anyone enjoys the process!). In Australia, the Labor and Liberal parties contest both state and national elections, meaning the Commonwealth Government and different state governments are often controlled by rival parties. Tensions between them permeate institutions such as the National Cabinet (where state and Commonwealth leaders sit around the same table). Cooperative federalism is also a misleading term because the pragmatic development of institutions enabling governments to work together to improve and coordinate policymaking has contributed to a centralisation of power. As Windholz (2011, 2) writes, the practice of federalism in Australia has shifted away from coordinate federalism and 'from relative equality to a system characterised by a constitutionally and fiscally dominant Commonwealth'.

FEDERALISM AS A SHAPING INFLUENCE

The shaping influence of the Australian Federation on its politics and society is little noticed but very real. The Federation serves to fragment key political institutions. Interest groups trying to work with government or influence public policy are often organised into state and Commonwealth bodies. For example, trade unions are represented at the national level by a peak association, the Australian Council of Trade Unions. But because state governments play an important role in regulating industrial relations, in each state and territory, unions also form state-level representative labour councils (such as the Queensland Council of Unions or the Victorian Trades Hall Council). In New Zealand, which has a unitary rather than federal system and where unions need deal only with the national government, there is a single peak association representing unions, the New Zealand Council of Trade Unions.

Other interest groups, professional associations and community organisations are similarly organised. There are Councils of Social Service giving voice to people experiencing poverty and social disadvantage in each state and an overarching Australian Council of Social Services which lobbies at the national level. The Australian Dental Association aspires to influence government policies affecting its members and 'maintains an active presence in every state and territory via its Branches' as well as a national secretariat to engage with the Commonwealth Government. Sports organisations often follow this pattern too; for example, the Australian Weightlifting Federation has a national body and a series of state associations. There are numerous other examples of groups shaping their activities and organisation to mirror the federal structure of government.

The logic of federation (which creates multiple and overlapping power centres) obliges interest groups wishing to influence policy to mirror it. This same fragmentation is apparent in the organisation of political parties. Strange as it seems, citizens cannot join the national ALP or Liberal Party of Australia. Rather they must join a state or territory branch or division of these federated organisations. We are accustomed to thinking of them as single entities, but the major parties are loose federations of separately constituted state and territory organisations. Each state or territory Liberal Party division and state or territory ALP branch has its own membership and network of local sub-branches. Each has its own constitution and is separately registered with the Australian Electoral Commission. Each has its own parliamentary team and internal factional politics. Each provides delegates to conferences who guide the policy direction that the national-level organisation will take. The national-level Liberal and Labor parties have their own office bearers and administrative staffs. In Labor's case, the central party organisation has the constitutional authority to intervene in failing state branches; but even in the ALP, individual state branches are differently organised.

The rivalry between the two major parties plays out differently in each state and at the national level. The Liberal Party's coalition with the National Party, which is an entrenched feature of national politics, is not automatically reproduced at the state level. In some states, the National Party does not operate. In Western Australia, the two parties have an uneasy relationship. Indeed, at the 2017 Western Australian state election, the Liberals opted to preference One Nation candidates ahead of National Party candidates. A different set of circumstances applies in Queensland, where the Liberals and Nationals have merged to form one party in order to be electorally competitive at the state level. The creation of this Liberal–National Party (LNP) has had a curious side effect: although it is formally the Queensland Division of the Liberal Party of Australia, LNP members in the Commonwealth Parliament can sit in either the Liberal or Nationals party rooms! This messy arrangement underscores the different ways that politics plays out in individual states and at the national level. Liberal divisions and ALP branches often get caught up by the state-level politics and priorities. Party organisations get pulled in different directions. In this way, the Federation imposes a different pattern on parties than is apparent in comparable unitary systems such as New Zealand.

REFLECTION QUESTION 2.3

Federalism is an ingrained feature of Australian political life. Make a list of the different illustrative examples used in this chapter. Can you add some examples of your own?

Response prompt is available at www.cambridge.org/highereducation/isbn/9781009108232/resources

FISCAL FEDERALISM

How the Commonwealth emerged as fiscally dominant is a key part of the story of Australia's evolving federal system. The Constitution established taxation as a concurrent power available to both state and the Commonwealth parliaments. In the late 19th century and immediately after Federation, customs and excise duties provided the major source of revenue available to governments. However, with Australia's subsequent economic transformation and development, personal income and company taxation grew increasingly important. In addition, High Court decisions have consistently increased the revenue-raising powers available to the Commonwealth (more on the role of the High Court in reshaping federalism can be found in Chapter 5).

Most notably the High Court upheld the Commonwealth Government's 1942 *Uniform Taxation Act*. Introduced during the Second World War, this Act secured control of income and company taxation for the Commonwealth while providing for tax reimbursement grants to the states. The Commonwealth subsequently acted to retain its monopoly of these increasingly important revenue streams by requiring that the states not levy income taxes as a condition for receiving tax reimbursement grants. When Victoria challenged this arrangement in 1957, in the *Second Uniform Tax* case, the High Court again ruled in favour of the Commonwealth, upholding its constitutional power to attach conditions to reimbursement grants. Today, income tax and company tax are the most lucrative taxes in Australia, raising more than all other taxes combined. In other decisions, the High Court has ruled in ways that prevented the states from imposing taxes on goods and challenging duties they had imposed on tobacco, alcohol and petrol.

As a result, the states have been left with a limited capacity to raise revenue via lesser and inefficient means such as stamp duty, payroll and land taxes. This means the states can only deliver the health, education, transport and other services and infrastructure for which they are responsible with additional funding from the Commonwealth. In 1902, Alfred Deakin, one of the framers of the Australian Constitution and a three-time prime minister, had foreseen this problem when he argued that the Constitution left the states 'legally free, but financially bound to the chariot wheels of the central government. Their need will be its opportunity' (James 2000).

REFLECTION QUESTION 2.4

What do you imagine Australia's Federation (and politics) would look like if, as was the case until the Second World War, the Commonwealth and states each collected income and company taxes?

Response prompt is available at www.cambridge.org/highereducation/isbn/9781009108232/resources

VERTICAL FISCAL IMBALANCE

Today Australia's federation features a pronounced '**VERTICAL FISCAL IMBALANCE**'. Fiscal imbalance refers to a mismatch between a government's spending responsibilities and its ability to raise the revenue it needs. In turn, vertical fiscal imbalance describes circumstances within a federation where one tier of government faces a revenue shortfall and depends upon a transfer of funding from the other to meet its commitments. Usually, it is subnational governments that depend upon central government disbursements. Australia fits this pattern. Indeed '[i]n Australia, taxation power is more centralised than in other federations' (Ratnapala 2014, 76). The Commonwealth collects four of every five tax dollars paid, which is more revenue than it needs to fund its own policy programs; meanwhile, the states and territories are unable to raise the revenue needed for their recurrent spending obligations.

The extent of vertical fiscal imbalance within the Australian Federation can be measured by the revenue transferred by the Commonwealth to the states as a proportion of their total revenue. Table 2.1 shows both the reduced capacity of states to raise their own revenue and the extent of their current dependence on Commonwealth transfers. Grants from the Commonwealth usually fund about half of state and territory general government spending. For example, in the 2017–18 financial year, the Commonwealth provided 43.9 per cent of the total revenue of the states. Smaller states are especially dependent on Commonwealth transfers: in 2017–18, South Australia, Tasmania and Northern Territory all received well over half their revenue this way. Commonwealth transfers have long 'been a large part of state budgets', accounting for 'around half since World War II' (CGC 2019, 3). That the Commonwealth financially underwrites the states helps explain the centralisation of power within the Australian Federation.

VERTICAL FISCAL IMBALANCE: A situation that arises in a federation where one tier of government lacks the revenue-raising capacity of the other and relies on grants to meet its policy commitments.

TABLE 2.1 REVENUE COLLECTED UNDER STATE LEGISLATION AND SUPPLEMENTARY COMMONWEALTH TRANSFERS

	PROPORTION COLLECTED UNDER STATE LEGISLATION	PROPORTION OF STATE REVENUE FROM COMMONWEALTH TRANSFERS
1901–02	59.0%	36.7%
1938–39	53.4%	13.9%
1946–47	15.1%	46.1%
1980–81	21.7%	62.0%
2000–01	22.2%	46.2%
2017–18	25.6%	43.9%

Source: Commonwealth Grants Commission (2019, 3).

Section 96 of the Constitution authorises the Commonwealth to provide funding to the states on the terms and conditions of its choosing. It is able to provide assistance conditionally in the form of 'payments for special purposes' and unconditionally as 'general revenue assistance'. The latter category of financial assistance to the states is inflated by the transfer of the proceeds of the lucrative GST. The GST was proposed in 1998 by the Howard Government, which pledged to hand over all of the monies raised as general revenue assistance (in return the states ended a number of inefficient state taxes). The automatic transfer of revenue raised by the GST commenced in 2000. It was intended to ameliorate vertical fiscal imbalance within the Federation by guaranteeing the states an efficient and expanding revenue source; however, while GST revenue is returned to the states to spend as they choose, the Commonwealth still provides significant amounts of additional funding with conditions.

SHORT-ANSWER QUESTION 2.3

What is the difference between horizontal and vertical fiscal imbalance?

Suggested response is available at www.cambridge.org/highereducation/isbn/9781009108232/resources

SPECIFIC PURPOSE PAYMENTS

There is a long history of national governments providing the states with funding conditional upon their adoption of the Commonwealth's own policy priorities and settings. Technically called specific purpose payments, the money is sometimes described as 'tied grants', because states must spend the funds on particular policy programs pursuant to agreements struck with the Commonwealth. Tied grants have allowed the Commonwealth to progressively exert influence over education, health, transport and other policy areas, which the Constitution's authors intended to be state responsibilities. This contributes strongly to Australia having one of the most centralised federal systems in the world. In a typical breakdown, the 2018–19 Commonwealth budget flagged $128 billion for the states, almost half ($60.8 billion) in the form of specific purpose payments (Australian Government 2019, 5).

The *Intergovernmental Agreement on Federal Financial Relations* adopted in 2008 significantly reduced specific purpose payments to the states and territories, instead allowing them greater flexibility in implementing their programs and in managing their budgets. The Agreement acknowledged that states have primary responsibility for service delivery across a range of areas, but also accepted the need for collaborative policy development and service delivery and for conditional funding of economic and social reforms of national importance. Where the Commonwealth and states and territories reached formal agreements (via COAG) setting out mutually agreed policy objectives and outcomes, as in the case of the Closing the Gap National Partnership Agreements, the Commonwealth Government would provide funding via a new category of national partnership payments.

Education provides a good example of the complex way in which policy works in the Australian Federation. Although the Commonwealth Government operates no schools, it nonetheless has a sizeable Department of Education and holds sway in shaping national policy. Similarly, there are Commonwealth and state departments of agriculture, health, environment and many others, suggesting the scale of the overlap between the tiers. On occasion, the Commonwealth Government has set quite specific conditions for special purpose payments; for example, in

2004 it 'tied school funding to flying the Australian flag. To get their slice of … Commonwealth funds, [state] schools had to have a functioning flagpole' (Ackland 2011). The NAPLAN tests that students in all states complete during their schooling is a similar example of a policy intervention to which Commonwealth Government funding is 'tied'. It is often suggested that the Commonwealth Government's capacity to impose its policy priorities through conditional funding has reduced the independence of state agencies; blurred who is responsible for policy; and limited the capacity of voters to hold governments accountable. In short, the complaint is that the manner in which taxation is raised and distributed has contributed to the centralisation of power within Australia's federal system.

SHORT-ANSWER QUESTION 2.4

Why is Section 96 of the Constitution important?

Suggested response is available at www.cambridge.org/highereducation/isbn/9781009108232/resources

HORIZONTAL FISCAL EQUALISATION

HORIZONTAL FISCAL IMBALANCE describes an inequity that arises where the various subnational governments within a federation have different capacities to raise revenue and face different service delivery costs. This is likely to occur where, as in Australia's case, there is significant variation in economic, demographic and geographic circumstances across a federation. In such circumstances federations typically develop mechanisms for horizontal fiscal equalisation – for transferring revenue to assist poorly-placed subnational governments.

As might be expected in a federation in which half of the population resides in New South Wales and Victoria and where the states range in physical size from 68 401 square kilometres (Tasmania) to 2 529 875 square kilometres (Western Australia), state governments face different challenges in funding and delivering education, transport, health and other services to their citizens. Regional variation across Australia means horizontal fiscal imbalance has long been a feature of its federation. Long-term structural causes of horizontal fiscal imbalance can be exacerbated by demographic change or by economic developments (such as the mining boom of the early 2000s from which Western Australia and Queensland especially benefited). As we have seen, horizontal fiscal imbalance proved a problem from the beginning, leading to several judicial inquiries, and then to the establishment of the quasi-judicial Commonwealth Grants Commission to advise the Commonwealth Government on the appropriate levels of top-up special assistance funding for disadvantaged claimant states.

Australians expect the same standards of education and health care from government irrespective of which state or territory they live in. To achieve this egalitarian outcome across the Federation, states must be treated differently, rather as horses in the Melbourne Cup are assigned different handicap weights to give all the best chance of victory. After 1910, the Commonwealth Government fell into the practice of supporting weaker states, including Western Australia. It soon found that providing a state with special financial assistance, and thus treating some more generously than others, was fraught with political difficulty. The creation of the independent Commonwealth Grants Commission in 1933 served to distance the processing of applications for special assistance by the states from day-to-day party politics. In 1976 the work of the Commonwealth Grants Commission was extended to advise the Commonwealth Government

HORIZONTAL FISCAL IMBALANCE: An inequity that arises in a federation where the various subnational governments have different capacities to raise revenue and face different service delivery costs.

on how it might best distribute general revenue assistance to remedy horizontal fiscal imbalance and ensure that states with different geographies, service costs and revenue-raising capacity were all able to provide the same level of education, health and other services to their citizens.

Today the Commonwealth Grants Commission investigates the 'relative fiscal capacities' of the states and territories and recommends how GST revenue raised by the Commonwealth Government on their behalf should be distributed among them. In this process it seeks the best available data, consults with states, and weighs their preferences against the available evidence. The process is transparent and the methodology it uses is regularly reviewed. The Commission calculates 'per capita relativities', which are updated annually. These scores (see Table 2.2) dictate the share of the GST collected that each state will receive; for example, in 2019–20, Western Australia's per capita relativity of 0.518 42 entitled it to 52 cents for every dollar of GST raised in Western Australia, making it the biggest loser in sharing the GST. Meanwhile, the Northern Territory received $4.26 for every dollar of GST raised in the Northern Territory, making it the biggest winner by a very large margin. The differences reflect the relative financial needs of the states and territories. Some state premiers, most notably from Western Australia, have been vocal critics, arguing that GST revenue should be shared more evenly. In the main, Australia has successfully quarantined the process of horizontal fiscal equalisation from the rough and tumble of politics.

TABLE 2.2 COMMONWEALTH GRANT COMMISSION PER CAPITA RELATIVITIES

JURISDICTION	2015–16	2019–20
NSW	0.947 37	0.870 13
Victoria	0.892 54	0.982 73
Queensland	1.127 53	1.053 70
WA	0.299 99	0.518 42
SA	1.358 83	1.465 52
Tasmania	1.819 06	1.755 76
ACT	1.100 12	1.237 59
NT	5.570 53	4.267 35

Source: Australian Government (2015, 80); Commonwealth Grants Commission (2020, 1).

REFLECTION QUESTION 2.5

Do you think it is reasonable for Australians to expect that government ensures people have similar standards of health care irrespective of where they live?

Response prompt is available at www.cambridge.org/highereducation/isbn/9781009108232/resources

RESEARCH QUESTION 2.1

What changes to horizontal fiscal equalisation did the Productivity Commission recommend in 2017?

FROM COAG TO NATIONAL CABINET: COORDINATING POLICY

Calls to reform how the federation is managed have long been a motif of Australian politics. From 1992 to mid-2020, much of Australia's intergovernmental relations was conducted through the Council of Australian Governments (COAG). Recognising its limitations, newly elected Coalition and Labor governments alike often came to power with plans to reform COAG and intergovernmental relations. Soon after being elected in late 2007, the Rudd Labor Government persuaded all Australian governments to embrace a wide-ranging national reform agenda including significant changes to Commonwealth–state funding arrangements. But it was during the 2020 coronavirus pandemic that Prime Minister Scott Morrison made the biggest shift of all, announcing that the initially temporary National Cabinet, created to deal with the pandemic, would be made permanent and replace COAG. In reality, rather than being a wholly new institution, the National Cabinet was a thoroughly re-vamped COAG; perhaps more of a rapid evolution than a revolution.

The importance of collaboration between Australian governments in addressing economic change loomed large in the late twentieth century as Australia faced the substantial pressures brought by globalisation and the opening of its economy to free trade and international competition. These pressures were for 'microeconomic reform' or the removal of barriers to Australia operating as an efficient single market. Against this backdrop, COAG was established in 1992 to better manage matters of national importance requiring a concerted policy response by Australian governments. Examples of such barriers included state legislation creating different haulage and road transport rules; setting in place different labour market regulations; fixing different food safety manufacturing and packaging requirements; or imposing different duty and other state revenue-raising measures. All were sources of economic inefficiency.

THE COUNCIL OF AUSTRALIAN GOVERNMENTS

COAG marked a step change in how intergovernmental relations were managed in Australia. It replaced the ad hoc Special Premiers' Conferences, providing a far more substantial set of arrangements, including a proper structure for intergovernmental processes with support from the public service, meaning it could pursue a more comprehensive agenda. COAG brought together leaders of the state, territory and Commonwealth governments as well as the president of the Local Government Association representing the third tier of Australia's Federation. It was then surrounded with various ministerial councils on specific policy areas. Leaders at COAG had the 'authority to negotiate on behalf of their jurisdiction and to strike and implement agreements which [were] binding' (Menzies 2013, 383).

In the 1990s and into the 2000s, COAG drove an extensive microeconomic reform agenda, including establishing National Competition Policy in 1994 to coordinate and accelerate the ambitious program. COAG also facilitated a variety of intergovernmental agreements where the 'the policy capacity of both levels of government needs to be harnessed' (Menzies 2013, 386). Among many areas of reform were establishing a national competitive electricity market, introducing a National Disability Insurance Scheme, standardising credit and consumer laws, trying to 'close the gap' by improving the lot of Indigenous Australians, introducing uniform counter-terrorism laws and managing gene technology. COAG was also instrumental in developing collective policy responses in the areas of early childhood development, gun control, affordable housing, educational and vocational training, natural disaster relief and climate change.

COAG met between one and four times a year, depending on the prime minister, so meetings became a big event. Meetings were preceded by meetings of state and Commonwealth public servants who tried to hammer out the details of agreements, for the first ministers to then formally agree to at the COAG table. This process was often criticised as slow and bureaucratic.

COAG is a good example of 'pragmatic federalism'. Neither 'constitutional nor statutory in origin or nature' but rather 'an administrative creation of executive will', COAG was 'constantly changing and adapting to political and other circumstances' (Blayden 2013).

Inevitably, COAG could be riven by politics, after all its members were political leaders, and COAG almost always contained leaders from rival political parties within a fiercely adversarial party system. Especially in the case of politically sensitive issues, very different ideological convictions and policy priorities could be on display. In these circumstances, there was frequently a reluctance 'to give any wins to a federal leader of an opposing party' where this might confer electoral advantage (Menzies 2013, 384).

Prime ministers were always in the driving seat of COAG. From the outset, different prime ministers used COAG in different ways to pursue their own political agendas. Some, such as Kevin Rudd, attached far greater importance to COAG than did others, like John Howard. Administrative support for COAG came from the Department of Prime Minister and Cabinet, and it met at the prime minister's request. The prime minister also chaired the meetings and oversaw the agenda, with states and territories only rarely raising matters for consideration.

SPOTLIGHT 2.2 COVID-19 AND FEDERALISM

The COVID-19 pandemic of 2020–21 provides a useful microcosm of the strengths and weaknesses of Australian federalism. Through the pandemic, Australia continued to operate as a federation, with powers divided between the federal and state tiers of government, and variation in policies between states. In many ways the pandemic highlighted the fact that Australia is a federation, for better or worse. On the one hand, federalism allowed each state to tailor responses to its own circumstances, to innovate in policy and to learn from each other. On the other hand, policy was not always consistent (e.g. in education), and when things went wrong, blame shifting emerged and there were occasional public slanging matches (e.g. on the vaccination roll out). Some policies, such as border closures, flowed directly from being a federal system and were controversial throughout. The vertical fiscal imbalance was also in evidence with, for example, the Commonwealth Government providing money to the states to fund additional hospital facilities. At the beginning of the pandemic, the National Cabinet was set up to coordinate responses across Australia's various governments including public health rules and examining expert modelling. A few months later, the National Cabinet was turned into a permanent body.

QUESTION

Overall, was federalism an advantage or disadvantage for Australia during the COVID-19 pandemic?

NATIONAL CABINET

As the COVID-19 pandemic started to unfold in 2020, leaders from around Australia decided a slimmer, nimbler, less formal forum was needed to manage and coordinate a rapidly changing and unknown crisis. While COAG may have been a decent forum for methodical, considered reform, the pandemic highlighted some of its inadequacies. A COAG meeting in March 2020 established the National Cabinet, comprising the prime minister, state premiers and territory chief ministers. The National Cabinet would be less formal and less driven by structures, processes and agendas. At some points, it met multiple times per week but at others once a week. On 29 May, Prime Minister Scott Morrison announced the leaders had agreed to build on the National Cabinet model and sweep away COAG.

The new system of intergovernmental relations, centred on the National Cabinet, would be designed to avoid the problems associated with COAG. The National Cabinet would:

- have monthly meetings rather than one to four a year that characterised COAG
- be a more informal forum, less driven by agendas and standing items
- have a reduced bureaucracy compared with COAG
- not be so reliant on senior public servants meeting beforehand to thrash out issues
- facilitate open discussions by applying Commonwealth Cabinet rules of confidentiality to deliberations and documents.[1]

Alongside the National Cabinet would be a similar body made up of federal, state and territory treasurers; several broad reform committees of relevant ministers (e.g. Health, Energy or Skills) and various expert advisory groups.

A National Federation Reform Council was also established to meet annually, comprising the National Cabinet, the treasurers' body and the Local Government Association (who were dropped in the switch from COAG to the National Cabinet). This Reform Council would have taskforces working on a very small number of key priorities.

These arrangements have real risks. Early in the pandemic, leaders put political differences aside and worked well together, in a genuinely cooperative and accommodating way. If trust is built, the new arrangements could be quicker, simpler and smoother. Alternatively, it may be that this was simply the result of the crisis and is not sustainable in ordinary times. The various competing interests and obvious political differences have not gone away, so removing the work of public servants could backfire and result in much more raw politics, grandstanding and showdowns. There is the further risk that the old problems of COAG could creep back over time. Problems of increased complexity, adding ever more committees and groups, rising levels of bureaucracy and politicisation would lead to the same slow and cumbersome system, but with a new name. The risks are compounded by the fact that the permanent institutions of the National Cabinet were designed in a hurry during a pandemic rather than in the methodical and considered way that COAG was designed (Prasser 2020, 151–2).

SHORT-ANSWER QUESTIONS 2.5

1. What is the National Cabinet?
2. Many people have pointed out that the National Cabinet is not a Cabinet in any conventional way. In what ways is it not a conventional Cabinet?

Suggested responses are available at www.cambridge.org/highereducation/isbn/9781009108232/resources

---

[1] At the time of writing, the future of this provision remains unclear. In mid-2021, the Administrative Appeals Tribunal determined National Cabinet was not bound by Cabinet confidentiality. The Morrison Coalition government then introduced legislation for this, but by early 2022 the legislation remained stuck in the parliament (Doran 2021).

MINISTERIAL COUNCILS

From the outset, COAG, and then the National Cabinet, has been surrounded by ministerial councils, which bring together Commonwealth, state and territory ministers with similar portfolios (such as health or environment) to work on issues requiring cross-border collaboration and decision-making. Ministerial councils often have responsibility for proposing reforms to, and for overseeing the implementation of, agreements.

As COAG grew in importance, 'a growing network of working parties and committees of officials operating across state borders' sprang up around COAG which Anderson (2008, 495–6) suggested can 'be characterised as a "nascent bureaucracy of federalism"'. Within a decade of COAG's creation in 1992, over 40 different ad hoc ministerial councils had been created, which had considerable autonomy in the areas they oversaw. Technically none was permanent. Starting in 2010, these were dramatically culled, and the survivors were formalised within COAG, but even so numbers were creeping back up again by the time COAG was scrapped in 2020. The switch to the National Cabinet included an attempt to strip away much of the bureaucracy and process, including many of the working parties and committees as well as ministerial councils.

In late 2020, the National Cabinet commissioned the Conran Review to make recommendations on ministerial councils and associated bodies, for the transition to the National Cabinet and the National Federation Reform Council. The National Cabinet accepted recommendations for significant changes including:

- just nine ongoing ministerial groups (with some other existing ministerial councils continuing for up to a year before disbanding)
- a review of all groups every two years
- new rules making it harder to create new ministerial groups
- no dedicated secretariat support provided by the Commonwealth Government (although there will still be public servants working in support of the ministerial groups)
- ministerial groups to focus on a smaller number (2–3) of key issues at a time and meet more regularly
- ministers will be in charge and will not have to report to the National Cabinet
- these ministerial groups are separate to the National Cabinet and its committees.

Of course, only time will tell whether these reforms stick or whether they join the list of failed attempts to streamline, focus and speed up intergovernmental relations.

Ministerial councils (and the senior public servants who advise them) have considerable decision-making power. This dominance of intergovernmental negotiation by the executive arm of government – along with the range and importance of policies they decide – points to the emergence of what some describe as 'executive federalism' (Anderson 2008, 496).

EXECUTIVE, COLLABORATIVE AND OTHER FEDERALISMS

It may be useful to review our account of the Australian Federation here. It was designed long ago to allow state and Commonwealth governments to operate side-by-side and largely independent of each other. But this prescription for a coordinate federalism proved impractical. It forced the pragmatic invention of institutions and processes to facilitate cooperation between governments. In short, Australia evolved an ad hoc system of cooperative federalism. The most recent steps along this path saw the transformation of COAG into the National Cabinet and reform of ministerial councils and the associated bureaucracy. Despite the many economic and other intergovernmental agreements, cooperative federalism does not imply harmony nor the absence of political tensions.

While COAG and now the National Cabinet 'began as a means of encouraging cooperative federalism', they have also quietly encouraged the centralisation of power and 'played a part in entrenching executive federalism' (Anderson 2008, 496). Executive federalism describes 'the channelling of intergovernmental relations into transactions controlled by elected and appointed officials of the executive branch' (Sharman 1991, 25).

Frameworks like the National Cabinet and COAG strengthen the hand of executive government and political leaders. The obligation to implement agreements reached by leaders diminishes both state and Commonwealth parliaments alike, reducing them to 'rubber stamping' any associated legislation. Anderson (2008, 506) suggests the particular 'form of executive federalism that COAG fostered is one which supported greater centralisation within the federation'. Prime ministers in particular benefit from this centralisation. It has been one cause of their growing power. Critics of the rise of executive federalism point to 'the "behind closed doors" character of intergovernmental decision-making' and to the resultant diminished scope for community consultation and parliamentary deliberation (Sawer 2009). Criticism resurfaced with the switch to the National Cabinet, with complaints the new body further strengthened the hand of executives, for example, with the imposition of Commonwealth Cabinet rules of confidentiality for the National Cabinet (Prasser 2020, 152).

Executive federalism is one of several concepts that political scientists have used to reframe our understanding of cooperative federalism and to explain the nature and shortcomings of the intergovernmental institutions and processes that have been devised to enable all Australian governments to liaise and to search for ways of addressing policy problems requiring a national approach. In keeping with the idea of 'pragmatic federalism', institutions such as COAG and the National Cabinet have not been developed to give expression to some 'grand theory' of federalism but as solutions to pressing problems and have often simultaneously placed greater power in the hands of the Commonwealth. Intergovernmental relations have evolved incrementally, in a process unencumbered by traditional arrangements or **'STATES' RIGHTS'** or similar ideological imaginations.

Australia has also been described as having a system of 'collaborative federalism'. Painter (1998, 1) depicts the Federation this way, arguing state and Commonwealth governments find themselves 'cooperating ever more closely on joint schemes of policy and administration', albeit often 'against their immediate wishes'. The creation of COAG 'greatly accelerated this trend' and blurred the distinctiveness of the states and Commonwealth: they are less and less 'separate political actors in a federal system'. The National Cabinet will not reverse any of this. At least partly this has happened because, since around the turn of the century, the Liberal Party has shifted decisively away from its traditional role as a champion of states' rights and towards the ALP's longstanding views that coordination and centralisation often make for good, effective, efficient policy.

'Coercive federalism' is a term that has also been used to describe the circumstances arising from vertical fiscal imbalance, which have allowed the Commonwealth Government to push states into accepting its direct involvement in areas such as education which ostensibly belong to the states (Hamill 2007, 43–56). Others argue Australia has produced a system not of cooperative federalism but of 'cooperative centralism', which has consolidated the dominance of the national government as policy 'instigator and coordinator and frequently as a policy driver' (Anderson and Parkin 2010, 111).

STATES' RIGHTS: In the Australian context, a political doctrine asserting the importance of protecting individual states from undue interference by the Commonwealth Government.

The centralisation of power within the Federation has been welcomed by some because it has facilitated integrated, national responses to pressing problems. But the financial dependency of states upon the Commonwealth Government and the extended role of the Commonwealth Government in developing uniform policy solutions also has its critics. Chief among those are scholars who prefer a more 'competitive federalism' in which states adopt their own approaches to policy problems, allowing them to compete with each other to minimise taxes and provide the best services possible at the lowest cost. Those same states can then also learn from one another's policy successes and failures.

The different ways in which the evolution of cooperative federalism has been represented point to the complexity of these changes (as well as to the propensity for political scientists to disagree). If there is a common thread to these different characterisations of intergovernmental relations that has been created outside of provisions of the Constitution, it is that states have lost out as the Commonwealth Government has established its dominance.

REFLECTION QUESTION 2.6

What are some of the different ways that political scientists have reframed cooperative federalism? (Is there fundamental disagreement about the nature of Australia's federal system?)

Response prompt is available at www.cambridge.org/highereducation/isbn/9781009108232/resources

SHORT-ANSWER QUESTION 2.6

What is executive federalism?

Suggested response is available at www.cambridge.org/highereducation/isbn/9781009108232/resources

REFORMING THE FEDERATION AND THE FUTURE OF STATES

It is difficult now to imagine an Australia in which premiers of the larger states were more politically influential than prime ministers, or in which powerful Liberal state premiers might force a Liberal prime minister from power – as happened to Sir John Gorton in 1971 – for pursuing centralist policies perceived as infringing 'states' rights'. Once a shibboleth of the Liberal Party, the concept of states' rights has few adherents today, with John Howard's prime ministership marking a real turning point in the Liberal Party's approach to federalism. The argument that federalism limits the power of government by dividing power has largely lost out to a contemporary view that the Australian federal system is costly, inefficient and anachronistic. A 2010 study found many Australians viewed the Federation negatively, and that three-quarters would prefer to see a different system in place (see Windholz 2011, 1). Their number includes former state and national leaders, as well as influential interest groups such as the Business Council of Australia who have advocated fundamental reform of the Federation.

Would-be reformers offer various reasons why wholesale reform of the Federation ought to be considered. The federal system is argued to be a source of duplication and inefficiency. The Business Council of Australia calculates that inefficiency within the Federation sees governments waste some $9 billion each year. A related complaint is that, with a Commonwealth Parliament plus six separate state parliaments, Australia is 'over governed' and oversupplied with politicians and competing laws and regulations. The range of economic, environmental, technological and other challenges facing Australia today mostly require a national or uniform policy response, something best achieved by the Commonwealth Government being formally handed control of policy areas presently handed to states by an antiquated Constitution. In short, the '19th Century constitutional division of powers is not capable of meeting the challenges presented by increasing globalisation, international economic competition and rapid advances in technology' (Windholz 2011, 1). Put another way: 'Our federal system was conceived in ... the age of the horse and buggy, and it shows' (Williams 2006). In this context, it may be worth replacing *ad hoc* intergovernmental processes and mechanisms with a constitutionally protected, 'permanent institution' serving this role (Menzies 2013, 387). As noted above, the Constitution offers very little guidance on managing federalism, aside from the largely ignored Inter-State Commission.

Some reformers believe improved intergovernmental processes ought to be matched by the reform of Commonwealth–state financial relations to correct vertical fiscal imbalance. Both tiers of government are increasingly entangled given that states and territories are only able to fund roads, schools and hospitals with significant support from the Commonwealth Government, which often makes funding available conditionally. This means it is often impossible for voters to hold governments accountable for policy failures because the authority of state and Commonwealth governments is not clearly delineated. Generally, the case for modernising federalism hangs on refashioning 'the role of the states' (Smith 2013, 362).

SPOTLIGHT 2.3 STATES' RIGHTS

There are few contemporary advocates of states' rights. Furthermore, the 19th century argument that federalism limits the power of government and protects freedom by dividing power has largely lost out to a contemporary view that the federal system is costly, inefficient and anachronistic. In particular, where once the Liberal Party was a champion and defender of states' right, the prime ministership of John Howard saw the party shift decisively towards the view that coordination and centralisation are essential for success in the modern world. In this century, when the nation faces environmental and economic challenges that require a concerted national policy response, some suggest Australia would be better off if states were scrapped in favour of a strong central government; however, there are constitutional obstacles that would likely prevent such a reform. If unitary government is not an option, then a practical solution is that suggested by the 2010 Senate Select Committee on the Reform of the Australian Federation: ending the pronounced gap in the revenue streams available to the Commonwealth and state governments, which it considered to be a principal source of the present dysfunction within the Australian Federation.

QUESTIONS

Why are there few contemporary advocates of states' rights? What are the arguments for decentralised government?

RECENT ATTEMPTS AT REFORM

As has been suggested already, Commonwealth governments frequently talk about reforming Australia's federal system, but the record of success is patchy at best. The reforms with the best chances are those which tinker with the ad hoc mechanisms for managing intergovernmental relations rather than those seeking to fundamentally shift the balance between the tiers of government by, for example, fixing the vertical fiscal imbalance or reshaping policy responsibilities.

Reform is possible. When the Rudd Government was elected in 2007, it quickly set about reforming the way the Federation worked, capitalising on the unprecedented moment of Labor controlling every state and territory government as well as the Commonwealth. For example, the use of tied grants was reduced, and national partnership payments were created. In ordinary times though, reform often seems doomed from the start.

Attempts at profound reform almost always end in failure. In 2014, then Prime Minister Tony Abbott established a full-scale Reform of the Federation White Paper process to overhaul the federal system and, in particular, to reduce the vertical fiscal imbalance and give the states more freedom in the areas they are responsible. The process included both centralising and decentralising ideas, from handing control of some policy areas to the Commonwealth to giving the states more capacity to raise taxes. The White Paper was killed by Abbott's replacement as prime minister, Malcolm Turnbull. In turn, Turnbull had a very short-lived tilt at fixing the vertical fiscal imbalance, when he informally proposed reducing Commonwealth income tax and then allowing states to levy their own modest income tax on top, collected for them by the Commonwealth. Despite being a system used in countries such as the United States and Canada, the idea was widely derided and quickly disappeared.

During the 2020 coronavirus pandemic, Scott Morrison swept COAG away and replaced it with the National Cabinet. But this was a return to tinkering with mechanisms and processes, rather than attempting to dramatically alter the shape or dynamics of Australian federalism.

FEDERALISM AS PART OF AUSTRALIA'S POLITICAL DNA

For some, the problem is the mismatch between Australia's regions and state boundaries. For instance, in 2016 the newly installed Minister for Northern Australia, Matt Canavan, endorsed calls for a referendum on the creation of a seventh Australian state in north Queensland (to be achieved by splitting Queensland in two). It was, he said, a proposal that had 'merit' and should be put to the people (Koziol 2016). Such calls for the creation of new states have periodically punctuated Australian politics. None has sustained any real momentum. One reason is that the creation of any new state must be 'put to the people' – to all the citizens of Australia in a referendum, not just those in the region seeking a separate future. Changing the Constitution is notoriously difficult and consumes a lot of political capital.

It is not clear even that the Northern Territory will smoothly fulfil its ambition to become Australia's seventh state (or that the Local Government Association will succeed in having the Constitution amended to formally recognise local government as a third tier of the Federation). Section 128 looms as a roadblock to anyone wishing to overhaul the Australian Federation. This may be why some suggest the question of whether or not the Federation 'is a sensible way to organise government and democracy' is 'a bit of a non-issue' (Cook, Walsh and Harwood 2009, 114). It is a non-issue because, like it or not, the Federation is 'constitutionally embedded' (Anderson 2008, 494). It is part of Australia's political DNA. This is not to say citizens today are passionately invested in the federal division of powers (as may have been the case in the 1950s and 1960s when premiers were able to invoke states' rights in their contests with Canberra).

Today most see themselves as Australians and 'state of origin' is more celebrated on the football pitch than in political life.

Whether citizens like it or not, the six founding states are very much a fixed feature of the Australian political system. Federalism is ingrained in all aspects of Australia's political system, which is a further barrier to change.

SUMMARY

Learning objective 1: Explain how and why federalism divides powers

Federalism is a prescriptive theory holding that we ought to prevent government from accumulating excessive power by constitutionally dividing it – by allocating the authority to decide policy in certain areas to a national government while giving a series of subnational governments responsibility to make decisions in other policy areas. While federalism shares the goal of preserving freedom by constitutionally constraining government, the federal division of powers between distinct tiers of government should not be confused with the separation of powers aiming to ensure that no single group controls the legislative, executive and judicial arms of government.

Learning objective 2: Analyse the Australian variant of federalism and explain how it has evolved

Understanding the Australian Federation begins with recognising that its Constitution embraces the theory of federalism and divides the authority to make policy between the Commonwealth and state governments. This was done for practical rather than theoretical reasons. The Constitution's framers intended these governments would operate largely independent of one another. But their 19th century prescription for coordinate federalism, underestimated the need for institutions that could satisfactorily manage intergovernmental relations. To correct this shortcoming, it proved necessary to invent additional institutions to allow governments to consult and collaborate. The evolution of the Australian Federation into a form of cooperative federalism unfolded in an unplanned patchwork fashion. It began with the resurrection of Premiers' Conferences almost immediately in 1901 and continues today with COAG being revamped into the National Cabinet.

Learning objective 3: Explain how the way states are funded enlarges the role of the Commonwealth

The Constitution's authors intended states would be an important seat of power. But this vision was dealt a blow by the High Court – most notably in the 1942 and 1957 Uniform Tax cases, which handed the Commonwealth Government control of income and company taxation. Its monopoly of these lucrative revenue sources enabled the Commonwealth Government to raise far more revenue than it required for its own policy programs. This introduced a pronounced vertical fiscal imbalance within the Australian Federation, which successive governments have exploited to expand the role of the Commonwealth Government. Section 96 of the Constitution empowers the Commonwealth to provide the states with financial assistance on its terms and conditions. In the past half century or more, the Commonwealth Government has attached conditions to the 'tied grants' it has offered the states in order to extend its influence into areas such as education and health, which the Constitution's authors imagined would remain in state hands. The result has been a greater integration of Commonwealth and state policymaking plus a 'creeping centralisation' of power.

Learning objective 4: Analyse bodies like the National Cabinet (and COAG before it) and explain their importance to contemporary politics and policymaking

In 2020, the National Cabinet replaced the Council of Australian Governments (COAG), which had been created in 1992. It meets monthly and gathers government leaders – the prime minister, state premiers and territory chief ministers. The National Cabinet and its associated bodies and ministerial councils built on the old COAG architecture, aiming to be less bureaucratic and faster moving than COAG. It will focus on fewer issues at any one time, remove much of the work done by senior public servants around meetings and have a smaller number of ministerial councils and other supporting bodies. The National Cabinet should continue COAG's central role in achieving intergovernmental agreements across areas such as economic reform, climate change and reform of health and education.

Learning objective 5: Make an informed judgement about the need for, and prospects of, reforming the Federation

Australia's federal system has, and will continue to, evolve. Some treat the 'creeping centralism' associated with the evolution of cooperative federalism as inevitable, even welcome. After all, problems governments increasingly grapple with require a national approach and a coordinated policy response, which is something more likely to be achieved within a federation in which the Commonwealth Government carries most weight. But a rival view holds that there are regional variations across Australia that may require state governments to adopt different solutions to environmental, economic and other such challenges as they arise. Those advocating reform have quite different aims. While some see federalism as an anachronism and advocate for greater centralisation at the expense of the states, others wish to free states from the heavy hand of Commonwealth Government interference by reducing their dependency on financial assistance from the Commonwealth Government. Yet others champion a more clearly delineated division of powers between the states and the Commonwealth. Reform does not have to involve the onerous task of altering the Constitution, but some reformers have argued for strengthening intergovernmental arrangements by enshrining them in the Constitution. All that said, today there is little popular enthusiasm for seriously reforming the Federation. Such demands come largely from within the ranks of government policymakers and are primarily about institutional design which does not resonate with the wider public. There is no grassroots groundswell for reform of the Federation itself. Federation is so ingrained in Australian political life that it is taken for granted despite being a central feature of a political system which mixes federal and parliamentary forms of government.

DISCUSSION QUESTIONS

1. What is the core difference between a de facto federal system and the Australian Federation?

2. What was COAG and how did it shape contemporary Australia?

3. What might an understanding of the process leading to Federation in 1901 add to understanding the Australian federal system today?

4. What arguments are made in favour of federalism? Are there any countering arguments that ring true in the Australian setting?

5. What factors do you think make serious reform of federalism in Australia so difficult?

FURTHER READING

Fenna, A. (2012). Centralising dynamics in Australian federalism. *Australian Journal of Politics and History*, **58**(4), 580–90.

Hollander, R. (2014). Federalism and intergovernmental relations. In C. Miller and L. Orchard (eds), *Australian Public Policy*, Chicago: Policy Press.

Kildea, P., Lynch, A. & Williams, G. (eds). (2012). *Tomorrow's Federation: Reforming Australian Government*, Annandale: Federation Press.

Tiernan, A. (2015). Reforming Australia's federal framework: Priorities and prospects. *Australian Journal of Public Administration*, **74**(4), 398–405.

Zimmerman, A. & Finlay, L. (2011). Reforming federalism: A proposal for strengthening the Australian Federation. *Monash University Law Review*, **7**(2), 190–231.

REFERENCES

Abbott, T. (2008). Speech Notes. Australian Federalism: Rescue & Reform Conference, *Griffith University & Institute of Public Administration Australia*, Tenterfield, 24 October. Retrieved from https://www.griffith.edu.au/__data/assets/pdf_file/0019/206560/Abbott2008-tenterfieldspeech.pdf

Ackland, R. (2011). Religiously follow the rules, or catch church in bed with state, *The Sydney Morning Herald*, 4 February. Retrieved from http://www.smh.com.au/federal-politics/political-opinion/religiously-follow-the-rules-or-catch-church-in-bed-with-state-20110203-1afbf.html

Anderson, G. (2008). The Council of Australian Governments: A new institution of governance for Australia's conditional federalism. *UNSW Law Journal*, **31**(2), 495–6.

Anderson, G. & Parkin, A. (2010). Federalism: A fork in the road? In C. Aulich and M. Evans (eds), *The Rudd Government: Australian Commonwealth Administration 2007–2010*, Canberra: ANU E-press.

Anderson, L.M. (2010). The paradox of federalism. In J. Erk and W. Swenden (eds), *New Directions in Federalism Studies*, London: Routledge.

Australian Government. (2015). *Budget Review 2015–16*. Retrieved from http://www.aph.gov.au/About_Parliament/Parliamentary_Departments/Parliamentary_Library/pubs/rp/BudgetReview201516/GSTDist

—— (2019). *Budget Paper No 3 2019–20*. Retrieved from https://budget.gov.au/2019-20/content/bp3/download/bp3_01_states.pdf

Australian Local Government Association (ALGA). (2021). *Local Government Key Facts and Figures*. Retrieved from https://alga.asn.au/facts-and-figures/

Beramendi, P. (2009). Federalism. In C. Boix and S.C. Stokes (eds), *The Oxford Handbook of Comparative Politics*, Oxford: Oxford University Press.

Blayden, L. (2013). *COAG*. Briefing Paper No 6/2013 NSW Parliamentary Research Service. Retrieved from http://www.parliament.nsw.gov.au/researchpapers/documents/coag/coag.pdf

Business Council of Australia (BCA). (2007). *A Charter for New Federalism*. [Policy Paper] 18 December. Retrieved from http://www.bca.com.au/publications/a-charter-for-new-federalism/view-all-related-publications

Commonwealth of Australia Constitution Act [Constitution of Australia]. (1900). Retrieved from http://www.austlii.edu.au/cgi-bin/viewdoc/au/legis/cth/consol_act/coaca430/s24.html

Commonwealth Grants Commission. (2019). *Commonwealth–state Financial Relations*. Retrieved from https://www.cgc.gov.au/sites/default/files/commonwealth-state_financial_relations.pdf

—— (2020). *Report on GST Revenue Sharing Relativities*. Retrieved from https://www.cgc.gov.au/sites/default/files/r2020_report_-_volume_1_-_gst_relativities.pdf

Cook, I., Walsh, M. & Harwood, J. (2009). *Government and Democracy in Australia*, 2nd edn, South Melbourne: Oxford University Press.

Doran, M. (2021). Why is the government debating a bill to keep National Cabinet secret? *ABC News*, 27 September. Retrieved from https://www.abc.net.au/news/2021-09-27/national-cabinet-foi-secrecy-exemption-bill-explained/100494880

Galligan, B. (2008). Comparative federalism. In R.A. Rhodes, S.A. Binder and B.A. Rockman (eds), *The Oxford Handbook of Political Institutions*, Oxford: Oxford University Press.

Hague, R. & Harrop, M. (2013). *Comparative Government and Politics: An Introduction*, Basingstoke: Palgrave.

Hamill, D. (2007). W(h)ither federalism. In *Upholding the Australian Constitution*, 19. The Samuel Griffith Society, pp. 43–56.

Hollander, R. (2014). Federalism and intergovernmental relations. In C. Miller and L. Orchard (eds), *Australian Public Policy*, Chicago: Policy Press.

Hollander, R. & Patapan, H. (2007). Pragmatic federalism: Australian federalism from Hawke to Howard. *Australian Journal of Public Administration*, **66**(3), 280–97.

Howard, J. (2005). Reflections on Australian federalism (Speech delivered at the Menzies Research Centre, Melbourne, 11 April). Retrieved from http://www.mrcltd.org.au/research/economic-reports/australian_federalism_final.pdf

James, D. (2000). *Federal-state Financial Relations: The Deakin Prophecy*. Retrieved from https://www.aph.gov.au/About_Parliament/Parliamentary_Departments/Parliamentary_Library/pubs/rp/rp9900/2000rp17

Koziol, M. (2016). Northern Australia Minister Matt Canavan backs poll plan for new North Queensland state, *The Sydney Morning Herald*, 28 March.

Martinez-Vazquez, J. (2011). *The Impact of Fiscal Decentralization: Issues in Theory and Challenges in Practice*, Mandaluyong City, Philippines: Asian Development Bank.

Menzies, J. (2013). Reducing tensions in Australian intergovernmental relations through institutional innovation. *Australian Journal of Public Administration*, **72**(3), 382–9.

Official Record of the Debates of the Australasian Federal Convention. Second Session. Sydney, 2 to 24 September, 1897. Retrieved from http://www.aph.gov.au/About_Parliament/Senate/Powers_practice_n_procedures/Records_of_the_Australasian_Federal_Conventions_of_the_1890s

Official Report of the National Australasian Convention Debates. Sydney, 2 March to 9 April, 1891. Retrieved from http://www.aph.gov.au/About_Parliament/Senate/Powers_practice_n_procedures/Records_of_the_Australasian_Federal_Conventions_of_the_1890s

Painter, M. (1996). The Council of Australian Governments and intergovernmental relations: A case of cooperative federalism. *Publius*, **26**(2), 101–20.

—— (1998). *Collaborative Federalism: Economic Reform in Australia in the 1990*, Melbourne: Cambridge University Press.

Parliamentary Education Office (PEO). (2020). *Federation.* Retrieved from https://peo.gov.au/understand-our-parliament/history-of-parliament/federation/the-federation-of-australia/

Prasser, S. (2020). A funny thing happened on the way to the National Cabinet – out goes good policy, one, two, three. *Australasian Parliamentary Review*, **35**(1), 141–56.

Ratnapala, S. (2014). Fiscal federalism in Australia: Will *Williams v Commonwealth* be a pyrrhic victory? *University of Queensland Law Journal*, **31**(3), 63–82.

Riker, W.H. (1975). Federalism. In F.I. Greenstein and N.W. Polsby (eds), *Handbook of Political Science, Vol. 5 Governmental Institutions and Processes*, Reading: Addison-Wesley, pp. 93–172.

Sawer, M. (2009). The trouble with federalism, *The Canberra Times*, 8 April. Retrieved from http://apo.org.au/node/6253

Sharman, C. (1991). Executive federalism. In B. Galligan, O. Hughes and C. Walsh (eds), *Intergovernmental Relations and Public Policy*, Sydney: Allen & Unwin.

Smith, D. (2013). How should we govern our big brown country? In T. Wilson, C. Carli and P. Collits (eds), *Turning Left or Right: Values in Modern Politics*, Ballarat: Connor Court Publishing.

Tiver, P.G. (1978). *The Liberal Party: Principles and Performance*, Milton: Jacaranda Press.

Wanna, J., Phillimore, J., Fenna, A. & Harwood, J. (2009). *Common cause: Strengthening Australia's cooperative federalism*, Final Report to the Council for the Australian Federation, May.

Williams, G. (2006). There's no denying the old buggy has lost a wheel, *The Sydney Morning Herald*, 5 July.

Windholz, E. (2011). Federalism in Australia: A concept in search of understanding. *Journal of Contemporary Issues in Business and Government*, **17**(2), 1–18.

CHAPTER 3
THE LEGISLATURE
Representative democracy

LEARNING OBJECTIVES

After reading this chapter, you should be able to:

1. Understand the historical evolution of legislatures in Australia
2. Explain for what purpose the institutions of state exist
3. Describe the key legislative functions of Australian parliaments
4. Understand the process through which laws are made
5. Identify the limits and variations of Australian legislatures

INTRODUCTION

When we think about parliaments and the legislature, we often find ourselves casting our minds back to the first 'parliaments', such as the fora of Ancient Greece or the Althing of Norse Iceland. Broadly speaking they were similar – a group of people coming together to make laws. Parliaments and legislatures have developed considerably since those times to be complex bodies, but the key idea of a group coming together to make laws remains. At the same time, we might also think that this collection of people is also somehow representative of democracy – but we need to be clear that just having a legislature does not itself mean you are democratic. A variety of other conditions need to be met before we would usually say that a country is 'democratic', though in the case of Australia this is generally a given. While other chapters will discuss the way parliaments are elected – the electoral system – and who gets to choose who the candidates are – the parties or individuals – this chapter will discuss the role, purpose and operation of the Australian Parliament, as it is the legislature that citizens, members of parliament (MPs) and parties all aim to attend and control.

Parliaments themselves are in reality a collection of people, however chosen, who represent the broader population. They are a key element in a democracy as they allow for deliberation and debate about the decisions that affect the lives of citizens. In this, parliament exists to make laws that govern the nation, regulate its citizenry, and raise and expend money. It is an advance upon the previous feudal system, which relied on fealty and payment of taxes and rent to Lord and King but provided very few with any say in who governed them or how they were governed. We call our own democracy a 'representative democracy' in recognition of the representative nature of the parliament, but it could just as easily be called a 'parliamentary democracy' in recognition of the primacy of the role of parliament (Heywood 2000, 172–4). Parliament as an institution is one that has developed over a long period of time. Importantly, parliaments are intended to provide 'good government', to provide the framework for the administration of law and justice, and to work for the general benefit of citizens.

The early parliaments had a restricted group of people who could be a member of the legislature, just as there was a restricted group of people who could vote in elections. They also provided the governing executive to run the colony, later Commonwealth and states (see Chapter 4). Originally the exclusive domain of property-owning men, the parliaments of early 21st century Australia now have remarkably few restrictions on those who can sit and serve (Parliament of Australia 2009). Where such bars to representation do exist, they are more a product of the party system (see Chapters 8 and 9) or of the vagaries of electoral representation (Chapter 7) than deliberate attempts to prescribe who might sit in parliament, or even vote in elections. The one clear exception has been Section 44 of the Constitution (Constitution of Australia 1900), which has at various times tripped up MPs who failed to comply with its provisions.

SPOTLIGHT 3.1 SECTION 44 AND AUSTRALIAN POLITICS

Section 44 exists within the Constitution to ensure that people who might be considered 'unfit' for parliament are not able to take their seat in the parliament even if elected. While this section of the Constitution was rarely invoked prior to the 1980s, since then several would-be parliamentarians have been caught out by its provisions. This was most obvious in 2017 when more than a dozen MPs resigned or were declared to be in violation of this section of the Constitution.

> **Disqualification**
>
> Any person who:
>
> (i) is under any acknowledgment of allegiance, obedience, or adherence to a foreign power, or is a subject or a citizen or entitled to the rights or privileges of a subject or a citizen of a foreign power; or
>
> (ii) is attainted of treason, or has been convicted and is under sentence, or subject to be sentenced, for any offence punishable under the law of the Commonwealth or of a State by imprisonment for one year or longer; or
>
> (iii) is an undischarged bankrupt or insolvent; or
>
> (iv) holds any office of profit under the Crown, or any pension payable during the pleasure of the Crown out of any of the revenues of the Commonwealth; or
>
> (v) has any direct or indirect pecuniary interest in any agreement with the Public Service of the Commonwealth otherwise than as a member and in common with the other members of an incorporated company consisting of more than twenty-five persons;
>
> shall be incapable of being chosen or of sitting as a senator or a member of the House of Representatives. (Constitution of Australia 1900)
>
> The MPs disqualified in 2017 were caught by subsections (i), (ii) and (v), with five being found to have dual citizenships in a large case before the High Court sitting as the Court of Disputed Returns in 2017 (see *Re Culleton* [2017] HCA 3 (31 January 2017), *Re Day [No 2]* [2017] HCA 14 (5 April 2017) & *Re Canavan; Re Ludlam; Re Waters; Re Roberts [No 2]; Re Joyce; Re Nash; Re Xenephon* [2017] HCA 45 (27 October 2017)). This has itself raised the question of who should be eligible to stand for parliament. The key question was whether you should have to renounce all other citizenships to be an MP – which in a country such as Australia with half the population either born overseas or with a parent born overseas, raised interesting questions about what it means to be Australian.
>
> **QUESTION**
>
> Do you think that Section 44 should be amended to allow those with dual citizenship to serve in parliament?

THE EARLY COLONIAL LEGISLATURE

Australia's electoral history is naturally entwined with that of the country that provided the bulk of the first white arrivals in Australia, the United Kingdom. Previous visitors to Australian shores were a wide and diverse group, from Macassan trepangers to Dutch explorers, but it was with the arrival of the British First Fleet in 1788 that colonisation began. The British parliament at Westminster provided a model for early colonial parliaments, and the basic principles were adopted as the colonies gradually reached a suitable size to need more formal government than can easily be provided by a governor. The first governments in Australia were military in nature, with Governors ruling the colony in New South Wales, initially alone and then with the aid of advisers, the Governors being the Monarch's representative. The advisers were appointed and served at the Governor's pleasure to assist in providing good government in the newly established colonies. The advisers themselves were first military men but were gradually supplanted by citizens in good standing with the Governor. From 1823 these advisers formed the first Legislative Council.

Through the early part of the 19th century the colony grew considerably. The increasing need for good governance, past that which could be provided solely by a Governor, meant expanding the original Legislative Council until it numbered between 10 and 15 at any one time. The Governor met with the Council to pass Acts to regulate such things as excise and currency, criminal justice, schools and the postal system. At the same time, new colonies were being founded in Tasmania (military outpost established in 1803, separate colony in 1825), Western Australia (military outpost in 1827, separate colony in 1829) and Victoria (first colonised in 1835, separate colony in 1850) (see Moon and Sharman 2003).

As the colonies grew, the demands to provide law, order and effective management escalated. Although the Parliament at Westminster in London still controlled affairs in the colonies, this was largely confined to external affairs (soldiers, navies, foreign relations and the like), even as English law was received as part of Australian law. However, the very different landscape and conditions required innovative thinking – whether to navigate the rivers, police the town and countryside over considerable distances, or provide services to far-flung settlements.

This necessity for an expanded bureaucracy brought with it a need to manage the colonies' finances. In doing so, the colonies developed tax and excise regimes to raise the funds needed to provide the various services. This required laws and an expanded legislature. The growing colonies established the new legislative frameworks as they expanded from the early coastal settlements and pushed into the outback.

The first of the colonies, New South Wales, established a Legislative Council in 1823 to advise the colony's Governor, which became a **BICAMERAL** legislature following the passage of the *1855 Constitution Act*. The creation of the colony of Victoria in 1850 allowed Victoria to implement a Westminster-style Legislative Assembly and Legislative Council, which began functioning in 1856. Tasmania created its own bicameral system in the same year. The other colonies, hived off from the original New South Wales colony, each founded their own legislative bodies. By 1890 all six colonies had a functioning legislature. When Australia was created as a self-governing nation in 1901, the colonial legislatures continued operating as they had done so previously, only now as state parliaments.

These legislative bodies were at first wholly appointed. However, these soon gave way to elected bodies, first as Legislative Councils and then as operating Assemblies, modelled on the English House of Commons. Suffrage (the right to vote) was at first restricted to men, with a 'property' bar ensuring that only those men who owned property could be engaged in parliamentary affairs, with only South Australia (from 1894) and Western Australia (from 1899) allowing women to vote prior to Federation. With the passing of the *Commonwealth Franchise Act 1902*, women gained the right to vote and stand at Commonwealth elections. At the state level this process was slower, with Victoria being the last to allow women to vote (1908) and stand for state parliament (1923). The 'property bar', where you had to possess property over a certain value, slowly disappeared, with Western Australia finally abolishing this requirement for Legislative Council electors in 1964. Various forms of racial qualifications also continued to exist until well into the 1960s, with Queensland the last state to eliminate restrictions on Aboriginal voting in 1965. While some restrictions on the right to vote still exist, 'universal suffrage' has largely been achieved, with the only significant restriction being the age at which a person can vote, along with some restrictions on prisoners.

BICAMERAL: A parliament that has two houses, such as a Legislative Assembly (the lower house or 'house of government') and a Legislative Council (the upper house – sometimes called a 'house of review'). The two houses of parliament are usually elected via different electoral systems.

REFLECTION QUESTIONS 3.1

1. How powerful is parliament?
2. Who should be allowed to be a candidate for parliament?

Response prompts are available at www.cambridge.org/highereducation/isbn/9781009108232/resources

THE STRUCTURE OF THE LEGISLATURE

As noted above, the early Australian parliaments consisted of a single house (styled as Legislative Councils), acting as advisory bodies to the Governors. However, this soon gave way to dual houses, with Legislative Assemblies being elected from the citizenry and the Legislative Councils being appointed. By the beginning of the 20th century most Legislative Councils were now elected, the exception being in New South Wales. The last appointed Council in New South Wales became a fully elected assembly following reforms in 1978. All legislatures in Australia are now elected, even though the manner of election varies between states and territories.

The powers and existence of upper houses were not, however, always accepted as positive or even useful. Former Prime Minister Paul Keating once described the Senate as 'unrepresentative swill'. The Labor Government in Queensland abolished the Legislative Council in 1922, and Labor attempted to do this twice in New South Wales (failing on both occasions). For the Labor Party, Legislative Councils were a conservative bulwark against progressive government, especially when fully appointed bodies. Following many reforms and the mostly failed attempts at abolition, proportionally elected Councils have now been accepted by Labor as part of Australia's institutional arrangements.

The houses of parliament

Most states, and the Commonwealth, have two houses of parliament. The original Legislative Councils continue to live on as the state upper houses in New South Wales, Victoria, Tasmania, South Australia and Western Australia. The upper house at the Commonwealth level is called the Senate. Most involve some level of proportional representation (except Tasmania), and so non-major parties have found it easier to be elected to them.

The lower house of parliament is called the Legislative Assembly (in Queensland, Victoria, New South Wales and Western Australia) or House of Assembly (South Australia and Tasmania). The Commonwealth version is called the House of Representatives. Each of these houses of parliament, with the exception of Tasmania, are elected from single-member electorates.

The two territories (the Northern Territory and Australian Capital Territory) are distinctive. They were not part of the original Federation but were created by Acts of the Australian Parliament. Neither are therefore 'states' as defined in the Constitution, but are considered self-governing territories, subordinate to the Commonwealth Parliament. Both have a single house of parliament, in the Australian Capital Territory a House of Assembly, and in the Northern Territory the Legislative Assembly. The Australian Capital Territory House is elected by proportional methods, and the Northern Territory Parliament with single-member electorates. Table 3.1 outlines the election methods for the houses of parliament for the Commonwealth, states and territories.

TABLE 3.1 HOUSES OF PARLIAMENT – ELECTION METHODS

JURISDICTION	UNICAMERAL OR BICAMERAL	METHOD OF ELECTION	
		ASSEMBLY/ REPRESENTATIVES	COUNCIL/SENATE
Commonwealth	Bicameral	Single member	Proportional
Queensland	Unicameral	Single member	(abolished 1922)
New South Wales	Bicameral	Single member	Proportional
South Australia	Bicameral	Single member	Proportional
Tasmania	Bicameral	Proportional	Single member
Victoria	Bicameral	Single member	Proportional
Western Australia	Bicameral	Single member	Proportional
Australian Capital Territory	Unicameral	Proportional	–
Northern Territory	Unicameral	Single member	–

Even within this, there is variation in methods used to elect MPs. As will be seen in Chapter 7, each state and territory electoral system has been a process of experimentation and evolution. For instance, while a number of states elect the Assembly in single-member districts, some (New South Wales and until recently Queensland) have non-compulsory allocation of preferences. While a number of Councils use a proportional method of election, some (New South Wales and South Australia) use a system where the whole state is treated as an electorate, whereas others (Victoria and Western Australia) use a system with a number of multi-member electorates (in Western Australia, 6; in Victoria, 8), with each electorate electing a certain number of MPs (in Western Australia, 6; in Victoria, 5). These electorates vary in size and in the number of electors.

Two important points to note are that parliament is often considered a 'gendered' institution and has only ever had a limited number of Indigenous representatives within it. When the Commonwealth Constitution was being negotiated at the Constitutional Conventions of the 1890s, all the participants were men. The Constitution, legislation and the informal conventions of parliament were all written, drafted and adopted with the considerations of men in mind, even while women could vote at the Commonwealth level from 1902. It was not until 1943 that a woman was elected to the federal parliament, and the structure and nature of parliament as a gendered institution remained largely unchanged. The variety of complaints from women MPs (such as Prime Minister Julia Gillard in her famous 'Misogyny Speech' in 2012) extended to the lives and travails of female staffers within parliament, culminating in the 2021 'March4Justice' campaign, after revelations of widespread sexism, discrimination and sexual violence within the Commonwealth parliamentary precinct.

For Aboriginal and Torres Strait Islander peoples, representation took a little longer. Neville Bonner is recorded as the first Indigenous MP, nominated to fill a casual vacancy in the Senate in 1971; although, a non-identifying Indigenous MP David Kennedy was elected in 1969. In all, 14 Indigenous MPs have been elected to the Commonwealth parliament, all since 1969. At the state or territory level, MP Hyacinth Tungutalum was elected to the Northern Territory parliament in 1974, the first of just 36 Indigenous MPs elected at that level (see Bennett 2017).

SHORT-ANSWER QUESTIONS 3.1

1. Why did state parliaments change from appointed to elected Legislative Councils?
2. Why do the territories and Queensland not have upper houses?

Suggested responses are available at www.cambridge.org/highereducation/isbn/9781009108232/resources

PARLIAMENTS IN OPERATION

Now that we have set out the differences in the various Australian parliaments, we should consider what is similar within them. Being a **WESTMINSTER SYSTEM** means that there are certain common features across the various parliaments.

First, bills are passed through both houses (except Queensland, Australian Capital Territory and Northern Territory, where there is only a single house) before becoming law as an Act. The set process for this, derived from the process used in the UK Parliament, means that a bill has three 'readings', during the second of which amendments may be made to the bill. The two houses must also agree on the bill when it is passed for it to become an Act. Finally, the Governor of each state (or Governor-General for the Commonwealth) must sign the bill – this last step being '**ROYAL ASSENT**'.

Following the Westminster precedent, the person who presides over the business of the various lower houses is called the **SPEAKER**. At the first sitting of parliament after an election, the initial task is to elect the Speaker, as the person who controls debate and generally manages the lower house. In the United Kingdom, the Speaker is generally considered non-partisan (although may well be a member of a party prior to election). The UK tradition is that the Speaker is not opposed by the existing opposition when he or she stands in elections, but of course after the election the Speaker may be changed. This tradition does not exist in Australia, although a number of Speakers have been well respected for their impartiality. The governing party usually nominates one of its own as Speaker.

In the upper houses, the person who presides over business is the **PRESIDENT**. The President is also elected after each election, in the same way as the Speaker, with the convention that the President will come from the same party as is in government. This may lead to the situation of the presiding officer of the upper house being from a party that does not have a majority in the upper house, and this has generally been the situation in the Senate since the 1980s.

In terms of seating, from the standpoint of the Speaker's chair, the government is always seated on the right, the **OPPOSITION** on the left, and minor parties and independents sit opposite the Speaker. This is mirrored in the upper house, on either side of the President. Ministers and shadow ministers sit at the front, with other government MPs arranged behind. From this arrangement derives the term the '**FRONTBENCH**', signifying the senior ministers. Opposition or shadow ministers also sit at the front (the 'opposition frontbench'), while those MPs not in the government or in the main opposition party are called the '**CROSSBENCH**', because of their position in the benches between the two main parties and opposite the Speaker. This particular seating arrangement is said to have originated at the time of the French Revolution, when the three 'Estates' were arrayed in front of the King (see Goodsell 1988, 296).

WESTMINSTER SYSTEM: A system of government in which there are two Houses of Parliament, and the chief minister and the Cabinet are drawn from one of the Houses. The model for this form of government is the parliament of Westminster in the United Kingdom. Not all Westminster-based systems have two Houses, but all have the executive drawn from the parliament.

ROYAL ASSENT: All bills must receive Royal Assent to become Acts of Parliament. This involves the Governor-General, or their equivalent at the state and territory level, signing the bill so that it becomes law. From this comes the phrase 'signing a bill into law'.

SPEAKER: The Speaker is elected from the members of parliament to act as the 'presiding officer' for the House. The Speaker's role is to allow for the orderly operation of the House, and the president of the Senate or Legislative Council is responsible for the conduct of the parliament as a whole.

PRESIDENT (OF THE SENATE OR LEGISLATIVE COUNCIL): The senator or legislative councillor elected by the Senate or Legislative Council to be presiding officer for the upper house. Like the Speaker, the president is responsible for the orderly operation of the Senate or Council, but also has additional responsibilities as the person who welcomes foreign dignitaries and the reigning Monarch to parliament.

REFLECTION QUESTION 3.2

What do parliaments do, and who controls them?

Response prompt is available at www.cambridge.org/highereducation/isbn/9781009108232/resources

THE LEGISLATURE AS AN INSTITUTION

WESTMINSTER 'CHAIN OF RESPONSIBILITY'

Parliaments based on the Westminster model, such as Australia, the United Kingdom and Canada, rely on the notion of lines of **RESPONSIBILITY** between the Sovereign (the reigning monarch) and the citizenry. This is sometimes referred to as the 'Westminster Chain of Responsibility' and forms the basis of 'responsible government'. At its simplest form, it is the idea that the Monarch is linked to the citizens via the ministers and parliament (Marshall 1963).

However, the idea of responsible government is more complicated, as even though the ministers act as 'Ministers of the Crown' – an advisory role to the Sovereign – they are drawn from the elected parliament and remain responsible to the people. The same can be said for the prime minister, who exists as a chief minister – also known as the 'first among equals' – and although nominally the second most important person in the nation, after the Sovereign or their representative, is the person whom we would normally call the leader of the nation. So, while the Sovereign (in the form of Queen or King of Australia – currently Queen Elizabeth II) is the Head of State, for all practical purposes the prime minister (in 2022 Anthony Albanese) remains the head of government.

Tied to the notion of the chain of responsibility is the debate around the 'reserve powers' of the Governor-General. As the Sovereign's representative, the Governor-General has the power to dismiss a government if required. It is their signature on election writs that dissolves parliament and begins the election process. It is the Governor-General who formally appoints the prime minister and ministers. The additional power is to dismiss governments. This power, a remnant of the days of powerful monarchs ruling their Cabinet, is generally only used on the advice of the prime minister. The dismissal of the Whitlam Government in 1975, part-way through its term, is the only example at the Commonwealth level, and Governor-Generals generally avoid engagement in overtly political actions.

The dismissal of the Whitlam Government raised an issue around how government could be made accountable to the people when there was no election scheduled. Allied to this is the question of how ministers are held responsible for their portfolio responsibilities. The notion of ministerial responsibility, whether as an individual minister or collectively as Cabinet, encompasses the idea that the minister is responsible for the actions or inactions of their department. The idea of ministerial responsibility is a long-standing convention in Westminster-based parliaments but is not legislated or constitutionally entrenched. This can also extend to whether they breach the relevant Ministerial Code of Conduct, or whether they are a suitable person to undertake the role. The intent is to ensure that ministers take responsibility for the actions of their departments, and particularly do not act in a corrupt, dangerous or damaging manner when conducting themselves personally or in their capacity as a minister.

OPPOSITION:
Generally taken as referring to the largest party not part of the government. The opposition members are seated to the left of the Speaker.

FRONTBENCH:
The collective term for those members of parliament (MPs) holding ministerial responsibilities. Those MPs in the opposition who 'shadow' ministers (that is, who have responsibility of covering that portfolio area) are referred to as shadow ministers and sit on the 'opposition frontbench'.

CROSSBENCH:
A group of members of parliament who are not members of either the government or the opposition parties, so referred to as they sit at the bottom of the parliament facing the Speaker.

RESPONSIBILITY:
The notion that ministers are responsible and answerable for their actions to parliament, and ultimately to the people.

However, it can be argued that in Australia at least this notion has been somewhat in abeyance since the second Howard ministry in 1998. Ministers in the Fraser, Hawke, Keating and first Howard ministries resigned over issues as relatively minor as a non-declaration of a colour TV to customs – which led to the resignation of the minister in charge of customs. Since that period ministers have tended not to resign unless there is significant public outcry. This raises the question of whether ministerial responsibility is now seen as only applying when it becomes public or when a minister has a serious political disagreement with the prime minister.

CASE STUDY 3.1 WHO GOVERNS AND WHY

The first Prime Minister of Australia, Sir Edmund Barton, was not the first choice for the position. The first Governor-General, Lord Hopetoun, had preferred Sir William Lyne, a prominent opponent of federation. However, Hopetoun was prevailed upon that this would be an inappropriate choice. Barton appeared to be the obvious and best choice, and so he was asked to form the first ministry and to lead the new country to its first election.

In what was called the 'Hopetoun blunder', Lord Hopetoun, charged by the Colonial Office with establishing the first Government of Australia, but with no knowledge of Australian colonial politics, followed the Canadian precedent and chose the premier of the most populous state to be the inaugural prime minister. The premier of New South Wales, the newly appointed Sir William Lyne, who had just taken over from George Reid, was commissioned to form the new government, but he found that the other colonial politicians would not accept him. Lyne returned the commission to Hopetoun a week prior to Federation and, along with future Prime Minster Alfred Deakin, advised Hopetoun to call for Barton, who was quite able to form a government within that week.

The question of who has the right to determine who governs was tested again in 1975 with the dismissal of the Whitlam Government. In that instance, the Whitlam Government had lost its majority in the Senate and found itself unable to pass the budget. The Governor-General, Sir John Kerr, then dismissed the government and called for the opposition leader, Malcolm Fraser, to form government until an election could be called. What had precipitated this was the death of an Australian Labor Party (ALP) senator from Queensland, who was then replaced by a person not chosen by the party but the premier and parliament of Queensland. While legal, this was at odds with the convention of the day which saw the party choose the replacement, which was then endorsed by the state parliament.

The Whitlam dismissal again highlighted the 'reserve powers' of the Governor-General that allows them to dismiss a government, appointing either a new government or appointing a caretaker government until an election is called. The Governor-General, although a representative of the Crown, retains the power to appoint a new or caretaker government should they believe that an existing government cannot fulfil their constitutional duties. (Parliament of Australia n.d.)

QUESTIONS

Should the Governor-General have the power to dismiss the government of the day? How should a government be held accountable to the Constitution?

PARTIAL SEPARATION OF POWERS

Allied to the chain of responsibility is a partial separation of powers. Following the lead of earlier democratic theorists who proposed a separation of executive and legislative functions, the 18th century political philosopher Montesquieu formulated the notion of the 'separation of powers' to balance the various competing institutional powers against each other, as a bulwark against tyranny (see Kurland and Lerner 1987).

The notion itself is fairly straightforward and can be seen most clearly in the operation of key institutions in the United States. The three key powers are designated as the executive, the legislative and the judicial. They are located, respectively, in the government administration (the ministers and departments), the parliament and the judiciary. In the United States, the executive is controlled by the president, who nominates cabinet members (the ministers in charge of departments). The legislative body is the Congress, and the president's appointees to the Supreme Court are ratified by the Senate representing the states of the Union. The US Supreme Court can make judgements on the constitutionality of bills passed by the Congress, which also have to be signed by the president. The idea is that the three power centres (executive, legislature, judiciary) are a check against each other.

RESEARCH QUESTIONS 3.1

1. Are all systems of government the same?
2. Why should the executive, legislature and judiciary be separate?

RELATIONSHIP TO THE EXECUTIVE AND THE JUDICIARY

Since Montesquieu wrote of the necessity of the separation of powers to prevent tyranny, there has been a debate regarding the proper relation of parliament to the executive and the judiciary. This relationship, in an Australian context, is based on precedent and convention. Some specific elements do remain. The parliament is the maker of laws but requires an administration to oversee and implement those laws. It is therefore incumbent upon the administration (through the executive and ministers) to provide for the proper functioning of government.

Parliament also retains the role of oversight of the various government departments, and generally performs this role through its various committees. Because of the partisan nature of the lower house, this generally tends to be a more limited oversight in Assemblies and the House of Representatives. However, given that most upper houses in Australia are not usually controlled by the government of the day, a significant committee system has developed within them. For example, the Senate committee system allows senators to question both ministers and senior bureaucrats on what has happened in their department, whether funds have been well spent and whether policy has been implemented effectively. This can and has been used by opposition parties to probe the running of government, and at times to embarrass governments that may have wished for some policies to remain hidden or at best not discussed. The functioning of committees will be discussed in more depth in the next section, but it is important to note that probing by committees has led to changes in how departments function and can cause problems for ministers if wrongdoing or waste is uncovered.

However, the growth of what might be called 'executive government' has constrained the role of parliament as an accountability instrument and has meant that debates on legislation are often constructed around attacks from the government benches directed towards the opposition. The problem has arisen as government in general has grown. When government administrations were relatively small, dealing primarily with taxation, the court system and armies there was not a great need for complex administrative arrangements. When Edmund Barton became Australia's first prime minister he relied almost wholly on the previous colonial administrations, which themselves were primarily concerned with the regulation of trade and commerce. The first cabinet in 1901 had seven portfolios and the prime minister. The growth of government administration has created a new tension over how much responsibility a minister can actually have in respect of everything a ministry does. The creation and expansion of the politically appointed cabinet and prime ministerial offices now places an extra layer of staff in senior policy roles, on top of departments with thousands of staff. As a whole, this has led to the expansion of the role of the executive to effectively manage the business of government, and a corresponding delinking of the chain of responsibility (for a fuller description of executive dominance, see Chapter 4).

In relation to the judiciary, parliament has a more restrained role. Although the Attorney-General and Cabinet (all of whom are members of parliament) advise the prime minister on the nomination of High Court justices for appointment by the Governor-General, once judges are appointed the role of parliament in oversight of their judgments and duties is very limited. The Attorney-General retains a direct relationship with the judicial system as the portfolio holder and controls the administration of the court system. This has led to the Attorney-General, as the head of the justice system, being referred to as the country's 'first law officer', although the Commonwealth Solicitor-General is the person who leads Commonwealth cases on important issues, and particularly in the High Court. Each state has control of its own court system, so the states' Attorneys-General are in an analogous position.

SHORT-ANSWER QUESTIONS 3.2

1. What is the Westminster Chain of Responsibility?
2. What is the difference between the executive and government?

Suggested responses are available at www.cambridge.org/highereducation/isbn/9781009108232/resources

THE FUNCTIONS OF PARLIAMENT

Parliaments function on a number of levels, the most obvious being the operation of the modern nation-state. While parliament in Montesquieu's schema forms part of the three great institutions of the state, parliament in a Westminster system has other discrete functions (Kurland and Lerner 1987). First, the party or faction with the largest number of seats within parliament forms government. Second, parliament passes legislation. Third, parliament allows for the views of electors to be represented. Last, parliament scrutinises the operation of government and holds government accountable for its actions. In relation to the first point, the number of parties in parliament is in part a function of the electoral system. The political scientist Maurice Duverger formulated this as three key outcomes:

1. a majority vote on one ballot is conducive to a two-party system

2. proportional representation is conducive to a multiparty system
3. a majority vote on two ballots is conducive to a multiparty system, inclined toward forming coalitions. (Duverger 1972, 23)

Duverger was noting that Westminster systems, such as Australia, where members of parliament are elected from single-member districts, tend to produce a two-party system. This is not an iron law, but certainly it tends to reduce the number of effective parties in parliament, and governments tend therefore to be made up of one or two parties. One of parliament's key functions is to determine who governs. In Australia's case this has been relatively straightforward, with the effective grouping of parties into the ALP, Liberal Party and Country/National Party since the Second World War. In only one instance since the Second World War has a Commonwealth Government not formed almost immediately after an election, with the clear result being between the ALP on one side and on the other the Liberal and National parties. In the period prior to the Second World War this was more complicated, but the strongest tendency since 1909 was for government to be formed by the ALP or a combination of non-Labor parties.

IMPACT OF THE ELECTORAL SYSTEM

The electoral system tends to deliver majority to either of the two main political groupings, but this is not necessarily the case. For example, after the 2010 federal election, there was no overall majority for either the ALP or the Liberal–National Party Coalition. Negotiations ensued to allow the Governor-General to have **CONFIDENCE** that one side or another can pass legislation and provide for government. This is known as guaranteeing 'confidence and supply', where 'supply' is the money to pay for government services. These negotiations with minor parties and independents allowed Julia Gillard to form government, and as the Leader of the Parliamentary Labor Party to become prime minister. If Gillard had been unable to negotiate effectively with the minor party MPs or the independents, then Tony Abbott, as leader of the Liberal Party (and as such de facto head of the Coalition), would have had a chance to try to form government.

The formation of government involves choosing the ministry. In the Australian election system for the House of Representatives, as a preferential single-member system (see Chapter 7), the leader of the party that controls a majority of the House chooses the ministers. As noted above, this has been the leader of the parliamentary Labor or Liberal Party since the Second World War. The leader would then become prime minister, after advising the Head of State (in this case represented by the Governor-General) that he or she has the confidence of the House. The leader can then choose their ministry, who are formally appointed by the Governor-General. The same method has been used since the 17th century in the United Kingdom and is similar to how many parliamentary systems operate around the world.

CONFIDENCE/NO CONFIDENCE: If a party (or coalition) has the majority of seats in the lower house, it is usually tested by a 'no confidence' motion, which if passed means that a new government must be formed, perhaps with a new group of members of parliament or parties, or a new election being held.

CASE STUDY 3.2 FORMING GOVERNMENT AFTER THE 2010 ELECTION

The 2010 federal election took place to the backdrop of strongly contested policy framework and a newly installed prime minister, Julia Gillard. On 23 June 2010, the then prime minister, Kevin Rudd, announced that there would be a leadership spill. This had been precipitated by several weeks of uncertainty around first the Climate Pollution Reduction Scheme, meant to tackle climate change, and then the outcome of the Henry Tax Review, intended to instigate major reform taxation arrangements in Australia. Opinion polling at the time showed the Rudd Government being passed by the Tony Abbott-led Coalition. A furious 24 hours of internal politicking saw Julia Gillard emerge unchallenged as the new Labor leader and prime minister. On 17 July, Gillard announced that an election would be held on 21 August 2010.

The outcome of the election was to be a surprise to both sides of politics. While Abbott had been gaining in the polls up to Rudd's departure as prime minister, to the extent that the election was too close to call three months prior to the election, Gillard had been sufficiently ahead to be able to overcome the Coalition. The final results, however, surprised nearly all poll watchers (see Table 3.2 for the results of the 2010 federal election).

TABLE 3.2 RESULTS OF 2010 FEDERAL ELECTION

PARTY	% OF VOTE	SEATS
Australian Labor Party	37.99	72
Liberal–National Party Coalition	43.62	73*
Australian Greens	11.76	1
Independents	2.54	4†
Family First	2.25	0
Others	1.85	0

* Tony Crook was elected as a National for WA but sat on the crossbench.
† Andrew Wilkie, Rob Oakeshott, Tony Windsor and Bob Katter.
Source: Adapted from *Australian Politics and Elections Archive 1856–2018*, University of Western Australia (https://elections.uwa.edu.au/elecdetail.lasso?keyvalue=1577&summary=false).

The result was a virtual tie. While the ALP clearly had the most votes of any single party (the Liberal Party had polled 30.46 per cent nationally), this was partly complicated by the Queensland Liberal and National parties having merged as the Liberal–National Party (LNP). The LNP total above included Tony Crook who sat separately from the rest of the National Party, as a 'Nationals WA', on the crossbenches alongside the independents and Adam Bandt from the Australian Greens. This left the major parties tied on 72 seats with six crossbench seats, the first time since the Second World War this had happened.

Gillard as caretaker prime minister was, however, the more successful negotiator, successfully gaining agreement from three independents (Wilkie, Oakeshott and Windsor) and the Australian Greens to form a new 'coalition' government, with Gillard free to choose her ministry, and with the four crossbenchers extracting formal agreements for particular actions.

(See Holmes and Fernandes 2012 for a full description of the process.)

QUESTIONS

Should the party with the most votes or the most seats choose the prime minister? What if there is a coalition? Who should have the first opportunity to form government?

SHORT-ANSWER QUESTIONS 3.3

1. What are the key functions of parliament?
2. Apart from the Liberal–National Party Coalition are there any other coalition governments in Australia?

Suggested responses are available at www.cambridge.org/highereducation/isbn/9781009108232/resources

POLICY AND LEGISLATION

The second role of parliament is to determine policy and legislation. Any party or faction that has the largest number of MPs, with a majority of them providing confidence to form ministries, then passes legislation. While the government, as the operator of the public service (what would be termed in the United States 'the administration') can function on a day-to-day basis, it needs to formulate and pass Acts of Parliament. These Acts are devised to empower the various parts of the government to operate by paying their wages, causing actions to be undertaken or benefits to be made. Thus, an Act providing for education is required to first establish that there will be a public school system, then to build the schools, define how they will be run, and then to allow for the employment of teachers. This may be contained in one bill (what an Act is called before it is passed), but generally all the operations may not be covered because of the intersection of different parts of the public service.

The passing of Acts is often seen as the most important function of parliament, as it is what allows many of the public services that we often take for granted to operate. In Australia, with two levels of government constructed by constitutions (the Commonwealth by the Commonwealth Constitution, the states by the various state Constitution Acts) this means that both state and Commonwealth governments are empowered to pass legislation. Governments use this power first to collect taxes, and then to disburse those taxes to provide services and benefits. In the state governments and the Northern Territory government, legislation also empowers local governments (usually called councils) to make regulations for the management of local issues.

This leads to the broader activities of the parliament in terms of committees and public inquiries. The Australian Parliament, sitting in Canberra, can seem fairly remote from what the majority of Australians do on a daily basis. Canberra is a 'public service' town, with most people employed directly by the public service, or by organisations and businesses that support it. How then do members of parliament gain an understanding of the impact of their legislation? While some legislation may be seen as 'nation building', such as those to do with the establishment of banks, the Snowy Mountains Hydro Scheme or constructing the armed forces, most of the legislation considered within parliament is more mundane. Members of parliament have offices in their electorates and home states, but they do not see or hear from the bulk of their constituents, and they require some way of gauging the impact of (and desire for) legislation and regulation.

COMMITTEES

This is where committees and public inquiries come in. Both houses of parliament, the House of Representatives and the Senate, have **COMMITTEES**, either standing or select, that may be established by one or both houses (when both houses establish a committee it is known as a

COMMITTEE: Delegated group of members of parliament who meet to discuss and debate bills or matters of interest, so that parliament does not have to go through an investigatory or debate process as a whole. House committees are generally controlled by the government of the day, but upper house committees are sometimes controlled by the crossbench, so such committees often produce wide-ranging reports with more far-reaching recommendations.

joint committee). All committees are established with terms of reference passed by the house that establishes them and with a set time to report back to parliament. The operation of committees is governed by Parliament's Standing Orders, which covers the operation and proceedings of parliament (Parliament of Australia 2017). At the calling of an election all inquiries and committee proceedings are terminated on the issue of writs, irrespective of whether they have reported or not, with select committees being disbanded. Standing committees continue after the election, although the composition may change depending on who is in government and who has kept or lost their seats.

Standing committees can gather material, take submissions, and generally can look more deeply into the impact a piece of legislation might have, or whether it is even required. Standing committees can therefore work on existing or proposed legislation, and their reports are often used as the basis for new policy that may be enacted as legislation or regulation, or simply to propose better ways of government operating (see Phillips et al. 1998, 58–62). Standing committees can also hold inquiries into matters of public interest where an issue is of such contention that parliament decides it needs more information.

Either house can also establish select committees to look into particular issues on an ad hoc basis. The issues dealt with by a select committee are usually tightly focused on a specific issue. The select committee will also be established for a relatively short period of time, and it will report back to the parliament in which it was established. Select committees are often established to deal with new, fairly straightforward and specific issues, although they may also be established to provide a report that then forms the basis for legislation (see Halligan et al. 2007).

The House of Representatives and Senate also have a small number of joint standing committees that look at critical information that effects the operation of the state. One such committee is the Joint Standing Committee on Electoral Matters, which gathers evidence after each election and provides recommendations for amendments to the electoral system (the current Committee's work can be found at https://www.aph.gov.au/Parliamentary_Business/Committees/Joint/Electoral_Matters).

Of course, much of the discussion of committees relies on the notion that executive government really wants to know or understand the outcome of committees. The work of committees has expanded considerably over the previous 30 years, especially for senators who may spend up to 20 per cent of their time on committee work (Brenton 2009, 60–1), yet may be unwelcome news for the government. When committee findings do not accord with the government or party's agendas, they may be seen as obstructive. Equally, committee members may feel that the work they do on a committee is difficult, onerous and thankless. As the former Foreign Minister Senator Gareth Evans asked early in his parliamentary career: ' … is it enough that the committee … has simply created the preconditions for others to act rationally?' (1982, 83).

REFLECTION QUESTIONS 3.3

1. Are committees an effective way to test, review and revise legislation?
2. If committees are useful in determining the purpose and worth of legislation, why aren't all recommendations implemented?

Response prompts are available at www.cambridge.org/highereducation/isbn/9781009108232/resources

LEGISLATION

BEGINNING THE LEGISLATIVE PROCESS

In its simplest form, legislation consists of a title, a purpose, some definitions of terms used in the Act, and then what is being legislated. In the case of simple amendments or enacting bills, this may just be a few pages, or in the case of complex legislation, such as the various Tax or Social Security Acts, run to many hundreds of pages. Each piece of legislation, whether as a primary piece of legislation or as an amendment, has to pass through both houses of parliament (see Figure 3.1 showing the outline of the usual path of a bill). The process of constructing legislation, once done by MPs themselves, is now done by a legal team within the Commonwealth Parliament, called the Office of Parliamentary Counsel, and exists across a number of Westminster-based parliaments (Page 2009).

Most legislation, before it is proposed, will have gone through a lengthy policy process (see Chapter 12). That policy process will have discussed the reasons for the legislation, seen some debate among the public service and any other stakeholders, and potentially an inquiry on the matter. It will then be drafted by a team either within parliament or the department from which the policy originated (in the case of complex policy instruments), whose job it is to write legislation in such a way as for it to be interpreted to actually do what it is intended to do. The team that drafts the legislation generally involves skilled lawyers with a good understanding of the structure of law and, if necessary, a good understanding of the existing legislation in the policy area. The legislation is then sent to the MP who asked for it.

If the MP is happy with the draft bill, they may then decide to propose it to parliament. This is not as easy as simply standing up in parliament and requesting that the bill be heard. Because there are many MPs who may wish to put forward bills, and certainly a government and administration that wishes to turn policy into legislative action, the process is considerably longer. For bills proposed by the government, the process is such that their bills will get listed for debate. However, prior to a government bill being introduced to parliament, it will first have been through the Cabinet process. The relevant minister will have tabled first the policy underlying the bill, and then the bill itself if it is agreed to proceed. This gives the rest of the Cabinet an opportunity to debate the bill and any objections to be dealt with. The relevant party room will also meet to discuss major bills, although all government MPs will have been informed of the legislative agenda beforehand. For the ALP, it would go to caucus when the party is in government, or in the case of a Coalition Government, to the Joint Party Room – which is the combined party rooms of both the Liberal and National parties.

These processes are obviously the model, and contentious issues may obviate the party rooms, although there may then be significant party room debate if the issue becomes a *cause celebre* in the media.

WHIPS AND VOTING

After the bill has been decided on, and prior to its actual introduction into parliament, there will be a meeting of the group of people who are essential communicators between parties, the 'whips'. The whips are those MPs designated by the parties in parliament to negotiate with the other parties and to communicate between their own MPs. You may have heard, in relation to the UK Parliament, the phrase, 'the three-line whip'. This is in relation to another function of the whip, which is to get MPs to vote according to the agreed party line. While Australia doesn't use a

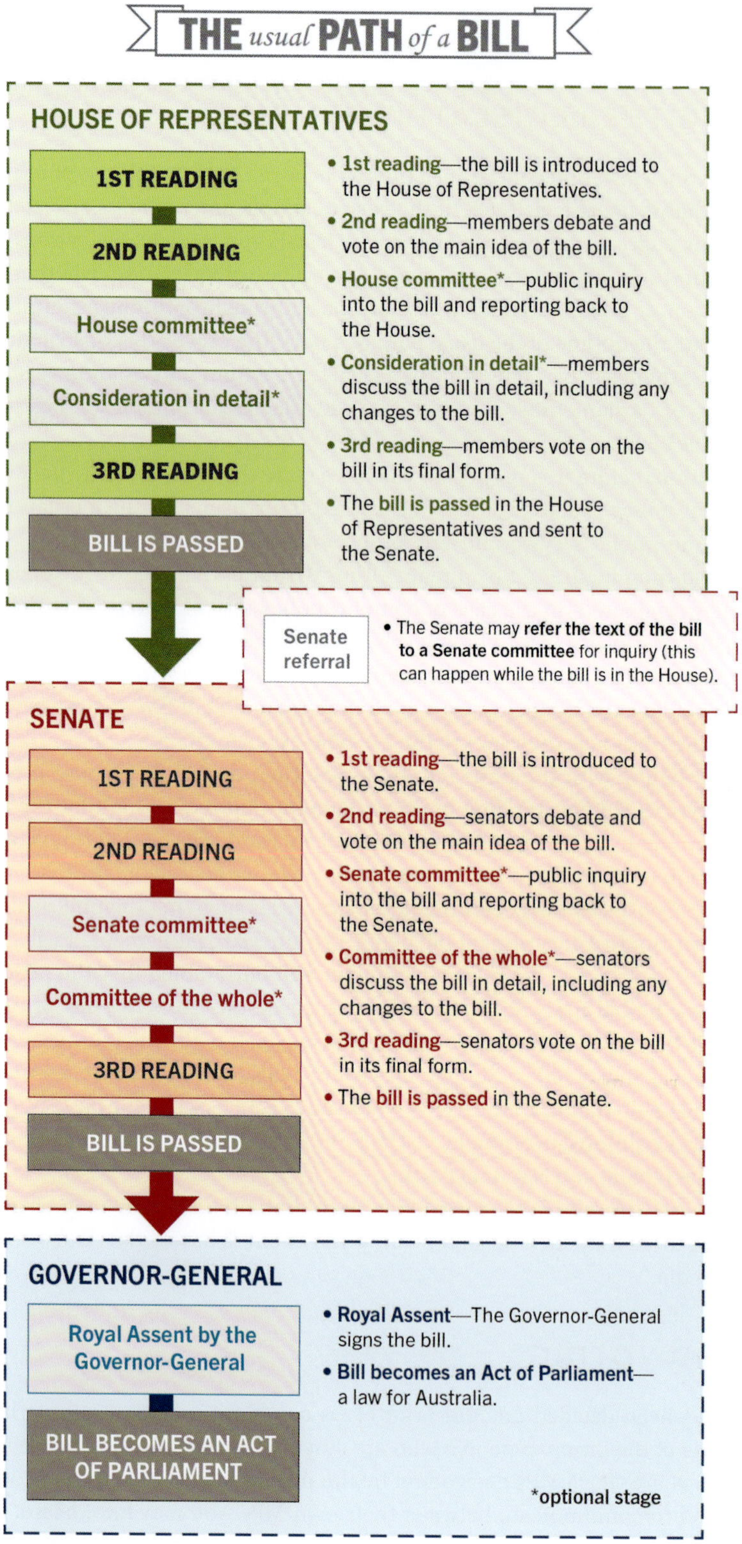

THE usual PATH of a BILL

HOUSE OF REPRESENTATIVES

- **1ST READING**
- **2ND READING**
- House committee*
- Consideration in detail*
- **3RD READING**
- BILL IS PASSED

- **1st reading**—the bill is introduced to the House of Representatives.
- **2nd reading**—members debate and vote on the main idea of the bill.
- **House committee***—public inquiry into the bill and reporting back to the House.
- **Consideration in detail***—members discuss the bill in detail, including any changes to the bill.
- **3rd reading**—members vote on the bill in its final form.
- The **bill is passed** in the House of Representatives and sent to the Senate.

Senate referral • The Senate may **refer the text of the bill to a Senate committee** for inquiry (this can happen while the bill is in the House).

SENATE

- **1ST READING**
- **2ND READING**
- Senate committee*
- Committee of the whole*
- **3RD READING**
- BILL IS PASSED

- **1st reading**—the bill is introduced to the Senate.
- **2nd reading**—senators debate and vote on the main idea of the bill.
- **Senate committee***—public inquiry into the bill and reporting back to the Senate.
- **Committee of the whole***—senators discuss the bill in detail, including any changes to the bill.
- **3rd reading**—senators vote on the bill in its final form.
- The **bill is passed** in the Senate.

GOVERNOR-GENERAL

- Royal Assent by the Governor-General
- BILL BECOMES AN ACT OF PARLIAMENT

- **Royal Assent**—The Governor-General signs the bill.
- **Bill becomes an Act of Parliament**—a law for Australia.

*optional stage

Figure 3.1 The usual path of a bill
Source: Parliamentary Education Office.

three-line system, the whips' role is essentially the same – to provide communication between the party leadership and its MPs, providing guidance and direction on voting in parliament.

The whips' meeting involves discussion of how the parliamentary agenda will be structured. In the House of Representatives, this is also the place where agreements about speaking orders and the introduction of non-government bills occurs. At this point, if there has not already been public discussion of the bill, the MPs get to see what will be introduced into parliament. Notice will then be given that at the next sitting of parliament a bill will be introduced.

For opposition and crossbench parties, the inclusion of any legislation they wish to put forward, or indeed in respect of questions or motions they wish to ask or move, is negotiated with the other parties at the whips' meeting. As the government has the numbers to pass legislation in lower houses, the opposition and crossbench business is usually far less regularly introduced or debated than government bills, questions or motions, but all are allocated some time. What this does mean is that it is rare that the opposition and minor parties get to introduce bills into the lower house, and they are far more likely to introduce bills in the upper house.

There are examples of Acts that have originated as non-government bills, called private members' bills – such as the bill to allow same-sex marriage in Australia – but these are rarely passed. There are also other types of bills where the whip is not applied as the bill is of a contentious nature. These bills, where party members can vote in any way they like, without fear of sanction from their party, are often called a conscience or free vote. An example of this was the debate and vote in 2016 on whether the Health Minister could regulate the drug RU486. Abortion law reform and voluntary euthanasia are two topics where conscience votes have occurred.

INTRODUCING THE BILL

Once a bill has a timetable for introduction, it moves forward to being formally introduced into parliament, with a 'first reading'. At this point, the bill is introduced by having its title read out by the Clerk of the House, and this is recorded in **HANSARD**. Usually, a motion will then be passed for the bill to be read a second time (the 'second reading'), and the relevant minister will give a speech about the general purpose of the bill. Debate on the bill is then adjourned until a later time to allow MPs a chance to see what is in the bill and to consider the consequences of passing the bill.

When the bill comes back from adjournment (which rarely happens for opposition or crossbench bills), this is called the 'second reading debate'. At this point the opposition will respond, with the relevant shadow minister or MP stating the opposition's position. Debate then occurs, with MPs speaking for or against the bill. At the end of the debate process, a vote is taken and so long as the bill is agreed the bill passes onto the committee stage.

HANSARD: The official record of the proceedings of each house of parliament.

THE COMMITTEE STAGE

On reaching this point, the bill may be referred to a committee for inquiry; the House may move into 'Committee of the Whole' – which allows the whole chamber to discuss the bill and agree on amendments – or the bill moves directly to the final stage. None of these options are specifically prescribed but will have been decided upon by the government and passed by a motion in the House. They will also occur in that order, such that if a committee inquiry is required, the bill will be sent to the relevant committee with a reporting timeframe for when it is to come back to parliament, at which time the report will highlight the findings of the committee and its suggested way to proceed. If the House moves into Committee of the Whole, the general outline of the bill is debated, but in a more informal setting than usual. At this point, each clause of the bill is debated in detail by the MP and parties, and amendments may be moved.

Once all committees have reported, amendments made, and debates had, the bill will be put to a vote. The vote in the lower house is generally a formality, assuming the government has a majority of the seats, but in the Senate this may not be the case. However, assuming that the government has the numbers, the vote will be taken, the bill passed, and the clerk then reads the title for the third time (the 'third reading').

RESOLUTION AND ROYAL ASSENT

The bill having passed through one house, must now move onto the other house. Assuming that the bill was a government bill, and so originated in the lower house, it now moves to the upper house. Debate then proceeds in the same order until the bill is finally agreed upon. At this point, the upper house may have made amendments to the bill as it was passed by the lower house. The changes are transmitted back to the lower house. Discussion then occurs between the two houses until a resolution is made and the final form of the bill is agreed.

The bill now makes its way to the Governor-General from whom it receives Royal Assent and becomes law as an Act of Parliament.[1]

As a corollary to this, the legislation passed as an Act can also delegate some of the powers of parliament to the executive to pass regulations and other statutes. These items are called delegated legislation. These regulations are formal powers of the government but must also be presented to parliament and they may be disallowed (that is, not agreed to) by either house. The term 'disallowable instrument' refers to these forms of delegated legislation.

SHORT-ANSWER QUESTIONS 3.4

1. How does a policy become a law?
2. Why are whips necessary to the process of passing legislation?

Suggested responses are available at www.cambridge.org/highereducation/isbn/9781009108232/resources

NEW CHALLENGES TO AN OLD PRACTICE

It is worthwhile thinking through these processes that parliament uses. The process outlined above has been in use since Federation. While parliament itself has a set of standing orders on the actual process, and can vary those orders as it desires, the general form of how parliament works has remained largely the same since the beginning of the 18th century. The question might then be asked whether these processes, developed in the English Parliament, are still appropriate or useful in the 21st century. The development of parties, disdained by the

---

[1] This process is covered in detail by the Australian Parliament House website: http://www.aph.gov.au/About_Parliament/House_of_Representatives/Powers_practice_and_procedure/00_-_Infosheets/Infosheet_7_-_Making_laws

writers of the Australian Constitution, has changed the process of debates. Developments in communication and travel have changed the way citizens can interact with their representatives, committees and even the government of the day. Governing in a globalised world has seen the number of bills being passed each year from less than 100 in the mid-18th century to over 200 in 2016, but with bills being increasingly complex and supported by regulation (Department of the House of Representatives 2016).

At the same time, the sitting hours of parliament have remained largely the same, even while constituency demands have increased immeasurably. Even if seats are not quite as big as whole states, the number of electors living in each electorate – well over 100 000 – means that MPs have many more constituents to meet, discuss, debate and interact with. The complexities of international trade, unthought of in the time of the British Empire, require large bureaucracies managed by ministers in the executive, still reporting and answerable to parliament.

REFLECTION QUESTIONS 3.4

1. Does the Westminster system help or hinder the operation of the executive in governing?
2. The process of parliamentary business is quite lengthy – why can't the executive just make the laws and the parliament ratify them?

Response prompts are available at www.cambridge.org/highereducation/isbn/9781009108232/resources

VARIATIONS BETWEEN STATES AND TERRITORIES

There are nine parliaments covering the nine Commonwealth, state and territory jurisdictions. They are different in size, structure and operation. For instance, the fact that Queensland, the Australian Capital Territory and the Northern Territory do not have upper houses means that the role and operation of the single chamber takes on a different importance from the other bicameral parliaments.

Table 3.3 indicates that as the population of a state increases so does the number of MPs in the lower house. This is because the key functions of government are assigned to elected ministers, and these ministers are preferably but not entirely drawn from the lower house. In the case of the three smallest parliaments, they are drawn almost exclusively from one house (in Tasmania, MPs elected to the Legislative Council are generally elected as independents). The number of seats required to govern –13 – is considered the minimum required to form a Cabinet, where there are enough MPs so that ministers are not allocated too many responsibilities. The minimum size of parliaments is in reality constrained by the necessities of government.

There is also no requirement for a set number of citizens per MP, so the representatives for some House of Representatives seats have electorates in excess of one million square kilometres (see Figure 3.2 for the size of the electorates for the 2016 federal election). The seats of Durack (1.38 million/km²) and Lingiari (1.35 million/km²) are currently the largest seats, but the former seat of Kalgoorlie (abolished in 2008) was 2.3 million/km² and encompassed some 90 per cent of the land area of Western Australia. If we consider that most inner-city seats are less than 50 km², the size disparity is extreme. This also brings difficulties for representatives from the largest districts as servicing constituent complaints – or even just visiting the various towns in the electorate – can be a major undertaking. Nonetheless, parliaments have resisted setting

TABLE 3.3 POPULATION AND SEATS BY JURISDICTION

JURISDICTION	POPULATION	LOWER HOUSE MPS	UPPER HOUSE MPS
Commonwealth	25 693 000	151*	76
New South Wales	8 166 000	93	42
Victoria	6 680 000	88	40
Queensland	5 184 000	89	-
Western Australia	2 667 000	59	36
South Australia	1 770 000	47	22
Tasmania	541 000	25	15
Australian Capital Territory	431 000	25	-
Northern Territory	246 000	25	-

* Commonwealth Parliament increased to 151 following 2017 redistribution
Source: Adapted from ABS (2020).

maximum sizes (or populations) for electorates, even as Western Australia and Queensland have used Large District Allowance[2] calculations as partial compensation for the lack of electors in the largest electorates.

During periods of electoral experimentation, seat sizes, district magnitudes and parliament sizes have all fluctuated. For instance, the Tasmanian Parliament has had as many as 37 seats (towards the end of the 19th century) and between 1959 and 1998 had 35. New South Wales Legislative Assembly elections between 1919 and 1926 were conducted in multi-member electorates. In respect of different chambers, Queensland itself had an upper house between the establishment of self-government in 1860 to its abolition in 1922 (Parliament of Queensland 2011). Single-member upper houses, present when both Western Australia and Victoria had dual-member seats where only one was elected at each election, have largely disappeared, and where there are two houses, they remain composed differently. Tasmania might be considered an exception, but with the Tasmanian Legislative Assembly being elected using a proportional system, the two houses remain differently elected.

Finally, the size of the Australian Parliament has grown from 75 to 151 members in the House of Representatives and from 36 to 76 senators. The ratio of members of the House of Representatives to senators is guaranteed by Section 24 of the Constitution of Australia (1900):

> The House of Representatives shall be composed of members directly chosen by the people of the Commonwealth, and the number of such members shall be, as nearly as practicable, twice the number of the senators.

The Constitution also makes provision that states may or may not be divided into divisions (electorates), and that the Commonwealth Parliament may increase the number of seats in parliament. Indeed, until 1948 Senate seats were allocated via block voting, not via proportional means, with a party winning all the Senate seats in a state if it won the largest vote in that state.

---

[2] http://www.boundaries.wa.gov.au/have-your-say-2015-proposed-boundaries-and-reasons/introduction-and-background

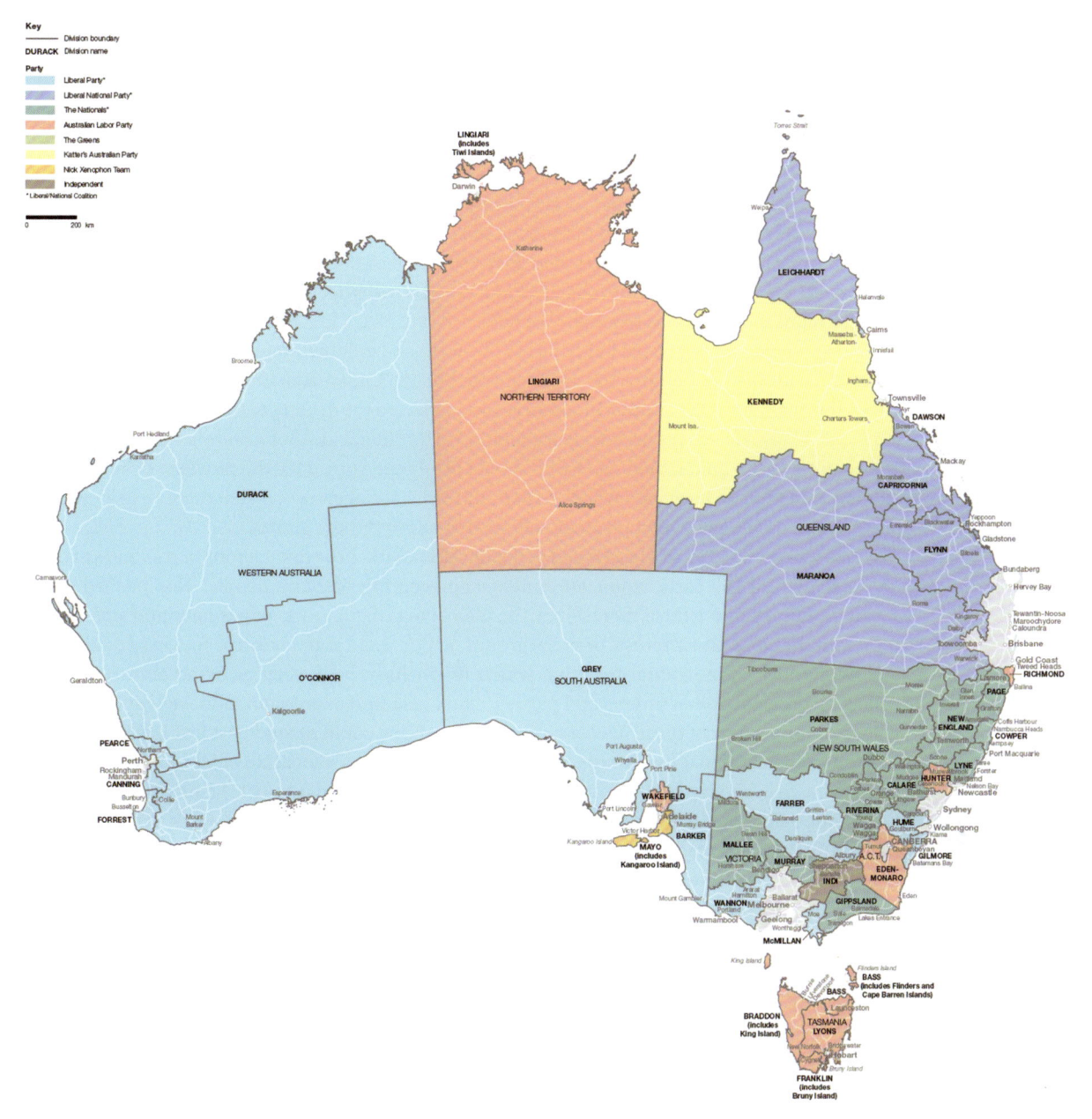

Figure 3.2 The AEC boundaries for the 2016 federal election
Source: © Commonwealth of Australia (Australian Electoral Commission) 2018.

REFLECTION QUESTIONS 3.5

1. Should the states and territories just have one electoral system?

2. Do single-member electorates help or hinder MPs doing their job?

Response prompts are available at www.cambridge.org/highereducation/isbn/9781009108232/resources

THE IMPACT OF ELECTORAL SYSTEMS

As we will see in Chapter 7 on elections, the nature of electoral systems, district magnitude and seat size can all affect the styles of campaigns and outcomes of elections. If we take Andrew Inglis Clark's desire for a fair electoral system at face value, and agree that parliaments should, as reasonably as possible, reflect the will of the people, then we need to consider how and why Australia went through a number of permutations, and why we have apparently settled on the systems we have now (Farrell and McAllister 2005).

The earliest English legislatures had MPs who represented town and city boroughs in the parliament. As boroughs grew and changed (and in some cases declined), it became clear that a solid basis for representations was required. The Reform Act of 1832 (first applied to England and then to Scotland and Ireland) began the long process of reform and enfranchisement of adults in the United Kingdom, with further Reform Acts being enacted in 1867, 1884 and 1918 (Phillips and Wetherall 1995). The Australian Constitution in some respects reflected the debates within the United Kingdom, but in other ways reflected a broader consideration of the liberal ideas of writers like John Stuart Mill. The changes in the understanding of who should be able to vote, once the province of landholders but now extending to business owners, renters and other social groups, meant there were increasing pressures on parliaments to implement policies that assisted these groups.

This was perhaps most clearly seen in the development of the first Labour parties in Australia, an outgrowth of the early union movement, representing working people. This pushed other social groupings to organise themselves, the idea being that a group of parliamentarians should represent the collective interests of social groups, which was a shift for former colonial politicians. The liberal idea of individual freedom, which might have been seen as being abridged in the collective organisation of unions and parties, could also find expression in the activities of those who chose to be part of these new organisations, and this could extend past just working men to include women and to other groups. The old English system of allocation of MPs by boroughs was replaced with even-sized electorates, use of the secret ballot, and from 1924 compulsory voting in Commonwealth elections. However, different states still adopted different rules over time, such that South Australia was the last to adopt compulsory voting in 1942.

While parties were quite fluid in the immediate years after Federation, and for a variety of reasons throughout the inter-war period, the impact of different electoral systems in the different states was not particularly marked in the post-Second World War period of party stability. There were long stretches of single-party domination, such as that which allowed Sir Robert Menzies to remain prime minister from 1949 to his retirement in 1966 (Brett 2003). At times, this single-party domination was due to gerrymandering (such as in the case in Queensland for much of the 20th century), but the good economic conditions in the long post-war boom meant that while there were occasional changes in government this was not generally the result of dramatic shifts in public opinion. Even when pressure to change the electoral system became overwhelming – as in the case of the Queensland gerrymander and Victorian and Western Australian province systems, all of which sought to entrench conservative majorities either in government or in upper houses – these did not necessarily indicate a desire by the public for wholesale change. However, this period of relative political stability began to break down with the arrival of significant minor parties in the 1980s and 1990s.

THE ROLE OF PARTIES

It is interesting to consider that in the writing of the Australian Constitution, the role and place of political parties was not considered desirable to have mentioned. In the early 21st century, as it was through much of the 20th century, Australian politics could not be thought of as anything but party politics (Jaensch 1989). While we will consider parties in more detail in Chapters 8 and 9, it is worth noting their role in particular developments within parliament. Aside from potentially making the formation of government far easier, they have also made the selection of who to vote for easier, by providing easy labels for electors to understand. However, they have also become gatekeepers as well, ensuring that some groups of people are not represented by the parties simply not selecting them to stand for election.

This is particularly true in respect of the role of women in Australian politics. The first woman elected to an Australian parliament was Edith Cowan, to the Western Australian Legislative Assembly in 1921. Women had only been given the right to stand for election in 1920, so this would seem to be a significant breakthrough, especially as Cowan was only the second woman to take a seat in parliament within the British Empire at the time. Despite this it would be another 22 years before women were elected to the Australian parliament, with Senator Dorothy Tangney and Dame Enid Lyons both being elected in 1943. Until the 1990s there had only been 13 women elected to the House of Representatives, with female representation only increasing markedly following the ALP's adoption of quotas for women, beginning in 1994. Since then, and with the ALP increasing the quota steadily from 25 per cent to 50 per cent, the number of women MPs elected from the ALP has now reached 40 per cent in the House of Representatives. However, the Liberal party has steadfastly opposed quotas arguing MPs should only be elected on 'merit', however defined. This has led to the situation where the number of women elected for the Liberal party has remained fairly stable at between 25 per cent and 30 per cent (Beauregard 2018). This pattern has been mirrored in the state and territory parliaments as well. While parties remain as gatekeepers to who may be selected to represent them, and with limited impetus or will to change, then the situation of women being represented on one side of politics but not the other will continue.

SUMMARY

Learning objective 1: Understand the historical evolution of legislatures in Australia

Parliaments do not generally spring to life fully formed – they have a historical base for their existence, and a rationale for the way they are constructed. This chapter briefly covers the historical formation of Australian parliaments from the colonial period onwards, and the path to the structures we are familiar with today. That also extends to the potential for ongoing change to how legislatures are elected and constituted, and possible paths leading forward.

Learning objective 2: Explain for what purpose the institutions of state exist

The institutions covered in this chapter sit at the heart of Australian constitutional life, as they are part of what we consider to be 'civic' life. They are critically important and are often considered the pivot (and veto) points for grand schemes and new ideas. The parliament is important in itself as the law-making vehicle, but then so are the courts as law interpreters and enforcers. Also, we need to recognise that systems are not static, and the history of Australian parliamentary politics is also a story of change, adaptation and experimentation.

Learning objective 3: Describe the key legislative functions of Australian parliaments

While Australia has a rich parliamentary history, it can also be confusing, and this chapter delineates those areas that can be most difficult in terms of understanding. In particular, attention is paid to the rationale of legislative control, as well as the processes of governing through parliament.

Learning objective 4: Understand the process through which laws are made

Laws do not magically appear – they have to be carefully constructed. The parliamentary process is at the end of a longer process of policymaking that extends into evaluation and future legislative changes. This process is iterative, and should involve debates, discussions and inquiry into what is best in terms of the Australian population and individual citizens.

Learning objective 5: Identify the limits and variations of Australian legislatures

That the state does have limits might seem self-evident – in so far that it has borders. However, the Constitution sits at the apex of the laws that govern Australian life, and so needs to be recognised as a guiding instrument that also limits what each element of the state can pursue. The variation between states – in size, electoral systems and policy processes – is itself both a response to and a test of those limits and is a challenge to governing Australia as a whole. Equally, the challenges that started in 2017 to MPs' eligibility to sit in parliament should be a warning that the Constitution covers all citizens, and that those at the heart of politics are perhaps doubly constrained in their ability to control the state.

DISCUSSION QUESTIONS

1. At various times, there are calls to make members of parliament (MPs) more accountable between elections – how might this be achieved, and what effect would it have on the operation of parliament?

2. If MPs are independent representatives, as in the Westminster conception of representative democracy, why is party cohesion and discipline so high, to the point of single parties being able to control the legislature?

3. Do parties all have similar policies? Is there genuine deliberation and debate over issues? Or is parliamentary business primarily a process of consensus and coalition building?

4. How is a parliament 'relevant' to most people – what makes any of the current parliaments in Australia work? Is it that parties have just grown stronger and are in control?

5. What is the potential effect of a more rigid role for the executive (the prime minister and the Cabinet) on the role of parliament, in the context of the Westminster system of responsible government, cabinet solidarity, and the role of the Senate as a house of review?

FURTHER READING

Clune, D. & Smith, R. (eds). (2012). *From Carr to Keneally: Labor in Office in NSW 1995–2011*, Crows Nest: Allen & Unwin.

Dryzek, J. & Dunleavy, P. (2009). *Theories of the Democratic State*, Basingstoke: Palgrave Macmillan.

Galligan, B., McAllister, I. & Ravenhill, J. (eds). (1997). *New Developments in Australian Politics*, South Melbourne: Macmillan.

Moon, J. & Sharman, C. (eds). (2003). *Australian Politics and Government: The Commonwealth, the States and the Territories*, Melbourne: Cambridge University Press.

Smith, R., Vromen, A. & Cook, I. (2006). *Keywords in Australian Politics*, Melbourne: Cambridge University Press.

REFERENCES

Australian Bureau of Statistics (ABS). (2020). *National, State and Territory population*. Canberra: Australian Bureau of Statistics. Retrieved from https://www.abs.gov.au/statistics/people/population/national-state-and-territory-population/latest-release#data-download

Beauregard, K. (2018). Partisanship and the gender gap: Support for gender quotas in Australia. *Australian Journal of Political Science*, **53**(3), 290–319.

Bennett, S. (2017). Indigenous voting rights in Australia. *Australian Parliamentary Review*, **16**(1), 16–20.

Brenton, S. (2009). *What Lies Beneath: The Work of Senators and Members in the Australian Parliament*, Canberra: Department of Parliamentary Services.

Brett, J. (2003). *Australian Liberals and the Moral Middle Class: From Alfred Deakin to John Howard*, Melbourne: Cambridge University Press.

Commonwealth of Australia Constitution Act [Constitution of Australia]. (1900). Retrieved from http://www.austlii.edu.au/cgi-bin/viewdoc/au/legis/cth/consol_act/coaca430/s24.html

Department of the House of Representatives. (2016). *Work of the Session*. Canberra: Department of the House of Representatives. Retrieved from https://www.aph.gov.au/About_Parliament/House_of_Representatives/Powers_practice_and_procedure/Work_of_the_Session#43P

Duverger, M. (1972). Factors in a two–party and multiparty system. In M. Duverger (ed.), *Party Politics and Pressure Groups*, New York: Thomas Y. Crowell, pp. 23–32.

Evans, G. (1982). Scrutiny of the executive by parliamentary committees. In J. Nethercote (ed.), *Parliament and Democracy*, Marrickville: Hale and Iremonger.

Farrell, D.M. & McAllister, I. (2005). 1902 and the origins of preferential electoral systems in Australia. *Australian Journal of Politics and History*, **51**(2), 155–67.

Goodsell, C.T. (1988). The architecture of parliament: Legislative houses and political culture. *British Journal of Political Science*, **18**(3), 287–302.

Halligan, J., Miller, R. & Power, J. (2007). *Parliament in the Twenty-first Century: Institutional Reform and Emerging Roles*, Carlton: Melbourne University Press.

Heywood, A. (2000). *Key Concepts in Politics*, Basingstoke: Palgrave Macmillan.

Holmes, B. & Fernandes, S. (2012). *2010 Federal Election: A brief history*, Research Paper No. 8, 2011–12, Parliamentary Library. Canberra: Department of Parliamentary Services. Retrieved from https://apo.org.au/sites/default/files/resource-files/2012-03/apo-nid28574.pdf

Jaensch, D. (1989). *Power Politics: Australia's Party System*, 2nd edn, Sydney: Allen & Unwin.

Kurland, P.B. & Lerner, R. (1987). The separation of powers. In P. Kurland and R. Lerner (eds), *The Founders' Constitution*, Chicago: University of Chicago Press. Retrieved from http://press-pubs.uchicago.edu/founders/documents/v1ch10I.html

Marshall, G. (1963). Ministerial responsibility. *The Political Quarterly*, **34**(3), 256–68. Retrieved from http://onlinelibrary.wiley.com/doi/10.1111/j.1467-923X.1963.tb01946.x/full

Moon, J. & Sharman, C. (eds). (2003). *Australian Politics and Government: The Commonwealth, the States and the Territories*, Melbourne: Cambridge University Press.

Page, E. (2009). Their word is law: Parliamentary Counsel and creative policy analysis. *Public Law*, **4**, 790–811.

Parliament of Australia. (n.d.). *House of Representatives Practice: Powers and Functions of the Governor General.* Retrieved from https://www.aph.gov.au/About_Parliament/House_of_Representatives/Powers_practice_and_procedure/Practice7/HTML/Chapter1/Powers_and_Functions_of_the_Governor-General

—— (2009). *The First Federal Election.* Website exhibition 'For peace, order and good government'. Retrieved from http://exhibitions.senate.gov.au/pogg/election/first_election.htm

—— (2017). *Annotated Standing Orders of the Australian Senate Chapter 5 – Standing and Select Committees.* Retrieved from http://www.aph.gov.au/About_Parliament/Senate/Powers_practice_n_procedures/aso/so025

Parliament of Queensland. (2011). *Legislative Council Chamber.* Retrieved from https://www.parliament.qld.gov.au/explore/history/parliament-house/inside-parliament-house/legislative-council-chamber

Phillips, H., Black, D., Bott, B. & Fischer, T. (1998). *Representing the People: Parliamentary Government in Western Australia*, Fremantle: Fremantle Arts Press.

Phillips, J.A. & Wetherall, C. (1995). The Great Reform Act of 1832 and the political modernisation of England. *American Historical Review*, **100**(2), 411–36. Retrieved from https://www.jstor.org/stable/2169005?seq=1#page_scan_tab_contents

CHAPTER 4
THE EXECUTIVE
Functions, power and accountability

LEARNING OBJECTIVES

After reading this chapter, you should be able to:

1. Explain what executive power is and distinguish between the political and administrative wings of the executive
2. Describe the main functions the political executive performs
3. Understand the key features of the role of the prime minister and the Cabinet and explain the relationship between them
4. Describe the tensions between executive power and accountability, and how they are manifested in Australia's system of government

INTRODUCTION

In Australia, executive power is concentrated in the roles of the prime minister and the Cabinet – the body of senior ministers who provide leadership for the government and departments of state. Executive power is the capacity to 'execute' or implement political decisions and legislation. Although the Australian Constitution formally vests executive power in the Queen, which is then 'exercisable by the Governor-General as the Queen's representative' (Australian Constitution, Chapter 2, article 61), this executive power is chiefly symbolic. Real executive power resides in the elected government of the day, led by the prime minister and the Cabinet. When political scientists and journalists refer to *The Executive*, it is this government leadership to which they are referring. The legitimacy of the prime minister and the Cabinet's executive function derives from the fact of being elected to parliament as part of a party or coalition who can command a majority in the House of Representatives. Yet in recent years this legitimacy, and Australia's executive government stability, has been called into question.

In the period between 2010 and 2018, for example, Australia changed prime minister five times. The replacement of Kevin Rudd by Julia Gillard, and then Gillard by Rudd, was later followed by elected Prime Minister Tony Abbott's ousting by Malcolm Turnbull who in turn was replaced by Scott Morrison. All these political executions were met with a degree of public irritation and hostility. How could it be that a prime minister, with a mandate to govern, is deposed outside of a new election? Is it not voters who choose an executive government led by a particular prime minister, rather than that prime minister's parliamentary colleagues? The frequency with which these sorts of questions are asked speaks to the degree to which Australia's prime ministers have become the focus of the public's political attention and preferences (Weller 2005, 35). This trend is sometimes identified with a growing 'presidentialisation', which is often viewed as a key challenge to Australia's parliamentary form of executive government. While there is undoubtedly much truth to such claims, they can sometimes underestimate the extent to which Australia's prime ministers are beholden to their party, parliamentary party room/caucus (all of their members of parliament (MPs) and senators) and the Cabinet. Between elections, it is the latter that ultimately determines if a prime minister remains in the top job.

In this chapter, we examine these issues in more detail. We begin with defining executive power and distinguishing between the political and administrative wings of executive government. We continue with a consideration of the functions that the executive government serves. The chapter then delves deeper into the heart of Australia's executive government, examining the key features of the roles of the prime minister and the Cabinet, and the relationship between them. We end by considering the tensions between executive power and accountability.

POLITICAL EXECUTIVE VS ADMINISTRATIVE EXECUTIVE

In discussing the executive in modern systems of government, it is helpful to make a distinction between its political and administrative arms. The former refers to that branch of the executive that has responsibility for making decisions about policy and, at the federal level, responding to national challenges as they arise. In Australia and other parliamentary systems, this is the **PRIME MINISTER** and the **CABINET** (in each Australian state, it is the premier and the Cabinet). In addition to the Cabinet, there is also an outer ministry composed of ministerial portfolios deemed to be of lesser importance, and whose ministers only attend Cabinet meetings when needed and invited. The **ADMINISTRATIVE EXECUTIVE**, by contrast, refers to the various branches of the state that have responsibility for administering policy and law in particular spheres. The public service or bureaucracy, as it is sometimes called, and its various subdivisions into health, education, finance, defence, trade, foreign affairs, police and justice and so on, constitutes the administrative wing of the executive. While there is a degree of overlap between the two wings – in that senior civil servants often play a substantial role in policy formulation – formal power resides in the elected **POLITICAL EXECUTIVE**.

SHORT-ANSWER QUESTIONS 4.1

1. What is a minister?
2. What is the difference between the political and administrative executive?

Suggested responses are available at www.cambridge.org/highereducation/isbn/9781009108232/resources

THE POLITICAL EXECUTIVE

As a constitutional monarchy, executive political power in Australia is formally vested in the Queen, who is also Head of State. The monarchy's formal **EXECUTIVE POWER** is 'exercisable by the Governor-General as the Queen's representative' (Australian Constitution, Chapter 2, article 61). The **GOVERNOR-GENERAL** acts on advice from his or her ministers, organised into a Federal Executive Council (FEC), which typically meets fortnightly to formalise or ratify decisions taken by the government (i.e. Cabinet). As the legal personality of the government of the day, and more specifically Cabinet, the FEC gives legal expression to the decisions governments make given the FEC is named in the Constitution and the Cabinet is not (Boyce 2007, 195). This is an institutional residue of the colonial governments prior to Federation, and before that the Westminster system in the United Kingdom as it had developed from the second half of the 17th century. At that time, executive power had shifted decisively from the monarch to parliament and its ministers. Increasingly, real executive power came to reside with parliament, while the monarch played a chiefly symbolic role as the personification of state unity.

THE GOVERNOR-GENERAL

A superficial reading of Australia's written Constitution can give the impression that it is the Governor-General, on behalf of the Queen, who exercises real executive power, rather than the prime minister and the Cabinet – neither of which is even mentioned in the Constitution. But this is not the case. Constitutional convention, which is no less a part of Australia's constitutional order than is the written Constitution, dictates that the Governor-General's role is chiefly symbolic, signifying unity of the nation and presiding over various ceremonial tasks such as swearing in ministers (Maddox 1996, 480–2). The Crown, whose local representative

PRIME MINISTER: The head of the political executive and government, by virtue of the fact that the party that they lead has the confidence of a majority of members in the House of Representatives.

CABINET: The government's central leadership and decision-making body that includes ministers responsible for government departments, and which is chaired by the prime minister.

ADMINISTRATIVE EXECUTIVE: The public service wing of the executive branch of government, which is responsible for the administration of the machinery of state.

POLITICAL EXECUTIVE: The wing of the executive that provides political leadership for the political community, which is distinguishable from the administrative executive.

EXECUTIVE POWER: The capacity to execute or implement political decisions on behalf of a given political community.

GOVERNOR-GENERAL: Australia's Monarch is represented in his/her absence by a Governor-General who has extensive, constitutionally given executive powers. Convention requires these be used only as the prime minister advises.

is the Governor-General, is above politics. Moreover, convention dictates that the Governor-General must take advice from his or her ministers – the elected government of the day, enjoying the confidence of a majority in the House of Representatives. This is why, among many other reasons, the 1975 dissolving of Gough Whitlam's democratically elected Labor Government by the unelected representative of a European hereditary monarch was so controversial (Sexton 2005, 239–62). In taking the decision to terminate Gough Whitlam's commission to form a government, while inviting Malcolm Fraser to be the interim prime minister despite leading a party/coalition that was in a minority in the House of Representatives, the Governor-General Sir John Kerr seemed to usurp executive powers that more properly belonged to the prime minister and the Cabinet. He did so without the advice of ministers from the party still enjoying a majority in the House of Representatives.

THE CABINET AND THE PRIME MINISTER

If the executive role of the Governor-General is chiefly symbolic and ceremonial in parliamentary democracies like Australia, then real executive power resides with the Cabinet and the prime minister. The Cabinet, as already intimated, is a body comprising senior ministers who make the key decisions about overall government policy. Each minister sits at the head of one or more government departments (such as finance, education, human services) and has responsibility for the effective functioning of that department and its implementation of government policy. Following the Westminster model, Cabinet ministers are always elected members of parliament and are ultimately responsible to parliament (this inevitably means the two are heavily intertwined, so some parts of this chapter are also explored in Chapter 3). This Westminster arrangement is unlike presidential systems such as the United States, where Cabinet secretaries are unelected officials appointed by and serving the president. This gives Cabinet ministers in Australia a legitimacy and power that their counterparts in the United States lack, especially as prime ministers lack the fixed term and personal mandate of presidents. That said, the prime minister powerfully shapes the composition of Cabinet in Australia's system of government.

The prime minister stands at the summit of executive power in Australia and is the head of government. Their power derives from being the leader of the party, or a Coalition of parties in the case of the Liberal–National Coalition, enjoying the confidence of a majority in the House of Representatives. This being so, the prime minister exercises both executive and legislative power, reflecting the fact that these functions are fused in the Australian system. In exercising these powers, the prime minister's key relationship and managerial challenge is with their own Cabinet and political party. Here the prime minister has historically been understood as first among equals (*primus inter pares*), though many have suggested that this has changed as recent prime ministers have concentrated greater power in their hands, often at the expense of the Cabinets that they lead (Kefford 2013; Weller 1985). This vexed issue is discussed below.

The biggest opposition party (or coalition of parties) in the House of Representatives presents itself as an alternative government. This takes the form of a **SHADOW CABINET** containing a team of shadow ministers, mirroring the government's ministerial team and developing their own policy program. The shadow Cabinet is led by the leader of the opposition who is effectively the alternative prime minister, should the opposition win the next election. The shadow Cabinet's other key role is to hold governments accountable, especially through parliament.

SHADOW CABINET: The team of spokespeople, known as shadow ministers, offered by the main opposition party, which scrutinises government and offers itself to the public as an alternative government at elections.

REFLECTION QUESTIONS 4.1

1. In the constitutional crisis of 1975, did the Governor-General usurp executive powers that more properly belonged to the prime minister and the Cabinet?

2. Does a prime minister's legitimacy as leader of the political executive derive from their success in a federal election, or from the support of a majority of their parliamentary colleagues, or some combination of both?

Response prompts are available at www.cambridge.org/highereducation/isbn/9781009108232/resources

THE ADMINISTRATIVE EXECUTIVE

The administrative executive is constituted by a public service organised into government departments that mirror the organisation of portfolios in the Cabinet and the outer ministry (a minister may have responsibility for more than one portfolio). Sitting within, or sometimes alongside, these departments are additional government agencies (for example, the Australian Federal Police, the Australian Security Intelligence Organisation, Centrelink) that are ultimately answerable to their political masters, in the form of ministers. Thus, there is a chain of responsibility and accountability, organised in a bureaucratic hierarchy where appointments are ostensibly made according to merit, which stops with a minister who is responsible to parliament and ultimately the electorate. This is why Australia, following its Westminster forebears, has what is known as a system of 'responsible' government. Public servants serve the public by serving the political executive that the public has elected to govern. As part of responsible government, the public service is supposedly politically neutral, which should draw a clear line between public servants and their political masters. Indeed, public servants sign up to the Public Service Code of Conduct that requires them to be apolitical (Maley 2012, 238). Reforms to employment terms, the appointment process and the organisation of services since the 1980s have generated much debate about the extent to which the modern public service can be genuinely apolitical. (For more on these issues, see Chapter 6).

THE CORE EXECUTIVE

Modern executives are huge. They comprise not just ministers (around 40 in the Commonwealth Government), but tens or hundreds of thousands of public servants and a range of arm's length bodies such as the Reserve Bank. Clearly not all parts of the executive are equally involved in decision-making and designing policy, and not all are equally powerful. This gives rise to the concept of the 'core executive'. The core executive refers to 'the complex web of institutions, networks and practices surrounding the prime minister, cabinet, cabinet committees and their official counterparts, less formalised ministerial "clubs" or meetings, bilateral negotiations and interdepartmental committees' (Rhodes 1995, 12). It also includes coordinating departments, such as the Department of Prime Minister and Cabinet, the Treasury, the Department of Foreign Affairs, as well as the senior law officers, security services and the Reserve Bank. This hints at an important point: the executive is not a homogeneous monolith with a single view of the world. It is made up of numerous agencies and individuals with sometimes competing ideas and interests. The executive is a site of multiple internal political conflicts and tensions. Before considering this, however, it is important to understand the roles of the executive.

EXECUTIVE POWER AND ITS FUNCTIONS

Executive power can be defined, in narrow formal terms, as the capacity to execute or implement law and policy (Heywood 2007, 358). In reality, the powers of modern executives extend far beyond what this formal definition suggests. Political executives do not just execute or give effect to laws passed in the legislature, they also initiate changes to the law, develop policy, craft communication strategies, navigate national crises, conduct diplomacy with other states, make decisions about war and peace, and much else besides. If governance is about 'steering the ship of state', executive power is about who, or what, controls the rudder of that ship.

KEY FUNCTIONS

The key function of the political executive is, as we have already seen, leadership. It stands at the summit of state power, and shapes the political, social and economic direction of a given country. It does so by *executing* law and policy, as its name implies, but also by initiating and refining law and policy, and navigating the many challenges that a country and its citizens face over a government's term in office. The political executive functions as a leader for the government of the day and also for the machinery of state more broadly conceived. Beyond this general leadership function, the political executive fulfils a number of more specific functions. These include symbolic and ceremonial functions; public leadership functions, including managing crises and national emergencies; policymaking functions; regulating Australia's interaction with its external, international environment; and providing leadership for the public service.

SYMBOL OF NATIONAL UNITY

One key function of political executives is to provide a symbolic personification of a national community's unity, which is periodically reaffirmed in public rituals and ceremonies. Presidents, monarchs, Governor-Generals and other heads of state represent the nation personally. They are central to the reproduction of what Benedict Anderson famously referred to as the 'imagined community' that is the nation (Anderson 1991). Because citizens in modern nation-states can only ever personally know a handful of their fellow citizens, mechanisms are necessary for producing a sense of national community and solidarity in the minds of those who are otherwise remote from each other. Such mechanisms include symbols, rituals and ceremonies that emphasise the continuity of the nation through time. Our political leaders often participate in these events, and indeed cultivate them for their own political purposes, which provide a focus for our national imaginings.

SHORT-ANSWER QUESTIONS 4.2

1. What is meant by executive power?
2. What is the main function of executive power?

Suggested responses are available at www.cambridge.org/highereducation/isbn/9781009108232/resources

LEADERSHIP TO THE PUBLIC

Another function of political executives is to provide leadership to the public, particularly in times of national crisis. Prime ministers, and to a lesser extent their senior Cabinet ministers, present themselves as providers of solutions to national problems, no matter how acute. This involves not just advancing pragmatic policy solutions, but also fashioning particular images of leadership appropriate to the circumstances being confronted.

In times of war, for instance, a prime minister, irrespective of gender, seeks to appear strong, stoic and resolute, in the way that Margaret Thatcher did during the Falklands War (1982), and Labor Prime Minister John Curtin did in the darkest days of the Second World War (Day 1999). Similarly, in the wake of the Port Arthur massacre in 1996, and again after the Bali bombing of 2002 in which 88 Australians were killed, prime ministerial leadership demanded that John Howard act in ways that expressed the emotions of his public. In the first case, Howard channelled national grief and harnessed it to bolster political support for a government gun buyback scheme, which was widely applauded as showing resolute leadership. The second case encompassed expressions of anger at the perpetrators, grief at the loss of life, and a determination to take action to ensure that it could never happen again. In his Bali memorial speech, Howard said he spoke for '19 and a half million Australians who are trying however inadequately to feel for you and to support you at this time of unbearable grief and pain'. He continued, 'I can on behalf of all the people of Australia declare to you that we will do everything in our power to bring to justice those who were responsible for this foul deed' (Howard 2002, 1). As prime minister, John Howard was channelling the emotions of the public, and in so doing providing a focus for Australians' grief and anger and their determination that these events should never occur again. Trauma was thereby transformed into a catalyst for national identification (Hutchison 2010, 65–8). At the same time, such crises are opportunities for political executives to concentrate greater powers in their hands, as was the case after both of these episodes. Crisis management often involves and invokes security anxieties. These in turn are readily translated into greater executive power – through means such as emergency legislation that suspends usual judicial protections for citizens – to meet real or imagined threats.

POLICY AND LEGISLATIVE LEADERSHIP

Political executives also, crucially, function to provide leadership in the policy and law-making process. They formulate broad political, economic and social programs (policy 'platforms') within which specific policies are developed. In Australia, the prime minister and the Cabinet are central in navigating the passage of these policies through both their party room and the legislature, though often having to make compromises along the way. Compromises are particularly necessary when the government does not have a majority in the Senate, or when there is significant opposition from within the prime minister's own party ranks. Nevertheless, the executive normally has a firm hold over the legislature in Australian policymaking, controlling the legislative agenda and parliament more generally. This is because it sits within a parliament where its party usually enjoys a majority in the House of Representatives (though not always – sometimes minority governments are formed with the support of independents, as with Julia Gillard's Government from 2010–13). This contrasts with a presidential system where the president and cabinet members do not sit in the legislature and cannot be sure of a majority in either house. (For more on policy and legislation, see the section in Chapter 3).

In most liberal democracies, this legislative function of the executive expanded over the course of the 20th century, in response to the greater complexity of modern societies and economies, and under the whip of stronger party discipline. It would be mistaken to think, however, that all policy is exclusively a function of the political executive. Senior civil servants play an important role in the development of much government policy, as their expertise and experience are often greater than that of their supposed political masters in the Cabinet. Furthermore, much policy is also initiated by interest groups and their lobbyists, and then embraced and sold to the public by executive politicians (see Chapter 12). The latter present policy as being in the universal, national interest, when in fact they often serve the narrow sectional interests of those groups and industries that promote them.

LEADERSHIP ON THE WORLD STAGE

An increasingly important function of the modern executive is managing a state's interactions with its external economic and political environment. As a country that has always been reliant on trade, the importation of capital for investment, and the security umbrella of powerful allies, Australia was, from its very inception, deeply involved in international politics and the global capitalist economy. With the acceleration of globalisation in the second half of the 20th century, this involvement deepened. Consequently, the function of managing Australia's bilateral relationships with other countries, fulfilling its obligations under international treaties, and overseeing its security alliances and trade relationships has become increasingly important for the modern executive. The political executive also makes decisions about taking the country to war, a prerogative that both Bob Hawke (Labor Prime Minister 1983–91) and John Howard (Liberal Prime Minister 1996–2007) energetically defended when they mobilised the Australian military in the first and second Gulf Wars, respectively. In fulfilling the function of leading Australia on the world stage, the political executive is hugely dependent on a vast array of public servants – ranging from ambassadors and other embassy staff, through trade officials and military officers, to scientific personnel and various international emissaries – who, formally led by the foreign minister, collectively constitute an administrative arm of the executive in the international field.

LEADING THE PUBLIC SERVICE

This brings us to the final function of the political executive, which is providing leadership to the administrative bureaucracy. In Australia's system of 'responsible government', the executive branch is organised into different departments, each with a minister at its head. That minister, as part of the political executive, has the responsibility for leading their department in accordance with the demands of law and the government's policy priorities. In discharging this responsibility, they play a key role in overall policy coordination and are ultimately accountable for departmental failings. The buck stops with the minister, in theory at least.

Ministers do not have it all their own way. Ministers are politicians who come and go. They are heavily reliant on their departmental secretaries and other senior bureaucratic staff who frequently have greater competence and experience than they do. In addition to greater experience in particular portfolios, these senior staff often also have superior skills in navigating the many pitfalls that bedevil all bureaucratic forms of organisation. Despite this, it is the political executive that ostensibly fulfils the function of leadership.

To better understand this and the other functions outlined, it is necessary to deepen our understanding of the roles of the prime minister and the Cabinet, and especially the relationship between them.

SPOTLIGHT 4.1 BUYING MINISTERIAL ACCESS?

In May 2014, the Fairfax media published articles with the provocative headline: 'Treasurer for sale: Joe Hockey offers privileged access'. Among other things, the articles argued that the then treasurer, Joe Hockey, was offering privileged access to business people and lobbyists in return for tens of thousands of dollars in donations to the Liberal Party (Nicholls 2014). Donors were members of a campaign fundraising group called the North Sydney Forum, which was run by Mr Hockey's North Shore FEC, an incorporated entity of the Liberal Party. The articles observed that in return for annual fees of up to $22 000, members were rewarded with 'VIP' meetings with the treasurer. In other words, money could buy access to a minister, with the implication being that perhaps it could also buy influence.

When Prime Minister Tony Abbott was queried about these fundraising activities, he responded that 'all political parties have to raise money. Typically, you raise money by having events where senior members of the party go and obviously they meet people at the events' (cited in Nicholls 2014). The alternative, he suggested, would be that taxpayers would have to fund party election campaigns; an alternative that was clearly not appealing to Mr Abbott or those sharing his small government ethos.

Mr Hockey subsequently made a defamation case against Fairfax media, which was upheld in the Federal Court, and he was awarded $200 000 in damages. Interestingly, the judgment of defamation related only to the headlines on advertising posters and tweets, which Justice Richard White found defamed Hockey by implying that he was corrupt. But the judge dismissed all of Mr Hockey's other claims, finding that the article's content was well researched and factually correct. Given those facts, we can conclude that the article had shone a light on the murky world of political donations in return for access to ministers or their shadow cabinet counterparts.

QUESTION

Given the scale of executive power and influence, is it acceptable for political parties to seek campaign donations in return for access to ministers?

REFLECTION QUESTIONS 4.2

1. Should decisions about taking the country to war be the exclusive function of the political executive, or should the question be debated in parliament?
2. Is there a universal, national interest, the advancement of which by the political executive is beneficial to all citizens, or are interests always sectional and partial?

Response prompts are available at www.cambridge.org/highereducation/isbn/9781009108232/resources

PRIME MINISTER AND CABINET GOVERNMENT

A political executive composed of a prime minister and the Cabinet that they lead, as already noted, dominates Australia's system of government. But we have not yet explored these roles in detail or examined the relationship between them. In this section we deepen the analysis of the roles of the prime minister and the Cabinet, and explore the sources of possible discord between them, and what this can mean when the relationship breaks down.

MAKING A CABINET

The process of putting together a Cabinet is far more complex than picking a football team where the captain simply picks the best players. Assembling a Cabinet is politically fraught because the prime minister must reward allies, try to keep enemies on side, balance states, balance regional and rural interests with big city interests, accommodate factions and tendencies, and ensure some ethnic, social and gender diversity. Cabinets always include ministers who believe they should be prime minister and others who support those rivals.

Ministers are generally not experts in the portfolios they oversee, instead needing skills like decision-making, juggling priorities, managing interests, mastering detail quickly, management skills, and solid political nous. Given all ministers come from parliament (and one side of parliament at that) it is unlikely there will ever be direct expertise in all areas of policy. You can find a list of all ministers and their portfolios (i.e. departments) on various websites, including the Australian Parliament House website (www.aph.gov.au) and the Department of Prime Minister and Cabinet website (www.pmc.gov.au).

There are some exceptions to this generalist model. The Attorney-General is always a lawyer and the Minister for Women is almost always a woman (Tony Abbott was widely derided when he put himself into that role!) It is only the last couple of decades that women have been more than an occasional feature of Cabinet. The Morrison government included a record seven women in Cabinet, which was still barely a third of Cabinet. This was subsequently beaten in 2022 when the incoming Albanese Labor government included 10 women in Cabinet – approaching half the total (Butler 2022). In 2019, Ken Wyatt made history when he became the first Indigenous person to become Minister for Indigenous Australians. With the increased representation of Indigenous people in parliament in recent years, it is yet to be seen whether this sets a new expectation that the portfolio should be held by an Aboriginal or Torres Strait Islander person. The signs are positive though: following the 2022 election Linda Burney, also an Indigenous MP, took over the portfolio from Wyatt (Butler 2022).

The major parties have different rules and processes for assembling their Cabinets. In the Labor Party, the parliamentary caucus (all the Labor parliamentarians) typically elect its Cabinet members, with the leader then distributing portfolios, making it a process much more subject to factional negotiation and bargaining. The ballot is in practice a ballot among Left members choosing Left candidates and among Right members choosing Right candidates. This changed in 2007 when Kevin Rudd insisted that he would pick his own Cabinet, which ended up looking much like one the factions would have handed him anyway. It was key figures in this Cabinet who then toppled him in 2010, demonstrating the constraints of prime ministerial power. Liberal Party prime ministers, by contrast, have a much freer hand in selecting their own Cabinet, giving them tremendous powers of patronage. They must accommodate the agreement with the Nationals which will name specific portfolios as 'belonging' to the party. Beyond that though, Liberal prime ministers can distribute the spoils of power, promote or demote, and thereby influence careers and political outcomes, but this is all tempered by the balancing act political reality demands.

That political reality has consequences, because Cabinet has the power to push back against the prime minister, including the ultimate option of engineering their removal. In recent years, Australia has been dubbed the 'coup capital' because it has had a high turnover of prime ministers but only one change triggered by an election. Since 2010, Kevin Rudd is not the only prime minister whose Cabinet was instrumental in removing them. The same fate befell Julia Gillard, Tony Abbott and Malcolm Turnbull. Unlike presidential systems, prime ministers only serve while they control the numbers in the lower house, so when their colleagues say it is time to go, they have no defence. The link between elections and prime ministerial changes is looser than most people imagine, with just four prime ministers both beginning and ending their prime ministership at the ballot box. Three died in office and some, like Robert Menzies, genuinely chose to go, but most are either removed by their colleagues or gently guided towards the exit (Lelliott 2013).

THE PRIME MINISTER, FIRST AMONG EQUALS

Australian prime ministers are at the heart of the political executive (Weller 2013). They lead the party or coalition that can secure majority support in the House of Representatives and thus dominate parliament. They shape the composition and policy agenda of Cabinet, chair Cabinet meetings, and have tremendous powers of patronage that can be deployed as leverage in bringing their party room and Cabinet to heel. Prime ministers have the massive resources of the Commonwealth bureaucracy at their disposal, and they can use the Department of Prime Minister and Cabinet as well as their large personal staff to oversee, and thus control, the performance of other ministers. The prime minister is the government's chief political communicator and the main focus of media attention. Voters may or may not recognise members of the Cabinet, but they are almost certainly familiar with the prime minister of the day. This is no surprise. The prime minister, after all, wields the largest microphone in the land, with ready access to a media enthralled by the leader's every utterance. Prime ministers can call snap elections at times that maximise their chances of victory, and then campaign from a position of prime ministerial authority, with all the advantages that this confers. They claim to speak on behalf of the nation, a claim that is at least tacitly accepted by millions. In times of national crisis, it is the prime minister who is the public face of the government's response. They salve national wounds and channel the emotions of their public, becoming the repository of both hopes and grievances. The prime minister is, in every sense of the word, the *chief* executive of the political executive. Arguably the power of the prime minister has grown in recent decades as they have become an increasing focus of the media and the public, have grown the bureaucratic and personal staff, and asserted their authority over party institutions. (For further discussion of these issues see Chapter 10).

Prime ministers as political agents

The manner in which different politicians have occupied the position of prime minister, however, has been very different (Grattan 2000; Weller 1992). These differences are shaped partly by personality, partly by the circumstances under which prime ministers have secured and kept power, and partly by the institutional constraints that they confront at any point in time. Prime ministers are political agents of change and/or continuity, and their choices and leadership matter, even if they are constrained by institutions and structures. Prime ministerial leadership makes a difference.

Some prime ministers, such as Robert Menzies (United Australia Party 1939–41 and Liberal 1949–66), Bob Hawke (Labor 1983–91) and John Howard (Liberal 1996–2007), accumulated authority and power over their Cabinets and parliament that other prime ministers could only dream of. Much of this authority was derived from their success in leading their parties to successive election victories. Even where a prime minister is not especially loved and admired by his or her colleagues, as was the case with Malcolm Fraser (1975–83), delivering election victory, and thus electoral seats to party candidates, ensures a solid core of party and Cabinet backing that is only diluted when electoral support wanes (Maddox 1996, 207–8).

In policy terms, some prime ministers such as Scott Morrison (Liberal prime minister since 2018) have taken a pragmatic, transactional and reactive approach while others such as Paul Keating (Labor 1991–96) have led strongly on shaping the big picture with transformational policy. In both instances, of course, success is at least partly defined by the ability to sell the style and the policies to the party, the media and the public.

Some prime ministers have been brilliant performers in the cut and thrust of parliamentary theatre. Paul Keating was certainly in this category, and Malcolm Turnbull (Liberal 2015–18) was also seen by many as a strong parliamentary performer. Others were underwhelming at best and embarrassing at worst, including William McMahon (Liberal 1971–72) who was widely viewed as a poor parliamentary performer.

Prime ministers also differ with respect to their approach to the Cabinet and Cabinet business. Julia Gillard (2010–13) and especially Bob Hawke (1983–91), for example, were well known for their 'Chair of the Board' style of leadership, in which they sought consensus and were comfortable with delegating authority to others. Kevin Rudd (Labor 2007–10 and 2013) and Tony Abbott (Liberal 2013–15), by contrast, gained a reputation for micro-managing and political centralisation, which contributed to their respective downfalls. John Howard's (1996–2007) approach to leadership and the Cabinet fell somewhere between these two poles. He was a 'Cabinet traditionalist' for whom all of the big issues had to be discussed by the Cabinet, although over time 'he increasingly worked with an inner circle' to make decisions (Bennister 2012, 41).

Presidentialisation?

The propensity to work with a trusted inner circle to make decisions implies a political centralisation around the prime minister, which some view as symptomatic of a broader 'presidentialisation' of Australian politics (Kefford 2013). The presidentialisation thesis argues that although the basic institutional arrangements remain the same, prime ministers in parliamentary systems increasingly exhibit features that have long been associated with executive presidents (Poguntke and Webb 2005). Executive presidents claim an indivisible personal mandate to govern, and secure that mandate on the basis of an electoral process that is highly personalised and focused on the particular qualities of presidential candidates. They appeal to voters directly, rather than through the mediation of their party. They construct a political 'brand' around themselves and gather an army of political and media advisers who are loyal only to the president.

Similarly, it is argued, prime ministers are now the supreme focus of electoral campaigns in countries with parliamentary systems. The modern media is preoccupied with, and almost exclusively focused on, the qualities of the respective leaders vying for power (also see Chapter 10). Consequently, these leaders often claim a personal mandate to lead the country if elected and gather around them hand-picked advisers who may have more sway over the prime minister than Cabinet ministers or departmental secretaries. Moreover, in most circumstances, prime ministers are increasingly able to dominate their Cabinets and the broader political agenda because as the leader of their party they are the focus of a preponderance of media attention.

Clearly, the presidentialisation thesis illuminates important developments in Australian politics. Few would disagree that prime ministers and their opposition counterparts are the main focus of media in and between modern elections, and that they are the chief political communicators for their parties. Moreover, voters may formally be electing a local member, but for most it is the party and the party's leader that is paramount when making their electoral choice. If a federal election were held tomorrow, the choice for most voters would be about which major party leader should be prime minister, not who should be their local MP.

Given all this, we can agree with some of the central propositions of the presidentialisation thesis, though with a couple of important qualifications. First, prime ministers have in some ways always been as powerful, or perhaps even more powerful, than presidents, especially with respect to the former's dominance of the legislature. After all, they lead the party enjoying the confidence of a majority in the House of Representatives. Second, prime ministers, for all of the political advantages that they enjoy, vis-à-vis their Cabinet colleagues, are still vulnerable to being removed by their own party, in a way that presidents are not. It is this relationship between the prime minister and the Cabinet, then, that is fundamental to Australia's executive government.

REFLECTION QUESTIONS 4.3

1. In what ways are Australian prime ministers more powerful than US Presidents, and in what ways are they less powerful?
2. To the extent that we can legitimately speak of the presidentialisation of Australian politics, what explains this development?

Response prompts are available at www.cambridge.org/highereducation/isbn/9781009108232/resources

CABINET GOVERNMENT

Australian Government is often described as Cabinet government (Weller 2007). It is perhaps more precise to describe the Australian system as prime minister and Cabinet government, given the centrality of leaders. Nevertheless, the importance of the Cabinet – the executive leadership team constituted by ministers at the head of key departments, plus the prime minister – cannot be underestimated. Cabinet comprises 18–25 senior ministers, while a further group of about 20 junior ministers are not part of Cabinet. Generally meeting weekly, sometimes more, it is the political body that steers the ship of state. Cabinet provides a general clearing house for a variety of aspects of government: it shapes policy; determines priorities; provides leadership to government departments; discusses and provides solutions to the most pressing issues facing government; deals with crises; and attempts to resolve disputes between ministers.

Despite the centrality to the system and the power the prime minister and Cabinet wield, neither the prime minister nor Cabinet is explicitly mentioned in the Constitution (although Cabinet is hinted at) and neither has any legislative underpinning. Instead, taking their cue from the Westminster model, Cabinet and Cabinet ministers are governed by a set of principles that are central to effective governance. Although they are sets of distinct ideas, together these are known as ministerial responsibility.

MINISTERIAL RESPONSIBILITY

The twin concepts of collective ministerial responsibility and individual responsibility are seen as essential conventions of any Westminster system, even if many question how strongly they are adhered to. The former comprises several interlocking conventions which together allow Cabinet to present a united front to the public, media and interest groups, as well as allowing parliament to hold ministers collectively accountable for the actions of the government. Collective responsibility does this while still allowing policy debate and disagreement internally. Individual responsibility is the mechanism, which means despite this outward unity, each minister is also personally accountable for the actions of their departments including allowing parliament to scrutinise or sanction individual ministers as necessary.

Since the early 1980s, some Westminster conventions relating to Cabinet have started to be written down, firstly in the *Cabinet Handbook* outlining processes and rules for Cabinet, and later supplemented with the *Ministerial Code of Conduct* setting out standards of behaviour expected of ministers (such as not using a public office for personal advantage). However, as none of this is enshrined in law the conventions cannot be upheld by the courts. This leaves enforcement of rules up to the whim of the prime minister, which can cause much controversy – repeatedly for some, such as John Howard's early years in office and for Scott Morrison with several ministers.

There are frequent complaints from the public and media about the erosion of these concepts, especially of individual ministerial responsibility. These complaints even spurred the previously sworn political enemies of former prime ministers Gough Whitlam and Malcolm Fraser to write an open letter to the newspapers on the subject (Whitlam and Fraser 2007).

Collective ministerial responsibility

The central principle of collective responsibility is solidarity, meaning outwardly displaying loyalty, identification with the group and shared interests with it. Ministers must act as one and promote government policy with a unified voice. Disagreement in Cabinet is always presented by the media and political opponents as evidence of divided and directionless government. Ministers are obliged to publicly defend Cabinet decisions even if they disagree with them and previously argued against them in Cabinet deliberations. Similarly, all ministers take responsibility for the decisions of government and for the government's successes and failures. When decisions are made, they must be executed and defended vigorously by all ministers, and all ministers must take responsibility for those decisions. Collective Cabinet decision-making implies collective accountability to the parliament, media, party members and voters. In turn this all makes confidentiality paramount, so Cabinet deliberations are conducted on the assumption of confidentiality, meaning ministers must not discuss the content of Cabinet deliberations outside of Cabinet. Without confidentiality, it would be impossible to maintain solidarity and the united defence of government actions and decisions. Cabinet documents are not released for 20 years. Taken together these are core principles of responsible government, but they are often seen to be some way from the contemporary realities of Cabinet disunity and dysfunction.

These principles have several benefits. They allow the fullest and most open debate possible in a body that is always composed of strong personalities and diverse opinions; they allow Cabinet to consider sensitive information such as security matters; and they allow parliament, the media and public to hold the government accountable for its actions. Of course, all this can look like devious politicians with something to hide, arguing publicly for ideas they might not even agree with (and sometimes of course they really do have something to hide!), but without collective responsibility government would be extremely unstable, unpredictable, hard to understand and largely unworkable.

If a minister is unable to act in this collective way, the convention is that they should resign as a minister and move to the backbench, where they have more freedom to publicly disagree with the government.

This does not always happen though and occasionally a dissenting minister or an ally leaks details of deliberations to the media, which is a sure-fire way of corroding solidarity and destabilising the government. We will see below how leaking provides negative proof of the importance of solidarity and confidentiality. The breakdown of Cabinet confidentiality is almost always evidence of a larger government crisis, particularly leadership tensions.

Individual ministerial responsibility

As well as being collectively responsible for the decisions and actions of Cabinet, ministers are also individually responsible for the policies and programs within their portfolio. In everyday language that means they are answerable for everything that happens in their department(s), and if things go wrong the buck stops with the minister. In theory, the minister is thus responsible for every action and decision by every public servant within their department(s), although over time the practice has changed and, in reality, the buck often stops with ministerial staff or senior bureaucrats. In the Westminster chain of accountability, the way individual responsibility occurs is through parliament with ministers held accountable via mechanisms such as answering questions in the chamber and attending Estimates hearings. It is also why misleading parliament is traditionally seen as such a serious offence. In the modern world, accountability to parliament is supplemented with media scrutiny of ministers.

Rewind to 1901 and the Treasury had 41 staff and External Affairs just 16, so ministers could be across the detail and activities of every member of staff in a way that ministers cannot be today when departments often have thousands of employees, across multiple sites and with many in highly technical roles. So where once ministers could reasonably expect to be fully in control of all decisions and all detail, this is no longer the case. Individual responsibility has evolved accordingly, and in recent decades it has been a generally accepted principle that ministers must make every effort to be across their portfolios, to ask questions and seek information, but their accountability only extends to what they could reasonably be expected to know or have enquired about. Prime minister John Howard summed this up 'one particular flaw in a departmental procedure can't automatically mean that the Minister has got to resign' (Raffin 2008, 234). There is much debate over where the boundaries are in this and there are frequent controversies over who should be held responsible for policy failures and other problems. The so-called Children Overboard affair in late 2001 is a classic case where many people felt Prime Minister John Howard and Defence Minister Peter Reith could have done more to find out the truth regarding claims their government had made of asylum seekers throwing their children from a boat into the ocean and then done more to correct the record (Weller 2002; Tiernan 2007, 175). The pattern in this story echoes that of many, with the government defending the minister and the opposition calling for their resignation (Raffin 2008, 226).

The clear consensus, though, is that if the minister is personally implicated in an error or wrongdoing then the minister is responsible, and if appropriate they should resign. In 2009, Labor Defence Minister Joel Fitzgibbon resigned when it was revealed his department held meetings with a private health insurer headed by Fitzgibbon's brother, including meetings in the minister's office (Rodgers 2009). In 2016 Stuart Robert resigned from the Turnbull Government after allowing the Chinese Government to treat him as an official visitor when he was not (Henderson 2016).

Again, the boundaries for what is a resigning matter or who is responsible are not always clear. Stuart Robert has been embroiled in other scandals that have not resulted in his resignation, for example, claiming expenses of over $2000 a month for home internet (nearly $38 000 in total) (Gladstone 2018). In early 2020 the Australian National Audit Office published a report into the

Community Sport Infrastructure Program which found Minister Bridget McKenzie had used her ministerial discretion to award a large number of grants in marginal and target electorates, against the advice of Sport Australia which had applied impartial guidelines and drawn up a list of recommended projects. In one round of the program, nearly three-quarters of recipients had not been recommended by Sport Australia. The accusation from opponents and commentators was that Minister McKenzie had deeply politicised what should have been a merit-based program. (Snape 2020). In the end she resigned over a technicality.

SPOTLIGHT 4.2 HOME INSULATION AND INDIVIDUAL MINISTERIAL RESPONSIBILITY

Months after the Rudd Labor Government came to power in 2007 the world was engulfed in the global financial crisis, and in late 2008 the government launched AU$52 billion of economic stimulus programs, including the Home Insulation Program (HIP). The HIP gave generous subsidies for homeowners to insulate their homes (effectively making it free for many). The HIP had been designed in the prime minister's department but was implemented by the Department of the Environment, Water, Heritage and the Arts, under Minister Peter Garrett. There was pressure to deliver the program quickly, and it proved very popular, sucking new companies and workers into an industry with light regulation and limited training (which were largely state government responsibilities).

By early 2010 the HIP was mired in controversy: four installers died on the job; poorly installed insulation caused a series of house fires; and there were accusations of widespread fraud. The speed of the rollout clearly accentuated the problems. Changes had been made to the program through 2009, but pressure mounted on Minister Garrett, with February and March 2010 seeing sustained calls from the opposition and media for his resignation (Tiffen 2010). Garrett claimed he had acted on advice, asked questions, sought information, and had written several letters to the prime minister as early as mid-2009 expressing concerns over the program. In late February 2010, the program was axed.

Prime Minister Kevin Rudd immediately took part of Garrett's portfolio from him and transitional arrangements from the program were overseen by another minister (Hall 2010). When Rudd reshuffled his Cabinet later that year, Peter Garrett was demoted again. His political career never recovered, and he left parliament at the 2013 election.

A report by the Commonwealth Auditor-General found many failings in the department, including when Minister Garrett asked questions, the answers were slow to come; information was often incomplete or contained errors; briefings were overly optimistic about the program; and critical issues were never raised with the minister (ANAO 2010). A Royal Commission in 2014 similarly found that the serious errors in the HIP were at the departmental level and made no adverse findings against Garrett. In his autobiography, Garrett's chapter on the HIP is titled 'Fall Guy' (Garrett 2017).

QUESTIONS

Can a minister really be responsible for everything that happens within their portfolio given the complexity of modern policy? Conversely, are there problems if we accept the idea that no one is ultimately responsible for a policy?

A DECLINE OF CABINET GOVERNMENT?

Despite general agreement that the conventions around Cabinet are central to the system of government, in recent decades many observers claim there has been a shift away from Cabinet as the centre of governing. The presidentialisation thesis discussed above is one way of thinking about this. More broadly, for many decades prime ministers have been accused of bypassing Cabinet and making decisions without it. Kevin Rudd was accused of relying on his 'gang of four' and Tony Abbott was known for his 'captain's calls', both examples suggesting Cabinet was handed a fait accompli. In both instances, their successors as prime minister arrived in office promising to restore proper Cabinet government.

Some commentators go so far as to talk of 'Court Government', not a reference to law courts and the judiciary, but to monarchs and courtiers of bygone eras. Court Government takes the idea of the core executive a stage further (see earlier in the chapter), with 'a shift from formal decision-making processes in cabinet and, as a consequence, in the civil service, to informal processes involving only a handful of key actors' (Savoie 2008, 16). Decisions are made by close, informal networks of senior ministers, select other politicians, senior public servants, trusted political advisers, with, of course, the prime minister at the centre (Boswell et al. 2021, 1260). Prime Minister Tony Abbott's former Chief of Staff Peta Credlin is a good example of someone unelected forming part of the prime minister's 'court', while Kevin Rudd's 'gang of four' illustrates how a small group of ministers can dominate decision-making. If Court Government is real, it raises serious questions about process, transparency, accountability, and democracy itself.

SHORT-ANSWER QUESTIONS 4.3

1. In politics, what is the Cabinet and what are its main functions?
2. What are the key principles on which Cabinet government rests?

Suggested responses are available at www.cambridge.org/highereducation/isbn/9781009108232/resources

THE PERILS OF CABINET DISUNITY

The sources of Cabinet discord are many and varied. All Cabinets comprise strong-willed and ambitious individuals, with at least some who have prime ministerial aspirations. Although in Australia ministers all come from the same side of politics, Cabinet is still a site of substantial political conflict. Ministers will hold differing views on a range of issues, which will reveal themselves in Cabinet discussions.

Some differences arise from philosophical worldviews which cause friction between ministers or blocs of ministers. In these cases, ministers routinely line up with like-minded ministers in arguing for particular positions. Similarly, the source of conflict may be between portfolio responsibilities, such as between the Minister for the Environment and the Minister for Resources, or between the Treasurer and Finance Minister on one side and ministers from high-spending departments on the other.

Alternatively, conflict can reflect electoral realities such as geographic differences. For example, between ministers representing conservative electorates and those representing socially liberal electorates, or between rural and urban electorates, or electorates with differing economic bases. Other issues will pit state against state.

Divisions can run right through the entire Cabinet, for example between conservatives and social liberals within Coalition governments, and between Left and Right factions within Labor governments. Unless the prime minister can skilfully manage and navigate these differences they can harden over time and be a source of considerable ongoing conflict, making Cabinet hard to control and undermining the prime minister's authority. In recent years, Cabinet disunity has occurred frequently when ministers are dissatisfied with their leader's performance. This takes many forms, including consistently poor opinion polls, or a feeling the prime minister is insufficiently consultative, or significant policy failures and backflips. As a prime minister's grasp on power weakens, a new factor kicks in as ministers think about who will replace them and jostling for position begins. When Cabinet is divided or the prime minister is weakened, there are often anonymous leaks of politically sensitive Cabinet information to the media, undermining the appearance of unity and the prime minister's hold on power.

Cabinet rolls a prime minister

In May 2015, for example, ministerial leaks to the Fairfax media revealed that Cabinet had rolled Prime Minister Tony Abbott on a proposal that he and his immigration minister, Peter Dutton, had belatedly brought to Cabinet. The proposal would allow the immigration minister to strip Australian citizenship from those they suspected of being terrorists or having links to terrorists without that proposition needing to be tested in a court against the usual standards of evidence.

The leaks were extraordinary in terms of the level of detail of Cabinet discussions. They revealed that senior ministers including Malcolm Turnbull, Barnaby Joyce, Christopher Pyne, George Brandis and Julie Bishop had all spoken out strongly against the proposal. One unnamed minister pointed out that, 'We are talking about executive detention without limit. It's an extremely dangerous proposal' (cited in Hartcher 2015a). Another questioned the propriety of stripping someone of citizenship, thereby making them stateless, when terrorism was suspected but not proven. This contradicted the rule of law and the principle that people are innocent until proven guilty. It also transgressed centuries of political and judicial development that protected citizens from the arbitrary exercise of executive power, by separating executive and judicial functions and thereby creating checks and balances against tyranny. By contrast, the Abbott/Dutton proposal, if successful, would concentrate in the hands of a single executive minister the functions of judge, jury and executioner.

As important as these issues of substance were, the fact that they were leaked was prompted more by Abbott's cavalier treatment of his Cabinet colleagues and his disregard for long-settled Cabinet conventions. The proposal was not presented to Cabinet in a written submission, and nor was it on the official agenda of the Cabinet meeting where it was raised. And yet the following morning Tony Abbott's messenger of choice, the *Daily Telegraph*, carried a report stating that the proposal had already been passed in Cabinet. This was despite the Prime Minister denying to his Cabinet colleagues that that media source had been briefed. As one minister complained, 'Ministers were genuinely shocked that something this important would be attempted to be put through without due process' (cited in Hartcher 2015b).

All of this manifested in broader tensions between Prime Minister Abbott and his Cabinet. The Prime Minister's propensity for micro-management and the making of what he called 'captain's calls', without Cabinet consultation, was symptomatic of an over-centralisation of decision-making in his own office. His Chief of Staff, Peta Credlin, became a particular source of irritation among those who viewed her as behaving in a high-handed way towards some Cabinet ministers, and generally acting beyond her proper role as a staffer. Such tensions were compounded when Abbott reacted to the leaks by making barely veiled threats that there would be 'personal and political consequences' for the leakers. But the leaks continued, Abbott's poll numbers dropped further, and we can see in retrospect that this was the beginning of the end of his prime ministership. Three months later, on 14 September 2015, colleagues informed him that he no longer enjoyed the confidence of a majority of his Cabinet. That night he lost a leadership ballot to Malcolm Turnbull by 54 to 44 votes. Tellingly, Prime Minister Turnbull's first promise was to lead a 'thoroughly traditional Cabinet government that ensures we make decisions in a collaborative manner' (cited in Bourke 2015).

This entire episode illustrates much that is central to discussions of prime ministerial and Cabinet government today. It highlights issues around presidentialisation in Australian politics, while also underlining the limitations of prime ministerial powers when confronted with Cabinet opposition; it highlights the norms of Cabinet government including group decision-making and collective responsibility, by illuminating an instance of their egregious violation; and, above all, it exemplifies the destructive impact of Cabinet disunity for executive government. Cabinet disunity and frictions with the prime minister are often prompted by falling public support for the government, which is then exacerbated by the appearance of disunity, which drives public support even lower. The prime minister's tenure can enter into a death spiral that only ends with their replacement. Such are the perils of Cabinet disunity for the political executive in general, and the prime minister in particular.

REFLECTION QUESTIONS 4.4

1. Is collective responsibility fair and reasonable where Cabinet ministers may not even be a party to decisions for which they are held to be responsible?
2. Is it possible to make generalisations about Cabinet disunity?

Response prompts are available at www.cambridge.org/highereducation/isbn/9781009108232/resources

SPOTLIGHT 4.3 PRIME MINISTER RUDD AND HIS CABINET

Interestingly, the dynamics between Prime Minister Tony Abbott and his Cabinet had played out in a similar way five years previously. Kevin Rudd had been elected in the so-called 'Rudd slide' of 2007, vanquishing an opponent who had been prime minister for 11 years. This success emboldened Rudd to demand he choose his own Cabinet, which broke with the usual Labor protocol of the caucus electing Cabinet and the leader distributing portfolios. After an initial period of popularity and significant policy success, the political landscape shifted in 2009–10. Prime Minister Rudd's poll numbers deteriorated, and he became the subject of dissatisfaction among Cabinet colleagues, who viewed his leadership as beset by the micro-managerial resulting in policy inertia due to the prime minister's office becoming a bottleneck. Lack of consultation with Cabinet, plus condescension and a perceived lack of respect from Rudd's personal advisers created frictions with Cabinet that would eventually doom Rudd, who had little factional backing (Evans

2011). When his colleagues moved against him, the numbers were clearly stacked against Rudd, and he did not even contest the leadership spill. Australia's first female prime minister, Julia Gillard, replaced him uncontested. While the personality foibles of Rudd, and later Abbott, were at play in the dynamics that eventually led to his downfall, political centralisation, and the Cabinet frictions to which it gave rise, might also be understood as a structural feature of a system undergoing presidentialisation. These cases also show that prime ministers are vulnerable to Cabinet machinations in a way that executive presidents are not.

QUESTION

Given that Kevin Rudd became prime minister with a significant mandate from the electorate, should his Cabinet and broader caucus have been able to force a leadership contest?

EXECUTIVE POWER AND ACCOUNTABILITY

The Westminster concept of responsible government sits at the heart of Australia's political system. It implies a chain of responsibility and therefore accountability, which ties the government to the governed – each part of the system is responsible to the part before it, with everything ultimately accountable to the people through parliament. The political executive is responsible to parliament for the successes and failures of their policies, with voters ultimately deciding whether to re-elect the government at the next election. As well as this, Australia's political system incorporates aspects of the US federal system (Thompson 1980). Both the British and US systems were deliberately framed to place limits on executive power, meaning both also developed institutions and conventions that would check executive power and make it accountable to the legislature and citizens. Australia is heir to these institutional arrangements, and although they provide protections against the abuse of executive power, there are also problems with the accountability mechanisms in the system.

THE RISE OF MINISTERIAL STAFF

An important development since the 1970s which impacts the relationship between the political and administrative arms of the executive is the growth in the number of ministerial advisers. All ministers (and most opposition shadow Cabinet members) now appoint a 'political staff' of partisan policy and media advisers whose careers rise and fall with the minister. These advisers create a layer of political rather than neutral advice between the administrative and executive arms of government. All documents pass through their hands on their way to the minister and they are closely engaged with the work of departments. In other words, they 'drive, sieve and skew advice; and they insist on what the minister wants as opposed to the public interest or the integrity of the policy process' (Walter and Strangio 2007, 54). While some defend this as providing more diverse sources of advice and therefore more informed final decisions, others say that it shields ministers from advice they may not want to hear but need to. (For more on the impacts of ministerial advisers on the policy process see the section 'Competition in the provision of policy advice' in Chapter 6).

The rising number of ministerial advisers and their obvious influence interferes with the responsible government model which should hold each piece in the system accountable. Despite their importance, there is little visibility of ministerial staffers, and they are not obliged to serve in the public interest. Furthermore, their presence muddies accountability where it is unclear exactly who in a minister's office took what decisions or actions or who received what information or advice. Although they are seen as speaking and acting on behalf of the minister, on some occasions advisers are used to shield their minister. In 2017 the media was tipped off about a police raid on the office of a trade union. Initially, the employment minister, Michaelia Cash, flatly denied any involvement from her office. When it was discovered that the tip-off had come from the minister's office after all, a senior adviser resigned but Michaelia Cash remained minister (Karp and Murphy 2017). Generally, there is limited accountability for political advisers, who unlike ministers are not accountable to parliament. Even then, although in theory ministers are accountable to parliament, in practice this can be very limited.

EXECUTIVE DOMINANCE OF PARLIAMENT

Scrutinising the executive is a central function of parliaments and is central to the Westminster responsible government model. Despite this, governments generally do not welcome scrutiny and avoid it where they can (Loney 2008, 160). There are many mechanisms for holding governments to account, including Question Time (for ministers and the prime minister), questions on notice, parliamentary committees, reports from bodies like the Australian National Audit Office and Senate Estimates hearings (for more on how scrutiny mechanisms work, see Chapter 3). Due to its centralisation of power, parliaments in the Westminster mould are frequently less good at scrutinising the executive than other parliamentary systems. Even within that context, the Australian parliament is particularly dominated by the executive, which significantly limits scrutiny.

The size of the executive in Australia has grown faster than the size of the parliament in recent decades meaning the proportion of parliamentarians with ministerial roles has grown and is larger than in comparable systems (Prasser 2012). In 2021, 42 of the 227 parliamentarians were also in the executive. Further, Australian political parties operate as very tight blocs, so 'discipline in Parliament is pronounced, even by high, Westminster standards' (Larkin 2012, 95–6). This means MPs and senators from the governing party or coalition are very constrained in their ability to criticise the executive, ask difficult questions or push back against its decisions. This means the government is in full control of the parliamentary agenda and how parliamentary time is used, and it also enables the government to write rules limiting the effectiveness of scrutiny mechanisms such as parliamentary committees.

Although executive dominance is pronounced in Australia, the silver lining in parliamentary scrutiny is the Senate, where governments rarely enjoy a majority. This means the Senate is better able to hold the executive to account, with for example Senate Estimates being one of parliament's best scrutiny mechanisms. However, the Senate has its own separate muddying effect on accountability by being able to frustrate the legislative program of the elected government.

FEDERALISM AND RESPONSIBLE GOVERNMENT

The problems of responsible government in the modern political world also conflict with political realities deriving from federalism. Although Australia's constitutional framers consciously blended the two systems, they are often in tension with each other.

Federalism intrudes directly into the Commonwealth Parliament in the form of the Senate, which is elected on the basis of state representation using proportional representation. For most of the recent past, governments have lacked a majority in the Senate and have thus typically relied on the support of minor parties and/or independents to get their legislation passed and, even then, often in modified form. Governments can plausibly blame Senate recalcitrance, rather than government incompetence, for policy failures. If a problem needs fixing but the Senate blocks or waters down the political executive's preferred solution, it can be difficult to hold the government accountable for the continuation of the problem. This problem does not arise in other Westminster systems because upper houses are, typically, either weaker than lower houses (e.g. the United Kingdom, Ireland, Jamaica) or are entirely absent (e.g. New Zealand, Solomon Islands, Malta).

A similar logic can be applied to the responsibility of ministers for their departments. Where ministers are unable to advance solutions to problems that their department encounters because of impediments in the Senate, they can deflect criticism and evade being held to account. Whether rightly or wrongly, they can lay responsibility for departmental failings at the feet of others, including political opponents with no access to the levers of executive power. Ministerial accountability, then, along with the accountability of the political executive more generally, is very slippery where the institutions of federalism are married with those of responsible government. The checks and balances of a federal system can prevent all-powerful executives from behaving badly but can also prevent the elected government from carrying out the program it was elected to enact.

But this is not the only or even the main area where there is a question mark over the accountability of the modern executive. In recent years, the '**SECURITISATION**' of a number of policy areas has restricted scrutiny of particular measures taken by the executive, and thus limited its accountability.

> **SECURITISATION:** The process of constructing particular issues as central to state security, which then become the subject of extraordinary government measures that often erode civil liberties.

SHORT-ANSWER QUESTIONS 4.4

1. What is meant by federalism?
2. What is meant by responsible government?

Suggested responses are available at www.cambridge.org/highereducation/isbn/9781009108232/resources

SECURITISATION AND ACCOUNTABILITY

In the middle of 2001, John Howard's Liberal–National Coalition Government had been trailing the Labor opposition by a wide margin in opinion polling and looked destined to lose the upcoming election. Then, in the space of less than a month, two events occurred that shook the very foundations of Australian politics, resurrected Howard's fortunes and strengthened the hand of the political executive in ways that are still being felt today.

First, in late August a Norwegian shipping vessel, the M.V. *Tampa*, responded to a distress signal from a sinking vessel carrying asylum seekers. It picked up 438 survivors and asked for permission to disembark them on the Australian territory of Christmas Island. The Howard Government refused and instead ordered special service military personnel to board the ship and take control.

In the days that followed, the so-called 'Pacific solution' was born (Marr and Wilkinson 2003), in which asylum seekers were placed in mandatory detention on Nauru and Manus Island in Papua New Guinea. The second event occurred two weeks later. The attacks on the World Trade Center and the Pentagon in September 2001 represented a watershed moment for Australian politics. Prime Minister John Howard immediately assured his US political counterparts that 'Australia will provide all support that might be requested of us' (cited in Summers 2007). Australia then joined the United States in its invasions of Afghanistan and Iraq and provided strong diplomatic support for George W. Bush's Global War on Terror.

These events and their aftermath provided the impetus for what political scientists refer to as 'securitisation'. This refers to the process whereby particular issues are constructed as central to state security and thus become the subject of extraordinary government measures that dilute civil liberties and judicial protections (Buzan et al. 1998, 25). Such measures often occur behind a veil of secrecy and executive privilege that is said to be necessary for both state security and the safety of those implementing the measures. Once successfully securitised, a policy area will attract disproportionate media attention and state resources, with the latter often being itself subject to secrecy. This in turn amplifies its gravity in the eyes of the public and thus perpetuates its usefulness to the political executive, which claims to be the most resolute public protector against the perceived security threat.

In this country, terrorism and maritime asylum seekers, and the frequent conjoining of the two, are the most obvious examples of securitisation at work. Since John Howard provided the political template for how these issues could be successfully exploited for political gain, Coalition *and* Labor governments have been at pains to continue highlighting the security aspects of these issues. With this, the various security agencies (Federal Police, Australian Security Intelligence Organisation (ASIO), Border Force, the Australian Defence Force) have been further empowered with an attendant diminution of civil liberties once considered sacrosanct. For example, in 2020 Home Affairs Minister Peter Dutton introduced legislation to parliament which would give the domestic intelligence agency, ASIO, expanded powers. This included an ability to question children as young as 14, authority to deploy tracking devices (for example, in someone's car or bag) without a warrant and to deprive people of a lawyer in some circumstances (SBS 2020).

Other bodies and institutions also provide important oversight and scrutiny of the political executive. These include Ombudsmen who investigate citizen complaints at various levels of government, a Human Rights Commission, and parliament itself. The latter includes the political opposition who, as well as presenting itself as an alternative government, is tasked with scrutinising government policy and legislation. There are also various parliamentary committees, which are useful watchdogs over executive power, even when they are chaired and controlled by members of the government. Finally, the media and investigative journalism remain crucial for shining a light on the darkest recesses of executive government and thereby providing some measure of executive accountability.

RESEARCH QUESTION 4.1

In what ways has the securitisation of the asylum seeker issue diluted the accountability of the political executive?

SUMMARY

Learning objective 1: Explain what executive power is and distinguish between the political and administrative wings of the executive

Executive power is the capacity to make political decisions and to put them into effect. This implies a political and administrative component of any executive. In Australia, the public service of neutral professionals constitutes the administrative executive, clearly distinguishable from the political executive which is composed of an elected prime minister and Cabinet. While Australia's Constitution formally vests executive power in the Queen, with that power being exercisable by her representative the Governor-General, this power is in fact only nominal and symbolic. Notwithstanding the extraordinary events of 1975, constitutional convention dictates that the Governor-General acts only on the advice of ministers (prime minister and Cabinet), who are elected representatives of the citizenry.

Learning objective 2: Describe the main functions the political executive performs

The main function of the executive is to provide political leadership. In doing so, it also functions as a symbol of national unity, a leader to the public, a body for making policy and providing legislative leadership, and a provider of national leadership on the world stage. It serves the important function of leading the public service, which is organised into departments that broadly mirror the portfolios of Cabinet ministers and junior ministers in the outer ministry. It also has the overarching function of providing a forum and clearing house for a wide range of policy and political issues.

Learning objective 3: Understand the key features of the role of the prime minister and the Cabinet and explain the relationship between them

The prime minister and the Cabinet constitute the real political executive and are responsible for making the most important decisions of government. The prime minister is at the apex of executive power and wields formidable powers in respect of the party, the Cabinet, the electoral process, the media and political opposition. This has contributed to what some have referred to as a presidentialisation of Australian politics. Despite this accumulation of powers, prime ministers are still vulnerable to being replaced by a majority vote of their parliamentary colleagues, should they falter in the polls and/or become subject to hostile action by influential Cabinet ministers. Cabinet refers to the collective leadership body, with the prime minister at its head, which ideally makes the most important government decisions. It ostensibly operates according to the principles of collective and individual responsibility. In reality, it often departs from these principles, which manifests a degree of disunity that can be very damaging for governments and prime ministers.

Learning objective 4: Describe the tensions between executive power and accountability, and how they are manifested in Australia's system of government

Finally, Australia's system of executive government has often been embroiled in concerns about a lack of accountability. This stems partly from tensions arising from the political traditions from which it has developed. The Westminster system tends to create strong executives at the expense of the parliament and its ability to scrutinise, which is especially true in Australia. This is compounded by adding in federalism which disperses power, including creating a strong Senate able to frustrate the government's program. The securitisation of particular areas of policy and law making also dilute the accountability of the political executive.

DISCUSSION QUESTIONS

1. Has Australia's executive accumulated greater powers in recent decades?
2. Is it right that Cabinet discussions and documents remain confidential?
3. Should there be legislated standards for ministerial behaviour?
4. Is federalism incompatible with the norms and conventions of responsible government?
5. What consequences does securitisation have for executive accountability and therefore democracy?

FURTHER READING

Bennister, M. (2012). *Prime Ministers in Power: Political Leadership in Britain and Australia*, Basingstoke: Palgrave Macmillan.

Kefford, G. (2013). The presidentialisation of Australian politics? Kevin Rudd's leadership of the Australian Labor Party. *Australian Journal of Political Science*, **48**(2), 135–46.

Raffin, L. (2008). Individual ministerial responsibility during the Howard years: 1996–2007. *The Australian Journal of Politics and History*, **54**(2), 225–47.

Tiernan, A. (2007). *Power Without Responsibility*, Sydney: UNSW Press.

Weller, P. (1985). *First Among Equals*, Hemel Hempstead: Allen & Unwin.

REFERENCES

Anderson, B. (1991). *Imagined Communities: Reflections of the Origins and Spread of Nationalism*, London: Verso.

Australian National Audit Office (ANAO). (2010). *Home Insulation Program.* Retrieved from https://www.anao.gov.au/work/performance-audit/home-insulation-program

Bennister, M. (2012). *Prime Ministers in Power: Political Leadership in Britain and Australia*, Basingstoke: Palgrave Macmillan.

Boswell, J., Corbett, J., Rhodes, R. & Salomonsen, H. (2021). The comparative 'court politics' of COVID-19: Explaining government responses to the pandemic. *Journal of European Public Policy*, **28**(8), 1258–77.

Bourke, L. (2015). Malcolm Turnbull defeats Tony Abbott in Liberal leadership spill to become Prime Minister, *The Sydney Morning Herald*, 15 September. Retrieved from http://www.smh.com.au/federal-politics/political-news/malcolm-turnbull-defeats-tony-abbott-in-liberal-leadership-spill-to-become-prime-minister-20150914-gjmhiu.html

Boyce, P. (2007). Executive Council. In B. Galligan and W. Roberts (eds), *The Oxford Companion to Australian Politics*, South Melbourne: Oxford University Press.

Butler, J. (2022). Anthony Albanese boasts of appointing 'largest number of women ever in an Australian cabinet', *The Guardian*, 31 May. Retrieved from https://www.theguardian.com/australia-news/2022/may/31/anthony-albanese-boasts-of-appointing-largest-number-of-women-ever-in-an-australian-cabinet

Buzan, B., Wæver, O. & de Wilde, J. (1998). *Security: A New Framework for Analysis*, Boulder: Lynne Rienner.

Commonwealth of Australia Constitution Act [Constitution of Australia]. (1900). Retrieved from http://www.austlii.edu.au/cgi-bin/viewdoc/au/legis/cth/consol_act/coaca430/s24.html

Day, D. (1999). *John Curtin – A Life*, Sydney: Harper Collins.

Evans, M. (2011). The rise and fall of the magic kingdom: Understanding Kevin Rudd's domestic statecraft. In C. Aulich and M. Evans (eds), *The Rudd Government: Australian Commonwealth Administration 2007–2010*, Canberra: ANU Press.

Garrett, P. (2017). *Big Blue Sky: A Memoir*, Crows Nest: Allen & Unwin.

Gladstone, N. (2018). Assistant treasurer bills taxpayers $2000 a month for data at home, *The Sydney Morning Herald*, 5 October. Retrieved from https://www.smh.com.au/national/nsw/assistant-treasurer-bills-taxpayers-2000-a-month-for-data-at-home-20181003-p507jx.html

Grattan, M. (ed.). (2000). *Australian Prime Ministers*, Sydney: New Holland.

Hall, L. (2010). Peter Garrett demoted after botched insulation program, *The Sydney Morning Herald*, 26 February. Retrieved from https://www.smh.com.au/environment/sustainability/peter-garrett-demoted-after-botched-insulation-program-20100226-p8jn.html

Hartcher, P. (2015a). Tony Abbott rolled by his own ministry over stripping terrorists of citizenship, *The Sydney Morning Herald*, 29 May. Retrieved from http://www.smh.com.au/comment/tony-abbott-rolled-by-his-own-ministers-over-stripping-terrorists-of-citizenship-20150529-ghcuxf.html

—— (2015b). Abbott only has himself to blame for Cabinet leaks over citizenship stripping proposal, *The Sydney Morning Herald*, 5 June. Retrieved from http://www.smh.com.au/comment/tony-abbott-only-has-himself-to-blame-for-cabinet-leaks-over-citizenshipstripping-proposals-20150605-ghhv0i.html

Henderson, A. (2016). Stuart Robert resigns from Turnbull ministry following probe into China trip, *ABC News*, 12 February. Retrieved from https://www.abc.net.au/news/2016-02-12/stuart-robert-to-resign-fom-ministry-abc-understands/7163226?utm_source=abc_news_web&utm_medium=content_shared&utm_campaign=abc_news_web

Heywood, A. (2007). *Politics*, 3rd edn, Houndmills, Basingstoke: Palgrave Macmillan.

Howard, J. (2002). John Howard's Bali Memorial Speech, *The Sydney Morning Herald*, 18 October. Retrieved from http://www.smh.com.au/articles/2002/10/18/1034561270521.html

Hutchison, E. (2010). Trauma and the politics of emotions: Constituting identity, security and community after the Bali bombing. *International Relations*, **24**(1), 65–86.

Karp, P. & Murphy, K. (2017). Michaelia Cash aide resigns over AWU raid tip-off to media, *The Guardian*, 25 October. Retrieved from https://www.theguardian.com/australia-news/2017/oct/25/michaelia-cash-says-her-office-did-not-tip-off-media-before-awu-raids

Kefford, G. (2013). The presidentialisation of Australian politics? Kevin Rudd's leadership of the Australian Labor Party. *Australian Journal of Political Science*, **48**(2), 135–46.

Larkin, P. (2012). Ministerial accountability to parliament. In K. Dowding and C. Lewis (eds), *Ministerial Careers and Accountability in the Australian Commonwealth Government*, Canberra: ANU Press, pp. 95–114.

Lelliott, J. (2013). PMs rarely begin and end with the people, *ABC News*, 23 August. Retrieved from https://www.abc.net.au/news/2013-08-23/lelliott-prime-ministerial-legitimacy/4908354

Loney, P. (2008). Executive accountability to parliament – reality or rhetoric? *Australasian Parliamentary Review*, **23**(2), 157–65.

Maddox, G. (1996). *Australian Democracy in Theory and Practice*, 3rd edn, South Melbourne: Longman.

Maley, M. (2012). Politicisation and the executive. In R. Smith, A. Vromen and I. Cook (eds), *Contemporary Politics in Australia*, Melbourne: Cambridge University Press.

Marr, D. & Wilkinson, M. (2003). *Dark Victory*, Crows Nest: Allen & Unwin.

Nicholls, S. (2014). Treasurer for sale: Joe Hockey offers privileged access, *The Sydney Morning Herald*, 5 May. Retrieved from http://www.smh.com.au/federal-politics/political-news/treasurer-for-sale-joe-hockey-offers-privileged-access-20140504-zr06v.html

Poguntke, T. & Webb, P. (2005). *The Presidentialization of Politics: A Comparative Study of Modern Democracies*, Oxford: Oxford University Press.

Prasser, S. (2012). Executive growth and the takeover of Australian parliaments. *Australasian Parliamentary Review*, Autumn 2012, **27**(1), 48–61.

Raffin, L. (2008). Individual ministerial responsibility during the Howard years: 1996–2007. *The Australian Journal of Politics and History*, **54**(2), 225–47.

Rhodes, R. (1995). From prime ministerial power to core executive. In R. Rhodes and P. Dunleavy (eds), *Prime Minister, Cabinet and Core Executive*, London: Macmillan.

Rodgers, E. (2009). Fitzgibbon resigns as Defence Minister, *ABC News*, 4 June. Retrieved from https://www.abc.net.au/news/2009-06-04/fitzgibbon-resigns-as-defence-minister/1703822?utm_source=abc_news_web&utm_medium=content_shared&utm_campaign=abc_news_web

Savioe, D. (2008). *Court Government and the Collapse of Accountability in Canada and the United Kingdom*, Toronto: University of Toronto Press.

SBS. (2020). Legal bodies concerned by Peter Dutton allowing Australian spies to question 14-year-olds, *SBS*, 13 May. Retrieved from https://www.sbs.com.au/news/legal-bodies-concerned-by-peter-dutton-bill-allowing-australian-spies-to-question-14-year-olds

Sexton, M. (2005). *The Great Crash: The Short Life and Sudden Death of the Whitlam Government*, Carlton North: Scribe Publications.

Snape, J. (2020). Federal government targeted marginal seats in potentially illegal sports grants scheme, auditor-general reports, *ABC News*, 15 January. Retrieved from https://www.abc.net.au/news/2020-01-15/government-sport-grants-targeted-marginal-seats-audit-office/11870292

Summers, A. (2007). The day that shook Howard's world, *The Age*, 17 February. Retrieved from http://www.smh.com.au/news/opinion/the-day-that-shook-howards-world/2007/02/16/1171405438845.html

Tiernan, A. (2007). *Power Without Responsibility*, Sydney: UNSW Press.

Tiffen, R. (2010). A mess? A shambles? A disaster? *Inside Story*, 26 March. Retrieved from https://insidestory.org.au/a-mess-a-shambles-a-disaster/

Thompson, E. (1980). The Washminster mutation. In P. Weller and D. Jaensch (eds), *Responsible Government in Australia*, Melbourne: Drummond.

Walter, J. & Strangio, P. (2007). *No Prime Minister: Reclaiming Politics from Leaders*, Sydney: UNSW Press.

Weller, P. (1985). *First Among Equals*, Hemel Hempstead: Allen & Unwin.

——— (ed.) (1992). *Menzies to Keating: The Development of the Australian Prime Ministership*, Melbourne: Melbourne University Press.

——— (2002). *Don't Tell the Prime Minister*, Melbourne: Scribe Publications.

——— (2005). Investigating power at the centre of government: Surveying research on the Australian executive. *Australian Journal of Public Administration*, **61**(1), 35–42.

——— (2007). *Cabinet Government in Australia 1901–2006*, Sydney: UNSW Press.

——— (2013). *The Prime Ministerial Condition: Prime Ministers in Westminster Systems*, Oxford: Oxford University Press.

Whitlam, G. & Fraser, M. (2007). Ministerial accountability transcends party politics, *The Herald Sun*, 12 November.

CHAPTER 5

THE 'RULEBOOK'
National governance and the Australian Constitution

LEARNING OBJECTIVES

After reading this chapter, you should be able to:

1. Understand the meaning of Australian 'constitutionalism' as a combination of the written constitution and Westminster practice
2. Identify some key sections of the Australian Constitution and their consequences for the system of federal governance
3. Understand the importance of the 1975 'constitutional crisis'
4. Identify the significance of the High Court
5. Understand how the Constitution can be altered and reflect on future constitutional reform

INTRODUCTION

On 1 January 1901, the newly constituted Australian Parliament met for the first time at the Royal Exhibition Building in Melbourne. This ceremonial meeting of the parliament marked the climax of a 'federation movement' that is usually associated with the advocacy of a national system of government by Sir Henry Parkes starting in the 1890s. It can also be argued, however, that the transition of Australian colonial governance from an exercising of executive power by governors acting as representatives of the British 'crown' to a system of parliamentary government had begun some time previously as some of Australia's first colonies – New South Wales, Van Diemen's Land (Tasmania), and the Port Phillip District (Victoria) – transitioned from convict settlements to free settler societies (Ward 1987). In each case, this transition required the creation of 'constitutions' – legal documents passed by the British parliament that provided the legal authority for the convening and exercise of parliamentary government, even while this is at odds with the lack of a constitution for the United Kingdom.

The Australian Constitution was to also draw upon some other constitutional developments in other places, including the United States. Arguably the most prominent American influences were over thinking about how the Australian colonies could structure a system of national government in which the states would remain relevant, and how the judiciary might be utilised to protect the federal arrangements that were to be incorporated into the emerging Australian Constitution. These ideas would find practical expression in the form of a parliamentary chamber to be called 'the Senate', distinct and powerful, with the states represented on an equal basis, and giving institutional expression to federation (Chordia and Lynch 2014). The High Court then acts as the legal guardian of the Constitution. These were profound outcomes, and this is the basis upon which some have labelled the Australian system as '**WASHMINSTER**' – the combination of American federalism and the British system of parliamentary government (Thompson 1980). This may be so, but it is also true that the Canadian constitution in the form of the *British North America Act (1867)* was used as a template for the Australian constitutional draft and was as influential on federalist thinking. Canada is, like Australia, a constitutional monarchy and a federation. The *Commonwealth of Australia Constitution Act (1900)* was similarly a bill passed by the British parliament at Westminster, though the drafting of the bill was undertaken by delegates of the Australian colonies themselves at a series of constitutional conventions held from 1891.

WASHMINSTER: Washminster blends 'Washington' and 'Westminster'. It flags the fusion of the US-style of federalism and Westminster parliamentary government, which is a feature of Australia's political system and sometimes a source of tension.

REFLECTION QUESTION 5.1

What is the purpose of a constitution?

Response prompt is available at www.cambridge.org/highereducation/isbn/9781009108232/resources

WHAT IS A CONSTITUTION?

Constitutions are simultaneously legal and political documents. They are legal in the sense that they are the foundation documents that provide the authority for the exercise of executive, legislative and judicial power, whose legal authority is usually reinforced by the fact that they are interpreted by the courts rather than by the legislature. Constitutions are also very political in that they allocate governmental powers and responsibilities, and they may also seek to extend rights and protections all of which profoundly affects the scope of the powers of government. In the case of liberal democratic states, constitutions tend to be seen as, among other things, protectors of individual liberty by placing legal constraints on the powers of government (King 2019).

In the case of federated nations (e.g. Australia, Canada, the United States), constitutions also outline the division of governmental powers between the national and subnational levels of government (in Australia, the subnational governments are 'state' governments). Constitutions also provide the basis upon which a system of government will be structurally arranged, particularly with regards to key institutions such as 'the executive' (that is, the 'government'), the legislature (the parliament), the judiciary (the courts) and the citizenry. In the case of representative democracies, one of the most important consequences of a constitution is to legally reinforce the power of the citizenry to be able to cast a vote, even as Australia has few other rights embedded within its Constitution. In this respect, constitutions are considered to be 'rule books' for the operation of government.

A WRITTEN CONSTITUTION

The Australian Constitution is a case study of how the federalist imperative – that is, the need to delineate the powers between the new national government and the powers of the federating states – dominated the way the document is drafted. Without such an agreement between the separate colonies, Federation might not have occurred. By the same token, for a document that is supposed to be a rulebook for the operation of parliament, the Australian Constitution is somewhat bereft. There is no direct reference to the notion that Australia is a 'Westminster' system (that is, a system based on the idea of parliamentary government), although there is an implication that the Westminster model applies by a passing reference in Section 64 to the need for Ministers of the Crown to be members of the parliament. This is a recurring theme in Australian constitutional practice, as the Australian Constitution and the six colonial/state constitutions that were passed by the British parliament prior to Australia's Federation, all shared this feature of leaving the essence of the Westminster system out of the written document.

These sets of unwritten rules that remain uncodified within the Constitution are known as **CONSTITUTIONAL CONVENTIONS**, and it is from this set of unwritten rules that we gain the practice of naming the most senior minister in parliament the prime minister (or premier in the states). While conventions do not have the legal weight of elements contained within the Constitution, they are however justiciable (i.e. a court can make a ruling based on them) (Barry, Miragliotta and Nwokora 2019). This therefore explains the structure of the Constitution, with each of the colonial/state and the national constitutions making explicit and extensive reference to the position of 'governor' (or, in the federal case, a Governor-General), as this clarifies the chain of responsibility from the Crown through to the colonial/Australian parliaments. There was never any mention of the positions of 'premier' or 'prime minister' as these positions were considered as a carry-over convention within the Westminster system.

Each Australian Constitution outlines a body called 'the Executive in Council' that is headed by a governor (or the Governor-General), and each delineates that Ministers of the Crown come from the parliament but that their authority as a minister derives from being appointed by the Governor. No Australian Constitution refers to a 'Ministry' or 'Cabinet', and nor do they talk about political parties that command a majority in the 'lower' parliamentary house being entitled to govern. Yet these are precisely the features of Australian Westminster practice that are assumed

CONSTITUTIONAL CONVENTIONS: Agreed, non-legal rules that impose expectations on how political actors should act, that, when violated, give rise to public and media criticism, which are the chief means by which conventions are enforced.

to apply. Understanding Australian constitutional practice requires more than a literal reading of Australia's national and state constitutions, with attention needing to be paid to the underlying assumptions and conventions that underpin a Westminster-based system.

SHORT-ANSWER QUESTIONS 5.1

1. Is the Governor-General a powerful office?
2. Does the Governor-General always need to act as the prime minister advises?

Suggested responses are available at www.cambridge.org/highereducation/isbn/9781009108232/resources

THE SIGNIFICANCE OF CONSTITUTIONALISM

In their discussion of the way Australia is governed, Hugh Emy and Owen Hughes preferred to refer to the idea of 'constitutionalism' rather than refer solely to the written constitution for insights into the way government and politics are done in Australia (Emy and Hughes 1988). Constitutionalism in this context was meant to refer to Australian constitutional practice in its totality, rather than just simply referring to the written word of the Australian Constitution. This is to identify the salience of those features of British constitutional practice that are assumed to apply in the Australian context notwithstanding their absence from the written document. Following Hobbes and Locke, constitutional practice defines the relationship between a parliament and the people via the rule of law (Loughlin 2015). In short, the things that are missing from the written constitution are the features of British parliamentary practice that are considered integral to Britain's constitutional heritage. Significantly, Britain does not have a single written constitution. Rather, British constitutionalism is considered to involve a host of unwritten constitutional assumptions (understood in Britain as 'conventions') derived from centuries of parliamentary practice and that exist alongside acts of parliament that were passed as part of the constitutional reform process.

REFLECTION QUESTION 5.2

Why do political scientists often define constitutions more broadly than do lawyers?

Response prompt is available at www.cambridge.org/highereducation/isbn/9781009108232/resources

WESTMINSTER CONVENTIONS

In the context of understanding Westminster 'constitutionalism', conventions are understood to be unwritten principles of constitutional practice. There are very many of these, although arguably the most important are those that seek to establish the relationships between the key institutions of a Westminster parliamentary system of government – specifically, the Crown, the Executive and the Parliament. To this list can be added the public service, who administer and enforce the laws created, and the judiciary, who interpret the laws. In the case of these last two, the notion of 'separation of powers' might be considered, as both the public service and especially the courts are assumed to require a certain degree of immunity from the more overtly political realms of the parliament and the executive that is drawn from the parliament (see Chapter 3; Kurland and Lerner 1987).

At its heart, the Westminster system revolves around the idea of 'parliamentary government' – known as 'responsible government' on the assumption that the ministry (or the 'the cabinet') is answerable and accountable to the parliament that selected it. This is based on the convention that the Crown only ever exercises executive authority on the advice of the person who leads a ministry or 'Cabinet' made up of members of parliament. As discussed in Chapter 4, Cabinet is the key to the administration of government and, as Bagehot famously noted, is the principal link between the executive (embodied in the Crown) and the parliament (Bagehot 1888). The person who leads this ministry is the 'first minister' (in Australia, this minister is referred to as the 'prime minister'). To be the first minister in a cabinet, the prime minister and the ministry must enjoy majority support in the 'lower' house of the parliament. Once again, this is a Westminster convention and derives initially from the events of the English Civil War of 1642–51 but principally advanced with the deposition of James II in 1688 and the invitation from the English Parliament to William of Orange to become King. This established the principle that the House of Commons, and not the King, exercised the power to govern (Moran 2012).

This is a convention of Westminster practice that remains relevant to this day and is an integral part of Australian constitutionalism. This provides the basis for Australian politics to involve actors such as the prime minister, the treasurer, the leader of the opposition and so on without any of these positions being mentioned – let alone extensively outlined – in the written Australian Constitution. However, there are other hints about the applicability of the Westminster conventions to the Australian system in the written document. The requirement that ministers be members of parliament outlined in Section 64 has been alluded to. The written constitution outlines the legal basis for the creation of a Commonwealth public service and indeed establishes a court – the High Court of Australia – to be the legal custodian of the Constitution. Section 44 (iv) states that anyone 'in receipt of profit from the Crown' shall not be allowed to be a member of parliament, thereby codifying a Westminster convention that a serving public servant cannot either run for election to the parliament let alone hold a parliamentary seat. Section 83 also outlines the legal requirement that the parliament must pass an appropriation bill before the Executive in Council may allocate public funds to government programs. This is a codification of the Westminster convention about the importance of 'supply' (meaning the 'supply' of funds to run the government) and the principle that a government that does not have parliamentary approval to spend money (that is, supply is denied) is unable to government and must resign.

If providing the confidence for a ministry is a core function of the House of Representatives (often styled as the lower house), through a vote or a single party being in the majority, what role is played by the Senate (the upper house)? As constructed in the Constitution, the Senate has almost equal power to the House of Representatives. This equality of power was still a feature of the British system at the time the Australian Constitution was being drafted (the power of the House of Lords to block legislation was removed in 1911) and can be seen most clearly in the power of the US Senate. Nonetheless, the framers of the Australian Constitution did see fit to place a deadlock provision in the Constitution (Section 57) that allowed for Parliament to be dissolved when there could not be agreement between the Houses.

The transferral of the power to determine who shall exercise the power of government to the lower house left the upper house acting as a **HOUSE OF REVIEW**. As was seen with the UK Parliament Act 1911, both the House of Lords and the Senate retained the power to block legislation

HOUSE OF REVIEW: The idea in Westminster systems of parliamentary government that an upper house (whether styled Legislative Council or Senate) shall act as a body to review legislation or matters of importance, separate from the government formed in the lower house.

and force the government of the day to negotiate, but while the House of Commons could force legislation through after presenting the same bill three times, the House of Representatives would need to call an election. Of course, the British House of Lords contains a mix of hereditary peers, life peers and 26 Church of England Bishops – all unelected – while the Australian Senate is wholly elected, so any election places senators in danger of losing their seat (Ballinger 2011; Mulgan 1996). Perhaps the clearest expression of the review function of the upper house lay in the Westminster conventions relating to how legislation would be made. A bill before the parliament would not become law until it had been approved by both houses of parliament, and also that there was a power to suggest amendments to a bill that had to be agreed upon by both houses. A bill without approval, or a bill whose amendments were not agreed to, would fail (see Chapter 3 for a full explanation of this process).

SPOTLIGHT 5.1 THE EVOLUTION OF A CONVENTION

A benefit of political institutions being governed by convention rather than law is that conventions can be adapted to suit changing circumstances. 'Individual ministerial responsibility' illustrates this point. It is the expectation that ministers be accountable to parliament for their own conduct and that of their departments. In the 19th century, this Westminster convention obliged ministers to answer to parliament and to resign from the ministry should public servants for whom they were responsible bungle the administration of public policy. A century ago, it may have been feasible to require ministers to take responsibility for the actions of public servants.

In 1905, Treasury had 41 employees, and the bigger department of Trade and Customs, 1100. Today the public service is far larger. Ministers can no longer be asked to closely supervise and be accountable for the actions of public servants. Last century saw 'a change in the perceptions of both ministers and informed commentators as to what is required by the convention of individual ministerial responsibility' (Wright and Fowler 2012, 50). Wright and Fowler have argued that 'the real practical limitations on strict adherence to the convention as it was traditionally conceived are now openly acknowledged' (2012, 50). Today, ministers are still asked to account to parliament for the administration of policy by departments they supervise; however, they do not 'bear the blame for all the fault'. They are not 'bound to resign or suffer dismissal' unless a failing arises directly from their own actions (2012, 51). But even this is an ambiguous rule, open to different interpretations (Wright and Fowler 2012).

Ministerial responsibility cannot be precisely defined. It is not decided and enforced by courts. Rather its meaning is largely established by political circumstance and the 'court of public opinion'. As conventions are, it is enforced by practitioners. Using parliament and the media as platforms, oppositions will demand that ministers resign where they have overseen policy failure or maladministration. But resignation (or removal) 'on these grounds is rare' (179). Governing parties, loath to pay the political cost of removing or losing a minister, incline toward more modest interpretations of any penalties that responsible ministers should pay (Mulgan 2012). Hence, what this convention means and requires of ministers is renegotiated and established in the hurly burly of such political brawls when they arise.

QUESTION

What are the advantages and disadvantages of having political institutions governed by convention rather than law?

REFLECTION QUESTION 5.3

Should upper houses (the Senate and Legislative Councils) operate as 'houses of review' or should they play an active role in the formation and operation of government?

Response prompt is available at www.cambridge.org/highereducation/isbn/9781009108232/resources

THE AUSTRALIAN CONSTITUTION

If so many important aspects of the Westminster system upon which the Australian system is based are absent from the written document, the question remains: what does the Constitution actually contain? To answer this, it is important to recall that the creation of a national system of government was the result of the previously autonomous self-governing entities known as 'the colonies' coming together to establish a system that would address the need for a national approach to a narrowly defined and specific set of governmental responsibilities. In short, there were four of these – specifically, the need for a national system of defence, a desire for a national approach to immigration, the wish to have a national system of communication particularly with respect to a postal service and the new technology (at that time) of telegraphs, and to achieve interstate free trade. These were the drivers of the federation movement. Emy noted that federal constitutions will always reflect the carve-up of powers between the two levels of government (Emy 1997). As such, Section 51 of the Australian Constitution outlines the powers the colonies were prepared to cede to the new national government. The special status of the interstate free trade debate is reflected in the inclusion of its own section, in the form of Section 92 and its provision of free movement of goods, trade and people, and Section 102 allowing the Commonwealth to forbid preference being given to particular states by other states – but with important limitations. Section 92 was tested recently by mining entrepreneur and former minister of parliament Clive Palmer when he was refused entry into Western Australia because of border closures due to the COVID-19 pandemic. The High Court found that interstate trade, commerce and concourse *could* be contravened when it was reasonable to do so – such as in the middle of a pandemic *(Palmer v The State Of Western Australia* [2021] HCA 5, 2021). Nonetheless, the importance of Section 92 has been reiterated in previous judgments and generally guarantees free movement between states.

The federalist imperative is also detected in so many other sections of the document including the parliamentary institutions that were to be established of which 'the Senate' was to be explicitly a house of 'the states' with equal representation and with co-equal powers with the House of Representatives (Section 53); the division of the number of lower house seats according to the population sizes of the federating colonies but always with a provision that the 'original states' would be guaranteed at least five seats regardless of population (Section 24); the location of the national capital (not Sydney nor Melbourne but somewhere in between (Section 125)); and how the Constitution could only be altered if a majority of voters nationally and in a majority of states were to agree to it at a referendum (Section 128). The double hurdle equates therefore to 50 per cent plus one of voters overall plus a majority in four of the six states. This is different to the mechanism used to alter the US Constitution, which does require a referendum but also requires agreement by two-thirds of both houses of Congress and three-fourths of states (Erikson 2017).

The constitutional framers were cognisant of the possibility of disputes between the representative 'lower' chamber and the Senate, and so they provided a disputes resolution mechanism of final resort in Section 57 and its provision of the 'double dissolution' election. The significance of this lay in the fact that, ordinarily, the tenure of a senator would be twice that of a member of the House of Representatives – six years compared with three – (Section 28) with Senate terms being staggered so that only half of the upper house would be up for election at around the time the lower house was to go to the polls. Even this was complicated by Section 13 that sought to establish the principle that five years of the six-year term of a senator had to expire before a fresh election could be called, and that the timing of a senatorial term would commence in the January (later changed to July) of the year after the year the Senate election was held. As Emy noted, the stated intention of the constitutional framers was to ensure the Senate was not controlled by the executive (Emy 1997). While this might be seen as reinforcing the idea that the Senate was to be a state house rather than a party house, Sharman points out that there has been very little evidence to support this notion, past the over-representation of the small states (Sharman 1977).

REFLECTION QUESTION 5.4

Does it matter that Section 51(xxvi) of the Constitution allows the Commonwealth Parliament to make laws for 'the people of any race for whom it is deemed necessary to make special laws'?

Response prompt is available at www.cambridge.org/highereducation/isbn/9781009108232/resources

A BILL OF RIGHTS?

Australia may be a democracy, but its paper Constitution does not expressly guarantee the right to freely engage in political debate or protest. Indeed, it secures few rights. Section 116 does provide for religious freedom. Section 80 secures a right to trial by jury, and Section 117 protects against discrimination based on state residence. Australia is a signatory to, and in 1948 had a prominent role in drafting, the UN **UNIVERSAL DECLARATION OF HUMAN RIGHTS** (UN 1948). But its Constitution does not expressly safeguard those civil and political rights (like the right to life, liberty, free speech and privacy), which the Declaration requires ratifying nations to protect. It does not expressly protect the right to vote, though the High Court affirmed an implied right from Section 24. It does not expressly safeguard against discrimination on gender or racial grounds. We use the word 'expressly' here advisedly.

The Constitution's authors imagined that the rights of citizens would be protected by common law (e.g. habeas corpus) and by parliament itself. They rejected a US-style Bill of Rights. However, a century later, the High Court appeared to reach a different conclusion about the wisdom of constitutionally entrenching political freedoms. During the 1990s, in Australia there were significant shifts in judicial interpretations, as well as legislative state manoeuvres (Galligan and Morton 2017). The High Court identified certain political rights that are implied by the way the Constitution is constructed although not specifically protected by its written passages. To find implied rights within the Constitution, the Court had to abandon the 'textual' judicial method (legalism) it had adopted in and used since the 1920 Engineers case.

UNIVERSAL DECLARATION OF HUMAN RIGHTS: The Declaration was proclaimed by the United Nations General Assembly in 1948 as the basis of fundamental human rights, and applied as the basis of numerous treaties globally. UN Member States undertook to inscribe the Rights covered into their own legal frameworks.

Several decades of advocacy having failed, Australia still has no bill or charter of rights and remains the exception among comparable parliamentary and common law countries. Parliament has passed various laws (e.g. the *Disability Discrimination Act*) which proscribe discrimination on the grounds of gender, race and disability. But this is ordinary law, which can be varied by governments. Section 128 – a much larger hurdle – would stand in the way of altering rights entrenched in the Constitution. Those who advocate adding a Bill of Rights to the Australian Constitution see this as an advantage. Opponents see it as a problem. Short of initiating a referendum – a difficult political process unlikely to succeed – there would be no way of correcting an expansive interpretation of constitutionally given rights by any future 'activist' court. Adding a Bill of Rights would expand the temptation for unelected, unaccountable courts to interpret legislation and the Constitution in ways which change its intended meaning.

CASE STUDY 5.1 A CIVILISED COUNTRY NEEDS A BILL OF RIGHTS BUT …

Extract from a lecture by Scott Reid in the Department of the Senate Occasional Lecture Series at Parliament House on 23 October 1998:

> It seems to me that even in as civilised a country as Australia, Canada, or the United States, there are a number of vital services that can be performed by a well-written, well-interpreted Bill of Rights. These are functions that cannot be performed by any other institution of which I am aware.
>
> This being said, however, I freely confess that I am a great deal less optimistic about either the willingness or the ability of courts to always serve as absolutely neutral defenders of the law and of the public interest. If Australia adopts a Bill of Rights, whether constitutionally as in Canada and the U.S. or by means of legislation as in New Zealand, it will be placing enormous potential power in the hands of the judiciary.
>
> The manner in which the judges choose to exercise this power will be entirely their own decision; Parliament will have lost the power to rein in the High Court, should the justices choose to begin the process of striking down legislation. As Gil Remillard, a Canadian cabinet minister, warned shortly after the 1982 adoption of the *Canadian Charter of Rights and Freedoms*, 'The Charter will be whatever the Supreme Court chooses to make it, because only a constitutional amendment … may alter a Supreme Court decision.'
>
> This would not be problematic, if:
>
> - judges could be counted upon to always enact decisions that are entirely impartial and entirely free of arbitrary content; and
> - impartial judgments always promoted justice, equity and other socially important goals.
>
> Sadly, neither of these two propositions is valid.
>
> … In the *course* of this talk, I hope to outline some of the dangers that can result from unchecked judicial supremacy, and also to suggest some potential solutions to these dangers. Intelligent observers have long recognized the concerns that I will be raising today. Ninety-one years ago, U.S. Chief Justice Charles Evans Hughes warned, 'We are under a Constitution, but the Constitution is what the judges say it is.'

Source: Reid (1998).

QUESTION

Do you think that Australia should have a Bill of Rights? Why? Why not?

THE FEDERAL–STATE BALANCE OF POWER

There is much in the written constitution (Chapter IV – Finance and Trade) that deals with public money, particularly with regards to how this money might be obtained from the community (revenue and taxation) and how it might be allocated to the various levels of government (expenditure and transfers). At Federation not only were the colonies the most important level of government, aside from the United Kingdom itself, but they were also entitled to keep what were at that time important sources of revenue – with one exception. While the newly created states were to be allowed to retain their alcohol taxes and duties, the Commonwealth obtained control over tariffs on imported goods by virtue of the trade-off over interstate free trade. While states retained their tariffs and duties derived from interstate trade, the Commonwealth obtained control of this previously colony-level revenue stream from external trade. It was assumed by the newly formed states that revenue obtained by the Commonwealth would be returned to the states, even as the Commonwealth retained control. Moreover, there was to be a provision for the Commonwealth to allocate funds to the states for specific purposes as outlined in Section 96.

At Federation, the prevailing view about Section 96 was that this was intended to be an emergency provision that would allow the national government to provide short-term assistance to any state that was in financial difficulty. There was, however, a nagging doubt about this arrangement in the mind of at least one delegate to these conventions. Former colonial parliamentarian, and later prime minister, Mr Alfred Deakin from Victoria foresaw the capacity of Section 96 and some of the taxation provisions to enable the Commonwealth to impinge on the powers and responsibilities of the states. While the states were allowed to keep their alcohol excise revenue, Deakin noted with disapproval that revenue from tariffs imposed on imports were to go to the Commonwealth (Shapiro and Petchey 1995). In conjunction with Section 96, Deakin warned these arrangements meant that states' financial arrangements were now attached to the 'chariot wheels of the central Government'. His concerns were dismissed at the time, but in the 1940s, during the Second World War, the federal government instituted the *Uniform Tax Act,* with the High Court ruling this to be within constitutional powers of the Commonwealth. The consequence of this decision was to give the federal government control of the vast bulk of Australia's income and company taxation revenue, thereby fulfilling Deakin's gloomy prognosis about the future fiscal integrity of the Australian Federation (Finlay 2012).

WIDENING THE COMMONWEALTH'S POWERS

JUDICIAL REVIEW: Courts engage in judicial review when they determine whether legislation passed by Commonwealth and state parliaments is a proper exercise of their constitutionally given powers.

To see why '**JUDICIAL REVIEW** is by its very nature political' (Galligan 1995, 164) and has shaped the Australian Federation we need to further delve into history. In the several decades that followed the Engineers case, the High Court umpired the federal compact in ways advantaging the Commonwealth, refusing to consider the framers' intentions, instead preferring 'textual' readings of the Commonwealth heads of power in the Constitution. Lasting to the mid-century, this second distinct phase of judicial review saw Commonwealth powers 'read broadly and without any overt consideration of federalism issues' (Selway and Williams 2005, 147). *R v Brislan* 1935 is an example of the High Court expanding the Commonwealth's reach. The best known and most significant example, as noted above, was the 1942 Uniform Tax case.

However, not all High Court decisions in this period favoured the Commonwealth. Notably the High Court overturned legislation by the Chifley Labor Government seeking to control the private banking system (in the 1948 Bank Nationalisation case). Legislation to nationalise interstate airlines met a similar fate in the 1945 Airlines case. Moreover, Chifley's *Pharmaceutical Benefits Act 1944*, opposed by the medical profession as nationalised healthcare, was found to exceed the Commonwealth's appropriation powers (in the 1945 First Pharmaceutical Benefits case). These rulings blocked the Chifley Labor Government's democratic socialist policy agenda – and provided Labor partisans with grounds to argue that the High Court represents a conservative political force.

Selway and Williams identify a further, third phase of judicial review from mid-last century onward during which the High Court 'provided a framework for the development of the Australian Federation' (2005, 467), reaching decisions in a range of cases that increased the relative importance of the Commonwealth. They are, though, reluctant to see the High Court as driving change. Rather their view is that the High Court *reflected* rather than caused the various changes within the Federation.

Since Federation something of a battle has ensued between the states and the Commonwealth over the power to make policy. With each major emergency (wars and depression in particular), the power of the Commonwealth government seemed to advance (Fenna 2019). As we shall see, the process could also be advanced by the High Court and its determination of disputes over the exercise of government powers. Observers of the High Court could identify 'federalist' or 'centralist' tendencies in the way these cases would be determined (Patapan 2000). Given the reluctance of Australian voters to change the balance of power between the two levels of government at referenda, judicial interpretation has been the main force behind the gradual erosion of the idea that the states would be the main source of government, with the Commonwealth dealing with the limited list of powers outlined in Section 51 of the Constitution.

SHORT-ANSWER QUESTIONS 5.2

1. How did the Australian Constitution come about?
2. Are High Court decisions from the 1930s and 1940s relevant today?

Suggested responses are available at www.cambridge.org/highereducation/isbn/9781009108232/resources

RESEARCH QUESTION 5.1

The High Court has issued several rulings that have had profound impacts on Australia's federal arrangements. What are the key decisions that significantly altered the balance between the Commonwealth and the states, and why were they so important?

THE EXECUTIVE IN COUNCIL

In addition to outlining the terms and conditions of the Australian federal contract, the Constitution also sets out the key institutions that make up the system of national government including the executive, the parliament, the public service and the courts. The question of where lies the power to govern the Commonwealth is complicated by the attempt to link the written constitution with the practices of Westminster governance. This difficulty in Australian constitutionalism can be best dealt with by identifying the formal arrangements for governance that are outlined in the written document and the practical arrangements derived from our understanding of Westminster conventions. The formal arrangements derive their authority from those sections of the Constitution that set out the powers of the Governor-General and provide for Executive in Council (see Chapter II). In the plain meaning of the words in the Constitution, the Executive Council comprises ministers who provide advice to the Governor-General presumably on executive matters (Section 62 and Section 64) (Secretariat, 2017). There is no stipulation that the Governor-General must accept that advice. Indeed, as we shall see, events in 1975 demonstrated the great extent of the Governor-General's power to act unilaterally in the event of what the vice-regal representative viewed as an otherwise irreconcilable political impasse in the parliament (see below).

The 1975 crisis notwithstanding, the more usual practice is for the formal body that advises the head of executive as outlined by Section 64 to discharge a ritual function and simply ratify decisions made by the practical body of government (the Cabinet) and the practical head of government (the prime minister). In so doing, the Governor-General normally conforms with the Westminster convention that requires the Crown to act on the advice of the prime minister, whose authority derives from having a majority of seats in the House of Representatives by virtue of the outcome of the last lower house election. If this convention is observed, the 'thread' of answerability and accountability runs down from the Crown through the ministry and the parliament to the citizens (the voters). In almost all circumstances it is the prime minister, and not the Governor-General, who is the most important person in Australian politics, and it is the Cabinet, not the Executive in Council, that governs the nation. It is also worth remembering that, while the appointment of the Governor-General is formally made by the British Monarch, this is done on the advice of the Australian prime minister – vividly exposed by the appointment of Sir Isaac Isaacs in 1930 over the objections of King George V (Waugh 2011). This is perhaps a further indicator of the practical superiority of the prime minister over the Crown in the Australian context.

THE 1975 CONSTITUTIONAL CRISIS

Between 1901 and 1975, the understanding of how the Australian system of parliamentary government worked tended to assume that the conventions of Westminster practice were key to its operation. After a very shaky start when the newly arrived first Governor-General, Lord Hopetoun, proposed to appoint William Lyne as prime minister despite the fact that Edmund Barton held a lower house majority (see Chapter 3), Governors-General have always respected the convention of taking advice from a prime minister who commanded a majority in the House of Representatives. However, on 11 November 1975, the then Governor-General, Sir John Kerr, dismissed the then prime minister, Mr Gough Whitlam, even though he was the leader of the parliamentary Labor Party that commanded an absolute majority in the lower house. Having dismissed Whitlam, the Governor-General then commissioned the leader of the Liberal–Country Party coalition, Malcolm Fraser, as prime minister. As part of this process, Kerr had asked Fraser if, on being appointed, he would be able to advise on the need for a new general election. Fraser stated that he would indeed so advise, and Kerr duly appointed him and then invoked Section 57 of the Constitution to dissolve both parliamentary chambers and hold fresh elections for December that year.

The matter that precipitated this action involved a long period of impasse in the Australian Parliament because of a seemingly unresolvable dispute between the House of Representatives and the Senate. At issue was the Appropriation Bill (known as 'supply') for 1975–6. The disputed

Bill that was the centrepiece of the Whitlam Labor government's budget had passed the House of Representatives where Labor had a majority. The Senate, however, was under the control of the opposition – a situation caused by the death of a Labor senator after the 1974 election after which the National Country Party Premier of Queensland, Joh Bjelke-Petersen, advised the Queensland Governor to appoint an anti-Labor replacement pursuant to Section 15 of the Australian Constitution as it was at that time.

With the number of senators being so finely balanced after the 1974 double dissolution election, the Queensland appointment gifted Opposition Leader Fraser a majority in the Senate. Under political pressure to advance the interests of his side of politics over those of his opponents, Fraser decided to utilise the supply power of the Senate to try to force Whitlam to call an early election. However, rather than block supply, the opposition undertook a procedural tactic of deferring consideration of the Appropriations Bill – at least until such time as Whitlam could advise the parliament that he had called a general election. With his party languishing in the opinion polls and reasoning that an early election would lead to the defeat of his government, Whitlam refused the directive.

The budget process in those days commenced in August, so the Senate's refusal to consider supply brought government to a halt in October. The Governor-General waited until 11 November – the last day the parliament could sit before being dissolved and writs could be issued for an election to be held before Christmas 1975 – before intervening. In his published reasons for his actions, Sir John Kerr argued that the dispute between the Australian parliamentary chambers had to be resolved by middle December so that Australians could enjoy their summer holidays without having to concern themselves with this political crisis. At the meeting that Kerr dismissed Whitlam, Whitlam was attempting to present Kerr a letter calling for a Half Senate election, but Kerr interrupted him and spoke first, dismissing the government.

'CONSTITUTIONALISTS' VERSUS 'LITERALISTS-FEDERALISTS'

That these events and the Governor-General's actions were controversial goes without saying. Labor partisans in particular were outraged not only because their party was on the receiving end of the decision, but also because it did not tally with their understanding of how the Westminster system was assumed to work. This 'constitutionalist' approach argued that the authority to be prime minister derived from the majority support a government received from the elected lower house, and that the bestowing of a commission to lead a government by the Governor-General was a formality that replicated the modern British situation where the Crown clearly only ever acted on the advice of the government that, in turn, had the confidence of the lower house. They argued that the House of Representatives was the chamber of executive power not least because it reflected the will of the citizens via a majoritarian voting system. The idea that Malcolm Fraser should be appointed prime minister by virtue of the fact that his party had a majority in the Senate seemed like a complete repudiation of the Westminster system. By refusing to accept these key Westminster conventions, the constitutionalists argued that Sir John Kerr had acted contrary to the spirit of Australian constitutionalism (Staveley 1976).

The argument against Whitlam and in support of the Governor-General, however, preferred to focus on the content of the words written in the Australian Constitution rather than on the more nebulous notion as to what the unwritten conventions of Westminster practice were supposed to provide for. This 'literalist' approach was also a 'federalist' argument, for it focused more on the concessions made to federalism in the Constitution, particularly with regards to what it had to say about the role and function of the Senate. The notion of a 'co-equal' status of the houses as outlined in Section 53 was the key here and turned out to be central to Sir John Kerr's reasons as to why he dismissed the Whitlam government (Sampford 1987). Kerr and other literalists pointed out that the power exercised by the Governor-General was legitimate because it was all written down in the Constitution. The literalists also pointed out that not only was the position of prime minister nowhere to be found in the document, but there was also no reference to the Governor-General having to be directed by advice from the Executive in Council. In other words, the literalist case revolved around the idea that not only was the Governor-General able to act unilaterally in dealing with political crises that might affect the operation of government, but also the words in the Constitution actually stated that such intervention to ensure 'good government' was required.

THE KERR DOCTRINE: 'PARLIAMENTARY RESPONSIBILITY'

This was only part of the argument for the dismissal, however. Given that he was the key actor in this event, the Governor-General's own reasoning behind his actions is worth reflecting upon given it stands as something of a precedent. Sir John Kerr based his argument on the fact that the Australian system of national government had been created as a federal system, with the Senate created as a chamber of co-equal status to the House of Representatives, with representatives also directly elected. This was what sat at the heart of the constitutional problem the Governor-General believed he was required to solve.

The Whitlam Government's failure to secure supply was the key to this problem, and this was due of course to the unwillingness of the Senate to pass the Appropriation Bill. Here Kerr's literalist approach was important: in assessing the legitimacy of the Senate's actions, Kerr was interested more in what the written constitution said about the Senate than in what the Senate was in political reality. The reality was (and is) that the Senate was hardly a state house but more a replica of the party system operating in the lower house. To the lay person, the Senate was deferring supply because it was controlled by the Coalition parties with a political leader anxious to get to an election before he was removed from the leadership, as had occurred to some before him. However, to a literalist such as Kerr the political nature of the Senate was irrelevant. What was important was the status accorded by the Constitution and the conventions derived from it, and it was on the basis of this that Sir John Kerr formulated his concept of the applicability of the idea of 'parliamentary responsibility'. This became the basis of assessing the extent of the problem presented by the Whitlam Government's inability to secure supply and what a Governor-General should do about it – even as scholars have noted that he failed to address the problem of convention ('responsible government') being subservient to the Constitution (Mayer 1980).

In outlining his reasons for dismissing Whitlam, the Governor-General considered the applicability of the Westminster model in a federal context. He noted that, while Australia did indeed replicate the Westminster system of parliamentary government as practiced in Britain, important points of difference existed between the two nations. Britain was a unitary state and not a federation, and no regional or geographic basis existed upon which the House of Lords could seek to counter the will of the House of Commons, and, besides this, the Lords was not an elected house compared with the direct election of the Australian Senate. Kerr argued that, in constructing the national system of federal government, the constitutional framers intended for the legislative process to carry the imprimatur of being approved by 'the people' (the House of Representatives) and of the federating states (the Senate). This included appropriation bills. Kerr argued that Australia's system of responsible government was modified by the federal reality: for appropriation to become law, he argued, the necessary bill had to be approved by the House of Representatives and the Senate. Failure for this to occur reflected a failure of government, and the applicable Westminster convention here required an election to resolve such irreconcilable disputes. This is not undisputed, and as Galligan pointed out after both Kerr and Whitlam put forward their own views in 1978 and 1979, respectively, Sir John Kerr acted with inappropriate haste, and not in full accordance with the Constitution (Galligan 1980).

As Kerr put it, having been unable to get appropriation approved by both the lower and upper houses, Prime Minister Whitlam had failed the test of responsibility and should have tended his resignation and asked for fresh elections accordingly. If, as was the case in 1975, a prime minister refuses to so advise, in Kerr's opinion the role of the Crown was to dismiss that prime minister. In Kerr's case, he did just that and then installed a parliamentarian (thus satisfying Section 64) who could pass the necessary appropriation bills though the house in question, prior to advising the Governor-General that Section 57 be invoked and fresh elections held. This happened to be Malcolm Fraser, notwithstanding the fact that at the time he was the leader of the opposition by virtue of a lack of a lower house majority. The problem of the caretaker prime minister lacking a lower house majority was resolved by Kerr through the dissolution process. The parliament was authorised to sit just long enough to get the Appropriation Bill through the Senate after which the parliament was 'prorogued'. Whitlam, for his part, failed to warn his own senators about the tactical shift, leading to the Labor senators supporting the very supply bill which legitimised the government's dismissal. By the time the House of Representatives was convened and voted a no-confidence motion in Fraser, the authority of the parliament to sit had been withdrawn. When the Speaker rang Buckingham Palace to inform Queen Elizabeth II about what had happened, he was politely reminded of the gross breach of protocol that he was embarking upon as Australian matters were only ever dealt with by the Governor-General. The Palace might have reminded the Speaker that he ought to have known this because the man in question, Sir John Kerr, had been appointed by the Queen on the advice of the then Australian prime minister, Mr Gough Whitlam. Unfortunately, the Palace might also have noted that they had known for two months that Kerr was contemplating dismissal ('The Kerr Palace Letters', 2020).

THE 1975 CRISIS: CONSEQUENCES

It is no overstatement to describe the 1975 constitutional crisis as the most divisive matter to arise in Australian politics since Federation, and the events of that year have precipitated many debates as to the legitimacy of the actions of all the key players. For the student of Australian constitutionalism, the understanding of how the Australian system of national government works must consider Sir John Kerr's actions as a precedent that influences our overview of the system regardless of our political standpoint. At the time, many Australians were quite shocked at the power that was exercised by two institutions that had previously been thought to be either moribund (the Governor-General), and/or of secondary importance (the Senate) to the role of the House of Representatives as the house of government and the assumption that the prime minister is the leading person in Australian politics. While perhaps not surprising, observers may also have been surprised at how flimsy the conventions of Westminster practice were when they came into conflict with the written words of the Constitution. Equally, the situation had not arisen previously and has not since, so those same conventions appear to still operate (Galligan and Brenton 2015).

Despite all of this, it is still the case that, notwithstanding a literal reading of the Constitution, the Australian system of national government is of the Westminster-type because it essentially involves parliamentary government. Furthermore, the position of prime minister continues to be central to the operation of the system not least because the first minister is so important to the interaction between the parliament and the Crown. The Australian system still requires elections for both houses of the parliament, and it is fair to say that, when an election is held and the count is completed, the community looks to the result in the House of Representatives to see which of the political parties has enough seats to be able to form a government. Moreover, the command of a lower house majority is the basis upon which the leader of the party or parties that have secured that majority will be entitled to liaise with the Governor-General to accept the commission to be prime minister and to present other members of the parliament who will be sworn in by the Governor-General to be Ministers of the Crown. This is the way the process worked at Federation and has continued to work since.

What the 1975 crisis showed was that the constraints on the power of the prime minister to dominate the operation of the parliament that were put into the system by Australia's nineteenth-century colonial lawyers and politicians have not been diminished by the passage of time. Though the notion of it being a 'state house' may have receded, the Senate, it turns out, continues to be a very powerful parliamentary chamber capable of denying government its ability to pass legislation and even being able to force the government out of power! The Senate's power to deny supply exists in the Australian Constitution. The decision to exercise it remains a political one. Were the numbers and conditions that led to the 1975 crisis to be replicated sometime in the future, the Senate would have the power to bring down a government if it so chose to do.

THE HIGH COURT

The provision of a judicial dimension as a part of the national system of government is outlined in Chapter III of the Constitution. At Federation this took the form of the High Court, although the ability for the parliament to create additional courts was provided for under Section 71, and, indeed, in 1976 the Federal Court was created to deal with the increasing administrative and litigative workload. Sections 75, 76 and 77 outline the jurisdictional remit of the courts, the most pertinent to a consideration of constitutionalism being the power to resolve disputes between the Commonwealth and the states over the creation of public policy. Here a matter of potential confusion can arise. Section 109 states that Commonwealth laws will prevail where there might be a conflict with state laws, and this gives the impression that the Commonwealth has a superior status to the states. The problem here, however, may relate to the constitutional authority the Commonwealth had to make those conflicting laws in the first place, and it is precisely at this juncture that the High Court (and now also the Federal Court) plays the crucial role in determining if the federal constitution did indeed provide the legal authority for the law.

It is important to understand that while the idea of a 'supreme court' capable of resolving constitutional disputes was an idea taken from the federal system of the United States, the High Court of Australia operates within the British legal culture. This includes the notion of the judiciary being separate from the political world of the legislature and in some sense depoliticised. That said, while the Australian High Court has not involved itself in some of the hyper-partisan debates seen in the US Supreme Court, it is not unpolitical. It has been the case that former parliamentarians have been appointed to the High Court. The first High Court, appointed in 1903, following the passage of the *Judiciary Act 1903*, included the former Prime Minister Edmund Barton, although there have also been appointees with extensive professional experience in the law before entering parliament. It is perhaps worth considering that while the appointment of

Supreme Court justices has generated considerable controversy over the past decade (in some cases many years before), justices considered both conservative and radical have sat on the High Court with only occasional protest.

High Court justices are appointed by the Governor-General on the advice of Cabinet, but thereafter a justice remains in place until the legislated retirement age of 70 years. The requirements of the *High Court of Australia Act 1979* regulates the appointment, such that the Commonwealth Attorney-General is required to consult with state and territory Attorneys-General on a new appointment, and that to be considered a person must already be a judge or be a barrister or solicitor of standing with a state Supreme Court or the High Court (Evans 2001). While the appointment of former politicians to the bench, such as former Attorneys-General Sir Garfield Barwick (Liberal) and Lionel Murphy (Labor), was the source of much controversy in the context of the way this seemed to politicise the bench, in general most justices are judged on their approach to extant law.

As already noted, judicial interpretation in constitutional disputes with the states, corporations or individuals has done more to alter the federal–state balance of power than changes made by the citizenry via the referendum process. Observers of the High Court tend to identify distinct periods of judicial 'activism' or 'conservatism' in the way particular courts have determined disputes (Galligan 1987; Patapan 2000). Activist courts are understood to be responsible for the most dramatic changes to the federal–state balance with decisions that more often than not enhance the powers of the Commonwealth. At the same time, conservative courts, as although nominally 'federalist' with a preference for constraining the power of the national government, have continued to provide judgments that constrain the scope of state government (Allan and Aroney 2008). The significance of the High Court to the policymaking process cannot be understated, for although it has been known for the court to nullify significant federal government initiatives such as the Chifley Labor Government's attempt to nationalise the private banking system in 1947, some judgments have dramatically shifted power between the states and the Commonwealth, such as the Tasmanian Dam case in 1983, and the overturning of the concept of 'terra nullius' in the Mabo Land-rights case of 1987. In such situations some critics have alleged that the courts appear to have overtaken the parliament as the institutional drivers of policy reform, and this is contrary to Westminster tradition. The Westminster model assumes a clear division of labour: the power to determine policy should rest with the parliament whereas the role of the courts should be confined to the task of applying policy as determined by the parliament.

SPOTLIGHT 5.2 THE SIGNIFICANCE OF JUDICIAL INTERPRETATION: THE TASMANIAN DAM CASE

There have been so many constitutional cases before the High Court whose determination was to have great consequence to the federal–state balance of powers. The Tasmanian Dam case was one of these. The case was brought by the Tasmanian Government to challenge the constitutional validity of legislation from the Commonwealth Parliament (in this case, the *World Heritage Properties Protection Act 1983)* that had been drafted to stop the Hydro Electricity Commission of Tasmania from proceeding with a hydro-electric scheme on the Franklin River in the state's south-west. Tasmania argued that the power to create land-use policy was a state responsibility. The Commonwealth argued that Section 51 gave it powers over 'external affairs' and that, as a signatory to a United Nations treaty on wilderness preservation, the national government had the power to stop the project.

The High Court found in favour of the Commonwealth. In so doing, it altered the previous balance of power in which the states were the determiners of land-use matters. It also opened the possibility for the Commonwealth to involve itself in many other matters irrespective of whether they were otherwise within the constitutional remit of the Commonwealth, provided it had signed a relevant international treaty. This case was to commence a period of unprecedented federal intervention into several other conservation matters. Prior to 1983 such matters had tended to be dealt with by state governments. The High Court had clearly altered the dynamics in national environmental policymaking by simply confirming the salience of the external powers subsection in Section 51.

QUESTION

Why is the Tasmanian Dam case significant?

SHORT-ANSWER QUESTIONS 5.3

1. Why might the High Court be considered a political actor?
2. How does the High Court make law?
3. What is the separation of powers?

Suggested responses are available at www.cambridge.org/highereducation/isbn/9781009108232/resources

---

CONSTITUTIONAL REFORM

The constitutional framers intended for the Constitution to be able to be altered, and the mechanism for doing so is outlined in Section 128. As already noted, concessions to Australia's federal system can be found in this section especially in the requirement that any change requires a referendum that must be approved by a majority of voters nationally and by a majority of voters in a majority of states. There have been 84 attempts at changing the Australian Constitution of which a mere eight have been successful. Of these, the majority of successful questions were minor adjustments to some of the mechanics of the system. Questions asking to transfer significant powers from the states to the Commonwealth usually fail, reflecting perhaps that the Australian people are very reluctant to make Canberra more powerful in the policymaking process. Despite this record of failure, political advocates of change persist with calls for constitutional reform and that inevitably requires use of the referendum process.

By far the greatest number of (generally unsuccessful) referendum questions have related to attempts to give the federal government more power than was originally intended by the constitutional framers. In among the unsuccessful questions were proposals to give the Commonwealth more power over incomes, prices, industrial relations and power over things as diverse as the party system (banning the Communist Party, for example) through to local government. The few successful questions tended to pass during times of national crises. Thus, a question to give the Commonwealth more leadership power over international finances was passed in 1925 (see Section 105A), and in 1942 powers over pharmaceuticals, health policy and financial assistance for tertiary students were included in Section 51 (see subsection xxiiiA). One of the most celebrated changes to Section 51 occurred in 1967 when a referendum agreed to strike out reference to Indigenous people in subsection xxvi that had had the effect of making policy on Indigenous people a state responsibility. This was the last time a referendum question proposing to alter the federal–state balance of power was approved of by way of the referendum process.

RESEARCH QUESTION 5.2

Just eight of 44 attempts to alter the written constitution have been successful. Look closely at some of the proposed changes that have failed in the past. What does this say about the political obstacles that referenda pose?

PROCEDURAL REFORMS

The next largest tranche of referendum questions has dealt with procedures and mechanisms involving the national parliament. These have included repeated attempts to resolve the tension between the Senate and the House of Representatives and this took on a particular urgency in the aftermath of the 1975 constitutional crisis. This has tended to take the form of trying to get the Australian people to accept fixed parliamentary terms (with the additional rider of increasing the tenure of the House of Representatives from three to four years). The extension of the parliamentary term is justified by its proponents to give the executive more time to create and apply 'difficult' (presumably, this means unpopular) policy decisions. It might also be argued that the constitutional guarantee of a fixed term would cancel the Senate's ability to force elections by blocking supply. Like questions that seek to alter the balance of power between the two levels of government, these questions typically fail. The last successful mechanical alteration occurred in 1977 when Section 15 was altered to require casual vacancies to be filled by candidates from the same political party as the vacating senator. Unlike matters to do with governmental powers, the High Court has been loath to get involved in such procedural matters.

NATIONAL SYMBOLISM

Presumably as a result of the consistent failure of questions seeking to alter the power balance between the two levels of government (and recognising that this is being done by the High Court anyway), more recent debates about constitutional reform have focused on the symbolic nature of the document. The questions on fixed parliamentary terms, the recognition of local government and 'free and fair elections' put to the Australian people in 1988 were the last procedural matters to be placed on the agenda. Since then, questions have been put about altering the preamble to the Constitution and making Australia a republic and were defeated. Republicanism continues to be debated notwithstanding the defeat at the 1999 referendum. So, too, does the matter of how Indigenous Australians are recognised. Under the terms of Section 51 in the Constitution as originally drafted, responsibility for Indigenous people was explicitly given to the states. It was this sentence that explicitly excluded Indigenous people as a policy concern for the Commonwealth that was removed by the celebrated 1967 referendum. It appears that the matter of Indigenous recognition will most likely be revisited in the future by way of proposed constitutional reform, although it is not clear just what form this recognition will take.

REFLECTION QUESTION 5.5

Considering the nature and interpretation of the constitution as a document most often regulating the relationship between the Commonwealth and the states, what explains more recent attempts at alteration of the constitution, concerning such things as republicanism and Indigenous recognition?

Response prompt is available at www.cambridge.org/highereducation/isbn/9781009108232/resources

SUMMARY

Learning objective 1: Understand the meaning of Australian 'constitutionalism' as a combination of the written constitution and Westminster practice

Australian constitutionalism involves a combination of a constitution that was drafted primarily to delineate the heads of powers (the 39 subsections of Section 51 of the Constitution) between the newly formed 'Commonwealth' and the federating states and the unwritten conventions of the Westminster system of parliamentary or 'responsible' government. The relatively long period of stable and, in the main, successful practice of state and national governance shows that this is generally a workable model. The Constitution that was drafted by colonial lawyers and parliamentarians back in the 1890s is the Constitution that is in use to this day and reflects a quite distinctly Australian approach to the idea of Westminster governance.

Learning objective 2: Identify some key sections of the Australian Constitution and their consequences for the system of federal governance

Remembering that the Australian Constitution is a bargain between those who would have a single nation and those that would retain state autonomy, key sections of the Constitution will be those relating to the powers of each. As noted above, Section 51 delineates the powers of the Commonwealth, while Chapter V concerns states powers and prohibitions. Section 109 allowed for Commonwealth law to override state law, but only to the extent that the Commonwealth had power in that area, thus preserving state's rights over those powers not included in the Constitution.

Learning objective 3: Understand the importance of the 1975 'constitutional crisis'

The onset of the 1975 constitutional crisis showed that there are indeed some contradictory principles associated with trying to combine a Westminster model within a federal system. The extent of the power that the Governor-General has to intervene in the event of a political crisis (albeit a political crisis occurring in the context of a lack of constitutional clarity as to whether the House of Representatives or the Senate are the pivot to the system) was also something of a surprise especially when compared with the clear subordination of the crown to the parliament in the modern British system.

Learning objective 4: Identify the significance of the High Court

The Constitution makes the High Court Australia's 'federal supreme court' and constitutional umpire. It has an original jurisdiction. Today much of its work entails hearing appeals from subordinate federal and state courts in cases where it believes that a law or the Constitution itself requires clarification. The High Court engages in judicial review where it is asked to determine whether executive actions or legislation passed by parliament comply with the Constitution. When the High Court has been asked to hear cases raising concerns about the proper application of the Constitution, often a question relating to the division of powers between the Commonwealth and the states has been involved. After all, the 1901 Constitution is substantially concerned with establishing Australia as a federation and contains no 'Bill of Rights' (which might otherwise engage the High Court in judicial review). In umpiring the federal compact, the High Court, over many decades and in many cases, has enlarged the authority of the Commonwealth at the expense of the states.

Learning objective 5: Understand how the Constitution can be altered and reflect on future constitutional reform

In the 21st century, Australia still has a Constitution that is largely silent on rights and freedoms that define liberal democracies and that entrenches a mix of federalism and responsible government that many argue ill-suits the challenge of governing a nation caught up in rapid technological, social and economic change. But updating the Constitution is no easy thing. Although Section 128 allows its amendment via a referendum process, changes have been difficult to achieve. Change first requires parliament to pass initiating legislation, and then that amendments be approved by a majority of voters and of the states.

Since Federation only eight amendments have been successfully prosecuted. This does not mean the wider constitution has not evolved. The High Court is able to change how the Constitution is interpreted, even if it cannot change the words on the page. And some rules governing government are open to alteration. Parliament can amend the *Electoral Act*. Conventions are ultimately decided in the court of public opinion and open to reinterpretation. But altering the formal Constitution is another matter. Often political obstacles stand in the way. This reminds us that constitutions are not only rules governing how political actors should behave. They are themselves the object of political struggle since they ultimately dictate who wins and loses in contests for political power.

DISCUSSION QUESTIONS

1. What is a constitution?

2. Is Australia's Constitution an 'anachronistic, dusty old book'?

3. Australian state constitutions can be changed without holding referenda elections. Should the Commonwealth Parliament be able to similarly amend the Australian Constitution?

4. Should the High Court 'make law'?

5. What are the arguments for and against adding a Bill of Rights to the Australian Constitution?

FURTHER READING

Fenna, A. (2013). The Australian system of government, especially. In A. Fenna, J. Robbins and J. Summers (eds), *Government and Politics in Australia*, Frenchs Forest: Pearson Australia, pp. 23–8.

Galligan, B. & Brenton, S. (2015). Constitutional conventions. In B. Galligan and S. Brenton (eds), *Constitutional Conventions in Westminster Systems: Controversies, Changes and Challenges*, Cambridge: Cambridge University Press, pp. 8–23.

Galligan, B. & Morton, F.L. (2017). Australian exceptionalism: Rights protection without a Bill of Rights. In T. Campbell, J. Goldsworthy and A. Stone (eds), *Protecting Rights Without a Bill of Rights: Institutional Performance and Reform in Australia*, Burlington: Ashgate Publishing Ltd.

Patapan, H. (2000). *Judging Democracy: The New Politics of the High Court of Australia*, Melbourne: Cambridge University Press.

Wright, B. & Fowler, P. (2012). *The House of Representatives Practice*, 6th edn, Canberra: Department of the House of Representatives.

REFERENCES

Allan, J. & Aroney, N. (2008). An uncommon court: How the High Court of Australia has undermined Australian federalism. *Sydney Law Review*, **30**(2), 245–94.

Bagehot, W. (1888). *The English Constitution*, 5th edn, London: Kegan Paul, Tench & Co.

Ballinger, C. (2011). Hedging and ditching: The Parliament Act 1911. *Parliamentary History*, **30**(1), 19–32. https://doi.org/10.1111/j.1750-0206.2010.00239.x

Barry, N., Miragliotta, N. & Nwokora, Z. (2019). The dynamics of constitutional conventions in Westminster democracies. *Parliamentary Affairs*, **72**(3), 664–83. https://doi.org/10.1093/pa/gsy027

Chordia, S. & Lynch, A. (2014). Federalism in Australian constitutional interpretation: Signs of reinvigoration? *University of Queensland Law Journal*, **33**(1), 83–107.

Commonwealth of Australia Constitution Act [Constitution of Australia]. (1900). Retrieved from http://www.austlii.edu.au/cgi-bin/viewdoc/au/legis/cth/consol_act/coaca430/s24.html

Emy, H. (1997). Unfinished business: Confirming Australia's Constitution as an act of political settlement. *Australian Journal of Political Science*, **32**(3), 383–400. https://doi.org/10.1080/10361149750814

Emy, H. & Hughes, O. (1988). *Australian Politics: Realities in Conflict*, Melbourne: Macmillan.

Erikson, B. (2017). Amending the US Constitution. *LegisBrief*, **25**(30).

Evans, S. (2001). Appointment of justices. In M. Coper, T. Blackshield and G. Williams (eds), *The Oxford Companion to the High Court of Australia*, Oxford: Oxford University Press.

Fenna, A. (2019). The centralization of Australian federalism 1901–2010: Measurement and interpretation. *Publius: The Journal of Federalism*, **49**(1), 30–56. https://doi.org/10.1093/publius/pjy042

Finlay, L. (2012). The power of the purse: An examination of fiscal federalism in Australia. *The Journal of Constitutional History/Giornale di storia costituzionale*, **24**(2), 81–93. https://doi.org/10.1400/201155

Galligan, B. (1980). The Kerr-Whitlam debate and the principles of the Australian Constitution. *Journal of Commonwealth & Comparative Politics*, **18**(3), 247–71. https://doi.org/10.1080/14662048008447363

—— (1987). *Politics of the High Court: A Study of the Judicial Branch of Government in Australia*, St Lucia: University of Queensland Press.

—— (1995). *A Federal Republic: Australia's Constitutional System of Government*, Melbourne: Cambridge University Press.

Galligan, B. & Brenton, S. (2015). Constitutional conventions. In B. Galligan and S. Brenton (eds), *Constitutional Conventions in Westminster Systems: Controversies, Changes and Challenges*, Cambridge: Cambridge University Press, pp. 8–23.

Galligan, B. & Morton, F.T. (2017). Australian exceptionalism: Rights protection without a bill of rights. In T. Campbell, J. Goldsworthy and A. Stone (eds), *Protecting Rights Without a Bill of Rights: Institutional Performance and Reform in Australia*, Aldershot: Ashgate Publishing, pp. 17–39.

The Kerr Palace Letters. (2020). Retrieved from https://www.naa.gov.au/explore-collection/kerr-palace-letters

King, J. (2019). The democratic case for a written constitution. *Current Legal Problems*, **72**(1), 1–36. https://doi.org/10.1093/clp/cuz001

Kurland, P.B. & Lerner, R. (1987). The separation of powers. In P.B. Kurland and R. Lerne (eds), *The Founders' Constitution*, Chicago: University of Chicago.

Loughlin, M. (2015). The constitutional imagination. *The Modern Law Review*, **78**(1), 1–25. https://doi.org/10.1111/1468-2230.12104

Mayer, D.Y. (1980). Sir John Kerr and responsible government. *Politics*, **15**(2), 50–8. https://doi.org/10.1080/00323268008401757

Moran, T. (2012). The challenges for the public service in protecting Australia's democracy in the future. In J. Wanna, S. Vincent and A. Podger (eds), *With the Benefit of Hindsight*, Canberra: ANU Press, pp. 177–87.

Mulgan, R. (1996). The Australian Senate as a 'House of Review'. *Australian Journal of Political Science*, **31**(2), 191–204. https://doi.org/10.1080/10361149651184

—— (2012). Assessing ministerial responsibility in Australia. In K. Dowding and C. Lewis (eds), *Ministerial Careers and Accountability in the Australian Commonwealth Government*, Canberra: ANU E-Press, pp. 177–93.

Palmer v The State Of Western Australia [2021] HCA 5 (High Court of Australia 2021).

Patapan, H. (2000). *Judging Democracy: The New Politics of the High Court of Australia*, Cambridge: Cambridge University Press.

Reid, S. (1998). *Curbing Judicial Activism: The High Court, the People and a Bill of Rights*. Papers on Parliament No. 33, May 1999, Canberra: Australian Parliament House. Retrieved from https://www.aph.gov.au/About_Parliament/Senate/Powers_practice_n_procedures/pops/pop33/reid

Sampford, C. (1987). The Australian Senate and supply-some awkward questions. *Monash University Law Review*, **13**(2), 119–48.

Secretariat, F.E.C. (2017). Federal Executive Council handbook. In *Department of the Prime Minister and Cabinet* (ed.), Canberra: Department of the Prime Minister and Cabinet.

Selway, B. & Williams, J. (2005). The high court and Australian federalism. *Publius: The Journal of Federalism*, **35**(3), 467–88. https://doi.org/10.1093/publius/pji018

Shapiro, P. & Petchey, J. (1995). Chariot wheels and section 90: A case for giving sales tax powers back to the states. *Policy: A Journal of Public Policy Ideas*, **11**(1), 13–16.

Sharman, C. (1977). The Australian senate as a states' house. *Politics*, **12**(2), 64–75. https://doi.org/10.1080/00323267708401617

Staveley, R. (1976). The conventions of the constitution: Kerr's folly. *Politics*, **11**(1), 16–19. https://doi.org/10.1080/00323267608401535

Thompson, E. (1980). The 'Washminster' mutation. *Politics*, **15**(2), 32–40. https://doi.org/10.1080/00323268008401755

United Nations. (1948). *Universal Declaration of Human Rights*. Retrieved from https://www.un.org/en/about-us/universal-declaration-of-human-rights

Ward, A.J. (1987). Exporting the British Constitution: Responsible government in New Zealand, Canada, Australia and Ireland. *Journal of Commonwealth Comparative Politics*, **25**(1), 3–25. https://doi.org/10.1080/14662048708447505

Waugh, J. (2011). An Australian in the palace of the King–Emperor: James Scullin, George V and the appointment of the first Australian-born Governor-General. *Federal Law Review*, **39**(2), 235–53.

Wright, B. & Fowler, P. (2012). *The House of Representatives Practice*, 6th edn, Canberra: Department of the House of Representatives.

CHAPTER 6
BUREAUCRACY
The APS and public policy

LEARNING OBJECTIVES

After reading this chapter, you should be able to:

1. Explain the origins and use of the term bureaucracy
2. Provide an overview of the contemporary Australian Public Service
3. Define public policy and describe the policy process
4. Understand the shift from 'government' to 'governance'
5. Outline some of the challenges for the public service and its possible future

INTRODUCTION

BUREAUCRACY: A mode of administration common in large organisations, but particularly associated with public sector agencies, based on hierarchical structures and adherence to processes, rules and routines.

NEW PUBLIC MANAGEMENT: A reform program applied to most public sector organisations in developed countries during the 1980s and 1990s based upon private sector management techniques and market logic.

PUBLIC POLICY: A core aspect of government activity involving governments committing resources to address public problems and issues.

GOVERNANCE: The broad process of governing comprising various strategies, processes and relationships and involving governments and/or a range of societal groups and institutions.

This chapter examines the role of the administrative arm of government known as the **BUREAUCRACY**, public service or civil service. Political scientists focus on bureaucracies because they are central components of government activity and the means by which governments put public policies into action. The first section of the chapter charts the origins and development of bureaucracy as a model of organisation, which contrasts with the popular, and largely negative, understanding of the term. Turning to the Australian context, the chapter then provides an overview of the Australian federal bureaucracy, the Australian Public Service (APS), from its embryonic status at Federation through to its development into a large, complex and multifaceted institution in the 21st century, including the huge **NEW PUBLIC MANAGEMENT** reforms to the public service during the 1980s and 1990s. In explaining the bureaucracy's role, the chapter outlines a key activity: policymaking. It examines definitions and stages of **PUBLIC POLICY**, noting that in practice these stages represent an idealised understanding of the policy work of the bureaucracy. In reality, the world of policymaking is often chaotic, ad hoc and subject to opportunities and political leadership.

New Public Management reforms and modern policymaking are then placed in a broader context of a shift from government to **GOVERNANCE** that has taken place in recent decades. Public sector organisations and their policymaking roles have been transformed from relatively monolithic entities into a complex array of public, civil society and business organisations all contributing to policy development and delivery. The degree to which state institutions including bureaucracies are strengthened or weakened by these new arrangements is a source of debate among political scientists. The chapter concludes by discussing the challenges the public service faces in the 21st century. Although large-scale reform has eased, the public service faces issues such as debate over its size and efficiency, its status as the pre-eminent source of policy advice to governments and use of digital technology.

WHAT IS BUREAUCRACY?

The 18th century economist Vincent de Gourney defined bureaucracy in its modern sense as 'a form of government in which officials dominate' (Bevir 2010, 143). But while the term bureaucracy is relatively new, the concept is said to have originated with early empires seeking to exert rule over expanded territories (Crooks and Parsons 2016). Bureaucracy was utilised in the Qin and Han dynasties in China, the Inca Empire and the Ottoman Empire to name just a few, for tasks such as determining and collecting taxes, governing trade and providing early forms of policing.

In the contemporary context, bureaucracy has been defined in a number of ways: as 'a hierarchical organisation of officials appointed to carry out certain public objectives' (Etzioni-Halevy 2010, 85); an 'organisation characterised by hierarchy, fixed rules, impersonal relationships, strict adherence to impartial procedures, and specialisation based on function' (Bevir 2009, 37); or simply as behaviour that rigidly applies general rules to particular cases. A central aspect of bureaucracy is that it is a form of organisation that prioritises rules and processes as an approach to administering human activity.

Inevitably, some degree of bureaucracy is essential for managing large numbers of people effectively or developing plans where there is a need to establish authority, order and systems.

While elected politicians are responsible for decision-making, the government bureaucracy provides the essential institutional machinery for formulating policy options and implementing government decisions.

In contemporary Australia, there is a permanent layer of bureaucracy associated with each tier of government at the local, state and territory, and federal levels. In broad terms, the bureaucracy is active across three general policy arenas: (1) law and order, including defence and foreign affairs; (2) economic management; and (3) social welfare such as health, education, arts, and aged care. Local government bureaucracies undertake activity associated with town planning and development, roads maintenance and waste collection. At the state and territory level, bureaucracies deliver education and health services, as well as managing infrastructure, water resources and electricity generation, to name a few areas. At the national level, the APS is the bureaucracy supporting the federal government and is most active in national policy areas including economic management, social security, overseeing inter-governmental relations, defence and foreign affairs.

SPOTLIGHT 6.1 WESTMINSTER AND APS VALUES

Because public servants undertake important work on behalf of governments and the broader public, a strong set of values and principles are critical to maintaining trust.

The basic principles of the APS and state/territory public services derive from the 1854 Northcote-Trevelyan Report, which established the modern British civil service and the model exported to Australia. In 2018–19, a government-commissioned review of the APS stated 'the modern Westminster principles of government remain essential: an apolitical, merit-based, and open public service, underpinned by integrity, serving the Government, Parliament and the people of Australia. These principles must be reinforced and supported' (DPMC 2019, 8).

Section 10 of the *Public Service Act 1999* outlines in detail the expectations of public sector employees in terms of performance and standards of behaviour (APSC 2020). The Australian Public Service Commission's website (APSC 2020) summarises these:

- *Impartial*: the APS 'is apolitical and provides the Government with advice that is frank, honest, timely and based on the best available evidence'
- *Committed to service*: the public service is 'professional, objective, innovative and efficient, and works collaboratively to achieve the best results for the Australian community and the Government'
- *Accountable*: the public service 'is open and accountable to the Australian community under the law and within the framework of Ministerial responsibility'
- *Respectful*: the public service 'respects all people, including their rights and their heritage'
- *Ethical*: the public service 'demonstrates leadership, is trustworthy, and acts with integrity, in all that it does'.

QUESTIONS

What makes the work of the public service different to that of the private sector? How might the principles and values above be the same or different in the two sectors?

BUREAUCRACY AS A MODEL OF ORGANISATION

In establishing the notion of bureaucracy as an organisational model, the scholarly work of German sociologist Max Weber has been most influential, particularly his foundational 1922 book *Economy and Society*. According to Weber, bureaucracy is the institutional form of rational-legal authority whereby power is exercised on the basis of expert knowledge, rather than on the basis of patronage, kinship or some other arbitrary preference (Weber and Andreski 1983). Indeed, bureaucracy was viewed in the early 20th century as an efficient, rational and modern form of organisation that would inevitably replace these more traditional governing approaches. During the 20th century, bureaucracies in most industrialised countries were modelled on principles derived from Weber's work. These include the dominance of hierarchy, specialisation, processes and rules; a permanent and merit-based staff; and the separation of administration from politics. It should be noted that although Weber was instrumental in developing the 'ideal-type' bureaucratic model, he was decidedly not enamoured with its implications. Instead, he saw bureaucracy as ultimately constituting an 'iron cage' antithetical to individuality and creativity (Mitzman 1970).

BUREAUCRACY AS A PEJORATIVE TERM

From the 19th century onwards, with the rise of modern industrial and political systems, government bureaucracies flourished. By the mid to late 20th century, it was common to equate bureaucracy with any large organisation, public or private. During this period, bureaucracy was a defining characteristic of developed countries – people were born, educated, employed, and spent their leisure time in bureaucracies. The Weberian model of bureaucracy formed something of an ideal type.

WELFARE STATE: A manifestation of the state during the 20th century whereby governments play a central role in promoting the wellbeing of citizens via health, education, social and economic programs.

As bureaucracy became pervasive, it was increasingly viewed in negative terms. By the 1970s, when criticisms of big government and the **WELFARE STATE** rose to prominence, bureaucracy was often portrayed as monolithic, uncontrollable, invasive, costly and curtailing individuality. It also became associated with 'red tape', meaning an obsessive focus on rigid and obstructive official procedures, processes, rules and regulations. The term comes from the coloured tape traditionally used to bind government documents in the United Kingdom (Bozeman 2000). Bureaucrats were parodied as a 'fragmented set of individuals so bound with red tape and rulebooks that they don't know what they are about at any one time, sending television sets to people who lack electricity and doing research on the optimal shape of toilet seats' (Peters 1989, 251). In the 21st century, 'bureaucracy' continues to be employed as a pejorative term.

While the term bureaucracy often has negative connotations, it is also a useful catchall for the activities of the public service. Terms such as policy development, program management and administration are more neutral but tend to refer to specific parts of the work of the public service.

SHORT-ANSWER QUESTIONS 6.1

1. What is the purpose of bureaucracy?
2. What activities do contemporary bureaucracies perform?

Suggested responses are available at www.cambridge.org/highereducation/isbn/9781009108232/resources

THE AUSTRALIAN PUBLIC SERVICE

In Australia, as for other developed nations, the bureaucracy grew substantially through the 20th century. However, Australia is unusual in that bureaucracy has been a central component of its governance since the arrival of the British in 1788. As a British outpost and penal colony Australia required authorities to administer the convict system, provide law and order, allocate property rights, establish trade, and build transport systems and other infrastructure. During this period Aboriginal and Torres Strait Islander peoples' relationship with bureaucracy was through reserves and missions (colonial, then state and territory governments administered the reserves and churches administered the missions). Australia's vast size and small population meant government provided many services which elsewhere had been provided by private enterprise (Bell and Hindmoor 2009). In this respect, Australians have long relied on governments and their bureaucracies.

At Federation in 1901, the Commonwealth Public Service was established consisting of seven departments with 12 000 staff drawn from the former colonial administrations (Spann 1959). These departments were Postmaster-General, Trade and Customs, Defence, External Affairs, Home Affairs, Attorney-General and Treasury. The Postmaster-General's Department employed 10 000 people and Trade and Customs a further 1100. By contrast, the Attorney-General's department had ten employees, External Affairs had 16 and Treasury 41 (Ward and Stewart 2010, 71). Like the colonial (later state) public services, the Commonwealth Public Service was based on the Westminster model and principles, which has proved enduring and highly effective. A 2019 report shows four of the top five performing public services in the developed world follow the Westminster model, including Australia at number five (InCiSE 2019).

THE PUBLIC SECTOR VS THE PUBLIC SERVICE

There is an important distinction to be made between apparently similar terms: the public sector and the public service. The public sector is broad and includes public servants as well as others who are paid by any tier of government including public school teachers, immigration officers, nurses, council workers, university staff and military personnel. It also includes those employed within public corporations, non-profit institutions controlled by government, government marketing boards, and legislative courts (ABS 2020). The public service is a subset of the public sector and refers to the people that the public typically imagine: staff in city centre offices, developing policies, overseeing programs, having meetings with stakeholders, and providing advice and options to ministers. The number varies over time, but in 2015 the public sector represented approximately 13 per cent of all employed people in Australia (ABS 2015).

To get more technical, at the Commonwealth level the Australian Public Service refers to all departments and agencies staffed under the *Public Service Act 1999*. The Act outlines the responsibilities and powers of agency heads, provides the legal framework for employing APS employees, and details employees' rights and obligations. The Commonwealth public sector includes the APS and anyone else paid by the government under other legislation. A similar distinction exists in the states and territories, and in local government (see Table 6.1 for the number of employees in all Australian public sector employment, 2019–2020).

TABLE 6.1 AUSTRALIAN PUBLIC SECTOR EMPLOYMENT, 2019–2020

LEVEL OF GOVERNMENT	EMPLOYEES (JUNE 2020)
Commonwealth	246 000
State and territory	1 609 100
Local	186 000
Total public sector	**2 041 200**

Source: ABS (2020).

Table 6.2 lists the main government portfolios at the Commonwealth level. These are frequently re-structured according to government's evolving requirements, but the list indicates how the federal bureaucracy is organised. Within each portfolio, there are specialist agencies that ultimately report to the relevant minister/s. Table 6.2 also provides the 2016–17 staffing level within each portfolio. Government departments like those listed in Table 6.2 are overseen by a minister, while organisations like the Australian Bureau of Statistics, the Commonwealth Scientific and Industrial Research Organisation and many others are government bodies, but kept at arms-length from ministerial control.

TABLE 6.2 AUSTRALIAN GOVERNMENT PORTFOLIOS AND AVERAGE STAFFING LEVELS, 2016–2017

PORTFOLIO	STAFF
Agriculture and Water Resources	5384
Attorney-General	14 631
Communications and the Arts	7815
Defence	99 035
Departments of the Parliament	1185
Education and Training	2676
Employment	3757
Environment	4350
Finance	2759
Foreign Affairs and Trade	7064
Health	6441
Immigration and Border Protection	13 445
Industry, Innovation and Science	10 889
Infrastructure and Regional Development	2535
Prime Minister and Cabinet	4841
Social Services	33 158
Treasury	25 508
Total 2016–17	**245 474**

Source: Adapted from Commonwealth of Australia (2017).

GROWTH OF THE APS

Over the 20th century, Australia adopted a similar pattern of bureaucratic expansion to other industrialised nations, with the size, scope, and complexity of the bureaucracy growing dramatically. A ratchet effect meant government grew by increments but never contracted. The APS acquired new functions as Australia consolidated and was then hit with the Great Depression. The Second World War prompted a 'war economy', with new national institutions, significant centralised planning and mobilising citizens for the war effort. Post-war, Australia's population increased, technology advanced, international trade expanded, and national development became a key objective, so government expanded again.

Following the Second World War, governments adopted **KEYNESIAN ECONOMIC MANAGEMENT**, requiring large bureaucracies to manage the national economy and extensive social policies. Keynesianism argues governments should actively intervene in the economy through taxing and spending to smooth out the tendency of free markets to swing strongly between 'boom' and 'bust' (Keynes 1957). In part this means highly interventionist policies in large sections of the economy. Keynesianism aligned with the dominant social democratic ethos of the post-war decades. Australia developed an array of economic and social policy programs requiring large, specialised and professional bureaucracies (Ward and Stewart 2010, 68). Hierarchical or bureaucratic governance consequently became a dominant aspect of Australian public life.

KEYNESIAN ECONOMIC MANAGEMENT: An approach to economic management based on government intervention through monetary and/or fiscal policies (taxing and spending) to lessen the extreme tendencies of unmitigated capitalism.

SHORT-ANSWER QUESTIONS 6.2

1. What key factors make the Australian experience of bureaucracy unusual?
2. What key events and ideas promoted the growth of bureaucracy in the 20th century?

Suggested responses are available at www.cambridge.org/highereducation/isbn/9781009108232/resources

PUBLIC SECTOR REFORM

By the 1970s, this Keynesian and social democratic model was under substantial pressure. The critique of 'big government' was informed by **PUBLIC CHOICE THEORY**, which argues governments are self-interested and seek benefits for themselves, rather than serving the public interest (Buchanan and Tullock 1965). In this view, bureaucrats will always try to enlarge their departments and the scope of their work regardless of any benefit to citizens. By the 1970s, it was increasingly argued the public sector was bloated, inefficient, unaffordable, difficult to steer, and was crowding out private sector activity (Sawer 1982). This critique was reinforced by severe economic problems including 'stagflation' (a combination of rising unemployment, high inflation and slow growth), which Keynesian economics seemingly could not fix.

In response, governments in most industrialised nations initiated controversial reforms to streamline and modernise their bureaucracies, as well as adopting market economic policies which were seen as more efficient and innovative. The reforms to government were labelled 'New Public Management' (Hood 1991) and in Australia, 'economic rationalism' was applied to the broader reform program (Pusey 1991). A central aim was to let market-based strategies guide both the internal operation of government and the programs they delivered. The reforms sought to improve government efficiency by introducing competition, shifting the focus from process to

PUBLIC CHOICE THEORY: An economic approach to political phenomena emphasising the self-interested and utility-maximising behaviour of individuals and organisations.

outcomes, encouraging innovation, and improving the accountability and transparency of the public service. The reforms were highly contentious as they shifted the balance between 'market' and 'state' in favour of market-based approaches. Indeed, this was viewed as ushering out an era of governmental benevolence to citizens to make way for the brave new world of economic growth over economic equality.

The shape of government changed significantly with the privatisation of public utilities, contracting out of service delivery to the private sector and not-for-profit groups, introduction of 'user-pays' systems to allocate public services, and the development of public–private partnerships to fund and deliver infrastructure. Public sector entities were to operate more like those in the private sector, for example introducing performance management systems to measure productivity.

New Public Management

Since the 1980s, New Public Management (NPM) has created a new paradigm of public sector management, with economic efficiency and a more business-like approach becoming primary goals (see Davis and Rhodes 2000; MacDermott 2008; Pollitt and Bouchaert 2011). Along with the shift to 'governance' (see below), NPM was part of the shift away from the post-war era of big government.

Transformation of the APS began with the Royal Commission into Australian Government Administration (the 'Coombs Commission'), established by the Whitlam Government in 1973, with similar reviews conducted at the state level (Simms 2009, 177). Many of the Commission's recommendations were implemented by the Fraser and Hawke governments during the 1970s and 1980s. The initial wave of reform included new administrative law to provide greater oversight of public servants' activity, offset administrative complexity, and improve transparency and accountability. New institutions were created including the Office of the Ombudsman; the Administrative Appeals Tribunal; the Administrative Review Council; and the *Freedom of Information Act 1982*. From the mid-1980s, new procedures were developed to make public sector employment more equitable for women, migrants, and Indigenous people, and the Howard Coalition Government introduced further diversity programs (Singleton et al. 2013, 251). Complex employment structures were abolished, encouraging greater mobility within the public service. These early reforms did not reduce the size of the bureaucracy.

A larger program of 'managerial' and 'marketisation' reforms then followed. As Prime Minister Hawke stated in a media release, '[a]lthough the primary impetus for these fundamental changes is efficiency and the better delivery of government services, there will be substantial savings arising from amalgamations, through economies of scale and the removal of duplication' (Hawke 1987). The reforms included:

- reorganising and reducing the number of departments
- formalisation of political advisers to support ministers in exercising control over agencies
- the creation of a Senior Executive Service employed on a fixed-term basis to provide professional management skills (see the following section)
- rules allowing greater employment flexibility and offering redundancies
- strategic management and corporate planning techniques from the private sector
- new budgeting and accountability frameworks to demonstrate cost effectiveness and provide forward estimates of expenditures.

Marketisation meant privatising public enterprises such as Qantas, Telecom and the Commonwealth Bank; introducing National Competition Policy to expose public utilities to market conditions; creating various semi-autonomous agencies within government; user-charges for previously free services such as university education and dental services; and contracting-out public service delivery. This set of reforms to the Australian bureaucracy starts to move into the 'government to governance' reforms (see below).

In parallel with NPM, was the rise of the '**CENTRAL AGENCIES**': Department of Prime Minister and Cabinet; Department of Finance; and Treasury. Where '**LINE AGENCIES**' deliver programs and services (such as schools, environmental care or business support), central agencies allocate resources, coordinate activities, manage budgets, monitor programs and performance, and ensure decisions are implemented. Although NPM argues for devolution to line agencies, and in many ways achieved this, the central agencies have simultaneously grown in authority, status, resources and power (Ward and Stewart 2010, 80).

While these reforms were extensive, the greatest changes occurred in the top echelons of the public service, which was fundamentally reshaped in an attempt to make it less powerful, more responsive, more engaged with the outside world and less siloed.

CENTRAL AGENCIES: Agencies that do not deliver services to the public themselves but rather take on coordinating, resourcing and monitoring functions.

LINE AGENCIES: Agencies that oversee the delivery of services to society such as healthcare, policing and infrastructure – all under the watchful eye and guidance of the central agencies.

SPOTLIGHT 6.2 THE 'FEMOCRATS'

Until the 1970s, the Australian public service was resolutely male, like those in many countries, and the top echelons in particular were a cosy club of men who had spent their entire working life in the public service (Davis and Rhodes 2000, 78). Women were pushed into specific roles, struggled to build careers and, as improbable as it seems, until 1966 married women had to give up their job (Sawer 2016).

Unsurprisingly, issues affecting women's lives were little considered in public policy, but with the rise of feminism and consciousness of 'women's issues' pressure grew for changes in policy, and more importantly in how policy was developed. The election of the Whitlam Labor Government in 1972 after 23 years of Liberal–National government saw a radical shift. Where once Labor had been hostile to feminism, Whitlam's program promised action in areas many women had been arguing for such as childcare, support for single mothers, greater employment rights for women and parental leave (Lever 2019).

Australia blazed a trail with the rise of the so-called Femocrats, second wave feminists who entered the public service (Arrow 2019, 63). In a world-first, Whitlam appointed Elizabeth Reid as his Women's Affairs Advisor and other Femocrats entered the upper reaches of the public service pushing a new policy agenda (Arrow 2019, 63–6). Reid's appointment opened the floodgates for women to express their concerns and needs to government, and it was difficult to prioritise and act on so many issues (Lever 2019).

Despite a significant backlash, Femocrats and the Whitlam Government made many significant changes in just a few years. As well as hostility from conservatives, some radicals accused the Femocrats of focusing too much on white middle-class women. Feminists also grappled with the question of whether it was even possible to reshape 'the state' to work in the interests of women. The debate is still not settled.

Although highly controversial, in the longer-term the policy issues have remained on the political agenda. There is still a long way to go, but women enjoy far greater rights, employment opportunities and support today than in 1970.

QUESTIONS

Does it matter whether the public service 'looks like' the country at large? What benefits accrue from an open public service employing people from a range of backgrounds?

REFLECTION QUESTION 6.1

What factors prompted a rethink of the bureaucratic model in the 1970s?

Response prompt is available at www.cambridge.org/highereducation/isbn/9781009108232/resources

THE SENIOR EXECUTIVE SERVICE

As noted in the reforms listed by Prime Minister Hawke (above), the senior ranks of the public service were also overhauled. The aim was to 'put ministers back in charge' and create a more unified top tier of public servants with greater world experience.

The Whitlam Labor Government of 1972–1975 came to power after 23 years of Liberal–Country Party rule and in that time many senior public servants had developed strong relationships with conservative politicians. Many public servants were suspicious of Labor's novel economic and social agenda. Although subsequently aware of its own failings, the ALP believed strongly the APS had deliberately frustrated parts of the Whitlam Government's program (Whitlam 1985; Simms 2009, 177).

Having ministers firmly in charge was a priority for the incoming Labor Government of 1983. Initially Labor wanted to overtly politicise the top ranks of the public service along American lines (Halligan 1997) but was dissuaded from this to maintain the Westminster ideal of neutrality. Instead, the top public service tiers would remain notionally neutral, but in 1984 were transformed into a Senior Executive Service (SES) (Simms 2009, 179). SES staff would no longer have permanent jobs, but be placed on renewable five-year contracts, appointments would be approved by Cabinet (rather than the Public Service Board), and SES staff could be sacked without notice and with no reason required. Echoing the corporate sector, SES staff would be continually audited against quantitative criteria like budget savings or customer satisfaction surveys. It was claimed senior public servants would become more responsive to ministerial needs and be focused on the government's priorities. Critics suggest these reforms simply made public servants more susceptible to political pressure (Mulgan 1998).

In a further break with tradition, SES staff were encouraged to move between departments, to reduce 'silos' and give broader knowledge and experience, as well as to generate a whole-of-government approach. The downside is that institutional knowledge was eroded and the hand of the public service weakened in the face of poor policy choices from ministers. Furthermore, recruitment was opened up, with the public service encouraged to appoint SES staff from outside government, helping broaden the experience and views of those creating policy, making it more relevant to the areas affected and bringing in the private sector thinking trumpeted by NPM.

The creation of the SES has led to widespread accusations that the public service has been politicised. Most obviously, some people with strong political links are appointed to SES jobs, although not all are seen as then acting politically. For example, in the 2000s Liberal Party apparatchik and Howard Government staffer Michael L'Estrange became Secretary of the Department of Foreign Affairs and Trade, but he was kept by Labor for several years after its return to power (Maley 2012, 240). Conversely, in 2018 Scott Morrison controversially appointed Phil Gaetjens, his long-term staffer, first as head of Treasury and later head of Department of Prime Minister and Cabinet. This was seen by many as a highly partisan appointment which was unlikely to survive any change of government (Mulgan 2019). As expected, when Labor won the 2022 election, incoming Prime Minister Anthony Albanese immediately sacked Gaetjens and replaced him with Glyn Davis, a more traditional appointment (Coade 2022). Despite these high-profile cases, most SES staff do not have political links and are recruited through the public service and approved by Cabinet on a purely merit basis. However, this does not free them from questions around politicisation.

REFLECTION QUESTION 6.2

How was the Australian bureaucracy reformed in the 1980s and 1990s?

Response prompt is available at www.cambridge.org/highereducation/isbn/9781009108232/resources

ALLEGED POLITICISATION

As part of the Westminster responsible government model, the public service is supposed to be politically neutral. Indeed, public servants sign a Public Service Code of Conduct requiring them to be apolitical (Maley 2012, 238). In other words, the political opinions and preferences of public servants should be private and should not be brought to work. Employees within the public service should be neutral with respect to political parties when discharging their duties, conscientiously implementing policy. Afterall, ministers have an electoral mandate, unlike public servants. At the senior levels, public servants should offer 'frank and fearless' advice to their masters in the political executive, regardless of the latter's political complexion (Mulgan 2007, 570). The measure of professionalism for public servants is the extent to which they can personify this neutrality and meet their obligation to 'serve the government of the day', even when dealing with politicians they disagree with or policies they find morally difficult and not in the public interest.

Historically, political neutrality within the public service has been promoted by security of tenure and promotion according to merit (Maley 2012, 240–41). But this ideal has increasingly separated from political realities over several decades (MacDermott 2008). A public servant can do their job more effectively if they do not have to worry about personal and career consequences, such as losing employment or a stalled career. This is particularly important in the SES where employees provide advice to ministers. Put bluntly, it is easier to tell a minister what they need to hear but do not want to when one is protected from reprisals.

There is a risk senior public servants end up being too keen to please the minister (Maley 2012, 244). In 2020, an inquiry into whether Jackie Trad, Deputy Premier of Queensland, had interfered in the appointment of a school principal found that rather than the deputy premier interfering, senior public servants were 'overresponsive' to her perceived wishes without her knowledge (Stone 2020). The various conflicts at the ABC in 2017–18 between the Chair and senior management are another example of being too keen to please the government, or possibly of direct political interference, illustrating the point that it is not always easy to see exactly what has happened (Fernando and Smith 2018).

Partisanship within the public service can take subtle ideological forms. In his classic account *Economic Rationalism in Canberra* (1991), Michael Pusey argues that during the Hawke governments of the 1980s, senior bureaucrats in the central agencies were overwhelmingly committed to free market solutions to problems. Ideological assumptions about the desirability of deregulation, corporatisation and privatisation masqueraded as impartial, technical advice to ministers who were often out of their depth in debating the finer points of economic policy. Seemingly dry economic advice was a part of a broader neo-liberal political project. Bureaucrats were not formally deciding policy, but they were arguably playing a larger role in Australia's economic reorientation than a politically neutral public service should.

Perceptions of increased politicisation can make governments, especially incoming governments, suspicious of the public service. When the Liberal–National Coalition came to power in 1996 after 13 years of Labor rule, Prime Minister John Howard sacked six departmental heads who some believed were too close to the outgoing Labor Government, in what was dubbed a 'night of the long knives' (Ward and Stewart 2010, 75). But on returning to power in 2007, the Rudd Labor Government made a virtue of retaining all departmental heads.

All of this throws up difficult questions for public servants as boundaries are not always clear (Maley 2012). Public servants have to find a balance between 'frank and fearless' advice and 'serving the government of the day'. They grapple with the issue of when loyally working for the government of the day morphs into helping the party in power get re-elected. These issues must be managed in a situation of greater career vulnerability than previously existed.

At a more profound level is the thorny question of whether a public servant's ultimate loyalty is to the government of the day or to the public interest. A well-known example of this occurred in the build-up to the second Iraq War in 2003. An analyst with the Office of National Assessments, a government agency analysing raw intelligence on national security matters, believed the government had already decided to join a war against Iraq and was misusing intelligence information about weapons of mass destruction to help build the case. The analyst, Andrew Wilkie (who subsequently became an independent MP in the federal parliament), went to the media to voice his concerns about the way intelligence was being used, sparking a heated debate pitting those who saw his behaviour as disloyal and dangerous against those who saw him as brave and ethical. Either way, the case highlights that the relationship between the political and administrative executives can be difficult. (See e.g. Kingston 2003 for more on the case).

REFLECTION QUESTION 6.3

Can the advice of senior public servants to the political executive ever be completely neutral? Are there factors beyond security of tenure which impact the nature of the advice offered?

Response prompt is available at www.cambridge.org/highereducation/isbn/9781009108232/resources

PUBLIC POLICY AND THE POLICY PROCESS

Public policy is a core activity of governments and their bureaucracies. The study of public policy, as a sub-discipline of political science, aims to improve understanding of critical areas of government activity, particularly bureaucracies, the governmental process, and the skills and tools required for improving policymaking. However, like many concepts in the social sciences, including 'politics' (discussed in Chapter 1), the definition of public policy is contested: there is no single agreed-upon meaning. In general terms, however, public policy comprises a relationship or interaction between governments, problems, resources and values. Public policy has thus been variously defined as: '[a] course of action or inaction chosen by public authorities to address a given problem or interrelated set of problems' (Pal 1992, 3) or 'the process by which a society makes and enforces decisions on what behaviour is acceptable and what is not' (Wheelan 2011, 7).

Policy work by the bureaucracy in Australia and elsewhere is consequently a complex affair encompassing a range of activities including the formulation of policy advice, designing policy instruments, policy coordination across agencies, consulting with stakeholders, policy implementation, evaluation and service delivery, to name a few key areas.

THE POLICY PROCESS

One of the more influential ways in which public policy is understood is as a process involving a series of steps or phases. In this regard, policymaking has been compared to applied problem-solving. Harold Lasswell was the first to propose a model of the policy process comprising the following elements: (1) intelligence gathering; (2) promotion of particular options; (3) prescription of a course of action; (4) the invocation of the prescribed option; (5) application of the policy through legislation and bureaucracy; (6) termination once it had run its course; and (7) appraisal and evaluation against original goal/s (Lerner and Lasswell 1951).

In Australia, the most influential version of the staged approach to understanding the policy process is Bridgman and Davis's 'policy cycle', first proposed in 1998, which 'brings a system and a rhythm to a world that might otherwise appear chaotic and unordered' (Althaus, Bridgman and Davis 2013, 32). Originally designed for new public servants in the Queensland Government, the model divides the policy process into nine steps comparable with Lasswell's approach.

As Althaus et al. (2013) argue, the policy cycle is an idealised sequence of activities and a tool for policy development and analysis rather than an accurate description of policymaking in action. A key strength of a cyclical staged approach to understanding public policy is that it portrays the process as dynamic whereby a policy may evolve, going through several iterations. In doing so, it recognises policymaking as a process that is rarely complete; following implementation and evaluation, the process often restarts with the discovery of new problems, issues and ideas for refinements.

Despite their practical benefits, policy process models are criticised on several fronts that are useful for understanding the complexity of policymaking and the nature of public sector work. In reality, it is difficult to map the policy work of public servants onto the policy cycle model. Public servants always work in a heavily constrained world where 'bounded rationality' means resources and information are limited, work has to be prioritised and political imperatives dominate (Simon 1997). In the real world, Ministers, advisers and bureaucrats often develop policy 'on the run' and policy ideas and advice frequently emanate from sources outside of the public service. Secondly, the point at which to move from one component of the cycle to the next is not clear from the model and some steps might be compressed or ignored altogether (Everett 2003). Thirdly, the policy cycle portrays a rather 'top down' approach whereby decision-makers are assumed to exert control over those who will ultimately implement the policy without factoring in the interpretations and discretion exercised by public servants and private contractors engaged in service delivery (Lipsky [1980] 2010). Finally, the model does not fully consider the added complexity of inter-governmental relations, which is a prominent part of the policy context in Australia. Indeed, the interaction between local, state and Commonwealth bureaucracies is, for many policy areas, crucial, particularly given the financial dominance of the Commonwealth.

Despite all these limitations and a general lack of realism, the policy cycle is still a useful tool for introducing students to the field of public policy.

SHORT-ANSWER QUESTIONS 6.3

1. What are the key stages that form a process view of policymaking?
2. What are the advantages and disadvantages of the process view of policymaking?

Suggested responses are available at www.cambridge.org/highereducation/isbn/9781009108232/resources

FROM GOVERNMENT TO GOVERNANCE

For much of the 20th century, political scientists saw their field of study as centred on the formal state and government including various components such as the public service. This focus on government bureaucracies was due to the formal legal authority and legitimacy of the state, its role as the major actor in international relations and, as outlined earlier in the chapter, post-war optimism about modern bureaucracy and the welfare state. Towards the end of the 20th century, in a context of deep reform of government across much of the developed world, political scientists increasingly spoke of 'governance' to describe the work of governments. The decline of Keynesian economic management in the 1970s, the associated reform of public sector bureaucracies, and the challenges of an increasingly globalised world had brought about a conceptual and practical rethinking of the role of governments, and with it a process of 'decentering' the state. Consequently, the term 'governance' grew in popularity to describe contemporary public administration, policymaking and service delivery. (See Bell and Hindmoor 2009, Chapter 2).

This sounds similar to New Public Management (discussed above) because 'new public management' and 'government to governance' are heavily intertwined. While NPM is directed towards large-scale reform of the internal arrangements of the public service and relations with ministers, the government to governance narrative focuses more on concurrent and broader shifts in the ways policy is developed and services are delivered. The boundaries can be unclear, especially as NPM is sometimes seen as part of the broader government to governance changes.

WHAT IS GOVERNANCE?

The meaning of the term governance is disputed. At the broadest level it is 'the tools, strategies and relationships used by governments to help govern' (Bell and Hindmoor 2009, 2), or in longer form: 'the exercise of economic, political and administrative authority to manage a country's affairs at all levels. It comprises mechanisms, processes, and institutions, through which citizens and groups articulate their interests, exercise their legal rights, meet their legal obligations, and mediate their differences' (UNDP 1997, 9). Governance therefore incorporates and transcends the associated concepts of the state, government and public policy. In this respect, governance is not the eclipse of governments but a way of governing via a wider group of actors, processes and methods, beyond simply the bureaucracy. This is evident in Mark Bevir's definition of governance as 'all processes of governing, whether undertaken by a government, market or network, whether over a family, tribe, formal or informal organization or territory and whether through laws, norms, power or language' (Bevir 2013, 1). The term governance often indicates the shifting boundaries between the public, private and community sectors in contemporary policymaking (Rhodes 2017, 166).

There are three core elements of governance. First, governance is broader than simply a focus on formal government and its components. In fact, governance is usually defined by contrasting it with the traditional approach, where authority is centralised and exercised hierarchically, exemplified by the traditional public service (sometimes called the 'command and control' model). Second, governance concerns the rules and management of society's common affairs and the processes for developing these rules and implementing policies and programs. It thus involves the organisation, development and application of processes for solving public problems and allocating society's resources by governments and/or other actors. Third, governance not only considers non-state actors, institutions, processes and structures within the political system that exercises authority, legitimacy, influence and control in public life but also focuses attention on the nature of relationships between governments and these actors. Relevant governing actors may include business associations, firms, trade unions, professional associations, private consultants, non-profit groups, community groups, lobbyists, wealthy individuals and activist organisations. Given all this, it is not entirely surprising to discover there is an ongoing debate about who is really in charge in the world of 'governance' and the extent to which traditional government can assert its will.

If governance is understood in this broad sense, much contemporary policymaking is illustrative of governance in action. For example, public–private partnerships, routine relationships between business, trade unions and government, contracting non-profit groups to deliver public services, certification systems for product labelling (e.g. organic food), the creation of markets by governments (e.g. private health insurance) may all be described as governance because they involve governments working in concert with other actors to address policy problems.

SPOTLIGHT 6.3 THE APS AND INDIGENOUS PEOPLES

Following the 1967 referendum, Aboriginal Affairs (now referred to as Indigenous Affairs) was established as a Commonwealth policy area. Post-1967, Aboriginal and Torres Strait Islander people could be counted in the census and the federal government could make laws on their behalf. The Whitlam Labor Government (1972–1975) adopted the policy of 'Self-Determination', this continued with the Fraser Liberal Government's (1975–1983) adoption of 'Self-Management' and the Hawke Labor Government's (1983–1991) adoption of both concepts. These policy eras were the catalyst for Indigenous peoples' participation in the APS and the Indigenous representative body, the Aboriginal and Torres Strait Islander Commission. Since the 1970s successive governments have committed billions of dollars into addressing the socio-economic disparities between Indigenous people and other Australians, yet the result has been the further decline in socio-economic indicators.

Aboriginal scholar Lyndon Murphy (2000) highlights the ways that Australia's political culture and political institutions focus on the symptoms of the problem rather than the problem itself. The problem being the mismatch between Indigenous cultural values and bureaucratic processes grounded in the values of non-Indigenous Australia that continues to perpetuate contemporary acts of dispossession and assimilation (see also the Report of the Royal Commission into Aboriginal Deaths in Custody – Dodson et al. 1991). Indigenous people in the APS have daily experiences of racial microaggressions that impede their elevation into senior positions (see Bargallie 2020). They are often overlooked as staff who bring valuable lived experience and social capital to inform the process of developing and delivering policies and programs (see Ganter 2016).

> In 2019, the Australia and New Zealand School of Government (ANZSOG) collaborated with senior Indigenous public servants to identify three priorities to action:
>
> 1. Establish a cross-jurisdictional community of practice to focus on best practice and cross-jurisdictional learning among Indigenous public servants.
> 2. Workshop ways to create a shift in the cultural mindset of non-Indigenous public servants.
> 3. Examine ways to support Indigenous staff to succeed in the public sector while staying on Country. (ANZSOG 2019)
>
> ANZSOG's submission (2019) to the Australian Public Servants Review to re-set the APS's relationship with Indigenous peoples advocated for Indigenous values and concepts to be incorporated into the *Public Service Act 1999*. Drawing from the work of Aboriginal Elder and scholar Dr Mary Graham the submission proposed included caring for country, kinship, consensus decision-making, understanding that process is important, and honesty and humility.

GOVERNANCE IMPLICATIONS

'Governance' is used to describe the process of governing in all its complexity, but there are several implications arising from this notion. First, the term implies that the formal power of governments is limited and therefore inadequate for addressing difficult and intractable policy problems ranging from homelessness, child poverty, Indigenous disadvantage, and climate change. The second implication is that rather than being considered as separate, stand-alone entities, governments are in fact embedded in society. Indeed, members of parliament are drawn from the community and governments should respond to community expectations. By contrast, the traditional view sees government as above and detached from the wider society. Governance instead implies that government is part of the social fabric and is one of many actors with influence over public policy. Because governments are dependent on the social environment, and many other actors, in delivering public policies, much of the new governance scholarship focuses on the interdependencies between governments and other actors.

In broad terms, the shift to governance means the role of governments has changed from 'rowing' (providing public services in their entirety) to 'steering' (determining overall goals, strategies and directions) (Osborne and Gaebler 1992). The interdependencies this demands were interpreted by some in the 1990s as meaning the state was diminished and 'hollowed out' (Rhodes 1994), although that position was somewhat revised subsequently. Others, meanwhile, contended that governments had not been weakened by governance but instead simply had to approach the task of policymaking differently (Pierre and Peters 2000). Effective governance is now more dependent on governments developing policy networks, market-based strategies and community collaboration alongside the traditional, hierarchical approach to governing favoured for much of the 20th century (Bell and Hindmoor 2009).

RESEARCH QUESTION 6.1

Examine an area of public policy and consider how it informs your understanding and views of 'governance'.

THE APS TODAY AND TOMORROW

In the 21st century, the public sector reform agenda in Australia relaxed, with a period of consolidation rather than radical experimentation. The basic model of the APS is agreed and the broad NPM and governance approach seems to be here to stay. Inevitably though the APS still faces challenges and further reform will happen.

21ST CENTURY CHALLENGES FOR THE APS

Public sector organisations still face criticisms and challenges, despite the zeal for more radical reform subsiding. First, the appropriate size and efficiency of the public service is an ongoing point of contention. Second, questions surround the roles of various actors in policy advice including the public service, consultants and political staffers. Third, technological change and the bureaucracy's use of digital technology in service delivery is challenging the regulatory and data safety capacity of government agencies.

Size, cost and efficiency?

There is a long-running debate in Australia about the appropriate size, cost and efficiency of the public sector, stemming from the criticisms of big government in the 1970s.

Critics argue the public sector consumes too much taxpayers' money and uses its resources inefficiently: 'citizens need to ask whether the bureaucrats we employ are working at maximum efficiency and whether the country is getting maximum bang for its buck' (Carr 2015). Yet by international standards, Australia has a low tax-to-GDP ratio, which is a reasonable proxy for the size of the public sector (OECD 2020). In 2015, the public sector accounted for about 13 per cent of the Australian workforce, down significantly from 2000 when the figure was 20 per cent (ABS 2015).

The Rudd and Gillard governments' economic stimulus packages and budget deficits following the global financial crisis exacerbated criticisms, with the Liberal–National Opposition Leader Tony Abbott complaining loudly of government waste and inefficiency. Having won the 2013 election, the Abbott Coalition Government commissioned a report *Towards Responsible Government*, which included drastic recommendations for the public sector and a path back to Budget surpluses (National Commission of Audit 2014). The Abbott Government's 2014 Budget included deep cuts to spending on aged pensions, health, unemployment benefits and higher education among many other areas, but much of the program was abandoned following widespread public discontent and Senate opposition.

With the onset of the coronavirus pandemic and consequent economic crisis in 2020, the Morrison Liberal–National government abandoned trying to return the Budget to surplus. The 2021 Budget forecast deficits for at least ten years and debt peaking at nearly a trillion dollars, smashing various records in the process. While there was consensus between the major parties on the need to spend, there were still prominent voices warning about excessive spending (Kehoe 2021).

Through recent decades and continuing into the pandemic, there has been pressure for ever-greater efficiency within the public service. Since 1987, governments have constrained the size and performance of the public sector through annual 'efficiency dividends'. Budgets are frequently reduced, typically in the range of 1 to 4 per cent but usually spanning a range of 1 to 1.25 per cent (Hamilton 2015). Depending on your perspective, these 'dividends' force agencies to make ever deeper cuts or they encourage innovation in carrying out government business. The Department of Finance and the Australian Public Service Commission also closely monitor staffing levels across the APS.

Despite the rhetoric, international evidence shows Australia's government bureaucracies compare favourably with similar countries. For example, the World Bank's Worldwide Governance Indicators listed Australia's level of government effectiveness as greater than the Organisation for Economic Co-operation and Development average for 2015, ahead of the United States, France, Belgium and Ireland, but trailing Canada, Denmark, Germany, Japan and the United Kingdom (World Bank Group 2017).

Competition in the provision of policy advice

While government agencies were the primary source of policy advice for governments prior to the NPM reforms, this has changed dramatically in the 21st century. In the modern policy world, 'ministers now access advice from think tanks, consultants, academics/researchers, professional lobbyists, interest groups and other advocates, political parties, ministerial staff, expert advisory committees/panels, taskforces, inquiries, media, social media, and their own personal and professional networks … This means that some ministers no longer regard the APS as their primary or even preferred source of advice' (Tiernan et al. 2019, 13).

Political advisers or 'staffers' are increasing powerful. They are employed directly by politicians and consider political and media angles as well as offering policy advice. In the 1970s, the Whitlam Government paved the way for the rise of staffers by forcing a change allowing ministers to appoint and control the staff in their offices. Their role was consolidated by the Hawke Government with the *Members of Parliament (Staff) Act 1984*. Between 1984 and 2014, the number of advisers more than doubled and now hovers around 900 (Ng 2016), giving Australia the world's largest cohort of political advisers (Creighton 2014). Initially, most advisers were senior public servants on secondment but are increasingly from political backgrounds, often with their own political ambitions. This is a far cry from the traditional model (Maley 2018) and forms a large group of political operators between elected representatives and public servants, producing their own research and advice as well as acting as gatekeepers to the minister. Political advisers are not obliged to serve in the public interest and are not accountable to parliament.

Private and non-profit sector consultants contracted by the APS have similarly become an increasing presence in public administration, with governments of all stripes now engaging consultants extensively. The Rudd Labor Government spent almost $800 million on consultants in its first 18 months (Whelan 2011, 11), and in 2014–15, the Abbott Liberal–National Government spent $10 billion on consultants while thousands of APS jobs were lost (Towell 2015). The number of 'management and organisation analysts' has grown steadily to 60 000 people across Australia which 'creates a shadow public sector that doesn't show up in government budgets' (Creighton 2017).

The growing ranks of political advisers, external consultants and others pose a considerable challenge for the public service. This is often intensified by 'governments believing that officials are resisting change or insufficiently skilled and knowledgeable, and officials believing that political leaders are ignoring sound advice to executive preconceived or ill-thought out ideas' (Lindquist and Tiernan 2012, 445). In addition to the budgetary, transparency and accountability implications, the growing reliance on alternative sources of policy potentially offers politicised, rather than 'frank and fearless', advice. These changes are arguably hollowing out robust policy capacity in the public service.

REFLECTION QUESTIONS 6.4

1. Why has public service work become increasingly complex in the 21st century?
2. To what degree do political advisers and external consultants undermine the core roles of the public sector?

Response prompts are available at www.cambridge.org/highereducation/isbn/9781009108232/resources

---

DIGITAL TECHNOLOGY

The rapid development of digital technology has proved challenging for public sector agencies to utilise and regulate, not just in Australia but worldwide. Although Australian governments have promoted the digital economy and built the National Broadband Network, government agencies have proved less adept in employing digital technology. The key aspects of this challenge are delivery of public services online and the complex task of regulating online activity.

Digital government (or e-government) is increasingly prevalent, offering a potentially lower cost, more efficient method for government agencies to conduct business as well as greater transparency. In Australia, MyGov is the main online platform for citizens to access public services including Medicare, the Australian Taxation Office and Centrelink. In 2015, the government established the Digital Transformation Agency to facilitate the use of digital technology and provide oversight across government agencies. Progress in e-government in Australia has been slower than anticipated with, for example, a 2019 report showing Australia ranked 15th out of 38 countries for government digital services (InCiSE 2019, 26). Various reports and inquiries, including the final report of the 2019 independent review of the APS, have recommended the APS speed up the transition to online service delivery and offered recommendations for achieving this (DPMC 2019).

While it offers many efficiency benefits, the Australian Government has encountered some high-profile problems stemming from the use of digital technology. In 2017, the human services portfolio came under fire when Centrelink, the nation's welfare agency, used an automated debt raising and recovery system to assess overpayment of benefits, resulting in the issue of thousands of letters incorrectly requiring welfare recipients to repay benefits. According to the Ombudsman's investigation, the 'implementation problems could have been mitigated through better project planning and risk management, including more rigorous user testing with customers and service delivery staff, a more incremental rollout, and better communication to staff and stakeholders' (Glenn 2017, 3). The 'Robodebt' debacle damaged the reputation of government and public sector agencies, thereby also eroding public trust.

The other challenge is for geographically defined national governments to regulate new technologies that are essentially global and borderless. Governments everywhere have struggled to regulate enormous global businesses with purely digital models (such as Microsoft, Uber, Airbnb, Google, Amazon). A more serious problem for the digital world is online crime. As well as online fraud, hacking and other obvious criminal activity, policing the 'dark web' where websites trade illegal goods and services, such as child pornography, weapons and stolen identities, is extremely difficult. More mundane online criminal behaviour, such as illegally downloading games and films, has sparked discussion of how to protect intellectual property and copyright.

New regulation has generated conflict over issues like liberty and privacy. For example, in 2017 there was widespread debate when the Australian Government's data retention scheme was established to store the metadata of citizens' mobile and online activity and allow it to be scrutinised by national security agencies.

The 2018–19 review of the APS

Like other political institutions, the APS is constantly evolving. This may come from new policy challenges, priorities of the executive or changes in society's expectations. On other occasions, governments try to impose order and chart a course for the future. This was the case with the Royal Commission into Australian Government Administration in the 1970s, which triggered two decades of reform.

More recently, then Prime Minister Malcolm Turnbull announced the Independent Review of the Australian Public Service in May 2018, the largest review since the 1973 Royal Commission. Describing it as a 'health check', Turnbull asked the review panel to 'examine the capability, culture and operating model' to ensure the APS was responsive, neutral, innovative and a good place to work (Turnbull 2018; Mannheim et al. 2018). The terms of reference gave huge scope for radical recommendations, sparking complaints that the opposition had not been consulted and unions feared further job losses and outsourcing (Mannheim et al. 2018).

In late-2019, the final report, *Our Public Service, Our Future*, was published (DPMC 2019). It claimed, 'the APS is not ready for the big changes and challenges that Australia will face between now and 2030' (DPMC 2019, 16), but the recommendations pointed to further incremental change rather than radical reform. The 40 recommendations were divided into core themes of needing to:

- Work more effectively together, guided by a strong purpose and clear values and principles
- Partner with the community and others to solve problems
- Make better use of digital technologies and data to deliver outstanding services
- Strengthen its expertise and professional skills to become a high-performing institution
- Use dynamic and flexible means to deliver priorities responsively, and
- Improve leadership and governance arrangements. (DPMC 2019, 8)

Although the government accepted most recommendations relating to the APS itself, it rejected key ones around the way the political executive operates (Grattan 2019).

Arguably, minor adjustment is all that is required anyway. The APS performs well, with a 2019 report ranking it the fifth best performing public service in the developed world. A mild warning though came from the fact the APS had slipped two places since the previous report in 2017 (InCiSE 2019).

CASE STUDY 6.1 DR KEN HENRY: REFLECTIONS ON POLICYMAKING IN AUSTRALIA

The APS attracts many talented people with an interest in good public policy; economic, social and environmental. A lot of policy commentary seems to assume that policy advisers operating across these various domains are in constant battle with political leaders forced into difficult trade-offs among competing policy goals: having to trade off conservation against development; and social equity against economic efficiency. I can recall some such battles in my 28 years in the APS; but by the mid-1990s APS policy advisers, for the most part, were keen to work cooperatively to develop ideas that offered progress simultaneously, in all three dimensions.

During the 1980s and 1990s, the role of the APS in the development of policy advice became increasingly contested, with economic consultancies emerging to offer their services directly to politicians, especially those in opposition. The ranks of advisers sitting in offices in Parliament House also grew strongly, as did the numbers employed by special interest advocacy groups and think tanks. All of these added to the more traditional contributions from academics and media commentators. In response, government departments were required by their ministers to develop capabilities in 'issues management'; perversely, in some cases this function was outsourced. Most of the economic consultancies offered policy perspectives similar to those to be found within departments. Differences were usually confined to second-order matters of detail, though these tended to be amplified in the media, and almost always manipulated to somebody's political advantage.

The manipulation of policy to political advantage has been the dominant theme of the period since the mid-1980s. Throughout that entire period, the most significant determinant of the success of a policy reform proposal has been the quality of political leadership, and not just within government.

The late 1980s and 1990s were characterised by audacious politicians making careers out of disproving conventional political wisdom. Reform options provided vehicles for journeys in political leadership that seemed to prove that good policy is also good politics.

But there have always been easier ways to achieve political success, and they have been much less favourable to the cause of good policy. In the 21st century, several significant politicians have realised their personal ambition by undermining sensible reforms championed by their opponents, often within their own parties; in some cases, even by attacking policies championed by their former selves.

Political leadership of optimism and policy ambition has been replaced by negativism, fear-mongering and policy choices that generally wouldn't be considered even second-best by the public servants tasked with their implementation. In the 21st century, the political contest, thus far at least, has been largely destructive of good policy.

[Dr Ken Henry AC was Secretary, Department of the Treasury (2001–11) and Special Advisor to the Prime Minister (2011–12).]

QUESTION

Why has it become more difficult in the 21st century to align 'good policy' with 'good politics'?

SUMMARY

Learning objective 1: Explain the origins and use of the term bureaucracy

This chapter introduced the idea of bureaucracy as an organising principle for public administration. It charted the origins of the concept, Max Weber's ideal-type model and the growth of government over the course of the 20th century. Indeed, by the latter half of the century, bureaucracy had become a pervasive feature of modern industrialised nations, and Australia was no exception.

Learning objective 2: Provide an overview of the contemporary Australian Public Service

The second part of the chapter examined the development and contemporary roles of the APS. While bureaucracy was employed by colonial administrators from the time of British arrival, the size, scope and complexity of Australian government agencies grew dramatically through the 20th century. From the 1970s onwards, criticism of big government triggered reform of government agencies in most developed countries. Later called New Public Management, these reforms included reshaping the bureaucracy and trying to make it more dynamic, responsive, transparent and accountable. At the same time, parts of the administrative executive were sold, commercialised or turned into semi-autonomous agencies.

Learning objective 3: Define public policy and describe the policy process

Next, the chapter unpacked the concept of public policy as comprising interactions between governments, problems, resources and values. One popular way in which policymaking is understood is as a process or cycle consisting of a number of stages. While this is a good introductory approach to the world of policymaking, government activity is often significantly more complex, value-laden and irrational than such models suggest.

Learning objective 4: Understand the shift from 'government' to 'governance'

Towards the end of the 20th century, the concept of governance came into vogue among political scientists and policy practitioners. It implies the rise of new strategies in public administration including market, community and network modes of governance, additional to the previously favoured bureaucratic approaches. The rise of governance has made policy development and delivery of services hugely complicated. The broader impact of governance strategies on the capacity and role of governments in the 21st century remains contested.

Learning objective 5: Outline some of the challenges for the public service and its possible future

In the 21st century, debate about the size and efficiency of the public service continues as governments seek to implement various measures to boost the performance of government agencies. Where once the public service was the sole source of advice to the political executive, there is now competition between many players in providing policy advice to ministers. The challenges of advancing digital technology have brought Australian Government agencies into unchartered waters providing both new opportunities and challenges. While reform of the public service on the scale of earlier decades seems unlikely, minor reforms are inevitable.

DISCUSSION QUESTIONS

1. How does the scholarly definition of bureaucracy differ from its use in the contemporary media?

2. How did the APS develop over the course of the 20th century and why was it reformed in the 1980s and 1990s?

3. What is public policy and what do process models of policymaking reveal?

4. Why is the contemporary term 'governance' increasingly employed by policy practitioners and political scientists?
5. Why does the public service constantly change and evolve?

FURTHER READING

Althaus, C., Bridgman, P. & Davis, G. (2013). *The Australian Policy Handbook*, 5th edn, Crows Nest: Allen & Unwin.

Bargallie, D. (2020). *Unmasking the Racial Contract: Indigenous Voices on Racism in the Australian Public Service*, Acton: Aboriginal Studies Press.

Bell, S. & Hindmoor, A. (2009). *Rethinking Governance: The Centrality of the State in Modern Society*, Melbourne: Cambridge University Press.

Mulgan, R. (2016). Goodbye, Westminster: Is our political system dying or just evolving? *The Canberra Times*, 30 July. Retrieved from: https://www.canberratimes.com.au/story/6046080/goodbye-westminster-is-our-political-system-dying-or-just-evolving/

Simms, M. (2009). New public management in Australia. In S. Goldfinch and J. Wallis (eds), *International Handbook of Public Management Reform*, Cheltenham: Edward Elgar.

REFERENCES

Althaus, C., Bridgman, P. & Davis, G. (2013). *The Australian Policy Handbook*, 5th edn, Crows Nest: Allen & Unwin.

Arrow, M. (2019). *The Seventies: The Personal, the Political, and the Making of Modern Australia*, Sydney: NewSouth Publishing.

Australian Bureau of Statistics (ABS). (2015). *Labour Force, Australia, Detailed*, quarterly, November 2015 (cat. no. 6291.0.55.003). Retrieved from http://www.abs.gov.au/AUSSTATS/abs@.nsf/Previousproducts/6291.0.55.003Main

—— (2020). *Employment and Earnings, Public Sector, Australia, 2019–20*. Retrieved from https://www.abs.gov.au/statistics/labour/employment-and-unemployment/employment-and-earnings-public-sector-australia/latest-release

Australian and New Zealand School of Government (ANZSOG). (2019). *Indigenous Leadership in a Changing Public Sector: ANZSOG Senior Indigenous Public Servant Forum Summary Report 2019*.

Australian Public Service Commission. (2020). *APS Values*. Retrieved from https://www.apsc.gov.au/working-aps/integrity/aps-values

Bargallie, D. (2020). *Unmasking the Racial Contract: Indigenous Voices on Racism in the Australian Public Service*, Acton: Aboriginal Studies Press.

Bell, S. & Hindmoor, A. (2009). *Rethinking Governance: The Centrality of the State in Modern Society*, Melbourne: Cambridge University Press.

Bevir, M. (2009). *Key Concepts in Governance*, Los Angeles; London: Sage.

——(2010). *Encyclopaedia of Political Theory*, Thousand Oaks: Sage Publications.

——(2013). *Governance: A Very Short Introduction*, Oxford: Oxford University Press.

Bozeman, B. (2000). *Bureaucracy and Red Tape*, Upper Saddle River: Prentice Hall.

Buchanan, J.M. & Tullock, G. (1965). *The Calculus of Consent: Logical Foundations of Constitutional Democracy*, Ann Arbor: University of Michigan Press.

Carr, A. (2015). The cost of a bloated bureaucracy, *The Australian*, 17 April. Retrieved from http://www.theaustralian.com.au/business/business-spectator/the-cost-of-a-bloated-bureaucracy/news-story/81859a3c1e89f18f00ddbce75140a4f8

Coade, M. (2022). Albanese chooses new DPMC head, *The Mandarin*, 30 May. Retrieved from https://www.themandarin.com.au/191019-albanese-chooses-new-dpmc-head/

Commonwealth of Australia. (2017). *Budget Papers 2016–2017, Budget Paper No. 4, Part 2: Staffing of Agencies*. Retrieved from http://www.budget.gov.au/2016–17/content/bp4/html/09_staff.htm

Creighton, A. (2014). How many staff members does it take to change the country? *The Australian*, 28 June. Retrieved from http://www.theaustralian.com.au/business/opinion/how-many-staff-members-does-it-take-to-change-the-country/news-story/e4d9bf4c90d73a521648d57f1c18747a

——(2017). Paying consultants to do public servants' jobs is waste of money, *The Australian*, 22 June. Retrieved from http://www.theaustralian.com.au/business/opinion/adam-creighton/paying-consultants-to-do-public-servants-jobs-is-waste-of-money/news-story/64a4c794e7fac3aa02242999e89158a3

Crooks, P. & Parsons, T.H. (2016). *Empires and Bureaucracy in World History: From Late Antiquity to the Twentieth Century*, Cambridge: Cambridge University Press.

Davis, G. & Rhodes, R.A.W. (2000). From hierarchy to contracts and back again: Reforming the Australian public service. In M. Keating, J. Wanna and P. Weller (eds), *Institutions on the edge?* Abingdon: Allen & Unwin.

Department of Prime Minister and Cabinet (DPMC). (2019). *Our Public Service, Our Future*. Independent Review of the Australian Public Service. Retrieved from https://www.pmc.gov.au/resource-centre/government/independent-review-australian-public-service

Dodson, P., Wootten, H., O'Dea, D., Wyvill, L. & Johnston, E. (1991). *The Report of the Royal Commission into Aboriginal deaths in Custody*.

Etzioni-Halevy, E. (2010). *Bureaucracy and Democracy: A Political Dilemma*, 3rd edn, Abingdon; New York: Routledge.

Everett, S. (2003). The policy cycle: Democratic process or rational paradigm revisited? *Australian Journal of Public Administration*, **62**(2), 56–70.

Fernando, G. & Smith, R. (2018). 'I've never called for anybody to be fired': Turnbull denies reports he interfered with ABC staffing, *News.com.au*, 27 September. Retrieved from https://www.news.com.au/finance/business/media/we-need-to-save-the-abc-secret-email-shows-public-broadcasters-chairman-wanted-to-fire-emma-alberici/news-story/2d7f69dccfbea7209a186f7ab1439c21

Ganter, E. (2016). *Reluctant Representatives*, Canberra: ANU Press.

Glenn, R. (2017). *Centrelink's Automated Debt Raising and Recovery System: A report about the Department of Human Services' online compliance intervention system for debt raising and recovery*. Retrieved from http://www.ombudsman.gov.au/__data/assets/pdf_file/0022/43528/Report-Centrelinks-automated-debt-raising-and-recovery-system-April-2017.pdf

Grattan, M. (2019). Morrison won't have a bar of public service intrusions on government' power, *The Conversation*, 13 December. Retrieved from https://theconversation.com/view-from-the-hill-morrison-wont-have-a-bar-of-public-service-intrusions-on-governments-power-128880

Halligan, J. (1997). Labor, the Keating term and the senior public service. In G. Singleton (ed.), *The Second Keating Government: Australian Commonwealth Administration 1993–1996*, Canberra: Centre for Research in Public Sector Management.

Hamilton, P. (2015). *Australian Public Service Staffing and Efficiencies: Budget Review 2015–16 Index*. Retrieved from http://www.aph.gov.au/About_Parliament/Parliamentary_Departments/Parliamentary_Library/pubs/rp/BudgetReview201516/APS

Hawke, R. (1987). Prime Minister: For media [Press release]. Retrieved from http://pmtranscripts.pmc.gov.au/release/transcript-7197

Hood, C. (1991). A public management for all seasons? *Public Administration*, **69**(1), 3–19.

InCiSE. (2019). *International Civil Service Effectiveness Index*. Retrieved from https://www.bsg.ox.ac.uk/sites/default/files/2019-04/InCiSE%202019%20Results%20Report.pdf

Kehoe, J. (2021). Decade of deficits a 'big risk', *Australian Financial Review*, 13 May. Retrieved from https://www.afr.com/policy/economy/decade-of-deficits-a-big-risk-20210513-p57rir

Keynes, J.M. (1957). *The General Theory of Employment, Interest, and Money*, London; New York: Macmillan; St. Martin's.

Kingston, M. (2003). Wilkie-v-Howard: who's the villain, who's the hero? *The Sydney Morning Herald*, 14 September. Retrieved from http://www.smh.com.au/articles/2003/09/14/1063478071549.html

Lerner, D. & Lasswell, H.D. (1951). *The Policy Sciences: Recent Developments in Scope and Method*, Stanford: Stanford University Press.

Lever, S. (2019). The decade of thinking dangerously, *Inside Story*, 8 March. Retrieved from https://insidestory.org.au/the-decade-of-thinking-dangerously/

Lindquist, E. & Tiernan, A. (2012). The Australian Public Service and policy advising: Meeting the challenges of 21st century governance. *The Australian Journal of Public Administration*, **70**(4), 437–50.

Lipsky, M. (2010). *Street-level Bureaucracy: Dilemmas of the Individual in Public Services*, New York: Russell Sage Foundation.

MacDermott, K. (2008). *Whatever Happened to 'Frank and Fearless'? The Impact of New Public Management on the Australian Public Service*, Canberra: ANU Press.

Maley, M. (2012). Politicisation and the executive. In R. Smith, A. Vromen and I. Cook (eds), *Contemporary Politics in Australia*, Melbourne: Cambridge University Press.

—— (2018). Understanding the divergent development of the ministerial office in Australia and the UK. *The Australian Journal of Political Science*, **53**(3), 320–35.

Mannheim, M., Dingwall, D. & Whyte, S. (2018). Turnbull unveils independent review of federal bureaucracy, *The Canberra Times*, 4 May. Retrieved from https://www.canberratimes.com.au/story/6018131/turnbull-unveils-independent-review-of-federal-bureaucracy/

Mitzman, A. (1970). *The Iron Cage: An Historical Interpretation of Max Weber*, New York: Knopf.

Mulgan, R. (1998). Politicising the Australian Public Service? *Parliamentary Library Research Paper*, **3**, 1998–9.

—— (2007). Truth in government and politicisation of public sector advice. *Public Administration*, **85**(3), 569–86.

—— (2019). Public Sector Informant: Labor sharpens its knives for Phil Gaetjens … and others? *The Canberra Times*, 8 May. Retrieved from https://www.canberratimes.com.au/story/6094671/labor-sharpens-its-knives-for-phil-gaetjens-and-others/

Murphy, L. (2000). Who's afraid of the dark? Australia's administration in Aboriginal Affairs. Master's Thesis, University of Queensland.

National Commission of Audit. (2014). *Towards Responsible Government*. Report of the National Commission of Audit phase one. Retrieved from http://www.ncoa.gov.au/report/docs/phase_one_report.pdf

Ng, Y.F. (2016). *Ministerial Advisers in Australia: The Modern Legal Context*, Sydney: The Federation Press.

Organisation for Economic Co-operation and Development (OECD). (2020). *Revenue Statistics 2020 – Australia*. Retrieved from https://www.oecd.org/tax/revenue-statistics-australia.pdf

Osborne, D. & Gaebler, T. (1992). *Reinventing Government: How the Entrepreneurial Spirit is Transforming the Public Sector*, Reading: Addison-Wesley Pub. Co.

Pal, L. (1992). *Public Policy Analysis: An Introduction*, 2nd edn, Scarborough: Nelson Canada.

Peters, B.G. (1989). *The Politics of Bureaucracy*, 3rd edn, New York: Longman.

Pierre, J. & Peters, G. (2000). *Governance, Politics and the State*, Basingstoke: Macmillan.

Pollitt, C. & Bouchaert, G. (2011). *Public Management Reform: A Comparative Analysis – New Public Management, Governance and the Neo-Weberian State*, 3rd edn, Oxford: Oxford University Press.

Pusey, M. (1991). *Economic Rationalism in Canberra: A Nation-building State Changes Its Mind*, Melbourne: Cambridge University Press.

Rhodes, R.A.W. (1994). The hollowing out of the state: The changing nature of the public service in Britain. *The Political Quarterly*, **65**(2), 138–51.

—— (2017). *Network Governance and the Differentiated Polity: Selected Essays, Volume 1*, Oxford: Oxford University Press.

Sawer, M. (1982). *Australia and the New Right*, Sydney: Allen & Unwin.

—— (2016). The long, slow demise of the 'marriage bar', *Inside Story*, 8 December. Retrieved from https://insidestory.org.au/the-long-slow-demise-of-the-marriage-bar/

Simms, M. (2009). New public management in Australia. In S. Goldfinch and J. Wallis (eds), *International Handbook of Public Management Reform*, Cheltenham: Edward Elgar.

Simon, H. (1997). *Administrative Behavior: A Study of Decision-making Processes in Administrative Organizations*, 4th edn, New York: Free Press.

Singleton, G., Aitkin, D., Jinks, B. & Warhurst, J. (2013). *Australian Political Institutions*, Frenchs Forest: Pearson.

Spann, R.N. (1959). *Public Administration in Australia*, Sydney: Govt. Printer.

Stone, L. (2020). Text messages show public servants feared Trad 'didn't like' principal, *Brisbane Times*, 2 July. Retrieved from https://www.brisbanetimes.com.au/national/queensland/text-messages-show-public-servants-feared-trad-didn-t-like-principal-20200702-p558ih.html

Tiernan, A., Holland, I. & Deem, J. (2019). *Being a Trusted and Respected Partner: The APS' Relationship with Ministers and Their Offices*. Retrieved from https://www.apsreview.gov.au/resources/aps%E2%80%99-relationship-ministers-and-their-offices

Towell, N. (2015). Australian Public Service spends $10 billion on consultants, *The Canberra Times*, 14 December. Retrieved from http://www.canberratimes.com.au/national/public-service/australian-public-service-spends-10b-on-consultants-20151214-gln4lj.html

Turnbull, M. (2018). *Review of the Australian Public Service* [PM Transcript 41613]. Retrieved from https://pmtranscripts.pmc.gov.au/release/transcript-41613

United Nations Development Programme (UNDP). (1997). *Governance for Sustainable Human Development*. Retrieved from http://www.pogar.org/publications/other/undp/governance/undppolicydoc97-e.pdf

Ward, I. & Stewart, R.G. (2010). *Politics One*, 4th edn, South Yarra: Palgrave Macmillan.

Weber, M. & Andreski, S. (1983). *Max Weber on Capitalism, Bureaucracy and Religion: A Selection of Texts*, London: Allen & Unwin.

Wheelan, C.J. (2011). *Introduction to Public Policy*, New York: W. W. Norton & Co.

Whelan, J. (2011). *The State of the Australian Public Service: An Alternative Report*. Retrieved from https://cpd.org.au/wp-content/uploads/2011/08/CPD_OP12_2011_State_of_APS_Whelan.pdf

Whitlam, G. (1985). *The Whitlam Government 1972–1975*, Ringwood: Penguin.

World Bank Group. (2017). *Worldwide Governance Indicators*. Retrieved from http://info.worldbank.org/governance/wgi/#reports

CHAPTER 7
ELECTIONS, THE ELECTORAL SYSTEM AND THE AUSTRALIAN VOTER

LEARNING OBJECTIVES

After reading this chapter, you should be able to:

1. Understand the history of elections in Australia
2. Describe the key electoral elements of Australian democracy
3. Understand the role and place of political parties in Australian elections
4. Explain why people vote the way they do

INTRODUCTION

When we come to think about what a democracy is, and how a nation might go about constructing a democratic government, an election is often the first thing we think is important in that process. While elections do not in themselves guarantee democracy, they are certainly seen as a key element, without which any regime will have a hard time calling itself a democracy. While democracies can conceivably have forms of decision-making other than elections (through such mechanisms as choosing by lot or with deliberative processes), elections are certainly the easiest way to gauge opinion on who should head the formal administration of the state. However, we need to be aware that there are a number of important provisos that allow us to call an election democratic or 'free and fair':

1. elections are held on a regular basis
2. a range of candidates and parties can participate
3. as many people as possible can vote freely for the candidate or party of their choice
4. a wide range of policies are debated in the public arena
5. there is a potential for a change in government at any given election.

These elements are often considered the baseline requirements for a democratic election.

As a western, liberal democracy, Australia has periodic elections at all three levels of government. We should also remember that Australia is firstly a constitutional monarchy. This means that the Head of State (which in some other systems would be a president) is the Queen of England, styled as 'the Queen of Australia'. This is a historical position, and the last effort to change the situation, in 1999, failed to gain a majority of votes to change the Constitution. So, we must first acknowledge that the Head of State is not elected. However, as discussed in Chapter 4, the Queen as Head of State plays a limited role in the day-to-day affairs of Australian politics. Her representative, the Governor-General, is the one who signs and receives the writ to call an election, heads the Federal Executive Council, and provides Royal Assent to Acts.

When we talk of elections in Australia, we are talking about the elections for the Commonwealth Parliament in Canberra, the state and territory parliaments, and at a local level for the councils and shires. We need to also keep in mind that the six colonies that federated in 1901 already had decades of experience in running elections and testing with electoral systems. The provisions for elections at the national level represent this to some extent, as well as the desire for a hybrid between the US and Westminster systems. Each of these jurisdictions has an elected body overseeing the administration of government (the operations of the various parliaments being covered in Chapter 3). For each of these elected bodies there must therefore also be elections. This chapter will explore the nature of those elections and some of the challenges facing the systems we use.

SHORT-ANSWER QUESTION 7.1

If you think about Australian elections what are the important aspects that make for a 'good' election?

Suggested response is available at www.cambridge.org/highereducation/isbn/9781009108232/resources

AUSTRALIAN ELECTORAL SYSTEMS

WHO GETS TO VOTE?

FRANCHISE:
The legal right to vote. 'Enfranchisement' refers to the process of being given that right.

The first thing we need to do, before an election is held, is determine who can vote. At the time of the first General Election those who had the right to vote (known as the '**FRANCHISE**') were all men over the age of 21 and women over 21 in South Australia and Western Australia. The peculiarity of women being able to vote in the Commonwealth election of 1901 only in these two states was because the Constitution deferred to state law in this respect, and only these two states had enfranchised women (Parliament of Australia 2009). Figure 7.1 shows the Womanhood Suffrage League of NSW, who would be granted the right to vote in 1902. As also discussed in Chapter 3, this situation changed with the passing of the *Commonwealth Franchise Act 1902*, with the franchise being granted to all women for Commonwealth elections. By 1908 all jurisdictions had passed similar laws and women could vote in all Australian states and territories, although it would be many years before a woman was elected to the federal parliament. However, it was not until 1973 that the voting age was finally lowered to 18 (McAllister 2014).

Figure 7.1 The Womanhood Suffrage League of NSW
Source: Wikimedia Commons, State Library of New South Wales.

Citizens, residents, people?

While women gained the vote across Australia by 1908, this was not the case in the United Kingdom nor the United States. The United Kingdom did not pass amendments granting the right to vote for women until 1918, and the US Nineteenth Amendment was not ratified until 1920, after a long process at the state level, with many states first providing then revoking the voting rights of women through the 19th century. The Nineteenth Amendment itself failed at the first attempt to pass it in 1918 by two votes, but the momentum continued to the eventual ratification in 1920.

The history of women gaining the vote is one based very much on the notion that you cannot reasonably exclude half the population from voting. That notion begins to break down when you start to think about minority voting rights, citizens versus residents, and who gets counted as a 'person' in the first place.

There is no question that citizens over the age of 18 have voting rights, but what about people who have a right to live in Australia but are not citizens? They may be a permanent resident, a refugee or on a number of temporary visas that allow people to work and perhaps eventually settle here. They may also have left school and be working from the age of 16. Should they be allowed to vote, especially if they pay taxes and are good members of the community? Compounding this is the situation of dual citizens, people who have the right to hold citizenship of several countries – at present they can vote (as citizens) but cannot run for federal office. At what point do we draw the line between people who live here and people who qualify for citizenship? This issue has become increasingly problematic over the last 40 years as the High Court has made a series of judgments increasingly restricting who may be considered a citizen for the purpose of elections, and under what circumstances, particularly in relation to dual citizenship.

The situation for Indigenous people is in many respects a microcosm of this situation. Although some Aboriginal people had the right to vote in 1901, through having the right to vote in their state, this was terminated by the *Commonwealth Franchise Act 1902*. Indigenous people in the United States gained the vote in 1924 (when they were granted citizenship), but Aboriginal Australians did not receive the vote at the Commonwealth level until 1962, when amendments were finally passed to the *Commonwealth Electoral Act 1918*, which had replaced the original Act. The situation was varied at the state level, with some Aboriginal people being able to vote throughout this period, but the passage of the 1962 Act, coupled with the 1967 referendum, ensured that Aboriginal people were counted as part of the population and expected to register to vote (Bennett 2001). This was somewhat analogous to the situation of First Nations people in Canada, who could vote from 1867 but only if they gave up any treaty rights and Indian status – essentially becoming assimilated into the white population – and only obtained unrestricted voting rights in 1960.

But does the franchise extend to everyone, including people convicted of crimes? The question around whether prisoners in jails should have the right to vote is a vexed one. Arguments range from the need to provide for universal suffrage for all people, irrespective of their status as people who are part of a society, to one of restricted franchise, based on the notion that only citizens can vote, and even then only citizens who meet certain criteria (Orr 2011). Thus while some would argue for the voting age to be lowered to 16, for prisoners to have the vote, and even the accepted notion that a person should only be able to exercise one vote ('**ONE VOTE, ONE VALUE**'), the counter arguments are also strenuously argued.

ONE VOTE, ONE VALUE: Where a person's vote is equal to another. This means that within a given state or nation all electorates are as close as possible to having the same number of electors. Where this is not the case, this is called 'malapportionment'.

SPOTLIGHT 7.1 VOTING RIGHTS

This issue of voting rights for prisoners was last argued in the High Court when the Howard Government attempted to restrict the right to vote for prisoners to those serving sentences for crimes that had a maximum sentence of one year or more. This would have been a change to the previous three-year maximum sentence. In *Vicki Lee Roach v Electoral Commissioner and Commonwealth of Australia* [2007] HCA 43, the High Court ruled that the change was unconstitutional, but also significantly did not rule on the existing restriction.

The case for 16-year-old people to vote has been raised previously in various examinations of the conduct of elections (and during inquiries into electoral reform such as *Electoral Distribution Repeal Bill 2001* and the *Electoral Amendment Bill 2001 (Electoral Reform Bills) – Report 8* by the Western Australian Legislative Council (Legislative Council 2001, 163–4), but at present 16 and 17-year-old people may only pre-register to vote (and then be able to vote as soon as they turn 18). This momentarily became an issue again during the 2017 national survey on same-sex marriage, when the original directions for the survey to allow 16 and 17-year-old people on the roll to take part, required some rapid changes by government ministers (Koziol and Whitbourn 2017).

The right to vote in elections therefore remains a vexed question, and not just in Australia. While the right to vote is covered by Article 25 of the International Covenant on Civil and Political Rights (General Assembly of the United Nations 1948), this does not mean that its application is universal. Just as other human rights can be abridged, so to can the right to vote. Nonetheless, for those who do have that right to vote, as do the vast majority of Australian citizens over the age of 18, this is exercised in elections.

QUESTION

Is the right to vote a right that cannot and should not be curtailed or withdrawn?

SHORT-ANSWER QUESTIONS 7.2

1. Who in Australia has a right to vote?
2. Why do we use voting to determine government?

> Suggested responses are available at www.cambridge.org/highereducation/isbn/9781009108232/resources

---

STRUCTURES IN CONTEMPORARY AUSTRALIA

PROPORTIONAL: A system of voting where multiple members of parliament (MPs) are elected for the same electorate, and the number of MPs a party or group wins is based on the party's share of the vote. Thus, a party getting 40 per cent of the vote would get 40 per cent of the seats. The way this is determined depends on how many MPs are to be elected, but the intent is to clearly represent voters as an aggregate.

PREFERENTIAL: A system of voting where voters number a square against each candidate in the order of their preference for the candidates or parties contesting the election. Votes are then counted in the order they are numbered until one is declared the winner.

To begin with, we need to recognise that Australia has a variety of electoral systems – in fact there are nine electoral systems – one for each of the states, the two territories and the Commonwealth, and that's before we get to the ever-changing systems used at the local government level. Having said that, it's not as if each system is entirely different, as each of the systems shares some common features. However, there is considerable difference in the structures and operation of each of the systems used, to the extent that they can appear quite dissimilar.

We also need to distinguish between two most significant system features used in Australia – the use of both **PROPORTIONAL** and single-member **PREFERENTIAL** voting to elect members of parliament (MPs) to seats in parliament (see Table 7.1 comparing the voting system used in the Commonwealth and each state). The first, proportional, describes the system used in most of the states' (NSW, SA, Victoria, WA) upper houses and the Commonwealth Senate, as well as the Tasmanian lower house and the Australian Capital Territory Assembly. The second describes the system used in most of the lower houses (NSW, NT, Queensland, SA, Victoria, WA), the Tasmanian upper house and the Commonwealth House of Representatives. We then have to remember that Queensland and the two territories have no upper houses. If we were then to consider local council elections, we would have to consider even further variation. So already we can see that there are very mixed and different electoral systems being used across Australia.

TABLE 7.1 STATE AND COMMONWEALTH HOUSES COMPARED

STATE/COMMONWEALTH	LOWER HOUSE	UPPER HOUSE
Commonwealth	Single Member	Proportional
Australian Capital Territory	Proportional	[no house]
New South Wales	Single Member	Proportional
Northern Territory	Single Member	[no house]
Queensland	Single Member	[no house]
South Australia	Single Member	Proportional
Tasmania	Proportional	Single Member
Victoria	Single Member	Proportional
Western Australia	Single Member	Proportional

You might ask why this is the case, and wouldn't it be easier to simply legislate for just one system? Indeed, it would be easier to simply have one system in place, except that electoral systems are designed for more than just electing someone to sit in a parliament. For that we have to consider what the purpose of the electoral system actually is. If we are to think about the purpose of the system, we might want equally to think about the purpose of democratic systems more broadly; but for now, we will restrict ourselves to discussing how do the Australian set of systems operate and why they were chosen.

One last point before we discuss the electoral systems for the Commonwealth and states. Australia has, since 1926, had **COMPULSORY VOTING**. This means that it is compulsory to register to vote once a citizen turns 18, and then it is compulsory to cast a vote at elections. This is relatively unique around the globe, with only six countries having compulsory voting. Also, votes are cast at polling places in a polling booth. These are just small booths where a person can mark their ballot paper in favour of particular candidates in secret, before placing their ballot paper in the ballot box. Now, most countries have secret voting, but this was once called 'the Australian ballot' – in that it was only done in Australia because voting was done openly in town halls and in caucuses, or by handing a pre-printed ballot paper to the election official. A person's vote might then be known – and voters could be intimidated into not attending or not voting. The first places to use the secret ballot were the then-colonies of Victoria and South Australia, from 1856 onwards, with other states following suit shortly after, and then the secret ballot was enshrined in the Australian Constitution.

COMPULSORY VOTING: In Australia, this refers to the requirement to first register to vote once you are 18 years old and then, having registered, to vote in all elections after that.

RESEARCH QUESTIONS 7.1

1. Which countries have compulsory voting and why do other countries not?
2. Why are there differences between the states and the Commonwealth as to whether to have 'fixed' election dates?

The Commonwealth

The Commonwealth electoral system is defined in the Australian Constitution, in so far as there are seats allocated to both the House of Representatives and the Senate. The designation of certain numbers of seats to each of the states for the House of Representatives is based on population, the number of seats representing the proportion of the population that the state has compared to the whole of Australia. There is an exception that states are not to have fewer than five seats, which is applied to Tasmania due to its continued small population, but other than that the calculation is applied after every election to check if changes need to be made. The reservation of five seats does not apply to the territories, but they are allocated seats on a population basis. Originally there were 75 seats in the House of Representatives, but this has been expanded to the current 150 seats. The Senate, on the other hand, has a set number of senators per state, irrespective of the state's population. The territories are allocated two senators each as they are not classed as states, so do not enjoy the full allocation of senators. Currently there are 76 senators, 12 from each state, and two each from the two territories.

The way each seat is elected, however, differs between the House of Representatives and the Senate. The House of Representatives seats return one member each – that is, one person represents the electorate. The electorates themselves are divided such that each seat has roughly the same number of people in it, while respecting the state boundaries. The exception is, of course, Tasmania, which retains five House of Representatives seats irrespective of the population of the state. It therefore takes fewer individual votes to elect a person in Tasmania than in other states. Each registered elector gets a single vote and is required to cast that vote – although this extends only as far as attending the polling place and placing the ballot paper into a ballot box, as the vote is secret and so what exactly a person marks on their ballot paper is known only to that individual.

Commonwealth elections are held according to the Constitution, which stipulates that House of Representatives elections must be held three years after the first sitting of the last parliament. It does not specify a minimum time, but equally it takes time to organise, so this has to be taken into account. The Senate has a more fixed timetable, with senators being elected for six years, with a fixed starting date (1 July) for terms, although the terms themselves depend on whether an election is held before or after that date. There is nothing to say that House of Representatives and Senate elections have to be held at the same time – and indeed up until the 1970s were often not – but given the cost of elections it has just been much cheaper to do so. The timing of an election is actually governed by the government of the day, and so does not fall on a specific date like in the United States. The prime minister sets in train the election by visiting the Governor-General and asking for parliament to be dissolved. The Governor-General then issues the writs for the election, which authorises the Australian Election Commission (AEC) to conduct an election. Elections can then potentially be called quite quickly if a government wishes (often called a 'snap election'). Once an election is called, the AEC has to run to a set timetable.

In the election itself, the requirement for voters in House of Representatives elections is to number all the boxes opposite candidate names in ascending order (1, 2, 3, 4, etc.), until all the boxes are filled, starting with a '1' next to the most preferred candidate. This is where the name 'preferential voting' comes from, and it affects the way a vote is counted. Essentially, the candidate with the least number of 1s next to their name is eliminated, and the vote transfers to the candidate marked next (i.e. with a '2') on the ballot paper. If there are still three or more candidates in the count, the same process is used again, with the candidate with the least total votes being eliminated, and their votes being transferred – in the order the voter has marked the ballot paper – to the remaining candidates. This continues, with votes being allocated from eliminated candidates, until only two candidates are left and the one with the most votes is declared elected.

SPOTLIGHT 7.2 COUNTING THE VOTE

When the AEC conducts an election, it does so using a set of rules and regulations, and it publishes the processes it uses along with the results. At 6 p.m. on polling day, the doors of the polling place are closed and no more voters are allowed in. Representatives of candidates may also be present (although not the candidates themselves), and these people are called 'scrutineers'. Scrutineers can observe and challenge ballot papers or process where they think an error has occurred but cannot under any circumstances touch the ballot papers.

Once the doors are shut and the last voter has left, polling officials are able to begin their job for the night, which consists of three key tasks:

- count all the House of Representatives first preferences
- conduct a two-candidate-preferred count for House of Representatives
- count all the Senate first preferences.

The only votes counted here are the votes cast on the day for the electorate in where the polling place is situated.

The process

1. The polling officials open and empty the House of Representatives ballot boxes. Inside are the green ballot papers used for the House of Representatives, and these are all emptied onto tables. They are sorted into separate piles, with the number '1' votes (first preferences) for each candidate put together and counted. Once this is done the result is phoned through to the polling official for the whole electorate and the result appears on the AEC Tally Room site.

2. The process is then repeated, but this time with just two of the candidates predetermined by the AEC as the most likely winners. This is usually the Australian Labor Party (ALP) or one of Liberal or National parties. The votes are sorted by who has the lowest number marked on the ballot paper (the likely winner of the contest). This is also phoned through to the tally room. This is not the same as the '**TWO-PARTY-PREFERRED**' vote sometimes referred to, as that is solely between the ALP and Liberal–National Party Coalition – the two-candidate-preferred count may have (as in the seat of Melbourne) the contest between a number of candidates and parties.

3. Finally, the Senate first preferences are counted and phoned through.

This completes the activity on the night, and often a good idea of who has won will emerge. Nonetheless, this is not the end: the ballot papers are next transported to the divisional office, where the votes are checked again, before heading into a central counting centre (usually in a warehouse) and the process is conducted in full, with all preferences being distributed for the House of Representatives, and all preferences being entered into computers for the Senate. The Senate counting can take up to two weeks to finalise, but the entering of the votes means that the process is both quicker and more accurate.

For further information, visit the AEC website: www.aec.gov.au.

TWO-PARTY-PREFERRED: A system of representing the vote after it is counted that allocates all votes to the two major parties (the ALP and the Liberal–National Party Coalition). This may be different to the 'two-candidate-preferred' vote, which represents the final result in an electorate (i.e. the winner and the last person left who has not been elected).

QUESTIONS

How much did you know about the counting of the vote before reading this section? Were you surprised by its complexity?

The Senate elects half of its senators at any one time, the exception being a double dissolution when all seats are declared vacant and elected as one lot. The state in which the Senate seats are elected is considered to be one electorate. Again, each registered voter has one vote, and marks the ballot paper preferentially, but when the votes are counted six people are to be elected. The total number of votes cast is divided by seven (the number of seats to be elected (6) + 1). The resulting number is the quota, which is the number of votes that must be reached to be elected. Counting is considerably more complicated than in the House of Representatives, but the seats won will mostly end up being more proportional to the actual percentage of votes that a candidate or group of candidates receives (Farrell and McAllister 2003). If, as in many European countries, the voter just has to mark a '1' for the group or party of their choice this form of voting is called proportional voting, but in Australia, where we allocate preferences it is '**PROPORTIONAL PREFERENTIAL**' voting.

PROPORTIONAL PREFERENTIAL: A system of voting where multiple members of parliament (MPs) are elected for the same electorate but where the elector allocates a preference for candidates, and that preference determines in what order MPs may be elected.

The states and territories

States each have their own systems for electing MPs, with considerable variation in counting, optional or compulsory preference distribution, multi- or single-member electorates, and fixed or variable timing of elections. Table 7.2 shows the distribution of seats and electorates between the various Legislative Assemblies and Legislative Councils. One further difference that might be noted here is the system of counting the votes. The description above for the House of Representatives holds true for those states with single-member electorates, although unlike the Commonwealth, not all states use compulsory preferential voting. In New South Wales from 1981, and in Queensland from 1992 to 2016, the marking of preferences for candidates past '1' is optional. In Tasmania and the Australian Capital Territory, five preferences need to be marked for a vote to be valid, but no more if an elector does not wish to.

TABLE 7.2 SEATS, ELECTORATES AND TERMS

STATE OR TERRITORY	ASSEMBLY			COUNCIL		TERMS
	SEATS	ELECTORATES	YEARS	SEATS	ELECTORATES	YEARS
Australian Capital Territory	25	5	4	[no house]	25	5
New South Wales	93	93	4	42	1*	8
Northern Territory	25	25	4	[no house]		
Queensland	93	93	3	[no house]		
South Australia	47	47	4	22	1*	8
Tasmania	25	5	4	15	15	6
Victoria	88	88	4	40	8	4
Western Australia	59	59	4	36	6	4

* Both South Australia and New South Wales elections for the Legislative Councils are every four years, with half the Council elected at each election. Both Councils are whole-of-state electorates.

The method of counting the votes also varies. While single-member electorates are quite straightforward, multi-member electorates pose some problems. The Western Australian Legislative Council uses a complicated 'Weighted Inclusive Gregory' method (see Miragliotta 2002), while the Tasmanian and the Australian Capital Territory Legislative Assemblies use the

'Hare-Clark' method. The South Australian Legislative Council and the Commonwealth Senate use identical systems for allocating votes, while the Victorian and Western Australian Legislative Councils still use group voting tickets (abolished in the Senate in 2016 and South Australia in 2017). The use of group voting tickets is a source of quite a bit of argument, focused on whether you should force people to number an increasingly large number of candidate boxes or allow the party to do this. The argument goes 'Does the voter choose who gets their vote or does the party?'.

This maze of variation might seem like a very confusing way to run elections. **'FIRST-PAST-THE-POST'** elections (where voters only have to mark a 1 against the candidate of their choice, and the person with the most votes wins) in the United Kingdom and the United States are very easy to administer and count, so the question might be asked, why don't we use a similar system? Simply put, electoral administrators and state politicians (when not looking for particular political advantage) have tended to consider which system would be the fairest to use to properly represent the wishes of electors. This is an important point to understand as representation is key to the kinds of systems you might wish to use. This explains why Andrew Inglis Clark, Tasmanian barrister, Attorney-General, and principal author of the Australian Constitution, modified an earlier proportional system designed by Sir Thomas Hare to come up with the eponymous Hare–Clark system in the late 19th century, currently used in Tasmania and the ACT. That this system of electing MPs isn't used more widely has as much to do with what we might want or expect from our MPs, as it does about the fairness of the system.

Today we mostly see MPs as representing constituents in an electorate, based on a geographical area. This owes a considerable amount to the Westminster system and relies on a perceived connection between people who live in a place and their local representative. Yet it is entirely possible for a system to be conceived that represents particular groups of people *not* based on geography but on another basis – perhaps class, ethnicity, language or religion. These **SOCIAL CLEAVAGES** are at least partly the basis of many European political parties that are represented in parliaments through proportional systems.

FIRST-PAST-THE-POST: A system of voting (also called 'plurality voting') where the person with most first preference votes wins the election, even if they did not win 50 per cent of all votes.

SOCIAL CLEAVAGES: Division in society that reflects core divisions, such as ethnicity, class, language and religion/belief. This is different from ideologies based on guiding principles.

SHORT-ANSWER QUESTIONS 7.3

1. What is the difference between proportional and preferential voting systems?
2. Why is voting secret?

Suggested responses are available at www.cambridge.org/highereducation/isbn/9781009108232/resources

REFLECTION QUESTIONS 7.1

1. When we think of electoral systems, we tend to think of where we live. How is it that Australia has so many different systems and practices?
2. Should whether a system is 'fairer' be the basis for electing representatives?

Response prompts are available at www.cambridge.org/highereducation/isbn/9781009108232/resources

AUSTRALIAN ELECTIONS

The question of representation is important when we come to view the post-Second World War stability in the Australian political system. What we might otherwise take for granted – stable elections with mostly two parties battling it out, and occasionally other parties or people winning a seat – was not the norm prior to 1945. In the colonial period, MPs were elected to represent particular groups of people, originally landed and male. As the franchise grew, so did the demands for wider representation. By the time of Federation in 1901, the ALP had formed and won seats. It had 'the Pledge' where members of the party pledged to follow the party's policies irrespective of their own feelings, on pain of losing the endorsement of the party, and thus potentially their seat in parliament. The question of larger, national issues, which motivated democracy campaigners and theorists such as Edmund Burke (see Figure 7.2) were less the concern of the ordinary ALP MP as were issues of the wages and conditions of workers (McKinlay 1981, 20).

Figure 7.2 Edmund Burke

On the other side of the political divide there were a variety of MPs and groups. In the colonial period, these were often grouped around individuals, but could equally represent themselves as 'Ministerialists', 'Nationalists' or 'Oppositionist' to demonstrate what they thought should be the key issues of representation. In the first federal parliaments, the two key non-Labor groupings were the 'Free Traders' and 'Protectionists', who argued over trade policy. The 1909 formation of the first Liberal Party (following the earlier 'Fusion' group) brought together a core of these people around free trade, with protectionists drifting towards the ALP, and later to the Country Party when it formed in 1919 (Weller and Fleming 2003).

The First World War brought its own problems with the ALP prime minister of the day, Hughes, arguing for conscription. The defeat of conscription plebiscites led to the first split in the ALP and the formation of a coalition of parties to take government. This coalition collapsed in 1928 with the defeat of the Bruce Government. The short-lived Scullin ALP Government suffered from being in office during the collapse of Wall Street and the subsequent Great Depression, leading to a second split in the party and the formation of a new coalition called the United Australia Party. First under the leadership of former Tasmanian ALP Premier Joseph Lyons, then under Prime Ministers Fadden and Menzies, the non-Labor parties held power until 1941, when Labor was returned to the ministerial benches under John Curtin. Curtin was to govern through much of the Second World War.

POST-WAR STABILITY, CONTEMPORARY VOLATILITY?

The Second World War marked a turning point in the Australian political culture. Sir Robert Menzies brought the many disparate right of centre groupings together again as the second Liberal Party, building 'a great movement of Liberal deliverance in Australia' (Brett 2003, 17), a party which has continued to flourish through to today. Out of government after the 1949 federal election, the ALP continued on, only to split again in 1955 over the perceived internal threat from the Communist Party, yet still remained the dominant left of centre party.

Electoral stability under the Liberal–Country Party coalition lasted from the 1949 election through to the election of Gough Whitlam in 1972. This period covered the formation of the

TABLE 7.3 ELECTION RESULTS 1946–2019

ELECTION	ALP	COALITION	FORMED GOVT
28.09.46	54.1	45.9	ALP
10.12.49	49	51	Coalition
28.04.51	49.3	50.7	Coalition
29.05.54	50.7	49.3	Coalition
10.12.55	45.8	54.2	Coalition
22.11.58	45.9	54.1	Coalition
09.12.61	50.5	49.5	Coalition
30.11.63	47.4	52.6	Coalition
26.11.66	43.1	56.9	Coalition
25.10.69	50.2	49.8	Coalition
02.12.72	52.7	47.3	ALP
18.05.74	51.7	48.3	ALP
13.12.75	44.3	55.7	Coalition
10.12.77	45.4	54.6	Coalition
18.10.80	49.6	50.4	Coalition
05.03.83	53.23	46.77	ALP
01.12.84	51.77	48.23	ALP
11.07.87	50.83	49.17	ALP
24.03.90	49.9	50.1	ALP
13.03.93	51.44	48.56	ALP
02.03.96	46.37	53.63	Coalition
03.10.98	50.98	49.02	Coalition
10.11.01	49.05	50.95	Coalition
09.10.04	47.26	52.74	Coalition
24.11.07	52.7	47.3	ALP
21.08.10	50.12	49.88	ALP
07.09.13	46.51	53.49	Coalition
02.07.16	49.64	50.36	Coalition
18.05.19	48.47	51.53	Coalition

Source: Results drawn from AEC (2021).

Democratic Labor Party following the 1955 split in the ALP, much of the Vietnam War, and a long period of economic prosperity. The oil crisis of 1974 ended the long period of post-war economic growth, and the formation of the Australian Democrats in 1977, from dissident Liberals allying with minor parties, ended the effective two-party duopoly in the Senate. Nonetheless, we still characterise the post-War period as being one dominated by the 'two-party' system, as it has only been the ALP or Liberal–National Party Coalition who have formed government since 1941.

Even while the history of Australian governments, portrayed as a contest between the Liberal and Labor parties, is seen as being about a stable two-party system, we equally have to keep in mind that most governments in Australian history have been coalitions of two or more parties. While the Liberal Party and Country (later National) Party were often seen as one grouping, the two parties have remained separate entities, in organisational and representational terms, in most states.

What we should be aware of is that the period from the mid-1990s to today has seen a destabilising growth in parties of the left, centre and right, each vying for some form of electoral and political relevance. However, the structure of most lower houses in Australia has ensured that the two-party system is not in any immediate danger of breaking down. This has been aided in part by the attempts of various state and federal governments limiting the impact of minor parties (although not directly eliminating them) upon the operation of parliaments. The major parties are still capable of large and significant wins in elections.

SHORT-ANSWER QUESTIONS 7.4

1. Noting the results in Table 7.3, how is it possible for a party to win less than 50 per cent of the two-party preferred vote and not be in government?
2. Is the 'two-party preferred vote' still a reasonable indicator of who should form government?

Suggested responses are available at www.cambridge.org/highereducation/isbn/9781009108232/resources

REFLECTION QUESTIONS 7.2

1. Given that the Coalition of the Liberal Party and National Party contains two separate parties, is it reasonable to say that Australia has a 'two-party system'?
2. Do people vote the same way at state and federal elections?

Response prompts are available at www.cambridge.org/highereducation/isbn/9781009108232/resourcess

THE DEVELOPMENT AND ROLE OF POLITICAL PARTIES

Parties are seen by most Australians as important for the functioning of parliaments, and indeed politics in general. That said, they are also widely distrusted by the same population. The many and widespread scandals and mis-steps by prime ministers and MPs alike lead citizens to consider politicians and their parties fairly lowly, with trust in MPs being similar to talk-back radio announcers, journalists and union leaders. Even though during the COVID-19 pandemic party leaders experienced sharp rises in public confidence, this could be rapidly eroded by new scandals, indicating the new-found trust in them to handle a crisis was transient in respect of politics more generally. Yet political parties have not only survived, but they have also proliferated as vehicles for individuals and groups, and essential to political campaigning.

Dean Jaensch (1989) once suggested that 'Politics in Australia is party politics'. This neatly sums up the idea that parties are intrinsically linked to the functioning of both parliamentary politics and the functioning of government. However, while we might take political parties for granted, they were not always revered organisations. In the debates around the Constitution, political parties were considered for inclusion but then disregarded as undesirable. That the Labor Party had formed and was operating at the time of the formation of the Commonwealth of Australia, and that the United Kingdom had a long history of essentially 'cadre' parties, did not endear them to the original framers of the Constitution. As Dahl (1998, 86) notes, early political 'factions' were 'generally viewed as dangerous, divisive, subversive of public order and stability, and injurious to the public good'. This extended to them not even being included within the Constitution – they were essentially seen as private organisations, and not key to the functioning of parliament or government.

We should then consider the evolution of parties in Australia to be a pragmatic development, as much to do with the organisation of class and social interests as with the organisation of parliament and elections. We can see this in the development of political parties across Europe and in other liberal democracies. Parties had their origins in bodies seen as key elements in organising not just political but also social life – as Duverger notes (1959), a wide variety of organisations, including those with philosophical, religious, labour, business and sporting bases, are responsible for the birth of parties. Once almost a normalised part of social life, many now see them as something of a necessary evil, tolerated as part of the operation of parliamentary politics, declining in social power and importance, yet still seen as a key institution to manage an increasingly complex political problem (Rose 2014). We might say that this is an interesting time in the life of parties.

One point that we must consider is the changing nature of what we consider a political party to be. There is a considerable number of descriptions of what parties are, or do, from Edmund Burke's (1770, 530) description of them being 'a body of men united, for promoting by their joint endeavours the national interest, upon some particular principle in which they are all agreed', through to Joseph Schumpeter (1942/2013, 283), who in dismissing Burke's philosophical description instead, suggesting a more pragmatic purpose for a party being 'a group whose members propose to act in concert in the competitive struggle for political power', to Giovanni Sartori suggesting (1976, 64), 'a party is any political group that presents at elections, and is capable of placing through elections, candidates for public office'. Between these descriptions there are a myriad more, some more descriptive than others.

SPOTLIGHT 7.3 POLITICAL PARTIES

As we have already noted there are many definitions of what a political party is or what it should do. Some more are listed below:

- Robert Michels (1911/1959, 78): 'The modern party is a fighting organisation in the political sense of the term, and as such must conform to the laws of tactics.'
- Max Weber (cited in Gerth and Mills 1948, 194): 'Parties live in a house of "power", their action is oriented toward the acquisition of social "power", that is to say toward influencing communal action no matter what its content may be'.

- John Aldrich (1995, 19): 'Political parties can be seen as coalitions of elites to capture and use political office. [But] a political party is more than a coalition. A political party is an institutionalized coalition, one that has adopted rules, norms and procedures.'

One of the key elements most theorists agree on is that parties must have members, and that those members must be active for the party to be able to get elected. Although some parties rely on charismatic figures to lead them (think of Nick Xenophon or Pauline Hanson), most parties still need members to be active, distribute material and campaign for elections. This leads us to realise that party members are important to the electoral success of political parties.

QUESTION

Thinking about the various definitions provided here (and any more you can find), how important do you think party members are to electoral success?

As we know from previous discussion, one of the key elements of democracy is open competition between political parties and candidates. Arguments and debates around policy and social outcomes become the norm as parties compete, and the elector's choice is then represented within the state and national parliaments. This points to a further relationship between parties and the state, but that relationship is far more dependent on the political and legal structures around parties. For some parties in Europe, those structures embedded parties within the state, and in doing so lessened the impact of unfavourable electoral outcomes. *Partitocracy* describes where the state structures and laws enable the key parties to govern, usually in coalition, without necessarily having to deliver key election promises, but at the same time drawing on state resources to fund and organise the party and providing positions on key state institutions for important party members. At the same time, the state defines and regulates the parties, describing their activities in statutes as if they were an institution of the state. Australia does not have a system that provides benefits in that way, and still does not regulate parties' behaviour other than how it directly relates to elections.

We need also consider that parties see themselves as important to the democratic process and seek to control and direct how politics in Australia operates. The activities that parties might engage can be described in several ways:

- Parties are institutions (potentially regulated by the state) that bring citizens together for the purpose of exercising power within the state.
- Parties seek and use legitimate means for pursuing their ends.
- Parties will contest elections in the state whenever they are able to.
- Parties are institutions that seek to represent more than a single, narrow interest in society.
- Parties are groups of citizens with similar beliefs, attitudes and values.

Do parties really do this? We normally see parties acting as a link between citizens and the state, whether that linkage derives from other non-government organisations, such as business and social groups, or more formalised bodies, such as unions. So, the ALP has its strong links to the union movement, the Liberal Party to business organisations such as the Business Council of Australia, the National Party to groups representing rural interests such as the National Farmers Federation, and the Greens to the many environmental non-government organisations. Each of these parties acts as an interest aggregator and articulator for the organisations or movements they are linked to. This allows multiple ideas to be formulated into single demands upon government – and thus also act to assist in the functioning of parliament by providing focused points of policy debate around specific bills.

Parties also play the role of recruiting suitable people to politics. While much is made at times of the 'pay peanuts, get monkeys' analogy as to why politicians sometimes seem unable to govern effectively, parties do recruit citizens with excellent creativity and ability. These particular people, whether a self-educated man such as former Prime Minister Paul Keating or the well-educated Malcolm Turnbull, are able to act in what they see as the best interests of the nation and its people.

A further important role of parties generally is that they facilitate political participation. This can be done through the party's activities or organisation – such as attending meetings, rallies and events, or by engaging with non-members in everyday life. These particular functions are mainly seen as the purpose of party members and activists – to be the front line of the party, whether dealing with people outside the party, engaging and bringing people to the party, or communicating with them before, during and after elections. As part of that broader community engagement function (and intrinsically linked to the function of the party), the party undertakes a political communication and education role, building up the knowledge of its own members on issues of civics and the political system, acculturating them to both the party and the democratic system, and then passing this information on to non-members outside the party. This role is often overlooked in thinking about parties, but much of our political knowledge comes from family, friends and colleagues, as much as it does from school, television or the internet.

We can use these functions of political parties to analyse different types and structures of political parties according to their priorities, and to assess their strength and effectiveness. And last, but not least, we should not forget that parties are campaign vehicles for the political aspirations of individuals and groups in Australian society.

REFLECTION QUESTIONS 7.3

1. What are the political issues that motivate you to want to take some form of action?
2. Would you be prepared to join or support a party?
3. What key functions do parties exist for? Must they always be registered for elections?
4. How should we define what a 'party' is?

Response prompts are available at www.cambridge.org/highereducation/isbn/9781009108232/resources

THE IMPACT OF PARTIES ON PARLIAMENT

WESTMINSTER (MOSTLY) INTACT

The impact parties have had on Australian democracy is quite profound. Although the framers of the original Australian Constitution knew of political parties, they sought to distance the new Commonwealth from them by not formalising them in the Constitution. This follows a long tradition within the Westminster system of using convention and common law to maintain political and social rights. Just as the Australian Constitution contains no provisions guaranteeing rights, such as the US Bill of Rights, no provision was made for either political parties or even a prime minister. All were covered by convention and common law. The idea that parliament was the primary source of all authority, derived directly from the Crown, meant that Acts of Parliament could define all those roles.

For the early years of the new Commonwealth's existence this worked quite well, with there being only one organised party actively campaigning as a relatively unified body – the Australian Labor Party. However, its unity soon caused other parties to emerge to defend the interests of other groups within Australian society. Thus, the Liberal Party, the Country Party and the United Australia Party emerged. The inter-war period saw a variety of splits and re-formulations of the major parties, but after the Second World War the major parties took on their recognisably contemporary form. Although there have been splits and defections since, the strength of the party system has meant that the three main parties have maintained a tight grip on the House of Representatives.

The Senate as a filter

The Senate voting system itself, originally a 'block' voting system where the winner of the Senate ballot in the state collected all the senators for the state, allowed for unbalanced control of the Senate and the unimpeded passing of legislation, almost as a rubber stamp to the government of the day. This changed in 1948, following adoption of proportional representation, with the effect being the Senate was now divided between the two voting blocks. The role of major party MPs was to be disciplined and provide the numbers for the passage of legislation.

However, the late 20th century, particularly after parliament was expanded and Senate elections further reformed, saw a growth in the number of parties competing for seats. While the ALP and Coalition maintained control of the House of Representatives, the Senate became a place where minor parties could have a significant influence. Beginning with the Democratic Labor Party in the 1950s and 1960s, the Australian Democrats in the 1980s and 1990s and the Australian Greens in the 2000s, a series of parties have been able to have the final say over government legislation (see Weller and Fleming 2003, 27–34).

What the early impact of parties amounted to, though, was the influencing of the passage of legislation, but not necessarily the halting or undermining of government. Arguably the most successful of the minor parties in this period was the Australian Democrats, who for the whole of the Hawke and Keating ALP governments, from 1983 to 1996, controlled the flow of legislation through the Senate. While the ALP would naturally have preferred to pass legislation unimpeded, much legislation was passed without amendment. The Democrats' lasting contribution during this period was not 'keeping the bastards honest' as their famous slogan claimed, but in building the Senate Committee system to inquire into and scrutinise legislation that came before the Senate.

WESTMINSTER IN THE 21ST CENTURY

The key role of parties in the Westminster system – to make it easier to form government and to pass government legislation through the parliament – remained relatively intact until the 21st century. The splintering of cohesive vote blocks and the declining identification by voters with the major parties (driven at least in part by the changing nature of the Australian workforce) led to the creation of multiple small parties.

The proliferation of minor parties has at least partly destabilised the major parties, at least as far as upper house votes are concerned. The sheer number of seats and necessary resources required to contest all the House of Representatives electorates has proven largely prohibitive for many of the smallest parties, with only parties that have a sizable vote or specific sectoral influence can seriously contest lower house seats. This clearly limits the possibilities for most smaller parties, who tend to confine themselves to campaigning for the upper house and to gain some exposure for their policy proposals.

Parties with clearly defined ideologies, causes or constituencies are then able to contest seats with a vague sense that it may improve their upper house vote, or even give them a chance of winning the seat. The Greens' ability to first win the lower house seat of Cunningham in a 2002 by-election, and then win and hold the seat of Melbourne in 2013 and 2016, has demonstrated that a concentrated vote can allow a minor party to succeed – and this has borne fruit at the state level in New South Wales, Victoria and Queensland in recent elections. The capacity of another minor party – the Shooters, Fishers and Farmers Party – to win not just upper house seats, but rural lower house seats in New South Wales, equally demonstrates that major parties ignore key voting groups and issues at their electoral peril.

In the midst of this, the 2010 federal election generated a 'hung' parliament, where neither the ALP nor Coalition had a majority. Although this situation had arisen after state elections on a number of occasions, this was the first time since the 1940s that this had occurred at the Commonwealth level. The crossbench, four independents, one Green and one Western Australian National Party MP deliberated, with three of the independents and the Greens eventually siding with the ALP. This allowed Julia Gillard to form a new ministry, although it also required Gillard to make concessions that she explicitly ruled out during the election campaign – specifically that there would be a price on carbon, which was the price for the Greens' support. While Gillard was able to govern for the next three years, the promise haunted her through the next election, with Tony Abbott leading the Coalition to a massive victory in 2013.

RESEARCH QUESTION 7.2

Are minor parties and independents a threat to parliamentary democracy?

VOTING AND THE INTERNET

In all this discussion of the system, the parties and who gets to vote, we have to also consider one of the most significant changes of the 21st century – the internet. While books have been written on the impact of the internet on life in the new century, in respect of elections three elements are important: (1) the impact for parties on targeting voters through various media (this will be covered in Chapter 11); (2) how citizens engage in electoral politics (Chapter 12); and, (3) how the electoral system itself has adapted to the internet.

This last element, the impact on the electoral system, represents perhaps the greatest challenge to electoral politics in Australia. Parties have turned to the internet as they would to any other communication tool, and citizens have seen it as a liberating vehicle (although perhaps without considering the full ramifications). However, the electoral system is still struggling with how to use the internet without compromising the integrity (and some would say *sanctity*) of the vote. Some change has been inevitable, such as using the internet to allow people who are sight impaired to vote through braille keyboards from home, but broadly, internet or electronic voting has not been adopted in anywhere near the volume that it has in the United States, and confidence in electronic voting is still lower than in the paper-based voting system (Smith 2016).

Even though it might be assumed that the COVID-19 pandemic might encourage internet voting, most of the state and Commonwealth electoral commissions continue to restrict electronic voting to a very specific group of people. The exception is in the Australian Capital Territory, where the use of electronic voting machines has occurred in increasing numbers since 2001.

The implication of all this is that it may be some time before electronic voting is more widely used in Australia, even as the internet improves the ease of communicating issues and concerns.

PERSONALISATION AND PRESIDENTIALISM

One issue that has exercised the minds of Australian political scientists is the question of the importance of party leadership, and the impact parties have had on election outcomes when the leader of the party is seen as a proxy for the whole party. We have seen that the horse race analogy is the trope most used to describe many electoral races in lower houses, but when we come to federal or state elections, we begin to see the race as really being between two leaders – the argument being that if they can't persuade you of the party's message then the party is going to perform poorly in government. At the same time, we have seen the rise of the 'preferred prime minister' or 'preferred premier' ratings appearing in opinion polling – and being given increasing prominence.

This increased focus on party leaders and their capacity to sell a party's message is not exactly new, but it does undermine the idea that voters are casting a vote based solely on self or group interests. Perhaps tellingly, however, the emphasis on leadership affects right of centre parties more than left of centre parties – that is, left-wing voters who might support the ALP or Greens are more motivated by policy, while more conservative voters such as might support the Liberal and National parties are more motivated by leadership.

The counter-argument is that Westminster systems place natural brakes on the increased focus on paramount leaders – after all, local candidates also need to win election, so the debate is really about the personalisation of politics as opposed to any undermining of the Westminster notion of cabinet government (Dowding 2013). So while Australian voters may look to party leaders to provide effective control of Cabinets, parliament and the nation, they will also consider the policies being proposed and the capability of the candidates in the local electorate.

THEORISING THE AUSTRALIAN VOTER

BEHAVIOURALISTS: Political scientists who examine the actions and behaviours of individual actors, as opposed to the actions of institutions such as legislatures and executives.

To properly understand why elections have the kinds of outcomes that they do, some understanding of why people vote the way they do is important. Academics who study why people act the way they do are sometimes described as **BEHAVIOURALISTS**, and they look for patterns in the way electors vote for some parties and not others. The key motivation for many voters was thought for a long time to be due to their socialisation; that is, how they grew up, what they learned from their parents, friends and from school. So, for example, people who grew up in conservative households, went to elite private schools, and lived and worked in circles of conservative occupations such as the legal profession were more likely to vote for a conservative party such as the Liberal Party. Equally, people who grew up on farms, went to school and socialised with friends who also lived on farms were more likely to vote for a party like the National Party.

Yet socialisation does not explain the many people who are apparently NOT voting the way their parents or friends may be voting. If we consider the high level of stability in the vote for the major parties through the 1950s and 1960s, what caused this to decline in the 1980s and 1990s, particularly in the Senate? Once upon a time we might have tried linking this to class-based voting – that is, that workers voted for Labor, while business and the middle classes voted for the Liberals. Yet, John Howard's wins across Western Sydney in the late 1990s suggests that many 'workers' were no longer identifying with the 'workers' party'. The classic social cleavages of Europe have been, and perhaps still remain, ethnicity, language, class and religion (Elff 2007), yet none of these appear to have much traction in Australia in the 21st century, even while the myth of class-based voting continues.

In part, this non-cleavage voting has to do with Australia's demographic makeup. The census of 2016 pointed to the fact that a quarter of the Australian population was born overseas, with a further quarter having parents born overseas (Phillips and Simon-Davies 2017). This suggests that a significant proportion of Australians do not necessarily fit the white, Christian vision of Australia that existed at Federation and was prevalent in politics and culture through to the early post-war period. On top of this, many Australians do not have strongly held religious beliefs. While the Indigenous population may be growing, it still accounts for only three per cent of the general population, and Australia generally has limited evidence of race-based voting.

The American political scientist Ronald Inglehart, in the 1970s, identified what he called '**POST-MATERIALISTS**' – people who were not motivated to vote by traditional material concerns of jobs, wages and conditions (and the corollary of health and education). The group of young people growing up in the 1950s and 1960s (particularly the late 'baby boomers') grew up in a period of relative abundance, with those material concerns being relatively well taken care of for most. While pockets of poverty and deprivation certainly existed in Australia and other Western nations (especially among the Indigenous populations of North American and Australia), for most Australians this period was relatively affluent. Drawing on the work of psychologist Abraham Maselow and his 'hierarchy of needs', Inglehart (1977) proposed that with material conditions now being fulfilled, there was a growing group of citizens who were looking past these material needs to issues of identity, social self-awareness and social collectivity.

Inglehart's post-materialism thesis certainly goes some way to explain why the Labor, Liberal, and National parties began to see their core votes being eroded, as voters began to ask for more than material benefits. However, other social and political scientists, including Inglehart, noticed that rather than post-materialists overwhelming 'materialists', most citizens became mixed in their views, looking for ongoing, stable material certainty, even while pushing increasingly for change around social and environmental concerns.

At the same time as these shifts in what voters had begun to seek from society, and with growing levels of education broadening many Australian's social and political horizons, institutional shifts within parties and the electoral administration opened up opportunities for new parties and political groupings. The delinking of politics from specifically material concerns also saw Australians turn away from existing social organisations such as unions, churches and

POST-MATERIALISTS: People who consider that their material conditions are such that their vote is determined by other factors, such as the environment or whether other groups in society have rights. This is different to materialists, who are concerned primarily with their own material conditions of life. Most people now identify as 'mixed', meaning they wish to balance both material and post-material concerns.

charity organisations. These shifts both within society and institutions allowed voters to express their concerns around a range of issues.

HOW DO PARTIES ATTEMPT TO INFLUENCE THE VOTER?

However, being able to express your views on a significant range of issues is not the same as parties being able to act in their role as **POLICY AGGREGATORS**. Parties such as the ALP or Liberal Party act to collect and synthesise a range of views on topics as diverse as industrial relations, health, education and the environment. Their political remit is to have policies across all these areas, but these policies will broadly reflect their voter base. The Liberal Party can therefore be expected to have policies that would benefit people engaged in business and small enterprise, but also people who are concerned about large government, civil liberties and personal freedom.

Newer parties, such as the Greens or Pauline Hanson's One Nation, do not, however, act as broad policy aggregators but are more tightly focused on issues and concerns around the environment (for the Greens) or immigration and social cohesion (in the case of One Nation). The policies of parties such as these, large enough to stand in most electorates at both state and Commonwealth elections, are more targeted to what the parties believe are their broad constituencies. For One Nation this is to people who are disaffected by rapid social and economic change, and the messages from the parties' candidates and spokespeople is that the party is there to make things right again. All the usual mechanisms of campaigning are used, from printed material delivered to letterboxes, to paid advertising and media statements, but several high-profile members of the party (Pauline Hanson being just one example) have made a point of maintaining a visible public profile by expressing opinions that might be considered outside the mainstream to attract media attention. Their positions can be amplified on social media platforms through the use of 'influencers' and core supporters. Irrespective of their personal beliefs, this has the effect of maintaining name recognition (so voters do not feel they are voting for a complete unknown) and a sense that they speak from outside what is often called 'the Canberra bubble'. In this way they create the impression they are outsiders to the political process and can therefore speak for those who feel in any way marginalised. Parties who rely on this form of projection and policymaking are often called populist, or of peddling **POPULISM**. The ubiquity of social media campaigning has changed what were once the norms of political campaigning – reaching electors through advertising and meeting them face to face – to the point where a tweet can reach more electors than thousands of dollars and many miles of walking. The triumph of Donald Trump in 2016 the United States is often seen as the epitome of this form of campaigning.

Equally, the ability of many smaller parties, sometimes referred to as 'micro' parties on account of their very small membership and voter base, have arisen representing groups as diverse as sporting shooters, recreational fishers, bicyclists, and the arts community. While the issue of Australian parties and their formation is dealt with more extensively in Chapters 8 and 9, the fact these parties exist within an institutional framework, run at elections, and collectively attract a significant vote means that the policy aggregation function, relied upon to give coherence to parliament and allow government to work more efficiently, has declined over time. The advent and rise of the micro party, aimed at sectional voting interests normally indicated in their name (though this relies upon a certain truth-telling on the part of parties, not always in evidence), might also be seen as an adjunct of the rise of personalisation of politics as much as it is about a desire to promote particular policies or ideas.

POLICY AGGREGATORS: The idea that parties bring together many ideas, and in sifting through them find the ones that the majority of members within the party can agree on.

POPULISM: A form of politics based around a high-profile leader who styles themselves as someone standing with the mass of people against a corrupt elite, and as a person who needs to be able to act outside complicated democratic processes to get things done.

For the voter, this means that their choices have expanded when it comes time to vote. Equally, we need to see that voters themselves have changed in respect of their motivations for voting in elections and on particular issues. We can then go further and consider how citizens engage in politics more generally, particularly in terms of how it impacts their voting choice. We know that Australians have a declining view of their 'democracy', especially those engaged in protest activity (Jackson and Chen 2015), and a low opinion of the political institutions of parliament and parties (Brenton 2008), so how does this affect their voting choices and indeed the way they engage in politics and political life more generally?

> **SPOTLIGHT 7.4** ARE WE ALL 'EVERYDAY MAKERS'?
>
> Political theorist Henrik Bang (2004) has argued that political actors, outside of those engaged at the core of political life in the institutions of parliament and parties, can be divided into two broad groups: 'everyday makers' and 'expert citizens'. Expert citizens are an interesting group in themselves, as they are those elite individuals travelling between non-government organisations, policy bureaus and political institutions, operating generally without partisan affiliation, even while driven by a desire for particular social and political outcomes. Expert citizens are not ordinary citizens, but an elite group, with specific expertise and knowledge. Everyday makers, on the other hand, are that broad raft of people who might consider themselves 'apolitical', in so far as their engagement with formal politics and institutions is concerned, but who do hold views on a range of social and political issues. They are also generally engaged in the general workforce, not the specialised and politicised workforce of the expert citizen. The everyday maker dips in and out of politics and political campaigns, engaging in those that are of interest and disengaging from the organisations or issues that are of less interest to them.
>
> In this way, everyday makers are able to fulfil some of those desires noted by Inglehart, of identity and self-awareness, but also maintain their engagement in their general social life. Of course, they are unreliable partisans for parties and political groups, but they are certainly more typical of how citizens engage in political activity than the existing idea of the active party member – and go some way to explaining why voters may shift from catch-all major parties and instead vote for single issue or 'lifestyle' parties.
>
> **QUESTIONS**
>
> Now that you understand the term 'everyday makers', reflect on the title of this spotlight. Are we all everyday makers? Why or why not?

REFLECTION QUESTIONS 7.4

1. What are the reasons Australians vote the way that they do?
2. What about trust in politicians/leaders?

Response prompts are available at www.cambridge.org/highereducation/isbn/9781009108232/resources

SUMMARY

Learning objective 1: Understand the history of elections in Australia

This chapter outlines the broad movement from pre- to post-colonial electoral structures, up to the current structures and processes. This covers the two main political party groupings – the ALP and Coalition, and their respective electoral trajectories. Importantly the key contests for government have all been between the ALP and the Coalition parties, and this defines Australian post-Second World War politics.

Learning objective 2: Describe the key electoral elements of Australian democracy

The Australian electoral system is complicated by nine different systems, and understanding their evolution requires some knowledge of the evolution of Australian democratic practices. This chapter covers the evolution of the Australian vote, the use of proportional and preferential electoral systems, and the methods of counting the votes.

Learning objective 3: Understand the role and place of political parties in Australian elections

Political parties are essential players in the electoral system, organising candidates and then making it easier to form a stable government. In this chapter we also see that parties act as policy aggregators, sifting through the many possible policy ideas to arrive at ones most likely to pass and be enacted.

Learning objective 4: Explain why people vote the way they do

Voters cast their ballots according to many different reasons. For some it is because the leader of a party appeals to them, while for others the policies are most important. The rise of the post-material voter concerned with issues of identity and broad social goals has occurred because many material demands of working class parties, such as the Australian Labor Party, have been met. At the same time, populist parties and leaders, such as One Nation, have appealed to voters who may feel marginalised or ignored.

DISCUSSION QUESTIONS

1. When elections are described in the media it is often using 'horse-race' analogy of a contest between two parties, the ALP and the Coalition. How realistic is this analogy given the range of parties contesting elections and the ability of minor parties to influence the formation of government or even be part of government?

2. When we think of how elections are run in Australia, we usually consider them as being efficiently and securely run by independent bodies – the Australian Electoral Commission and their state equivalents – yet other countries have had significant problems with elections. What does it mean for an election to have 'integrity', and what are the various issues that need to be considered if we are to trust organisations that run elections?

3. Today we consider parties to be an integral part of elections and government, but what if there were no parties? How would elections be run under those circumstances, and what does this mean for government formation? Can you find examples of this situation?

4. Many different groups and organisations have an interest in who governs Australia. These organisations include churches, unions, environmental groups and business associations. Should these groups be able to try to influence the outcomes of elections?

5. Australia has compulsory voting, which means that if you are over 18 and an Australian citizen you are required to register to vote, and then when elections occur go to vote. However, most other countries do not. Should Australia have compulsory voting and why/why not?

FURTHER READING

Hay, C. (2007). *Why We Hate Politics*, Cambridge: Polity Press.

Kriesi, H., Koopmans, R., Duyvendak, J.W. & Giugni, M.J. (eds) (1995). *New Social Movements in Western Europe: A Comparative Analysis* (Vol. 5), Minneapolis: University of Minnesota Press.

Lipset, S.M. (1981). *Political Man: The Social Basis of Politics*, Expanded edition, Baltimore: John Hopkins University Press.

Marsh, I. (1995). *Beyond the Two Party System: Political Representation, Economic Competitiveness and Australian Politics*, Cambridge: Cambridge University Press.

Ware, A. (1996). *Political Parties and Party Systems*, Oxford: Oxford University Press.

REFERENCES

Aldrich, J. (1995). *Why Parties? The Origins and Transformation of Political Parties in America*, Chicago: University of Chicago Press.

Australian Electoral Commission (AEC). (2021). Australian Electoral Commission. Retrieved from http://www.aec.gov.au/

Bang, H.P. (2004). Everyday makers and expert citizens: Building political not social capital. Discussion Paper, ANU School of Social Sciences. Retrieved from https://openresearch-repository.anu.edu.au/handle/1885/42117

Bennett, S. (2001). Indigenous voting rights in Australia. *Australian Parliamentary Review*, **16**(1), 16–20.

Brenton, S. (2008). *Public Confidence in Australian Democracy. Democratic Audit of Australia*, Canberra: Australian National University.

Brett, J. (2003). *Australian Liberals and the Moral Middle Class*, Melbourne: Cambridge University Press.

Burke, E. (1770). Thoughts on cause of the present discontents. In *The Works of the Right Honourable Sir Edmund Burke*, London: John C Nimmo. Retrieved from: http://www.gutenberg.org/files/15043/15043-h/15043-h.htm#Page_433

Dahl, R.A. (1998). *On Democracy*, New Haven: Yale University Press.

Dowding, K. (2013). Presidentialisation again: A comment on Kefford. *Australian Journal of Political Science*, **48**(2), 147–9.

Duverger, M. (1959). *Political Parties*, 2nd edn, trans. B & R North, New York: Science Editions.

Elff, M. (2007). Social structure and electoral behavior in comparative perspective: The decline of social cleavages in Western Europe revisited. *Perspectives on Politics*, **5**(2), 277–94.

Farrell, D.M. & McAllister, I. (2003). The 1983 change in surplus vote transfer procedures for the Australian Senate and its consequences for the Single Transferable Vote. *Australian Journal of Political Science*, **38**(3), 479–91.

General Assembly of the United Nations. (1948). *The Universal Declaration of Human Rights*. New York: General Assembly of the United Nations. Retrieved from http://www.un.org/en/documents/udhr/

Gerth, H. & Mills, C. (1948). *From Max Weber: Essays in Sociology*, New York: Oxford University Press.

Inglehart, R. (1977). *The Silent Revolution: Changing Values and Political Styles in Western Publics*, Princeton: Princeton University Press.

Jackson, S. & Chen, P.J. (2015). Rapid mobilisation of demonstrators in March Australia. *Interface*, **7**(1), 98–116.

Jaensch, D. (1989). *Power Politics: Australia's Party System*, 2nd edn, Sydney: Allen & Unwin.

Koziol, M. & Whitbourn, M. (2017). Government unsure if marriage survey will exclude 100,000 voters, rules out 16-year-olds loophole, *The Sydney Morning Herald*, 11 August.

Legislative Council. (2001). *Report of the Standing Committee on Legislation in relation to the Electoral Distribution Repeal Bill 2001 and the Electoral Amendment Bill 2001* (Electoral Reform Bills). Report 8. Hon John Ford MLC, Chair. Presented 26 November 2001. Retrieved from http://www.parliament.wa.gov.au/parliament/commit.nsf/all/F39F41917D6860BB48257831003B0396?opendocument&tab=tab3

McAllister, I. (2014). The politics of lowering the voting age in Australia: Evaluating the evidence. *Australian Journal of Political Science*, **49**(1), 68–83.

McKinlay, B. (1981). *The ALP: A Short History of the Australian Labor Party*, Richmond: Drummond/Heineman.

Michels, R. (1911/1959). *Political Parties: A Sociological Study of the Oligarchical Tendencies of Modern Democracy*, trans E. and C. Paul, New York: Dover.

Miragliotta, N. (2002). *Determining the Result: Transferring Surplus Votes in the Western Australian Legislative Council*, Perth: Western Australian Electoral Commission.

Orr, G. (2011). The voting rights ratchet: *Rowe v Electoral Commissioner*, University of Queensland, TC Beirne School of Law Research Paper No. 12–3. Retrieved from https://ssrn.com/abstract=1926493 or http://dx.doi.org/10.2139/ssrn.1926493

Parliament of Australia. (2009). *The First Federal Election*. Website exhibition 'For peace, order and good government'. Retrieved from http://exhibitions.senate.gov.au/pogg/election/first_election.htm

Phillips, J. & Simon-Davies, J. (2017). *Migration to Australia: A quick guide to the statistics*. Research Paper Series 2016–17. Canberra: Department of the Parliamentary Library. Retrieved from http://parlinfo.aph.gov.au/parlInfo/download/library/prspub/3165114/upload_binary/3165114.pdf

Rose, R. (2014). Responsible party government in a world of interdependence. *West European Politics*, **37**(2), 253–69.

Sartori, G. (1976). *Party and Party Systems: A Framework for Analysis*, Cambridge: Cambridge University Press.

Schumpeter, J. (1942/2013). *Capitalism, Socialism and Democracy*, Abingdon: Routledge.

Smith, R. (2016). Confidence in paper-based and electronic voting channels: Evidence from Australia. *Australian Journal of Political Science*, **51**(1), 68–85.

Weller, P. & Fleming, J. (2003). The Commonwealth. In J. Moon and C. Sharman (eds), *Australian Politics and Government*, Cambridge: Cambridge University Press, pp. 12–40.

CHAPTER 8
THE ORIGINS AND EVOLUTION OF THE MAJOR PARTIES

LEARNING OBJECTIVES

After reading this chapter, you should be able to:

1. Understand where Australia's major parties came from and why they emerged
2. Explain how the relationship between the major parties and voters has changed
3. Recognise some of the ways the major parties have been theorised
4. Describe how Australia's major parties are different to major parties in other comparable advanced democracies

INTRODUCTION

The Australian Labor Party (ALP) and the Liberal Party of Australia (LPA) (who, at the federal level, are in a formal Coalition with the National Party) dominate Australian politics. In its modern guise this dominance extends back to the 1940s, though with Labor/non-Labor party electoral competition extending right back to Federation (albeit in a more complex form until 1909). Despite recent evidence of falling support for the two main parties, they will almost certainly remain dominant for the foreseeable future and are the only serious contenders to lead any government at federal or state/territory level. It is important to understand where these parties came from, how they have changed, and the contemporary political and organisational challenges they confront.

Despite their ritualistic claims to represent all Australians, the origins of both the ALP and LPA were decidedly *sectional*. That is, they arose from and represented the interests of certain sections of the population. To simplify greatly, the ALP grew out of and represented the interests of organised labour, while the LPA represented the interests of employers and the middle class. This picture of a crude, binary structural division was always somewhat simplistic but has become much more so in recent decades. Voting patterns have changed, and some suggest there has been a degree of policy convergence between the ALP and the LPA. It is also frequently claimed these parties work together to prevent competitors from disrupting their dominance of the political landscape. This idea, commonly associated with the 'cartel thesis', suggests these parties are prepared to put their competition with one another to one side, so they can continue to rotate between government and opposition as they have done for decades. Debates like these go to a larger issue: whether the relationship between voters and these parties has changed, with trust in the major parties on the decline (as it is with many other institutions). These problems are, of course, not uniquely Australian. Major parties in Australia face technological, social, cultural and political challenges which are common across most advanced industrial democracies.

The first section of this chapter examines the history and evolution of the major parties. In doing so, we explore their organisation and ideology and then consider how, if at all, the relationship between the major parties and voters has changed. The chapter concludes by examining the ways Australia's major parties have been classified, and how they might differ from those in other advanced democracies such as the United Kingdom and the United States.

AUSTRALIA'S MAJOR PARTIES: HISTORY AND EVOLUTION

The history of institutions and organisations always continues to live in the present. To fully understand the present, and alternative futures, we need some understanding of the past. This is certainly the case with political parties. Without some understanding of Australia's major parties and their history, it is nearly impossible to understand Australian politics. They are influential in the politics of the nation at every level of government – local, state and territory, and federal – and the ALP and LPA brands appear ubiquitous (unlike, e.g. Canada where different parties operate at different levels of the system (Lecours et al. 2021, 517)). Yet, around the time of Federation there was deep scepticism among voters, politicians and constitutional framers as to whether parties, let alone large strong parties, were desirable (Gauja 2015, 164). Despite this view, large strong parties quickly emerged and dominated the system, today playing critical roles in organising and shaping politics as well as making the system workable. 'If every member of parliament was an independent with no institutionalised links with other members – the result would be something close to chaos' (Gallagher, Laver and Mair 2005, 308).

Major party dominance is due in part to the electoral systems employed in lower houses across Australia. This hints at the fact parties do not exist in a political vacuum but form a **PARTY SYSTEM** influenced by various factors. The dominance of the major parties is also a product of historical legacy and the socialisation of voters into politics. In part this is driven by the relationship the parties have with different units of civil society, but it is also driven by partisanship and the effect colleagues, families, schools and workplaces have on how we perceive the world around us, including the political parties contesting for power. Whether this dominance is in the public interest and can be sustained is a matter of great importance. To better understand the major parties, then, it is important to consider the origins and evolution of these parties.

> **PARTY SYSTEM:**
> The interactions between political parties in a democratic system, as well as the interactions between parties with voters and the electoral system.

THE AUSTRALIAN LABOR PARTY

Labor's election defeat in 2013, and the six turbulent years in government preceding it, exemplified many of the issues punctuating its history (alongside those of personality and ambition). These issues include the role of factions, the relationship between the parliamentary and non-parliamentary wings of the party, the extent to which Labor is or should be a workers' party, and the related issue of union involvement in shaping party policies. This can all be condensed into two questions which confront all ALP members and leaders, past and present: What is the ALP, and what does it stand for? The varying answers given to these questions have been shaped by the party's history.

The early years: From unions to party

The ALP was a creation of the union movement that developed in the Australian colonies in the 1880s and 1890s. The labour movement grew from small beginnings earlier in the 19th century, and it represented a collective effort to improve workers' lives in a context where the economy and politics were dominated by big pastoralists and urban business interests. Despite many successes, the limitations of purely union activity were starkly illuminated during the economic crisis that shook the colonies in the early 1890s. Deteriorating economic conditions contributed to social hardship and a spate of industrial conflicts. These ultimately ended in humiliating defeats for unions involved in shipping, the wharves, mining and shearing (Macintyre 2001, 25). Colonial governments, in which workers had little or no representation, sided decisively with employers to crush worker resistance. This bitter lesson was the catalyst for the formation of various labour political organisations in the different colonies. Their purpose was the pursuit of parliamentary representation to advance the interests of workers, chiefly by gaining concessions in return for their support of non-labour politicians. By the end of the century, all the mainland eastern colonies had realised this objective. A short-lived Labor ministry had even formed in the Queensland parliament in 1899 – a world first.

In the early years after formation, Labor was an ideological amalgam of various socialist and radical liberal ideas, within a labourist party. It was committed to notions of equality, solidarity and social justice, but also constitutionalism and personal freedom. Its socialism was – from the outset – of the incremental, reformist variety. Far from fighting for the revolutionary overthrow of the existing system, the party sought parliamentary representation to affect gradual social change that could mitigate the worst excesses of capitalism, by providing industrial and social protections for workers and the elderly. Members and parliamentarians pledged themselves to the 'Democratic socialisation of industry, production, distribution and exchange', but only 'to the extent necessary to eliminate exploitation and other anti-social features of these fields' (ALP 2011). This pragmatic socialism was coupled with ideas drawn from the liberal tradition. These included a commitment to the rule of law and constitutionalism, a defence of freedom of thought and expression, and a strong belief in the separation of church and state. Labor also worked with other political groupings around shared beliefs, for example on tariffs. To its shame and embarrassment today, it also worked with others to introduce and sustain the racist White Australia policy, which protected the privileges of white workers against non-white, imported labour (Castles 1988; Bongiorno 2001). The newly formed ALP was a workers' party, with its social base firmly entrenched in working class trade unions. It is a matter of ongoing debate, though, whether it still is a party of the working class.

The early years of the ALP also brought into sharp focus organisational issues, which ultimately are also political issues – ones that continue to be sources of intra-party controversy to this day. Central here were the related questions of: (1) how to ensure Labor parliamentarians would continue to advance the interests of, and policies endorsed by, the broader membership and their unions, and (2) how to balance the personal beliefs and judgements of members with the need to act collectively in a disciplined, centralised, and politically effective fashion.

The answer to the first of these questions involved organising the party in such a way that power and legitimacy emanated from below, at least formally (Warhurst and Parkin 2000). As Australia's first mass party, Labor organised branches within each state and federal electoral area. Members in these branches had the right to vote on but also to initiate policy proposals and to nominate as delegates to higher bodies. If they secured the necessary votes, they could represent their branches and electoral areas in higher party bodies, up to and including state and federal conferences. These conferences, now held biennially, were where the supreme decision-making of the party took place. Importantly, these state and national conferences also reserved a certain percentage of delegates and therefore votes to member unions of the ALP (today unions have 50 per cent representation at National Conference). The party's structure, which has changed surprisingly little in over a century, is a transmission belt for union influence on the party and its parliamentarians.

The answer to the second of the questions complements the first. The mechanism for balancing the preferences of individual members with the political necessity of acting in unison entails members accepting the obligation of party discipline, in return for the right of democratic participation in decision-making. Members have the right to argue for their position and to vote on important decisions, but once a decision is taken by a majority vote all members are bound by the decision, whether they agree with it or not. They are obliged to implement the decision and to defend it in public. This is assumed to create a unity of purpose and thus a maximisation of political efficacy. Future Labor Prime Minister Billy Hughes eloquently summed up the principle in 1908 when he wrote:

> Nothing can more conform to the principles and ideals of Democracy and at the same time more effectively promote the interests and secure the objects for which a party contends than an institution which, enabling all to be heard, ensures that after due deliberation the party should speak with one voice. (Quoted in Lloyd and Weller 1975, 5)

That the party *should* speak with one voice, however, does not mean the party *does* speak with one voice. Hughes himself prompted a split in the Labor Government in 1916, when he supported military conscription despite broader opposition in his parliamentary caucus and among the ALP rank and file (Bongiorno and Dyrenfurth 2011, 61–6). A Labor government would again split in 1931 over Depression era austerity, which portended the deeper and more damaging split of the 1950s.

SHORT-ANSWER QUESTIONS 8.1

1. What provided the impetus for the formation of the ALP?
2. What is the highest decision-making body in the ALP?

Suggested responses are available at www.cambridge.org/highereducation/isbn/9781009108232/resources

From split to modernisation

Between the post-war period and the 21st century, three key developments have shaped the ALP's evolution: the split in 1954–55; the Party's modernisation under Gough Whitlam's leadership in the late 1960s; and the dramatic change in policy direction during the Hawke and Keating years (1983–96), which followed and was influenced by the 1975 dismissal of Whitlam's government. The first of these, the split, was a manifestation of deep divisions within the ALP, which were exacerbated by the Cold War and anti-communist hysteria (Costar and Strangio 2005; Bongiorno and Dyrenfurth 2011, 107–19). An undeclared conservative faction had crystallised in the 1940s and early 1950s, alarmed by what it viewed as growing communist influence within the labour movement. Largely Catholic in origin, it organised itself into so-called 'industrial groups' (or 'groupers') to combat alleged communist influence in the unions. It severely disrupted Labor's own union work and plunged the party into a state of almost permanent civil war with itself. This led to the expulsion of groupers and their fellow travellers in 1954–55, and the subsequent creation of the conservative Democratic Labor Party in 1957. The latter would win enough votes away from the ALP to help keep it from federal government for the next decade and a half.

In the latter years of that period, the ALP underwent a significant modernisation. The transition of the Labor leadership from Arthur Calwell to Gough Whitlam in 1967, symbolised a shift from the working class, blue collar, masculine and largely Anglo-Celtic party that Labor had been to a more middle class, white collar, feminised and ethnically diverse party it was to become (Warhurst 1996). Modernisation was intimately linked to combatting the perception that unions and shadowy backroom numbers men controlled Labor parliamentarians, which had frequently been used against the party (Kefford 2015, 52–4) and continues to be today. Before the ALP would return to government in 1972, Whitlam (and others) would go on to wage an internal struggle to modernise the party by diluting the power of unions within the National Conference and the ALP more generally, by breaking the resistance of those still hostile to the Australia–US alliance, and by ensuring the parliamentary leadership was represented on the ALP's Federal Executive. Whitlam and his supporters would eventually succeed, professionalising the party and broadening its electoral appeal. This was based on more sophisticated use of research, marketing and media techniques that had been pioneered in the United States. Labor increasingly became a **'CATCH-ALL' PARTY**, fighting for the support of middle class and other swing voters (voters who switch between parties from one election to another, rather than consistently voting ALP or LPA) who determine election outcomes.

CATCH-ALL PARTY: Parties which lack a clear ideological direction and, instead, promote policy preferences from across the ideological spectrum in a broad pitch to voters.

SPOTLIGHT 8.1 LABOR AND THE DISMISSAL

The dismissal of the Whitlam Government on 11 November 1975 by the Governor-General, Sir John Kerr, is without question the most controversial day in the history of Australian federal politics (Sexton 2005). At the time, the Australian economy was experiencing the same stresses and strains that were sweeping the rest of the developed world. Economic stagnation and rising unemployment were coupled with sharply higher inflation and increased industrial conflict. The opposition and conservative media presented these developments as the chaotic outcomes of misplaced Labor policies. This came to a head with the notorious 'loans affair', where Labor Minister Rex Connor misled parliament about having ended the unconventional channels through which he had explored securing an international loan. This would become part of the pretext for the Senate withholding supply (the money needed to run government) and demanding Whitlam call an early election. Whitlam refused, presenting both the Senate and its demands as being illegitimate and unconstitutional (Whitlam 1979). A crisis ensued, and eventually the Governor-General intervened, sacked Whitlam and replaced him with the leader of the opposition, Malcolm Fraser. An election was held in December, and Labor lost in a landslide. The entire episode seemed to exemplify the axiom that Labor could be in government but not necessarily in power. The dismissal, along with further election defeats in 1977 and 1980, chastened the ALP and made its leaders more circumspect about advancing policies that could be construed as radical. Thus, when Labor swept back into government in March 1983, it was with a very different agenda to that of its predecessors. This new agenda ultimately transformed the party and, many would argue, made it more remote from those it claimed to represent.

QUESTIONS

How did the ALP of 1983 differ to that of the Whitlam era? Why do some argue that this shift moved the party further from those they claim to represent?

The Labor administrations of Bob Hawke (1983–91) and Paul Keating (1991–96) are often presented as governments of neo-liberalism or, in the more Australian vernacular, 'economic rationalism' (Pusey 1991). By this, commentators mean that the Hawke and Keating Labor governments had shifted from state interventionism and market regulation that had previously characterised Labor to a free market, small government-oriented administration. There is much truth to this observation. Treasurer Paul Keating had commented in 1985 that Australia had to become more internationally competitive if it was to avoid becoming a 'Banana Republic' (Langman 1992, 75–90). In the language of 'governnment to governance', the Australian Government needed to start 'steering not rowing' (see Chapter 6 for more on this transformation). The 'rowing' would now be done by a private sector liberated from the shackles of government regulation, bureaucracy, and high corporate taxes. 'Sound economic management', which became a euphemism for fiscal conservatism, became the new mantra of Labor leaders. Consequently, in its 13 years in office, Labor comprehensively restructured the Australian economy. It deregulated financial markets, replaced centralised wage fixing with enterprise bargaining, lowered tariffs, privatised many state-owned industries and floated the Australian dollar, thereby exposing the country to the constraining judgements of global financial markets. Much of this was accomplished with the acquiescence, if not the active support, of union leaders. The instrument

PRICES AND INCOMES ACCORD: The Accord, as it is commonly known, was a series of agreements between trade unions and the Hawke and Keating Labor governments, which led to the union movement reducing their wage demands in return for increased social provisions such as health and education entitlements.

through which union cooperation was secured by the Labor Party and its government was a series of agreements called the **PRICES AND INCOMES ACCORD** (Stilwell 1986).

Critics claimed the accords tethered the unions to the parliamentary party's right-wing agenda, to the detriment of members (Beilharz 1994). Union leaders agreed to wage restraint, limitations on industrial action, and the restructuring of the economy, in return for a place at the negotiating table and the maintenance of the 'social wage'. The social wage refers to those socialised services that benefit workers but which they do not pay for directly. These include healthcare, education and welfare, the foundations of which were largely maintained, albeit with some reductions in certain areas (such as tertiary education, where users now had to pay a certain proportion of their fees). From a political perspective, this strategy was tremendously successful. Labor won five consecutive elections while undertaking transformative change and preserving its union support. But the very success of the strategy sowed the seeds of longer-term problems for Labor, expressed in and compounded by Labor's 11 years in opposition (1996–2007). The party is still grappling with these problems.

Contemporary challenges for Labor

Labor was resoundingly defeated in the September 2013 federal election, after six tumultuous years in power. Kevin Rudd had led the party to a compelling victory in 2007, but soon faced an economic and political storm which, coupled with Rudd's leadership style, ultimately led to his replacement by Julia Gillard. The way Gillard became Australia's first female prime minister in June 2010 placed a cloud over her leadership, with many viewing it as a perfidious act betraying not only a sitting first-term prime minister but also the electorate that had voted him into power. Nevertheless, it is doubtful a male politician would have faced the same criticism in similar circumstances. Indeed, when Malcolm Turnbull replaced Tony Abbott as prime minister in 2015, there was barely a ripple of condemnation, other than from staunch Abbott supporters. It would seem, therefore, the denunciations of Gillard had more to do with her gender than her leadership. Regardless, under Gillard's leadership the ALP limped back into government after the 2010 federal election, forming a minority administration with backing from three independents and the Greens. But she would lose the leadership back to Rudd just months before the 2013 election loss. This loss ended a political era for Labor, exemplifying many of the challenges the contemporary ALP faces. These include ideological tensions and the loss of electoral support on both their left and right, changes in the labour market that dilute its traditional support base in the unions, and damaging factionalism. Linking and strengthening these issues is an ongoing tension over control of the party. In theory (and unlike the Liberals) the broader party controls the parliamentary team, but since the Whitlam years, leaders have exerted more and more autonomy in decision-making (Gauja 2015).

Labor has always been a party with overlapping and competing worldviews including social democracy, labourism, social liberalism and democratic socialism (see e.g. Manwaring and Robinson 2020, 7). These sometimes pull in different directions and tensions have been evident in recent decades. While Labor maintains the support of its union base, its embrace of the market from the 1980s has strained its credentials as a party of the left and alienated some of its traditional supporters. This has manifested in a long-term decline of Labor's primary vote at federal elections. On the left, many progressive urban voters who would once have been expected to vote for Labor have become disenchanted – on cultural as much as economic issues – and drifted towards the Greens, who now receive around 1 in every 10 votes at federal elections. On the right, some of Labor's traditional working-class support has leaked to the Coalition, apparently attracted by its more conservative messages on national security, asylum seekers, multiculturalism and the role of government generally. Liberal Party Prime Minister John Howard accelerated this development in the late 1990s and early 2000s, through his politically adroit appeals to suburban 'battlers' (Brett 2004, 81–2). The effect was to wedge Labor and magnify internal divisions, particularly around national security and refugees arriving in Australia by boat. In recent years, Labor has tried to neutralise the issue by sticking close to the Coalition's political playbook. But in doing so they risk further alienating some of their progressive support. This is a political challenge Labor will have to manage for the foreseeable future.

Another challenge for Labor has been the precipitous decline in workers' union membership. In the early 1950s around 65 per cent of the workforce was unionised. Even as late as 1980, union density was still over half. Today the figure is less than 20 per cent. Membership has gradually shifted towards white-collar public-sector employees, and today less than 10 per cent of private sector workers belong to unions. Structural changes to the Labor market mean this trend is likely to continue and even deepen. The growth of casualisation, the 'gig' economy and automation make it ever more difficult to unionise workers. The problem for the ALP is two-fold. On the one hand, a decline of unionism represents a decline of Labor's traditional base – a base that provides funds, members and talent. On the other hand, Labor's parliamentary wing still contains many former union figures, while union members are a smaller and smaller proportion of Australia's population. This makes Labor vulnerable to the oft-made charge it does not fully reflect the entire Australian community and is instead a party of sectional interests.

Another challenge for Labor is destructive factionalism. **FACTIONS** are smaller organised groups of like-minded individuals within a political party that organise to win influence, offices and positions of power. There is nothing wrong with factions per se. In some ways, they are effective for managing conflicts that invariably arise within broad political parties. Factions were formalised in the ALP in the mid-1980s (left faction, unity [right] faction and the centre-left faction) but this did not cause undue harm to Labor's cause. In fact, some suggest they enhanced Labor's position because conflict was largely managed out of the public spotlight and power was shared in Labor's parliamentary caucus, with the distribution of portfolios largely a function of factional bargaining (Faulkner 2001, 216). But these undoubted benefits also have costs, which came to the fore during Labor's period in opposition (1996–2007).

The frustrations of being in opposition during the 11 years of the Howard Government exacerbated factional division and conflicts, with widespread allegations of faction-led branch stacking at state and federal level (Jaensch 2006, 39–41). The allegation was that large groups of new members would be recruited at short notice for no other reason than to provide the numbers for factional power plays, especially around pre-selections (choosing candidates to run in state and federal elections). This was particularly notable in the NSW state branch, where the manoeuvrings of factional power brokers led to the making and unmaking of a series of state premiers (Cavalier 2010). This had disastrous consequences for the public image of the state branch, ultimately being realised in a landslide electoral defeat. This exemplified the problems that arise when factions become ends in themselves, exclusively pursuing the spoils of power within the party, at the expense of the party's main objective of winning or keeping government. The success of one's faction is placed before the success of one's party.

In 2010, the factions had engineered the replacement of Prime Minister Rudd by Julia Gillard, who just months before the 2013 election was replaced following more manoeuvring by the same factional powerbrokers who reinstalled Rudd. A rule change demanded by Rudd remodelled the system for choosing leaders, making the job much better defended against challengers and factional powerplays. In the wake of the 2013 election loss, Bill Shorten, one of

FACTIONS AND TENDENCIES: In Australian politics, factions are organised sub-groups within a party which vie for dominance and positions. While formalised factions exist in the ALP, they are informal in the Liberals and other parties, and are often known as 'tendencies'.

those powerful factional figures, became the new parliamentary Labor leader under these rules. Under Shorten's leadership, the party seemed to have learned from the Rudd–Gillard–Rudd years' disunity and came very close to toppling the Coalition government at both the 2016 and 2019 federal elections. Following the 2019 loss, the party turned to Anthony Albanese, one of the few senior figures to come out of the Rudd–Gillard–Rudd years with their reputation enhanced. Albanese immediately faced the thankless task of being opposition leader during a long crisis, with the COVID-19 pandemic. Despite this, the ALP crawled across the line at the 2022 election, managing to form a government with a narrow majority and a limited set of policy promises.

SHORT-ANSWER QUESTIONS 8.2

1. Why are the Hawke and Keating years so contentious for some ALP voters?
2. What about this period is similar to that of more recent ALP governments, for example, the Rudd and Gillard governments?

Suggested responses are available at www.cambridge.org/highereducation/isbn/9781009108232/resources

THE LIBERAL PARTY

The Liberal Party too has had its own divisions and leadership volatility while in office. In August 2018, Scott Morrison replaced Malcolm Turnbull as Liberal Party leader and prime minister after a long internal war in the party. Against almost everyone's expectations, Morrison went on to win the 2019 election, albeit by the narrowest of margins. This broadly mirrored Turnbull's arrival in office three years before when he defeated fellow Liberal Tony Abbott and became party leader and prime minister, going on to win an exceptionally narrow election victory in 2016. In 2022, after further internal divisions, Morrison led the party to arguably the worst election defeat in its history and ended nine years of turbulent Coalition rule. These leadership battles reveal the deeper political truth about the Liberal Party of Australia (LPA) and its historical forebears. The various centre-right, anti-Labor parties have always exhibited a degree of tension between their liberal and conservative wings. In the last decade these divisions have been shown in ongoing battles for the party leadership between different tendencies in the party.

The early years: Anti-socialism and liberalism

Since 1909, interparty competition in Australia has been structured around a core Labor/non-Labor divide. The first Liberal Party – not to be confused with the modern LPA, which only came into existence in 1944 – was a fusion of free trade and protectionist non-labor politicians, who came together in 1909 to combat Labor's socialist leanings and its capacity to dominate the federal sphere (Brett 2003, 20–7). This pattern continued after 1944 with today's Liberal Party, which is in an enduring coalition with the Nationals (originally known as the Country Party). While the Liberals and Nationals maintain separate party organisations and identities in all states excluding Queensland, they form united Cabinets and shadow Cabinets, make binding agreements on the distribution of ministerial portfolios, and have mutually agreed policy platforms on major issues. The LPA is clearly the senior partner, though, and always has been.

In the decades of colonial self-government before the 1890s, politics was a highly personalised affair. Fluid alliances of individuals and factions rather than parties dominated parliaments (Loveday and Martin 1977). Colonial legislatures were filled by (almost exclusively) men of ambition drawn largely from landed and commercial interests and from the professions (especially law). Commentators at the time would attempt to politically locate and label these early politicians by drawing on British experiences. 'Liberals' were those who typically supported universal male suffrage, land reform, state sponsored compulsory secular education, the separation of church and state, and limits on the power of upper houses. Moreover, they championed a significant role for government in advancing economic development, which was a key issue in all the colonies. Men drawn from the professions and commercial classes, especially manufacturers, were over-represented among Liberals and their supporters. 'Conservatives', on the other hand, sought to preserve existing power, institutions and privilege. They resisted liberal causes, were hostile to the democratic ideal of one vote one value, favoured religious education, and sought to preserve the veto powers of legislative councils (upper houses) over legislative assemblies (lower houses). There were many wealthy landowners among Conservatives, as well as men drawn from trade and commerce.

This Liberal/Conservative divide partly overlapped with one of the most contentious economic issues of the period: tariffs versus free trade (Starr 1980). Nascent manufacturers, especially in Victoria under the leadership of Alfred Deakin, favoured government-imposed protectionist measures to help incubate emerging industries from foreign competition. They cooperated closely with Labor on this and related issues. This was fiercely opposed by farmers and some merchant interests who viewed such measures as artificially raising their costs and thus undermining profits and being anathema to a free society. Consequently, the non-Labor forces in Australia's first three parliaments were evenly divided between Protectionists and Free Traders. Yet as deep as these divisions were, they proved not to be as fundamental as the threat both Liberals and Conservatives, protectionists and free traders, perceived in the rise of organised labour. The leader of the Free Traders, George Reid, summed up the danger when campaigning for the 1906 federal election:

> I have not manufactured an election cry, but have discovered a real and increasing national danger, which must some day compel all liberals, whether in one camp or the other, to bury their differences and rally their forces to free parliament from the determination of the secret caucus, and to defend the industrial and political liberty of Australia from the attack of socialism. (Quoted in Starr 1980, 6)

Hence, it was in response to the growing success of the ALP that anti-Labor politicians came together in the 'fusion' of 1909 and contested (unsuccessfully) the federal election of the following year under the banner of the Liberal Party.

From the outset, then, the Liberal Party was defined as much by its opposition to Labor and socialism, as by any common ideological platform. While all Liberal Party politicians could agree on abstract commitments to constitutionalism, the rule of law and the primacy of the individual and personal responsibility, they would remain divided over various social questions (religion, education, welfare and industrial arbitration) and over the extent to which the state should be active in protecting and shaping the economy. These divisions would remain an irritant in the conservative Nationalist governments of the 1920s, into which the Liberals dissolved themselves after 1917. They also resurfaced periodically in the United Australia Party (UAP) governments in the 1930s, which takes the centre-right story from the Nationalists to the modern LPA. It was the weaknesses and limitations of the UAP that led one of its leading lights, Robert Menzies, to conclude a new Liberal Party was needed.

SHORT-ANSWER QUESTIONS 8.3

1. What was the 'Fusion' of 1909?
2. Who was Alfred Deakin?

Suggested responses are available at www.cambridge.org/highereducation/isbn/9781009108232/resources

The Liberal Party of Australia and the 'forgotten people'

The LPA was formed in December 1944, after a conference had been called in October of that year to rally support for a new non-Labor Party. The UAP had fallen into disarray after losing government in October 1941, and then being crushed in the election of 1943. But the UAP's problems were not only political; they were also organisational. Any new party would need a stronger and more authoritative federal executive plus greater organisational capacities at the level of individual electorates, which the UAP lacked (Starr 1980, 24). The central figure in the formation of such a new party was the former Prime Minister Robert Menzies, although he was by no means the only important player, which is the impression sometimes given in political mythology.

Menzies had become prime minister in 1939, after UAP leader Joe Lyons had died in office. This first tenure as prime minister, on the eve of the Second World War, had not been particularly successful or inspiring. He had earned the epithet 'Pig Iron Bob', when he clashed with waterside workers over his insistence pig iron continued to be shipped to Japan, just months before the outbreak of the Pacific War. Moreover, his government's preparations for war had been haphazard, and many viewed him as being aloof, arrogant and overly subservient to Britain. He would later resign the leadership of his government in favour of Country Party leader Arthur Fadden, who quickly lost the government's majority in the House of Representatives when it could no longer depend on the votes of two independents (Maddox 1996, 333). Labor was invited to form government, which it did, consolidating its majority in the 1943 election.

Having lost the prime ministership, Menzies turned his mind to clarifying his own political philosophy. In a series of radio broadcasts in 1942, he set out his vision for Australia, including most famously a speech on what he referred to as the nation's 'forgotten people' (Brett 2007). The speech is more than a political manifesto. It is a moral vision of the good society and, at the same time, a polemic against those on the left for whom social class is the organising principle of modern politics. In Australia, unlike Britain, 'the class war must always be a false war', Menzies says. Yet he continues by acknowledging the existence of social classes and clarifying the class that he, and later the LPA that he led for more than two decades, claimed to represent:

> But if we are to talk of classes, then the time has come to say something of the forgotten class – *The Middle Class* – those people who are constantly in danger of being ground between the upper and the nether millstones of the false class war; the middle class who, properly regarded, represent the backbone of this country. (Menzies cited in Brett 2007, 21)

It was this constituency to which the LPA would orient itself right from its inception. Previously, the UAP had been, and was perceived to have been, closely aligned with the interests of big business, to the detriment of the middle class. Menzies was clear that if the new party was to be electorally appealing to a broad layer of the population – if it was to be a truly *national* party rather than a party of sectional interests as the ALP was assumed to be – it would need to avoid such a perception. This was reflected in the very name *Liberal* Party, which was adopted 'because we were determined to be a progressive party … ' (Menzies cited in Starr 1980, 79). But the LPA's progressive credentials, especially in respect of civil rights, would be put to the test in the period immediately after winning office for the first time in December 1949.

In those years, the early years of the Cold War, the Liberal Party energetically set about trying to undermine the civil rights of those on the political left. In 1950, the Menzies Government introduced the Communist Party Dissolution Bill. This legislation aimed to ban the Communist Party of Australia and the freedoms of speech, assembly and association of its members, which Liberals rhetorically uphold as sacrosanct. The law would later be rejected as unconstitutional by the High Court, but the damage was done. Lives were disrupted, and reputations destroyed, and Labor was hopelessly split over the issue of communism and civil rights, eventually leading to their split in 1955.

The split in Labor helped the Liberal Government continue for another 17 years, and for that reason Menzies' willingness to play the red scare card was effective politics, if not good policy. It also underlines the profound ambivalence LPA leaders have with liberal principles, when the temptations of political opportunity are periodically aroused around national security issues. Similar questions would later be directed at John Howard, Tony Abbott and Malcolm Turnbull's commitments to liberal principles in the context of national security challenges. It would be wrong, however, to think it was only political opportunism that accounts for the LPA's 23 years in power till 1972. The Liberals also enjoyed, and some would argue were the architects of, an unprecedented period of economic prosperity that would see the national economic pie grow, employment expand, real wages increase and educational opportunities, especially in universities, multiply (Starr 1980). Coalition governments accomplished all of this while maintaining most elements of the welfare state, and while being broadly committed to the post-war, Keynesian economic consensus.

After the retirement of Menzies in 1966, the Liberal Party went through a period of leadership instability, with Harold Holt, John Gorton, William McMahon and Billy Snedden filling the leadership in relatively quick succession. This instability underlined the importance for the LPA of a strong parliamentary leader, who could provide focus and political cohesion for a party room frequently encompassing diverse political tendencies. As the distribution of ministerial or shadow-ministerial portfolios is not beholden to factions, with the leader being free to choose their Cabinet and shadow Cabinet, LPA leaders theoretically wield more power within their party than do their Labor counterparts. It is no coincidence, therefore, that the party's most successful periods have all been under strong and authoritative leaders – Menzies (1949–66), Fraser (1975–83) and Howard (1996–2007).

SHORT-ANSWER QUESTIONS 8.4

1. Who was Robert Menzies?
2. What was the Communist Party Dissolution Bill?

Suggested responses are available at www.cambridge.org/highereducation/isbn/9781009108232/resources

The Liberal Party in transition

Malcolm Fraser became prime minister in 1975 under the most controversial of circumstances, but he consolidated and legitimised his hold on power in subsequent elections. The Fraser Government embodied the contradictions between social liberalism and conservatism evident in the LPA from its founding (Weller 1989). On the one hand, his government will be remembered for accepting refugees arriving by boat from Vietnam and for advancing multiculturalism. On the other hand, Fraser and his ministers were harsh critics of unions and welfare recipients, with the latter being vilified as the authors of their own misfortunes. These contradictory impulses also found expression on the economic front, in the division between so-called 'wets' and 'dries'. The former were those ministers who accepted a significant role for government in regulating the economy – a position that was in keeping with the long years of Menzies' leadership. The latter advanced a starker free market ideology, focused on the alleged necessity of economic deregulation, corporatisation, privatisation and industrial relations reform, to tackle the intractable economic problems the country faced in the form of high unemployment and inflation. Fraser was criticised by the 'dries' for not using his control of government, including periods with a Senate majority, to advance market-oriented economic reform. These divisions were starkly exposed in the years after the Coalition lost power in 1983.

It is no exaggeration to say that the long years in opposition (1983–96) created something of an identity crisis for the LPA. The Labor governments of Hawke and Keating adopted policies of economic reform more typically associated with the Liberal side of politics, leading some to speak of a 'convergence' in party politics. Regardless of the merits of this thesis – and it certainly needs to be qualified (Goot 2004) – the shift in Labor policy did create difficulties for Liberal leaders in terms of distinguishing themselves from Labor who seemed to have stolen their ideological clothes. As a result, the tensions between social liberals and conservatives, and economic wets and dries, intensified, giving rise to fierce LPA leadership battles through the 1980s and early 1990s. It was not until after the 1990 election, when John Hewson became the leader of the LPA, that the party embarked on a concerted effort to position itself for government. The result was *'Fightback'* – a long and dense document which outlined a neo-liberal blueprint for transforming the Australian economy (Simms 1994). At its heart was a regressive 15 per cent goods and services tax, which would be offset by income tax cuts. These would favour high-income earners and disadvantage those on more modest incomes. Prime Minister Paul Keating exploited this fact mercilessly and ended up winning the apparently unwinnable election of 1993.

That election loss taught the Liberal Party a valuable lesson in electoral politics: a 'small target' campaign, consisting of very modest and non-threatening proposals for change, is electorally preferable to the type of expansive, ideologically charged program represented by *Fightback* (this was echoed at the 2019 election when Labor lost an apparently unlosable election, fighting on what many saw as an overly ambitious and detailed platform). Consequently, after winning back the Liberal leadership in 1995, the great political survivor John Howard took the Coalition to victory in 1996 on a promise to make us 'relaxed and comfortable' (Manne 2004). This was the start of 11 years of unbroken Coalition rule that again revealed tensions within the LPA between its conservative and socially liberal wings.

Although a pragmatist, when it came to issues that could electorally damage the Coalition, John Howard essentially governed as a cultural conservative, once boasting he was the most conservative leader the Liberal Party had ever had. The effect was to marginalise liberal voices within his caucus and the Cabinet and drag the Coalition further to the right (Barns 2003). Howard dismissed those who acknowledged the white invasion of Australia, and the dispossession of Indigenous people, as proffering a 'black armband' view of Australian history. He articulated a traditional, conservative view of family and gender relations. He refused to receive more than 400 asylum seekers who had been rescued at sea by a Norwegian ship (the *Tampa*), which was the first act in the so-called 'Pacific solution'. Finally, the Howard Government skilfully exploited understandable concerns around national security after the terrorist attacks on the World Trade Center and the Pentagon in September 2001 and the Bali terrorist attacks in 2002. Along with mistaken intelligence about Saddam Hussein's supposed weapons of mass destruction and his support for terrorists – which Howard still insists was the best intelligence at the time, even though it would later be shown to be false – these became pretexts for Australia's support for an American-led invasion of Iraq (Kelton 2008, 131–5; Bamford 2004, 333–65).

On the domestic front, the Howard Government undertook welfare reforms that raised the threshold for receiving many forms of welfare for Australia's most disadvantaged (Disney 2004). At the same time, his government was also criticised for its enthusiastic support of middle-class welfare – government programs and handouts that disproportionately flowed to middle and high-income earners. These were accompanied by significant income tax cuts, which were paid for by the billions of dollars that were rolling into Australia's Treasury courtesy of the mining boom. Tax reform was regressive in that it cut income taxes and introduced a 10 per cent goods and services tax on consumption. The Coalition Government also sought to transform Australia's industrial relations landscape through its introduction of *WorkChoices* – legislation that was successfully portrayed by its critics as further dis-empowering unions and workers, and tilting the Australian workplace playing field even more in favour of employers (Peetz 2006). It was this policy, more than any other, that destroyed the Coalition's chances at the 2007 election. It embodied one of the challenges the Coalition has faced historically, and that it continues to face today.

These reforms reflect a deeper shift in the Liberal Party. Once the champion of states' rights (see Chapter 2), the modern Liberal Party has joined Labor in placing greater faith in the abilities of the federal government and the desire for central control and coordination. Despite this and in contrast to Labor, the Liberal Party itself retains an organisational structure that is a loose federation where the national organisation has little ability to intervene in the affairs of state divisions.

REFLECTION QUESTIONS 8.1

1. Why has the LPA often, if not always, contained within it socially liberal and socially conservative elements?
2. What is the political and moral vision embodied in Robert Menzies' notion of the forgotten people?

Response prompts are available at www.cambridge.org/highereducation/isbn/9781009108232/resources

Contemporary challenges for the Liberal Party of Australia

In 2014, the Abbott Government brought down a budget that was widely perceived as being harsh and unfair to many sectors of the community – particularly those on welfare and low incomes. In the following year, there was a public backlash against his leadership and government, expressed in falling poll numbers, which ultimately led to his replacement by Malcolm Turnbull in 2015. Turnbull sought to soften the party's image, while also trying to manage and, in some instances, placate conservative resentment in his party room. But this satisfied neither conservatives nor moderates in his party, and the ensuing controversies around same-sex marriage, energy, banking and climate policy eventually cost him the prime ministership with the Liberal Party replacing him in 2018 with the more conservative Scott Morrison. These developments well illustrate the challenges the contemporary LPA and its leaders face. These include reconciling the interests of its base constituency with those of the broader electorate, overcoming the deep divisions between its conservative and liberal wings, and managing more general issues of factionalism within the party.

As we have seen, the LPA has historically been a party that has championed the interests of the business community and middle to high-income earners in the Australian community. The underlying premise is that supporting business encourages investment, employs more workers, increases wages and grows the overall economic pie in a way that benefits all Australians. But, despite 26 years of unbroken economic growth (1991–2017), and an investment environment that is advantageous to employers, underemployment remains stubbornly high, income growth has long been stalled, and there is a crisis of housing affordability. Moreover, economic inequality has grown since the 1970s, as it has in other developed countries. By the time of the 2022 federal election, the unprecedented government spending during the COVID-19 pandemic had still done little to address these issues. Even during the pandemic when huge government spending was popular with the public, there was a vocal minority in the LPA, both within the parliament and beyond, who had deep misgivings about the extent of the spending and enhanced welfare programs (as well as the impact on civil liberties).

This is intimately related to a second challenge: managing the political and ideological gulf between the LPA's socially liberal and socially conservative wings. For much of the past quarter century, it has been the conservatives who have been ascendant, dominating the parliamentary party and the federal executive. Since the loss of the 2007 election, there has been an occasional reassertion of the more moderate social liberals, with Brendon Nelson and then Malcolm Turnbull, but efforts to reposition the party in a more moderate direction has angered conservatives, and some of the harder line conservatives seem willing to destroy the party's electoral chances rather than tolerate a moderate Liberal leader. The party perhaps entered a new phase with the 2022 federal election, which saw a handful of key moderate Liberal MPs in heartland seats lose to so-called 'teal' independents and even to the Greens in Brisbane (see Chapter 9 for more on this).

REFLECTION QUESTIONS 8.2

1. When John Howard lost his seat and the 2007 federal election, he had been the prime minister for 11 years and the member for Bennelong for 33 years. Do you think there should be time limits on either of these roles?

2. In what way is the Liberal Party a party of liberalism, and in what way is it a party of conservatism?

Response prompts are available at www.cambridge.org/highereducation/isbn/9781009108232/resources

SHORT-ANSWER QUESTIONS 8.5

1. What are some of the more controversial decisions the Howard Government took during its period in government?

2. What were the key advantages the four Howard administrations had during this period of office?

Suggested responses are available at www.cambridge.org/highereducation/isbn/9781009108232/resources

SPOTLIGHT 8.2 LIBERAL DIVISIONS AND SAME-SEX MARRIAGE

Nowhere was the balancing act between social liberals and social conservatives more on show than in the debate around same-sex marriage. Despite being a long-time supporter of same-sex marriage, Prime Minister Turnbull, under pressure from the right of his party, refused to bring the issue to a parliamentary vote. Instead, he advocated a plebiscite and then – when the Senate blocked that – a non-binding voluntary postal survey. The latter was widely viewed as a cynical ploy by conservatives in his party to delay the seemingly inevitable. It satisfied the desires of conservatives, led by Tony Abbott, to buy time in which they could agitate to sow doubts in the minds of a populace that, polls suggested, supported same-sex marriage by a considerable margin. Supporters of same-sex marriage viewed such a postal vote as being not only unnecessary but as being positively dangerous. It would be making a discomforting public judgement about people's sexuality and could unleash hate speech against the LGBTQI community under the guise of open debate and freedom of expression. This is in fact what did happen, though it was largely downplayed in media reporting. As events transpired, the yes-vote for marriage equality did get up by a decisive margin that was very close to what the polls predicted. As Prime Minister Turnbull sought to take credit for the result, however, many conservatives in his own party tried to place further obstacles in the path of marriage equality. Under the pretext of protecting religious freedoms, they sought amendments that would allow discrimination against same-sex couples seeking to marry. These were largely unsuccessful, but they did highlight the deep divisions within the LPA, and the challenges this poses for any potential Liberal leader. Despite following the path set by the conservative wing of the Liberal Party, this seemingly wasn't enough and within a few months those same conservatives toppled the Turnbull prime ministership.

QUESTION

How can a party with members holding a wide range of views avoid this kind of intra-party conflict?

AUSTRALIA'S MAJOR PARTIES AND VOTERS

When considering the relationship Australia's major parties have with voters, it is important to recognise the crucial role electoral systems play. The Alternative Vote system used for the House of Representatives tends to boost big parties, so the ALP and the Liberals are in a very strong position to win the overwhelming majority of seats in the 151-seat chamber. By contrast, the use of the Single Transferable Vote system (a form of proportional representation) in the Senate is more even-handed, so generally means the government – the largest party or coalition of parties in the House of Representatives – is rarely in control of the Senate. Governments then have to conduct often complex and difficult negotiations with the Senate crossbench to secure passage of their legislation. If these negotiations fail, blame can often fall at the government's feet rather than those opposing the government's proposals. The flipside to this story is governments are rarely rewarded for negotiating the passage of legislation; this is merely seen as the task at hand. Hence, the major parties, especially when they are in government, are held to a high standard and are expected to 'get on with the job', no matter the political circumstances they find themselves in.

PARTIES, ELECTIONS AND VOTERS

The relationship between particular constituencies and the major parties can be usefully understood through the lens of processes that shape voter behaviour and perceptions. In particular, the concepts of 'Socialization', 'Immunization' and Party Identification are critical. All three emerged from research originally published in 1960 in the ground-breaking book *The American Voter*. In it, and a number of related books, political scientists started to theorise the relationships between voters and political parties standing for elected office. Socialisation is 'the mechanism by which most norms and values are acquired' (Van der Eijk and Franklin 2009, 49). What this means for the relationship between voters and the major parties is that during early life, we learn certain behaviour patterns which become habitual. These patterns come from a variety of socialising agents around us: our family, friends, people we go to school or work with, play sport with or practice religion with. As Van der Eijk and Franklin (2009, 49) suggest, 'if these influences reinforce each other, then young adults are virtually certain to enter the electorate with a partisanship consistent with those influences'.

Once the voting age is reached, immunisation effects take place. Put simply, this arises from the practice of going to the polling place and voting. The act of voting for a specific party, if repeated over and over, can affirm the psychological identification voters have with the party they cast the ballot for. According to Butler and Stokes (1974), once a voter supports the same party three times, they are immunised against change. This effect is, arguably, even more pronounced in Australia, as compulsory voting ensures most voters are 'immunised' at an early age. As a result of these processes, voters become partisan and identify with one party over another. This is referred to in the literature as party identification.

The concept of party identification has been revised since the early forays into political behaviour. First, as McAllister (2011, 35) notes, if the party a voter is aligned to introduces a policy particularly offensive to the voter, they may vote for another party. However, party identification theory predicts the 'homing tendency' will eventually lead that voter back to the party they identify with. Second, it has become accepted that party identification is used as a short-cut for many voters. With an avalanche of information available to voters to digest when considering which party to vote for, identifying with one party over another simplifies the voter's decision. For Australia's major parties, these voting processes have ensured the ALP and LPA have remained the dominant choices for Australian voters for decades. However, the strength of these ties is weakening.

Australia had long been seen as an outlier when it came to partisanship as the levels of identification with the major parties remained high, while elsewhere significant declines were evident (McAllister 2002, 387). In recent years, however, two important changes have occurred which means Australia is now less an outlier; partisanship is declining and the strength of the ties between the partisans and their party is weakening. The major parties are certainly still dominant, but this dominance is now under threat from forces that seem beyond their control. The global anti-establishment movement sweeping advanced democracies is showing signs of contagion here like it has in North America and Western Europe. To date, this has not been enough to shake the foundations of Australian parliamentary democracy like it has in some places, but the effect is certainly evident. The capacity for parties to respond to the depth of the democratic crises sweeping the globe will be fundamental to their long-term success. In the last couple of years, the COVID-19 pandemic has made prediction even harder. On the one hand, voters' faith in institutions and governments in many countries rose sharply through the pandemic. On the other, it is unclear anything has changed at a fundamental level, so the effects may be temporary.

THEORISING AUSTRALIA'S MAJOR PARTIES

Liberal democracy is often referred to as party-based democracy. Political parties play a critical role in aggregating and articulating the views of the electorate at large as well as acting as representatives of the people in the legislature, which is decided via the mechanism of the democratic election. The centrality of parties in the liberal democratic tradition has meant they have received significant theoretical attention. This has not only been about the evolution in how political parties are organised and structured, but also focuses on the ways they can affect one another as part of the party system. Yet for all the theorising about political parties, including Australia's major parties, it is important to remember they are a relatively new phenomenon, as discussed earlier in this chapter. While recent years have seen some debate on whether the major parties' stranglehold on Australian politics is being weakened, we know from political history in Australia and internationally they will attempt to evolve as necessary to ensure their survival.

ELECTORAL SYSTEMS AND AUSTRALIA'S MAJOR PARTIES

It is also important to recognise that a strong relationship exists between the type of electoral system a jurisdiction uses and the type of party system and parties that are likely to emerge. This includes how dominant the major parties are likely to be in numbers of seats in the legislature. For example, consider the results of the 2019 UK General Election to those of the 2019 Australian federal election as shown in Table 8.1. While the United Kingdom utilises the Single Member Plurality electoral system (often referred to as first-past-the-post) for the House of Commons (with an appointed House of Lords), Australia uses a mixed electoral system consisting of the Alternative Vote system in the House of Representatives and a form of proportional representation known as Single Transferrable Vote (PR-STV). It is easy to see how these different electoral systems have a significant effect on the votes to seats ratio for the major parties. It is particularly worth noting how proportional representation alters the dynamics within the legislature. While the use of PR-STV in the Senate is now widely seen as one of the checks and balances employed to limit executive over-reach and ensure a wider range of views are present in this chamber, it also produces a result more consistent with the wishes of voters.

TABLE 8.1 MAJOR PARTIES AND ELECTORAL SYSTEMS COMPARED

COUNTRY AND ELECTION	NATIONAL VOTE FOR MAJOR PARTIES IN %	% OF SEATS WON
United Kingdom 2019 General Election	75.8% 43.6% – Conservative Party 32.2% – Labour Party	568/650 = 87.4% of the seats
Australia 2019 Federal Election House of Representatives	74.78% • 41.44% – Liberal/National • 33.34% – Labor	145/151 = 96.0% of the seats
Australia 2019 Federal Election Senate*	66.78% • 37.99% – Liberal/National • 28.79% – Labor	32/40 = 80.0% of the seats

* The 2019 federal election was a 'half Senate' election, meaning half of seats were contested for the states and all seats for the territories (total 40 out of 76 seats).
Source: Based on AEC (2019a; 2019b); BBC (2019).

While there are many who suggest proportional representation should be introduced for all major elections to best capture the will of voters, the effect of these reforms on the functioning of the chamber is also important. Introducing proportional representation for elections to the House of Representatives would almost certainly lead to minority governments and governments based on temporary coalitions becoming a regular feature. Whether this would be the right approach considering the system already in place in the Senate is open to some debate. The Gillard-led minority government demonstrates minority governments can work and are not necessarily an impediment to the passage of legislation (Prosser and Denniss 2015), yet the public and politicians remain hostile. Indeed, the relationship between electoral systems and the representation of Australia's major parties goes to much larger questions about whether the dominant two-party model, which is a Westminster legacy, remains an appropriate model for governing the nation. A plausible argument can be made that if politics is going to become less polarised and confrontational it needs also to be more **DELIBERATIVE**. As it stands, with the current electoral system the major parties have no incentive to engage with a diverse range of voices and views. Given the long-term steady decline in primary votes for the major parties, their hand may be forced, and electoral reform may be required.

What 'type' of party are Australia's major parties?

One of central theoretical debates about political parties is about how to classify them. This debate has many dimensions including what characteristics can be used to distinguish one party from another, whether parties are generally evolving in a particular direction, and what constitutes a new type of party. While there have been some notable Australian contributions to this scholarship (for example, Jaensch and Mathieson (1998) have identified 13 different types of parties in Australian political history), much of this debate has occurred in the international scholarship, as summarised by Katz and Mair (1995) (also see Krouwel 2006).

When thinking about what type of parties Australia's major parties are, party scholars often compare them to some of the **IDEAL-TYPES** proposed in the academic literature. The most common ideal-types used include the elite or cadre party, the mass party, the catch-all party and the cartel party. When compared, as is displayed in Table 8.2, these ideal-types are often used to show the evolution of political parties in modern democracies starting with the emergence of the elite or cadre parties in the 19th century all the way up to the present-day cartel parties. Debates about this story of the evolution of political parties are hotly contested and some party scholars contend this narrative about party change being linear, oversimplifies significant complexity and diversity. Nonetheless, thinking about how contemporary parties in Australia have changed since Federation is a useful exercise to determine the ways parties are able to adapt to changing economic and political conditions, and whether parties really are the drivers of social and political change or they are merely the effect.

Australia's major parties are relatively easy to classify when compared in such a way. The ALP, as discussed earlier in this chapter, came into being as a proto-typical mass party. Some scholars contend the ALP then became a catch-all party as their policies became focused more on winning the middle-class suburban vote. Others, however, argue the party reflects many of the characteristics of the cartel party (Jaensch 2006, 30). In contrast, the Liberal Party under the leadership of Robert Menzies was never truly a mass party in the same way the ALP was. The Liberal Party was created as an anti-Labor Party to represent the interests of business and a 'forgotten' middle-class and to win elections. Hence, the Liberal Party is seen by many as a

DELIBERATIVE: Processes based on considered and reasoned discussion among those who will be affected by a decision, leading to a collective decision. Proponents argue deliberative democracy can improve collective decision-making.

IDEAL-TYPES: In the political science literature, ideal-types are often used as a heuristic device which aims to explain how, for example, parties have changed over time. Ideal-types are not identifiable empirically as they are often based on evidence from hundreds of different cases.

TABLE 8.2 IDEAL PARTY TYPES IN THE COMPARATIVE POLITICS SCHOLARSHIP

CHARACTERISTICS	ELITE OR CADRE PARTY	MASS PARTY	CATCH-ALL PARTY	CARTEL PARTY
Time-period	19th century	1880–1960	1945–	1970–
Nature of party work and party campaigning	Irrelevant	Labour intensive	Both labour intensive and capital intensive	Capital intensive
Principal source of party's resources	Personal contacts	Members' fees and contributions	Contributions from a wide variety of sources	State funding for electoral participation and success
Relations between ordinary members and party elite	The elite are the 'ordinary' members	Bottom up; elite accountable to members	Top down; members are organised cheerleaders for elite	Mutual autonomy
Character of membership	Small and elitist	Large but not very diverse	Membership open to all	Small

Source: Adapted from Katz and Mair (1995, 18).

catch-all party. This is primarily because while there are strands of conservatism and liberalism within the Liberal Party, neither is entirely dominant. The same scholars who refer to the ALP as a cartel party, naturally make this claim about the Liberal Party as well and this debate is worth considering in more detail.

REFLECTION QUESTIONS 8.3

1. Do you think one or more of these ideal-types could be used to describe Australia's major parties?
2. If you had to think about other ways to describe the major parties, in two to three words, how would you do this?

Response prompts are available at www.cambridge.org/highereducation/isbn/9781009108232/resources

ARE AUSTRALIA'S MAJOR PARTIES A CARTEL?

The cartel party thesis is the single most important – and hotly debated – contribution to the study of political parties since the 1990s. Its creators, Richard Katz and Peter Mair, had spent years considering hundreds of individual cases of how political parties had changed, primarily in Western Europe, but also in North America. The argument they put forth suggested two fundamental changes had occurred. One of these relates to the way political parties are organised and structured. The second, which is related to the first, is that party systems have also evolved due to the changes to parties. At its core, the cartel thesis is about the historical evolution of political parties, making it similar to earlier stories of parties changing from elite or cadre parties into mass parties and so on. But it is also about how parties cooperate and compete within democratic competitive party systems.

The cartel party, as a theoretical party type, has few party members meaning party campaigns have to be capital intensive, which generally means spending money on expensive advertising. As the party has very few party members, it cannot rely on membership fees as mass parties do to fund their activities. Instead, cartel parties are heavily reliant on the state funding their participation in the electoral process. In most countries, this means that after elections, the relevant electoral authority – in Australia, the Australian Electoral Commission – will provide funding to parties based on their share of votes. The second part of the thesis considers the cooperation and competition between the major parties. When we think about cartels in business, we generally think of a group made up of competitors who form to fix prices. This analogy is useful for considering this thesis for the major parties. Do the major parties act in unison to prevent competitors entering the market or taking market share? There is significant disagreement about this. Whether they form a cartel or not, the major parties certainly have significant advantages over other parties at elections (Sawer 2021).

RESEARCH QUESTION 8.1

With reference to Table 8.2, what economic or social changes do you think may have contributed to changes in the way political parties were organised?

UNDERSTANDING AUSTRALIA'S PARTIES FROM A COMPARATIVE PERSPECTIVE

The ALP and the LPA share a pattern of family resemblances with political parties in other wealthy liberal democracies. An understanding of the similarities and differences with these parties helps to illuminate what is distinctive about Australia's major parties, and the historical and political contexts in which they have developed. The ALP, for example, is often compared with Labour parties in the English-speaking world, and with social democratic parties in Europe and Scandinavia. The similarities with the former are especially striking. Like their Australian counterpart, the British and New Zealand Labour parties grew out of the union movement, still have significant union involvement, and were and are subject to many of the same pressures as the ALP. These parties have been agents of progressive social change – universal public health systems, mass public housing projects, welfare safety nets and regulated labour markets – but they have also had the difficult task of reconciling the interests of their working-class constituents with the demands of the profit system. This has periodically led to splits in the Labour movement and allegations these parties betray the interests of those they claim to represent.

This was especially the case in the Australian and New Zealand Labour parties in the 1980s and 1990s. Unlike in Britain, where it was Margaret Thatcher's Conservative Party who spearheaded the neo-liberal restructuring of the economy and welfare state, it was Labour governments that initiated these policies in Australia and New Zealand (see the sections on New Public Management and on Government to governance in Chapter 6). This demoralised many party members and put pressure on the link between the industrial and political wings of the labour movement, though without severing it. But the process in the two countries was not identical. Federalism and bicameralism in Australia, as opposed to the unitary and unicameral system of government in New Zealand, meant ALP parliamentarians were more constrained than their New Zealand counterparts. The latter could radically overhaul the welfare state, whereas the ALP's project of restructuring was slower and more incremental, and was undertaken with the support of the union leadership under the auspices of the Accords (Cox 2006). Today, the union movement retains more influence over the ALP than do unions over the New Zealand Labour Party. This speaks to the importance of institutions in shaping what parties can and cannot do.

The ALP is also often compared to the US Democratic Party. It is sometimes assumed the Democratic Party is to the Republican Party what the ALP is to the Liberal Party. This is very misleading. Although it is true many American unions support the Democratic Party, and that the latter has often advocated welfare measures and state involvement in the economy, the differences with the ALP are more important than any superficial similarities. Historically, the US Democratic Party was the party of white supremacy in the southern states of the United States. It has never had the organic links with the union movement that is a core feature of the ALP. Unions are not an integral part of the Democratic Party's form or function, and nor do they exercise a strong influence over the Party's political platform. Membership is not dependent on joining one's relevant union, if available, as it still is with the ALP. Politically, the Democratic Party is probably closer to Australia's Liberal Party than to the ALP.

The LPA is also often compared with its non-Labour counterparts in other wealthy countries. As one of the two major parties, structurally the LPA does indeed perform a similar function to Britain's Conservative Party, New Zealand's National Party, and the US Republican Party. Even in multi-party European systems of government, one can note certain similarities between Christian Democratic parties (e.g. in Germany, Italy and Austria) and the LPA. Most obvious here is the explicitly pro-business, pro-free market bias these parties exhibit, which places them on the centre-right of an ideological continuum. They are all, to varying degrees, committed to an anti-collectivist ideology that emphasises the virtues of small governments and individual responsibility. More fine-grained comparisons, however, reveal very significant differences, reflecting divergences in the political cultures and institutional contexts in which they developed.

For example, while bearing certain similarities to the British conservatives, the LPA is very different. The British Conservative Party has its roots in British landed interests of the 18th and 19th centuries, and still strongly bears the imprint of its aristocratic, class heritage. While its detractors would say the same of the LPA, the latter has always been more of an urban-based, middle-class party. Historically, although it has had its conservative moments as under Howard's leadership, the LPA has more typically sought to position itself as a liberal rather than conservative party, as we saw with Menzies' determination that the LPA should orient to the middle class and be 'a progressive party'. The LPA has also been shaped by a broader political culture that values, at least rhetorically, egalitarianism, even if many would argue the LPA's commitment to it is only skin deep.

If the LPA is different from the British Conservative Party, it is even more different from the modern US Republican Party. Although the US Republicans emerged in the mid-19th century as a progressive anti-slavery party, they would go on to become the party of Wall Street and big business, and by the early 1980s a party increasingly wedded to the ultra-conservative ideas of the Christian Right. By contrast, the LPA has always been, broadly speaking, a secular party, even if those holding deep religious views can exercise considerable influence within its ranks, including as leaders and prime ministers. Once again, this reflects a political culture in Australia that is relatively secular and intolerant of religious meddling in politics.

Westminster systems, like those in Australia, the United Kingdom and Canada, tend to produce big, strong parties with parliamentarians who generally toe the party line. 'Discipline in Parliament is pronounced, even by high, Westminster standards' (Larkin 2012, 95–6), and more broadly Australia's 'political parties exhibit some of the highest rates of party cohesion in the world' (Gauja 2015, 163). Going against the party line is a rare and newsworthy event. There are several reasons for this, not least the fact Australia's parliaments are small by international comparison, meaning the vote of every parliamentarian is more likely to matter. Lower houses generally use some form of single-member electorate, creating a logic for big cohesive parties. Further, the ALP's formal pledge, which binds its parliamentarians to always voting with the party (on pain of being expelled) has created a cross-party culture of very strong discipline.

In keeping with many other countries, Australia has seen changes in the profile of its parliamentarians. On the one hand, politicians are now more diverse in terms of religious and ethnic background, and women are far better represented than before (although they are nowhere near half of MPs). But at the same time, educational and professional backgrounds have narrowed, especially on the Labor side (Miragliotta and Errington 2012). Parliamentarians are 'predominantly middle-aged, well-educated men, likely to have been employed in politics-related occupations, business or law before entering parliament' (Lumb 2013). So, the stereotyped MP is essentially correct, and many voters inevitably find this alienating.

RESEARCH QUESTION 8.2

What impact do you think bicameralism has had on the major parties in Australia, compared with New Zealand's unicameralism system?

REFLECTION QUESTIONS 8.4

1. Do you consider the apparent weakening of the major parties a threat to stability or an opportunity for renewal in the Australian political system?
2. To what extent are the major parties their own gravediggers considering the rise of minor parties?

Response prompts are available at www.cambridge.org/highereducation/isbn/9781009108232/resources

SUMMARY

Learning objective 1: Understand where Australia's major parties came from and why they emerged

In this chapter, the history and evolution of the major parties were discussed. What is evident from this is that the major parties each emerged in response to a distinct set of political and economic challenges. The ALP emerged because of the desire of working-class trade unions to have a more direct say in decisions, while the modern Liberal Party created by Robert Menzies responded to the crisis in conservative politics after the demise of the UAP in 1943 and as an avenue for non-Labor forces to promote their agenda.

Learning objective 2: Explain how the relationship between the major parties and voters has changed

The relationship between the major parties and voters has changed significantly as a result of changing economic, cultural and social conditions in Australia. Most notably, the vote share that the major parties could previously rely on is under pressure as other parties and candidates gain support. The strength of the bonds between many Australian voters and the major parties has also weakened. This is not to say these voters will not return to the major parties, they certainly could, and this phenomenon may be cyclical. However, there are certainly serious challenges for the major parties in maintaining their unparalleled dominance of Australian electoral politics.

Learning objective 3: Recognise some of the ways the major parties have been theorised

Like major parties across advanced industrial democracies, scholars of political parties frequently try to theorise what type of parties Australia's major parties are. Australia's major parties have, at times, been referred to as mass parties, catch-all parties, electoral-professional parties as well as cartel parties. While debate about this will continue unabated, in thinking about how we understand and theorise Australia's major parties, two facets remain critical: how they are organised and their ideologies. Thinking about the combination of these two facets allows us to categorise Australia's major parties and compare them internationally.

Learning objective 4: Describe how Australia's major parties are different to major parties in other comparable advanced democracies

Australia's major parties may appear like those in New Zealand, the United States and elsewhere, but there are clear differences. In each country, the parties are products of the environment they work in. Hence, institutional, social and cultural differences need to be accounted for in any discussion of how they are similar or different. For example, Australia's major parties are different for the simple reason they work in a federal, bicameral parliamentary system as opposed to a federal presidential system in the United States or a unitary, unicameral parliamentary system in New Zealand. This has a significant impact on the way these parties are organised.

DISCUSSION QUESTIONS

1. What does the history of Australia's major parties tell you about the institutional structure of Australian federal politics?

2. Is contemporary federal politics just a continuation of a battle between Labor and non-Labor forces like it was from 1910 onwards?

3. How could Australia's major parties improve their standing in the eyes of most voters? Or is this impossible?

4. What technological, cultural or economic forces are altering the relationship between the major parties and young voters?

5. Are Australia's major parties now so similar that Australian federal politics has become nothing more than a battle between competing brands?

FURTHER READING

Brett, J. (2005). *Relaxed and Comfortable: The Liberal Party's Australia*, Quarterly Essay number 19, Melbourne: Black Inc.

Gauja, A. (2015). The presidentialisation of parties in Australia. In G. Passarelli (ed.), *The Presidentialisation of Political Parties: Organizations, Institutions and Leaders*, Hampshire: Palgrave Macmillan.

Johnson, C. (2011). Gillard, Rudd and Labor tradition. *Australian Journal of Politics & History*, **57**(4), 562–79.

Marsh, I. (2006). *Political Parties in Transition*, Sydney: Federation Press.

Sawer, M. (2021). The concept of the level playing field: Assessing fairness in electoral competition. *Australian Journal of Public Administration*, **80**, 29–45.

REFERENCES

Australian Electoral Commission. (2019a). *2019 Federal Election, House of Representatives Results*. Retrieved from https://results.aec.gov.au/24310/Website/HouseResultsMenu-24310.htm

——— (2019b). *2019 Federal Election, Senate Results*. Retrieved from https://results.aec.gov.au/24310/Website/SenateResultsMenu-24310.htm

Australian Labor Party. (2011). *National Platform*. Retrieved from www.alp.org.au/austraian-labor/our-platform/

Bamford, J. (2004). *A Pretext for War: 9/11, Iraq, and the Abuse of America's Intelligence Agencies*, New York: Anchor Books.

Barns, G. (2003). *What's Wrong with the Liberal Party?* Melbourne: Cambridge University Press.

BBC. (2019). Election 2019: Results. Retrieved from https://www.bbc.com/news/election/2019/results

Beilharz, P. (1994). *Transforming Labor: Labour Tradition and the Labor Decade in Australia*, Cambridge: Cambridge University Press.

Bongiorno, F. (2001). The origins of caucus: 1856–1901. In S. Macintyre and J. Faulkner (eds), *True Believers: The Story of the Federal Parliamentary Labor Party*, Crows Nest: Allen & Unwin, pp. 3–17.

Bongiorno, F. & Dyrenfurth, N. (2011). *A Little History of the Australian Labor Party*, Sydney: UNSW Press.

Brett, J. (2003). *Australian Liberals and the Moral Middle Class: From Alfred Deakin to John Howard*, Melbourne: Cambridge University Press.

——— (2004). The new liberalism. In R. Manne (ed.), *The Howard Years*, Melbourne: Black Inc, pp. 74–93.

——— (2007). *Robert Menzies' Forgotten People*, Melbourne: Melbourne University Press.

Butler, D. & Stokes, D. (1974). *Political Change in Britain: Basis of Electoral Choice*, Basingstoke: Palgrave Macmillan.

Castles, S. (1988). *Mistaken identity: Multiculturalism and the Demise of Nationalism in Australia*, United Kingdom: Pluto Press.

Cavalier, R. (2010). *Power Crisis: The Self-destruction of a State Labor Party*, Melbourne: Cambridge University Press.

Costar, B.J. & Strangio, P. (2005). *The Great Labor Schism: A Retrospective*, Melbourne: Scribe Publications.

Cox, L. (2006). The Antipodean social laboratory, labour and the transformation of the welfare state. *Journal of Sociology*, **42**(2), 107–24.

Disney, J. (2004). Social policy. In R. Manne (ed.), *The Howard Years*, Melbourne: Black Inc, pp. 191–215.

Faulkner, J. (2001). Splits: Consequences and lessons. In J. Faulkner and S. Macintyre (eds), *True Believers: The Story of the Federal Parliamentary Labor Party*, Crows Nest: Allen & Unwin.

Gallagher, M., Laver, M. & Mair, P. (2005). *Representative Government in Modern Europe*, London: McGraw-Hill.

Gauja, A. (2015). The Presidentialisation of Parties in Australia. In G. Passarelli (ed.), *The Presidentialisation of Political Parties: Organizations, Institutions and Leaders*, Hampshire: Palgrave Macmillan.

Goot, M. (2004). Convergence of the major parties and the emergence of minor parties: A response to Lavelle. *Australian Journal of Political Science*, **39**(3), 651–5.

Jaensch, D. (2006). Party structures and processes. In I. Marsh (ed.), *Political Parties in Transition?* Sydney: Federation Press, pp. 24–46.

Jaensch, D. & Mathieson, D. (1998). *A Plague on Both Your Houses: Minor parties in Australia*, St Leonards: Allen & Unwin Academic.

Katz, R. & Mair, P. (1995). Changing models of party organization and party democracy the emergence of the cartel party. *Party Politics*, **1**(1), 5–28.

Kefford, G. (2015). *All Hail the Leaders: The Australian Labor Party and Political Leadership*, Melbourne: Australian Scholarly Publishing.

Kelton, M. (2008). *'More than an Ally'? Contemporary Australia–US Relations*, Aldershot: Ashgate.

Krouwel, A. (2006). Party models. In R. Katz and W. Crotty (eds), *Handbook of Party Politics*, Thousand Oaks: Sage Publications, pp. 249–69.

Langman, J. (1992). The Labor government in a de-regulatory era. In B. Galligan and G. Singleton (eds), *Business and Government Under Labor*, Melbourne: Longman Cheshire, pp. 75–90.

Larkin, P. (2012). Ministerial accountability to parliament. In K. Dowding and C. Lewis (eds), *Ministerial Careers and Accountability in the Australian Commonwealth Government*, Canberra: ANU Press, pp. 95–114.

Lecours, A., Beland, D., Fenna, A., Fenwick, T.B., Paquet, M., Rocco, P. & Waddan, A. (2021). Explaining intergovernmental conflict in the COVID-19 crisis: The United States, Canada, and Australia. *Publius*, **51**(4), 513–36.

Lloyd, B. & Weller, P. (1975). *Caucus Minutes, 1901–1949: Minutes of the Meetings of the Federal Parliamentary Labor Party*, Carlton: Melbourne University Press.

Loveday, P. & Martin, A. (1977). *The Emergence of the Australian Party System*, Sydney: Hale & Iremonger.

Lumb, M. (2013). *The 43rd Parliament: Traits and Trends Parliament of Australia*. Retrieved from https://www.aph.gov.au/About_Parliament/Parliamentary_Departments/Parliamentary_Library/pubs/rp/rp1314/43rdParl#_Toc368474618

Macintyre, S. (2001). The first caucus. In S. Macintyre and J. Faulkner (eds), *True Believers: The Story of the Federal Parliamentary Labor Party*, Sydney: Allen & Unwin, pp. 17–29.

Maddox, G. (1996). *Australian Democracy in Theory and Practice*, 3rd edn, Melbourne: Longman.

Manne, R. (2004). The Howard years: A political interpretation. In R. Manne (ed.), *The Howard Years*, Melbourne: Black Inc, pp. 3–53.

Manwaring, R. & Robinson, G. (2020). What is 'Labor' about Labor state governments in Australia? *The Australian Journal of Politics and History*, **66**(1), 3–21.

McAllister, I. (2002). Political parties in Australia: Party stability in a utilitarian society. In P. Webb, D. Farrell and I. Holliday (eds), *Political Parties in Advanced Industrial Democracies*, Oxford: Oxford University Press, pp. 379–408.

—— (2011). *The Australian Voter: Fifty Years of Change*, Sydney: UNSW Press.

Miragliotta, N. & Errington, W. (2012). Legislative recruitment and party models: Evidence from Australia. *Journal of Legislative Studies*, **18**(1), 21–40.

Peetz, D. (2006). *Brave New Workplace: How Individual Contracts are Changing Our Jobs*, Sydney: Allen & Unwin.

Prosser, B. & Denniss, R. (2015). Minority government and marginal members: New issues for political and policy legitimacy in Australia. *Policy Studies*, **36**(4), 434–50.

Pusey, M. (1991). *Economic Rationalism in Canberra: A Nation-building State Changes Its Mind*, Melbourne: Cambridge University Press.

Sawer, M. (2021). The concept of the level playing field: Assessing fairness in electoral competition. *Australian Journal of Public Administration*, **80**, 29–45.

Sexton, M. (2005). *The Great Crash: The Short Life and Sudden Death of the Whitlam Government*, Melbourne: Scribe Publications.

Simms, M. (1994). The end of pragmatism? The coalition parties in the early 1990s. *Australian Journal of Political Science*, **29**(1), 28–41.

Starr, G. (1980). *The Liberal Party of Australia: A Documentary History*, Richmond: Drummond/Heinemann.

Stilwell, F. (1986). *The Accord… and Beyond: The Political Economy of the Labor Government*, Sydney: Pluto Press.

Van der Eijk, C. & Franklin, M. (2009). *Elections and Voters*, Hampshire: Palgrave Macmillan.

Warhurst, J. (1996). Transitional hero: Gough Whitlam and the Australian Labor Party. *Australian Journal of Political Science*, **31**(2), 243–52. https://doi.org/10.1080/10361149651210

Warhurst, J. & Parkin, A. (2000). *The Machine: Labor Confronts the Future*, St Leonards: Allen & Unwin.

Weller, P. (1989). *Malcolm Fraser PM: A Study in Prime Ministerial Power in Australia*, Sydney: Penguin Books.

Whitlam, G. (1979). *The Truth of the Matter*, Ringwood: Penguin Books.

CHAPTER 9
THE MINOR PARTIES AND INDEPENDENTS

LEARNING OBJECTIVES

After reading this chapter, you should be able to:

1. Identify and reflect on the significance of parties other than the two main parties to the Australian party system
2. Identify the key 'minor parties' and understand their organisation and impact
3. Consider the role of independents in the Australian system

INTRODUCTION

The Australian party system comprises many more parties than just the Australian Labor Party (ALP) and the Liberal–National Party coalition. As dominant as the big two parties are, they do not exercise a complete duopoly over the House of Representatives or the Senate. Indeed, with its **MULTI-MEMBER PROPORTIONAL ELECTORAL SYSTEM**, the Senate has always offered greater potential for a much more diverse set of political parties to win representation, although this was not realised until the 1980s. The major parties have tended to be more predominant in the House of Representatives, but even here in recent years non-major parties have succeeded in winning seats. The array of other political parties that form to contest elections also poll rather small shares of the primary vote and usually do not win lower house seats. Generally, a party is considered 'minor' not only because of a small vote share, but also because of a lack of representational success in the lower house contest, or where success is confined to the proportionally representative Senate. While this labelling is contested (Kefford 2017), it is a useful counterpoint to the 'major' party tag of Labor and the Coalition.

The problem with this rule of thumb is that, in recent times, the Labor and Liberal–National dominance of representational outcomes in the House of Representatives has been successfully challenged by other parties and that rather difficult sub-set of parliamentarians referred to as 'independents'. Since 2002 – when the Greens won the seat of Cunningham in a by-election – parties other than Labor, Liberal and the Nationals have regularly held lower house seats. These parties have included the Katter Australia Party, the Palmer United Party, the Nick Xenophon Team/Centre Alliance, as well as the Australian Greens. Each of these non-major party successes were in part noteworthy for the precarious hold these representatives had on their seats (Adam Bandt in Melbourne being an exception) and the importance of their titular leader. In this way, these 'minor' party successes seem to replicate the occasional success for an independent candidate in House of Representatives elections. There have been a number of these successful independents, many former major party MPs, and some have played important roles in government formation. After the very close election result in 2010, the potential for independents to wield real power was on display when three such members – Andrew Wilke in Denison (now Clark) in Tasmania, Tony Windsor in New England (NSW) and Rob Oakeshott in Calare (NSW) – held the balance of power and supported a **MINORITY GOVERNMENT** between 2010 and 2013 (Costar 2012).

The Senate represents a different proposition, and it has been the case that since 1961 a government majority in the upper house has occurred on only two occasions – specifically, after the 1977 and 2004 federal elections. At all other times, a minor party has held the **BALANCE OF POWER**. Between 1961 and 1984, the number of minor parties in the Senate was not great and were primarily created out of a split from a major party (Sharman, 1999). This included the Democratic Labor Party (DLP) (created in the aftermath of Labor's 1955 split), the Liberal Movement (created following internal tensions within the South Australian division of the Liberal party) and the Australian Democrats (the natural successor to the Liberal Movement). The earlier minor parties may be described as 'secessionist' deriving as they did from groups seceding from existing parties (Ghazarian 2012).

Following changes to the Senate voting system and the introduction of the group voting ticket in 1984, a variety of minor parties have found their way into the Senate with at least one, the Greens, having achieved quite a significant presence in the upper house (Economou 2016). Unlike the earlier minor parties, the new parties tended to focus more on particular issues, whether broad social divisions around religion, the environment and class or tightly focused on very specific issues such as nuclear disarmament, gambling, arts funding and the

MULTI-MEMBER PROPORTIONAL ELECTORAL SYSTEM: An electoral system that has votes within multi-member electorates, and then allocated on a proportional basis to the number of votes cast for a party or candidate.

MINORITY GOVERNMENT: Government by the largest party in a legislature where that party does not command an overall majority of seats in the lower house.

BALANCE OF POWER: A situation where neither the major party nor the coalition has a controlling majority in the upper house, and the passage of legislation is controlled by one or more smaller parties.

like (Ghazarian 2012). Having secured their Senate seats, the minor parties in the upper house have been able to exercise some power over legislation, particularly where the major parties are opposed, that in turn has required governments to work with them should they wish to achieve their legislative program.

THE POINT AND PURPOSE OF MINOR PARTIES

Assessments of the impact of minor parties tend to fall into two broad camps – those who venerate the phenomenon as a confirmation of the vibrancy of a diverse liberal democracy and those who condemn minor parties as an attempt by a minority to try to derail the aspirations of majority politics as expressed via the two-party system – this last approach once summed up by Henry Mayer as manifestations of big party 'chauvinism' and minor party 'romanticism' (Mayer 1980). In this romantic view, a minor party may either claim their party will displace one or other of the major parties and dominate the lower house or achieve their goals through crossbench representation and negotiation to win concessions. When Dr Bob Brown, former leader of the Australian Greens, claimed only the Greens had a vision for future Australia, he echoed the claim of major party leaders (Rogers 2010). The reality is, of course, that minor parties rarely achieve this objective as they do not have the required electoral support.

By the same token, long-term voting trends have indicated a gradual decline in total voter support for the two major political parties, particularly for the ALP, which dropped from primary vote of 50 per cent in 1983 to 33 per cent in 2019 (Manwaring 2020). The rate of voter decline for the major parties is even stronger in national Senate voting trends (Green 2018). The reasons for these trends are diverse and varied, but the noticeable increase since 1984 in the number of parties being formed to contest national elections, and the use of the **GROUP VOTING TICKET**, is an important consideration. In 1984, a total of 20 parties registered with the Australian Electoral Commission (AEC) to contest both House of Representatives and Senate seats. By 2013 the number of parties formed to contest Commonwealth elections had risen to over 50, although by 2022 this had declined to less than 40 with the end of the use of Group Voting Tickets in 2016. This still presents electoral authorities with the problem of potentially fitting all the parties and candidates on to a single ballot paper.

GROUP VOTING TICKET: A mechanism on a ballot paper for multi-member electorates whereby the elector need only number the box next to a party, with the vote and preferences allocated according to prior determination of the party.

REFLECTION QUESTION 9.1
Should group voting tickets be maintained or abolished?

Response prompt is available at www.cambridge.org/highereducation/isbn/9781009108232/resources

SPOTLIGHT 9.1 HOW MANY PARTIES ARE TOO MANY?

The significant increase in the number of minor parties running for the Senate in 2013 alarmed the major parties and the Greens, especially when a number of candidates from what the press dubbed as 'micro-parties' secured Senate seats. Most of the newly elected senators were from Clive Palmer's Palmer United Party (PUP), but also elected were Ricky Muir from the Australian Motor

Enthusiasts Party in Victoria and Wayne Dropulich of the Australian Sports Party in Western Australia. The Western Australian results were eventually voided when the AEC admitted to losing some 1400 ballot papers, and Dropulich did not win in the ensuing Senate by-election. The election of Muir and Dropulich caused particular outrage among commentators due to their election on 0.5 per cent and 0.23 per cent of the vote, respectively. The parliament's Joint Standing Committee on Electoral Matters recommended changes to the electoral laws designed to discourage 'micro parties' (JSCEM 2014). These recommendations included the abolition of the group voting ticket vote (thereby denying preference trading between these parties), changes to preferencing requirements, and new rules about registering parties to deal with the apparent phenomena of 'front' parties – parties with limited support, established to 'harvest' preferences for better-known candidates and parties. The use of front parties was noted in the 1999 New South Wales state election and saw major changes to the manner of election in the NSW Legislative Council (Lovelock 2009). In both cases party registration fees and the number of members a prospective party needed to be registered were increased and group voting tickets were abolished (see also Chapter 7).

Clearly the desire of politically active people to get into parliament can be very strong. A party organisation is one of the ways in which this attempt to get a parliamentary presence can be made (the alternative would be to run as an independent). As a proportional system based on allowing voters to cast preferences for all candidates, the Senate's Single Transferable Vote system has previously been seen by most minor party candidates as providing the best opportunity to win a seat, and thus parties and candidates cluster around the Senate contest. In all but the rarest occasions, the best a minor party candidate can hope to achieve in a single-member district election for the House of Representatives is to try to influence the result through the recommendation of preferences via the how-to-vote card – and perhaps be blessed with the surplus Senate votes from the major party of their choice in the Senate (Sharman 1999). The non-major parties could, however, engage in 'trading' preferences in the Senate, essentially corralling their preferences by ensuring that a group or cartel of parties preference themselves above the major parties. This is a function of the preferential voting system. The hope then is that one of the parties is able to corral enough votes to achieve a quota and thus election (Sharman, Sayers and Miragliotta 2002). Of course, the way a minor party would seek to utilise the preference system to impact on a result will be influenced by the minor party's own ideological position (Bowler and Denemark 1993). It is worth remembering that the Australian Democrats began with a policy of not directing preferences to either major party, but by the 1990s were prepared to make exceptions where it was particularly advantageous to themselves (Gauja 2010).

There is no denying the empirical evidence of a significant rise in the rate of party formation in Australian politics. The enthusiasm for those creating parties is not, however, necessarily matched by electors willing to support their particular electoral vehicle. Most parties fail to win enough primary votes to be able to retain the deposit they must pay to be a candidate (1 per cent), let alone obtain public funding (4 per cent). On those rare instances where a minor party has secured a seat in either house, it has proven difficult for them to retain that seat. Quite often the minor party implodes, as the One Nation party did after the 1998 election, and the Palmer United Party did after the 2013 election. Notwithstanding this, it is still possible to identify a handful of minor parties that have defied or are still defying the conventional notion that minor party politics are short-term and volatile.

QUESTIONS

Should there be a minimum threshold of votes a party must receive before the party can take a seat in parliament? Do you think this would reduce the number of parties appearing on the ballot paper?

THE KEY MINOR PARTY PLAYERS

While the origins and politics of parties such as the Nationals, the DLP, the Australian Democrats, the Australian Greens, and One Nation are very different, these minor parties have all had a major impact on Australian politics. The Nationals, whose vote share has declined significantly, remain a key part of the party system due to their ongoing coalition with the Liberal Party of Australia (LPA), but equally they are struggling to maintain a separate identity. Their inclusion here is as much a counter-point to their identity as a Coalition partner as much as a minor party. The DLP, created in the ALP split of 1955, kept the ALP out of office through the late 1950s and 1960s, but collapsed and disappeared in the mid-1970s. While important in understanding the long ALP electoral drought in the 1950s and 60s, the DLP's importance is now more historical. The other three parties have shared a similar structural position within Australia's political landscape, while also grappling with many of the same issues. These have included how to remain politically relevant while maintaining a voice distinct from the big parties; how and for what ends to use their Senate representation, especially when holding the balance of power; and how, or indeed whether, they should seek to extend their influence beyond the confines of the Senate. For that purpose we will focus primarily on the latter three as parties who have had a substantial and enduring impact on Australian politics at the state and federal level over the past 40 years, even as other, personality-based parties, such as the Nick Xenophon Team (NXT) and the PUP/ United Australia Party (UAP), have risen and fallen on the fading (or resurgence) of their leader.

REFLECTION QUESTION 9.2

What is the key difference between the structural position in Australian federal politics that the Nationals have played on the one hand and the DLP, Democrats and Greens have played on the other?

Response prompt is available at www.cambridge.org/highereducation/isbn/9781009108232/resources

THE NATIONALS

While sharing similarities with other minor parties, the National Party of Australia (NPA) is unique in two respects: first, it operates as part of a more or less permanent Coalition with the Liberal Party of Australia, which gives it power and influence beyond the relatively modest vote that it receives in elections; second, the NPA positions itself as the conservative political voice of rural and regional Australia, with support particularly concentrated in New South Wales and Queensland (in 2008, the Nationals and Liberals merged in Queensland). It is a self-consciously agrarian party, one of the oldest in the world (Davey 2010; Costar and Woodward 1985). Although it is the junior party in the Coalition, the NPA's history is longer, and arguably its roots in its favoured constituency are deeper than those of the LPA. That history begins a century ago.

Origins

The Country Party, as the NPA was called up until 1975, officially formed in 1920. Representatives of state-based Farmers and Settlers' Associations that had coalesced in the previous decade constituted the new party (Graham 1966). These organisations viewed both the Liberal and Labor parties, and the new Nationalist Party that formed after the split in Labor in 1916, as representing essentially urban-based interests, although the ALP was clearly regarded with greater hostility. The ideology of the new party was firmly rooted in agrarian myths of rugged individualism and personal responsibility, and thus it has imbibed a conservative moral ethos that has animated the party's policies throughout its history. Australia's prosperity was, the Country Party claimed, derived from the sheep's back and the soil that the farmers' labour tendered. These were the core constituents of the Country Party, although it tried to broaden its appeal in 1975 by changing its name to the National Country Party, and then dropping 'Country' altogether in 1982 and simply becoming the National Party.

The Country Party first won the balance of power in the 1922 election, and soon after would enter into a coalition with Stanley Bruce's nationalist government. The Coalition did not survive the loss of government in 1929, nor did it immediately reconvene when the United Australia Party won and kept government in its own right after 1931. It would not be until the formation of the modern LPA in 1944 that the Liberal–Country Coalition would take on its contemporary form.

Organisation

At the founding of the new Liberal Party in 1944, its leader Robert Menzies was clear that a stable Coalition with the Country Party was essential to the fortunes of the non-Labor side of Australian politics (Costar 1994). The price that Menzies and subsequent Liberal leaders have been prepared to pay to preserve a stable Coalition Agreement has not been trivial. The Nationals' leader is always deputy leader of the joint party caucus, which means they are deputy prime minister when the Coalition is in government (this tradition has been in place since 1968, when the position of Deputy Prime Minister was formally created). Moreover, some key ministerial portfolios in Cabinet are reserved for the Nationals – such as trade and agriculture – irrespective of the talents and experience of Liberal contenders for these coveted positions. The National Party has also had a strong track record of extracting concessions from its Coalition partner that the latter might not always be predisposed to giving, in the absence of having to preserve the Coalition. Thus, the NPA has a strong track record of winning government subsidies and other handouts for farmers and miners, which more free-market oriented Liberals may not have given if they were governing alone (Maddox 1996, 327).

A related issue has revolved around tariff protection. From the 1950s, under leader John 'Black Jack' McEwan, whose name became synonymous with protectionism, the party moved to a position of supporting high tariffs (Davey 2010, 110–11). In an effort to broaden its appeal beyond rural sectional interests, it argued that city workers and their manufacturing employers provided the customers for rural goods, and therefore manufacturing should be protected from foreign competition. This position was eroded in the 1980s and 1990s, often under pressure from a Liberal Coalition partner enamoured with free trade and globalisation. This speaks to one of several challenges that the contemporary NPA faces.

At least one of those challenges, aside from other insurgent parties, is the uneven-ness of the National Party as an organisation across Australia, primarily derived from a very strong state-centric organisational base. While the NPA is particularly strong in Queensland and performs well electorally in New South Wales and Victoria, the party has consistently struggled in South Australia, has been perceived at times as very much the junior party in Western Australia, and is all but non-existent in Tasmania, the Northern Territory and the Australian Capital Territory. The party is therefore primarily driven by the politics of Queensland and New South Wales and not by the smaller, more peripheral states and territories. While not permanently damaging, it has meant that, for instance, the first West Australian NPA member to be elected to the House of

Representatives in 36 years, Tony Crook, won after challenging Wilson Tuckey, the sitting Liberal MP. Crook then sat outside the NPA party room during his three-year tenure and for two years sat on the crossbench. He was succeeded by a LPA member rather than a National.

Support base

From the outset, the new party campaigned within parliament for the interests of land-owning primary producers. As such, it rejected the commitment to high tariffs from both the main parties (a position that shifted considerably in the decades after the Second World War), rejected government price fixing, argued for reduced government spending and championed the rights of returned servicemen, many of whom had roots in rural and regional Australia.

If the NPA's relationship with the LPA has enabled it to win certain concessions for its rural and regional constituents, that same relationship has also led it to make compromises that have alienated some of those same supporters. The Coalition's general commitment to market-oriented solutions to economic and social problems has frequently had losers in rural and regional Australia. This has periodically led to charges that the National Party has sold its soul to the LPA, and in so doing betrayed the bush. The NPA is said to have subsumed itself to the interests of its Coalition partner, thereby diluting what is distinctive about its politics and making itself largely irrelevant. Consequences have been occasional bitter recriminations against the NPA's parliamentary leadership and the splitting away of some high-profile figures who have run against the Nationals as independents or as representatives of new parties (e.g. Bob Katter).

The Nationals have also had to contend with the political challenge posed by One Nation since the late 1990s and more recently the Shooters Fishers and Farmers Party (SFF). One Nation, an anti-immigration populist party, has appealed to some traditional NPA voters, which has meant that the National Party has had to position itself further to the right of the political spectrum than it otherwise would. SFF has claimed that the Nationals have positioned themselves too far away from their origins and their rural, farming-based, constituency and have caused considerable concern for the NPA at a state level. Finally, a longer-term structural challenge to the NPA has been demographic change. There has been an ongoing decline in the population of rural and regional Australia relative to urban areas, which threatens to further dilute NPA representation in Australia's federal parliament in the future.

Despite these challenges, the NPA has exhibited a resilience that has proved its detractors and doomsayers wrong more than once. As long as they remain an integral part of the Coalition, they will remain an important force in Australian politics for the foreseeable future.

THE AUSTRALIAN DEMOCRATS

Although it is now more or less moribund, the Australian Democrats is worthy of consideration not only for the way the party's appearance marked the beginning of a new era of minor party politics but also because of the way the party was able to link its raison d'être with the potential for the Australian Senate to discharge its role as a house of review. While the Democrats aspired to winning seats in the House of Representatives, as they had done in South Australia state elections on two occasions, the party was primarily a Senate party.

Origins

At its very beginning the party coined the phrase 'keeping the bastards honest' as its political rallying cry based on the assumption that 'the bastards' were the two major political parties and that the place to keep them honest was in the Senate (Warhurst 1997). Interestingly, and innovatively, the party passed up wheeling and dealing roles with preferences by promising to never direct them – at least, not to the major parties. The experience of the 1975 removal of the Whitlam Government through the blocking of money bills ('Supply') by the Senate led directly to another promise to never use its numbers to block supply (Millar 1981).

The party was quite successful in winning Senate representation. By 1981 the party was in the balance of power, a position it occupied solely to 1993, and then shared with other minor parties including the Greens between 1993 and 2004. For the period 1981–1993, covering the Fraser and Hawke governments, it held this position alone. The outcome for this period was that governments were required to deal with the Democrats whenever opposed by the other major party if they sought to have their legislative program get through the parliament. The Democrats could be amenable to passing things they agreed with, such as the Hawke government's legislation to prevent the Franklin Dam in Tasmania in 1983 (indeed, the bill had originally been drafted by the Democrats in 1982) (Spindler 2005). The Democrats could also refuse governments, such as the time the party would not countenance the Hawke Government's attempt to bring in a national identity card. Most of the time the Democrats would seek to moderate the legislative program of the government of the day usually by way of negotiation that would lead to amendments being proposed in the Senate. The Howard Government's goods and services tax (GST) was an example, with the Democrats only agreeing to pass this bill if certain goods and services were to be exempt from the consumption tax.

Organisation

The Democrats were also seen as having an innovative approach to organisation, although the aspect of the party's rules that tended to capture the most attention was its mechanism for selecting its parliamentary leader. At the time, the party was the only one to put the power to choose its leader in the hands of the ordinary members (albeit by way of a complicated nomination process). The mechanism had to be invoked several times, as leadership instability became something of a recurring theme in the party. The party's first leader was former Liberal parliamentarian Don Chipp who served from 1977 until his retirement in 1986. He was succeeded by Janine Haines who became the first female party leader in Australian parliamentary history. Haines' leadership seemed stable enough until an unsuccessful bid to win the South Australian lower house seat of Kingston led to her retirement from politics. After Haines, the party was subjected to a series of leadership battles. Of those who led, arguably the most significant were Cheryl Kernot (until her defection to the Labor Party), Meg Lees (who oversaw the GST negotiations and was removed from the leadership soon after) and Natasha Stott-Despoja (who was also removed as leader in the dramas that followed internal division within the party over the role it had played in expediting the GST legislation through the Senate).

Support base

Over its existence, the Australian Democrats party tried to develop into something beyond its original remit as a Senate-based party to which voters who either disliked the major parties or who were attracted to the Democrat mantra of keeping the Senate out of the hands of the government of the day could align their support. The party's campaign for greater relevance was based on identifying with issues it saw as important to the electorate, most of which resonated as socially progressive agenda items such as women's politics, Indigenous affairs and the environment (Gauja 2010). In so doing, the party expanded its appeal past disaffected major party electors to include a socially progressive constituency that might have otherwise voted for the ALP. Consequently, Democrat gains in the Senate came at the expense of Labor, although the political consequences of this was mitigated by the fact that Labor could often rely on Democrat support to get its bills through the Senate. Arguably the biggest threat to the Democrats, however, came in the form of green party politics. In 1984 the Nuclear Disarmament Party (NDP) ran on an antinuclear and disarmament policy similar to one promoted by the Democrats. By the 1990s the Democrats floated the idea of merging with the nascent Australian Greens although this was strongly opposed by the Democrat Senators Meg Lees and Cheryl Kernot plus a large section of the party's membership (Brown and Singer 1996; Kernot and Walters 1995). The proposal came to nought and Janet Powell was removed as party leader in a members-initiated leadership contest in 1992 (Economou and Ghazarian 2008). By 2004 the Greens had displaced the Democrats as the party capable of winning Senate seats at the expense of Labor, and by 2007 the Democrats' failure to win any Senate seats marked the end of the party as a parliamentary presence at a federal level.

SHORT-ANSWER QUESTIONS 9.1

1. Which of the more recent minor parties that have been successful do the Democrats resemble?
2. Do you think that, like the niche that the Democrats exploited, that there is room for another party that fills that gap between social conservatives and social liberals in Australian federal politics?

Suggested responses are available at www.cambridge.org/highereducation/isbn/9781009108232/resources

RESEARCH QUESTION 9.1

What were the key challenges that the DLP and the Democrats, as key minor parties who have disappeared from parliament, were unable to overcome?

THE AUSTRALIAN GREENS

The emergence of the Greens party is arguably one of the most significant developments in the Australian party system since the appearance of the Australian Democrats in the 1970s. Like the Australian Democrats, the Australian Greens at the federal level is primarily a Senate party with the majority of the party's parliamentary wing being elected to the Senate. At the state level, the party's most consistent electoral performances in terms of seats secured have been under proportional electoral systems. However, unlike the Democrats, the Greens have enjoyed lower house success in the national electoral contest as well as at the state level. The election of a Greens' representative in the federal division of Cunningham in 2002 was the first lower house success, albeit in a by-election in which the LPA did not field a candidate (Cahill and Brown 2008). Consequently, Michael Organ – the Greens' first ever member of the House of Representatives – was unable to retain his seat at the following general election. In the 2010 general election, however, the Greens' Adam Bandt was elected in the federal division of Melbourne and has held that seat ever since. Perhaps to the disappointment of the party, this inner-urban success has not been replicated at the federal level in other states. The Greens have, however, been able to win single-member district contests in state parliaments, particularly in the inner city of Melbourne, Sydney and Brisbane, as well the 'tree-change' seat of Ballina on the New South Wales north coast.

This record of lower house electoral success points to a demographic specificity to the 'green vote' that rather replicates the dynamic at work in the vote for the National Party. The demographic clustering of the vote, which for the Nationals is largely rural, is key to a success based off a low overall vote (Costar 2015). In the case of the Greens, support is highest in inner urban electorates with a lower median age and much higher rates of tertiary education than the national averages and is replicated in the party's membership (Gauja and Jackson 2016). Indeed, the proximity of a tertiary educated electorate to seats in which the Greens have been successful is a recurring theme. In addition to inner city Melbourne, Sydney and Brisbane, strong support for Greens' candidates has also occurred in the New South Wales seats of Cunningham, Newcastle and Richmond. All three of these regional seats have universities within them and, indeed, the first Greens' member of the lower house, Michael Organ, had been a lecturer at the University of Wollongong. In short, if **POST-MATERIALISM** counts as an acceptable socio-economic measure, the Greens would appear to be very much a post-materialist party (Grant and Tilley 2019).

Origins

According to the party's own narrative, the Australian Greens are the direct descendants of the United Tasmania Group (UTG) that was formed out of the conservation protest movement that was mobilised to campaign against the construction of hydro-electricity schemes deep within wilderness areas on the west coast of Tasmania (Kiernan 1990). The UTG is widely thought of as the world's first conservation-oriented political party and it was the first political party to which Dr Bob Brown, one of Australia's most prominent environmental activists, had previously been a member.

Bob Brown himself was elected to the Tasmanian House of Assembly on a countback following the resignation of Australian Democrat Norm Sanders over the Franklin Dam. Brown had run at the previous election as a Green Independent but had not been successful, and indeed was in Hobart's Risdon jail, having been arrested at the Franklin Dam site, when he received the news he had been elected (Brown and Singer 1996; Lines 2006).

Brown was to lead the first fledgling Green Independents in the Tasmanian parliament, then the Tasmanian Greens, before finally becoming the leader of the Australian Greens. This occurred slowly, with the Green Independents from his election in 1982 through to 1993, when he resigned to run in the federal election in the seat of Denison. He lost that election but was ultimately successful in being elected to the Senate in 1996 (Manning 2019).

When he took up his seat as a member of the Australian Greens, there were already senators present who also used the term 'green' in their party nomenclature. This other green party was the Greens (WA) whose lineage could be traced back to the Nuclear Disarmament Party – a party formed to contest the 1984 election at which Jo Vallentine, the lead candidate in the Western Australian ticket for the Senate, was elected. Senator Vallentine was returned as a Vallentine Peace Group candidate in 1987, but this was also the election in which the NDP's Robert Wood secured a Senate seat from New South Wales (his win would later be overturned by the High Court as he did not hold Australian citizenship). The NDP was a party connected to the anti-nuclear and peace and disarmament movements (Vallentine and Jones 1990).

At the same time as Jo Vallentine was being elected to the Senate for the NDP, a new set of parties, loosely affiliated, were forming across Australia. These were the various green parties utilising the original AEC registration to circumvent the rules regarding membership thresholds

> **POST-MATERIALISM:** The notion that once voters have achieved material satisfaction through wages, conditions and basic standards, they will turn to non-material satisfaction such as through caring for the environment, identity rights and the like.

for party registration (Harris 2010). Beginning in Sydney in early 1985 (shortly after running their first candidate, Daphne Golan, in the 1984 federal election as an independent), these new Green parties were at first fiercely independent, jealously guarding their separate identities. However, by 1992 they had coalesced into state parties and were able to formally found the Australian Greens as a single entity – although without the Greens (WA). For all their rhetoric about their common aspirations, the two political parties continued to operate as separate entities until 2003 when the Greens (WA) finally voted to become part of the Australian Greens (Jackson 2016).

Organisation

The task of consolidating and coordinating what was a diverse and quite localised collection of parties using the word 'green' in their nomenclature commenced in 1992 when the Tasmanian Greens sought to bring other green parties together in order to create a national organisation. This proved to be only partially successful especially given that the West Australian Greens party – the only other green party to have won seats in the Senate – opted to remain outside of the national body. The putative national organisation proceeded nonetheless and decided to develop a federal structure in order to have an organisation that could coordinate national election campaigns but still accommodate the state-based diversity of green party politics. The consolidation process was finally completed in 2003 when the West Australian Greens finally agreed to join the national organisation, a decision that had been long delayed – there had been two previous internal referendums to join – but which was now driven by the necessity of building a united party across Australia.

The Australian Greens prefer to use the term 'confederation' to describe its organisation in order to re-enforce the notion that the party stands apart from the way the other main parties in the Australian system are organised. The party's own rhetoric likes to utilise claims that its organisation is 'innovative' and that it reflects a commitment to 'grass roots democracy', although a comparison between the four main parties and indeed the way the Australian Democrats party was organised suggests the Australian Greens are different, they respond in the same manner as the other parties to Australia's federal structures (Miragliotta and Jackson 2015). The decentralised nature of the organisation makes it rather similar to the way the right-of-centre parties are organised. Similarly to the LPA, the Australian Greens' paramount internal organ, the National Conference, originally comprised equal numbers of delegates from each state and territory branch as well as various officials who are given ex officio status (they can attend but not vote). Each of the state and territory branches, meanwhile, have their own peak bodies and can decide upon their own rules. Most of the state branches eschew external organisations, but the Tasmanian party allows The Wilderness Society to affiliate in a manner similar to union affiliations to the ALP.

The real difference between the Australian Greens and the other main parties manifests itself in the party's operational culture. The National Conference lacks formal policy-setting power, although disputes over policy rarely occur to the extent that they can be problematic. One interesting incident occurred in 2002 and was a rare moment of disjuncture within the party over a matter of policy. Following the 2001 federal election at which Brown was joined in the Senate by Kerry Nettle from New South Wales, Brown indicated he had some sympathy for a proposal to use the proceeds of the sale of Telstra to halt the logging of old growth forests and broad acre land clearing (Manning 2002). The various state branches of the party made it clear that they did not support this proposal and Brown soon shifted his position. This was an insightful moment that highlighted that the parliamentary leader of the Australian Greens could be brought to account on a policy matter notwithstanding the lack of the organisation's formal power to direct on policy.

It should also be noted that this was a rare occurrence. The Greens appear to operate from a strong internal consensus about where the party stands on policy issues, be they social policies or issues directly relevant to the 'green' agenda (Cunningham and Jackson 2014; Jackson 2016). When they arise, internal disputes tend to derive from structural concerns rather than ideological divisions, even though it is commonly held by commentators that tensions exist within the party between pragmatists and idealists.

This, in turn, highlights the rather problematic relationship the Greens have with the idea of leadership due to the party's link with what is often referred to as 'new social movement' politics (Kitschelt 1989). The environmental, peace and disarmament and antinuclear movements all identify as activist-oriented politics to which protest and mass mobilisation are viewed as defining characteristics that set them apart from the bureaucratic politics of more traditional interest group activity (lobbying and negotiation). It is also thought that a more activist-oriented approach is more attractive to the political ambitions of the young compared to the more bureaucratic politics of the major parties. This is one of the reasons why the Greens readily identify with and project themselves as a form of youthful politics – noting the party's constant reference to traditional political parties and activities as 'old politics' – a narrative that appears to resonate with the comparatively more youthful inner-city electorates of Melbourne and Sydney. Having said this, it is still the case that the political system places a high value on party leadership and this, in turn, has been one area of the party's operation where internal tensions have occasionally occurred (Cunningham and Jackson 2014).

Internal politics

Like all political parties the Australian Greens have internal divisions reflecting the importance of the diversity of the party at the state level and, on occasions, also reflecting differences of opinion on what should or should not be included in policy. According to some recent academic analysis, ideological divides within the party are based on differences of opinion on how ecological matters should be dealt with, but the prominence of more traditional left-right issues (economics, internationalism, welfare, etc.) have become increasingly evident (Holloway 2019). The dominant narrative here revolves around identification of 'fundamentalists' (or 'fundos', according to the internal party vernacular) and 'realists' (or 'realos'). These two categories might actually be reflecting a long-standing tension within green politics between those whose political experience was garnered via the peace and disarmament campaigns of the 1970s and 1980s, and those who were at the forefront of the great conservation campaigns in Tasmania at about the same time. The dichotomy is based on the view that some within the Greens can accommodate working within the policymaking system to achieve policy objectives (in the manner in which conservationists operated in the 1980s and 1990s), while others come from a more radical approach to politics that reflects the primacy of activism and ideological commitment to a 'new politics' (Miragliotta 2006).

It has also been the case that the Australian Greens party has been remarkably stable and unified notwithstanding the presence of activists and ideologues within its ranks. Disputes within the parliamentary ranks have thus far been relatively minor and are usually about personality differences or competing aspirations for leadership positions. At the local level, disputes have arisen over preselection decisions, and there has been an allegation that the creation of the Animal Justice Party in Victoria was the result of a split between radicals and pragmatists with some of the former group deciding to create their own party. There was also a simmering tension between party elder Dr Bob Brown and the then New South Wales Senator Lee Rhiannon whose former membership of the now defunct Communist Party of Australia was sometimes seized upon by some commentators of proof of the 'red' interior of the Green party, but this has only slowly dissipated with the retirement of both senators (Neighbour 2012).

It would appear to be the case that the Australian Greens is a stable and unified party notwithstanding its decentralised organisational structure and its strong ideological approach to politics. Those internal tensions that arise replicate tensions that happen in all parties and reflect occasional disjuncture between the organisation and the parliamentary wing, the importance of personality politics when the question of parliamentary leadership arises, and a sense that an incremental balance of power situation occurs between the key state branches, each of which is quite different in structure and organisation. The incorporation of the West Australian Greens was an important moment in the party's development, after which time there occurred a shift from the Tasmanian to the Victorian branches as arguably the most influential regarding leadership of the federal branch. In the meantime, the Australian Greens party has displaced the Australian Democrats as arguably the most important minor party in the Australian party system especially with respect to the Senate.

In the context of 'wing' parties (Siaroff 2003), it is useful to consider that the left side of politics has now been substantially consolidated, with the Australian Greens as the principal party of the left on the Australian political spectrum and the ALP on the centre-left. This is reflected not only in the party's ideological position, but it is also evident in the success it has had in appealing to many voters who might have previously been a Labor constituency. While the Australian Greens party itself likes to claim an ability to attract Liberal voters as well, in terms of seats won – both in the House of Representatives and the Senate – Green gains have so far largely been at the expense of Labor. The Australian Greens party has also succeeded in consolidating what had previously been a diverse and fragmented array of left-of-centre minor parties that emerged in the 1980s and early 1990s and by 2007 had assumed the mantle of 'third party' in the Senate with the redundancy of the Australian Democrats party.

SHORT-ANSWER QUESTIONS 9.2

1. What electoral strategies have contributed to the Australian Greens gradual improvement to become the third force in Australian federal politics?
2. In what ways is the organisational structure of the Australian Greens an advantage and a disadvantage?

Suggested responses are available at www.cambridge.org/highereducation/isbn/9781009108232/resources

REFLECTION QUESTION 9.3

The Greens are part of a network of global Green parties, the Global Greens. How might the Australian Greens be similar or different to other Green parties, and why might this be the case?

Response prompt is available at www.cambridge.org/highereducation/isbn/9781009108232/resources

ONE NATION

When considering the emergence of a right-of-centre party as a 'wing' party to match the Australian Greens, no single minor party has emerged as the primary minor party of the right, and certainly not to the extent to which the Australian Greens party has for the left, although this has not been for the want of party formation. Since 1984, an array of right-of-centre minor parties have been created and some have won seats in the Senate, including the Family First Party (a revived version of the Democratic Labor Party), the Liberal Democratic Party, the Palmer United Party, the Australian Motor Enthusiasts Party, and the One Nation party (also sometimes referred to as Pauline Hanson's One Nation (PHON). Of these, it has been the One Nation party that has arguably been the most consistent performer in that it has succeeded in winning Senate seats on more than one occasion.

Origins

The appeal of One Nation, and Pauline Hanson in particular, has been the source of some discussion, but it might generally be described as 'right populism'. Right populism can be defined as having a particular formulation of nativism, authoritarianism and populism, and in the case of Australia and One Nation, due to the structural changes occurring within the political economy of Australia since the 1980s (McSwiney and Cottle 2017). Those most affected by changes in the economic structures of Australia, particularly in manufacturing, have a strong need to look for explanation for their economic woes, in Australia's case brought on by the slow removal of firstly tariffs coupled with an increasingly globalised market (Moore 2019). The appeal of One Nation, and Pauline Hanson at the centre of the party, is not the same as for say Donald Trump, Nigel Farage or Emmanuel Macron (or Marine Le Pen for that matter), as Hanson was not part of an existing economic or political elite. One Nation and Hanson was able to appeal to a seemingly economically disadvantaged rural and regional blue collar sector and the self-employed middle-class electorate that was no longer being serviced by the major parties (Economou 2001).

Pauline Hanson appeared first as a disendorsed Liberal candidate in the safe outer-Brisbane electorate of Oxley. She had lost Liberal Party endorsement due to her inflammatory comments about perceived Aboriginal entitlement but remained on the ballot paper as a Liberal as the disendorsement came after the close of nominations and the printing of the ballot papers. Hanson stormed to victory in the seat with a 22 per cent swing against the sitting ALP member. Her maiden speech was noted for its xenophobic, anti-Asian sentiments. Although Hanson lost her seat at the next federal election, at the 1998 Queensland election the party polled over 22 per cent of the vote.

Internal politics

The party appeared to have arrived – yet as rapidly as it had gained votes, the party's internal tensions soon tore it apart. For a time, Pauline Hanson, the central figure of the One Nation story, was not even a member of the party that she helped found and spent time in jail, and even at one stage she ran against the party in New South Wales. Between 2001 and 2013, the party seemed constantly on the brink of a complete implosion.

After its extraordinary success in winning 11 seats in the 1998 Queensland state election, five of the parliamentary members of the party resigned to create their own party (the Country City Alliance) within months of taking up their seats. By the 2001 state election, the party saw its vote more than halved from 22.7 per cent to 8.7 per cent and reduced to three seats. Their vote fell further in 2004 to less than 5 per cent, retaining just one MP, Rosa Lee Long, in the seat of Tablelands. At the same time, the West Australian branch of the party had managed to win three seats in the 2001 state election, though by 2004 none of the three MPs elected in 2001 were members of One Nation, with one sitting as an independent and two sitting as New Country Party MPs.

In 2002, an aggrieved One Nation candidate, supported secretly by sections of the Liberal Party (Kingston 2012), alleged that the party had inappropriately used public election funding in that election. This led to a further police investigation and court trial resulting in 2002 Hanson and the One Nation party secretary David Ettridge being convicted for breaches of the electoral law (Warner 2003). Both served time in prison until the conviction was overturned on appeal. In the meantime, the One Nation candidate elected to the Senate from Queensland in the 1998 federal election was disqualified by the High Court on the grounds that she was not an Australian citizen. This was in the early days of the party. In 2002 Ms Hanson had been expelled and a splinter party formed around another executive member of One Nation, and by 2004 the party had lost all its seats either at election or through resignation.

Yet the party did not die, even as other right-of-centre parties emerged to try to replicate what was seen as Hanson's success of tapping into the disillusionment of regional voters. Although Clive Palmer and PUP appeared to be a worthy successor at the 2013 federal election, that party could not replicate its success. Hanson herself returned to the party she founded in 2013, and in 2016 she was re-elected to the Senate. In state elections in Western Australia and Queensland (both in 2017), One Nation MPs were elected, and in 2017 former ALP Leader Mark Latham joined the party and was elected to the New South Wales Legislative Council. Hanson has demonstrated that, while not able to fully recapture the success she enjoyed in the late 90s, there is still an electorate available to exploit.

RESEARCH QUESTION 9.2

What other parties internationally are similar to PHON?

OTHER INSURGENT PARTIES

Party success for other right-of-centre minor parties has largely occurred in the Senate, although Katter Australia Party (KAP) and the PUP won seats in the House of Representatives, with United Australia Party (UAP) gaining an MHR after the sitting MP for the seat of Hughes, Craig Kelly, joined the Party in 2021. Apart from former National Party member Bob Katter in the Queensland federal division of Kennedy, and One Nation in the Senate, most other right-of-centre minor parties have been unable to defend their seats. These minor parties often appear designed to serve the political ambitions of a prominent individual, with examples including One Nation (Pauline Hanson), the PUP/UAP (Clive Palmer), the KAP (Bob Katter), the Justice Party (built around Victorian and former media personality Derryn Hinch) and the Jacqui Lambie Network (built around former Tasmanian PUP senator, Jacqui Lambie). These organisations tend to be quite limited and prone to internal instability demonstrating the difficulty in managing the tensions between leader-centric populism and grassroots (yet individualised) grievance politics, where there is a lack of any unifying ideological position or policy platform. One Nation members appear continually in dispute with the Party's executive. Clive Palmer was incapable of keeping his Senate team together after the PUP's quite strong performance at the 2013 election, with all MPs leaving the Party or being defeated at the 2016 election, and the PUP was deregistered in 2017. Palmer's new venture, the UAP, was created with former One Nation Senator Brian Burston being appointed its parliamentary leader on formation in 2018. Family First had to continually deny claims that it was a secretive organisation with links to evangelical churches, or a preference harvesting vehicle for the Liberal Party under former leader Bob Day. Family First eventually merged into former Liberal Senator Cory Bernardi's Australian Conservatives, even as its last remaining senator, Lucy Gichuhi, joined the Liberal Party.

For all this volatility and instability, the accumulated national vote for the right-of-centre minor parties contesting the upper houses has been rising. The proliferation of parties has tended to mask this growing support, as very few of those parties contesting poll more than 1 to 1.5 per cent of the primary vote. The accumulated effect of all these party tickets securing such a small share of the vote has been significant, however, especially if preferences are aggregated and accumulated to one of these parties. Having noted the impact and potential of a party being elected on a small percentage of the vote, the Commonwealth and states have begun adapting their methods of election to their respective upper houses, eliminating group voting tickets. Nonetheless, it is still possible for a party to win a seat without polling a full quota. It is therefore still possible that a party capable of polling above 2 to 3 per cent of the primary stands a chance of winning a seat by virtue of being well ahead of competing parties in the count. Clearly the party that is most likely to achieve this is One Nation, especially in states such as Queensland, Western Australia and New South Wales where the party performs best.

SPOTLIGHT 9.2 WHAT IS THE PROCESS FOR POLITICAL PARTIES REGISTERING TO CONTEST AN AUSTRALIAN FEDERAL ELECTION?

If an individual or group of individuals want to start their own party and stand as a candidate or group of candidates for election to the Commonwealth parliament, they have to follow a registration process administered by the AEC. As part of this process, a party constitution needs to be created which sets out at least some of the aims of the party, who the registered officers of the party will be and what the party will be known as.

Before this occurs, however, the new party needs to meet the conditions for registration. Recent changes to the *Commonwealth Electoral Act 1918* mean that the party now needs to have over 1500 members who are on the electoral roll to be registered and not a member of another party. Alternatively, a new party may register if their membership includes a current member of the federal parliament. This is the way that a number of relatively new minor parties have been created. For example, the Jacqui Lambie Network and the Nick Xenophon Team. The party then needs to complete an application for party registration form, attach all documents plus a $500 application fee.

If the AEC accepts that these documents are in order, they will advertise that an application for new party registration has occurred on their website as well as in major newspapers. During this period, objections can be lodged with the AEC about the new party registration. Objections generally relate to whether the name of the party is too similar to other parties or if there is a challenge to whether the party has met the requirements for registration. If the party successfully passes this stage, they can be officially registered as a party that can contest Australian federal elections.

QUESTION

Do you think parliamentarians who have defected from other parties, like Jacqui Lambie and Cory Bernardi did, should be allowed to start their own parties?

REFLECTION QUESTION 9.4

Have Australia's minor parties only been successful when the major parties have ignored key social issues?

Response prompt is available at www.cambridge.org/highereducation/isbn/9781009108232/resources

INDEPENDENTS

Technically, an independent candidate is the antithesis of a party candidate. Independent candidates focus on the specific electoral region in which they campaign and eschew the organisational demands of trying to run candidates across a number of other districts or jurisdictions. The independent candidate is a throw-back to Burkean notion of the House of Commons as the house that sought to allow for the representation of 'communities' by inviting the residents to choose their representative to speak on their behalf in that forum known as the parliament. In the modern context, the independent seeks to attract support from voters who have become disillusioned with the major political parties, in particular.

There is a rich history of independents holding seats in the Australian parliament, at both the state and federal level (Smith 2006). In the case of the House of Representatives, however, independents have rarely been able to exercise any substantial impact other than to try to counter the dominance of the major parties. Arguably the two most celebrated instances of independent significance were in 1941, when two independents, Alex Wilson and Arthur Coles, shifted their support from Arthur Fadden to John Curtin and thus expedited a minority Labor Government (Grattan 1941), and in 2010 when Rob Oakeshott, Andrew Wilkie and Tony Windsor – all independents – agreed to support Julia Gillard's minority Labor Government. The rate of independent success in the Senate has not matched that in the lower house, but the close numbers in the upper chamber have arguably allowed those who do get elected to have more influence with regards to determining the balance of power. In recent times, Tasmanian Senator Brian Harradine and South Australian Senator Nick Xenophon either held the balance of power or were part of a power bloc whose support was necessary to secure the passage of legislation.

Confusion can arise when so-called independents seek to utilise organisation in a bid to impact in contests beyond their specific locale. At the Tasmanian state election of 1989, for instance, five members were elected to the lower house under the banner of 'Green Independents'. Eventually this group became the Tasmanian Greens with the formalisation of their active state-wide organisation (Haward and Smith 1990). More usually a successful independent will form an organisation to try to achieve representational gains elsewhere. Thus, former independent federal member for Kennedy, Bob Katter, created his Katter Australia Party to run candidates in other states. Former 'No Pokies' Senator Nick Xenophon – who ran for and was successful on the No Pokies ticket for the South Australian upper house – similarly formed the NXT to contest the 2013 federal election, with NXT rewarded with gains in the Senate as well as winning the federal South Australian seat of Mayo. Former independent member for the federal Victorian seat of Indi, Cath McGowan, had a support group called to later lend its experience and resources to other independent candidates contesting the 2019 election, including the successful candidate in Wentworth, Zali Steggall, as well as McGowan's successor in Indi, Helen Haines. This was further expanded in the lead up to the 2022 election with a group of candidates, dubbed by some media outlets as 'teal' independents as they were all running to unseat conservative incumbents, who received initial campaign funding from the Climate 200 organisation. While these candidates had the initial appearance of being a group, each was very clear that they were independent, even though united on the need for action on climate change.

Previously, those who were successful in securing a seat have been a small proportion of the total number of independent candidates who nominate for both houses. This was usually a problem for the major parties (Labor, Liberal and National), as the vast majority of independents elected to the lower house are returned from what would have otherwise been a very safe major party seat. That situation changed in 2022 with the election of seven independent candidates in high profile conservative leaning seats. Their victory was part of a larger campaign involving 17 lower house and three Senate candidates, plus three sitting independents, backed by the pro-climate action group Climate 200, and principally targeting seats held by the Liberal Party. Like the incidence of voter support for minor parties, independent success resonates as an expression of voter disillusion with the major political parties (Economou 2021). Given the extent to which independent successes occur in safe seats, this disillusionment appears felt most acutely among former party-partisan supporters rather than swinging voters – as it was in Liberal heartland seats on the issue of climate change.

SPOTLIGHT 9.3 INDEPENDENTS AND HOLDING THE 'BALANCE OF POWER'

Independents have been an occasional presence in the House of Representatives on very many occasions, but rarely do they figure in the crucial question of determining who might be able to form a government. The transition from the United Australia Party to Labor in 1941 was caused by two independents shifting their support, with this being the last occasion independents were so pivotal to the formation of a federal government until 2010 – although independents in the Senate were at the heart of the 1975 constitutional crisis and the collapse of the Whitlam Government. In the 2010 election, the incumbent Labor Government lost its majority, but the Coalition was unable to secure enough seats to be able to govern. The balance of power was held by the minor parties (KAP, Greens) and the independents (Andrew Wilkie, Rob Oakeshott and Tony Windsor) on the crossbench. These three, along with Adam Bandt from the Greens, decided to back Julia Gillard's prime ministership, Windsor and Oakeshott judged a Gillard-led Labor Government with a Green–Labor Senate majority, likely be the most stable. Katter ruled himself out, being deeply uncomfortable with the Green–Labor agreement. Labor was now able to form a minority government (Costar 2012). The trade-off for this support came in the form of policy concessions – in particular, the commitment of better telecommunications resources for regional areas (Windsor and Oakeshott holding rural seats), support for action on gambling (Wilkie), and support for more practical policies to deal with climate change (Bandt). The Green–Labor agreement led to the Gillard Government introducing what was dubbed a 'carbon tax' and the broader unpopularity of this, in turn, probably led to the downfall of both Gillard and the Labor Government at the 2013 election, and with both Windsor and Oakeshott not contesting their seats. If nothing else, the ability of the independents to secure policy outcomes acted as an inspiration to other potential independents who could foresee achieving similarly agreeable policy outcomes for their communities.

QUESTION

Should independent MPs support the major party with the most votes or seats or support (or not support) parties based on other factors?

SHORT-ANSWER QUESTIONS 9.3

1. What challenges beyond the electoral system do Australia's minor parties and independents face in being elected to the Commonwealth Parliament?
2. What role beyond holding the major parties to account can minor parties and independents play in Australian federal politics?
3. Why have independents been successful in Australian federal politics?

Suggested responses are available at www.cambridge.org/highereducation/isbn/9781009108232/resources

REFLECTION QUESTION 9.5

Minor parties are said to have a 'blackmail' position, most pronounced in the Senate where parties may be in balance of power positions. Can you think of examples where minor parties have blocked or amended key pieces of legislation?

Response prompt is available at www.cambridge.org/highereducation/isbn/9781009108232/resources

SUMMARY

Learning objective 1: Identify and reflect on the significance of parties other than the two main parties to the Australian party system

Minor parties are those parties that, unlike the major parties, do *not* expect to form government in their own right or in most cases to even be part of government. In upper houses they may hold balance of power or veto positions, so can negotiate legislative programs with governments. Dependent on the electoral system they may also shape the nature of party competition. The array of parties that exist beyond the two major political parties provides the basis upon which Australia can be considered to be a multi-party liberal democracy, even though the vast majority of electors vote for the major parties that, in turn, dominate representation in both the House of Representatives and the Senate. This has been a longstanding feature of Australian politics, although it is also true that, in more recent national elections, the record of representational success for minor parties has been improving in both houses. This seems to correspond with evidence of weakening voter loyalty towards the major political parties, with these trends also having occurred alongside increasing rates of party formation – especially with the intention of contesting the Senate. The transfer of a vote from the major parties might reflect the greater choice voters have at elections as much as it might be a sign of increasing disillusion with the major parties among a growing minority of voters. The shift in voter alignments to minor parties that can be more readily identifiably ideological in their approach to the debate is another interesting trend in contemporary minor party politics.

Learning objective 2: Identify the key 'minor parties' and understand their organisation and impact

Since the use of proportional representation in 1949, three phases of minor party impact on the Senate can be identified. In the first phase, minor parties that took up Senate seats such as the DLP and the Liberal Movement, split from one of the major parties. The rise of the Australian Democrats from 1977 indicated a second phase in which the dominant minor party was a centrist party espousing the virtues of checking and balancing executive power. By 2004, this phase was coming to an end as the Australian Democrats lost votes and seats while being overtaken by much more ideological parties from the left – the Greens – and the various minor parties of the right, including One Nation. The rise of a set of more polarised and issues-oriented parties marks the third phase in the minor party system. The rise of issue-oriented and/or dogmatic political parties is a consequence of shifting voter alignments. This is where the decline in total support for the major political parties is particularly relevant, especially with regards to the contest for the Senate as this shift in voting alignments is having representational consequences.

Learning objective 3: Consider the role of independents in the Australian system

The ability of minor parties to win lower house seats is much more constrained by the electoral system. This applies to most of the lower houses in Australia, with the exception of Tasmania and the Australian Capital Territory. For independents, on the other hand, the chances of winning a seat in the lower house under a single-member electoral district system are better than the state-wide challenge of running for the Senate. This is particularly the case in electoral districts that might be otherwise considered very safe for the major parties. For independents, a strong sense of voter disillusion with the major parties is the key to representational success, but this disillusionment may not extend to the independent supporting governments or policies at odds with the preferences of the electorate. Unfortunately, an independent's power, whether at the state or federal level, is generally constrained to representing their district's interests in parliament and to ministers, and only in rare instances may they be called upon to adjudicate the formation of government.

DISCUSSION QUESTIONS

1. To what extent are minor parties an expression of voter disillusionment with the major parties? Is this reflected more in the vote or in the rate of party formation?

2. What are the most important drivers for minor parties' formation?

3. What are the explanations for successful independent candidates? Where has the greatest incidence of independent success occurred, and what are the reasons for that?

4. Are minor parties a reflection of a healthy democracy?

5. Do minor parties undermine good government?

FURTHER READING

Gauja, A. (2016). *Political Parties and Elections: Legislating for Representative Democracy*, Abingdon: Routledge.

Ghazarian, Z. (2015). *The Making of a Party System: Minor Parties in the Australian Senate*, Melbourne: Monash University Publishing.

Manning, P. (2019). *Inside the Greens: The Origins and the Future of the Party, the People and the Politics*, Carlton: Black Inc.

Miragliotta, N., Gauja, A. & Smith, R. (eds). (2015). *Contemporary Australian Political Party Organisations*, Melbourne: Monash University Publishing.

REFERENCES

Bowler, S. & Denemark, D. (1993). Split ticket voting in Australia: Dealignment and inconsistent votes reconsidered. *Australian Journal of Political Science*, **28**(1), 19–37. https://doi.org/10.1080/00323269308402223

Brown, B. & Singer, P. (1996). *The Greens*, Melbourne: Text Publishing Company.

Cahill, D. & Brown, S. (2008). The rise and fall of the Australian Greens: The 2002 Cunningham by-election and its implications. *Australian Journal of Political Science*, **43**(2), 259–75. https://doi.org/10.1080/10361140802035770

Costar, B. (ed.). (1994). *For Better or for Worse: The Federal Coalition*, Carlton: Melbourne University Press.

—— (2012). Seventeen days to power: Making a minority government. In M. Simms and J. Wanna (eds), *Julia 2010: The Caretaker Election*, Canberra: ANU Press.

—— (2015). The National Party: The resilient party. In N. Miragliotta, A. Gauja & R. Smith (eds), *Contemporary Australian Political Organisations*, Clayton: Monash University Press, pp. 24–36.

Costar, B. & Woodward, D. (eds). (1985). *Country to National: Australian Rural Politics and Beyond*, Sydney: Allen & Unwin.

Cunningham, C. & Jackson, S. (2014). Leadership and the Australian Greens. *Leadership*, **10**(4), 496–511. https://doi.org/10.1177/1742715013498407

Davey, P. (2010). *Ninety Not Out: The Nationals 1920–2010*, Sydney: UNSW Press.

Economou, N. (2001). The regions in ferment? The politics of regional and rural disenchantment. *Alternative Law Journal*, **26**(2), 69–74. https://doi.org/10.1177/1037969X0102600204

—— (2016). Electoral reform and party system volatility: The consequences of the group vote ticket on Australian senate elections. *Australasian Parliamentary Review*, **31**(1), 117–30.

—— (2021). Kicking against the majority. In A. Harkness and R. White (eds), *Crossroads of Rural Crime*, Bingley: Emerald Publishing Limited, pp. 135–47.

Economou, N. & Ghazarian, Z. (2008). *Vale the Australian Democrats: Organisational failure and electoral decline*. Paper presented at the Australian Political Studies Association Conference, Brisbane.

Gauja, A. (2010). Evaluating the success and contribution of a minor party: The case of the Australian Democrats. *Parliamentary Affairs*, **63**(3), 486–503. https://doi.org/10.1093/pa/gsp055

Gauja, A. & Jackson, S. (2016). Australian Greens party members and supporters: Their profiles and activities. *Environmental Politics*, **25**(2), 359–79.

Ghazarian, Z. (2012). The changing type of minor party elected to parliament: The case of the Australian Senate from 1949 to 2010. *Australian Journal of Political Science*, **47**(3), 441–54. https://doi.org/10.1080/10361146.2012.704007

Graham, B.D. (1966). *The Formation of the Australian Country Parties*, Canberra: ANU Press.

Grant, Z.P. & Tilley, J. (2019). Fertile soil: Explaining variation in the success of Green parties. *West European Politics*, **42**(3), 495–516. https://doi.org/10.1080/01402382.2018.1521673

Grattan, C.H. (1941). Australia's new Labour government. *Current History*, **1**(4), 333–9.

Green, A. (2018). The Senate results. In A. Gauja, P. Chen, J. Curtin and J. Pietsch (eds), *Double Dissolution: the 2016 Australian Federal Election*, Canberra: ANU Press, pp. 185–210.

Harris, T. (2010). Regulating the Greens: Federal electoral laws and the emergence of Green parties in the 1980s and 1990s. *Labour History*, **99**(1), 71–6.

Haward, M. & Smith, G. (1990). The 1989 Tasmanian election: The green independents consolidate. *Australian Journal of Political Science*, **25**(2), 196–217. https://doi.org/10.1080/00323269008402118

Holloway, J. (2019). *Measuring Minor Party Impact: The Australian Greens in a Changing Party System*. (Doctor of Philosophy), Bedford Park, SA, Flinders University, College of Business, Government and Law. Retrieved from https://www.researchgate.net/profile/Josh-Holloway/publication/334107931_Measuring_Minor_Party_Impact_The_Australian_Greens_in_a_Changing_Party_System/links/5d16f949a6fdcc2462ae9bc1/Measuring-Minor-Party-Impact-The-Australian-Greens-in-a-Changing-Party-System.pdf

Jackson, S. (2016). *The Australian Greens: From Activism to Australia's Third Party*, Melbourne: Melbourne University Publishing.

JSCEM. (2014). *Interim Report on the Inquiry into the Conduct of the 2013 Federal Election: Senate Voting Practices*. Canberra: Parliament of the Commonwealth of Australia.

Kefford, G. (2017). Rethinking small political parties: From micro to peripheral. *Australian Journal of Political Science*, **52**(1), 95–109. https://doi.org/10.1080/10361146.2016.1246650

Kernot, C. & Walters, T. (1995). The Democrats and an alliance. In R. Leach (ed.), *The Alliance Alternative in Australia: Beyond Labor and Liberal*, Annandale: Catalyst Press, pp. 154–74.

Kiernan, K. (1990). I saw my temple ransacked. In C. Pybus and R. Flanagan (eds), *The Rest of the World is Watching*, Chippendale: Pan Macmillan.

Kingston, M. (2012). How Abbott funded the fight against One Nation, *New Matilda*. Retrieved from https://newmatilda.com/2012/12/10/how-abbott-funded-fight-against-one-nation/

Kitschelt, H. (1989). *The Logics of Party Formation: Ecological Politics in Belgium and West Germany*, Ithaca: Cornell University Press.

Lines, W.J. (2006). *Patriots: Defending Australia's Natural Heritage*, St Lucia: University of Queensland Press.

Lovelock, L. (2009). The declining membership of the NSW Legislative Council cross bench and its implications for responsible government. *Australasian Parliamentary Review*, **24**(1), 82–95.

Maddox, G. (1996). *Australian Democracy in Theory and Practice*, 3rd edn, South Melbourne: Longman.

Manning, H. (2002). The Australian Greens and the handicap of left legacies. *Australian Quarterly*, **74**(3), 17–40.

Manning, P. (2019). *Inside the Greens: The Origins and Future of the Party, the People and the Politics*, Carlton: Black Inc.

Manwaring, R. (2020). The Australian Labor Party. In A. Gauja, S. Marian and M. Simms (eds), *Morrison's Miracle: The Australian Federal Election*, Canberra: ANU Press, pp. 277–93.

Mayer, H. (1980). Big party chauvinism and minor party romanticism. In H. Nelson and H. Mayer (eds), *Australian Politics: A Fifth Reader*, Melbourne: Longman Cheshire, pp. 345–60.

McSwiney, J. & Cottle, D. (2017). Unintended consequences: One Nation and neoliberalism in contemporary Australia. *Journal of Australian Political Economy*, (79), 87–106.

Millar, T.B. (1981). Conservatives triumph on a slender base. *The Round Table*, **71**(281), 44–8. https://doi.org/10.1080/00358538108453499

Miragliotta, N. (2006). One party, two traditions: Radicalism and pragmatism in the Australian Greens. *Australian Journal of Political Science*, **41**(4), 585–96. https://doi.org/10.1080/10361140600959791

Miragliotta, N. & Jackson, S. (2015). Green parties in federal systems: Resistant or compliant to centralizing pressures? *Government and Opposition*, **50**(4), 549–77. https://doi.org/10.1017/gov.2014.21

Moore, T. (2019). Once as tragedy and again as farce: Hansonism, backlashers, and economic nationalism after 20 years. In B. Grant, T. Moore and T. Lynch (eds), *The Rise of Right-Populism*, Singapore: Springer.

Neighbour, S. (2012). Divided we fall. *The Monthly*, (Feb 2012), 20–8.

Rogers, E. (2010). Greens seek to capitalise on voter frustration, *ABC News*, 1 August. Retrieved from https://www.abc.net.au/news/2010-08-01/greens-seek-to-capitalise-on-voter-frustration/927818

Sharman, C. (1999). The representation of small parties and independents in the Senate. *Australian Journal of Political Science*, **34**(3), 353–61. https://doi.org/10.1080/10361149950272

Sharman, C., Sayers, A. & Miragliotta, N. (2002). Trading party preferences: The Australian experience of preferential voting. *Electoral Studies*, **21**(4), 543–60.

Siaroff, A. (2003). Two-and-a-half-party systems and the comparative role of the half. *Party Politics*, **9**(3), 267–90. https://doi.org/10.1177/1354068803009003001

Smith, R.K. (2006). *Against the Machines: Minor Parties and Independents in New South Wales, 1910–2006*, Canberra: Federation Press.

Spindler, S. (2005). Senate safeguard: Come back! We didn't mean it! [The development of third party politics in Australia.]. *Dissent*, (19), 51–4.

Vallentine, J. & Jones, P.D. (1990). *Quakers in Politics, Pragmatism Or Principle?* Alderley: Margaret Fell Quaker Booksellers and Publishers.

Warhurst, J. (1997). *Keeping the Bastards Honest: The Australian Democrats' First Twenty Years*, St Leonards: Allen & Unwin.

Warner, K. (2003). Sentencing review 2002–2003. *Criminal Law Review*, **27**(6), 325–40.

CHAPTER 10
FOLLOW THE LEADER
Political leadership in Australia

LEARNING OBJECTIVES

After reading this chapter, you should be able to:

1. Understand the tension between leadership and liberal democracy
2. Recall some of the theoretical debates on leadership and the importance of leaders
3. Explain the different arenas leaders work in and the different skills they require
4. Summarise the debate about Australia's 'leadership problem'
5. Describe the leadership gender gap and some of the methods employed to remedy this

INTRODUCTION

POLITICAL LEADERSHIP: Leadership involves more than occupying a leadership position; it is the capacity to take and build support for difficult policy decisions by motivating followers.

In a democracy the people are said to lead. And yet within Australia's liberal democracy, the people elect individuals to represent them. This sets up a unique role for **POLITICAL LEADERSHIP**. Ideally, a collaborative leadership results in a democracy in which all citizens are given the opportunity to participate and vote, ideas are exchanged freely, and policy debate encouraged. This democratic process ensures citizen participation and the election of representatives who lead in line with the majority. But is it these representatives who lead the people the most important part of the political process or, alternatively, are the institutional and structural contexts in which leaders work the key determinant of success and failure? This question has long been debated in political science and scholars have sought to understand the relationship between actors and the agency they possess and how structures shape, mould and bend to the will of actors. Debates about leadership churn are especially relevant in Australia given the number of political leaders that were replaced in the decade following the 2007 federal election.

While questions about leadership can appear abstract at first, understanding the friction between leadership and liberal democracy provides scholars and students with a deeper grasp of our institutional setup. Hence, questions about whether it really matters who the leaders of the major parties are, or even the prime minister, are not merely theoretical or philosophical pursuits. In considering political leadership in Australia, this chapter begins by considering the tension that exists between leaders in liberal democracies and the democratic institutions they work within. It then outlines some of the theories about leaders and leadership. It goes on to investigate and discuss Australian political leadership by considering the different types of political leadership in Australia. This extends beyond the parties and includes the bureaucracy, interest groups and non-governmental organisations (NGOs). Following this, debates about recent leadership failure and supposed 'poor leaders' in Australia will take place. This chapter also deals with questions related to structure and **AGENCY** as well as the political leadership gender gap in Australia.

AGENCY: The ability of social actors to act freely and independently. Social scientists debate the extent to which agency is restricted by context and structure – by the institutions and processes which define social roles. This is usually called the 'structure/agency' problem.

LEADERSHIP AND DEMOCRACY

Is it possible to both lead and be a representative of the people? This seemingly simple question goes to the central conundrum for political leaders in liberal democracies. They are meant to represent electorates, parties and nations by acting as the delegate for these different groups with disparate interests, but they are also required to demonstrate their initiative and capacity to drive political and policy progress. While not impossible, the tension between the need to represent and to lead are often incompatible. This explains many of the problems that leaders in liberal democracies face. Indeed, when we think about what democracy means, this problem is further illustrated. Democracy literally means rule by the people and 'democracy is about an autonomous **DEMOS** governing itself as a collective, which entails that rulers who control the coercive power of the state need to be constrained' (Hendriks and Karsten 2014, 41).

DEMOS: Effectively refers to the population of a democratic state and was used to refer to the citizens of the Ancient Greek states.

While there are alternatives, such as rule by an elite few (aristocracy) or the rule by an individual with absolute power (autocracy), it has long been accepted that democracy is the best of the options available – as famously stated by Winston Churchill: 'Indeed it has been said that democracy is the worst form of Government except for all those other forms that have been tried from time to time …' Moreover, many studies in related fields, such as management and education, claim democratic leadership to be the most effective form (Gastil 1994). Yet combining popular rule with organisational structures to maintain the social and political order that allows nations to try to resolve complex problems is extremely challenging. Democratic leadership is therefore inherently problematic, as how can societies be simultaneously governed by the people and by their leaders? Indeed, this reveals the difference between modern representative or liberal democracy and earlier types of democracy. In its original Athenian form, democracy involved the direct participation of a small number (500) of male citizens in their government. However, today's democracy is more often understood as rule by the people's representatives and is marked by popular elections, political parties and parliamentary representation. Like elsewhere, these are the institutions and processes that characterise the Australian political system.

According to Kane and Patapan (2012, 14), leadership has often been overlooked by scholars and students of democracy, and 'inherent in this neglect is the suspicion that leadership, if inevitable, is inevitably "elitist"'. This is particularly prescient for a number of reasons. First, considering the focus on freedom or liberty in liberal democracies this suspicion is, in part, understandable. Liberal democracies like to compare themselves to authoritarian regimes to highlight how good their citizens have it. Second, the rise of various populist parties and movements around the globe have shown that this suspicion is felt strongly by many voters who espouse democratic but illiberal values. This means that these voters may support democracy, but they seek greater direct influence over decisions by the 'people', who they perceive to have been shut out of the decision-making (Mudde and Kaltwasser 2014, 385).

The tension between leadership and democracy and how this tension should be resolved has been an endless source of debate by political scientists and philosophers. Kane and Patapan (2012, 15) suggest that 'democratic theory since 1915 can be interpreted as a variety of attempts to affirm, modify, or transcend what Robert Michels then described as the iron law of oligarchy'. Michel's (1962) thesis is that all organisations, including those with democratic ideals, will inevitably become dominated by a few elites. Other theorists have sought to redefine liberal democracy as not rule by the people but elite rule with public approval (Schumpeter 1961, 246). But this particular view inverts the logic of representative democracy. It rejects the suggestion that voters choose a parliament which, in turn, chooses and holds leaders accountable. Instead, leaders are thought to manufacture public opinion and shape the electoral choices voters will make.

While these approaches show that there are a variety of theories about how leadership and democracy shape one another, they generally consign voters to the passive role of bystanders. This is a step too far for those who emphasise the importance of the participation of citizens in their government in so far as this is possible in a complex, diverse society such as Australia's. In a representative democracy, voters must be able to determine who governs, both by electing representatives to parliament to form and then hold governments accountable and – in between elections – by actively participating via grassroots activism in various units of civil society, through expressing their views in opinion polls, surveys, petitions or via social media. Leadership is absolutely necessary in all of these processes and forums as will be discussed in the rest of the chapter. However, the tension between these leaders and those who are led are as acutely felt in these organisations as they are in society as a whole.

SHORT-ANSWER QUESTIONS 10.1

1. In what ways is there a tension inherent within liberal democracy in regard to political leadership?

2. In what ways have we seen more direct forms of democracy used recently in Australia and what impact did that have on the parliamentary leaders?

Suggested responses are available at www.cambridge.org/highereducation/isbn/9781009108232/resources

THE EXECUTIVE AND THE SEPARATION OF POWERS IN AUSTRALIA

By convention, the prime minister is accepted as the leader of Australia. However, this role is not recognised by the Constitution. Instead, our sovereign is the Queen of England who forms the head of executive by appointing and then delegating these functions to the Governor-General (Section 61 of the constitution). The Governor-General, in turn, is selected by the prime minister, who advises the sovereign to make this appointment. The Governor-General represents the Queen as head of executive government and acts as advised by the Federal Executive Council. So, by convention, the Governor-General should in all matters act as advised by the prime minister and ministers. Nevertheless, the Governor-General has reserve powers to act independently in emergencies, though the extent of these powers and the way they should be exercised are not agreed on. While these powers have not been exercised fully, the sovereign may disallow an Act of Parliament. Outside of these exceptional circumstances, in practice, the sovereign's role remains largely ceremonial as the Head of State. **THE WHITLAM DISMISSAL**, however, showed the extreme outcomes the exercise of this form of power may have (see Chapter 5). These constitutional complexities raise the fundamental question: who *really* is the leader of Australia?

In a parliamentary system, the prime minister is the senior-most member of Cabinet in the executive of government. In Australia, they are the leader of the party which has the support of the most members of the House of Representatives. The prime minister is sworn in by the Governor-General as a Minister of State to become, in practice, the head of the executive government. The prime minister chairs Cabinet, which is composed of senior ministers who each administer a significant government department. Like the prime minister, the Cabinet is also not recognised in the Constitution, and yet in practice, Cabinet is the heart of the executive government making all major policy and legislative proposals. This raises important issues around the nature of executive power in Australia and its role in leading the nation.

The roles of the 'leader' of a nation are not just internal, such as leading political parties and ministries. Externally they are the sovereign representative of the State. In Australia, this important leadership role is shared by the prime minister, the foreign minister and the official Head of State, the Governor-General. These offices lead the nation in international affairs, foreign policy and even in making the determination of when and where to lead the nation into war.

As outlined in Chapter 4, the executive is the arm of government that implements, enforces and administers the law. The executive powers of government in Australia have been steadily growing in the last two decades, which means an expansion of leadership roles as well. Some suggest this corresponds to a decline in parliamentary power, such as oversight and law-making. The most important reasons why there has been an increase in executive powers has been the focus on border security and control issues, such as the highly politicised issue of asylum seekers

THE WHITLAM DISMISSAL: Also known as the 1975 Australian constitutional crisis, refers to the dismissal of Prime Minister Gough Whitlam of the Australian Labor Party by Governor-General Sir John Kerr, who then commissioned the leader of the opposition, Malcolm Fraser of the Liberal Party, as caretaker prime minister.

arriving by sea and combatting terrorism in the post-9/11 world. This has expanded the role of the Australian Security Intelligence Agency (ASIO), the Australian Federal Police and the Minister of Home Affairs, among others. These developments raise fundamental concerns about the sufficiency of checks and balances on abuses of executive power in Australia. As expressed by Robert French AC (2018, 16):

> Non-statutory executive power, sourced directly from the Constitution, engenders particular anxiety because it is not easy to attach to it justiciable constraints of the kind that can be derived from the text, subject matter and purpose of a statutory grant of power.

As warned by Prasser (2012, 48) 'the growing proportion of parliamentarians serving in executive government roles ... threaten the independence of parliament, reduce its capability to scrutinise executive government and undermine Westminster notions of accountability'.

At the core of the Westminster approach to responsible government 'is the relationship between the executive and a sovereign parliament, reinforced by the authority of independent courts to resolve disputes over the lawfulness of executive action and the meaning of legislation' (Saunders 2013). While Australia has incorporated important institutional structures from the Washington system, we have Ministers of State drawn from the parliament that firmly ties the executive to the legislature. This forms the unique separation of powers through a range of 'checks and balances' within our political system that limit the power of each of the three branches of government (legislature, executive and judiciary). In his book *The Spirit of Laws* (1748), Montesquieu enunciated this idea, arguing that if any two powers are combined in the same arm of government it may lead to a tyrannical exercise of power and jeopardise the liberty of the people. However, the Constitution does not strictly maintain the separation between legislative and executive power, and the High Court has allowed the executive to be invested with the power to make delegated legislation such as regulations.

The dangers of executive power overstepping its bounds was expressed by Sir Owen Dixon in a landmark High Court case *Australian Communist Party v Commonwealth* (1951, 187) where he held:

> History and not only ancient history, shows that in countries where democratic institutions have been unconstitutionally superseded, it has been done not seldom by those holding the executive power.

Operation Fortitude provides a recent example of the potential for such executive overreach in civilian affairs. This called for a 'coalition of the willing' named by Australian Border Force (2015) who would be placed 'at various locations around the Melbourne CBD speaking with any individual we cross paths with' warning that 'if you commit visa fraud, you should know it's only a matter of time before you are caught' (ABF 2015). The operation was cancelled after public protests because of the obvious dangers for racial profiling, but as Triggs (2015) questioned, the various state and federal executive agencies never asked whether such an operation was consistent with Australian liberties or constitutional protections.

Another example is the worrying expansion of ASIO powers. For example, Amendments to the *Australian Security Intelligence Organisation Act 1979* sought to weaken a range of common law protections such as the questioning of minors (as young as 14), the rights of legal advisers, and permitting individual tracking. For some, such examples highlight the need for a legislated charter of rights (see Triggs 2015; Barns 2020). This is doubly important when viewed against the lack of any constitutional provisions for executive offices like the prime minister and Cabinet and the potentially dangerous reliance on convention to protect against executive overreach. In fact, the system largely relies on the personal leadership style acting in conformity with convention to ensure responsible government.

THEORISING POLITICAL LEADERSHIP

The theoretical literature on political leadership is incredibly diverse. It traverses a variety of areas in political science with little consensus on why and how leaders are important. Nonetheless, there are a number of theories which are helpful in unpacking the opaque nature of leadership in liberal democracies. One such theory comes from Heywood (2013, 301–3), who suggests leadership can be understood in four ways: as a natural gift, as a sociological phenomenon, an organisational necessity and as a political skill. The idea that leadership is a natural gift is an ancient premise that men, as they all were at this time, were born with some special attributes that allowed them to change the course of history. Very few, if any, social scientists would still subscribe to such a view, which would be seen as simplistic as it underestimates the institutions, history and social forces that shape political contexts. As Heywood notes (2013, 302), from this perspective leaders 'do not so much impose their will on the world as act as a vehicle through which historical forces are exerted'. Hence, the personalities of individuals are not as important as the conditions these leaders find themselves working in.

A more instrumental view of leadership is to view it simply as a necessity that needs to be met. In this view, leadership is part of bureaucratic politics and the more complex and bureaucratic that politics becomes, the more that leaders and leadership will be required. The final theory of leadership, that it is a political skill, suggests that leadership is something that can be learned, whereby leaders can try to use their personality as well as the resources available to them to convince others of their position and to drive political and policy outcomes. Whichever we think best describes leadership, it is evident that attempts to create theoretical models are likely to be contested.

Nineteenth and early 20th century German sociologist and philosopher Max Weber asked in what circumstances followers accept the authority of leaders. He concluded that authority takes three pure forms:

1. Traditional authority derives from tradition and custom, such as monarchs
2. Rational-legal authority attaches to office
3. Charismatic authority attaches to an individual who, through sheer force of personality, commands the loyalty and trust of others who follow him/her because they believe in them. (Weber 1978, 226–45)

Weber understood that, in practice, leaders possess overlapping kinds of authority. A prime minister will have a formal-legal authority, such as the right to convene Cabinet meetings, appoint ministers and call elections. But the authority and the loyalty they command may also derive from their personal charm and have a charismatic component. Moreover, one form of authority might morph into another.

Given the rise of populism across many liberal democracies, it is important to note the dangers Weber noted with charismatic leaders. He said that if the leader's charisma is accompanied by accountability to parliament, it is likely to ensure its autonomy via political parties and also the bureaucracy. However, as stated by Pakulski and Higley (2008) where this does not occur 'there is either a "passive" democracy controlled by professional politicians and bureaucrats or a volatile "plebiscitary" democracy' (see Pakulski and Higley 2008, 47 citing Weber 1978,1460) – then the dangers for unconstrained leadership may result.

One popular approach to understanding leadership has been to focus on the traits of individual leaders. This trait-centred approach looks to the characteristics of the individual leader to predict leadership style and quality or effectiveness. Typically, it is a top-down approach to leadership, examining the individual leader's power, skills, charisma and persuasion to inspire their followers. However, many studies have been unable to identify a common, agreed set of attributes to determine a good leader (see Stogdill 1948). Indeed, some of the most effective and popular leaders have been facilitation centred. Such leaders push things forward as part of the group having followers agree to goals, direction and change. Moreover, the GLOBE project (2020) has revealed how notions of effective or desirable leadership traits are linked to culture, with Australians valuing a 'captain-coach' approach consistent with the idea of 'mateship' (BTLi 2011).

Other approaches suggest that a successful leader's characteristics is one relevant to the demands of the leadership situation, rather than their individual traits. As an example, Burns (1978) distinguished between transactional and transformational leaders. Transactional leaders are leaders who exchange tangible reward/s for the work and loyalty of followers. It is a managerial style of leadership devoted to securing and retaining power, using directives and creating dependency. Transactional leaders motivate followers by appealing to their self-interest – compliance is achieved through a mix of reward and punishment. Prime ministers who offer voters tangible benefits such as tax cuts or subsidies for their support, or who reward their party room supporters with ministerial positions are exercising transactional political leadership.

In contrast, transformational leaders enhance the motivation and engagement of followers by directing their behaviour toward a shared vision/goal, causing wider changes in individuals and social systems. Burns (1978, 4) considered that transformational leadership involves processes (rather than a series of discrete transactions) in which 'leaders and followers raise one another to higher levels of motivation and morality'. Transformational leadership is characteristic of periods of challenge and reform where the opportunity exists for a leader's intellectual, moral and heroic capacities to impact the solution of larger societal problems.

PRIME MINISTERS AND POWER

Prime ministers, as the most well-known face of political leadership in Australia, have received significant academic scrutiny. While this literature has a number of dimensions, one important theoretical and empirical debate is about whether the capacity of political leaders to 'get their way' and to lead with little interference from colleagues and institutions has increased. While there has been much written in recent decades about how and why leaders may have more power or authority than they once had, Bennister (2008, 336–7) argues that:

> In contrast to the burgeoning study of leadership in other disciplines, political science has been slow to make systemic analyses of political leadership. The keenness of scholars to concentrate on institutions and structures has led to a downplaying of the role of leadership. Prime Ministers, in particular, are viewed as constrained actors, dependent and contingent.

SPOTLIGHT 10.1 PM SCOTT MORRISON AS TRANSACTIONAL LEADER

Here, leadership theory from Max Weber and James McGregor Burns is used to analyse leadership in Australian federal politics by focusing on the current prime minister, Scott Morrison, and his use of transactional leadership in response to the COVID-19 crisis.

The beginning of 2020 was calamitous for Australia: catastrophic bushfires, drought, and the global outbreak of COVID-19. Scott Morrison had been named the 'Miracle Man' because of his Pentecostal faith and after winning an unlikely 2019 election. He had been heralded as a pragmatist, focused on delivery, and a master of political spin. In distinction to some of the more recent prime ministers like Gillard or Turnbull who aspired to be more transformational, Morrison was transactional. Morrison said, 'You get things done by mobilising large numbers of people to do things, to go in the direction you're seeking to take them. That's what the job is' (quoted in Williams 2020). In a comment made to Senator Xenophon, he was even more blunt: 'I'm purely transactional' (quoted in Murphy 2020).

Yet across January 2020, Morrison was under mounting public pressure over his handling of the bushfires, forced to release a public statement of 'regret' for his actions in taking leave to Hawaii during the climate emergency (Remeikis 2019). The hashtag #ResignMorrison trended on Twitter. Things worsened as the COVID-19 pandemic spread. There was a $60 billion black hole in government costings and he officially abandoned the disastrous Robodebt program that faced a Federal Court challenge.

Initially, Morrison rejected COVID-19 lockdown measures and seemed to abdicate federal responsibilities for quarantine, a federal power under the Constitution. Instead, Morrison created the National Cabinet to increase influence with the states and premiers. This was a new paradigm, creating a more centralised authority that has been credited with effectiveness by sharing the capacities of the Commonwealth and the states to combat COVID-19 (Saunders 2020, 1). However, it has also been criticised as a form of executive federalism, allowing it to make political decisions with little legislative oversight and lack of accountability. Different policies on state border closures and lockdowns have exposed the tensions in Australia's Federation and the lack of nationally consistent, designated quarantine facilities has shown the problems of relying on the private sector for public health.

The most contentious issue, however, has been the slow national vaccination role out. Here, the limitations of transactional leadership have been revealed. Originally, reliance was placed on procuring enough doses of AstraZeneca and a locally developed University of Queensland (UQ) vaccine – both of which could be manufactured in Australia. However, in the highly competitive international environment, Morrison's transactional powers had very little purchase and he was unable to obtain requisite amounts of the vaccine, being effectively boxed out of the market by Australia's allies the United States and the United Kingdom. The UQ trials were unsuccessful. Morrison's skills of spin also caused undue public confusion when in an April 2021 address on the potential for blood clots if taking AstraZeneca seemed to contradict the entire national plan. In light of the numerous transactional failures, the official national targets changed dozens of times, causing further uncertainty.

QUESTIONS

What are the benefits and limitations of transactional leadership? Which contemporary leaders of Australia have shown transformational or transactional leadership?

This has certainly been true of how leaders, but specifically prime ministers, have been viewed in Australia. But these debates are not new. In fact, they have a long and storied history. Within Westminster parliamentary democracies, this can be traced back to debates in the United Kingdom that considered whether cabinet government remained an accurate description of how the executive functioned. Critics contended that, in fact, a better description was prime ministerial government (Bennister 2008, 337; Honeyman 2007, 4; Crossman 1963). These debates continued for decades in Westminster settings, but two important theoretical contributions have emerged since. The first of these is known as **PERSONALISATION**, while the second is referred to as **PRESIDENTIALISATION**.

While these will be discussed in more detail in the section that follows, it is worth considering the language we use to describe governments. It has now become commonplace that when we talk about Australian federal governments, that we refer to them as the 'Rudd Government', the 'Abbott Government' or the 'Turnbull Government'. By doing this, we are assigning the success and failure of these governments to the prime minister and the leader of one of the major parties. In one way, this makes sense as the responsibility stops at the top, or at least it should. However, it also simplifies the complexity of the system, the way parties and parliament work. Depending on who you ask, this may or may not matter, but it is a simplification of some of the features of the personalisation debate, which is where we will now turn.

PERSONALISATION:
A theory that suggests that individual political actors have become more prominent at the expense of political parties and other collective actors.

PRESIDENTIALISATION:
A theory that suggests that the expanding powers of the office, the media attention they command, and their pivotal place in election campaigns has seen prime ministers accrue a now considerable authority and autonomy.

REFLECTION QUESTIONS 10.1

1. How much authority and control do you think prime ministers have in Cabinet meetings and over their Cabinet colleagues?
2. Why do you think we refer to governments that consist of the members of one or more political parties as the 'Howard Government' or the 'Rudd Government'? What are the impacts of this?

Response prompts are available at www.cambridge.org/highereducation/isbn/9781009108232/resources

A PERSONALISED OR PRESIDENTIAL POLITICS?

Explanations vary widely about the causes of personalisation. However, the media is generally seen as central. According to McAllister (2007), 'the electronic media have been seen as crucial in shaping the way that governments communicate with voters and seek to convert them; at the same time, party leaders have exploited their exposure in the electronic media in order to attract votes'. While there is considerable debate about it (Karvonen 2010), a weakening of the major parties is often seen as contributing to personalisation, the effect of which is said to be that potential leaders will attempt to build a support base outside the party as well as within it. Most important in this regard was the evolution of the media landscape and this starts with the rise of television. From the 1960s onward television gave a new prominence – and new political opportunities – to leaders. But the media is no magic bullet and broader changes to democratic politics and our societies also need to be considered. Indeed, in the view of McAllister, 'whatever the importance of the media in this process, no single explanation accounts for the increasing personalisation of politics in democratic societies' (McAllister 2007, 573).

While related to the idea of personalisation, presidentialisation goes much further (Kefford 2013; Dowding 2013a; 2013b). According to Poguntke and Webb (2005, 1), presidentialisation describes circumstances in which leaders acquire more resources and autonomy within the institutional parameters of their regime. Poguntke and Webb (2005) perceived that this process has three distinct faces: the executive face, the party face and the electoral face. In their view, each 'revolves around the tension between political parties and individual leaders' (Poguntke and Webb 2005, 7). The crux of the claim is that prime ministers have accumulated presidential-like powers in that they can govern over or around their Cabinet and party. Thus, the executive face of presidentialisation is supposedly apparent in the expansion of the Department of Prime Minister and Cabinet as well as an array of advisers working in close contact with the prime minister. Some have argued that the formation of the National Cabinet in 2020 is such an example of presidentialisation (Tulich et al. 2020). The party face of presidentialisation involves a shifting balance of power within parties to the advantage of leaders and can be seen in the political leverage prime ministers today have because they carry extra responsibility to sell their party to voters. The electoral face of presidentialisation is evident in the pivotal role that party leaders have in modern-day election campaigns; in the ready-made opportunity they have to speak directly to voters, which flows from the focus that news media give to leaders; and the increasing tendency for voters to rely upon their perceptions of leaders in choosing which party to support at the ballot box.

Not all political scientists agree that parliamentary politics has become presidentialised. There are after all fundamental structural differences between presidential and parliamentary systems. Tiffen (2017, 155) points out that in Australia 'party leadership is, first of all and inescapably, leadership of the party room, of a relatively small group of MPs'. Relations in the closed party room are 'crucial to the leader's survival'. The circumstances of presidents are very different. They are directly elected by voters, which can be advantageous but have the problem of dealing with a legislature that they often have little control over. Compare this to a prime minister in Australia, who will already have control of the House of Representatives, and this is why many scholars argue that prime ministers are more powerful than presidents already, so describing the phenomenon as presidentialisation is misleading (Dowding 2013b). There are many dimensions to this debate, and they are hotly contested. Their importance is that they allow us to think about the ways that political actors respond to incentives in the Australian political system, and the ways that norms develop and are abandoned.

SHORT-ANSWER QUESTIONS 10.2

1. What campaigning techniques do political parties use which personalise politics?
2. What campaigning techniques do political parties use that reduce the level of personalisation?

Suggested responses are available at www.cambridge.org/highereducation/isbn/9781009108232/resources

NO, PRIME MINISTER

In considering the ways that political leaders exercise power, James Walter and Paul Strangio (2007) investigated five Australian prime ministers seeking to explain the growing importance of the office. Their study examined the (different) leadership styles of Whitlam, Fraser, Hawke, Keating and Howard and sheds light on what distinguishes leadership from holding office. Their analysis also draws attention to long-term structural factors that explain the growing importance of prime ministers – factors such as the growing web of ministerial advisers, the expanding influence of the Commonwealth vis-á-vis the states, the politicisation of the public service and the changing nature of parties. They consider that democracies require both leaders who are able to provide the political community with direction and the support of robust institutions including advisers and an independent public service able to say 'no, prime minister' along with an effective opposition able to provide alternative policy advice.

One maxim often repeated in the large literature on leadership is that 'the most effective leaders surround themselves with the right people' (Rath and Conchie 2008, 2). Walter and Strangio (2007) also make this point. While the capacity of prime ministers to lead is shaped by institutional context and by their personality, style and skill, governing inescapably entails working with a wide range of other players. Prime ministers do not govern alone, and prime-ministerial leadership is always co-dependent on colleagues and followers. Their relationship with their party is a 'critical source of leadership empowerment and constraint' (Strangio, 't Hart and Walter 2013, 2–3). Put another way, the capacity of prime ministers to exercise the authority their office brings – their *agency* – is both enhanced and contained by *structure* and by their dependence on public servants, advisers, ministers and their party. This may seem contradictory; however, this is part of the chimerical nature of leadership and why successful leaders accrue and exercise power in different ways (Heifetz 2010, 16).

Ultimately, there are no recipes for success for Australian prime ministers. While there are some templates that are often cited, such as the way that John Howard or Bob Hawke managed their Cabinets, what works for one leader may not necessarily work for another. Prime ministers are dependent on their colleagues, the public service and those within their party. As leaders, prime ministers will not always have a determining influence on issues (Strangio, 't Hart and Walter 2013, 11). To further complicate matters, prime ministerial leadership is also conditional on the 'historical moment', on the political climate and current institutional conditions. For all their informal authority, style and skill, prime ministers may find themselves unable to exercise the leadership they would like (Strangio, 't Hart and Walter 2013, 9).

REFLECTION QUESTIONS 10.2

1. Do you agree with the critique that recent political leaders have not had a clearly articulated vision for the future of Australia?
2. Are contemporary political leaders constrained by globalisation and international economic conditions?

Response prompts are available at www.cambridge.org/highereducation/isbn/9781009108232/resources

POLITICAL LEADERSHIP IN AUSTRALIA

While parliamentary leaders, and especially prime ministers, are important and deserve significant attention, political leadership in Australia should never be seen simply as the purview of parliamentarians. Political leadership crosses cultural, social and economic lines and should not be seen as simply a top-down, hierarchical phenomena. Political leadership is evident in everyday grassroots politics within social movements, NGOs, interest groups and any number of other disparate units of civil society. Leadership is therefore not just about managing the people or institutions of the state.

Equally important to understand is that political leadership is not just about administration and decision-making by political elites behind closed doors. There is quite evidently a rhetorical aspect to political leadership. Structures and the institutional context are no doubt important but so is the capacity to use language to persuade, cajole and negotiate colleagues, political opponents as well as the citizenry.

It would be expected then that this broader view of what constitutes political leadership in Australia should be evident in any of the recent lists of Australia's greatest political leaders. However, disappointingly, in many of these, leadership is viewed through a very narrow prism. For example, one such list was devised by John Adams, former political adviser and public servant. In designing his list, Adams said he hoped to kick-start public debate about the nature of genuine leadership. Australia's 'current political class', he worried, were 'obsessed with obtaining and maintaining power', unprepared 'to lead and take significant political and personal risks', attached to 'deeply ideological agendas' which do not align with 'the pressing public policy concerns of the Australian people', and are addicted to 'hyper-partisan divide and conquer tactics'. In his view, great political figures show the qualities of personal courage, willingness to act in the public and national interest, leadership, foresight, and their tenure is marked by consistency and impact (Adams in Hildebrand 2017).

Adams' complaint about the dearth of leadership within Australia's political class will resonate with many. There is a deep disappointment with the current crop of political leaders, which is evident in the growing support for anti-establishment, outsider and protest parties. Yet his account has been criticised as lacking diversity (especially gender), as well as maintaining an overtly masculine and aggressive style of leadership in Australia (Davis, Musgrove and Smart 2011).

The reality is that political leadership is on display every day in public service departments and agencies, in non-government organisations and social movements, in Indigenous communities, and in bodies such as the Reserve Bank of Australia (which sets monetary policy at arm's length from the government of the day). Leadership is also highly visible within industry sectors, in trade unions and the business community. For example, governments have recruited business leaders to provide policy leadership such as David Gonski who was asked in 2010 to lead efforts to find a better model for school funding.

Parliament may be the institution from which our most visible political leaders emerge, but there are many who do not hold public office, with vision and influence, who are shaping and moulding Australia's future. Of course, there are also more concerted attempts by individual leaders and groups of leaders to influence politics via the interest groups they are a part of as well. The Business Council of Australia, comprising the CEOs of some 100 of Australia's largest companies, sets out to steer policy debate – to exercise leadership – across issues ranging from tax reform to remaking Australia's Federation. The Australian Council of Trade Unions similarly try to influence debate around industrial relations. Nonetheless, in asking what are the qualities that an effective political leader displays, it is important to consider the unique set of institutions they work in. Take, for example, the Aboriginal activist, leader and founder of the Cape York Institute for Policy and Leadership, Noel Pearson. Some of the methods that prime ministers or opposition leaders use, Pearson also uses, but he is free of the millstone of party and parliamentary representation. This provides Pearson with the capacity to utilise other sets of skills and to engage with a wider set of stakeholders.

In other instances, however, there is a distinct lack of institutions that stunt how leadership can emerge. Continuing with Indigenous politics, a key example is the dissolution of the Aboriginal and Torres Strait Islander Commission (ATSIC) and its lack of a suitable replacement. Established in 1989, ATSIC was intended to combine both representative and executive roles through an organisation of regional councils and a national board elected by Indigenous people. It was dissolved by Prime Minister Mr Howard in April 2004 – something he had championed since its foundation when he warned the body would 'create a black nation within the Australian nation' (cited in Pratt and Bennett, 2005). In its place the Howard Government created the National Indigenous Council comprised of distinguished Aboriginal people appointed by the government who would provide 'advice' on Indigenous affairs. This ended in 2008 without any replacement. This was a shift from self-determination and any meaningful institutions for representative of Indigenous leadership (see Bennett 1999, 66–7). So, despite the personal qualities of exemplary figures in Indigenous leadership (like Noel Pearson), structures supportive of representatives of the Indigenous community have been actively curtailed.

REFLECTION QUESTIONS 10.3

1. What are the skills or traits you think successful leaders should possess?
2. Are there any skills that political leaders in elected office require that political leaders outside of parliament do not need?

Response prompts are available at www.cambridge.org/highereducation/isbn/9781009108232/resources

CHALLENGES FOR POLITICAL LEADERS

If we accept that political leaders are an inevitable feature of representative democracy, the question then is what types of demands are placed on them. This is not just a theoretical or abstract pursuit. 'Political leaders in democracies face a multitude of demands, which are hard to reconcile' (Hendriks and Karsten 2014, 42). Prime ministers require the support of political parties to win regular elections and to secure the support of parliament for their legislative program. To retain this support, they may need to make decisions that reward their party supporters and that will not be seen as being in the wider public interest. For example, when Malcolm Turnbull replaced Tony Abbott as prime minister in 2015, it was widely anticipated that he would pursue some of the 'small' liberal policies with which he had previously advocated (such as introducing same-sex marriage and support for an emissions trading scheme to deal with climate change). But he was hamstrung by the need to placate a conservative bloc within the Liberal party room. Inevitably this weakened Turnbull's authority as prime minister and added to a growing public disillusionment with his leadership and also his government.

Another challenge for those leaders who work in the daily cut and thrust of Australian federal politics has been the ever-growing number of new players that have appeared in parliament. All recent prime ministers have had to deal with a Senate in which a historically large number of minor party and independent senators have been able to block legislation when they work together. Prime ministers have either been unable to legislate policies they had promised to introduce or been forced to engage in 'horse trading' to pass modified versions of laws they had initially proposed. In the view of many critics, this shows why the institutional structure of Australian politics no longer works the way it should as senators, some elected on tiny numbers of votes, should not dictate policy to the major parties who have received millions of votes. Leaving this to one side, the point is that political leadership, especially at times when there is a fragmentation in the political landscape, is hard. It requires expert negotiation skills and interpersonal skills. Moreover, the Westminster-inspired majoritarian politics, which has been dominant in Australia for decades, is largely incompatible with the new realities that leaders face.

Claims that political leaders are beholden to opinion polls has been presented as another challenge. In 2007 Kevin Rudd declared climate change 'the greatest, moral, economic and environmental challenge of our generation' (Van Onselen 2010). This was an appeal to Australians to put higher ideals and values ahead of narrow self-interest that James MacGregor Burns (1978) might recognise as an attempt at transformational leadership. And indeed, as prime minister, Rudd was able to convert lofty ideals into meaningful policy that would deal with climate change. Had Rudd been able to secure a Senate majority, worked harder to get a deal done with the Greens or even gone to a double dissolution election on the issue, events may have followed a different course. Instead, he was forced into a policy retreat, which proved especially damaging because of expectations raised by his earlier efforts at transformational leadership. Indeed, the harm to Rudd's public standing was such that his party colleagues would conclude that the Australian Labor Party's (ALP) best chance of retaining power lay in replacing him as party leader and prime minister.

Changing public opinion to support good policy is therefore not so easily done. Leaders will not always be able to bring their party or the electorate with them. They may not always be fairly or accurately reported in the media. When public opinion is polarised, they will inevitably face a trenchant opposition able to freely voice its concerns online and in the news media. Democracy itself can therefore create circumstances that prevent transformational leadership.

SHORT-ANSWER QUESTIONS 10.3

1. It has become commonplace to say that leading a major political party has never been harder. In what ways do you think this is correct?
2. In what ways have recent leaders of the major political parties used different parts of the media to connect with traditional and even new voters?

Suggested responses are available at www.cambridge.org/highereducation/isbn/9781009108232/resources

DOES AUSTRALIA HAVE A LEADERSHIP PROBLEM?

An election defeat in 2007 ended John Howard's (11 years, 267 days) tenure as prime minister. In the decade that followed, the prime ministership changed hands five times. Rudd, Gillard, Rudd again, Abbott and then Turnbull all held the office. Three of these – Rudd, Gillard and Abbott – were overthrown by their own party. In the entire previous century, this had occurred on just three occasions. More noteworthy still, in the politically turbulent decade following Howard's defeat, each major party removed an election-winning prime minister before they had completed a full term. Labor replaced Rudd in 2010 after two years and 76 days, and the Liberal Party of Australia replaced Abbott one year and 327 days into his first term. It appears that prime ministers today are indeed 'more vulnerable to being displaced by their own side' (Tiffen 2017, 2). If we look at the evidence in the state and Commonwealth parliaments between 1970 and 2016, the evidence suggests that leaders are viewed as dispensable – seemingly consistent with a democratic theory of leadership. Rather than being rejected by voters or allowed to retire, 68 of the 138 leaders who have headed major parties were overthrown by their colleagues (Tiffen 2017, 2).

R.G. Menzies' 16-year tenure as prime minister is unlikely to be matched. It is equally unlikely that we will ever again see a state premier stay in office as long as Tom Playford did in South Australia (from 1938 to 1965). Internal wars over the leadership of political parties and the prime ministership are not new. Similar battles were fought in the 1980s and 1990s on both sides of politics. In the ALP, Hawke and Keating fought for the leadership and the keys to the Lodge; while in the Liberal Party, Howard and Peacock were the central protagonists in the battle for the leadership. Today party leaders are more closely scrutinised by the news media and on social media, and their performance is routinely measured by opinion polling and low favourability ratings, encouraging both voters and their party room colleagues to question their leadership.

When a leadership challenge occurs, it has also become common for the media to report voters saying that they voted for the leader and their colleagues should not be able to replace them. Leaders will often invoke this direct relationship they share with voters too. For example, when Abbott was replaced by Turnbull he said, 'It's the people that hire, and frankly it's the people that should fire' (Bourke 2015). However, there are a few problems with this analysis. To begin with, this is not how liberal democracy works in a parliamentary system. But more than this, while voters might say this is their view at the time, longitudinal survey data tells us that when voters express why they voted the way they did, individual leaders usually fall well behind a long list of policy preferences. Hence, while we need to recognise that some voters do feel that they develop a bond with various leaders, it is equally important to recognise that the evidence suggests that whether voters like or are comfortable with a particular leader's style, does not determine the way they vote. Nonetheless, cutting down leaders, especially when it is seen as unnecessary, is unlikely to be rewarded by Australian voters.

RESEARCH QUESTIONS 10.1

Since 1949, when R.G. Menzies became prime minister, how many Australian prime ministers have, as Menzies eventually did, voluntarily retired from office? How many prime ministers lost office after being defeated in an election, and how many were removed by their own party? What does this tell you about prime ministerial leadership in Australia?

SPOTLIGHT 10.2 IS THE RECENT LEADERSHIP CHURN UNUSUAL?

Australia has been described as the 'coup capital of the democratic world' for the manner and the frequency that political leaders are replaced (Bryant 2015). But is this just hyperbole? Is the recent period all that different to earlier periods of Australian politics? See Table 10.1 for leadership changes from November 2007 to June 2021.

While it is hard to dispute that there have been a significant number of leadership changes, whether this period is unique is worth considering. One example in modern times has been the Liberal Party during the period that the Hawke and Keating governments were in power. After the Hawke-led ALP defeated the Fraser Government at the 1983 federal election, Andrew Peacock was elected as leader of the Liberal Party. He would subsequently be replaced by John Howard in 1985, who would then be replaced again by Andrew Peacock in 1989. In 1990 it was John Hewson's turn. By 1994, Alexander Downer was the leader. And then in 1995, Howard returned to lead the Liberal Party again. He would remain as leader till the defeat of

TABLE 10.1 LEADERSHIP CHURN IN CONTEMPORARY AUSTRALIAN POLITICS

DATE	AUSTRALIAN LABOR PARTY	LIBERAL–NATIONAL COALITION
29 Nov 2007		Brendan Nelson becomes leader of the Liberal Party and Opposition Leader following the 2007 election loss
3 Dec 2007	Kevin Rudd sworn in as PM after leading ALP to 2007 election victory	
15 Sept 2008		Malcolm Turnbull replaces Brendan Nelson as Opposition Leader
1 Dec 2009		Tony Abbott replaces Malcolm Turnbull as Opposition Leader
24 June 2010	Julia Gillard replaces Kevin Rudd as PM	
26 June 2013	Kevin Rudd replaces Julia Gillard as PM	
18 Sept 2013		Tony Abbott sworn in as PM after leading the Coalition to the 2013 election victory
13 Oct 2013	Bill Shorten becomes leader of the ALP and Opposition Leader after 2013 election loss	
14 Sept 2015		Malcolm Turnbull replaces Tony Abbott as PM
21 Aug 2018		Malcolm Turnbull defeats challenge by Peter Dutton
24 Aug 2018		Scott Morrison replaces Malcolm Turnbull as PM
4 Feb 2020		Michael McCormack replaces Barnaby Joyce as leader of the Nationals
21 June 2021		Barnaby Joyce replaces Michael McCormack as leader of the Nationals

his government at the 2007 federal election, where he also lost his own seat of Bennelong. Nonetheless, while in opposition, the party changed leaders six times across the space of 12 years. While the ALP was in government, there was also significant ongoing friction about leadership although the leadership of the party and the government only changed hands once in 1991. When the most recent period is compared to this earlier period, you could argue there is a slight increase in leadership turnover but to call it unique in Australian politics is an exaggeration. The important questions are whether the turnover of leaders is healthy for Australian politics and what is driving such turnover?

QUESTION

What are the different types of justification given for leadership changes in Australia and which of these are the most defensible? For example, personality, electoral success or failure, or ideology.

WHY HAS THERE BEEN A 'REVOLVING DOOR' OF LEADERS?

The larger question is whether the institutional structure and political culture incentivise the 'coup culture' that has dominated Australian federal politics from 2007 onwards. While there is much discussion about politicians being in it for themselves, the reality is that the pressure and sacrifices to serve as an elected official in the federal parliament are enormous and should not be underestimated. Who would want to be away from friends and family for over half the year and who would want to be working seven days a week and, in many cases, 16–18 hours per day? Clearly this has some effect on not only who is elected to parliament, but also the types of personalities that are incentivised in the Australian political system.

While in Spotlight 10.2, we suggested that the major parties changing their leader frequently is not unique, we do need to recognise that leaders are remaining in their positions for shorter periods than previously. According to Gauja (2015), this is partially attributable to domestic factors and that the nature of party politics is changing: 'Citizens are less engaged with formal political institutions; are more likely to use social media and act as citizen reporters and run their own issue campaigns; are more educated and likely to be more critical of, and less loyal to, parties'.

Another factor is how Australia's political parties select their leaders. Increasingly, who votes for the party leader has changed in other parliamentary democracies. An interesting counterpoint here is the way the UK parties select their party leaders. In the case of the United Kingdom's three biggest parties – the Conservatives, the Labour Party and the Liberal Democrats – leaders are selected by a broader range of people than simply the political representatives in parliament. While it differs in each case, party members, supporters and affiliated groups have a say over who will be the parliamentary leader. Broadening the number of people who are involved in making leadership decisions does a few things. First, the process takes more time, so this slows down any 'night of the long knives', as has been common in Australia. Second, it changes the relationship between potential leaders and the grassroots of the party, as being a 'factional powerbroker' in and to itself is no longer enough. Third, it allows those beyond the elected officials to prevent what they see as overreach and the removal of a leader that the base support. For example, this may have saved Kevin Rudd in 2010 and Julia Gillard in 2013.

Only the ALP has moved toward such a model in Australia. The structural differences in the major parties may explain this difference. After the Gillard–Rudd spills, at the initiative of Rudd, the party endorsed giving more power to the party membership allowing for votes by the Federal Parliamentary Labor Party (its Caucus) and the party membership to be weighted equally. Any challenge to the leader would require 60 per cent Caucus support – and the 2018 ALP National Platform sets this process out in s27. Following the 2013 election defeat, this process was used for the first time resulting in a win for Bill Shorten (52.02 per cent compared to Anthony Albanese's 48.98 per cent). While Shorten received 63.95 per cent of the votes of his parliamentary colleagues, he only received 40.08 per cent of those of the broader membership (Griffiths 2013). It was estimated that 30 000 ALP members voted in the 2013 leadership ballot. In 2019 Albanese was formally appointed the leader after he was the only one to declare candidacy. In distinction, s52 of the Liberal Party Federal Constitution provides that the parliamentary party shall appoint its leader. In response to the spate of leadership challenges in 2018, Prime Minister Morrison clarified this rule to mean that a prime minister could only be removed by a special majority two-thirds vote by the party – which increased the likelihood that challenges would not be successful but did not democratise the process (for more information see Madden 2019/2020).

SHORT-ANSWER QUESTIONS 10.4

1. The 'leadership churn' that followed the 2007 election is widely seen as evidence of leadership failure, a source of instability, and as contributing to a wider disillusionment with mainstream politics and parties. All this may be true. But are such leadership changes always damaging and harmful?

2. How does allowing party members and supporters to vote in parliamentary leadership contests alter the nature of party politics?

Suggested responses are available at www.cambridge.org/highereducation/isbn/9781009108232/resources

GENDER AND LEADERSHIP

While the question, 'Does Australia have a leadership problem?' has been answered so far in terms of the institutional environment and processes used to select leaders, there is another way to answer this question. Australia has a leadership problem for the simple fact that in well over a century Australia has had one female prime minister, 11 female state premiers or territory chief ministers, one female High Court chief justice and one female Governor-General. Neither the ALP nor Liberal–National Party have ever chosen a woman as federal opposition leader. Just three of the 30 Speakers of the House of Representatives, and just one of the 36 Attorneys-General of the Commonwealth Parliament have been women. Women remain under-represented in the senior ranks of the Commonwealth public service. One state – South Australia – has never had a female premier. The federal Liberal Party has never had a female leader. This list could go on and on. Table 10.2 shows the gender diversity in Commonwealth Parliament as of 15 November 2021.

TABLE 10.2 COMMONWEALTH PARLIAMENT GENDER DIVERSITY AS OF 15 NOVEMBER 2021

PARTY	M	F	%F
Australian Labor Party	48	46	48.9
Liberal Party of Australia	66	24	26.7
Nationals	15	6	28.6
Greens	4	6	60
Centre Alliance	1	1	50
Jacqui Lambie Network	0	1	100
Katter's Australian Party	1	0	0
Pauline Hanson's One Nation	1	1	50
United Australia Party	1	0	0
Independents	2	2	50
Total	**141**	**86**	**37.9**

Source: Adapted from Hough (2021).

Similar observations might be made about the dearth of Indigenous Australians in Australian Parliaments: only 38 have ever sat in a national, state or territory legislature and only two in the House of Representatives. So too with ethnic minorities, for example, it took until 2010 before a Muslim was elected to the Commonwealth Parliament. But it is the failure to recruit women into leadership roles in Australian politics which is especially striking, since, at its birth, Australia was a pioneer in progressing the enfranchisement of women. The fact that women are notably absent from Australia's political leadership ranks points to gender bias and to a particularly insidious leadership problem.

The experiences of Julia Gillard as Australia's sole female prime minister are worthy of further analysis. While Gillard endured significant attacks from within parliament, as Summers (2012) has shown with great detail, the attacks from parts of the community were disturbing. This included violent and sexually explicit images of the prime minister that were distributed widely. In reflecting on her time in office, Gillard (2014, 106–7) said:

> As early as 1975, in her book Damned Whores and God's Police, feminist and author Anne Summers explained that during our nation's history, women were always categorised in one of these two roles. It felt to me as prime minister that the binary stereotypes were still there, that the only two choices available were good woman or bad woman. As a woman wielding power, with all the complexities of modern politics, I was never going to be portrayed as a good woman. So I must be the bad woman, a scheming shrew, a heartless harridan or a lying bitch.

While some will attest that the attacks on Gillard were no more or less than any other prime minister has endured, this overlooks the gendered nature of much of the material disseminated about Gillard. Ultimately, the way that the Gillard's prime ministership is defined and what it says about Australian democracy is in the eye of the beholder: some view it as the end of a bad era of ALP government; others view the personal and misogynistic attacks on Gillard as key to understanding the period; and there are many views between and beyond this. No matter the view, there can be little doubt that there are likely to be significant challenges for Australia's next female prime minister.

REFLECTION QUESTIONS 10.4

1. What were the key challenges for Gillard as prime minister? Were they primarily institutional, contextual or about her gender?
2. Why is the proportion of females elected to the Senate higher than the House of Representatives?

Response prompts are available at www.cambridge.org/highereducation/isbn/9781009108232/resources

AFFIRMATIVE ACTION AND THE KEYS TO THE LODGE

Between them the two major parties have controlled the keys to the Lodge since the Country Party provided a stop-gap prime minister in the summer of 1967–68. Each has taken a different approach to encouraging women to enter the national parliament, which is the first hurdle that every future leader must leap. In 1994, the ALP adopted a quota and set itself the challenge of endorsing women in at least 35 per cent of winnable seats by 2002. This has since been refined. Labor's constitution presently provides for 'comprehensive affirmative action' and requires that men and women each fill a minimum of 40 per cent of seats in parliament, with candidates of either sex able to occupy the remaining 20 per cent. Legislated or voluntary quota systems (such as Labor's 40:20:40 scheme) operate in a number of countries (McCann 2013). But such schemes have their critics. For critics, fixed quotas for women are seen as incompatible with merit. This is the view that has prevailed within the Liberal Party.

Sussan Ley, for example, has said she wants to be seen 'to be here for my ability, for my merits' (Mills 2014). Instead of introducing quotas, the Liberal Party has sought to provide networked support and encourage women to stand for preselection to enable them to crash through the '**GLASS CEILING**'. However, the evidence suggests that quotas have been the only effective mechanism that has improved female representation. One Australian study, which analysed female representation in 250 parliaments in 190 countries, found that when the three common strategies employed to deal with representation gaps were analysed – namely, no targets, targets, or quotas – that the only strategy that led to increased female representation were quotas. Moreover, targets had the same effect as having no target at all (Sojo et al. 2016). Increasing female representation will not by itself solve the issue of a lack of female leaders. Clearly, there are deeper cultural and social issues at play. Nonetheless, by increasing the number of female-elected officials, it raises the prospect for these women, who otherwise may not have had the opportunity to make their case for the leadership of their respective parties.

> **GLASS CEILING:**
> An invisible but very real pattern of discrimination that prevents women rising to the top of hierarchical organisations such as corporations, government agencies and political parties.

CASE STUDY 10.1 JULIA GILLARD SPEAKS IN LONDON IN MEMORY OF JO COX MP, 11 OCTOBER 2016

Let me share with you what that gender discrimination can look and feel like. As Prime Minister, day after day, time after time, I would find myself in a room, often a business boardroom, where I was the only woman, apart perhaps from a woman serving coffee or food.

Because politics at senior levels … has been almost always the pursuit of men, the assumptions of politics have been defined around men's lives – not women's lives. It is assumed a man with children brings to politics the perspective of a family man, but it is never suggested that he should be disqualified from the rigours of a political life because he has caring responsibilities. This definitely does not work the same way for women.

Even before becoming prime minister, I had observed that if you are a woman politician, it is impossible to win on the question of family. If you do not have children, then you are characterised as out of touch with 'mainstream lives'. If you do have children then, heavens, who is looking after them? I had already been chided by a senior conservative senator for being 'deliberately barren' …

Before becoming prime minister, I had also worked out that what you are wearing will draw disproportionate attention. … Undoubtedly a male leader who does not meet a certain standard will be marked down. But that standard is such an obvious one: … a well-tailored suit, neat hair, television-friendly glasses. … Being the first female prime minister, I had to navigate what that standard was for a woman.

It is galling to me that when I first met NATO's leader, predominantly to discuss our strategy for the war in Afghanistan, where our troops were fighting and dying, it was reported in the following terms: 'The Prime Minister, Julia Gillard, has made her first appearance on the international stage, meeting the head of NATO, Anders Rasmussen, in Brussels. Dressed in a white, short jacket and dark trousers she arrived … and was ushered in by Mr Rasmussen …' This article was written by a female journalist. It apparently went without saying that Mr Rasmussen was wearing a suit …

This gender stereotyping was at the very benign end compared to much of what I faced: 'Ditch the witch' on placards at rallies. The ugly ravings about how 'women are destroying the joint' from a conservative and cantankerous radio shock jock. The pornographic cartoons circulated by an eccentric bankrupt. The vile words on social media.

It may be easy and comforting for you to conclude that all this is something about the treatment of women in Australia. I regret doing this but I have to disabuse you of that notion. Indeed, some of the sexist insults thrown at me were not original. Rather they had originally been hurled at Hillary Clinton … in 2008.

Source: Gillard (2016).

QUESTION

In this extract from a speech she made in 2016 in tribute to the slain British MP Jo Cox, Julia Gillard reflects on some of the challenges she faced as prime minister. Are gender stereotypes still embedded in our understanding of political leadership?

RESEARCH QUESTION 10.2

Will Australia's Commonwealth Parliament always have an under-representation of women unless the Liberal Party adopts quotas like the ALP has?

SUMMARY

Learning objective 1: Understand the tension between leadership and liberal democracy

Ultimately their party colleagues will regard prime ministers as successful if they are winning elections or they retain the confidence and majority support of the voting public. Democracy and the need for popularity poses leaders with a particular dilemma. Leaders who follow public opinion are seen as 'weak'. Leaders who steer their own policy course and seek to bring the public along with them risk being seen as autocratic and 'out of touch'. Political theorists have long reminded us that while leadership is vital, it always sits uncomfortably with the democratic principle of popular sovereignty.

Learning objective 2: Recall some of the theoretical debates on leadership and the importance of leaders

What makes a good leader is much debated. Prime ministers need a variety of strengths, skills and talents to manage the Cabinet; to rally supporters in Question Time; to understand and explain complicated legislation; to negotiate with powerful vested interests; to outmanoeuvre opponents; and to identify and win support for public policy solutions to the problems Australia faces. Unsurprisingly, there is little agreement about the particular attributes successful leaders require. But there have been some theoretical approaches that have dominated. The 'great man' tradition imagined that, when needed, leaders would emerge to change the course of history. Political psychologists search for the personality and other traits that mark individuals out as charismatic leaders. Political scientists are more prone to ask about the relations of leaders with Cabinet and party colleagues, advisers, public servants and others on whom they depend – to emphasise that the structures of executive government restrict the agency of leaders. While Burns (1978) distinguished between transactional leaders who cultivate supporters by appealing to their self-interest and by offering rewards and threatening punishment and transformational leaders able to articulate and build support for their vision of a better society.

Learning objective 3: Explain the different arenas leaders work in and the different skills they require

Leadership is not easily defined, but we intuitively recognise that it is central to politics and government – and often complain that the current crop of leaders fail the test of making and explaining difficult but necessary decisions. While it is party leaders and prime ministers who first spring to mind, leadership is displayed in the public service, in industry, in communities and displayed by NGOs and interest groups.

Learning objective 4: Summarise the debate about Australia's 'leadership problem'

The perceived problem that Australia has with leadership relates to both the number of leadership changes and the process that leads to these changes. In the period 2007–14, there were a large number of changes in the leaders of the major political parties. Australia, until recently, stood largely alone in the way that leadership changes occurred. Most other comparable parliamentary systems have changed the process whereby leaders can change in the middle of a term. The changes the ALP introduced in 2013 are similar to changes in other countries like the United Kingdom and Canada.

Learning objective 5: Describe the leadership gender gap and some of the methods employed to remedy this

Just one woman – Julia Gillard – has served as Australian prime minister. Her party turned to her – as in the case of several of the women who became state premiers – at a time of flagging political fortunes and then later turned on her when her own political fortunes appeared to be falling. In the two major parties, women are under-represented – even in the ALP which employs a quota system to boost the numbers of women in Caucus. This under-representation reduces the likelihood that female political leaders will soon be commonplace. The evidence suggests that targets that are often advocated for in the Liberal Party have no effect on increasing the representation of women and will, therefore, have no effect on the number of women in leadership positions either.

DISCUSSION QUESTIONS

1. What makes an effective leader?
2. Who are some of Australia's most important political leaders outside of parliament?
3. What agency do prime ministers have?
4. Have prime ministers become more presidential-like figures?
5. Why have there been very few female prime ministers and state premiers?

FURTHER READING

Daly, F. (1977). *From Curtin to Kerr*, South Melbourne: Sun Books.

Grattan, M. (ed.). (2003). *Australian Prime Ministers*, Sydney: New Holland Publishers.

Helms, L. (ed.). (2012). *Comparative Political Leadership*, Basingstoke: Palgrave Macmillan.

Kane, J., Patapan, H. & 't Hart, P. (eds). (2009). *Dispersed Democratic Leadership: Origins, Dynamics, & Implications*, Oxford: Oxford University Press.

Kefford, G. (2013). The presidentialisation of Australian politics? Kevin Rudd's leadership of the Australian Labor Party. *Australian Journal of Political Science*, **48**(2), 135–46.

REFERENCES

Australian Border Force. (2015). ABF Joining Inter-Agency Outfit to Target Crime in Melbourne CBD. Media Release, 28 August 2015.

Australian Communist Party v Commonwealth (1951) 83 *CLR* 1, 187.

Barns, G. (2020). New ASIO law one more step towards a totalitarian state, *The Sydney Morning Herald*, 13 May. Retrieved from https://www.smh.com.au/national/new-asio-law-one-more-step-towards-a-totalitarian-state-20200513-p54smi.html

Bennett, S. (1999). *White Politics and Black Australians*, Sydney: Allen & Unwin.

Bennister, M. (2008). Blair and Howard: Predominant prime ministers compared. *Parliamentary Affairs*, **61**(2), 334–55.

Bourke, L. (2015). Only voters have the right to 'hire and fire' their leaders, says embattled Tony Abbott, *The Sydney Morning Herald*, 2 February. Retrieved from http://www.smh.com.au/federal-politics/political-news/only-voters-have-the-right-to-hire-and-fire-their-leaders-says-embattled-tony-abbott-20150202-133xno.html

Bryant, N. (2015). Australia: Coup capital of the democratic world, *BBC News*, 14 September. Retrieved from http://www.bbc.com/news/world-australia-34249214

BTLi. (2011). *Australian Cultural Imprints at Work: 2010 and Beyond* – Report, East Melbourne, March 2011.

Burns, J.M. (1978). *Leadership*, New York: Harper & Row.

Crossman, R. (1963). Introduction. In *The English Constitution*, London: Fontana, pp. 1–57.

Davis, F., Musgrove, N. & Smart, J. (2011). Introduction. In F. Davis, N. Musgrove and J. Smart (eds), *Founders, Firsts and Feminists: Women Leaders in Twentieth-century Australia*, eScholarship Research Centre: University of Melbourne.

Dowding, K. (2013a). The prime ministerialisation of the British Prime Minister. *Parliamentary Affairs*, **66**(3), 617–35.

—— (2013b). Presidentialisation again: A comment on Kefford. *Australian Journal of Political Science*, **48**(2), 147–9.

French, Robert A.C. (2018). Executive power in Australia – Nurtured and bound in anxiety. *University of Western Australia Law Review*, **43**(2), 16–41.

Gastil, J. (1994). A definition and illustration of democratic leadership. *Human Relations*, **47**(1), 953–75.

Gauja, A. (2015). This is why Australia churns through leaders so quickly, *Monkey Cage Blog*, 18 September. Retrieved from http://www.washingtonpost.com/news/monkey-cage/wp/2015/09/18/this-is-why-australia-churns-through-leaders-so-quickly/?utm_term=.6953a5f1096b

Gillard, J. (2014). *My Story*, Melbourne: Random House.

—— (2016). Julia Gillard speaks in London in memory of Jo Cox MP. Retrieved from http://juliagillard.com.au/articles/julia-gillard-speaks-in-memory-of-jo-cox-mp/

Global Leadership and Organizational Behavior Effectiveness (GLOBE). (2020). Retrieved from https://globeproject.com/

Griffiths, E. (2013). Bill Shorten elected Labor leader over Anthony Albanese after month-long campaign, *ABC News*, 13 October. Retrieved from http://www.abc.net.au/news/2013-10-13/bill-shorten-elected-labor-leader/5019116

Heifetz, R. (2010). Leadership. In R.A. Couto (ed.), *Political and Civic Leadership: A Reference Handbook*, Thousand Oakes: Sage.

Hendriks, F. & Karsten, N. (2014). Theory of democratic leadership. In R.A.W. Rhodes and P. 't Hart (eds), *The Oxford Handbook of Political Leadership*, Oxford: Oxford University Press, pp. 41–56.

Heywood, A. (2013). *Politics*, 4th edn, Basingstoke: Palgrave.

Hildebrand, J. (2017). Assange, Keating named among Australia's top 10 figures of all time, *News.com.au*, 3 June. Retrieved from http://www.news.com.au/finance/work/leaders/assange-keating-named-among-australias-top-10-figures-of-all-time/news-story/5152c5c6dc20c0382d5246b97514cb17

Honeyman, V. (2007). Harold Wilson as measured using the Greenstein criteria. Paper presented to PSA Conference, University of Bath, 11–13 April. Retrieved from http://www.psa.ac.uk/2007/pps/Honeyman.pdf

Hough, A. (2021). Gender composition of Australian parliaments by party and gender: A quick guide. *Research Paper Series*, 2021–21. Retrieved from https://parlinfo.aph.gov.au/parlInfo/download/library/prspub/3681701/upload_binary/3681701.pdf

Kane, J. & Patapan, H. (2012). *The Democratic Leader: How Democracy Defines, Empowers and Limits its Leaders*, Oxford: Oxford University Press.

Karvonen, L. (2010). *The Personalisation of Politics: A Study of Parliamentary Democracies*, Colchester: ECPR Press.

Kefford, G. (2013). The presidentialisation of Australian politics? Kevin Rudd's leadership of the Australian Labor Party. *Australian Journal of Political Science*, **48**(2), 135–46.

Madden, C. (2019/2020). *Party Leadership Changes and Challenges: A quick guide*, 29 July 2019 updated 14 April 2020. Retrieved from https://www.aph.gov.au/About_Parliament/Parliamentary_Departments/Parliamentary_Library/pubs/rp/rp1920/Quick_Guides/PartyLeadershipChangesChallenges

McAllister, I. (2007). The personalisation of politics. In R.J. Dalton and H. Klingemann (eds), *The Oxford Handbook of Political Behavior*, Oxford: Oxford University Press.

McCann, J. (2013). *Electoral Quotas for Women: An international overview*, 14 November. Parliamentary Library. Retrieved from http://www.aph.gov.au/About_Parliament/

Parliamentary_Departments/Parliamentary_Library/pubs/rp/rp1314/ElectoralQuotas#_ftnref47

Michels, R. (1962). *Political Parties: A Sociological Study of the Organizational Tendencies in Modern Democracies*, New York: Free Press.

Mills, T. (2014). Sussan Ley rejects gender quota call, *Border Mail*, 10 March.

Montesquieu, C. (1748). *The Spirit of Laws*, Covent Garden: George Bell & Sons.

Mudde, C. & Kaltwasser, R. (2014). Populism and political leadership. In R.A.W. Rhodes and P. 't Hart (eds), *The Oxford Handbook of Political Leadership*, Oxford: Oxford University Press, pp. 376–88.

Murphy, K. (2020). The End of Certainty: Scott Morrison and Pandemic Politics. *Quarterly Essay*, QE79, September 2020.

Pakulski, J. & Higley, J. (2008). Towards Leader Democracy? In P. t'Hart and J. Uhr (eds), *Public Leadership: Perspectives and Practices*, Canberra: ANU E-Press, pp. 45–54.

Poguntke, T. & Webb, P. (2005). *The Presidentialisation of Politics in Democratic Societies: A Framework for Analysis*, Oxford: Oxford University Press.

Prasser. S. (2012). Executive growth and the takeover of Australian parliaments. *Australasian Parliamentary Review*, Autumn 2012, **27**(1), 48–61.

Pratt, A. & Bennett, S. (2005). *The End of ATSIC and the Future Administration of Indigenous affairs*, Current Issues Brief no. 4 2004. Retrieved from https://www.aph.gov.au/About_Parliament/Parliamentary_Departments/Parliamentary_Library/Publications_Archive/CIB/Current_Issues_Briefs_2004_-_2005/05cib04

Rath, T. & Conchie, B. (2008). *Strengths Based Leadership*, Omaha: Gallup Press.

Remeikis, A. (2019). Scott Morrison's Hawaii horror show: How a PR disaster unfolded, *The Guardian*, 21 December.

Saunders, C. (2013). *The Scope of Executive Power*, Papers on Parliament No. 59 April 2013. Retrieved from https://www.aph.gov.au/~/~/link.aspx?_id=C8C131542382464EB28135A33F9EA201&_z=z

—— (2020). *A New Federalism? The Role and Future of National Cabinet, Governing During Crises*, Policy Brief No. 2, Melbourne School of Government, University of Melbourne, 1–10. Retrieved from https://government.unimelb.edu.au/__data/assets/pdf_file/0011/3443258/GDC-Policy-Brief-2_National-Cabinet_final01.07.2020.pdf

Schumpeter, J. (1961). *Capitalism, Socialism and Democracy*, London: Allen & Unwin.

Sojo, V.E., Wood, R.E., Wood, S.A. & Wheeler, M.A. (2016). Reporting requirements, targets, and quotas for women in leadership. *The Leadership Quarterly*, **27**(3), 519–36.

Stogdill, R. (1948). Personal factors associated with leadership: A survey of the literature. *Journal of Psychology*, **25**(1), 35–71.

Strangio, P., 't Hart, P. & Walter, J. (eds). (2013). *Understanding Prime-ministerial Performance: Comparative Perspectives*, Oxford: Oxford University Press.

Summers, A. (2012). Her Rights at Work (R-rated version). Retrieved from http://www.annesummers.com.au/speeches/her-rights-at-work-r-rated-version/

Tiffen, R. (2017). *Disposable Leaders*, Sydney: UNSW Press.

Triggs, G. (2015). Human Rights and the overreach of executive discretion: Citizenship, asylum seekers and whistleblowers. Annual Tony Blackshield Lecture delivered at Macquarie Law

School, Macquarie University, 5 November. Retrieved from https://humanrights.gov.au/about/news/speeches/human-rights-and-overreach-executive-discretion-citizenship-asylum-seekers-and.

Tulich, T., Reilly, B. & Murray, S. (2020). The National Cabinet: Presidentialised Politics, Power-sharing and a Deficit in Transparency, *AUSPUBLAW*, 23 October. Retrieved from https://auspublaw.org/2020/10/the-national-cabinet-presidentialised-politics-power-sharing-and-a-deficit-in-transparency

Van Onselen, P. (2010). Politics trumps a moral challenge, *The Australian*, 29 April.

Walter, J. & Strangio, P. (2007). *No, Prime Minister*, Sydney: UNSW Press.

Weber, M. (1978). *Economy and Society*. G. Roth & C. Wittich (eds), Berkley: University of California Press.

Williams, P. (2020). How Scott Morrison learnt to filter out the noise, *Financial Review*, 2 October. Retrieved from https://www.afr.com/politics/federal/how-scott-morrison-learnt-to-filter-out-the-noise-20200819-p55n91

CHAPTER 11
THE FOURTH ESTATE
News media in the digital age

LEARNING OBJECTIVES

After reading this chapter, you should be able to:

1. Understand the production, content, and audience of the news media and its role as the Fourth Estate in a democratic society
2. Understand what the public sphere is, how the news media is said to contribute to it, and its connection to political discourse
3. Differentiate between various theories of news media, especially its affect, use and reception
4. Explain key changes to the Australian media landscape from the 20th to the 21st century
5. Describe the opportunities and challenges digital technologies present to media organisations and their journalism

INTRODUCTION

PUBLIC SPHERE: A communicative space where public opinion about politics and policy are formed. Freely expressed and diverse voices are regarded as a precondition for a healthy democracy.

FOURTH ESTATE: In Britain, the media's reputation as providing this monitorial role of state power was coined the Fourth Estate, reportedly when Thomas Carlyle used the word in reference to House of Commons politician Edmund Burke: 'Burke said there were Three Estates in Parliament; but, in the Reporters' Gallery yonder, there sat a *Fourth Estate* more important far than they all' (Carlyle 1840, 392). Today it refers to the function of the news media to act as a guardian of the public interest and as a watchdog on the activities of government, forming an imponent component of the checks and balances vital to a modern democracy.

FAKE NEWS: The Collins English Dictionary (2018) defined fake news as 'false, often sensational, information disseminated under the guise of news reporting'. The Harvard's First Draft at Harvard's Shorenstein Centre suggests it encompasses different types of misleading content (misinformation, disinformation and mal-information).

According to liberal democratic theory, a free press is necessary for a well-functioning democracy. In its 'ideal' form, the news media play an essential role in informing the **PUBLIC SPHERE** by mediating the exchange of ideas, providing diverse political communications, and allowing for broad public knowledge and participation in the political process. In these ways, the media has often been labelled a **FOURTH ESTATE**, a phrase attributed to the conservative theorist Edmund Burke, that refers to the capacity of media to frame political issues by distributing information, serving the people with access to the 'truth', and providing a crucial check on the actions of the state.

However, there are a range of factors that reveal how this ideal notion of the media can fall short (Davies 2014). First, there is declining resources and funding for journalism, alongside reductions in ethical standards. For example, the United Kingdom was struck in 2011 by revelations of phone hacking of celebrities, citizens and police by the Murdoch-owned *News of the World*. The Leveson Report (2012) showed the extent of decline in journalistic ethics, recommending a new independent body with sanction capacities to protect the public interest. This legislation was never enacted, and the second part of the inquiry into the extent of unlawful or improper conduct by media organisations was dropped entirely. Second, media ownership has become highly concentrated – or monopolised – in many Western states. For example, the Australian news media has one of the most concentrated press ownership structures of any liberal democracy (Finkelstein and Ricketson 2012, 60). This raises serious concerns about the number and diversity of voices, and the operation of power in this public space that may restrict critical debate. Third, Ivor and Tiffen (2018) have shown an increased volatility in the contemporary media landscape, leading to widespread public distrust and cynicism. The Reuters Institute's Digital News Report 2017 found that trust in the news in Australia was at a low 42 per cent (Newman et al. 2017). Finally, there remains an inherent tension between the need for national security and a thriving press to report on the extent of state activities. The Department of Home Affairs and Attorney-General's Department *submission* to the 2020 inquiry into freedom of the press in Australia (Parliamentary Joint Committee on Intelligence and Security 2020) was revealing. It stated: '… press freedom is not absolute … The freedom to publish has always been subject to other considerations such as laws concerning defamation, criminal offences, the right to a fair trial, and national security.' In the increasingly securitised political environment, especially since the War on Terror, the state has been expanding its security agenda, encroaching on many civil freedoms, including of the press and information.

In plotting these dynamic shifts in the Australian media landscape, this chapter provides an overview of the challenges and opportunities for media institutions and political journalism in the digital age. The emergence of social media and other online communications has both positive and negative consequences for newsrooms. The negative includes the viral spread of **FAKE NEWS** that leaves people unsure of what is true, and what is not, and can damage public trust in news. As used by politicians, non-mainstream media, hoaxers, and other political actors, fake news undermines the public's confidence in mainstream news (McNair 2018, 91). Studies show this phenomenon is causing the public to be confused about basic facts (Barthel et al. 2016). On the positive side, the digital era enables journalists to reach new audiences beyond traditional geographical boundaries. Journalists can source information and reach audiences more cheaply and quickly than before. Online communication technologies serve politicians, political parties and interest groups to communicate directly with citizens and – importantly for their organisational survival – to recruit volunteers and to fundraise.

This chapter aims to provide a better understanding of the Australian media's contribution to the public sphere and its role to critically inform Australians about politics and policy. We do this, firstly, by examining the media sphere, including its production, content, and audience within various 'models' of media. We then look at a range of theories of media that accounts for its affect, use, and reception, discussing two largely contrasting views about how the media functions in society: the chaos (pluralist) and control (propaganda) paradigms. We consider questions of media ownership and the question of whether having fewer media proprietors affects diversity of voices or the quality of journalistic practice in the public sphere. Finally, we turn to the 'new media' political landscape by exploring not only how networks and social media platforms have affected the public sphere but also how media technologies have led to an increased form of surveillance of the public. Along the way we will ask questions such as: How much does the news we read, watch and listen to affect how we, as individuals, think about everyday issues? Are certain stories missing or some issues or groups in society under-represented? How does Australia's concentrated media ownership affect the quality of information of the Australian public sphere? And has 'new media' changed the relationship between security, the news, and the public?

We begin by focusing on what news media is.

WHAT IS NEWS MEDIA?

For the purposes of this chapter, we are largely reflecting on the news media. This includes newspapers, television and radio news programs and online content, such as Facebook, Twitter or Reddit, that is concerned about the news of the day, current affairs and events. Other forms of media such as film, literature, art and written music also form part of the media environment that surrounds us every day (Croteau and Hoynes 2014, 2) but are outside the scope of what we consider here as news media. News, as the name suggests, is describing happenings, phenomenon or events that are new. It is difficult to define exactly as news can be described in terms of its production processes, its content, or its function in society. Here are some examples of different approaches.

SPOTLIGHT 11.1 WHAT IS NEWS?

Media scholar Michael Schudson argues that news is the product of journalistic activity (2011, 5). This might have been true in the past, but we should consider if this will be so in the future. For example, technology companies such as Google are partnering with media outlets in Europe to fund artificial intelligence news machines to produce news stories (Williams 2017). Is this to be considered journalistic activity if it is automated by robots? Some describe news as providing a shared experience of the world. In this case, news is 'new information about a subject of some public interest that is shared with some portion of the public … News is, in effect, what is on a society's mind' (Stephens 1988, 9). Another way to think about news is as a 'manufactured good' like other consumable goods in society. Schudson (2011, 6) sees this good as 'the product of a set of social, economic, and political institutions and practices'.

Yet, if news can be fashioned like a product, who or what determines what is news? Why are some stories considered news and others not? This way of thinking about news is helpful because it introduces the notion that news makers have power in society: to emphasise some issues over others and to frame how society understands an issue. This also underscores that news is produced, as opposed to the news being a 'mirror of reality'. This idea relates to groups and voices in society that are under-represented in news coverage because newsrooms often consist of similar types of people who think about news in similar ways. Studies of the types of journalists and values that dominate newsrooms in the United Kingdom and the United States show that white middle-to-upper-class men dominate the people behind the news (Conboy 2013, 46). From this perspective, news is seen as a construction 'dependent on professional routines and also on broader forces such as ideological powers exercised by elites within society' (Wall 2005). Following this logic, news reproduces society's dominant paradigms and power structures (Hall et al. 1978). Geoffrey Craig, for example, reminds us that the news media is not just any old business but has the important role of informing the public sphere: 'The media are businesses and yet they are ascribed a special function in the democratic health of a society' (2004, 3). Schudson warns us to be wary of smuggling 'democracy' into the description of journalism but does define it as 'information and commentary on contemporary affairs taken to be publicly important' (2011, 7).

QUESTIONS

What are the different ways that researchers have thought about how to define news? What do these different ways of thinking tell us about the idea that news can be 'objective'?

THE 'MEDIA SPHERE'

Sarah Oates offers a highly useful way of beginning to understand news media and politics by examining what she calls the 'media sphere' that contains three aspects: production, content and the audience (Oates 2008, 3). Dividing news media in this way helps us to analyse the diverse factors that influence news media's role in a democratic society, like Australia, more effectively.

News *production* refers to all the factors and filters by which news/media is made. This includes the political environment of the country, such as whether it follows a libertarian, socially responsible, or authoritarian media model (Seibert et al. 1984/1956). For instance, Australia follows a commercial model in which news media is (with the exception of the ABC and SBS) privately owned, whereas the Russian Federation follows an authoritarian model in which media is largely controlled, either directly or indirectly, by the state. As a commercial media model, Australian media laws are premised on fiduciary obligations to shareholders and not necessarily for the public interest in information or 'truth'. The political environment includes all the laws and regulations that binds how media can be produced within its borders, including constitutional powers (like the Commonwealth's power to make laws with respect to electronic communications under Section 51(v) of The Constitution) and human rights obligations (such as Article 19 'freedom of expression' of the United Nations Covenant on Civil and Political Rights that protects the 'freedom to seek, receive and impart information and ideas of all kinds'). Importantly it includes laws on media ownership, that is, who can own media outlets, how much coverage these owners can hold, and balancing the needs of the public and commercial interests in news media. Production is also impacted by normative standards of the country, including what role the society believes the media should play in the community and journalistic professional standards or ethics. Of course, these norms are contested and shift overtime.

Content refers to what is actually transmitted or contained within the news/media, for example, what information is made available through a TV channel or newspaper or an online provider. Schudson (1995, 31) writes that what journalists 'produce and reproduce is not information – if there is such a thing; it is what is recognised and accepted as public knowledge given certain political structures and traditions'. This means that evaluating the content of media is a crucial question for understanding what stories are told and why and conversely those stories that are marginalised or even silenced in news media. Finally, the *audience* refers to the public and individuals affected by the news media. It not only includes how people take in such information and react to it but also fundamental questions about who can hear, see, access, and participate in news media and how.

Using this approach provides a useful lens into Australian politics and news media. For example, if we examine coverage of the 2019 Federal election through Oates' 'media sphere' approach (2008, esp. Chapter 2), we could look at how Australia's commercial news media model permitted all News Corporation Australia newspapers, and most of its masthead papers, to produce content that endorsed the Coalition (Australian Associated Press 2019). In terms of content, we could look at the influence of editors in choosing content and editorialisations that focused the election discourse on things like balancing the budget and responsible spending, rather than broader social issues or climate change. In terms of the audience, we could examine how this election coverage was received: how were the public exposed to news media? Was coverage and access greater or lesser for some communities? Did audiences change their voting preference in accordance with information received from news media?

THE PUBLIC SPHERE

German sociologist Jürgen Habermas outlined a concept of the public sphere in his 1962 book *The Structural Transformation of the Public Sphere* (translated into English in 1989). It contributes to democratic theory by critically examining the role of mass media in political debates, public opinion formation, and legitimacy of state power in the 17th through to the 20th centuries. Habermas's thesis focused on the role of private persons coming together in rational-critical debate about public issues (Calhoun 1992, 1). This contest of ideas by private people in a public space was important because it compelled 'public authority to legitimate itself before public opinion' (Habermas 1989, 25–6). In other words, it allowed the governed to have opinions of their rulers and their laws, and publicly airing these views was one way to hold authority to account. Until this time, 'public opinion' was not a well-known phrase and arose at about the same time as the emergence of the public sphere (Habermas 1989, 26). An early sociological study by Lang and Lang (1952) suggested news media shaped political outcomes and public opinion, but the movement between this general social consensus, public debate, and a subsequent change in social action or values remained under-explored. These same authors (1983) would go on to call this process a 'battle' over public opinion in the news media, following the Watergate scandal.

In Europe, the public sphere's 'preeminent institution' for exchanging ideas was the press (Habermas 1989, 181). This was made possible by political conversations in British coffee houses, French tea salons, scholarly German journals and academic societies. In the United States, the public sphere emerged in the political and professional pamphlets like Thomas Paine's *Common Sense* in 1776 (Schudson 2011, 66). The production of newspapers and related publications was made possible by Johannes Gutenberg's much earlier invention of the printing press, in 1440.

The press provided a means for freely sharing diverse viewpoints. Habermas (1989, 171) chronologically plots the rise and fall of the public sphere, finally characterising it in the 20th century as little more than an illusion, corrupted by the commercialisation of the mass media. His later writings revise this very pessimistic conclusion, finding that the media in the digital age could still serve as the backbone of the public sphere but with significant qualifications including that, for democracy's sake, the state must undertake to 'protect the public good of the quality press' (Habermas 2010, 136).

REFLECTION QUESTIONS 11.1

What is meant by the public sphere? How well do you think Australia's media serve the public sphere by providing space for the exchange of ideas that informs democracy? Do you accept Habermas's view that the commercialisation of media has harmed the public sphere?

Response prompt is available at www.cambridge.org/highereducation/isbn/9781009108232/resources

---

NORMATIVE: The expression of value judgements or prescriptions. In relation to the media, it refers to the expression of its 'ideal' role, how media *should* function, as opposed to how the media actually performs.

There has been much thoughtful scholarly criticism of both the historical and **NORMATIVE** aspects of Habermas's conception of the public sphere (see Calhoun 1992 for details). These collectively tackle underlying assumptions of, or lack of attention to, class, gender, religion, culture and ethnicity (Calhoun 1992, 466). Historians and political scientists also question the neglect of the role of social movements and the overestimation of the degeneration of the public sphere, especially the uniform negativity applied to the modern media (Calhoun 1992, 33 and 37). Some criticise Habermas's distinction of the public from the private, while others are concerned with how the public sphere is conceived as being singular rather there being multiple public spheres that co-exist and may overlap or compete.

The existence of multiple public spheres could also be construed from how the Canberra press gallery reported former Prime Minister Julia Gillard's 'misogyny speech' compared to reactions of international and social media – here, we see different public spheres in action. In her speech, Gillard, under heavy opposition fire for appointing the controversial Liberal-turned-independent Peter Slipper as the Speaker of the House, accused Opposition Leader Tony Abbott of being a hypocrite and misogynist. While mainstream journalists mainly focused on the immediate political context of the speech, overseas media saw it from a broader perspective, labelling it as a watershed moment in public life against sexism.

REFLECTION QUESTIONS 11.2

1. What were the differences in the way that the Australian mainstream media depicted this moment in history compared to how the public and overseas media reacted to the speech?

2. What does the mainstream media reporting and 'framing' of Gillard's speech tell us about the treatment of women in the media more generally?

3. Does the different media and public reactions to Gillard's speech lend strength to the idea of the media serving the public sphere by providing a space (or spaces) for the exchange of diverse viewpoints?

Response prompts are available at www.cambridge.org/highereducation/isbn/9781009108232/resources

While it is contested that the public sphere should be conceived as a singular or plural space, the overall concept is useful here for considering the ideal role of the media in a democracy. It offers us a framework and starting point for thinking about how the Australian media should ideally inform our democracy in the digital or 'new media' age. It does this by providing us with the concept of a shared communicative space (or spaces) for Australians to engage in public debates and weigh up social and policy issues that may, in turn, inform who we vote for or participate in wider political actions. It is also important for informing us as to whether our political parties and leaders are using their power appropriately and in accordance with Australia's representative system.

RESEARCH QUESTION 11.1
Do you agree that journalism is a 'horribly white' profession? Select an issue of diversity such as race, disability or class and critique how the news media report such stories.

THE DIGITAL GLOBAL PUBLIC SPHERE

Since the commercialisation of the internet in the mid-1990s, and the development of digital technologies, the opportunities for connecting the peoples of the world have never been greater. The emergence of Facebook in 2004, YouTube in 2005 and Twitter in 2006, among other forms of social media, has further enabled citizens to participate, comment and engage with political ideas in various ways whether in comment sections of online newspapers, online forums or Tweets and status updates. The capacity of this digitised network information space is not just considered a digital public sphere but a globalised public sphere by some scholars (see McNair et al. 2016, ix; Volkmer 2014). It has changed the political landscape so much that one commentator claimed that the 2019 Federal Election was Australia's first social media election, in which 'no longer is the debate shaped by the major parties into a narrative mediated through newspapers and broadcasting' (Warren 2019).

For Manuel Castells (2008, 89), 'the contemporary global public sphere is largely dependent on the global/local communication media system'. This media system includes both the traditional media of television, radio and the press, as well as digital communications, including what Castells labels 'mass self-communication'. This is using communication networks for the many-to-many transmission and reception of messages in ways capable of bypassing mainstream media and often government controls (2008, 90).

If, as Castells argues, the public sphere is where citizens come together to express their 'autonomous views' to influence the political institutions of society, then civil society is the 'organised expression of these views' (2008, 78). In a democracy, the relationship between the state and civil society is key as 'without an effective civil society capable of structuring and channelling citizen debates over diverse ideas and conflicting interests, the state drifts away from its subjects'

INFORMATION AND COMMUNICATION TECHNOLOGIES: A broad term that refers to technologies that provide access to information through communication technologies that include the internet, wireless networks, mobile phones and other communication forms to give society new communication capabilities.

(Castells 2008, 78). Castells (2008) argues that the digital communication tools and networks available to us in the 21st century pave the way for the formation of global civil society enabling 'ad hoc forms of global governance' to address problems that transcend the nation-state.

The development of **INFORMATION AND COMMUNICATION TECHNOLOGIES** has for some time lifted hopes of a more inclusive public sphere that will allow greater democratic engagement between political parties, candidates, other political actors, and voters. Kellner (1999, 101) predicted that such technologies would 'advance the interests of oppositional social groups and movements that have been excluded from mainstream media and political debate'.

However, other scholars have highlighted how social media is failing to live up to this democratic promise of greater inclusion and deliberation. Cass Sunstein (2007, 1) identifies a narcissistic trend, colloquially named the 'DailyMe', whereby online users engage with a self-selected narrow range of interests to focus on themselves. This is commonly called the 'echo chamber effect'. In addition, Angela Nagle (2017) has traced how the culture of internet-based media in internet forums such as 4Chan promotes transgression, anonymity, misogyny and racist attitudes at odds with a deliberative public sphere. These simultaneously feed into and on the growing polarisation of the electorate.

SPOTLIGHT 11.2 WHAT ARE 'ECHO CHAMBERS' AND 'FILTER BUBBLES'?

An echo chamber is where like-minded participants group together to share similar viewpoints and are cordoned off from alternative views or information. The concern is that these groups can tend towards polarisation and hyper-political partisanship that, in turn, can foster division and intolerance towards others (Curran, Fenton and Friedman 2012, 10).

Studies suggest that this type of polarising online behaviour presents a challenge to mainstream politicians in at least two ways. First, because they seek to engage broadly without alienating any voters, politicians may be 'risk averse' in their online communications and tend toward broadcasting messages rather than engaging in dialogue with social media users. This involves *talking* rather than *listening* and does not fully utilise social media's capabilities to engage in conversations with voters (Macnamara and Kenning 2014; Lukamto and Carson 2016).

Second, an individual's filter settings on websites, along with digital platforms' algorithms, may result in a 'filter bubble'. This results in intellectual isolation. It is caused by algorithms personalising online content to filter information based on the user's past online behaviours (Pariser 2011). It can result in us missing out on information and debates contrary to our pre-existing views, which may reinforce our preconceptions and biases (Sunstein 2007, 116).

More recent studies suggest fears of the echo chamber effect are exaggerated. In 2016, a national survey by the US Pew Research Center during the US Presidential election campaign found that most users of Facebook and Twitter had a mix of people, with a variety of political beliefs, in their networks (Duggan and Smith 2016). Moreover, a fifth of those surveyed reported changing their minds about a political or social issue because of their engagement with social media (Duggan and Smith 2016, 18). This finding questions the echo chamber theory. In a multi-nation study, the Reuters Institute at the University of Oxford found social media users, and users of search engines, engage with more online news brands than non-users. This suggests that social media use might actually increase an individual's exposure to diverse news, rather than limit it (Newman et al. 2017, 43). In some Australian Twitter studies, the echo chamber effect has also been discounted, except for a minority of 'hardcore partisan online communities' (Bruns 2017).

However, as the Cambridge Analytica scandal has shown, social media platforms can be harvested for data – which can then be used by political groups to target and control the types of political messaging and information received by individuals on online platforms. This allows for secret political interests to amplify or distort certain views or information without the person knowing it. The lack of transparency around such data practices is of major concern for democratic processes and civil liberties. Moreover, as Kuehn and Salter (2020, 2595) have shown, the attention economy logics of social media platforms 'largely dictate information received, undermining rational debate and the context for making informed choices needed to sustain a vibrant, functioning democracy'.

QUESTION

Think about the way you use social media: do you engage with a wide range of political viewpoints online, or is the information you receive mainly about things you already agree with?

THEORIES OF MEDIA

So, somewhere between promises of inclusion and deliberation, and the problems of echo chambers and manipulation, the news media plays a key role in the public sphere. But what is the effect of news media on audiences? In this section we focus our attention on a range of theories of news media that helps explain questions such as how audiences choose or are exposed to news media? What is the effect of their exposure or consumption of news media? These are difficult questions to answer, and a range of different theories contest this relationship between media and audience.

THE CULTURE INDUSTRY AND THE SPECTACLE

Stewart et al. (2001, 25 cited in Bell 2010) claim that audiences are not unquestioning consumers as they were once seen to be. 'Far from being turned into "zombies"', they write, 'it has grown increasingly clear that audiences are in fact capable of a high degree of self-determination in the nature of the response that they make to products offered to them'. Nevertheless, there persists a deep suspicion of the interests behind mass media and today's news media giants. Writing in 1963, Theodor Adorno (1982) stated that mass media had a 'monopolistic character' and that its function was 'mass deception' and 'fettering consciousness'. Hardly a bastion like the Fourth Estate, mass media was simply 'the playthings of institutions', tailoring information about products for consumption by the masses. There were historical reasons for Adorno's pessimism. For example, we know 'soap operas' were created to target specific audiences to advertise cleaning goods to them. Guy Debord (1992) also drew an equivalence between the role of mass media and marketing, and how this process led to social alienation and cultural homogenisation in which marketing, and especially images, had supplanted real human interaction. In terms of news media, this was being produced for profit and therefore standardised and commodified through distribution and mechanical production. While critical, these theories suggest a direct and largely negative effect between news production and the audience. But how does this process operate?

MEDIA EFFECTS THEORY

Media effects theory attempts to provide an answer to precisely this problem. While a broad school of thought, such approaches suggest mass media can influence people directly by 'injecting' them with messages (hence other names include the hypodermic needle or magic bullet theory). So, like a needle that administers something directly to a patient, this theory believes there is a direct, one-way effect of news media onto the audience that is passive and powerless to prevent this influence of information transmission. We are like the character Alex DeLarge in *A Clockwork Orange* forced to watch news programs that fill our minds with messages that we can only but internalise. While studies have shown that humans are not blind automatons but are selective of and filter news media, there are nevertheless clear examples of effects theory in action. 'Moral panics' have been shown to be able to be promoted by news media to elicit mass fear across populations. In Australia, the Children Overboard Scandal (2001) is just such an example. In the lead up to the 2001 election, images were manipulated by the incumbent government and promoted by the news media that claimed asylum seekers had deliberately thrown children overboard as a ploy to secure rescue. The government was able to portray itself as 'strong' on border protection, even though it was shown that they had known that no children had been at risk, instead cynically exploiting voters' fears and moral outrage.

A variation on this approach, agenda-setting theory looks to how the media can frame political discourses within states. According to McCombs and Shaw (1972) the media not only tell people what to think about in broad terms but *how* to think about specific items or issues and then *what* to think. Dearing and Rogers (1996) further developed this theory. According to them, the agenda is a 'set of issues' that are regarded or framed as most worthy of media coverage. They claim that the agenda-setting process is fluid and multidirectional: a dynamic attempt to get the attention of the media, the public, and policymakers. New media functions as a gatekeeper, placing items on the agenda and removing or excluding others. While media can only influence rather than determine audience perception, its power rests in its ability to set the agenda. However, so-called priming theory, in contrast, contends that the media are responsible both for the ranking of issue importance and for the use of this issue importance by voters to judge their leaders (Borah 2016, 6 citing Cappella and Jamieson 1997).

USES AND GRATIFICATIONS MODEL

Another approach holds that people have far greater agency when it comes to consuming media, that they engage with particular media purposefully. This uses and gratifications model holds that we choose news media to meet a variety of our needs. For example, McQuail (1983) finds that media is used by audiences for a range of reasons: information, personal identity, integration/social interaction, and entertainment. According to this approach, humans do not blindly imitate the news media they are exposed to but filter information. Yet, this raises a quandary: people may willingly choose fake news for a range of gratifications it may give them. The rise of QAnon is a key example, that despite being shown to be false, misleading, and conspiratorial nevertheless gains traction of millions (NBC 2021) – against which more reliable and social-responsible news media must constantly compete. This means we need to understand more about reasons why media is used and the gratification/s certain audiences may desire or need (see West and Turner 2010), alongside the imperfect rationality of media consumers and the socio-economic structures that may influence or even pre-determine the exercise of their 'choice'.

RECEPTION THEORY

Given the neglect of socio-economic factors in various other approaches to media theory, some scholars began to look to what audiences do with the media, specifically, how they receive it – hence the name of this approach, reception theory. This approach focuses on how individuals and groups interpret or make meaning from media. In these models, media use is not passive but active, offering a counter-point to both the one-way directionality of media effects theory and the voluntary aspects of the use and gratification model too. It brings in a wider sociological field when examining the influence of news media on the audience such as the intersection of race, gender, class, culture and education.

A key part of reception theory is the idea of 'audience positioning'. This has two dimensions; that audiences read and understand a particular text according to their cultural upbringing, and, that texts contain certain meanings – they are encoded. Stuart Hall ([1973] 1980) first developed this idea of an encoding/decoding model of communication as a form of textual analysis that focuses on the scope of 'negotiation' and 'opposition' by the audience. 'Codes' refer to the culturally known meanings of words, symbols and conventions. And through theses codes, audiences may receive or 'read' the message from media in four ways. A *dominant reading* is where the audience decodes the message as the maker intended and accepts the social values of the text. A *negotiated* or *subordinate reading* is where audience filters the message through their own agenda. They may accept the values in the text but in negotiation with it. In contrast, an *oppositional* or *radical reading* is where the dominant code is recognised and rejected, along with its social values. Finally, there may be an *aberrant reading* where there is complete disjuncture between the code and its reception.

In all of these ways, the news media is seen to do something crucial: in the expression of Hall it 're-presents' something. The news is a 're-presentation' of some story, thing or event. In this construction, things are selected for inclusion, others are omitted; certain images and words are deployed, and others not. This 're-presentation' then stands in for 'the real' but is necessarily incomplete. Reception theory offers ways to study the gap between the meaning of the event, the representation of it, and how the audience receives it.

SHORT-ANSWER QUESTIONS 11.1

1. What are the main claims of media effects theory?
2. How does the uses and gratifications model contrast with reception theory?

Suggested responses are available at www.cambridge.org/highereducation/isbn/9781009108232/resources

LIBERAL DEMOCRATIC THEORY ('CHAOS' PARADIGM)

As discussed in Chapter 8, the liberal tradition emphasises the virtues of freedom and liberty. A democracy, briefly, is a political system that involves citizens in governing their own affairs. It is predicated on a commitment to the rule of law in which political leaders are elected in free and fair elections, which are contestable, and allows for the greatest possible adult public participation in the election process (suffrage), guaranteed by various civil and political rights.

Important elements of liberal democratic society include 'elections, competitive political parties, free mass media, and representative assemblies' (Almond et al. 2010, 23). It is the virtue of a 'free mass media' to inform public opinion in a democracy that is the foundation of liberal democratic theory of the media. Why is this considered so important? Italian political philosopher Norberto Bobbio argued that liberal democracy presumes that not only do citizens have the right to choose who governs them, but that they must be well informed to 'vote for the wisest, the most honest, the most enlightened of their fellow citizens' (1987, 19). Speaking broadly, the media is one means by which the public can be informed about rival political candidates' values, beliefs and the issues for which they stand. As the Fourth Estate, the media plays a crucial role for promoting openness, transparency and accountability of the elected representatives that have been considered central tenets of a well-functioning democracy. The media have been formally recognised for this role – for example, in the First Amendment to the US Constitution.[1] In Australia, this role is not codified in its Constitution but has been recognised by the High Court, most recently in *Smethurst v Commissioner of Police* [2020] HCA 14. The 'fourth estate' role of the media has also been acknowledged in successive inquiries into the print and news media.[2]

Further, in recognition of the media's role to provide diversity of voices, Australia and some European democracies, including the United Kingdom, Norway, Finland and Sweden subsidise or fund sections of the media. In Australia, this involves taxpayer funding of the Australian Broadcasting Corporation (ABC) and partial funding of the Special Broadcasting Service (SBS) though they have full editorial independence. Government funded, or subsidised, media is considered by one school of thought necessary for a commercially sensitive industry where popular and sensational news can be 'interesting to the public', but not necessarily 'in the public interest'. This corresponds to a socially responsible model (Siebert et al. 1984/1956). From this perspective, public broadcasting is regarded as important to a free public life (see Garnham 1990, 104–14). Democracy depends on the state accepting criticism of its power. Through the liberal democratic lens of the media, citizens should encounter diverse and multiple viewpoints, including those of dissenting and critical voices of the state, in the public sphere.

The 'ideal' role of media

Media scholar Brian McNair (1999, 17) draws on the defining characteristics of the liberal tradition broadly conceived as 'constitutionality, participation and rational choice'. Constitutionality refers to the rule of law and ensuring that the processes of democracy such as elections are lawful. Participation includes those of legal age able to vote, which should be as universal as possible. Rational choice is the notion that voters have enough information to choose what Bobbio (1987) calls the 'wisest' candidate. This implies also that voters have a sufficient choice of candidates. Bringing these three elements together in the context of the public sphere, McNair highlights the key normative roles of the news media in the public sphere of a democracy.

---

[1] The First Amendment to the US Constitution: 'Congress shall make no law respecting an establishment of religion, or prohibiting the free exercise thereof; or abridging the freedom of speech, or of the press; or the right of the people peaceably to assemble, and to petition the Government for a redress of grievances.'

[2] This includes the 'Norris Inquiry' by Sir John Norris on behalf of the Victorian Government in 1981; the report of the House of Representatives Select Committee on the Print Media, News & Fair Facts: The Australian Print Media Industry, Canberra: Australian Government Publishing Service, March 1992; and the 2012 'Report of the independent inquiry into the media and media regulation' by Ron Finkelstein QC with Professor Matthew Ricketson.

The news media is ascribed several specific functions in a democracy. Brian McNair (1999, 21–2) identifies five:

1. To inform citizens – this is the monitoring function of the media
2. To educate citizens as to the meaning and significance of the 'facts' – this role is often linked to the need for 'objectivity' or 'professional distance' in reporting rather than opinion or emotive reporting
3. To provide a platform for public political discourse – this is to enable public opinions to be formed by facilitating public conversations
4. To give publicity to governmental and political institutions – this puts the media spotlight on those with power and includes the accountability or watchdog role of the media
5. To serve as a channel for the advocacy of political viewpoints – this includes allowing parties and other political actors to say what they stand for. It also can include the media taking a stand on issues, sometimes called 'campaigning journalism'. These stories are usually labelled as having a particular editorial stance.

Investigative journalism

Of the above functions, a much-celebrated role of the media is its accountability role. This was made famous by the Watergate scandal, unearthed by *Washington Post* reporters Carl Bernstein and Bob Woodward in the early 1970s, leading Richard Nixon to resign the US presidency. Investigative journalism can provide a check on the excesses of government and on powerful private interests. Among others, de Burgh (2000), Ettema and Glasser (1998), and Schudson (2008) have argued that the investigative journalists have a responsibility to expose wrongdoing in the public interest. This may include exposing injury and injustice; revealing information that would otherwise not be made public; or promoting legal, policy or regulatory reforms to correct a wrong or close a loophole. Investigative journalism is not the only means of exposing transgressions – parliamentary hearings, police and whistleblowers do this too – but it is a powerful one. For example, Schudson (2008) argues the mere existence of investigative journalism in democracies serves as a deterrent to politicians and others against engaging in wrongdoing.

Twenty-first century examples of watchdog reporting in Australia, such as the 2017 exposure of the mistreatment of youths at the Don Dale Youth Detention Centre in the Northern Territory, highlight the investigative journalist's role to expose hidden information in the name of the public interest. Caro Meldrum-Hanna, an investigative reporter with the ABC's TV program *Four Corners*, unearthed videos showing several boys being maltreated by the centre's staff. The footage included a 13-year-old being stripped naked, and a 17-year-old boy strapped to a chair with a hood over his head. After screening of the program on 25 July 2016, a public outcry led the Prime Minister Malcolm Turnbull to announce a Royal Commission into the abuse of youths in the Northern Territory corrections system.

More recently, Mark Willacy and the ABC Investigations team conducted a 14-month investigation beginning in August 2019 into shocking allegations of war crimes by Australian special forces in Afghanistan. Some journalists had been under threat of criminal charges for the so-called 'Afghan Files' stories that led to Federal police raids on ABC headquarters. After examining Afghan Independent Human Rights Commission files, 10 hours of film footage from, and communicating with, an anonymous source culminated in the *Four Corners* program *Killing Field* (Four Corners 2020) that brought to public attention these alleged war crimes.

Nevertheless, the funding for such investigative journalism has been significantly cut. Moreover, in wider media outlets, especially Murdoch-controlled sources, there is a disturbing lack of reporting on related public interest and social justice issues. For example, the high incarceration levels, suicide rates, and police violence against Indigenous youth were muted by the mainstream press. Similar studies have shown how the Murdoch press reports on female political leaders with misogyny and sexism (Williams 2020). Instead, it was forms of social media that promoted these issues through #MeToo and the #BLM, linking these movements that emanated from the United States to the Australian context. In terms of Black Lives Matters, it was social media that promoted the linking of 474 Indigenous deaths in custody since the Fitzgerald Inquiry to the police violence in the United States. Of the coverage that was made in mainstream sources, even the more progressive outlets were highly criticised for their lack of diversity, including the ABC *Insider* program (7 June 2020) that aired an all-white panel on BLM and *The Age* that was shown to have hired only one Indigenous reporter in its 166 years of operation (Zhou 2020; ABC 2020).

CASE STUDY 11.1 'THE JOURNALIST'S PERSPECTIVE OF THE MEDIA'S ROLE IN DEMOCRATIC SOCIETY' – NICOLE CHVASTEK, ABC RADIO PRESENTER AND FORMER TV REPORTER, CHANNEL 7 AND ABC

When I think of journalism and its role in a democracy I think of game changing exposes like *Four Corners* Moonlight State, a story that shone a disinfecting sunlight on the corruption poisoning aspects of the Queensland government in the 1980s. I think of the Panama and Paradise Papers leak of millions of documents that shed light on how the rich and powerful set up systems to redirect their profits into tax havens to avoid paying the full tax rate.

It is the work of journalists who dig for information and report in hostile environments which have brought these stories to the surface, triggering debate and often action.

You will rarely be welcomed by the powerful when you work as a journalist. Nor should you be. Your role is to ask difficult questions, to scrutinize and to hold to account fearlessly, impartially and accurately.

If the story has revealed illegality or abuse, expect the backlash. It may be from lawyers. It may be from an angry spin doctor. It may be from an angry crook.

My advice: Fact check, get it right and report. And if you report in places where the rule of law doesn't hold as it does in Australia, and even here where it does, expect to be threatened. It won't happen for every story you write, but it's coming.

It is interesting to reflect on the roles of modern Australia's journalism greats. Chris Masters. Laurie Oakes. Kerry O'Brien. There's the TV, radio and newspaper investigative teams who put their own safety to one side to secure justice for total strangers. Witnesses to truth who hunt down and meticulously research strands of information from dark places. Reporters who sift the legitimate from the fraudulent and through publication bring that information into the light in order for you and I to truly understand the system we live under and the forces that construct and manipulate it or honour it. Only when we are informed can we make informed choices.

When I first started reporting I remember naively asking the manager of a building site for permission to film. He politely asked everybody including my TV crew to leave the room and then rushed at me, standing over me, his face contorted in menace, a hot breath near mine, roaring physical threats at me with wild eyes. I remember a union official doing much the same thing as I tried to report from a picket line. I remember a Bikie with a gun who answered the door when I knocked and a drug addict with nothing to lose wielding a needle my way as I reported on a stabbing at an inner-city housing estate.

A media adviser recently barked a series of ultimatums and insults at my new and impressionable junior producer because the minister he was advising was getting interview questions (asked by me) that the staffer didn't like. The politician tried to walk out of the interview. He lodged a complaint with my organization. He banned my program and favoured others. Not everyone operates like this, but you'll encounter the ones that do.

If you are operating within the law, fairly, accurately and in the public interest these tactics should be expected. Accept criticism with grace but understand the environment in which you operate. Be safe and always wary when you are reporting on the road. Understand that no-one has an obligation to speak to you, but you have a duty to shine that light.

And remember, journalism is not all *Moonlight State*. Recently Rose, a pensioner from Creswick rang into my radio show and explained with gentle fury how Centrelink had robo-called her demanding she repay $60 000 in welfare payments they alleged had been overpaid to her. Rose had never had $60 000 in her life and was never likely to. With gentle fury, she spoke about the trauma this had triggered in her as she fought for a year to prove she, in fact, owed them nothing. She detailed the months of tracking down documents and records from years ago while the powerful bureaucracy insisted she come up with the money.

As it happened, she didn't owe the money. But no one can return the peace of mind and the year she lost fighting them. Journalism gives people who do not have a giant bureaucracy at their disposal a voice and a chance to be heard. Not by a recorded robot message but by hundreds of thousands of other people who think and who act, and who respond.

We are fortunate in Australia that we rarely face threats to our lives when we take on the powerful. This is not Russia. It is not Syria. But here, in wealthy democratic Australia, lives can also be lost and diminished when people feel they are invisible and despair sets in.

So, when Rose goes on air she'll never have a million-dollar Public Relations machine behind her that studies focus groups for months before she speaks, and workshops a list of slogans for her to recite. Her voice is where the real people speak from. There's something about the polite but determined quiver in her delivery that tells you she's your neighbour, or your grandma.

And in that moment, like a thousand other moments when you work as a journalist, people hear Rose's story and respond, and the power imbalance is righted, just a little bit. And a 70-year-old pensioner knows her complaint is valid and her voice has been heard.

QUESTION

Using McNair's list of five 'ideal' functions of the media in democratic society, which functions are identified by the journalist here as central to how she sees the reporter's role?

The 'chaos' paradigm

Investigative reporting could be considered the highpoint of the liberal democratic role of the media. The way journalists can use media to inform the public sphere (audience) about the abuse of institutional power, fits within a pluralist (or chaos) model of the media in society.

The chaos model is a pluralist theory for understanding the democratic function of the news media. Coined by McNair, the term is often contrasted with control theories of media (see below), which have a top-down approach to the flow of power in society. The chaos approach rejects the idea that power only flows in one, and the same, direction all the time. Chaos theory's emphasis is on mechanisms of the media for 'dissent, openness and diversity rather than closure, exclusivity and ideological homogeneity' (McNair 2006, vii).

Media scholars referencing this stream generally view media technologies as liberating, providing citizens with greater opportunities for participation, engagement, and political accountability. Political scientist John Keane argued that the digital age is a time of 'communicative abundance' and provides exciting new opportunities for observing and reporting abuses of power in society. He argues that in the digital age, 'power-monitoring and power-controlling devices have begun to extend sideways and downward through the whole political order' (Keane 2010, xxvii).

The International Consortium of Investigative Journalists' (ICIJ) reporting of global tax evasion in the 'Panama Papers' in 2016, and the 'Paradise Papers' in 2017, are examples of 'new mechanisms for observing and reporting abuses of power' in the global public sphere. Reporting of the Panama Papers is the largest example to date of many journalists from different countries collaborating and using mass data leaks to convey a story of international importance. It tells the global story about how the world's rich and famous use offshore tax havens to cut their tax bills. Other mass data dumps to reporters have included Edward Snowden's National Security Agency file leaks about how governments spy on their citizens, and WikiLeaks' Iraq war files that showed how the United States covered up the killings of innocents in the crossfire of war. Julian Assange has been indicted in the United States for violating the *Espionage Act (1917)* by publishing these military documents in a case that challenges the First Amendment and threatens the freedom of the press. It is feared the case will have a chilling effect on investigative journalism and whistleblowers.

This type of collaborative reporting is in line with what Castells identified as the 'global/local communication media system'. In the case of the Panama Papers, 400 journalists from different nations, including Australia, worked together using digital tools to expose global tax evasion and corruption. By exposing wrongdoing, this new global collaborative journalism can strengthen democratic accountability and tell a local story about an individual or company's tax avoidance. At the same time, the reports tell a broader story of how the rich and powerful across the globe use these purpose-built offshore schemes to maintain their wealth and privilege. Collaborative investigative reporting challenges the top-down power of elites in the international political order.

The Panama Papers had many real-life impacts such as costing Icelandic Prime Minister Sigmundur Davíð Gunnlaugsson his job. It also highlighted the power of 'big data' leaks in the digital age. A year later, in 2017, the ICIJ again formed a collaboration of almost 100 media outlets including Australia's online *Guardian* newspaper and ABC TV's *Four Corners* program to reveal the leaked Paradise Papers. This leak of 13.4 million documents, mostly from Bermuda, revealed how companies and individuals – including royalty, politicians, rock stars and sporting heroes – use offshore entities to avoid paying their share of national taxes.

However, it is important to note that a challenge in the 'communicative abundance' era is that communications are not evenly distributed across the globe, and there exists a power gap between the information-poor and the information-rich. Keane has argued that the information-poor may suffer because they are deemed to be 'almost unneeded as communicators, or as consumers of media products' (Keane 2010, xxvii). Another contemporary challenge in the communicative abundance era is the rise of fake news. The technological advances that have engendered the global public sphere also allow for the 'weaponisation' of information.

POLITICAL ECONOMY THEORY (CONTROL PARADIGM)

In contrast to the chaos model, which views media reporting as diverse and as a public good, the control paradigm conceives news media as shaped by 'a number of influences, [which] all work in the same conservative direction' to reinforce the existing power structures in society (Miliband 1973, 203). It conceives the mass media as largely reflecting the 'corporate good' rather than the 'public good' by upholding the interests of elites and capital (see Herman and Chomsky 2002).

Walter Lippmann wrote in his 1922 book *Public Opinion* that the mass media were altering the nature of public political discourse. He argued that 'a revolution is taking place, infinitely more significant than any shifting of economic power … [through] the manufacture of consent' (Lippmann [1922] 1997, 158). Lippmann was among the first to describe the transformative role of the media and its power to create or recreate the way we see the world, and thus mediate reality. Having seen the effects of war propaganda in the First World War, Lippmann was cautious of the misuse of media power for political purposes. He warned 'the creation of consent is not a new art', nor was it a 'daring prophecy to say that the knowledge of how to create consent will alter every political calculation and modify every political premise' (Lippmann [1922] 1997, 158).

In a similar vein, and influenced by the context of the Cold War, Edward Herman and Noam Chomsky (2002) address the economic and political power of the mass media to act as **GATEKEEPERS** of information. They seized on Lippmann's famous phrase 'manufacturing consent' to write a significant account of how the media reinforce the economic, social and political agendas of the powerful in society through their construction of what is news. *Manufacturing consent: The political economy of the mass media* (Herman and Chomsky 2002) applies a propaganda model, through the lens of political economy, to understand the behaviour of the mainstream media in the 20th century.

Herman and Chomsky (2002) argued that Western media subliminally activate news filters to pander to powerful commercial and political interests when deciding what has news value. The essential elements informing their propaganda model were: (1) the size of the media outlet, its ownership structures and wealth; (2) the influence of advertising as the primary media income source for the mass media; (3) reliance on information provided by government and business 'experts' who reinforce the dominant paradigms, and reliance on information provided by perceived purveyors of propaganda, such as public relations specialists and government lobbyists; (4) 'flak' the concerted attempts to manage public information by negative responses to media statements that complain, threaten or discredit organisations or individuals who disagree with or cast doubt on the prevailing assumptions of established power; and finally, (5) what they termed anti-communism – the negative reaction to any news that seemed to support communist ideology (Herman and Chomsky 2002, 2). In the 21st century, anti-communist rhetoric is less prevalent, and this last point could be reasonably perceived as 'marginalising dissent', or those that challenge liberal ideology (i.e. Islamism) or threaten its dominance (i.e. leftist social movements).

Herman and Chomsky's work remains salient in the 21st century because, notwithstanding new media digital entrants, the owners of existing large media companies have continued to consolidate. In the 19th century, the press was likely to be family-owned enterprises. Then, as these businesses were acquired, society witnessed the rise of the media baron. In turn, in the 20th century, large numbers of these businesses were sold to corporate conglomerates. By the 21st century, media businesses had acquired further holdings to become global media empires such

GATEKEEPER: Someone who decides if access will be granted. In terms of the media, 'gatekeeping' refers to access to information. It occurs at many stages of the news gathering process including what sources a reporter decides to consult, who is quoted, how the sub-editors and editors arrange the story, and the prominence that it is given on the webpage or in the newspaper or television bulletin. Politicians' press secretaries also play a gatekeeping role by determining what information goes to which media outlet and how much information is released. Gatekeeping theory was conceptualised by social psychologist Kurt Lewin in 1943.

as the announcement of the US$52.4 billion merger of Disney Corporation and Rupert Murdoch's 21st Century Fox in late 2017.

Scholars such as Ben Bagdikian, Robert McChesney, Thomas McPhail and Eli Noam among others, have critiqued global media ownership structures, raising concerns about their increasing concentration and the associated cultural imperialism that may follow. For example, Bagdikian (2004, 3) found that from 1983 to 2004, due to media acquisitions and mergers, corporate media ownership in the United States had consolidated from 50 major media enterprises to just five including Time Warner, The Walt Disney company and Rupert Murdoch's News Corporation. All had commercial interests across different aspects of the supply chain (called 'vertical integration') and disseminated their media products across multiple media platforms and markets. Bagdikian's (2004, 3) conclusions were stark:

> They are American and foreign entrepreneurs whose corporate empires control every means by which the population learns of its society. And like any close-knit hierarchy, they find ways to cooperate so that all five can work together to expand their power, a power that has become a major force in shaping contemporary American life.

More than a decade later, the media corporations have been joined by social media giants in shaping contemporary society. In November 2017, the US Senate committee hearings in Washington into the 2016 US Presidential election heard how before and after the election of Donald Trump, 146 million Facebook users may have seen Russian disinformation about the election. Similarly, Google's YouTube bosses conceded that the platform had housed 1108 Russian-linked propaganda videos. Twitter also revealed it had been home to more than 36 000 Russian-linked accounts that generated 1.4 million election related tweets (*The Economist* 2017). While it is not easy to measure the impact this content had on how Americans voted in November 2016, the cultural power of these digital monoliths to spread all types of information is unprecedented. This global cultural power provides a new basis for taking note of Lippmann's warning about 'manufactured consent', and for revisiting Herman and Chomsky's structural analysis of media power.

SHORT-ANSWER QUESTIONS 11.2

1. According to political economy theories of the media, who benefits most from the types of stories that are considered news? What is a counter perspective to this view?
2. Social media companies allow billions of users to communicate every day, but what is a drawback of this global networked communication ecosystem? Explain why.

Suggested responses are available at www.cambridge.org/highereducation/isbn/9781009108232/resources

THE CHANGING AUSTRALIAN MEDIA LANDSCAPE

As in other developed economies, Australia's traditional media outlets of newspapers, radio and television are in a state of flux in the digital age. The rise in digital technologies has contributed to falls in Australia's traditional media outlets' revenues, as audiences and advertising have migrated online. Advertising revenue was the major income source for commercial news last century. Journalism was the lure to attract what Australian advertisers call 'eyeballs', or consumers, to its news pages. Today, non-media companies beyond Australia's borders attract advertisers, offering cheaper rates and data analytics for the sophisticated targeting of ads to consumers.

Australian newspapers that relied heavily on classified advertising revenues have been hardest hit with job losses, market write-downs and asset sales. Marshall McLuhan (1964, 207) predicted in his book *Understanding Media: The Extensions of Man*: 'The classified ads (and stock market quotations) are the bedrock of the press. Should an alternative source of easy access to such diverse daily information be found, the press will fold.'

However, it is important to note that as much as the internet and global companies such as Google and Facebook take the lion's share of the online advertising market, the reasons for the decline in the established media are multifaceted. Australian daily newspapers' hard-copy circulation declines began *before* the internet took hold, in the early 1990s (Simons 2007, 29). This suggests that other factors contributed to the falls in newspaper profitability such as changes to Australian ownership laws, political imperatives leading to those law changes, and cultural factors such as busy lifestyles leaving little time to buy and read a printed newspaper or to watch a television news broadcast at a set time. Also noteworthy is that the Organisation for Economic Co-operation and Development (Wunsch-Vincent et al. 2010) found that the decline of newspapers is not a worldwide trend. Less economically developed nations such as India have experienced growth in their newspaper markets, and the number of titles worldwide increased in the first decade of this century.

The changes to the media market and arrival of social media have important implications for the reporting of politics in Australia and elsewhere. Compared to last century, the news cycle is faster, continuous and ravenous for content. In the words of former British Prime Minister Tony Blair (2007, 477):

> Make a mistake and you quickly transfer from drama into crisis … A vast aspect of our jobs today – outside of the really major decisions, as big as anything else – is coping with the media, its sheer scale, weight and constant hyperactivity. At points, it literally overwhelms.

Almost 15 years later, the information available to us through social media, online sites and established media has increased. This highly competitive environment has made it more difficult for politicians to get a sustained message heard without the distraction of new stories competing for the audience's attention. The consequence of this, said Blair, is a more toxic relationship between politicians and the media that results in increased public cynicism of both. He argues that new forms of media have further blurred the line between fact and opinion:

> The new forms can be even more pernicious, less balanced, more intent on the last conspiracy theory multiplied by five … we are all being dragged down by the way media and public life interact. Trust in journalists is not much above that in politicians. (Blair 2007, 479)

REFLECTION QUESTIONS 11.3

1. How might it be a public concern that giant online technology and social media companies have gained advertisers at the expense of traditional Australian news providers such as newspapers and free-to-air television?
2. Consider how our fast-paced lifestyles, with the convenience of the mobile phone to look up information instantly, have impacted on how you get your information. How do you think

changes to the media landscape might impact on politicians' political messaging and subsequent media reporting?

Response prompts are available at www.cambridge.org/highereducation/isbn/9781009108232/resources

AUSTRALIAN MEDIA OWNERSHIP

Concurrent with technological and cultural change, Australian media ownership structures have altered profoundly since the latter part of the last century, resulting in fewer overall owners and a greater concentration of ownership. A recent study showed the predominance of News Corp (and to a far lesser extent Nine Entertainment) across Australia television, radio and print media is *unprecedented* in liberal democracies (Brevini and Ward 2021, 5). Moreover, in cross-media settings these corporations extend their control beyond direct ownership through extensive content licencing and affiliates.

Media diversity has plummeted since its high point in the 1920s, when '21 independent media owners owned 26 capital city daily newspapers' (Brevini and Ward 2021, 4). By the late 1980s, Australian media takeovers significantly contributed to Australia losing *all* its daily evening newspapers due to cross-media ownership law changes during the period. This caused irreversible falls in newspaper penetration by 50 per cent (Tiffen and Gittins 2009, 181). Whether it was the lack of newspaper choice, or the loss of a favourite masthead, many readers abandoned the newspaper-buying habit altogether during this time. Under a corporate structure, newspaper publishers must consider diverse internal interests, some of which are competing. These interests can include shareholder, advertiser and reader considerations, which need to be balanced alongside responsible economic management.

Concentration of media ownership is of interest to us because it can narrow editorial choices for readers. For example, watchdog reporting is generally more expensive and time consuming to produce than everyday news stories. Similarly, concerns about journalism standards such as a potential lack of plurality of opinion and diversity of stories can arise in cities with concentrated media ownership (House of Representatives Select Committee report 1992, xxi). As the 'anti-False News' scandal of the Sinclair Broadcast Group on 1 April 2018 showed in the United States, despite having a range of 'local' providers, as they were all owned by the same corporation, each network was made to read out the exact same message across all 200 channels.

Among liberal democracies, Australia has the most concentrated press ownership structure. It has two major metropolitan print media owners and a third smaller proprietor (Seven West Media). The second largest print proprietor is Fairfax Media, which is owned by investors and individual shareholders and has media interests in magazines, radio, online and metropolitan and regional newspapers. Fairfax Media owns the daily national financial masthead the *Australian Financial Review* and three capital city daily mastheads, *The Age*, *The Sydney Morning Herald* and *The Canberra Times*. The largest of Australia's print proprietors is News Corp. Like Fairfax, it is a multiplatform media company but with more interests in pay television, magazines, online and newspapers. It owns about 200 national, metropolitan, suburban, regional and Sunday print titles, including daily metropolitans sold in every state and territory except in Western Australia (Battersby 2017). News Corp owns Australia's only general news national daily broadsheet, *The Australian*.

One hundred years ago, Australia's print newspapers were flourishing. By 1848, there were 11 daily Australian newspapers (Mayer 1964, 10). By 1886 there were 48 daily papers, including regionals. In the 20th century, by 1958, the total number of dailies had grown to 55. This peaked at 56 in 1984 – when profits were high, and advertising revenues were considered 'liquid gold'. It was not to last, as Figure 11.1 shows.

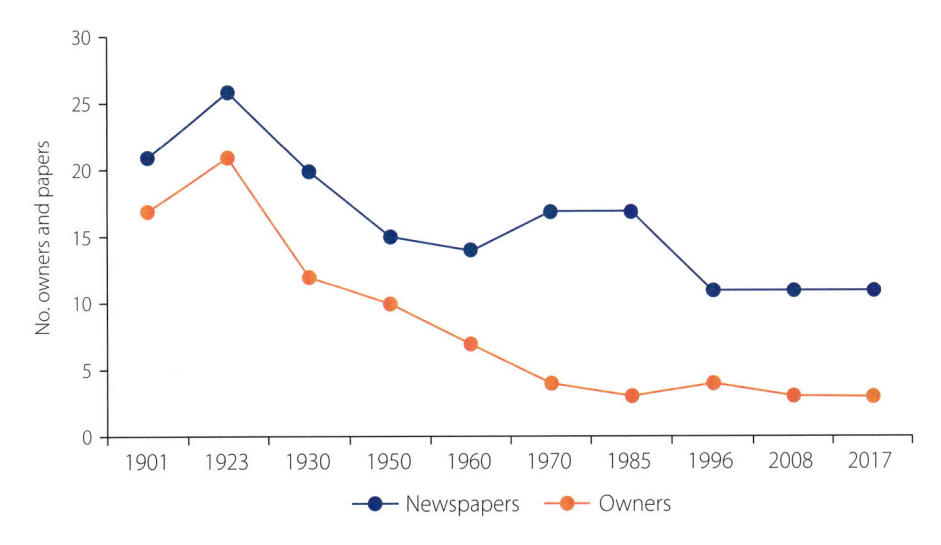

Figure 11.1 The number of Australian mastheads and newspaper owners over time

During the print media company acquisitions and mergers of the late 1980s, 12 of Australia's 19 metropolitan daily newspapers changed hands; two of them changed ownership twice, *The Canberra Times* and *The West Australian* (Tiffen 2015, 67). By 2008, the overall number of Australian daily papers – including regionals – slipped back to its late 19th century figure of 49. Twelve were daily capital city papers, half the number produced at the turn of the 20th century. By 2015, this number appeared to stabilise and Australia now has around 46 daily papers, regional and metropolitan (Tiffen 2015, 70) and 12 daily metropolitan papers. There are three proprietors of these 12 mastheads and two of them, News Corp and Fairfax Media, own 11 between them. This gives these owners a daily newspaper circulation share of about 85 per cent – the highest of any developed democracy (Tiffen 2015, 65).

RESEARCH QUESTION 11.2

What are the costs to the Australian public sphere of having the highest media concentration of ownership or monopolisation of any developed democracy?

However, there were significant changes made to Australia's media laws in 2017. Prior to this the regulatory framework sought to 'support competition policy, discourage concentration of media ownership in local markets, and enhance public access to a diversity of viewpoints, sources of news, information and commentary' (see Gardiner-Garden and Chowns 2001/2006). For example, *Broadcasting (Ownership and Control) Act 1987* that amended the *Broadcasting Act 1942* legislated for an audience 'reach rule' to limit any person controlling interests in licences serving a maximum of 75 per cent of the population. However, a dramatic shift took place with the passage of the Broadcasting Legislation Amendment (Broadcasting Reform) Bill 2017 that changed specific controls over media ownership. It abolished the 'reach rule' that had prevented a single broadcaster from reaching more than 75 per cent of the population, along with the 'two out of three' cross-media control rule which had prevented companies owning three media interests (print, radio and television) in one area. Revenue-based licence fees were also replaced by a lower spectrum charge. It did try to retain a concern with protecting local content in regional media with broadcasters required to provide at least 720 points of local content per six-week period. Nevertheless, the consequences of this legislation for media concentration are stark, allowing the biggest players, News Corp, to be able to buy *all* the print, radio and television in any single market.

The dangers of this increased media concentration were raised by former Prime Minister Rudd who circulated Australia's largest-ever parliamentary e-petition calling for a Royal Commission into media diversity in 2021. While the bid failed, his statements at Parliament House were damning. He claimed the 'Murdoch mob' were seeking 'compliant politicians' and that politicians were fearful of facing a 'systematic campaign'. 'Everyone's frightened of Murdoch', Rudd claimed. 'They really are. There's a culture of fear across the country.' Looking across the city papers of News Ltd, Rudd stated: 'Each paper has their own editors who claim they are not influenced by proprietors, and yet all newspapers have identical front pages – the only difference is the mastheads of the papers.' The making of Sky News Regional as freely available from August 2021 shows the dangers of concentrated ownership, allowing these views to penetrate into some rural communities that lack any alternatives.

Following the popularity of Kevin Rudd's petition, in November 2020 the Senate referred an inquiry into the state of media diversity, independence and reliability and this report was given on 9 December 2021 (Environment and Communications References Committee 2021). Here, the Senate Environment and Communications References Committee summarised the various government policies and regulation regarding media, before engaging directly with failures in the regulatory approach to standards, complaints, digital platforms, and disputes over content, among other things. Perhaps most importantly, it highlighted the concentration of media ownership and the weak regulation in this area (especially regarding News Corp) that required urgent reform. More constructively, it offered a number of policy recommendations to build more diversity into news media across all platforms in Australia and suggested a judicial inquiry would have the capacity for a more comprehensive investigation into media diversity than just a parliamentary inquiry.

MEDIA FREEDOM AND AUSTRALIAN DEMOCRACY

Australia's concentrated media ownership has implications for how the nation is evaluated in terms of its media freedoms. Two international watchdogs on media freedom, Reporters Without Borders (RSF) and Freedom House, assess freedom of the media in nation-states as one measure of a nation's democratic legitimacy. Both ranked Australia below other democracies in 2017 at 19th and 22nd, respectively. Freedom House has measured media freedom since 1979 and Australia has had a noticeable drop in its ranking, shifting from 8th place in 2002 to 22nd in 2017. It has remained ranked 25th by the RSF from 2013 to 2021, who considers press freedom in Australia as 'fragile' (RSF, 2021).

Australia is considered to have a free press but our ranking suffers because of its concentrated media ownership, combined with political and legal environments that restrict reporting in various ways. In the watchdogs' recent annual reports, they identified, as violations of press freedom, new laws related to national security. For example, the Australian Parliament passed a 2014 law that introduced jail terms for journalists who disclosed 'special' intelligence operations. The watchdogs also identified a 2015 law to compel internet and mobile phone providers to store user metadata for two years, which could threaten the ability of journalists to freely interact with sources (Freedom House 2016). Both organisations cite restricted media access into immigration detention centres, onshore and offshore at Nauru and Papua New Guinea, as harmful to Australia's media freedom. Further, Australia's legal environment does not allow for constitutionally guaranteed press freedom at the federal level (Freedom House 2016).[3]

Reporters Without Borders considers Australia's public broadcaster as a positive for media freedom but criticises Australia's heavily concentrated press ownership. It identified the raiding of Labor Party offices in federal police raids during the 2016 federal election campaign – initiated to determine the source of a leaked story about the National Broadband Network that embarrassed the Commonwealth Government – as a violation of confidentiality of sources. The organisation stated that it 'showed that the authorities were more concerned about silencing the "messengers" than addressing the issues of concern to the public that had been raised by their revelations' (RSF 2017). Its 2021 review claimed investigative journalism was 'in danger' across Australia, citing the Federal police raids in June 2019 on the home of a Canberra-based political reporter and the headquarters of the ABC in Sydney, how imperatives of 'national security' were used to intimidate investigative reporters, and that the 2018 defamation laws were 'the harshest of its kind in a liberal democracy'. Moreover, it found that Australia's terrorism laws were so restrictive that it made 'covering terrorism almost impossible' (RSF 2021).

The recent defamation case brought against satirist Jordan Shanks (of 'Friendlyjordies') by NSW Deputy Premier John Barilaro highlights the difficulty of balancing these public goods. While the defamation matter was settled in late 2021, the case also included the arrest of the show's producer, Kristo Langker, charged with stalking and intimidation under special police powers of the Fixated Persons Investigations Unit, which was intended for terrorist investigations. After a dramatic house arrest, the police dropped all charges and Mr Langker was awarded a five-figure payout. The case exemplifies the potential chilling effect such police powers could have on political commentary and freedom of political communication if misused (Ferri 2022).

REFLECTION QUESTION 11.4

In Freedom House's 'Freedom of the Press' (2017) index, Australia was ranked 22, behind New Zealand (19th). The RSF ranked Australia at 25th in the world. Should we be concerned by this ranking?

Response prompt is available at www.cambridge.org/highereducation/isbn/9781009108232/resources

IMPACTS OF MEDIA ECONOMICS

The political economy of media contributes to concentrated media ownership in Australia through company mergers and acquisitions. This has led to fewer professional journalists working in the major news outlets in Australia (MEAA 2017, 6). Newspaper companies, free-to-air (FTA) television and the national broadcaster, the ABC, have seen their newsrooms shrink in recent years due to cost cutting. After several rounds of editorial job cuts during the global financial crisis, the largest single cuts were in 2012 when Fairfax Media, Channel Ten and News Corp combined cut almost 3000 staff (Carson 2013). In March 2017, Fairfax's daily metropolitan mastheads *The Age* and *The Sydney Morning Herald* shed a quarter of its remaining editorial staff: 125 full time jobs (Ward 2017). In 2014, federal government budget cuts to the ABC caused it to shed 10 per cent of its workforce including journalists (Carson 2014). Cuts in 2020 meant another 250 staff were lost – despite the fact the ABC remains the most trusted news provider in the country (Park et al. 2020).

---

[3] It is explicitly protected in Victoria through the Charter of Human Rights and Responsibilities.

Regional towns and rural Australia are particularly vulnerable to cuts to local media services as large companies such as Fairfax find ways to cut costs to their holdings outside the capital cities. Regional television and radio news have also been affected with the ABC shutting five regional radio posts in 2014 and ending the popular national rural program 'The Bush Telegraph'. At the same time, the ABC closed Adelaide's television studio and wound back television production in smaller states.

Of the commercial television networks, Channel Ten has been hardest hit by media market changes. It was put into voluntary administration in mid-2017. The network had a last-minute reprieve when US TV network giant CBS made a winning bid to take over the company. Channels Nine and Seven have also reported massive losses with advertising revenue falls in recent years. Pay TV, streaming video on demand with services like Stan and Netflix, Apple TV and YouTube also impact FTA TV's advertising revenues. Top rating shows that would attract significant advertising dollars like *Stranger Things, Game of Thrones* and *Breaking Bad* are not available on free TV in Australia.

There have been many new digital media entrants to the Australian media market including international companies since the major newsroom job losses in 2012. These include *The Guardian, Daily Mail, Huffington Post, New York Times, Buzzfeed* and, the academic digest, *The Conversation*. These newsrooms are generally smaller than the newsrooms of the past. Thus, they do not attempt to cover everything but rather focus on more niche aspects of news. Generally, Australian politics is part of the reporting mix of these new entrants, although the tone of reporting tends to be more conversational and engaging than traditional outlets (Carson and Muller 2017).

OPPORTUNITIES AND CHALLENGES OF DIGITAL MEDIA TECHNOLOGIES

As we have discussed in this chapter, the development of digital technologies raises formidable challenges for newsrooms and the public sphere in the form of lost revenues, downsizing of newsrooms and fake news, yet the digital media environment also heralds unprecedented opportunities for journalists and political reporting. Three areas of opportunity arising from digital technologies that we will elaborate on here are media collaborations, the use of data reporting, and greater audience participation in public discourse.

OPPORTUNITIES FOR JOURNALISM

Collaboration

Internet connectivity and many-to-many digital networks are some of the conditions which allow for the viral spread of fake news. They have also enabled new collaborations between multiple newsrooms (and countries) to share information in order to reveal wrongdoing. We saw this with the example of the ICIJ and the worldwide collaborative reporting efforts that produced the Panama and Paradise papers. Another example is the not-for-profit US online newsroom *ProPublica*. Their newsroom of 50 journalists work with established media outlets in Europe and America to produce investigative journalism. *ProPublica* has partnered with more than 150 media outlets since its beginnings in 2008 and has won numerous Pulitzer Prizes. Its first Pulitzer was for working with the *New York Times Magazine* in 2010 to trace the devastating consequences of local hospital workers' decisions when cut off by Hurricane Katrina's flood waters (Fink 2009). Through media collaborations, *ProPublica* reduces costs by pooling resources and using different media platforms to reach bigger audiences for stories of public interest (Carson and Farhall 2017). This highlights how we can tell stories in different ways depending on the platform.

On a smaller scale, Australian media outlets are also starting to collaborate with each other, and with non-media outlets such as academia, and winning Walkley Awards for their efforts. These collaborations have been mainly between Fairfax Media and ABC journalists on investigative stories. They include, among others, exposing the Commonwealth Bank's unscrupulous tactics in providing life insurance to customers but avoiding insurance pay-outs. *The Guardian* Australia has partnered with the ABC and US whistleblower Edward Snowden to show how Australian spy agencies attempted to monitor the telecommunications of the Indonesian President Susilo Bambang Yudhoyono and his wife. While University of Technology Sydney journalism students collaborated with experienced *Sydney Morning Herald* reporters to reveal the free trips and gifts that Australian politicians receive. This won the 2012 Walkley Award for Best Digital Journalism.

These examples reveal an innovative adaptation by media outlets in times of cost-cutting to newsrooms. This trend is a major shift away from the 20th century model of reporting where single newsrooms competed against one another for 'scoops'. This century, journalists are seeing the value in collaborations to share resources, reach a bigger audience and to tell public interest stories across different platforms. These stories, as the awards recognise, can lead to important public outcomes such as policy and law reforms, criminal charges, public sackings and Royal Commissions (Carson and Farhall 2017).

Data journalism

The digital era also offers reporters new ways to use numbers to tell stories. In a data-rich age, it is possible for journalists to show their evidence behind a story to increase public trust in the veracity of a report. This might involve displaying original documents online, embedding data in news reports, or using data to produce infographics to tell the news in interesting and interactive ways. News stories about the 2021 Australian annual federal budgets are excellent examples of this type of interactive storytelling using numbers. Journalists are also using big data leaks to crowdsource stories by asking their audiences to help. An early example was Britain's *Guardian* newspaper inviting its readers to scrutinise politicians' expenses after the paper uploaded half a million leaked documents relating to the claimed expenses of members of parliament in 2009. In Australia, former *Sydney Morning Herald* journalist Linton Besser was awarded the 2010 investigative journalism Walkley Award for exposing the Department of Defence's spending of millions of dollars on luxury items that were unrelated to its role. The newspaper built a database to enable the public to trawl through 70 000 defence contracts and to report back any unusual findings.

Pulitzer Prize-winning investigative journalist David Barstow (quoted in Carson and Farhall 2018, 1907) of the *New York Times* argues that investigative reporting is of a higher quality than ever before due to new tools and use of data:

> The very best investigative reporting is a cut above what used to be the best. The highest levels are in part because we have a whole bunch of new tools, our ability to interrogate data, our ability to display original documents, to embed original documents online, digital presentations, our growing sophistication with graphics, growing sophistication with how to integrate all of the different forms of storytelling.

New audiences and participation

Modern newsrooms use data analytics to track audience receptiveness to stories. Academic research with Facebook in 2017 found that understanding the audience through analytics is central to the news process. In-depth case studies with seven Australian digital-only media outlets showed that data analytics allowed for a better knowledge of their audiences. When a story is uploaded, many newsrooms will have the live analytics on a big screen to see what the immediate interest is in the story. Outlets also track their individual page impressions each month to see if readers and viewers are growing (Carson and Muller 2017, 12) and to track what stories social media users engage with.

Social media enables two-way conversations. Through social media, audience interaction is an opportunity to source story ideas and for reporters to get more information and story tip-offs. The research found that social media played a vital role in decisions about how to shape and present the news. Shareability is a key criterion in news judgements, and for this reason video had become an increasingly popular means of presenting a story. The study found contemporary reporters need to consider the audience in every step of the news process: gathering information, posting the story and responding to comments (Carson and Muller 2017, 7).

Finally, scholars such as Wright (2012) and Wojcieszak and Mutz (2009) have revisited the concept of the public sphere in the digital age in their examination of how internet users' 'everyday talk' online can become political. They argue that these online spaces, which are varied and include comment sections of newspapers, online community forums for shared interests or advice forums on topics such as parenting, can become a space for political participation and deliberation that was not available last century.

CHALLENGES FOR JOURNALISM

It is important to acknowledge the challenges for journalism when considering news media in the digital age. These include funding journalism and ways that companies are addressing revenue shortfalls and the decline in public trust across democracies.

Funding journalism

Newspapers do attract new audiences by posting their stories online. In Australia their readership has never been larger; however, the problem is not size. Studies show that most people do not pay for online news; for example, Deloitte's Sixth Annual Media Review (2017) found 90 per cent of people surveyed did not pay for online news. Of those who did, they paid mainly for specialist news, in-depth reporting and trusted brands. Here is a conundrum. Liberal democratic media theorists would argue that newsroom cost-cutting that leads to the shedding of journalists who report on those who wield power – politicians, councils, corporates, statutory authorities and so forth – limits media's watchdog role and this has serious implications for the health of a democracy. The 2012 Finkelstein media inquiry stated that job cuts at Australian newspapers could affect democratic accountability:

> With the growing influence of the internet as an advertising medium and the consequential reduced capacity of newspapers to use advertising revenue to support news production efforts, there is a fear that the civic watchdog, or Fourth Estate, function of news organisations will be permanently weakened with consequential damage to democracy and society's wellbeing. (Finkelstein and Ricketson 2012, 305)

The question, then, is who is going to pay for professional journalists to maintain the Fourth Estate function while there is an expectation that online news is free?

This came to a spectacular head in 2021 when Australians woke up to find that they could not view or share news on Facebook after it blocked such content over proposed changes to Australia's News Media Bargaining Code. These changes were designed to regulate the commercial relationship between the digital giants and the mainstream media when content was shared on online platforms. Facebook cut off all news communication, even health and emergency services, preventing the sharing of public interest journalism. Prime Minister Morrison said this 'confirm(ed) the concerns that an increasing number of countries are expressing about the behaviour of BigTech companies who think they are bigger than governments and that the rules should not apply to them'. He continued that 'they may be changing the world, but that doesn't mean they run it' (Meade 2021). Whereas Google had made separate commercial deals to set up effective licensing agreements, Facebook had not. This led many to fear an increase in misinformation and fake news on its platform without access to quality journalism. Others claimed, however, that 'If Australians don't want to pay for news about their own country, it's hardly the responsibility of foreign companies to foot the bill for them' (Babones 2020). Others still suggested the legislation merely benefited existing Australian media monopoly owners such as News Corp. In the end, the code was watered down in terms of arbitration clauses, and Facebook made deals with significant players like Channel Nine and News Limited, who now had a mechanism to get some money out of social media companies. Nevertheless, small news outlets, regional newspapers, independent news outlets and the Australian public will find little benefit as these will unlikely have the ability to make such agreements. Media diversity will not be increased.

Twenty-first century business models

While there is, as yet, no single silver bullet funding model for journalism, there are some options such as finding a wealthy benefactor (though this raises potential conflicts of interest), relying on philanthropy and public donations, using a non-profit model or diversifying their business interests.

Analysis of new business models for newspapers by the Pew Research Center (Rosenstiel et al. 2012) found that 44 per cent of papers are looking at some form of non-traditional revenue. These included holding events, consulting and selling new business products. Yet, the news industry has not moved very far in finding a model that would replace the once thriving print advertising model of last century. This is a great challenge ahead for traditional news media organisations. Academic research with Facebook found that Australian digital newsrooms are using a hybrid business model to pay their journalists. This model combines several revenue-raising methods. The combination varies depending on the target audience. The most common methods were advertising, **NATIVE ADVERTISING**, building databases and selling access; hosting events related to the media content; using market research to develop and offer new media products; crowdsourcing funds and philanthropy (Carson and Muller 2017, 5); and the least popular model for digital newsrooms was the electronic **PAYWALL** (Carson and Muller 2017, 35). The study showed that this hybrid funding model was working for many online-only Australia news outlets and that consequently most had increased staff numbers in the past five years (Carson and Muller 2017, 48).

Fake news and public trust

Public confidence in the authenticity of public information is being challenged by fake news. The internet and computer algorithms make it easier for false information to spread, whether

NATIVE ADVERTISING: Where advertising has the same presentation style as news stories so that consumers feel like the ad belongs with the content. It can be hard to tell apart from news because it looks so similar.

PAYWALL: An electronic 'fence' used to charge for online content. A hard paywall requires readers to pay before they can access any story online. Soft paywalls allow some free access.

deliberately (fake news) or not (sloppy reporting). A century ago, the 'yellow press', so named because of the yellow pages of the newspapers, fostered scuttlebutt and sensationalism. What is different in the 21st century is that fake news stories, through digital technologies, spread further and faster than before. Since US President Donald Trump's election, public apprehension has intensified about Trump's 'alternative facts', his 'war' on journalists and fake news. Trump used the term to describe parts of the mainstream media with which he disagreed. A recent US Pew Research study found 88 per cent of Americans believe fake news confuses the public about basic facts (Barthel et al. 2016). The Oxford English Dictionary declared fake news its 'word of the year' for 2016, and in 2017 the Collins Dictionary followed suit. Collins defined it as 'false, often sensational, information disseminated under the guise of news reporting'. Brian McNair (2018, x) argues that it is a cultural phenomenon that 'is one expression of a wider crisis of trust in elites, including political and mainstream media elites'. McNair also makes the point that the term is deployed by a subsection of the elites, often on the fringe of mainstream politics, as an ideological weapon across the political spectrum.

Wrong information, whether deliberate (disinformation), malicious (mal-information) or incorrect (misinformation), in the public sphere matters because news needs to be accurate to inform the public and for the public to have confidence in the information they receive (Wardle and Derakhshan 2017). This is part of the normative functions that liberal democratic theorists ascribe to news media in democracies (Carson and Farhall 2018). Inaccurate reporting has consequences for media's role to provide for a well-informed citizenry, particularly during election campaigns when voters decide who to elect.

There were many examples of fake news during the 2017 Brexit campaign in the United Kingdom. One instance was the use of billboards on buses by the Leave campaign claiming that Britain's exit from the European Union would free up £350 million per week for allocation to their National Health Service. Official figures clearly showed this claim to be untrue. In fact, the accurate figure was £250 million per week, and even then, much of this funding returned to the country under various schemes. Once caught out in the lie, Leave campaigners denied that they had meant the £350 million figure to be taken literally (McNair 2018, 28). This is what McNair calls the 'weaponisation' of information for political gain. Consider what misinformation does for public trust in the media.

We know that public trust in the media is declining in Australia, as it is in other democracies. The Edelman Trust Barometer, which researches public trust in the media across 28 countries, found Australians' trust in the media had fallen to 32 per cent in 2017. This was a drop of 10 points from 2016 (Edelman 2017, 75). More recently, Elliott (2019) reported a 14 per cent net decline in Australian's trust in newspapers and magazines between 2014–15 and yet found trust in traditional media in Australia is much greater than the global average. More than half of Australians (57 per cent) trust television and radio, 54 per cent trust newspapers and magazines, and websites and platforms are the least trusted at 45 per cent (Elliott 2019). A 2020 RMIT study showed similar trends, with television deemed the most credible source of information and online news sources the least (Flew et al. 2020). It found news remained more trusted than business and government.

Australian research also finds trust in the Australian media across different outlets is falling, but confidence in some organisations is higher than others. For example, Essential Research (2017) polling found 63 per cent of surveyed Australians said they had 'a lot' or 'some' trust in the ABC compared to only 20 per cent having the same level of trust in blogs. This was confirmed again in 2020 with Flew et. al (2020) noting high levels of trust in the ABC and SBS.

One of the key policy areas that this lack of trust has had the most significant effect on has been climate change. The attempt to balance reporting by including climate scepticism on an equal footing, despite overwhelming scientific consensus, has confused the electorate. Moreover, the views of powerful lobby interests to discredit climate science are routinely embedded in media (see Taylor 2014, Chapter 7). Many other opinion-based platforms promote climate sceptics (i.e. Fox News, Bolt Report) without balance. Recent studies have shown that Australians do not believe the media is partial when it comes to reporting on climate change, with the result that Australians are more likely to dismiss the science of climate change than in most other developed countries and twice as likely to think it is not a serious problem (Park et al. 2020).

SHORT-ANSWER QUESTIONS 11.3

1. What are some of the opportunities for journalists and audiences in the digital age?
2. What are some of the challenges for journalists and audiences in the digital age?

Suggested responses are available at www.cambridge.org/highereducation/isbn/9781009108232/resources

MEDIA AND SURVEILLANCE

There are a range of developments, especially in regard to media technologies and surveillance, that while ancillary to the news media are relevant for the relation of media to democracy. These technologies can heighten the monitoring and control of information and people, raising dire implications for freedom, privacy and human rights. If one takes a closer look at the Freedom House (2020) score, Australia is ranked much lower on Internet Freedom with only 76/100. Why? A key reason has been the highly controversial pro-security legislation known as Australia's **METADATA** retention scheme, passed in 2015, that requires telecommunication and internet service providers (telcos) to retain customer metadata for a period of two years. Metadata is a highly sensitive form of information about the individual. The legislation allows for indiscriminate retention of metadata by telcos and access without a warrant, which goes against forms of due process of Australia's existing warrant-based system. In 2020, Commonwealth Ombudsman Michael Manthorpe admitted the legislation ambiguity had allowed law enforcement officials to access more metadata than originally promised – telcos had sometimes provided the full URLs to law enforcement officials, something supposed to be excluded. Evidence has revealed that police accessed the metadata of journalists and 3365 telecommunications users unlawfully (Karp 2019).

This is not just a question of the separation of powers with the executive overstepping their role, but the affect this might have on people seeking out information on their government. This information could be tracked and used against them. Australian legislators have shown little willingness to fulfil their obligations under the International Covenant on Civil and Political Right relating to privacy, information and association. As Churches and Zalnieriute (2020) have warned, Australia has been left with a 'system of metadata access and retention which does not protect the human rights of its citizens; [and] is disproportionate to the societal objectives sought to be achieved'.

METADATA: Defined as 'data that provides information about other data', online metadata shows a telecommunications user's contacts; location; date, time, duration and form of a communication; web browsing activity; URL accessed, among a range of other forms of data. It enables agencies a digital picture of individuals' movements, contacts, interests and associations.

SUMMARY

Learning objective 1: Understand the production, content, and audience of the news media and its role as the Fourth Estate in a democratic society

Edmund Burke famously claimed the media was the Fourth Estate, distributing information, giving people access to the 'truth' and providing a check on the state. However, resources for journalism are declining and the rise of fake news is spreading disinformation. Media ownership has become highly concentrated so that diversity of sources is constrained. How the news is made and what it covers has become highly politicised. News makers therefore have tremendous power in a society to exclude or include stories and to frame issues for the electorate. The media may offer commentary on current affairs that are taken to be publicly important, but this does not mean all publicly important affairs are on the agenda. By looking at the media sphere as containing production, content and the audience, we can analyse the diverse factors that influence news media's role in a democratic society and the challenges it faces today.

Learning objective 2: Understand what the public sphere is, how the news media is said to contribute to it, and its connection to political discourse

The public sphere is a normative concept regarding the role of the news media in providing the public with information so that they can ultimately make rational choices about who to elect to best represent them. It is a physical and figurative space for people to come together, engage in political discourse and form their opinions. In the 21st century, the public sphere extends to the online environment and, through social media and other digital networks, has the capacity to be global. Many scholars think of the public sphere as being plural rather than a singular space for discussing political issues and ideas.

Learning objective 3: Differentiate between various theories of news media, especially its affect, use and reception

There are a range of theories of media. Critical theory suggested media was a tool of domination, and that it formed a culture industry that produced passive, one-dimensional consumers. A broad school of thought then looked at the effects media has on audiences, positing ways in which mass media can influence people directly by 'injecting' them with messages and frame political discourses within states. Another approach suggested it was the audiences' agency that was important, looking at how they consume media purposefully to meet a variety of our needs. Reception theory, in distinction, looked at how audiences receive media; that is, how individuals and groups interpret or make meaning from media.

Media theorists also have different views on the news media's role in a democracy. There are many contending theories of the effect news media has on audiences. Liberal democratic theorists tend to view it as serving the public sphere in a positive way. Theorists such as McNair, Schudson, Kellner and Keane generally view the media as supporting the wellbeing of democracy through several functions including acting as a check on the (mis)use of power. They understand the media to be diverse and open with the power to disrupt the established social order. Conversely, control theorists such as Herman and Chomsky see the media as activating filters that serve to reinforce the interests of the wealthy and powerful.

Learning objective 4: Explain key changes to the Australian media landscape from the 20th to the 21st century

Australian media are in a state of flux. On one hand, the business model that linked advertising to journalism has broken, and the established media has suffered from cost cutting and professional journalism job losses. On the other hand, the digital age has lowered the barriers to entry to make it easier and cheaper for anyone to purport to be a journalist and to act as a check on power. This century has also seen many international media brands enter the domestic market giving Australians more media options, but these newsrooms tend to be smaller and do not attempt to cover every story as was the endeavour of 20th century newspapers. There has been recent public debate on how content should be shared and paid for between traditional and online platforms.

Learning objective 5: Describe the opportunities and challenges digital technologies present to media organisations and their journalism

As with other sectors, the development of digital technologies has affected media organisations. They provide both opportunities and challenges to journalism and the reporting of politics. On the positive side, digital technologies provide the communication and data sharing means for greater collaboration between journalists and newsrooms, domestically and abroad. Collaborations offer journalists greater resources, audiences and safeguards against persecution than going it alone. Software developments to parse large amounts of data have enabled data journalism to thrive. Journalists can tell stories using numbers in new and engaging ways. The use of data analytics means that the audience is central to every decision including what story to pursue, how to tell it and on which platform. Likewise, people have more options for engaging with stories, reacting to them, and for telling their own.

But media organisations also face challenges. Among the most pressing is finding a sustainable funding model to employ professional journalists. Every indication so far is that this is likely to be a hybrid model whereby media outlets rely on more than one revenue stream to finance their journalism. Another great challenge is how to address the proliferation of fake news and falling levels of trust in the media. Public confidence in journalism is declining in democracies and Australia is no exception.

DISCUSSION QUESTIONS

1. In what century was the Habermasian public sphere thought to have emerged, and how did it exist? In Habermas's view, what triggered its demise?

2. What balance, if any, do you think is required between news, opinion and commentary when reporting on politics and public policies in the digital age? How might this mix change the formation of public opinion in the public sphere?

3. Can you think of examples of how the media in the 21st century plays a role informing the global public sphere about matters in the public interest?

4. Where do Australian audiences get their news from in the 21st century? What concerns exist about contemporary sources of news?

5. What does it mean when voters are increasingly relying on social media to get news? What is the democratic 'promise' of 'new media'? Does the existence of alternative views mean they are equally influential?

FURTHER READING

Errington, W. & Miragliotta, N. (2011). The liberal democratic tradition and the media. *Media and Politics: An Introduction*, Melbourne: Oxford University Press, pp. 1–19.

Herman, E.S. (2000). The propaganda model: A retrospective. *Journalism Studies*, **1**(1), 101–12.

McNair, B. (2018). *Fake News: Falsehood, Fabrication and Fantasy in Journalism*, London: Routledge.

Parliamentary Joint Committee on Intelligence and Security. (2020). Inquiry into the impact of the exercise of law enforcement and intelligence powers on the freedom of the press, Commonwealth of Australia, August 2020. Retrieved from https://www.aph.gov.au/Parliamentary_Business/Committees/Joint/Intelligence_and_Security/FreedomofthePress/Report

Young, S. (2011). Creating election news: Journalists. *How Australia Decides: Election Reporting and the Media*, Melbourne: Cambridge University Press, pp. 107–25.

REFERENCES

Adorno, T.W. (1982). The culture industry reconsidered. *Media Studies: A Reader*, New York: New York University Press.

Almond, G.A., Powell, G.B., Dalton, R.J. & Strom. K. (2010). *Comparative Politics Today: A World View*, 9th edn, Longman: New York.

Australian Associated Press. (2019). Most Sunday papers back vote for Morrison, *The Canberra Times*, 12 May.

Australian Broadcasting Commission (ABC). (2020). Lacking Diversity, *Media Watch*, Episode 19, 15 June. Retrieved from https://www.abc.net.au/mediawatch/episodes/blm/12357278

Babones, S. (2020). Why Facebook is right to pull the plug on Australia, *Foreign Policy*, 20 February. Retrieved from https://foreignpolicy.com/2021/02/20/facebook-australia-media-law-advertising-profits/

Bagdikian, B.H. (2004). *The New Media Monopoly*, Boston: Beacon Press.

Barthel, M., Mitchell, A. & Holcomb, J. (2016). Many Americans believe fake news is sowing confusion, *Pew Research Centre*, 15 December. Retrieved from http://www.journalism.org/2016/12/15/many-americans-believe-fake-news-is-sowing-confusion/

Battersby, L. (2017). News Corp and the Murdochs starting 2017 with more news and influence than before, *The Sydney Morning Herald*, 14 January. Retrieved from http://www.smh.com.au/business/media-and-marketing/news-corp-and-the-murdochs-starting-2017-with-more-news-and-influence-than-before-20170110-gtoo2a.html

Bell, C. (2010). Audience responses. In B. Connell (ed.), *Exploring the Media*, New York: Columbia University Press.

Blair, T. (2007). Tony Blair's 'media' speech: The Prime Minister's Reuters speech on public life. *The Political Quarterly*, **78**(4), October–December, 476–87.

Bobbio, N. (1987). *The Future of Democracy*, Cambridge: Polity Press.

Borah, P. (2016). Media Effects Theory. *The International Encyclopedia of Political Communication*, London: Wiley.

Brevini, B. & Ward, M. (2021). Who controls our media? *GetUp*, 12 April. Retrieved from https://cdn.getup.org.au/2810-GetUp_-_Who_Controls_Our_Media_.pdf

Bruns, A. (2017). *Echo Chamber? What Echo Chamber? Reviewing the Evidence*, St Lucia: University of Queensland. Retrieved from http://snurb.info/files/2017/Echo%20Chamber.pdf

Calhoun, C. (1992). *Habermas and the Public Sphere*, Baskerville: MIT Press.

Cappella, J. & Jamieson, K. (1997). *Spiral of cynicism: The press and the public good*, New York: Oxford University Press.

Carlyle, T. ([1840] 1908). Lecture V: The hero as man of letters: Johnson, Rousseau, Burns. *On Heroes, Hero-Worship, & the Heroic in History. Six Lectures*, London: Dent.

Carson, A. (2013). Investigative journalism, the public sphere and democracy: The watchdog role of Australian broadsheets in the digital age. Unpublished doctoral thesis, University of Melbourne.

—— (2014). ABC cuts a tale of two Australias: Sydney-Melbourne and also-rans, *The Conversation*, 24 November. Retrieved from https://theconversation.com/abc-cuts-a-tale-of-two-australias-sydney-melbourne-and-also-rans-34424

Carson, A. & Farhall, K. (2017). The rise of global collaborative journalism in the 'post-truth' age. Presented at Future of Journalism 2017 conference, Cardiff School of Journalism, Media and Cultural Studies.

—— (2018). Understanding collaborative investigative journalism in a 'post-truth' age. *Journalism Studies*, **19**(13), 1899–911.

Carson, A. & Muller, D. (2017). *The Future Newsroom*, Sydney: Facebook. Retrieved from http://arts.unimelb.edu.au/__data/assets/pdf_file/0003/2517726/20913_fnreport_sept2017_web-final.pdf

Castells, M. (2008). The new public sphere: Global civil society, communication networks, and global governance. *Annals of the American Academy of Political and Social Science*, **616**(1), 78–93.

Churches, G. & Zalnieriute, M. (2020). A window for change: Why the Australian metadata retention scheme lags behind the EU and USA, *AUSPUBLAW*, 26 February. Retrieved from https://auspublaw.org/2020/02/a-window-for-change-why-the-australian-metadata-retention-scheme-lags-behind-the-eu-and-usa

Collins English Dictionary. (2018). *fake news*. Retrieved from https://www.collinsdictionary.com/dictionary/english/fake-news

Conboy, M. (2013). *Journalism Studies: The Basics*, Abingdon: Routledge.

Craig, G. (2004). *The Media, Politics and Public Life*, Sydney: Allen & Unwin.

Croteau, D. & Hoynes, W. (2014). *Media/Society: Industries, Images, and Audiences*, 5th edn, Thousand Oaks: Sage.

Curran, J., Fenton, N. & Friedman, D. (2012). *Misunderstanding the Internet*, Abingdon: Routledge.

Davies, N. (2014). *Hack Attack: The Inside Story of How the Truth Caught Up with Rupert Murdoch*, New York: Faber.

De Burgh, H. (2000). *Investigative Journalism*, London: Routledge.

Dearing, J.W. & Rogers, E.M. (1996). *Agenda-setting*, Thousand Oaks: Sage Publications.

Debord, G. (1992). *Society of the Spectacle*, London: Rebel Press.

Deloitte. (2017). *Media Consumer Survey 2017: Australian media and digital preferences*, 6th edn. Retrieved from http://landing.deloitte.com.au/tmt-media-consumer-survey-2017-inb-lp-ty.html

Duggan, M. & Smith, A. (2016). *The Political Environment on Social Media*, Washington: Pew Research Center. Retrieved from http://assets.pewresearch.org/wp-content/uploads/sites/14/2016/10/24160747/PI_2016.10.25_Politics-and-Social-Media_FINAL.pdf

Edelman Trust Barometer. (2017). Asia Pacific, Middle East and Africa, *Edelman Trust Barometer: Annual Global Study*. Retrieved from http://www.edelman.com/trust2017/trust-asia-pacific-middle-east-africa

Elliot, D. (2019). Australians trust the media less: Ipsos 'Trust in the Media' study, *IPSOS*, 25 June. Retrieved from https://www.ipsos.com/en-au/australians-trust-media-less-ipsos-trust-media-study

Environment and Communications References Committee. (2021). *Media Diversity in Australia*. Retrieved from https://apo.org.au/sites/default/files/resource-files/2021-12/apo-nid315537.pdf

Essential Research. (2017). Trust in media, *Essential Report*, 4 October. Retrieved from https://www.essentialvision.com.au/?s=media&searchbutton=Search

Ettema, J. & Glasser, T. (1998). *Custodians of Conscience: Investigative Journalism and Public Virtue*, New York: Columbia University Press.

Ferri, L. (2022). NSW Police drop charges against Friendlyjordies producer Kristo Langker, ordered to pay legal costs, *News.com.au*, 10 March. Retrieved from https://www.news.com.au/national/nsw-act/courts-law/nsw-police-drop-charges-against-friendlyjordies-producer-kristo-langker-ordered-to-pay-legal-costs/news-story/e5d2cd31127e5341c391117debf5729a

Fink, S. (2009). Deadly choices at memorial, *ProPublica*, 27 August. Retrieved from https://www.propublica.org/article/the-deadly-choices-at-memorial-826

Finkelstein, R. & Ricketson, M. (2012). Report of the Independent Inquiry into the Media and Media Regulation, Australian Government, DBCDE, 2 March. Retrieved from https://www.abc.net.au/mediawatch/transcripts/1205_finkelstein.pdf

Flew, T., Dulleck, U., Park, S., Fisher, C. & Isler, O. (2020). *Trust and Mistrust in Australian News Media*, Brisbane: Digital Media Research Centre.

Four Corners. (2020). Killing Field, *ABC Australia*, 20 March. Retrieved from https://www.abc.net.au/4corners/killing-field/12060538

Freedom House. (2016). *Freedom of the Press 2016*. Retrieved from https://freedomhouse.org/report/freedom-press/freedom-press–2016

—— (2017). *Freedom of the Press 2017*. Retrieved from https://freedomhouse.org/report/freedom-press/freedom-press–2017

—— (2020). *Freedom in the World 2020*. Retrieved from https://freedomhouse.org/country/australia/freedom-world/2020

Gardiner-Garden, J. & Chowns, J. (2001/2006). Media Ownership Regulation in Australia, E-Brief, updated 30 May. Retrieved from https://www.aph.gov.au/about_parliament/parliamentary_departments/parliamentary_library/publications_archive/archive/mediaregulation

Garnham, N. (1990). *Capitalism and Communication*, London: Sage.

Habermas, J. (1989). *The Structural Transformation of the Public Sphere*, trans. T. Burger, Cambridge: MIT Press.

—— (2010). *Europe: The Faltering Project*, trans. C. Cronin, Cambridge: Polity Press.

Hall, S. ([1973] 1980). Encoding/decoding. In Centre for Contemporary Cultural Studies (ed.), *Culture, Media, Language: Working Papers in Cultural Studies, 1972–79*, London: Hutchinson, pp. 128–38.

Hall, S., Critcher, C., Jefferson, T., Clark, J. & Roberts, B. (1978). *Policing the Crisis: Muggings, the State, Law and Order*, Basingstoke: Macmillan Education.

Herman, E.S. & Chomsky, N. (2002). *Manufacturing Consent: The Political Economy of the Mass Media*, New York: Pantheon.

House of Representatives Select Committee on the Print Media. (1992). *News & Fair Facts: The Australian Print Media Industry*, Canberra: Australian Government Publishing.

Ivor, G. & Tiffen, R. (2018). Politics and the media in Australia and the United Kingdom: Parallels and contrasts. *Media International Australia*, **167**(1), 27–40.

Karp, P. (2019). ACT police admit they unlawfully accessed metadata more than 3000 times, *The Guardian*, 26 July. Retrieved from https://www.theguardian.com/australia-news/2019/jul/26/act-police-admit-unlawfully-accessed-metadata-more-than-3000-times

Keane, J. (2010). *The Life and Death of Democracy*, London: Pocket Books.

Kellner, D. (1999). Globalisation from below? Toward a radical democratic technopolitics. *Angelaki: Journal of the Theoretical Humanities*, **4**(2), 101–13. https://doi.org/10.1080/09697259908572039

Kuehn, K.M. & Salter, L.A. (2020). Assessing digital threats to democracy, and workable solutions: A review of the recent literature. *International Journal of Communication*, **14**(2020), 2589–610.

Lang, G.E. & Lang, K. (1983). *The Battle for Public Opinion: The President, the Press and the Polls during Watergate*, New York: Columbia University Press.

Lang, K. & Lang, G.E. (1952). The unique perspective of television and its effects: A pilot study. *American Sociological Review*, **18**, 3–12.

Leveson, L.J. (2012). *An Inquiry into the Culture, Practices and Ethics of the Press – Report*. Retrieved from https://www.gov.uk/government/publications/leveson-inquiry-report-into-the-culture-practices-and-ethics-of-the-press

Lippmann, W. ([1922] 1997). *Public Opinion*, New York: Harcourt Brace.

Lukamto, W. & Carson, A. (2016). POLITWEETS: Social media as a platform for political engagement between Victorian politicians and citizens. *Communication Research and Practice*, **2**(2), 191–212.

Macnamara, J. & Kenning, G. (2014). E-electioneering 2007–13: Trends in online political campaigns over three elections. *Media International Australia Incorporating Culture and Policy*, **152**, 57–74. https://doi.org/10.1177/1329878X1415200107

Mayer, H. (1964). *The Press in Australia*, Melbourne: Lansdowne Press.

McCombs, M.E. &. Shaw, D.L (1972), The agenda-setting function of mass media. *The Public Opinion Quarterly*, **36**(2), 176–87.

McLuhan, M. (1964). *Understanding Media: The Extensions of Man*, New York: McGraw-Hill.

McNair, B. (1999). *An Introduction to Political Communication*, 2nd edn, London: Routledge.

—— (2006). *Cultural Chaos: Journalism, News and Power in a Globalised World*, London: Routledge.

—— (2018). *Fake News: Falsehood, Fabrication and Fantasy in Journalism*, London: Routledge.

McNair, B., Flew, T., Harrington, S. & Swift, A. (2016). *Politics, Media and Democracy in Australia*, London: Routledge.

McQuail, D. (1983). *With Benefits to Hindsight: Reflections on Uses and Gratifications Research. Critical Studies in Mass Communication Theory: And Introduction*, Beverly Hills: Sage.

Meade, A. (2021). Prime minister Scott Morrison attacks Facebook for 'arrogant' move to 'unfriend' Australia, *The Guardian*, 18 February.

Media, Entertainment and Arts Alliance (MEAA). (2017). Submission to the Senate Select Committee Inquiry into Public Interest Journalism, 14 July. Parliament of Australia. Retrieved from https://www.aph.gov.au/Parliamentary_Business/Committees/Senate/Future_of_Public_Interest_Journalism/PublicInterestJournalism/Submissions

Miliband, R. (1973). *Parliamentary Socialism*, London: Merlin.

Nagle, A. (2017). *Kill All Normies: Online Culture Wars from 4chan and Tumblr to Trump and the Alt-Right*, London: Zero Books.

NBC. (2021). Study #210016 – NBC News Survey, 10–13 January. Retrieved from https://assets.documentcloud.org/documents/20457943/210016-nbc-news-january-poll-1-17-21-release.pdf

Newman, N., Fletcher, R., Kalogeropoulos, A., Levy, D.A.L. & Nielsen, R.K. (2017). *Reuters Institute Digital News Report 2017*, Oxford: Reuters Institute for the Study of Journalism. Retrieved from https://www.digitalnewsreport.org/

Oates, S. (2008). *Introduction to Media and Politics*, London: Sage.

Pariser, E. (2011). *The Filter Bubble: What the Internet is Hiding from You*, London: Penguin.

Park, S., Fisher, C., Lee, Y.J., McGuinness, K., Sang, Y., O'Neil, M., Jensen, M., McCallum, K. & Fuller, G. (2020). *Digital news report: Australia 2020*, News and Media Research Centre, University of Canberra. Retrieved from https://www.canberra.edu.au/research/faculty-research-centres/nmrc/digital-news-report-australia-2020

Parliamentary Joint Committee on Intelligence and Security. (2020). Inquiry into the impact of the exercise of law enforcement and intelligence powers on the freedom of the press, Commonwealth of Australia, August. Retrieved from https://www.aph.gov.au/Parliamentary_Business/Committees/Joint/Intelligence_and_Security/FreedomofthePress/Report

Reporters Without Borders (RSF). (2017). *2017 World Press Freedom Index*. Retrieved from https://rsf.org/en/ranking_table

—— (2021). *2021 World Press Freedom Index*. Retrieved from https://rsf.org/en/australia

Rosenstiel, T., Jurkowitz, M. & Hong, J. (2012). *The Search for a New Business Model*, Pew Research Centre, 5 March. Retrieved from https://www.journalism.org/2012/03/05/search-new-business-model

Schudson, M. (1995). *The Power of News*, Cambridge: Harvard University Press.

—— (2008). *Why Democracies Need an Unlovable Press*, Cambridge: Polity Press.

—— (2011). *The Sociology of News*, 2nd edn, San Diego: Norton.

Siebert, F.S., Peterson, T. & Schramm, W. (1984/1956). *Four Theories of the Press: The Authoritarian, Libertarian, Social Responsibility, and Soviet Communist Concepts of What the Press Should Be and Do*, Urbana: University of Illinois Press.

Simons, M. (2007). *The Content Makers: Understanding the Media in Australia*, Melbourne: Penguin.

Smethurst v Commissioner of Police [2020] HCA 14.

Stephens, M. (1988). *A History of News*, New York: Viking Press.

Sunstein, C. (2007). *Republic.com 2.0*, Princeton: Princeton University Press.

Taylor, M. (2014). *Global Warming and Climate Change: What Australia Knew and Buried*, Canberra: ANU Press.

The Economist. (2017). Do social media threaten democracy? *The Economist*, 4 November, 19–22.

Tiffen, R. (2015). From punctuated equilibrium to threatened species: The evolution of Australian newspaper circulation and ownership. *Australian Journalism Review*, **37**(1), 63–80.

Tiffen, R. & Gittins, R. (2009). *How Australia Compares*, 2nd edn, Melbourne: Cambridge University Press.

Volkmer, I. (2014). *The Global Public Sphere: Public Communication in the Age of Reflective Interdependence*, Cambridge: Polity Press.

Wall, M. (2005). Blogs of war: Weblogs as news. *Journalism*, **6**(2), 153–72.

Ward, M. (2017). Fairfax Media to axe 125 editorial jobs as part of $30 m restructure, *Mumbrella*, 3 May. Retrieved from https://mumbrella.com.au/fairfax-media-axe-125-editorial-jobs-part-30m-restructure-442106

Wardle, C. & Derakhshan, H. (2017). Information disorder: Toward an interdisciplinary framework for research and policymaking. *The Council of Europe*. Retrieved from https://shorensteincenter.org/wp-content/uploads/2017/10/PREMS-162317-GBR-2018-Report-de%CC%81sinformation.pdf?x78124

Warren, C. (2019). Australia just had its first social media election, *Crikey*, 27 May. Retrieved from https://www.crikey.com.au/2019/05/27/social-media-2019-election/

West, R.L. & Turner, L.H. (2010). *Uses and Gratifications Theory. Introducing Communication Theory: Analysis and Application*, Boston: McGraw-Hill, pp. 392–409.

Williams, B. (2017). Journalists, look out: Google is funding the rise of the AI news machine in Europe, *Mashable*, 7 July. Retrieved from https://mashable.com/2017/07/07/google-ai-journalism-funding-europe/#cgw1ydf63sq8

——— (2020). It's a man's world at the top: Gendered media representations of Julia Gillard and Helen Clark, *Feminist Media Studies*, 1–20.

Wojcieszak, M. & Mutz, D. (2009). Online groups and political discourse: Do online discussion spaces facilitate exposure to political disagreement? *Journal of Communication*, **59**(1), 40–56.

Wright, S. (2012). From 'third place' to 'third space': Everyday political talk in non-political online spaces. *Javnost – The Public*, **19**(3), 5–20.

Wunsch-Vincent, S., Vickery, G., Serra Vallejo, C. & Youn Oh, S. (2010). Evolution of news and the internet. *OECD Working Party on the Information Economy*, Paris: Organisation for Economic Co-operation and Development.

Zhou, N. (2020). It dampens the conversation: No more excuses for Australian media's lack of diversity, *The Guardian*, 28 June.

CHAPTER 12
HAVING A VOICE
Citizen participation and engagement

LEARNING OBJECTIVES

After reading this chapter, you should be able to:

1. Describe the organisational landscape of political participation in Australia and the variety of tactics employed by citizens' groups
2. Outline and evaluate the ways in which Australian governments engage with citizens' groups
3. Discuss the challenges arising from the growing demand for political participation and engagement in the 21st century

INTRODUCTION

While conventional accounts of the political landscape highlight Australia's well-established formal institutions such as the electoral system, parliament, federalism, the public service and judiciary, a holistic approach to the study of Australian politics must also include the political contributions of a wider range of citizens and the various ways in which governments attempt to structure their input. In the 21st century, political participation by a diverse range of citizens' groups in Australia is expanding. In contrast, Aboriginal and Torres Strait Islander First Nations' groups have experienced a drastic change in political participation following the demise of two national Indigenous representative organisations this century.

Australian governments provide a range of opportunities for citizens to contribute to political debate and public policy. Key examples include invitations to submit written and/or oral statements; hosting public forums and conventions such as 'community cabinets'; forming issue-specific stakeholder groups; administering surveys and national votes; and establishing more formal **COLLABORATIVE GOVERNANCE** arrangements, particularly for managing natural resources. The relative merits and drawbacks of these government-initiated arrangements are discussed with reference to theoretical modelling of community engagement.

The chapter begins with a description of the organisational landscape of citizens' groups in Australian politics and an overview of the various terms used to describe them including **INTEREST GROUPS**, pressure groups, non-governmental organisations (NGOs) and the non-profit sector. It surveys the most common political strategies employed by groups seeking to influence political debate. These comprise the organisation of public protests and demonstrations, the dissemination of campaign material through various media, consumer activism, and engaging with formal institutional politics. The chapter summarises the main advantages and drawbacks for the political system arising from the active participation and engagement of citizens' groups.

The final section of the chapter examines the new challenges arising from the growing citizen participation and demand for community engagement in Australian politics. These comprise debates over the extent of representativeness and transparency of citizens' groups and their resulting legitimacy, the appropriate level of public funding for citizens' groups, state governments' legislative attempts to curtail public demonstrations, and the phenomenon of '**SLACKTIVISM**'. The discussion of these issues demonstrates how the participation and engagement of citizens' groups is evolving in 21st century Australia.

COLLABORATIVE GOVERNANCE: Governments transferring some degree of decision-making power to citizens' groups and/or other stakeholders, such as business actors and other levels of government.

INTEREST GROUPS: Associations of individual people or organisations with shared objectives which aim to influence the political process.

SLACKTIVISM: A pejorative term for activism conducted via online media.

THE ORGANISATIONAL LANDSCAPE OF CITIZEN PARTICIPATION

CIVIL SOCIETY

In Australia, a nation with relatively few restraints on political freedom, a vast array of citizens' groups is actively engaged in politics and public policy, both within formal processes as well as external to governments. Australian citizens' groups are extremely diverse, hailing from all facets of organised Australian social life, yet also having the common desire to advance their own sectional or altruistic interests. Many also have global linkages including, for example:

1. Australian Childcare Alliance
2. Australian Christian Lobby
3. Australian Conservation Foundation
4. Australian Council of Social Service
5. Australian Government Primary Principals Association
6. Australian Medical Association
7. Australian Red Cross
8. Australians for Constitutional Monarchy
9. Australians for Native Title and Reconciliation
10. Beyond Blue
11. Business Council of Australia
12. Civil Society Australia
13. Climate Action Network of Australia
14. Diversity Council Australia
15. Federation of Ethnic Communities Councils of Australia
16. GetUp!
17. Minerals Council of Australia
18. National Farmers' Federation
19. National Rifle Association of Australia
20. National Union of Students
21. Oxfam Australia
22. Save the Children
23. Smith Family
24. United Patriots Front
25. Wilderness Society of Australia

UNIONS

Australia has a long history of organisation among workers advocating for better pay and conditions, to the extent that colonial conflict between labour and employers provided the foundation for much of 20th century Australian politics. The earliest recorded strike action dates back to 1791, and one of the most substantial strikes before Federation was the 1854 Eureka Rebellion which led to the Battle of Eureka Stockade. This initial gold rush period resulted in an influx of migrants from nations other than England. They arrived with knowledge and experience of how to advocate and lobby for better work conditions, thus unions emerged (see Bertone,

Griffin and Iverson 1995). Today unions operate at the national and state level and represent workers across most industries – and include, for example:

- Australian Council of Trade Unions (ACTU)
- Australian Federation of Air Pilots
- Australian Maritime Officers Union
- Australian Education Union
    - New South Wales Teachers Federation
    - Queensland Teachers Union
    - State School Teachers Union of Western Australia
- Australian Nursing and Midwifery Federation
    - New South Wales Nurses and Midwifery Federation
    - Queensland Nurses & Midwives Union
- Australian Workers' Union
- Builders Labourers Federation Union
- Transport Workers Union
- Construction, Forestry, Mining and Energy Union (CFMEU)
- Community and Public Sector Union
- Health Services Union
- Media, Entertainment and Arts Alliance
- Textile and Clothing and Footwear Union of Australia.

INDIGENOUS ACTORS

Aboriginal and Torres Strait Islander peoples have a history of engaging with western organisational structures dating back to the early twentieth century. Aboriginal and Torres Strait Islander leaders learned the mechanisms of engagement with colonial administrations including various forms of advocacy, lobbying, and collective organising from black and white immigrants (see Attwood and Markus 2004; Goodall 1982; Maynard 2003; Sharp 1993). In the 1950s this knowledge and experience led to organisation and activism against exclusion and discrimination and culminated in a national movement for civil rights and constitutional reform. Constitutional changes in the 1967 referendum removed a constitutional prohibition on the counting of Aboriginal and Torres Strait Islander peoples in the census. After several years of more protest and activism in the 1970s, governments responded by distributing funds for Indigenous-specific programs and, by extension, the proliferation of Indigenous civil society organisations across Australia. Indigenous organisations advocate, lobby for and influence policy that directly affects their lives. Bradfield (2006, 80) notes 'Indigenous peoples in Australia enjoy less formal political autonomy than in any comparable settler society in the world'. Indigenous representative bodies that assert Indigenous rights, interests and status as First Nations people have struggled to survive in the broader political environment (see Bourne 2017). As a result of settlement and colonisation, Aboriginal and Torres Strait Islander peoples are **STRUCTURALLY DISADVANTAGED** and thus

STRUCTURAL DISADVANTAGE: Disadvantage experienced by individuals or groups in society because of the way society functions. For example, who has the privilege of deciding how resources are distributed, how laws are made, how institutions are organised, and which institutions are valued and upheld or reformed.

have a unique relationship with the state. This structural disadvantage is reflected in the way Indigenous organisations are constructed, often reliant solely on government funding and therefore at the whim and the will of governments (see Brigg and Curth-Bibb 2017). Since 1972 a range of government funded national Indigenous representative structures have existed with relatively short life spans (see Table 12.1).

TABLE 12.1 ABORIGINAL AND TORRES STRAIT ISLANDER PEAK ORGANISATIONS

ORGANISATION NAME	LIFE SPAN	ORGANISATION TYPE
National Aboriginal Consultative Committee	1973–1977	Advisory body to the Commonwealth government. Made up of an elected assembly of 41 Aboriginal and Torres Strait Islander people from 41 electorates estimated to represent the views of approximately 800 First Nation's communities.
National Aboriginal Conference	1977–1985	Advisory body to government. Made up of an elected 10-member national executive drawn from representatives elected to state branches.
Aboriginal and Torres Strait Islander Commission (ATSIC)	1990–2005	A statutory authority in the public sector. A comprehensive representative structure with elected regional and national councils., including service delivery responsibilities.
National Congress of Australia's First Peoples	2010–2019	A company limited by guarantee, a membership organisation, a civil society organisation. With three membership categories for peak bodies, organisational representatives and individuals, respectively. Forty representatives elected by the relevant members to form three chambers that formed a 120-member congress. The board of directors were elected through the chambers and the co-chairs were elected by all members of the organisation.
Coalition of Peaks	2019–current	A coalition of Indigenous health peak organisations with formal terms of reference. Not incorporated. Supported by a small secretariat hosted by the National Aboriginal Community Controlled Health Organisation.

After the demise of ATSIC, the National Congress of Australia's First Peoples provided a much smaller scale representative structure; however, successive governments have demonstrated a preference to engage with First Nations peoples through committees, expert panels and councils. These groups have largely had a combined membership of Indigenous and non-Indigenous membership. This has prompted First Nations leaders to explore options to achieve a more permanent arrangement; an arrangement that ensures Aboriginal and Torres Strait Islander peoples have a voice that can influence policies that directly affect their lives (e.g. Treaty, Voice to Parliament).

In political science, and more generally, a variety of terms are used to describe citizen-based groups. Among these are interest groups, NGOs, **CIVIL SOCIETY** groups, community organisations, pressure groups, associations, social enterprises, advocacy groups, lobby groups, non-profit organisations, social movements, charities, activist groups and cooperatives. While this seemingly crowded field indicates complexity in the realm of citizens' political participation, four common elements may be identified. First, citizens' groups attempt to exert influence from

CIVIL SOCIETY: The sphere of society that is distinct from governments and business, above the level of the family and distinct from the institutions of the state.

outside parliament and do not generally seek to become formal representatives. Second, they represent a relatively narrow set of citizens and/or limited issue-based concerns in contrast to major political parties, which tend to develop comprehensive sets of policies across most issue-areas. Third, participation in citizens' groups is voluntary. And fourth, the primary motivation for such groups is not usually to generate a financial profit. Citizens' groups are thus conceptually located above the level of the family but separate from government and the market.

The organising principle for citizens' groups is affiliation, or a sense of affiliation, that individuals may have with a broader set of citizens. Citizens' groups are organised at all levels of politics at the grassroots, municipal, regional, state/territory, national and global levels. They include groups such as local community clubs and churches to environmental NGOs, trade unions, professional bodies and business associations. It is important to note that business entities are increasingly engaged in public advocacy on a range of issues alongside regular citizens' groups, and in this sense, they may reasonably be included in such discussions. A prominent example is the more than 1300 businesses operating in Australia that had pledged support for marriage equality. Indeed, Qantas, Airbnb, Fairfax Media and Foxtel even produced and distributed marriage equality 'acceptance rings' to support the cause (Urban 2017). These groups can also be 'defensive' in nature, to campaign for the retention of particular policies or policy outcomes, such as the Minerals Council campaign regarding coal usage, or the Australian Hotels Association concerning alcohol sale and poker machine licenses.

CATEGORISING CITIZENS' GROUPS

Among the most common is the notion of 'insider' versus 'outsider' groups (Grant 1978). Outsiders are said to have little access to governments, few economic resources, and mainly focus on public channels to air their grievances and elicit support. Examples include animal liberation groups, anti-vaccination organisations or the Occupy Wall Street protesters. Outsider groups employ various tactics of persuasion, but they often rely on evocative language, images and public protest to generate support.

In contrast, insider groups enjoy relative ease of access to elected representatives and bureaucrats, considerable economic resources, and consequently employ less visible political strategies. Examples of Australian insider groups include the Australian Council of Trade Unions (ACTU), National Farmers' Federation, Australian Chamber of Commerce and Industry, and Returned Servicemen's League. Because members typically pay fees, insider groups often have a professional staff, management structure, annual budget and the capacity to undertake research to inform their policy positions.

While the insider/outsider typology provides insights into citizens' groups relative access to governments and economic resources, in practice, many groups straddle both camps according to the preferences of the government of the day. On occasions, the insider status of some groups fails to result in the desired level of influence, prompting instead media campaigns that seek to rally citizens to their cause and thereby pressure governments from the outside. In 2010, the use of a $22 million national advertising campaign by the Minerals Council of Australia to argue against the Rudd Government's proposed 'super-profits' mining tax is one such example (Davis 2011).

A second method for categorising citizens' groups is on the basis of their primary function. Distinguishing groups according to whether they serve a promotional (public interest) or sectional (private interest) role (Warhurst 2009, 329) highlights the political motivations of various groups and the range of citizens they aim to represent. For example, **PROMOTIONAL GROUPS** often publicise underreported dimensions of issues that they believe are neglected by

PROMOTIONAL GROUPS: Citizens' organisations working toward public interest rather than private, instrumental objectives.

the media and policymakers. Exit International, which advocates the legalisation of euthanasia, is one such organisation. Promotional groups often seek to make claims about the moral, rights-based or ethical dimensions of an issue and group membership is rarely restrictive. In fact, the primary aim of some promotional groups is not to represent a broader set of citizens but to publicise the philosophical merits of a principle or idea, regardless of the number of supporters. In contrast, **SECTIONAL GROUPS** are said to primarily exist to serve the interests of members and membership is often restricted by occupation, business type or industry sector. Examples include the Housing Industry Association, Pharmacy Guild of Australia or Transport Workers Union. Sectional groups are likely to be relatively well-funded due to the financial contributions of members.

> **SECTIONAL GROUPS:** Organisations that seek to represent the interests of a particular sector or cohort of society, often a particular profession or industry.

The promotional versus sectional typology is closely linked to the public/private dichotomy, which similarly distinguishes business associations, occupational lobby groups and trade unions from groups seen as representing the broader public interest. In other words, private interest groups are viewed as largely self-interested and instrumental organisations, while public interest groups are seen as selflessly working toward the betterment of society. In reality, however, the distinction between promotional (or public interest) and sectional (private interest) groups is murky. At face value, trade unions, for instance, are primarily sectional groups seeking to advance the rights of members, but they also play promotional roles that may serve the broader public interest. Groups such as the ACTU and the Australian Medical Association concurrently represent members while campaigning to promote social justice more broadly through their support for campaigns against domestic violence and gender discrimination. Meanwhile, business associations such as the Clean Energy Council, which officially represents the Australian renewable energy industry, may be understood as serving a simultaneous public interest function by promoting low emissions energy alternatives to fossil fuels. Further, business associations often engage in philanthropic causes not directly related to advancing their private interests. The Small Business Association of Australia, for instance, supports the Act for Kids support service, which aims to treat and prevent child abuse and neglect.

Classifying citizens' groups according to their orientation towards existing policy settings is yet another system for distinguishing between groups. Such a scheme might divide groups into the categories of 'conformer', 'reformer' or 'radical' (Scholte, O'Brien and Williams 1999, 112). Conformer groups seek to maintain the policy status quo and typical examples include some business groups, such as the Australian Hotels Association seeking to preserve existing policy approaches to poker machines, or religious groups striving to uphold the traditional conception of marriage. Alternatively, radical groups may wish to overhaul existing policies in their entirety and replace them with fundamentally different approaches to organising public life. Examples might include far-right nationalist groups such as United Patriots Front, 'deep green' environmental groups such as Earth First! Australia or the Socialist Alliance. Meanwhile, situated between conformers and radicals, reformer groups work within existing political frameworks to adapt policies according to their particular issues and priorities. Notable Australian examples include the Australian Conservation Foundation, Australian Council of Social Service and the ACTU. A strength of this classification method is that it avoids distinguishing between the moral and instrumental goals of citizens' groups, instead highlighting their degree of support for the status quo. However, the boundary between proposing reform and advocating radical change is open to interpretation. Some might view the harm minimisation objectives of the Australia Drug Law Reform Foundation as radical, while others perceive it as advocating sensible policy change.

In short, while there is no one recognised way to classify citizens' groups, the various typologies outlined above encourage consideration of citizens' groups' proximity to elected representatives, the main functions they undertake, and their general policy orientations. Together, these are important factors in understanding the varied roles and significance of citizens' groups in Australia and elsewhere.

POLITICAL STRATEGIES FOR PUBLICISING CITIZENS' CONCERNS

Citizens' groups employ an extensive repertoire of tactics in an effort to influence politics and public policy. These may be divided into four key strategies, often employed simultaneously: conducting public activities and performances, developing and disseminating documentation via a range of media, consumer activism, and engaging with formal political structures. While these generic political strategies are also used by elected representatives and governments to influence public life, they are cornerstones of citizens' groups' *modus operandi* given that they typically lack formal authority through which to realise their goals. In particular, the use of new media and consumer activism by citizens' groups has proliferated in the 21st century, which has proved challenging for governments.

Conducting public activities and performances

Citizens groups regularly engage in public activities or performances designed to attract media coverage. These activities include organising and participating in public demonstrations and protests; acts of civil disobedience; media appearances, such as interviews on news and current affairs programs; and staging press conferences.

Public demonstrations are a staple of Australian public life. They involve people marching in the streets or assembling at specific venues such as parliaments, armed with signs and slogans summarising their cause and a range of speakers rallying the crowd. In a globally coordinated event in November 2015, for instance, thousands of citizens participated in a Peoples' Climate Rally, comprising a march through city streets in Sydney, Canberra, Perth and Hobart, plus a number of regional Australian towns, to call for stronger measures to address global warming in the lead up to the Paris UN climate conference. In August 2017, citizens from trade union, youth, conservative Christian, and LGBTIQ groups clashed in Canberra's Civic Square advocating their opposing views about the Safe Schools program initiated by the Victorian Government, which promotes the inclusivity of same-sex attracted, intersex and gender diverse students. Similarly, Reclaim Australia supporters have repeatedly conflicted with anti-racism groups such as No Room for Racism at rallies around Australia in recent years. In short, public demonstrations attract media attention to an issue, demonstrate the strength and depth of concern among citizens, attract supporters and detractors, and may ultimately result in a governmental response in the form of policy change.

Acts of civil disobedience are another avenue for citizens' groups – and individuals – aiming to attract public attention in order to influence the political process. These may comprise 'sit-ins' or the chaining of individuals to buildings or equipment requiring a police presence and forcible removal. In essence, civil disobedience is a principled refusal to adhere to a particular law for moral or ethical reasons. Indeed, in 2016, the secretary of the ACTU, Sally McManus, contentiously stated that the right of citizens to defy 'bad laws' is an essential aspect of democratic participation (ABC News 2017). In the early 1980s, civil disobedience was prominently employed by environmental activists opposed to hydroelectric dams in Tasmania. It resulted in 1500 citizens arrested and a further 500 detained in prison for purposefully breaking a state law making 'lurking, loitering or secreting' in the Franklin River forests area illegal (Tierney 2003). More recently, in regard to health policy and illicit drug use, terminally ill people and those with chronic pain are challenging laws that criminalise the use of cannabis for medicinal purposes by continuing to source and administer cannabis for pain relief. Civil disobedience has also been employed by journalists refusing to reveal sources of information, gay law reform activists, and illegal workers' actions such as strikes.

Representatives of citizens' groups contribute frequent media appearances and even conduct their own press conferences and media forums to publicise their causes. Indeed, many news reports include input not only from government and opposition party spokespeople but community and stakeholder representatives from industry, trade unions and an array of other citizens' groups. In 2016, the proposed restrictions on lever-action shotguns, an issue that pitted civil libertarians and conservatives against gun control and greens groups, resulted in numerous media appearances by citizens' groups including Gun Control Australia, the Alannah and Madeline Foundation, the Australian Medical Association, the Sporting Shooters Association of Australia, Firearm Owners United, the National Farmers' Federation, and the National Rifle Association. In regard to hosting forums, ACOSS's (Australian Council of Social Service) regular NGO Media Forums bring together journalists, professional experts, and researchers to discuss the community services sector. And in 2012, Greenpeace and the Sydney Aquarium held a joint press conference to highlight the vulnerability of the Great Barrier Reef to coal mining in Australia (Greenpeace International 2012). Regardless of the particular format employed, media engagement is a crucial method for citizens' groups to publicise their concerns to governments and the wider electorate.

Producing and disseminating documentary material

Citizens' groups produce documentary material in many different forms in their effort to influence public debate. These include press releases, public statements, position papers, reports, newsletters, open letters, petitions, posters, pamphlets, advertisements, opinion pieces, letters to the editor, films, books and public announcements. Such materials are disseminated via newspapers, television, radio, citizens' groups' websites, social media, billboards, car bumpers and the postal service. Examples of these contributions are endless, but a number of recent noteworthy instances include:

- Lock the Gate's films about the social and environmental impact of coal mining and gas extraction *Fractured country: an unconventional invasion* and *Undermining Australia: coal vs communities*

- *Coal; making the future possible* and *Little Black Rock* advertising campaigns advocating the current and future requirement of coal for energy production, supported by mining companies and sections of the union movement (e.g. CFMEU, ETU, plus others)

- *Ban the super-trawler* car stickers and associated campaign material targeting factory fishing vessels in Australian waters involving Greenpeace, Stop the Trawler Alliance and recreational fishers' groups, among others

- *Without Trucks Australia Stops* car stickers and associated material advocating a nationally regulated road transport industry, supported by the various road transport (industry) bodies, the Transport Workers Union, and many trucking companies.

- Australia Defence Association's letter to the *Australian Financial Review* in November 2015 advocating that Defence Housing Australia remain in public hands

- United Voice's report *Who pays for our common wealth: tax practices of the ASC 200* and associated video advertisements about corporate tax avoidance and wealth inequality in Australia

- People with Disability Australia's Twitter, YouTube, Pinterest and Facebook pages advocating funding for the National Disability Insurance Scheme
- Australians Together four-episode DVD *Sharing our story* about Australian history and the current generation of Indigenous people
- Sustainable Population Australia's media releases, submissions, brochures, books, and articles available on their website.

Consumer activism

In the 21st century, consumer activism has emerged as a significant and increasingly common strategy for citizens' groups in promoting their causes. It involves groups promoting the purchase of ethically and/or sustainably produced goods that reflect a political belief or set of beliefs; or it may involve calls to boycott particular products or corporations on the basis of perceived deficiencies in their production processes. The rise of ethical investment, organically certified goods, free range meats and eggs, fair trade coffee and a host of global groups that set voluntary standards such as Fairtrade International, Forest Stewardship Council and Marine Stewardship Council are indicative of the recent surge in consumer activism. The market mechanism of consumption offers a potentially significant source of leverage because accusations made by citizens' groups about unethical and unsustainable production practices may affect corporate reputations and ultimately profitability. The eventual goal of consumer activism is to persuade governments to enhance their regulation of industrial activity to reflect contemporary community values about corporate production processes, although if business responds to community pressure this may also alleviate the need for a policy response.

In regard to ethical and sustainable consumption, there are numerous certification schemes administered by a range of groups. In addition to those mentioned above, notable examples include Rainforest Alliance certification, Aquaculture Stewardship Council certification, Fair Tax Mark, the UTZ Certified program, Ethical Clothing Australia certification and Responsible Investment Australia Association certification. These schemes typically involve the setting of standards and development of product labels by citizens' groups, applications by producers to be certified as compliant with a scheme's standards and use of the scheme's label on product packaging and in advertising material. Such labels are signposts to consumers seeking to align their political beliefs with their consumption choices, subject to their ability to pay premium prices. A recent example of a corporate boycott in Australia is the 'NoHarveyNo' campaign orchestrated by GetUp! and Markets for Change (GetUp! 2017). The groups demanded that retailer Harvey Norman cease selling furniture produced from native forest timber. In general, consumer activism strategies aim to pressure businesses to adhere to higher social and/or environmental production practices without necessarily resorting to the coercive power of the state.

Engaging with formal politics

Alongside the evolving strategies outlined above, many citizens' groups continue to employ more traditional advocacy methods. In broad terms, traditional advocacy may be understood as engaging with formal political structures – the agents and institutions of the state. This may take a number of forms. First, citizens' groups may use the legal system to test existing or proposed government policies and corporate activities. This is often referred to as 'lawfare'. In 2016, for example, the Australian Conservation Foundation sought to challenge Adani's Carmichael coal mine in Queensland's Galilee Basin in the Federal Court. Similarly, in 2017, Environmental Justice Australia initiated Federal Court proceedings against the Commonwealth Bank for not disclosing sufficiently the risk that climate change poses to its business and the resulting impacts on shareholders.

The contribution of financial donations to political parties and individuals running for office by citizens' groups is another aspect of citizen participation in formal politics. The National Shop, Distributive and Allied Employees' Association, for instance, donated $657 395 to the Australian Labor Party (ALP) in the 2015–16 financial year, while the Alliance of Australian Retailers donated $90 000 to the Liberal Democratic Party; the Australian Hotels Association SA branch donated $80 000 to the Liberal Party in South Australia; and the Sporting Shooters Association of Australia (Queensland) donated $75 000 to Katter's Australia Party (Elvery 2017).

Second, citizens' groups engage in behind-the-scenes lobbying, advice and policy provision, as well as the cultivation of personal relationships with members of parliament (MPs), ministers and bureaucrats. As Jacobs (2014) explains, parliamentarians see 'a steady stream of lobbyists through the door' making such relationships a routine aspect of day-to-day formal political life. The Australian Council for International Development, for example, has a long history of regular meetings with public servants, ministers and politicians to discuss existing and proposed foreign aid policy (Kilby 2015), while the Australian Women Against Violence Alliance lobbies parliamentarians at the state and federal levels in its efforts to positively influence gender equality. Other groups have firm preferences for relationships with particular parties. While trade unions and groups espousing progressive values have well-publicised relationships with the ALP, business, libertarian and conservative groups have traditionally been associated with the Liberal Party and the Nationals. The Institute of Public Affairs, for instance, has long standing informal links to the Liberal Party and several shared personnel (Kelly 2016).

Third, more visibly, citizen's groups schedule their campaigns to coincide with the electoral cycle to influence citizen's voting decisions. For the 2016 federal election (and again in 2019), the group GetUp! targeted the seats of conservative Liberal MPs. In 2016 in Tasmania, GetUp! spent close to $300 000 on campaign advertising alone to successfully unseat Andrew Nikolic MP (Morton 2016). In 2019 the campaign targeting Boothby MP Nicolle Flint was not successful and led to claims that attacking a female MP caused an upswing in attacks on other female candidates. For the 2013 federal election, the Australian Chamber of Commerce and Industry launched their campaign to promote the goals of small business, emphasise the need to reduce 'red tape', simplify the tax system, improve infrastructure and promote flexibility in employment. Similarly, Australian trade unions mobilised against the Howard Government at the 2007 federal election with the 'Your Rights at Work' campaign targeting the government's liberal approach to workplace flexibility. One of the most successful campaigns occurred in 2022 when the climate-focused group Climate 200 poured hundreds of thousands of dollars into an ultimately successful campaign to unseat conservative candidates. Their success combined significant donations with an excellent ground campaign to elect seven new independent MHRs and a Senator. This accords with the observation of Reece (2013) that, in the context of elections, 'advocacy groups are using all the campaign tools and techniques that were once the sole preserve of the political parties'.

The benefits and drawbacks of citizens' groups

Citizens' groups perform a range of roles and activities in Australian politics including agenda-setting, public education and service delivery, and therefore confer a variety of benefits on the political system at large. Indeed, democratic theorists praise open citizen participation, not just at election time, because citizens' groups are viewed as important intermediaries between communities and government (Dryzek 2000). They provide a channel for consultation about, and access to, the views of disadvantaged or marginalised groups, which may lead to the formulation of more effective policies (Maddison and Denniss 2013). Additionally, citizens' groups provide public commentary, feedback and evaluation of existing public programs as well as deliver government and privately funded programs in their own right. In doing so, they promote public debate and facilitate wider community understanding of, and input into, public policy (Yeatman 1998). Citizens' groups therefore serve an important accountability and policy effectiveness function in liberal democracies. Significantly, their participation may boost the legitimacy of government decisions by creating at least the veneer of democratic participation, representativeness and transparency, even while providing a mechanism for the exertion of citizen-based power separate from the state.

In contrast, there are a number of concerns about the roles and impact of citizens' groups in the political process. It has been argued that citizens' groups often seek to advance their own private interests, which they disguise as being in the public interest (see Hamilton and Maddison 2007). Citizens' groups may not be representative, and the internal structures of groups may not be transparent or democratic. The idea that some groups will have a disproportionate influence is a chief concern of public choice theorists who emphasise the self-serving, utility maximising behaviour of citizens' groups (Johns 2000). Critics are particularly wary of public funding for citizens' groups, which is seen to distort citizens' views, elevating some over others (Kelly 2014). Another issue is that citizens' groups are typically focused on one particular issue area, or group of issues, and therefore have the luxury of making niche demands that do not have to be weighed against competing priorities or whole-of-government objectives. A final criticism is that citizens' groups tend to consist of citizens who are willing and regular participants in the political process (Alver 2016). Often dubbed the 'usual suspects', these citizens, rather than being representative, are unique simply because they are willing and able to devote their time and resources to getting involved in public debate, while the vast majority of citizens are busy with their day-to-day lives.

SHORT-ANSWER QUESTIONS 12.1

1. What are the key features of citizens' groups?
2. Why is there no one accepted classification system for distinguishing among citizens' groups?
3. What are the main political strategies employed by citizens' groups to advance their goals?
4. What are the primary advantages and disadvantages of an active cohort of citizens' groups?

Suggested responses are available at www.cambridge.org/highereducation/isbn/9781009108232/resources

REFLECTION QUESTIONS 12.1

1. Do you or any of your family members belong to citizens' groups and, with reference to the private/public interest categorisation, what is your motivation for participating?
2. Select four of the citizens' groups that appear in the list in the chapter. How might each group be classified?
3. Of the four political strategies commonly employed by citizens' groups as outlined in the chapter, which is most influential and why?
4. Have you participated in any of the four political strategies outlined in the text and if so, what prompted your activity?

Response prompts are available at www.cambridge.org/highereducation/isbn/9781009108232/resources

SPOTLIGHT 12.1 CITIZEN GROUP IN PROFILE: AUSTRALIAN HOTELS ASSOCIATION

The Australian Hotels Association (AHA) is a membership-based industry association established in 1839. It currently represents over 5000 industry employers around Australia via a networked organisation of branches in each state and territory and a Canberra-based National Office. The aim of the AHA is to represent the interests of the hotel and hospitality industry on a range of state and federal policy issues including gambling and alcohol regulation, trade practices matters, taxation, workplace relations, tourism, music licensing and business regulation. It is governed by a National Board staffed by delegates from each of its state/territory branches. The number of delegates from each state/territory is based on the number of members located in each region.

The AHA works with other industry bodies whose interests coincide with the hotels and hospitality industry including the Australasian Gaming Council, Clubs Australia, and the Australian Chamber of Commerce and Industry. In recent years, the AHA has been active in public debates about several contentious policy issues. The AHA has advocated a reduction in the 'backpacker tax', supported the reduction of workers' penalty rates for weekend and public holiday work, opposed 'lockout laws' in Australian cities to target late night alcohol-related violence, opposed poker machine reform, opposed the 'plain packaging' tobacco laws and supported greater regulation of holiday accommodation via the sharing economy (e.g. Airbnb). The AHA's political strategies include employing lobbyists, maintaining a national office in Canberra, producing written submissions for governmental consultation processes, and financial donations to the major political parties. Indeed, various branches of the AHA are some of the largest donors among gaming and hospitality industry groups. In total, for 2015–16, the AHA donated close to $800 000 to the Coalition parties while the ALP received over $500 000 (Livingstone and Johnson 2017).

QUESTIONS

Discuss the influence of the AHA in Australian politics. How should this group be classified and what roles does it play in policy debates?

CASE STUDY 12.1 CITIZEN GROUP IN PROFILE: GETUP!

Paul Oosting, National Director, Getup!

GetUp! is a national-level campaigning group that brings together its one million members with experts, strategists and movement partners to promote progressive change in Australia. The organisation is independent and driven by values, rather than party politics. GetUp! aims to achieve its vision of a fair, flourishing and socially just Australia by campaigning on human rights, environmental justice, economic fairness and democracy.

One of the most notable successes of GetUp! was its influential 2016 federal election campaign, which saw conservative MPs lose their place in parliament, and several MPs were left clinging to once safe seats. GetUp! sought to be nimble with its campaign tactics, pivoting to focus on the issues most important to its members. It aimed to make the economic fight of the election about protecting Australia's 'world class' public health and education systems, the iconic Great Barrier

Reef, and the future of the clean energy industry. GetUp! aimed to shift votes away from MPs who failed to support action on these issues. It achieved:

- an average swing of 4.9 per cent against conservative MPs in its target seats
- eight conservative MPs or those considered to be opposing progress on GetUp!'s issues lost their place in parliament and swings were recorded against other notable conservative MPs George Christensen and Peter Dutton
- Australia-wide conversations from all sides of politics about investing in hospitals and renewable energy and addressing corporate tax avoidance.

Prior to the election, GetUp!'s nationwide phone banks saw 3736 volunteers donate 17 471 hours to have 40 218 conversations with swinging voters. These conversations were paired with the use of targeted social media, especially Facebook, which reached 6.2 million users over the course of the campaign. On election day, 3031 GetUp! members reached 1.1 million voters with 'how to vote' cards across 500 polling booths in marginal seats. The 'all-angle' combination of campaign tactics and the rapid mobilisation of members aims to keep GetUp! at the forefront of Australian political change.

However, the 2019 election was far less successful, with campaigns such as that against Boothby MP Nicole Flint drawing considerable controversy as an example of attacks on female candidates. This led to renewed pressure on GetUp!'s charitable status. While ultimately unsuccessful, the government managed to call into question exactly what forms of advocacy and lobbying activities are acceptable, and whether any civil society organisation campaigning during elections should be instead governed by the electoral act.

QUESTION

What key factors explain the rise in prominence of GetUp! in recent years?

BEYOND THE ELECTORAL CYCLE: GOVERNMENT MECHANISMS FOR ENGAGING CITIZENS

Aware of the potential benefits of, and increasing demands for, citizen participation in the political process in the 21st century, governments employ a range of techniques and measures to elicit community input into policymaking. These include inviting written and oral submissions, hosting public forums, establishing stakeholder groups, conducting surveys and polls on particular issues, and initiating formal collaborative governance arrangements that delegate decision-making authority to groups of citizens. These arrangements, which allow citizens to participate in various ways and to differing degrees, are discussed in more detail below.

WRITTEN AND ORAL SUBMISSIONS

Governments frequently employ the engagement strategy of inviting written and oral submissions from citizens' groups and individuals on a particular policy matter under consideration, often in response to a government produced 'issues paper'. For example, the Department of Foreign Affairs and Trade invited written submissions, ranging from short emails to entire analytical papers, from citizens' organisations and individuals on the potential impacts and opportunities of an Australian free trade agreement with Hong Kong. The Department provided possible key topics that it saw as significant in the proposed agreement and subsequently received submissions from the Australia China Business Council, the Australian Fair Trade and Investment Network, the Australian Forest Products Association, the Australian Red Meat Industry and Certified Practising Accountants Australia, among others (Department of Foreign Affairs and Trade 2017). In the interests of transparency, it is common practice for governments to publish all submissions unedited on their websites.

PUBLIC FORUMS

Public forums or 'town hall' meetings are typically hosted by governments to provide information to communities from a particular geographical area or policy sector. Such meetings allow large groups of citizens to come together to ask questions of elected representatives, senior public servants and/or consultants, and permit governments to gauge a community's reception to particular policies or programs. In reviewing its Disability Employment Framework, for example, the Department of Social Services hosted 38 public forums across 11 Australian cities with a total of 740 participants comprising people with disability and their families, carers, service providers, employers and industry associations (Department of Social Services 2015). From 2008, the Rudd Government conducted federal level 'community cabinets' in locations around Australia (a mechanism initiated in Queensland in the 1990s) as a method for bringing the workings of government closer to regular citizens (McCann 2012). Community cabinets typically include an hour-long public forum featuring the prime minister or state premier/territory chief minister plus several Cabinet ministers with opportunities for one-on-one meetings between citizens and ministers.

STAKEHOLDER GROUPS

Governments frequently construct policy stakeholder groups, small representative groups of citizens, that meet once or periodically over several months or even years as a method to elicit citizen feedback on programs and policies. In late 2016, for instance, the Turnbull Government announced a Forum on Western Sydney Airport, a project with vast economic benefits for the region, and called for community, stakeholder and local government nominations. Subsequently, in March 2017, it named a 22-member panel comprising representatives from the local community, relevant stakeholder groups and those nominated by the affected local governments (Department of Infrastructure and Regional Development 2016). According to the Department of Infrastructure and Regional Development (2016), the group 'will provide a communication channel for the community's engagement in the development of the airport and ensure community's views are taken into account [...][and] will play an important role in the airspace and flight path design process'. Not all attempts to form stakeholder groups, however, follow an effortless path. In 2010, Prime Minister Gillard's idea for a citizens' assembly on climate change consisting of up to 200 people to elicit community views on a carbon price was criticised as a 'community gobfest' and a stalling mechanism by groups wanting rapid and decisive governmental action to address climate change (Rodgers 2010), criticism's reminiscent of those provided regarding Kevin Rudd's 2020 Summit. Stakeholder engagement can also appear as a 'sham' or intended to provide a distraction from decisions already made. The more recently approved inland rail project from Queensland to Victoria is an example of consultation being conducted even while route changes cannot be considered as they are already decided. Stakeholder consultation in that instance provides some avenue for the venting of frustration, but only limited input into the decision-making processes.

SURVEYS AND POLLS

In Australia, plebiscites and referenda refer to one-off polls on issues of national significance. A referendum is a national yes/no vote on altering the Australian Constitution, while a plebiscite or advisory referendum is used to determine voters' will on a non-constitutional issue with verdicts not binding on governments. Plebiscites and referenda are the broadest possible citizen participation mechanism employed by governments because they give (indeed compel given Australia's compulsory system of voting) all citizens an opportunity to cast a ballot. Elected representatives, citizens' groups and individual citizens are often collectively involved in leading arguments for and against a proposed change.

Since Federation, Australian citizens have approved just eight of 44 proposed constitutional changes via 19 referenda (Parliamentary Education Office 2017). The most recent, the referendum on an Australian republic in 1999, was unsuccessful. The generally low rate of success is at least partly due to Australia's referenda rules, which require a double majority in order to be approved: this comprises a majority of voters across Australia *and* a majority of voters in a majority of states. Most recently, a possible referendum on recognising Indigenous people in the preamble of the Australian Constitution that received bipartisan parliamentary support was debated by Aboriginal and Torres Strait Islander representatives at a constitutional convention at Uluru in May 2017 (Zillman 2017). However, participants ultimately expressed a preference for representation measures beyond symbolic constitutional recognition. In regard to plebiscites, only two have been held, in 1916 and 1917 on military conscription, which were both defeated. The 2017 national postal vote on same-sex marriage is another such national vote, albeit non-compulsory and non-binding on parliament. Despite its informal status (as a 'plebiscite'), a wide majority of Australian citizens participating in the postal vote supported the change. As such the plebiscite acted as an indication of citizens' views and ensured that the Turnbull Government could proceed with legislative changes with broad community support. While national polls on specific issues bypass the problems of representative democracy by giving every citizen a voice, the minimum level of citizen participation required is simply a registering of support for, or against, change.

At the state and territory as well as local levels, governments regularly deploy voluntary surveys of relevant groups of citizens on particular issues that affect them. In Queensland, for example, the Queensland Government Statistician's Office conducts official surveys involving individual citizens, their households, businesses and other citizens' groups. The data generated by such surveys aim to reflect a representative cross-section of the community and, to the extent that surveys require greater than yes/no input, they may provide policymakers with more in-depth, nuanced understandings of citizens' views.

COLLABORATIVE GOVERNANCE

In the 21st century, governments are increasingly turning to 'collaborative governance' arrangements to enlist the active contribution of citizens in the political process to deal with increasingly complex policy and social issues. Such arrangements are similar in intent to the establishment of stakeholder groups, but the degree of decision-making authority conferred to citizens in collaborative governance is intended to be substantive, rather than simply advisory. Alternative descriptions of such arrangements include devolved or decentred governance, polycentric governance and participatory democracy (Gunningham 2009). For example, in the early 2000s, in regard to the governance of the Murray–Darling Basin, the New South Wales Government established local committees to develop recommendations for allocating water rights across competing industry sectors and the environment. Each of the 36 committees contained between 12 and 20 members with representatives of environmental groups, Indigenous people, elected representatives and local and state government public servants (Bell and Park 2006). In the area of social services, in 2010 the Rudd Government established a National Compact: a policy framework document setting out a new era of relations between government and the non-profit service and advocacy sector (Butcher 2010). The Tasmanian forest industry, business, union and environmental group representatives were involved in a collaborative 'forest peace process' arrangement for three years from 2010 to negotiate the future of the controversial sector (Schirmer, Dare and Ercan 2016). While collaborative governance processes, such as policy networks and various other forms, offer selected citizens a substantial degree of input, in practice, due to the degree of deliberation required, they are often difficult to administer due to value conflicts, accusations of non-representativeness and/or stalemate in negotiations. Consequently, it may be incumbent on governments to appropriately design and administer such arrangements from the outset in order to promote their effectiveness (Bell and Hindmoor 2009).

SPOTLIGHT 12.2 COLLABORATIVE GOVERNANCE IN PROFILE: NATIONAL CONGRESS OF AUSTRALIA'S FIRST PEOPLES AND THE COALITION OF PEAKS

The National Congress of Australia's First Peoples (The Congress) was a civil society organisation set up under the Rudd Government. The Congress grew to a membership base of 10 000 individual and 180 organisations. Through its membership base, The Congress collaborated with Indigenous peak organisations and Indigenous leaders to develop the Redfern Statement in 2016. The Redfern Statement provided a plan to address systemic inequalities and structural disadvantage experienced by Aboriginal and Torres Strait Islander peoples. The Congress' co-chair, Dr Jackie Huggins, presented the Redfern Statement to the Commonwealth Government, voicing that Aboriginal and Torres Strait Islander peoples have the solutions and governments need to harness the lived knowledge and expertise in Indigenous communities and organisations. The Australian Human Rights Commission and NGOs such as AnTAR, Oxfam and the Australian Council of Social Services assisted in the advocacy and lobbying work that followed. As a result of federal government funding cuts that started in 2013 under the Abbott government and continued with the Turnbull Government, the National Congress of Australia's First Peoples was forced to close its doors in June 2019. A group of 50 Indigenous peak health organisations formed to partner with governments on the health policy Closing the Gap. The Coalition continued to advocate for the sentiments shared in the Redfern Statement, highlighting the need for Aboriginal and Torres Strait Islander people to be involved in the policies and programs that affect their lives. In March 2019, the Coalition of Peaks formalised a partnership agreement with the Council of Australian Governments for a period of 10 years. The agreement commits to Aboriginal and Torres Strait Islander peoples having a leading role in a

> three-yearly review of Closing the Gap. The Coalition continues to advocate for the interests of its membership through representation by chief executive officers in The Coalition. The Coalition is a stand-alone unincorporated group that receives secretariat support from the National Aboriginal Community Controlled Organisation.
>
> **QUESTION**
>
> What does the demise of the National Congress of Australia's First Peoples and the formation of the Coalition of Peaks reveal about how governments want to collaborate with Aboriginal and Torres Strait Islander peoples?

EVALUATING CITIZEN ENGAGEMENT MECHANISMS

While community engagement is said to involve 'working collaboratively with and through groups of people affiliated by geographical proximity, special interest, or similar situations to address issues that affect them' (Lowe and Hill 2005, 170), not all engagement mechanisms are aptly described as collaborative. In order to assess the degree of citizen involvement in policymaking, Sherry Arnstein's 'ladder of citizen participation' model (1969) is one potential evaluative framework. It describes eight rungs or levels for evaluating the degree of engagement between governments and citizens comprising, from the bottom, manipulation, therapy, informing, consultation, placation, partnership, delegated power and, at the highest level, citizen control (Arnstein 1969). However, this model, as the pejorative terms of 'manipulation', 'therapy' and 'placation' for lower levels of citizen input attest, is geared towards dissecting *and* promoting citizen participation.

Another influential and more recently developed method for assessing citizen participation is the International Association for Public Participation's 'public participation spectrum' (2014) comprising a five-point continuum. The five nodes on the continuum range (from the lowest level of citizen participation to the highest) are informing, consulting, involving, collaborating and empowering (International Association for Public Participation 2014). The first node of *informing* involves governments sharing information with citizens. Contemporary examples may include regular newsletters from local governments to citizens, fact sheets published on departmental websites, government advertisements on TV or social media. *Consulting*, the second node on the continuum, additionally involves a process of feedback from citizens to governments, but only with the obligation by government to acknowledge rather than act upon citizen responses. Examples include surveys, calls for submissions and other public comment arrangements. Further along the continuum, the third node of *involving* involves some level of government action in response to citizen participation, even if this is marginal. Similar types of engagement could be involved as for the consulting stage, but with a greater level of government feedback. *Collaborating* is the fourth node and represents processes that join citizens with decision-makers whereby citizen input will be reflected in the final decisions made. The final, and highest node on the continuum, is *empowering*, whereby citizens are responsible for decision-making and governments will act upon citizen decisions. Empowering is said to guarantee that decision-making is delegated to citizens or citizens' groups. However, the real-world implications of such strategies, involving delegation of power and uncertain outcomes, has made the delegation of decision-making authority in Australia relatively rare. When it does occur, it tends to be difficult to administer and far from conflict-free. Indeed, most citizen engagement by governments in Australia is best described as informing, consulting and involving on the International Association for Public Participation's spectrum.

REFLECTION QUESTIONS 12.2

1. What factors motivate governments to select between various citizen engagement mechanisms?
2. Compared with other community engagement methods, why are collaborative governance approaches rarely employed in Australia?

Response prompts are available at www.cambridge.org/highereducation/isbn/9781009108232/resources

SHORT-ANSWER QUESTIONS 12.2

1. In what ways do governments structure citizen engagement?
2. How is citizen engagement evaluated?

Suggested responses are available at www.cambridge.org/highereducation/isbn/9781009108232/resources

KEY CHALLENGES FOR CITIZEN PARTICIPATION AND ENGAGEMENT

The contemporary field of citizen participation and engagement has given rise to a new set of issues and challenges for the Australian political system. These comprise debates over the extent of representativeness and transparency of various citizens' groups, the appropriateness of public funding for citizens' groups, recent governments' legislative attempts to minimise citizen protest at sites deemed workplaces, and the phenomenon of 'slacktivism'.

REPRESENTATIVENESS AND TRANSPARENCY

Among the key attributes of citizens' groups is that they offer marginalised people opportunities for political participation and publicise neglected issues and problems that might otherwise remain peripheral. However, the degree to which 'noisy' citizens' groups may dominate or distort debates about public issues is a concern for those who prioritise representativeness as a key value underpinning the participation of citizens' groups. Without a valid claim of representation, such groups, and their contributions to public debate, may be said to lack legitimacy. Compounding this issue is that citizens' groups are often accused of being staffed by elites and/or professional activists with few links to regular citizens (Johns 2000). Indeed, 'community representatives' are often atypical precisely because, unlike most people, they are willing to become involved. However, this affliction may also be true of elected representatives and party officials.

Further compromising the legitimacy of citizens' groups, at least in the eyes of critics, is the source of their funding. The Sunrise Project, for example, a group campaigning against Australian coal mining, is funded by a US-based organisation, the Sandler Foundation (Kelly and Shanahan 2016; Shanahan 2016). Such arrangements raise questions about the accountability of citizens' groups and the interests they serve, particularly where funding emanates from international sources. In contrast, other groups may have limited access to external funding and may suffer resource constraints that severely hamper their operations. State and Commonwealth governments seek to address such unevenness across the sector of citizens' groups by providing a variety of funding opportunities.

Another difficulty in the practice of citizen engagement is NIMBYism or 'not in my backyard' syndrome, which is a particular issue for governments in decisions about the siting of new commercial developments or industries, whereby citizens residing in close proximity to proposed developments protest most loudly. When such groups gain traction, governments may be motivated to put the public good on hold for a minority of citizens disproportionately affected by government projects or commercial activities. In Melbourne, the controversial Skyrail public transport project to replace congested level crossings, for instance, prompted a local protest group, Lower Our Tracks, to challenge the project in the Victorian Supreme Court (Willingham 2016).

For governments, a key challenge in mediating the input of citizens' groups is that they 'rarely speak with one voice' and, in fact, communities may be deeply fragmented (Foley and Martin 2000, 486). In regard to efforts to curb spending on gambling, drugs and alcohol by those receiving welfare payments, government attempts to introduce a welfare card have been simultaneously met with praise and opposition. At its worst, such fragmentation may result in endless consultation, delayed decision-making or governments watering down their policy positions in an effort to placate dissenting groups at the expense of robust public policy.

PUBLIC FUNDING FOR CITIZENS' GROUPS

While citizens' groups are considered separate to governments, the reality is that many, at least partially, rely on some degree of public funding. This may take the form of government contracts to deliver services, grants and/or the receipt by various groups of tax-deductible gift recipient (DGR) status, which incentivises citizens to contribute financial donations. Tax deductible donations alone are said to cost the government up to $1.3 billion per year (Martin 2017). The rationale for public funding is that it supports a pluralistic society in which a diverse range of voices and issues may be heard. In recent years, however, this status, particularly for environmental groups, has been subject to scrutiny by Coalition governments and conservative think tanks such as the Institute for Public Affairs (Kelly and Shanahan 2016). Scepticism about public funding for citizens' groups rose to prominence during the Howard Government, which initiated a process of defunding various citizens' groups, particularly those engaged in political advocacy over service delivery (Hamilton and Maddison 2007). More recently, a Parliamentary Inquiry into the Register of Environmental Organisations initiated in 2015 brought attention to environmental groups' DGR status and, currently, many environmental groups face the possibility of having their status revoked for engaging in political advocacy. However, a 2010 High Court decision on *Aid/Watch Incorporated v Commissioner of Taxation* upheld the notion that advocacy, lobbying and similar activities do in fact constitute charitable activity.

SPOTLIGHT 12.3 PUBLIC FUNDING FOR CITIZENS' GROUPS? THE PARLIAMENTARY INQUIRY INTO THE REGISTER OF ENVIRONMENTAL ORGANISATIONS

The Register of Environmental Organisations, established in 1992, is a Commonwealth tax deductibility scheme allowing eligible environmental groups to receive DGR status by the Australian Taxation Office. Donations made to organisations listed on the Register are tax deductible for the donors. There are currently more than 600 groups listed on the Register of Environmental Organisations.

The purpose of the Register is to increase the fundraising capacity of conservation groups by incentivising citizens and corporations to donate. As Friends of the Earth's Cam Walker contends 'like every environmental organisation across the country that employs staff, tax deductibility is the lifeblood of our organisation' (Duffy 2015).

In order to be eligible for DGR status, organisations must have a principal purpose of: 'the protection and enhancement of the natural environment or of a significant aspect of the natural environment; or, the provision of information or education, or the carrying on of research, about the natural environment or a significant aspect of the natural environment' (Department of the Environment and Energy 2017).

However, in recent years, environmental organisations have been accused of misusing their DGR status. Former MP Andrew Nikolic stated that '[t]here are some of those groups that unfortunately abuse that privilege, they engage in untruthful, destructive attacks on legitimate business and undertake political activism, which shouldn't attract those very generous concessions from the taxpayer' (ABC News 2014).

On the back of such criticisms, a 2016 Parliamentary Inquiry examined the Register in the context of how it supports citizens to preserve the environment. The Committee received more than 700 submissions, thousands of letters and other correspondence, met with representatives, held public hearings and conducted discussions (Standing Committee on the Environment 2016, 2–3).

The Inquiry report concluded that the Register should only approve DGR status for environmental non-government organisations involved with 'practical' conservation work. However, the federal government is yet to formally respond to the report beyond releasing a discussion paper on potential reforms.

QUESTION

What are the key arguments for and against government funding for citizens' groups engaged in political advocacy?

ANTI-PROTEST LAWS

The rights of peaceful assembly and freedom of expression are seen as core values within Australia and other liberal democracies and are included in the International Covenant on Civil and Political Rights (1966). However, a number of Australian states have recently developed anti-protest legislation to limit the locations at which activists can conduct political demonstrations. For example, in Tasmania in 2014, the Liberal Government introduced the *Workplaces (Protection from Protesters) Act* as a way to curb protest activity in forestry areas while the New South Wales Liberal Government recently granted police the power to stop, search and detain protesters, and shut down protests that disrupt traffic. Further, the New South Wales Government expanded the offence of 'interfering' with mining sites, including coal seam gas exploration and extraction (de Kretser 2016). Such legislation is criticised as curtailing a vital aspect of Australian democracy and prioritising business interests ahead of citizens' concerns relating to environmental conservation and social justice, as much as it is an attempt to curtail rival sources of power outside the state. In highlighting the trend to stifle citizen advocacy, in early 2016, a coalition of Australian citizens' groups collectively launched a report *Safeguarding Democracy* (Human Rights Law Centre 2016). According to the Human Rights Law Centre, the key architect of the report, since 2001, 'the Australian Parliament has passed over 200 new laws that infringe many of our basic fundamental freedoms. As a result, more and more government decisions are now made about peoples' lives by bureaucrats or Ministers behind closed doors' (Howie 2016).

SLACKTIVISM OR THE NEW CITIZEN ADVOCACY?

Also known as 'armchair activism', 'keyboard activism' or 'hashtag activism', slacktivism refers to political advocacy performed online, especially via social media. The most commonly used online platforms for such advocacy in Australia include Change.org Australia, GetUp! and Dosomething.org. Critics argue that unlike traditional forms of protest such as street demonstrations, strikes or hard-copy petitions, slacktivism does not require the same degree of effort and dedication on the part of citizens. Indeed, it is often derided because it requires minimal input, often just a 'click and share' on social media, which results in little real-world impact other than a 'feel good' effect for the contributor. In other words, people who support various causes in this way are criticised as not being truly engaged or sufficiently committed to social change. This has led critics to argue that internet campaigns or social media campaigns should not be treated with the same seriousness as campaigns conducted in real time involving face-to-face communication (Robertson 2014).

In support of internet advocacy, the Director of Change.org Australia, Karen Skinner, cites the increased number of citizens engaged in political advocacy that may previously have been politically inactive: '[p]eople talk about slacktivism and clicktivism or whatever term you want to use, but it's not the case. We're seeing 3.7 million Australians starting online petitions. It shows Australians have issues that they care about, and they want to see things change. We're also seeing a petition win every 24 hours. Change is being enacted. Slacktivism is just a dismissive term, it's not the reality' (Gillespie 2016). In this regard, the online public sphere may in fact facilitate an active citizenry by mobilising supporters to a cause and disseminating campaign material far more rapidly than traditional methods. For example, in 2016 an online petition succeeded in bringing about the cancellation of Australian meetings of the men's rights activist group Return of Kings, the capping of credit card surcharges by federal Treasurer Scott Morrison, specialised training for emergency department staff in Queensland on responding to suicidal patients, and a pay rise for the Australian Defence Force among many more instances.

Black Lives Matter (BLM) demonstrates that online advocacy is capable of generating a global movement and mobilising people to hit the streets across the globe. It began in response to fatal police shootings of African American men in the United States. In 2013, three citizens (Alicia Garza, Patrisse Cullors and Opal Tometi) used Twitter to voice their concerns using the hashtag #BlackLivesMatter. Further deaths of African American men and women following interactions with the police reignited the hash tag and to an increase in protests and demonstrations. In 2020, during the height of the COVID-19 pandemic George Floyd was killed by police in Minneapolis, Minnesota. This sparked world-wide demonstrations that resulted in citizens on every continent (except Antarctica) hitting the streets in protest.

Counter-movements with hashtags #AllLivesMatter and #BlueLivesMatter awakened public discourse about race among BLM supporters and critics (see Carney 2016; Stewart et al. 2017). In Australia it reignited discourse about the unexplained deaths of Aboriginal and Torres Strait Islander peoples in the justice system (see Whittaker 2021) and the health system (see Bond, Singh and Tyson 2021). Cartillier (2021, 3) compares the African American experience in the United States to the experience of First Nations peoples in Australia: 'Both groups face disproportionate incarceration rates, endure far more police brutality, and are far more likely to die in the case of an arrest than the rest of the population'. BLM facilitated growing awareness about its relevance in Australia by reigniting calls for governments to implement the 1987–91 Royal Commission into Aboriginal Deaths in Custody recommendations.

RESEARCH QUESTION 12.1

What roles do citizens' groups perform in the Australian political process?

SUMMARY

Learning objective 1: Describe the organisational landscape of political participation in Australia and the variety of tactics employed by citizens' groups

In the 21st century, the scale, scope and complexity of citizens' demands for political input in Australia has increased. A broad range of local, regional and national citizens' groups – many with membership of international groups – actively strive for political influence utilising an array of traditional and newly evolved strategies. Citizens' groups are thus becoming an increasingly ubiquitous force in Australian political life.

Citizens' groups employ four key strategies, often concurrently. These comprise public performances and activities, developing and disseminating documentation via a range of media including new media, consumer activism, and engaging with formal political structures. In doing so, citizens' groups confer a range of benefits on the political system at large. They may serve a public education function, broaden citizen participation and highlight neglected issues. Alternatively, critics often contend that they distort public debate, are self-serving, and do not represent regular citizens' concerns.

Learning objective 2: Outline and evaluate the ways in which Australian governments engage with citizens' groups

From the perspective of governments, citizens' groups may serve a functional role in providing local knowledge, expertise and feedback that may improve the quality of public policy. Governments therefore facilitate the involvement of citizens' groups in the political process in a number of ways. These include through advertising for written and oral submissions; arranging public forums, meetings and briefings; forming stakeholder advisory groups; administering surveys and votes on specific issues; and establishing formal collaborative governance processes with some degree of decision-making authority. Each consultation mechanism involves a different degree and style of citizen input, which can be assessed by various participation models such as the International Association for Public Participation's model.

Learning objective 3: Discuss the challenges arising from the growing demand for political participation and engagement in the 21st century

With the increase in demand for citizen participation in the 21st century, a number of new issues and challenges have arisen. First, the degree to which citizens' groups are representative of a broader set of citizens is an ongoing debate that goes to claims about their degree of legitimacy. This entails debates over funding sources, staffing, NIMBYism and fragmentation. Second, contention over public funding for citizens' groups has re-emerged with a Parliamentary Inquiry focused on environmental groups in particular. Third, since the 9/11 bombings in 2001, governments have sought to place limits on the location and extent of public protests permitted, ostensibly for security reasons. Finally, the merits of 'slacktivism' or online activism are variously derided as an inferior form of advocacy or hailed as the new face of citizen activism.

DISCUSSION QUESTIONS

1. What factors facilitate the active presence of citizens' groups in Australian politics?
2. Why is it difficult to classify citizens' groups?
3. What is the significance of the outsider/insider typology of citizens' groups?
4. Why do governments choose to engage with citizens between elections?
5. What is the biggest challenge for citizen engagement in 21st century Australia?

FURTHER READING

Baer, B.J. & Kaindl, K. (eds). (2018). *Queering Translation, Translating the Queer: Theory, Practice, Activism*, New York; Abingdon: Routledge, p. 242.

Bell, S. & Hindmoor, A. (2009). *Rethinking Governance: The Centrality of the State in Modern Society*, Cambridge: Cambridge University Press.

Bertone, S. & Griffin, G. (1992). *Immigrant Workers and Trade Unions*, Canberra: Australian Government Publishing Service.

Davis, M. & Langton, M. (2016). *It's Our Country: Indigenous Arguments for Meaningful Constitutional Recognition and Reform*, Melbourne: Melbourne University Press.

REFERENCES

ABC News. (2014). Liberal MP moves to strip charity status from some environmental groups, *ABC News*, 29 June. Retrieved from http://www.abc.net.au/news/2014-06-29/andrew-nickolic-moves-to-strip-charity-status-from-some-environ/5557936

—— (2017). ACTU boss Sally McManus has no problem with workers breaking 'unjust laws', *ABC News*, 15 March. Retrieved from http://www.abc.net.au/news/2017-03-15/actu-boss-happy-for-workers-to-break-unjust-laws/8357698

Alver, J. (2016). What makes participatory processes democratic? From external to internal inclusion, *The Policy Space*, 20 September. Retrieved from http://www.thepolicyspace.com.au/2016/20/144-what-makes-participatory-processes-democratic-from-external-to-internal-inclusion

Arnstein, S.R. (1969). A ladder of citizen participation. *Journal of the American Institute of Planners*, **35**(4), 216–24.

Attwood, B. & Markus, A. (2004). *Thinking Black: William Cooper and the Australian Aborigines' League*, Acton: Aboriginal Studies Press.

Bell, S. & Hindmoor, A. (2009). *Rethinking Governance: The Centrality of the State in Modern Society*, Melbourne: Cambridge University Press.

Bell, S. & Park, A. (2006). The problematic metagovernance of networks: Water reform in NSW. *Journal of Public Policy*, **26**(1), 63–83.

Bertone, S., Griffin, G. & Iverson, R.D. (1995). Immigrant workers and Australian trade unions: Participation and attitudes. *International Migration Review*, **29**(3), 722–44.

Bond, C.J., Singh, D. & Tyson, S. (2021). Black bodies and bioethics: Debunking mythologies of benevolence and beneficence in contemporary Indigenous health research in colonial Australia. *Journal of Bioethical Inquiry*, **18**, 83–92.

Bourne, J. (2017). National Indigenous organisations in Australia: Why governance environments matter. *Journal of Australian Indigenous Issues*, **20**(1), 71–86.

Bradfield, S. (2006). Separatism or status-quo? Indigenous affairs from the birth of land rights to the death of ATSIC. *Australian Journal of Politics & History*, **52**(1), 80–97.

Brigg, M. & Curth-Bibb, J. (2017). Recalibrating intercultural governance in Australian Indigenous organisations: The case of Aboriginal community controlled health. *Australian Journal of Political Science*, **52**(2), 199–217.

Butcher, J. (2010). An Australian compact with the third sector: Challenges and prospects. *Third Sector Review*, **17**(1), 35–58.

Carney, N. (2016). All lives matter, but so does race: Black lives matter and the evolving role of social media. *Humanity & Society*, **40**(2), 180–99.

Cartillier, V. (2021). The over-representation of First Nations People in the judicial system, *The Guardian*, 1946. Retrieved from https://cpa.org.au/guardian/issue-1946/the-over-representation-of-first-nations-people-in-the-judicial-system/

Davis, M. (2011). A snip at $22 m to get rid of PM, *The Sydney Morning Herald*, 2 February. Retrieved from http://www.smh.com.au/business/a-snip-at-22m-to-get-rid-of-pm-20110201-1acgj.html

de Kretser, H. (2016). NSW anti-protest laws are part of a corrosive national trend, *The Sydney Morning Herald*, 22 March. Retrieved from http://www.smh.com.au/comment/nsw-antiprotest-laws-are-part-of-a-corrosive-national-trend-20160321-gno10h.html

Department of Foreign Affairs and Trade. (2017). *Australia-Hong Kong Free Trade Agreement: Submissions and public consultations*. Retrieved from http://dfat.gov.au/trade/agreements/a-hkfta/pages/submissions.aspx

Department of Infrastructure and Regional Development. (2016). *Factsheet: Forum on Western Sydney Airport*. Retrieved from http://westernsydneyairport.gov.au/files/factsheet_fowsa.pdf

Department of Social Services. (2015). *Disability Employment Framework – Round One – Consultation report*. Retrieved from https://engage.dss.gov.au/disability-employment-framework/consultation-report/

Department of the Environment and Energy. (2017). *Register of Environmental Organisations*. Retrieved from http://www.environment.gov.au/about-us/business/tax/register-environmental-organisations

Dryzek, J.S. (2000). *Deliberative Democracy and Beyond: Liberals, Critics, Contestations*, Oxford: Oxford University Press.

Duffy, C. (2015). Environmental groups face tax deductibility loss in Government push, *ABC 7.30*, 10 April. Retrieved from http://www.abc.net.au/7.30/content/2015/s4214478.htm

Elvery, S. (2017). Who did the political parties receive donations from? Search the full dataset, *ABC News*, 1 February. Retrieved from http://www.abc.net.au/news/2017-02-01/australian-political-donations-searchable-database-2015-2016/8208090

Foley, P. & Martin, S. (2000). A new deal for the community? Public participation in regeneration and local service delivery. *Policy and Politics*, **28**(4), 479–91.

GetUp! (2017). The ad they don't want us to see, viewed. Retrieved from https://www.getup.org.au/campaigns/save-our-forests/no-harvey-no/the-ad-they-dont-want-us-to-see

Gillespie, K. (2016). The director of Change.org Australia explains how slacktivism is a myth, *VICE*. Retrieved from https://www.vice.com/en_au/article/bnkdad/the-director-of-changeorg-australia-about-medicinal-cannabis-gay-panic-and-the-myth-of-slacktivism.

Goodall, H. (1982). A history of Aboriginal communities in New South Wales, 1909–1939. PhD Thesis. Department of History. Sydney: University of Sydney.

Grant, W. (1978). *Insider Groups, Outsider Groups and Interest Group Strategies in Britain*, Department of Politics, University of Warwick.

Greenpeace International. (2012). *Press conference at the Sydney Aquarium*, Greenpeace International. Retrieved from http://www.greenpeace.org/international/en/multimedia/photos/press-conference-at-the-sydney-aquarium/

Gunningham, N. (2009). The new collaborative environmental governance: The localization of regulation. *Journal of Law and Society*, **36**(1), 145–66.

Hamilton, C. & Maddison, S. (2007). *Silencing Dissent: How the Australian Government is Controlling Public Opinion and Stifling Debate*, Crows Nest: Allen & Unwin.

Howie, E. (2016). *It's Time to Safeguard Our Democracy*, Human Rights Law Centre. Retrieved from https://www.hrlc.org.au/news/its-time-to-safeguard-our-democracy

Human Rights Law Centre. (2016). *Safeguarding Democracy*, Human Rights Law Centre. Retrieved from http://static1.squarespace.com/static/580025f66b8f5b2dabbe4291/5812996f1dd454018

6f54894/581299ee1dd4540186f55760/1477614062728/hrlc_report_safeguarding democracy_online.pdf?format=original

International Association for Public Participation. (2014). *IAP2's Public Participation Spectrum*, IAP2 International Federation. Retrieved from https://www.iap2.org.au/tenant/c0000004/00000001/files/iap2_public_participation_spectrum.pdf

Jacobs, C. (2014). The secret life of lobbyists, *Crikey*, 16 July. Retrieved from https://www.crikey.com.au/2014/07/16/the-secret-life-of-lobbyists/

Johns, G. (2000). NGO way to go: Political accountability of non-government organizations in democratic society. *IPA Backgrounder*, **12**(3), 1–16.

Kelly, D. (2016). With friends like these: Just how close are the Liberal Party and IPA? *The Conversation*, 6 June. Retrieved from https://theconversation.com/with-friends-like-these-just-how-close-are-the-liberal-party-and-ipa-60442

Kelly, J. & Shanahan, D. (2016). Eight biggest green groups net $685 m windfall over decade, *The Australian*. Retrieved from http://www.theaustralian.com.au/national-affairs/climate/eight-biggest-green-groups-net-685m-windfall-over-decade/news-story/2c5c2a5b7e2f553fc6c251394458cc09

Kelly, P. (2014). New climate change battlefront pits Abbott against the anti-coal brigade, *The Australian*, 17 October. Retrieved from http://www.theaustralian.com.au/opinion/columnists/paul-kelly/new-climate-change-battlefront-pits-abbott-against-the-anticoal-brigade/news-story/0d6e84ad0ae845a2f5f4d045a01e9808

Kilby, P. (2015). *NGOs and Political Change: A History of the Australian Council for International Development*, Canberra: ANU Press.

Livingstone, C. & Johnson, M. (2017). Gambling lobby gives big to political parties, and names names, *The Conversation*, 22 February. Retrieved from https://theconversation.com/gambling-lobby-gives-big-to-political-parties-and-names-names-73131

Lowe, J. & Hill, E. (2005). Closing the gap between government and community. In A. Rainnie and M. Grobbelaar (eds), *New Regionalism in Australia*, Aldershot: Ashgate, pp. 165–80.

Maddison, S. & Denniss, R. (2013). *An Introduction to Australian Public Policy: Theory and Practice*, 2nd edn, Melbourne: Cambridge University Press.

Martin, F.A. (2017). Explainer: Why are some donations to charities tax deductible? *The Conversation*, 15 March. Retrieved from https://theconversation.com/explainer-why-are-donations-to-some-charities-tax-deductible-72968

Maynard, J. (2003). Vision, voice and influence: The rise of the Australian Aboriginal Progressive Association. *Australian Historical Studies*, **34**(121), 91–105.

McCann, J. (2012). *Community Cabinets in Australia*, Parliament of Australia. Retrieved from http://www.aph.gov.au/about_parliament/parliamentary_departments/parliamentary_library/pubs/bn/2012–2013/communitycabinets

Morton, A. (2016). Election results: Abbott-backer Andrew Nikolic blames GetUp! for swing that cost him seat of Bass, *The Sydney Morning Herald*, 4 July. Retrieved from http://www.smh.com.au/federal-politics/political-news/election-results-abbottbacker-andrew-nikolic-blames-getup-for-swing-that-cost-him-seat-of-bass-20160704-gpy38y.html

Parliamentary Education Office. (2017). *Referenda and Plebiscites*, Parliamentary Education Office. Retrieved from https://www.peo.gov.au/learning/fact-sheets/referendums-and-plebiscites.html

Reece, N. (2013). *The Rise and Rise of Issues Campaigners*, Election Watch Australia, The University of Melbourne. Retrieved from http://past.electionwatch.edu.au/australia-2013/campaign-ads/rise-and-rise-issues-campaigners

Robertson, C. (2014). Slacktivism: the downfall of millennials, *HuffPost* (US edition), 14 October. Retrieved from https://www.huffingtonpost.com/charlotte-robertson/slacktivism-the-downfall-_b_5984336.html

Rodgers, E. (2010). Gillard defends climate change 'gobfest', *ABC News*, 23 July. Retrieved from http://www.abc.net.au/news/2010–07–23/gillard-defends-climate-change-gobfest/917416

Schirmer, J., Dare, M. & Ercan, S.A. (2016). Deliberative democracy and the Tasmanian forest peace process. *Australian Journal of Political Science*, **51**(2), 288–307.

Scholte, J.A., O'Brien, R. & Williams, M. (1999) The WTO and civil society. *Journal of World Trade*, **33**(1), 107–23.

Shanahan, D. (2016). Green campaign against Australian coal: Trail leads to John Podesta, *The Australian*, 28 October. Retrieved from http://www.theaustralian.com.au/opinion/columnists/dennis-shanahan/green-campaign-against-australian-coal-trail-leads-to-john-podesta/news-story/42784b8b30e0ab18d7386054189a0933

Sharp, N. (1993). *Stars of Tagai: The Torres Strait Islanders*, Acton: Aboriginal Studies Press.

Standing Committee on the Environment. (2016). *Inquiry into the Register of Environmental Organisations*, Canberra: House of Representatives.

Stewart, L.G., Arif, A., Nied, A.C., Spiro, E.S. & Starbird, K. (2017). Drawing the lines of contention: Networked frame contests within #BlackLivesMatter discourse. *PACM on Human-Computer Interaction*, **1**(96).

Tierney, J. (2003). Tassie's Franklin River – 20 years on, *ABC News*. Retrieved from http://www.abc.net.au/7.30/content/2003/s892579.htm

Urban, R. (2017). Firms ring in campaign for marriage equality, *The Australian*, 4 April. Retrieved from http://www.theaustralian.com.au/national-affairs/firms-ring-in-campaign-for-marriage-equality/news-story/0539ca1821754e570cd16a08dc7b6586

Warhurst, J. (2009). Interest groups and political lobbying. In D. Woodward, A. Parkin and J. Summers, (eds), *Government, Politics, Power and Policy in Australia*, 9th edn, Frenchs Forest: Pearson Australia.

Whittaker, A. (2021). Indigenous deaths in custody: Inquests can be sites of justice or administrative violence, *The Conversation*, 14 April. Retrieved from https://theconversation.com/indigenous-deaths-in-custody-inquests-can-be-sites-of-justice-or-administrative-violence-158126

Willingham, R. (2016). Sky rail: Supreme Court dismisses residents' bid to derail project, *The Age*, 20 December. Retrieved from http://www.theage.com.au/victoria/sky-rail-supreme-court-dismisses-residents-bid-to-derail-project-20161220-gtepu5.html

Yeatman, A. (1998). *Activism and the Policy Process*, St Leonards: Allen & Unwin.

Zillman, S. (2017). Symbolic constitutional recognition off the table after Uluru talks, Indigenous leaders say, *ABC News*, 27 May. Retrieved from http://www.abc.net.au/news/2017–05–27/uluru-calls-for-treaty-puts-constitutional-recognition-off-table/8565114

CHAPTER 13
CONCLUSION

LEARNING OBJECTIVES

After reading this chapter, you should be able to:

1. Outline some of the overarching challenges for Australian democracy
2. Consider whether domestic politics still matters or whether international politics governs what role states can play

INTRODUCTION

Contemporary Australia is buffeted by forces over which it has only limited control. The climate grows harsher and increasingly variable as a result of climate change, even while domestic policies seem to seek to ignore this new reality. The global refugee crisis, in which huge numbers of refugees seek a safe haven, has been driven by continuous conflict around the world but is now increasingly seeing people driven from homes and countries as a product of climate-induced destruction of livelihoods. The economy, interconnected with other nation-states via a system of bilateral and multilateral trade agreements and the free flow of capital, is continually impacted by economic developments elsewhere. A global pandemic has not only exposed Australia's reliance on trade networks but also the vulnerability of domestic populations. The erosion of trust in established modes of political communication and of core social and political institutions has upended liberal democracy. While a wealthy advanced industrial economy, Australia argues it has little capacity to act as a global change agent, even as it makes plays at being so. Abrogating our responsibilities to the international community would indicate that the closed-minded, colonial thinking that Australia had seemingly unshackled itself from still lingers within the national psyche.

The scale of international challenges is matched by domestic economic, political and social concerns, some of which would appear intractable. Economic inequality is on the rise. Corporate profits are enormous, yet wage growth is stagnant. Meaningful engagement with Australia's First Peoples is routinely sacrificed to political expediency. Home ownership, the bedrock of the 'Australian dream', is increasingly out of reach to young Australians, even as it powers the wealth of the oldest. The Constitution, the document which established Australia, remains unmodernised due to the difficulty in making changes to it. The simple fact of dual citizenship, now available to many Australians, caused the unseating of a series of federal politicians because the High Court found them to be in breach of an arcane section of the Constitution and therefore ineligible to sit in the parliament.

By highlighting some of the problems Australia faces, our goal is not to suggest that Australian democracy is broken beyond repair. All nations face similar issues, and so Australia is not unique in that sense. Indeed, we might still argue Australia is Donald Horne's *The Lucky Country* – in both the sense of being 'lucky' and in the sense Horne intended it (Horne 2008). But it is only by analysing the challenges we as a nation face, that students of Australian politics can truly evaluate the future of Australian democracy. This chapter provides an opportunity to engage in analysis of contemporary Australian politics and question some of the challenges chosen for further discussion in this chapter. It also aims to bring together much of the discussion through the previous 12 chapters.

SIX KEY CHALLENGES FOR AUSTRALIAN DEMOCRACY IN THE 21ST CENTURY

Some of the overarching problems that Australian democracy faces today are enduring challenges also faced by other liberal democracies. Working out how to, for example, best manage the institutions of the state or developing strategies to engage with and empower interest groups and non-government organisations (NGOs) are problems that democracies across the globe are confronted with. Equally, how well nation-states manage social and political inclusion and equality can define how successful and representative liberal democracies are. However, the domestic context remains important. Australia's unique mix of institutions, its history and culture ensure that the problems it faces and the challenges to its democracy are never quite the same as in other comparable countries like New Zealand, the United Kingdom or Canada.

Here we discuss the six key challenges facing Australian democracy in the 21st century. We can of course find many more challenges that may have an impact on how we progress more generally as a society. The effect of climate change might be considered one of the great existential crises of the 21st century, not just for Australians but for citizens globally – especially as farming and food production come under increasing pressure. Equally, what are we to make of the apparent crisis of democracy, whereby increasing numbers of citizens disengage from contemporary politics and politicians, and what is now referred to as 'anti-politics' (Humphrys, Copland and Mansillo 2020). The ensuing turn to populism surely presents a significant challenge to mainstream political institutions. However, the next section will focus on six specific areas of concern for governance and the state, not the least because, as Gerry Stoker put it 'politics matters because collective decisions matter' (Stoker 2017, 5).

The challenges discussed here are key to the functioning of Australia as a nation: governance and the role of the State; the Australian Federation; the place of First Nations; national security, the environment, and the pandemic; globalisation and economic inequality; and representation and participation.

GOVERNANCE AND THE ROLE OF THE STATE

As was discussed in Chapter 6, there has been a discernible shift from government to governance in recent decades. Changes to the Australian public sector and the ways that the government has delivered services since the 1980s has undoubtedly changed the way Australians understand what government does and what we can expect of it. One question that these changes has prompted is to what extent have more problems been created than the changes were intended to solve. Market-based approaches are now the favoured instruments of both major parties despite widespread concern for the effect of the 'market' when used in service delivery. The privatisation of government assets has become a source of agitation and anger among critics and voters alike, who consistently oppose sales of government assets, while favouring increased expenditure on services over tax cuts (Cahill and Toner 2018; Essential 2015). Bodies such as the staunchly pro-market Australian Competition and Consumer Commission (ACCC) now acknowledge the limited benefits of these approaches, with ACCC chairman Rod Sims arguing in 2016 that asset sales had damaged the Australian economy (Hatch 2016).

Discussions about the use of market-based mechanisms cannot be separated from discussions of ideology and evidence-based policy. However, these debates at their core are more often about the role and place of the State, whether as policymaker, implementation vehicle, or regulator. Since the 1980s Australian voters have been presented with free-market policies from the major parties in Australia, similar to those enacted in the United Kingdom, the United States and countries where structural reform was deemed essential.

Two case studies that can assist with understanding how States and parties have reacted and adapted to the free-market ideology are in Chile and the United Kingdom. Chile underwent major economic reforms in the 1970s and 1980s, heavily influenced by market economists such as Friedman and Hayek. Chile's Pinochet military regime suppressed all dissent, rapidly implementing a complete overhaul and privatisation of the Chilean economy. Initial economic indicators appeared to show increases in productivity and dramatic growth to the extent that Chile was described as a 'Latin Tiger', emulating East Asian economies. However, social inequality soared to be worse than that of the Asian Tigers, and the free-market reforms were of little assistance in diversifying export markets (Duquette 1998). Chile became increasingly and visibly segregated by class.

Overall, the market reforms were a mixed blessing, leading to an increasingly pragmatic approach to economic and social policy by Chilean political leaders (Santiso 2007). The second case is that of the British Labour Party under Jeremy Corbyn. Corbyn led the Labour Party into the 2017 UK general election with a set of policies that were some of the most radical in the Anglo-American democracies of the last 30 years (Manwaring and Smith 2020). This included re-nationalisation of key sectors of the British economy, reform of the health system to return it to being fully public, free education, and de-nuclearisation of the defence forces. While other factors contributed, the near 10 per cent swing to the Labour Party demonstrated the potential for parties to propose policies that contradict the bipartisan neo-liberal consensus.

The question then remains: how is it that the major parties – which are by their very nature, vote-seeking – continue to advocate a set of policies which polling shows the majority of voters oppose, and that have very real negative effects economically?

Breaking free of the ideological straitjackets the major parties in many countries are in is important for another reason too. Many of the radical-right populist political parties who pose a threat to liberal democracy are able to fill a niche in party systems by presenting themselves as not only the saviours of 'the people' from unaccountable political elites but also as the only parties who will smash the free-market consensus and deliver power back to the people. Few would dispute that free markets *can* work, but the challenge for Australia's political class is using market-based instruments when they are appropriate and not as panacea to *all* of our public policy problems.

SHORT-ANSWER QUESTIONS 13.1

1. Do you think that the key challenges for Australia in the 21st century are domestic or international in nature?
2. What are the key differences between the 'arena' and 'social process' views of politics?

Suggested responses are available at www.cambridge.org/highereducation/isbn/9781009108232/resources

THE AUSTRALIAN FEDERATION

Australian democracy in the 21st century still operates under the 19th century settlement of Federation. As discussed in Chapter 2, Australia, as a federation, needs to resolve issues such as the distribution taxes to and between states. However, the increasing centralisation of financial power at the Commonwealth level contrasts with the ongoing role that the states play in the heavy-lifting service-delivery areas of policing, transport, health and education. The years 2019–2020 brought two exemplars – severe bushfires across the country and the COVID-19 pandemic – of the importance of state governments and what can happen when the Commonwealth is unable or unwilling to play an effective coordination role. Scholars have noted that, around the globe, national governments – even unitary governments – are devolving policy responsibilities to subnational levels of government. This trend points to the impossibility of governing complex societies from national capitals. But it does not also mean that national-level governments wield less influence. In Australia's case, the Commonwealth has been content to see the states operate transport systems, schools and hospitals, but to use its own financial supremacy and authority to conditionally fund the states in order to direct transport, education and health policy. The ongoing challenge is to strike a balance between achieving national policy priorities while still allowing policy to be shaped to fit particular regional or local needs and circumstances.

Whether Australia has the right mix of national and regional-level political institutions is another matter. There is a widespread sense that Australia's particular federal structures need adjustment, if not wholesale reform. Various proposals for 'big picture' change have extended to creating new states, providing sovereignty and representation to Aboriginal and Torres Strait Islander peoples, embedding local government in the Constitution, and refashioning taxation responsibilities to end the financial dependence of states upon the Commonwealth. The creation of the National Cabinet during the COVID-19 pandemic is one example of an attempt to re-invigorate the previous Council of Australian Governments' process to deal with an issue that cut across state and federal lines of responsibility. Then there are those who would enlarge the scope and authority of the states and those who would replace them with more numerous, smaller-scale regional governments. The Uluru Statement looked to embed a formal process of political sovereignty through a separate representational body to provide advice to the Commonwealth Parliament, as well as a Makarrata Commission to work towards formal agreements between the government and Aboriginal and Torres Strait Islander people (McKay 2017).

But tempering the enthusiasm of all those who would reform Australia's Federation is a harsh political fact: the Constitution is not easily changed. In recent decades governments have shied away from seeking to amend the Constitution, fearing defeat and loss of face, especially given the reality that only 8 of the 44 proposals to amend the Constitution have been passed (Parliament n.d.).

Section 128 of the Constitution was put in place to ensure that the populous states of New South Wales and Victoria could not override the smaller states and reshape Australia's federal system to their advantage. This has effectively prevented constitutional amendment in circumstances where the major parties are not fully agreed on the merits of reform. Australia's Federation is unlikely to be altered unless ways can be found to overcome short-term vested interests and party rivalries. Invariably different political parties hold government in the various states and territories and at the Commonwealth level. The search for partisan advantage is ever-present in their dealings, as much as any centre-periphery struggle. Australia's form of federalism might instead be called pragmatic, where each prime minster needs to assess the political landscape and work out how best to engage state governments (Hollander and Patapan 2007).

FIRST NATIONS WITHOUT A VOICE?

One of the questions that has vexed Australians for the past 200 years is how to approach and reconcile non-Indigenous and Indigenous Australians. Australia's First Peoples have been campaigning (violently and non-violently) since the first arrival of white invaders, colonists and settlers. For the whole period since 1788, Aboriginal and Torres Strait Islander people have been arguing and demanding a voice as the people who were here at colonisation (Attwood and Markus 1999). That voice has been consistently, and at times explicitly, denied. Whether it is the almost constant changing of rules to deny them rights, even under white Australian law, to the theft of wages, children and culture, Australia's First People have been remarkably resilient – and consistent in their demand for a voice in the future of Australia (Attwood 2020).

From the first legal challenges over rights, through the Mabo High Court Challenge, the Reconciliation March across the Sydney Harbour Bridge in 2000 and the Uluru Statement from The Heart, a movement has been growing for a more formal set of arrangements between the current legal structures – those of the coloniser – and Australia's First Peoples. Whether this takes the form of a formal treaty recognising the place of Australian Aboriginal people as both First Nation Peoples and dispossessed or the encompassing of Indigenous voices with the formal structures of the state. The idea of treaty is not new – think of the New Zealand Treaty of Waitangi, signed in 1841 and more recently formally enforced within New Zealand law. Neither is Indigenous representation – think of any number of European nations that provide rights and representation to indigenous and ethnic minorities. So why then is the idea of either (or both) a treaty or indigenous representation so seemingly anathematic to some in Australia?

The answer might be found by at least looking at the arguments of those who would either undermine efforts toward sovereignty or who would see Indigenous Australians assimilated. The Bennelong Society, which existed from 2001 to 2011, argued in respect of traditional lands and communities that 'strong leadership will be required to overcome the separatist policy, not by imposing solutions but by encouraging movement into the wider community' (Howson 2001). The broader program amounted to what might otherwise be described as assimilation. Johns argues directly for integration into white society, concluding '(b)ut if the problem is differently conceived – that is, that Aborigines must learn to adapt to their new environment – it will resolve itself more quickly and with less pain' and that retention of culture, especially in remote or regional communities, is a barrier to meaningful integration. (Johns 2008, 81). Treaty, sovereignty or any form of separate representation is cast as a form of separatism from mainstream Australian society and therefore wrong.

NATIONAL SECURITY, THE ENVIRONMENT, AND THE PANDEMIC

Central to many debates in political science is the ongoing role of the state in our lives. This is also true of the challenges Australia faces in the 21st century. We live in an era of securitisation. Not only is national security high on the agenda for governments but decision-making in this and many other areas, such as how we deal with asylum seekers, are securitised.

As discussed in Chapter 4, this is the process whereby particular issues are constructed as central to state security, and thus become the subject of extraordinary government measures that dilute civil liberties and judicial protections (Buzan, Wæver and De Wilde 1998). The 2001 terrorist attacks on the World Trade Center and Pentagon in the United States, quickly followed by the Bali bombing in 2002, elevated the belief that Islamic terrorism posed a real threat to Australia. Coupled with a series of further bombings in Madrid (2004) and London (2005), each with significant loss of life, Australia moved to introduce stricter anti-terrorism laws in the belief that terrorist attack was both possible and imminent. Beginning with legislation pushed through the parliament in 2001, then followed by numerous other pieces of legislation including the 2005 Anti-Terrorism Acts enacted across states and territories, Australian governments dramatically enhanced the power of police and security forces to combat terrorism (Gelber 2013).

Between 2013 and 2022, various Liberal–National Party governments (under Abbott, Turnbull and Morrison) have enacted a string of ostensibly anti-terrorist measures including the capacity of security agencies to detain and hold Australians not even suspected of a crime but who those agencies consider may be material to an action (that is, may be involved in any way, even if not known by the individual concerned), introduced a range of penalties for the advocating of terrorism, amended penalties for journalists and whistleblowers deemed to be acting 'against the national interest' (especially where that may involve the disclosure of intelligence operations), and dramatically expanded the powers of the Australian Security Intelligence Agency (Hardy and Williams 2021). Data retention laws were also amended to ensure that internet service providers must keep all details of electronic traffic through their service for a period of two years, and to make the metadata available for security services.

The rapid securitisation of Australian democracy, including freedoms Australians may have thought were automatic – speech, communication and even anti-government commentary – may be thought of as an overreaction. Certainly, by the standards of many other accidental (or intentional) deaths in Australia, the increased security presence in Australian lives has increased dramatically. Perhaps more surprisingly, however, is the parliamentarianisation of security – whereby security issues, once the purview of executive government, have become increasingly the province of parliament (Neal 2021) – at once ensuring a form of public knowledge while also ensuring that security issues are no longer solely the realm of security forces but now encompass all of society, existing in the 'commonplace' rather than as the 'exceptional' (Chambers and Andrews 2019). The challenge this securitisation represents, however, is potentially very real, when taken in the light of the increased pressure on the media to comply with government under the guise of 'national security'. The question that arises is then: at what point does securitisation, as encompassed by the panoply of laws, restrict or become a threat to democratic behaviour (Ananian-Welsh, Kendall and Murray 2021)?

Free speech and open political communication are not ideas that we can simply consign to the realm of 'old-ideas'. They may seem irrelevant when argued for by commentators claiming censorship when columns are withdrawn for making false statements, but in the realm of day-to-day information passage they are critical concepts that allow citizens to understand what is happening around them. Far from being an abstract ideal of liberal democracy, open political communication is part and parcel of active engagement in democracy enabling citizens to freely discuss and debate issues of concern. As Gelber notes, 'effective democracy is dependent on citizens' ability to criticise the government and to participate actively in deliberation over issues affecting them' (Gelber 2010).

Yet free speech and the limits of democracy are also connected to the debate around both climate change and pandemics. Over the past 30 years, a variety of individuals and organisations have argued that climate change is not real, the effects are overblown, or that we will find the appropriate technical fix for the problem and therefore can continue as before (Uscinski, Douglas and Lewandowsky 2017). This occurred against the backdrop of ever-increasingly dire warnings from scientists and agencies. During the pandemic, those who questioned the efficacy of vaccines or who argued that the pandemic was an attempt by the powerful to control free citizens were at times given equal billing to health and medical specialists. Does the free flow of information mean giving equal standing to all opinions and comments? This brings us to Hannah Arendt and the difference between what she described as 'rational truths' (those of science, mathematics and philosophy) and 'factual truths' (that determined by events, circumstances, witnesses and testimony). If factual truth is contingent, and that lying can destroy truth by substituting alternative truths, then freedom of opinion is a false premise unless facts are themselves not in dispute (Bernstein 2018; Watts 2014). As philosophers might note, being entitled to an opinion is not equal to that opinion being treated as a serious candidate for the truth.

RESEARCH QUESTION 13.1

With reference to the idea of securitisation, in what ways is the issue of asylum seekers securitised?

GLOBALISATION AND ECONOMIC INEQUALITY

In 2019, 41 million people travelled to and from Australia, up from 27 million in 2010. One in four Australians are overseas born, with half of all Australians having parents born overseas. These may be taken as measures of **GLOBALISATION** – of the trend toward an increasingly complex interdependency between Australia and other countries. Globalisation, whether facilitated or caused by population movements, global trade patterns, financial flows, and communication technologies, is a process that transcends national boundaries. In the post-Second World War period, globalisation has transformed Australian society by changing our view of the world and forcing our politics to adapt to a new world of connectivity. While many may welcome globalisation, it is also resented by a significant proportion of Australians who perceive themselves as 'losers' in the process. Exasperation and a loss of identity has been given as reasons for the rise of Pauline Hanson and One Nation, as globalisation produces winners and losers, particularly centred on industrial and technological change (Goot and Watson 2001). That minor parties recorded Senate votes of 34 per cent and 35 per cent in the last two federal elections – primarily for parties promoting a shift from current economic practices – suggests that this exasperation is more widely felt, although with markedly different drivers. For at least some, the changes in society over this period, including rising economic inequality, has given rise to a major break in traditional voting patterns (Inglehart and Norris 2017).

The ending of significant import tariffs (a significant trade barrier, and bulwark of protectionism since Federation) started with a major reduction in tariffs in 1973, followed by the continued withdrawal from the mid-80s onwards. Trade protection policies, seen as by Kelly as a part of the Australian Settlement which allowed for the founding of the Australian Federation (Kelly 1992), allowed for Australian wages and standards of living to rise, even as they may have conversely allowed productivity to stagnate. The lowering of the tariffs in the 1980s saw a rapid decline in Australian manufacturing, which was unable to compete with cheap imports from low-wage nations – yet conversely saw at the same time a rapid increase in extractive industries such as mining and forest products (Anderson 2020).

At the same time as tariffs were being lowered, a further fundamental change was occurring in the provision of services by governments. During the 1980s and 1990s, large parts of what were core elements of previous governments were first corporatised and then privatised. The process started with enterprises that had previously been important in the development of Australia as a nation, such as state development banks and the Commonwealth Bank, but went further to governments divesting themselves of the bulk of state enterprises that might be considered to be in competition with private business, including Qantas, telephony services (rebadged as Telecom then Telstra), railway services, and power generation. The process is still ongoing – note the recent privatisation of bus services in NSW – even as the Commonwealth, states and territories have become aware that they have effectively passed on their control of large sections of the economy. As part of this process, many former government workers faced disruption, job losses and wage contraction.

While we might then blame globalisation for the removal of trade barriers and the shift in manufacturing industries to cheaper wage areas of East Asia, we might also argue that the trade liberalisation increased profitability for many in the Australian service sector, as much as it generated huge profits for the mining industry. Even as large-scale manufacturing, such as in the former Australia car-industry, were slowly shuttered, new jobs were being created in areas such as education services and tourism. The nature of the labour market in Australia was fundamentally changing (ABS 2012). These changes were also seen within other high-waged areas in North America and Europe, along with a shift from jobs rural, regional and ex-urban

GLOBALISATION: A process of growing inter-connectedness across the globe; in particular, the ease of movement of people, ideas and capital are cited as examples.

to increased employment in urban areas close to the major cities. Australia's economy entered a sustained period of growth and consumers benefited enormously from cheaper imported goods. At the same time, union density declined as the large single-site manufacturers closed as dispersed workshops, offices and retail areas became key employment sites, and industry-specific semi-skilled blue-collar work shifted toward low-skill white-collar jobs in the service industries.

It has also become clear that economic divisions within Australian society have deepened since the 1980s. There is now an emerging view that inequality has reached unacceptable levels matching those last seen in the 1940s, although the measures of inequality differ between who is asked. The Productivity Commission, the body that provides microeconomic advice to government in Australia, acknowledges there have been increases in inequality in Australia, though describes the changes as slight (Productivity Commission 2018). The Australian Council of Social Services (ACOSS) argues that it is considerably more severe. What is clear is that while the absolute wages of the poorest workers have risen at comparable rates as other workers, those of the highest wage-earners have skyrocketed. The ACOSS study found that Australians in the top quintile (20 per cent) of income earners now earn around five times as much as Australians in the bottom quintile (Davidson, Saunders and Phillips 2018). At the extremes of income inequality, the wealthiest 1 per cent of Australians earns 26 times what a person in the lowest 5 per cent does. In terms of wealth inequality, the top 20 per cent improved their overall wealth during the period 2003 to 2016, while the bottom 20 per cent saw theirs decrease by 9 per cent. As you might expect, the top 5 per cent saw a 60 per cent growth. These figures underscore the significant structural changes in Australia that have occurred during the past 30 years.

A deepening economic inequality (which is visible in the high cost of housing and in static or falling wage levels) presents a significant challenge to Australian democracy in the 21st century. There is a growing body of work that points to perceived income inequality being negatively correlated to happiness and, as we have noted, the previous dislocations during the 1980s has increased dissatisfaction with mainstream Australian politics. The combination of political detachment and dissatisfaction with government performance are both posited as potential explanations for general mistrust of Australian politics, and when linked to rising inequality should pose a longer term question as to the political legitimacy of existing Australian political institutions (Cameron 2020; Dassonneville and McAllister 2021).

SHORT-ANSWER QUESTIONS 13.2

1. What is the political effect of economic inequality?
2. In what ways is economic inequality evident in Australia?

Suggested responses are available at www.cambridge.org/highereducation/isbn/9781009108232/resources

REPRESENTATION AND PARTICIPATION

As noted in several chapters, who is represented in Australian politics is a vexed question. Certainly we know that Australian parliaments do not necessarily reflect Australian society in terms of gender, ethnicity, class or culture (Hough 2021; Lewis 2019; Richards 2021). That they do not may at least be part of the reason as to why Australians are disengaged from the democratic process. The leadership changes, after Kevin Rudd's election victory in 2007 – which broke 11 continuous years of John Howard as prime minister – in both major parties might also be taken as both cause and reaction to an apparent new era in politics.

Others see more serious problems. One diagnosis is that, alongside a rise in populism, there has been a commensurate rise in '**ANTI-POLITICS**'. While populism might be described as a process where political leaders curry favour with the electorate by actively projecting themselves as anti-establishment and anti-elitist, anti-politics derives from below, from the mass of citizenry who can be seen to be disengaged, disenchanted and generally alienated from formal political processes (Humphrys et al. 2020). Populist leaders utilise these sentiments in their political campaigning in an attempt to place themselves at the centre of politics. Whether they are pundits or academics there are a raft of commentators who are prepared to diagnose the issue and then provide the solution. Yet is the Australian political system 'broken' as some might argue?

First and foremost, the Australian system of electoral management is seen as one of the best globally. It is extremely difficult to manipulate votes such that outcomes are corrupted. However, the system of choosing representatives itself is one that, while serving the interests of mainstream parties and electors alike, has started to generate outcomes that are now less welcome. Legislative majorities may have once been desired by the electorate, but this is by no means certain. As discussed in Chapters 7–9, Australian voting patterns have diverged significantly from the days of their being few parties or candidates to vote for. The rise of the minor party and independent vote in both houses of parliament suggests electors want considerably more from their parliamentary representatives, but the system of single-member electorates does not serve that outcome well. The real problem might then be that, instead of voters being seen as disenchanted and alienated, the electoral system itself might do with some changes to allow for effective representation. Various suggestions from multi-member electorates to lowering the voting age have been suggested at times, but the dynamic of the major parties having control of the legislative framework means there is limited desire from them to change things (Miragliotta, Murray and Drum 2021).

We need also consider that the Australian Parliament, as noted at the beginning of this section, does not replicate the Australian population in respect of its age, gender, ethnicity or class. While Australia was an early adopter of votes for women, that a little over one-third of parliamentarians in the lower houses are women – so often argued as the 'House of Government' – suggests there is still a failure to select women into winnable seats. The picture for those who are of non-Anglo backgrounds is hardly better, with over 87 per cent of members of parliament (MPs) being of Anglo ancestry.

The one area of representation that does appear to come close to community population levels is that for Aboriginal and Torres Strait Islander people, making up 2.2 per cent of parliamentarians while being 3.3 per cent of the total Australian population. We should recognise that the 2.2 per cent is an aggregate figure, with representation being strongest in the Northern Territory where there has been a total of 22 Indigenous MPs elected over the years, and Aboriginal and Torres Strait Islander people make up 30 per cent of the population. Yet as we have seen in Chapter 12, it is also among this population that a demand for stronger representation, not just to have MPs but to have a stronger voice in affairs concerning them, whether this is through a representative body or via enforceable agreements. While the Apology to Stolen Generations by Prime Minister Rudd in 2008 was a powerful statement, encouraging engagement and participation in the political processes requires more than this. The challenge to Australian democracy is to maintain an active and engaged civil society that goes beyond election campaigns, political slogans and institutional inquiries that have few results.

> **ANTI-POLITICS:** Political activity external to formal political process involving a broad rejection of elite structures and political institutions.

REFLECTION QUESTIONS 13.1

1. In what ways is the composition of Australia's parliament unrepresentative of the voters who the elected officials represent?

2. Does it make sense to suggest, as numbers of commentators recently have, that the Australia political system is 'broken'?

3. By most measures Australian parliaments are unrepresentative of the wider population? Do you think this is important?

Response prompts are available at www.cambridge.org/highereducation/isbn/9781009108232/resources

DOES DOMESTIC POLITICS MATTER? HAS GLOBALISATION CONSTRAINED GOVERNMENTS?

An oft-repeated mantra during the latter part of the 20th century was that national governments were not relevant, even while we ourselves might think of Australia as a democracy in which voters elect governments to implement policies that they wish to see enacted. However, the inexorable march of globalisation has meant Australia being drawn into an interconnected and interdependent world. Various Australian governments have found themselves obliged to comply with the variety of international agreements covering, for instance, trade, defence, human rights and environmental conservation. One direct expression of globalisation is that Australia is, as other countries are, evermore engaged in negotiating and implementing both bilateral and multilateral agreements with other countries that allow them to jointly or collectively address the many economic, environmental, social and political problems that require an integrated policy response. The conventions and treaties that Australia has signed may influence the way it behaves, both domestically and internationally, but the ratification of an international agreement has not meant handing over **SOVEREIGNTY** to a supranational body or government.

The first two decades of the 21st century will have hopefully shown that, far being irrelevant, national governments have become more relevant for citizens than ever before. After the global financial crisis (GFC) in 2008, in which global economic structures lead to a collapse of banks and industry in many countries, it was national governments that stepped in to guarantee both struggling businesses (consider the situation of one of the largest car manufacturers in the world, Chrysler, in the United States) and prop up an ailing financial sector. Chinese investment in domestic growth during the immediate post-GFC period kept the Australian mining sector afloat, and with it, investment in jobs and domestic industry, allowing Australia to weather the worst of the crisis.

The advent of the pandemic at the beginning of 2020 has meant national and subnational governments have again been at the forefront of working to protect the workforce while keeping the wheels of industry turning. Although global responses to the pandemic have come in the form of a wide variety of vaccines and a commitment from wealthier nations to supply vaccines to developing nations, it has been left to individual nation-states to determine how to combat the

SOVEREIGNTY: Governments are said to be sovereign when they exercise an authority over their people and territory which is not constrained by external influences.

worst effects of COVID-19. For wealthy nations of the North, this has meant lockdowns, vaccine distribution and subsidies to both business and workers, but this form of response is far harder among working and rural poor of many nations. The global economy has continued but with far lower growth rates during parts of the pandemic, and often with multiplying state debt levels.

The key to understanding Australia's responses to first the GFC and then the pandemic is to understand that Australia, as a commodity exporter, is somewhat buffered by dramatic increases or falls in share markets linked to manufacturing. Not just Chinese investment but also Chinese industrial output was important. Relatively cheap Australian iron ore flowed to Chinese steel mills. Relatively cheap Australian liquefied natural gas also flows from the North West Shelf off Western Australia. During the pandemic, the nature of the Australian Constitution has been revealed, with state governments now carrying the weight of caring for those afflicted, as well as administering responses to it. The Australian Government's role has been largely reduced to acting as a coordinating body, via the National Cabinet, for vaccine purchase and distribution, as well as external border control. State governments have asserted their authority when it comes to interstate border closures as health measures – an action affirmed by the High Court. Have state governments been strengthened by the pandemic? Perhaps, but a more likely situation is that federation structure has allowed varied responses in different states according to conditions on the ground, something the Commonwealth Government would have struggled to achieve.

REFLECTION QUESTIONS 13.2

1. How has globalisation influenced Australian politics?
2. Australia is a signatory to international agreements, treaties and conventions. Do these involve surrendering sovereignty?

Response prompts are available at www.cambridge.org/highereducation/isbn/9781009108232/resources

SUMMARY

Learning objective 1: Outline some of the overarching challenges for Australian democracy

Australian democracy faces a number of significant challenges in the 21st century. While we could choose from an expansive list, six key examples were provided in this chapter that have underpinned much of the previous discussion throughout this text. These include governance and the role of the state; the Australian Federation; the place of First Nations; national security, the environment, and the pandemic; globalisation and economic inequality; and representation and participation. You will notice, perhaps unsurprisingly, a degree of overlap between the different challenges. Economic, cultural and historical forces all shape political outcomes. Likewise, Australia's institutional architecture has an influence on political outcomes long after forces driving their need has changed from when those institutions were established. Indeed, this is one of the central challenges that Australian democracy faces: managing significant challenges at a time when its institutional structure is largely the same as it was over a century ago.

Learning objective 2: Consider whether domestic politics still matters or whether international politics governs what role states can play

International politics may seem to dominate the headlines, particularly at times of international crisis, whether that be intense conflicts, environmental disasters, financial collapses or critical matters of security. However, domestic politics should never be underestimated. Between the blaring headlines are the many other stories of what is happening in Australia, some of which is just as important, if not more so, to the passage of our lives. Beyond the dealings in the various corridors of power, we can see democracy in action in the meetings of NGOs, fledgling political parties, interest groups, right down to the neighbourhood action group. While this may not be what we first consider as we ponder questions of sovereignty or representation, it is through this active civil society that democracy is at work. The reality is that while Australia may be a signatory to a range of international agreements, treaties and conventions, it is still in the realm of domestic politics that these are enabled and enacted. So, while international events in Europe, the Americas or Asia do have a direct impact on Australia, the domestic political context remains central to political and policy outcomes for Australian citizens.

REFERENCES

Ananian-Welsh, R., Kendall, S. & Murray, R.J. (2021). Risk and uncertainty in public interest journalism: The impact of espionage law on press freedom. *Melbourne University Law Review*, **44**(3).

Anderson, K. (2020). Trade protectionism in Australia: Its growth and dismantling. *Journal of Economic Surveys*, **34**(5), 1044–67. https://doi.org/10.1111/joes.12388

Attwood, B. (2020). *Rights for Aborigines*, Abingdon: Routledge.

Attwood, B. & Markus, A. (1999). *The Struggle for Aboriginal Rights: A Documentary History*, Sydney: Allen & Unwin.

Australian Bureau of Statistics (ABS). (2012). *Fifty Years of Labour Force: Now and Then*. Canberra: Australian Bureau of Statistics. Retrieved from https://www.abs.gov.au/ausstats/abs@.nsf/Lookup/1301.0Main+Features452012

Bernstein, R.J. (2018). The illuminations of Hannah Arendt, Opinion, *The New York Times*, 20 June. Retrieved from https://www.nytimes.com/2018/06/20/opinion/why-read-hannah-arendt-now.html

Buzan, B., Wæver, O. & De Wilde, J. (1998). *Security: A New Framework for Analysis*, Boulder: Lynne Rienner Publishers.

Cahill, D. & Toner, P. (2018). *Wrong Way: How Privatisation and Economic Reform Backfired*, Carlton: Black Inc.

Cameron, S. (2020). Government performance and dissatisfaction with democracy in Australia. *Australian Journal of Political Science*, **55**(2), 170–90. https://doi.org/10.1080/10361146.2020.1755221

Chambers, P. & Andrews, T. (2019). Never mind the bollards: The politics of policing car attacks through the securitisation of crowded urban places. *Environment and Planning D: Society and Space*, **37**(6), 1025–44. https://doi.org/10.1177/0263775818824343

Dassonneville, R. & McAllister, I. (2021). Explaining the decline of political trust in Australia. *Australian Journal of Political Science*, **56**(3), 280–97. https://doi.org/10.1080/10361146.2021.1960272

Davidson, P., Saunders, P. & Phillips, J. (2018). *Inequality in Australia 2018*. Sydney. Retrieved from https://www.acoss.org.au/wp-content/uploads/2018/07/Inequality-in-Australia-2018.pdf

Duquette, M. (1998). The Chilean economic miracle revisited. *The Journal of Socio-Economics*, **27**(3), 299–321. https://doi.org/10.1016/S1053-5357(99)80092-4

Essential. (2015). Privatisation of government services. In *Essential Report* (13 October 2015 edition), Essential Research.

Gelber, K. (2010). Freedom of political speech, hate speech and the argument from democracy: The transformative contribution of capabilities theory. *Contemporary Political Theory*, **9**(3), 304–24. https://doi.org/10.1057/cpt.2009.8

—— (2013). Secrecy provisions in Australian counter-terrorism policy: Violating international human rights standards? *Australian Journal of Human Rights*, **19**(2), 25–46. https://doi.org/10.1080/1323-238X.2013.11882125

Goot, M. & Watson, I. (2001). One Nation's electoral support: Where does it come from, What makes it different and How does it fit? *Australian Journal of Politics & History*, **47**(2), 159–91. https://doi.org/10.1111/1467-8497.00226

Hardy, K. & Williams, G. (2021). Press freedom in Australia's constitutional system. *Canadian Journal of Comparative and Contemporary Law*, **7**(1), 222.

Hatch, P. (2016). Privatisation has damaged the economy, says ACCC chief, *The Sydney Morning Herald*, 26 July. Retrieved from https://www.smh.com.au/business/privatisation-has-damaged-the-economy-says-accc-chief-20160726-gqe2c2.html

Hollander, R. & Patapan, H. (2007). Pragmatic federalism: Australian federalism from Hawke to Howard. *Australian Journal of Public Administration*, **66**(3), 280–97. http://doi.org/10.1111/j.1467-8500.2007.00542.x

Horne, D. (2008). *The Lucky Country*, Melbourne: Penguin.

Hough, A. (2021). *Composition of Australian Parliaments by Party and Gender: A Quick Guide*. Canberra: Australian Parliament. Retrieved from https://www.aph.gov.au/About_Parliament/Parliamentary_Departments/Parliamentary_Library/pubs/rp/rp2021/Quick_Guides/CompositionPartyGender

Howson, P. (2001). The Objectives of the Bennelong Society. Retrieved from http://archive.ipe.net.au/Bennelong.html

Humphrys, E., Copland, S. & Mansillo, L. (2020). Anti-politics in Australia: Hypotheses, evidence and trends. *Journal of Australian Political Economy*, (86), 122–56.

Inglehart, R. & Norris, P. (2017). Trump and the populist authoritarian parties: The silent revolution in reverse. *Perspectives on Politics*, **15**(2), 443–54. https://doi.org/10.1017/S1537592717000111

Johns, G. (2008). The Northern Territory Intervention in Aboriginal affairs: Wicked problem or wicked policy? *Agenda: A Journal of Policy Analysis and Reform*, **15**(2), 65–84.

Kelly, P. (1992). *The End of Certainty: The Story of the 1980s*, Sydney: Allen & Unwin.

Lewis, A. (2019). *The Way in: Representation in the Australian Parliament*, Melbourne: Per Capita. Retrieved from https://apo.org.au/node/216161

Manwaring, R. & Smith, E. (2020). Corbyn, British Labour and policy change. *British Politics*, **15**(1), 25–47. https://doi.org/10.1057/s41293-019-00112-9

McKay, D. (2017). *Uluru Statement: A quick guide*. Canberra: Australian Parliament. Retrieved from https://www.aph.gov.au/About_Parliament/Parliamentary_Departments/Parliamentary_Library/pubs/rp/rp1617/Quick_Guides/UluruStatement

Miragliotta, N., Murray, S. & Drum, M. (2021). Values, partisan interest, and the voting age: Lessons from Australia. *Politics & Policy*, **49**(5), 1192–215. https://doi.org/10.1111/polp.12413

Neal, A.W. (2021). The parliamentarisation of security in the UK and Australia. *Parliamentary Affairs*, **74**(2), 464–82. https://doi.org/10.1093/pa/gsaa012

Parliament, C. (n.d.). *House of Representatives Practice: Constitution alteration*. Retrieved from https://www.aph.gov.au/About_Parliament/House_of_Representatives/Powers_practice_and_procedure/Practice7/HTML/Chapter1/Constitution_alteration

Productivity Commission. (2018). *Rising inequality? A stocktake of the evidence*, Commission Research paper, Canberra. Retrieved from https://www.pc.gov.au/research/completed/rising-inequality

Richards, L. (2021). *Indigenous Australian Parliamentarians in Federal and State/Territory Parliaments: A Quick Guide*. Canberra: Australian Parliament. Retrieved from https://www.aph.gov.au/About_Parliament/Parliamentary_Departments/Parliamentary_Library/pubs/rp/rp2021/Quick_Guides/IndigenousParliamentarians2021

Santiso, J. (2007). *Latin America's Political Economy of the Possible: Beyond Good Revolutionaries and Free-marketeers*, Cambridge: MIT Press.

Stoker, G. (2017). *Why Politics Matters: Making Democracy Work*, London: Palgrave.

Uscinski, J.E., Douglas, K. & Lewandowsky, S. (2017). Climate change conspiracy theories. In *Oxford Research Encyclopedia of Climate Science*, Oxford University Press.

Watts, R. (2014). Truth and politics: Thinking about evidence-based policy in the age of spin. *Australian Journal of Public Administration*, **73**(1), 34–46.

GLOSSARY

administrative executive: The public service wing of the executive branch of government, which is responsible for the administration of the machinery of state.

agency: The ability of social actors to act freely and independently. Social scientists debate the extent to which agency is restricted by context and structure – by the institutions and processes which define social roles. This is usually called the 'structure/agency' problem.

anti-politics: Political activity external to formal political process involving a broad rejection of elite structures and political institutions.

balance of power: A situation where neither the major party nor the coalition has a controlling majority in the upper house, and the passage of legislation is controlled by one or more smaller parties.

behaviouralists: Political scientists who examine the actions and behaviours of individual actors, as opposed to the actions of institutions such as legislatures and executives.

bicameral: A parliament that has two houses, such as a Legislative Assembly (the lower house or 'house of government') and a Legislative Council (the upper house – sometimes called a 'house of review'). The two houses of parliament are usually elected via different electoral systems.

bureaucracy: A mode of administration common in large organisations, but particularly associated with public sector agencies, based on hierarchical structures and adherence to processes, rules and routines.

Cabinet: The government's central leadership and decision-making body that includes ministers responsible for government departments, and which is chaired by the prime minister.

catch-all party: Parties which lack a clear ideological direction and, instead, promote policy preferences from across the ideological spectrum in a broad pitch to voters.

central agencies: Agencies that do not deliver services to the public themselves but rather take on coordinating, resourcing and monitoring functions.

civil society: The sphere of society that is distinct from governments and business, above the level of the family and distinct from the institutions of the state.

coalition: A group of two or more parties who agree to a common leader and platform for government. Coalitions may be formed prior to or after elections, but when in government all MPs of the parties agree to be bound by decisions of the Cabinet.

collaborative governance: Governments transferring some degree of decision-making power to citizens' groups and/or other stakeholders, such as business actors and other levels of government.

committee: Delegated group of members of parliament who meet to discuss and debate bills or matters of interest, so that parliament does not have to go through an investigatory or debate process as a whole. House committees are generally controlled by the government of the day, but upper house committees are sometimes controlled by the crossbench, so such committees often produce wide-ranging reports with more far-reaching recommendations.

compulsory voting: In Australia, this refers to the requirement to first register to vote once you are 18 years old and then, having registered, to vote in all elections after that.

confidence/no confidence: If a party (or coalition) has the majority of seats in the lower house, it is usually tested by a 'no confidence' motion, which if passed means that a new government must be formed, perhaps with a new group of members of parliament or parties, or a new election being held.

constitutional conventions: Agreed, non-legal rules that impose expectations on how political actors should act, that, when violated, give rise to public and media criticism, which are the chief means by which conventions are enforced.

cooperative federalism: A type of federalism where the different levels of government consult and collaborate in developing policy solutions to their common problems.

coordinate federalism: A theory which holds that regional and national governments within a federation should be substantially independent of one another and free to exercise their allocated powers without interference from each other.

crossbench: A group of members of parliament who are not members of either the government or the opposition parties, so referred to as they sit at the bottom of the parliament facing the Speaker.

deliberative: Processes based on considered and reasoned discussion among those who will be affected by a decision, leading to a collective decision. Proponents argue deliberative democracy can improve collective decision-making.

demos: Effectively refers to the population of a democratic state and was used to refer to the citizens of the Ancient Greek states.

division of powers: Found in federal systems, where the responsibility for some policy areas is allocated to a national government and other policy areas are reserved for subnational governments.

executive power: The capacity to execute or implement political decisions on behalf of a given political community.

factions and tendencies: In Australian politics, factions are organised sub-groups within a party which vie for dominance and positions. While formalised factions exist in the ALP, they are informal in the Liberals and other parties, and are often known as 'tendencies'.

fake news: The Collins English Dictionary (2018) defined fake news as 'false, often sensational, information disseminated under the guise of news reporting'. The Harvard's First Draft at Harvard's Shorenstein Centre suggests it encompasses different types of misleading content (misinformation, disinformation and mal-information).

federalism: 'The principle of sharing sovereignty between central and state (or provincial) governments' (Hague and Harrop 2013, 255), each with a defined set of powers and neither with authority over the other. The alternative is a unitary system, where sovereignty is held by one central government which devolves power to others as it sees fit.

federation: One of three common systems of government used in organising modern nation-states (unitary and confederal being the others). It involves a division of power between a central government and subnational governments. There are generally three layers of government: federal, state/provincial and local. Unitary systems, in contrast, have no division between central and subnational units, while confederal systems imply states that have come together under an overarching body which has limited power.

first-past-the-post: A system of voting (also called 'plurality voting') where the person with most first preference votes wins the election, even if they did not win 50 per cent of all votes.

Fourth Estate: In Britain, the media's reputation as providing this monitorial role of state power was coined the Fourth Estate, reportedly when Thomas Carlyle used the word in reference to House of Commons politician Edmund Burke: 'Burke said there were Three Estates in Parliament; but, in the Reporters' Gallery yonder, there sat a *Fourth Estate* more important far than they all' (Carlyle 1840, 392). Today it refers to the function of the news media to act as a guardian of the public interest and as a watchdog on the activities of government, forming an imponent component of the checks and balances vital to a modern democracy.

franchise: The legal right to vote. 'Enfranchisement' refers to the process of being given that right.

frontbench: The collective term for those members of parliament (MPs) holding ministerial responsibilities. Those MPs in the opposition who 'shadow' ministers (that is, who have responsibility of covering that portfolio area) are referred to as shadow ministers and sit on the 'opposition frontbench'.

gatekeeper: Someone who decides if access will be granted. In terms of the media, 'gatekeeping' refers to access to information. It occurs at many stages of the news gathering process including what sources a reporter decides to consult, who is quoted, how the sub-editors and editors arrange the story, and the prominence that it is given on the webpage or in the newspaper or television bulletin. Politicians' press secretaries also play a gatekeeping role by determining what information goes to which media outlet and how much information is released. Gatekeeping theory was conceptualised by social psychologist Kurt Lewin in 1943.

glass ceiling: An invisible but very real pattern of discrimination that prevents women rising to the top of hierarchical organisations such as corporations, government agencies and political parties.

global financial crisis: Also known as 'the great recession', emerging in 2007–08 to refer to the global downturn in economic growth resulting from the collapse of several US and European financial institutions.

globalisation: A process of growing inter-connectedness across the globe; in particular, the ease of movement of people, ideas and capital are cited as examples.

governance: The broad process of governing comprising various strategies, processes and relationships and involving governments and/or a range of societal groups and institutions.

Governor-General: Australia's Monarch is represented in his/her absence by a Governor-General who has extensive, constitutionally given executive powers. Convention requires these be used only as the prime minister advises.

group voting ticket: A mechanism on a ballot paper for multi-member electorates whereby the elector need only number the box next to a party, with the vote and preferences allocated according to prior determination of the party.

Hansard: The official record of the proceedings of each house of parliament.

horizontal fiscal imbalance: An inequity that arises in a federation where the various subnational governments have different capacities to raise revenue and face different service delivery costs.

house of review: The idea in Westminster systems of parliamentary government that an upper house (whether styled Legislative Council or Senate) shall act as a body to review legislation or matters of importance, separate from the government formed in the lower house.

ideal-types: In the political science literature, ideal-types are often used as a heuristic device which aims to explain how, for example, parties have changed over time. Ideal-types are not identifiable empirically as they are often based on evidence from hundreds of different cases.

information and communication technologies: A broad term that refers to technologies that provide access to information through communication technologies that include the internet, wireless networks, mobile phones and other communication forms to give society new communication capabilities.

interest groups: Associations of individual people or organisations with shared objectives which aim to influence the political process.

judicial review: Courts engage in judicial review when they determine whether legislation passed by Commonwealth and state parliaments is a proper exercise of their constitutionally given powers.

Keynesian economic management: An approach to economic management based on government intervention through monetary and/or fiscal policies (taxing and spending) to lessen the extreme tendencies of unmitigated capitalism.

liberal democracy: Representative democracy, rather than direct democracy, that includes free and fair elections with individual rights enshrined in a constitution and an active civil society.

line agencies: Agencies that oversee the delivery of services to society such as healthcare, policing and infrastructure – all under the watchful eye and guidance of the central agencies.

metadata: Defined as 'data that provides information about other data', online metadata shows a telecommunications user's contacts; location; date, time, duration and form of a communication; web browsing activity; URL accessed, among a range of other forms of data. It enables agencies a digital picture of individuals' movements, contacts, interests and associations.

minority government: Government by the largest party in a legislature where that party does not command an overall majority of seats in the lower house.

multi-member proportional electoral system: An electoral system that has votes within multi-member electorates, and then allocated on a proportional basis to the number of votes cast for a party or candidate.

nation-state: A geographically defined area in which sovereignty is claimed over the area and its citizens.

National Cabinet: A forum for intergovernmental collaboration, established in mid-2020, which brings together the leaders of state, territory and Commonwealth governments. It is a significantly overhauled version of the Council of Australian Governments, which it replaced.

native advertising: Where advertising has the same presentation style as news stories so that consumers feel like the ad belongs with the content. It can be hard to tell apart from news because it looks so similar.

New Public Management: A reform program applied to most public sector organisations in developed countries during the 1980s and 1990s based upon private sector management techniques and market logic.

normative: The expression of value judgements or prescriptions. In relation to the media, it refers to the expression of its 'ideal' role, how media *should* function, as opposed to how the media actually performs.

one vote, one value: Where a person's vote is equal to another. This means that within a given state or nation all electorates are as close as possible to having the same number of electors. Where this is not the case, this is called 'malapportionment'.

opposition: Generally taken as referring to the largest party not part of the government. The opposition members are seated to the left of the Speaker.

party system: The interactions between political parties in a democratic system, as well as the interactions between parties with voters and the electoral system.

paywall: An electronic 'fence' used to charge for online content. A hard paywall requires readers to pay before they can access any story online. Soft paywalls allow some free access.

personalisation: A theory that suggests that individual political actors have become more prominent at the expense of political parties and other collective actors.

policy aggregators: The idea that parties bring together many ideas, and in sifting through them find the ones that the majority of members within the party can agree on.

political actors: Individuals who seek to influence the distribution of power either directly or indirectly, whether by standing for election, lobbying politicians or campaigning on issues.

political executive: The wing of the executive that provides political leadership for the political community, which is distinguishable from the administrative executive.

political institutions: Bodies that influence the distribution of power, and can be formal, informal, bureaucratic or cultural such as parliament, federalism, political parties, churches and the state.

political leadership: Leadership involves more than occupying a leadership position; it is the capacity to take and build support for difficult policy decisions by motivating followers.

populism: A form of politics based around a high-profile leader who styles themselves as someone standing with the mass of people against a corrupt elite, and as a person who needs to be able to act outside complicated democratic processes to get things done.

post-materialism: The notion that once voters have achieved material satisfaction through wages, conditions and basic standards, they will turn to non-material satisfaction such as through caring for the environment, identity rights and the like.

post-materialists: People who consider that their material conditions are such that their vote is determined by other factors, such as the environment or whether other groups in society have rights. This is different to materialists, who are concerned primarily with their own material conditions of life. Most people now identify as 'mixed', meaning they wish to balance both material and post-material concerns.

pragmatic federalism: A willingness to unsentimentally adapt or replace institutions to suit particular needs is a hallmark of Australian federalism (Hollander and Patapan 2007). In the absence of clear direction from the Constitution, Australia has relied on ad hoc arrangements, such as National Cabinet, the Council of Australian Governments and the Murray–Darling Basin Authority.

preferential: A system of voting where voters number a square against each candidate in the order of their preference for the candidates or parties contesting the election. Votes are then counted in the order they are numbered until one is declared the winner.

President (of the Senate or Legislative Council): The senator or legislative councillor elected by the Senate or Legislative Council to be the presiding officer for the upper house. Like the Speaker, the president is responsible for the orderly operation of the Senate or Council, but also has additional responsibilities as the person who welcomes foreign dignitaries and the reigning Monarch to parliament.

presidentialisation: A theory that suggests that the expanding powers of the office, the media attention they command, and their pivotal place in election campaigns has seen prime ministers accrue a now considerable authority and autonomy.

Prices and Incomes Accord: The Accord, as it is commonly known, was a series of agreements between trade unions and the Hawke and Keating Labor governments, which led to the union movement reducing their wage demands in return for increased social provisions such as health and education entitlements.

prime minister: The head of the political executive and government, by virtue of the fact that the party that they lead has the confidence of a majority of members in the House of Representatives.

promotional groups: Citizens' organisations working toward public interest rather than private, instrumental objectives.

proportional: A system of voting where multiple members of parliament (MPs) are elected for the same electorate, and the number of MPs a party or group wins is based on the party's share of the vote. Thus, a party getting 40 per cent of the vote would get 40 per cent of the seats. The way this is determined depends on how many MPs are to be elected, but the intent is to more clearly represent voters as an aggregate.

proportional preferential: A system of voting where multiple members of parliament (MPs) are elected for the same electorate but where the elector allocates a preference for candidates, and that preference determines in what order MPs may be elected.

public choice theory: An economic approach to political phenomena emphasising the self-interested and utility-maximising behaviour of individuals and organisations.

public policy: A core aspect of government activity involving governments committing resources to address public problems and issues.

public sphere: A communicative space where public opinion about politics and policy are formed. Freely expressed and diverse voices are regarded as a precondition for a healthy democracy.

responsibility: The notion that ministers are responsible and answerable for their actions to parliament, and ultimately to the people.

Royal Assent: All bills must receive Royal Assent to become Acts of Parliament. This involves the Governor-General, or their equivalent at the state and territory level, signing the bill so that it becomes law. From this comes the phrase 'signing a bill into law'.

Section 96: The section of the Constitution that empowers the Commonwealth to set conditions on how states must spend any grants that it provides them.

sectional groups: Organisations that seek to represent the interests of a particular sector or cohort of society, often a particular profession or industry.

securitisation: The process of constructing particular issues as central to state security, which then become the subject of extraordinary government measures that often erode civil liberties.

shadow Cabinet: The team of spokespeople, known as shadow ministers, offered by the main opposition party, which scrutinises government and offers itself to the public as an alternative government at elections.

slacktivism: A pejorative term for activism conducted via online media.

social cleavages: Division in society that reflects core divisions, such as ethnicity, class, language and religion/belief. This is different from ideologies based on guiding principles.

sovereignty: Governments are said to be sovereign when they exercise an authority over their people and territory which is not constrained by external influences.

Speaker: The Speaker is elected from the members of parliament to act as the 'presiding officer' for the House. The Speaker's role is to allow for the orderly operation of the House, and with the president of the Senate or Legislative Council is responsible for the conduct of the parliament as a whole.

the state: A political entity that exercises sovereign jurisdiction over a defined area and the population residing within it, via institutions that structure and organise public life.

states' rights: In the Australian context, a political doctrine asserting the importance of protecting individual states from undue interference by the Commonwealth Government.

structural disadvantage: Disadvantage experienced by individuals or groups in society because of the way society functions. For example, who has the privilege of deciding how resources are distributed, how laws are made, how institutions are organised, and which institutions are valued and upheld or reformed.

two-party-preferred: A system of representing the vote after it is counted that allocates all votes to the two major parties (the ALP and the Liberal–National Party Coalition). This may be different to the 'two-candidate-preferred' vote, which represents the final result in an electorate (i.e. the winner and the last person left who has not been elected).

Universal Declaration of Human Rights: The Declaration was proclaimed by the United Nations General Assembly in 1948 as the basis of fundamental human rights, and applied as the basis of numerous treaties globally. UN Member States undertook to inscribe the Rights covered into their own legal frameworks.

vertical fiscal imbalance: A situation that arises in a federation where one tier of government lacks the revenue-raising capacity of the other and relies on grants to meet its policy commitments.

Washminster: Washminster blends 'Washington' and 'Westminster'. It flags the fusion of the US-style of federalism and Westminster parliamentary government, which is a feature of Australia's political system and sometimes a source of tension.

welfare state: A manifestation of the state during the 20th century whereby governments play a central role in promoting the wellbeing of citizens via health, education, social and economic programs.

Westminster system: A system of government in which there are two Houses of Parliament, and the chief minister and the Cabinet are drawn from one of the Houses. The model for this form of government is the parliament of Westminster in the United Kingdom. Not all Westminster-based systems have two Houses, but all have the executive drawn from the parliament.

the Whitlam dismissal: Also known as the 1975 Australian constitutional crisis, refers to the dismissal of Prime Minister Gough Whitlam of the Australian Labor Party by Governor-General Sir John Kerr, who then commissioned the leader of the opposition, Malcolm Fraser of the Liberal Party, as caretaker prime minister.

REFERENCES

Carlyle, T. (1908) [1840]. Lecture V: The hero as man of letters: Johnson, Rousseau, Burns. *On Heroes, Hero-Worship, & the Heroic in History. Six Lectures*, London: Dent.

Collins English Dictionary. (2018). *fake news*. Retrieved from https://www.collinsdictionary.com/dictionary/english/fake-news

Hague, R. & Harrop, M. (2013). *Comparative Government and Politics: An Introduction*, Basingstoke: Palgrave.

Hollander, R. & Patapan, H. (2007). Pragmatic federalism: Australian federalism from Hawke to Howard. *Australian Journal of Public Administration*, **66**(3), 280–97.

INDEX

Abbott, Tony
   Cabinet and, 90, 95, 96–7
   federal elections and, 64, 175
   on federalism, 28
   on fundraising, 87
   leadership spills and, 192
Abbott Government, 46, 147, 148, 197
Aboriginal and Torres Strait Islander Commission (ATSIC), 247, 302
Aboriginal people, 17, 55, 161, 246
   see also Indigenous Australians
accountability, executive power and, 98–101
   see also responsible government (Westminster system)
activism, consumer, 307
Acts of Parliament, 65
   see also legislation; specific Acts
Adams, John, 246
administration, public, see governance
administrative executive, 81
   see also Australian Public Service (APS)
Adorno, Theodor, 269
advertising, native, 287
advisers, political, 98–9, 148
advocacy, traditional, 307–8
   see also citizens' groups
affirmative action, in political parties, 253–4
'Afghan Files' stories, 273
African American people, 319–20
agency (social actors), 236, 245
agenda-setting theory (media), 270
Albanese, Anthony, 192, 251
Alternative Vote system, see preferential voting
anti-politics, 335
Appropriation Bill (1975–6), 118–19, 120–1
Arendt, Hannah, 332
Assange, Julian, 276
asylum seekers, 16, 93, 100, 101, 270
Attorney-General, 62, 88, 123
audience (news media), 265, 269–78
audience positioning, 271
Australia, as the 'lucky country', 12
Australia Party, 308
Australian Agriculture Council (1934), 31
Australian Broadcasting Corporation (ABC), 283–4, 288
Australian Capital Territory
   electoral system in, 57, 163, 166
   electronic voting in, 176
   population and seats in, 72
   as self-governing, 25, 56
Australian Communist Party v Commonwealth (1951), 239
Australian Conservative Party, 226
Australian Constitution, see Constitution, Australian
Australian Democrats, 174, 212, 214, 217–19
Australian Education Council (1936), 31
Australian Electoral Commission (AEC), 73, 226
Australian Federation, see Federation, Australian
Australian Greens, see Greens, The
Australian Hotels Association (AHA), 310
Australian Labor Party (ALP)
   2010 federal election and, 64
   affirmative action in, 75, 253
   APS views by, 140
   Cabinet assembly by, 88
   challenges for, 190–2
   changes in, 188–90
   classification of, 202
   comparative perspective on, 204–5
   declining support for, 190–1
   donations to, 308
   factionalism in, 191–2
   Greens Party agreement with, 228
   history, 10, 168–70, 186–90
   ideology, 186–7
   leadership changes in, 191, 248, 250, 251
   organisation of, 187
   origins, 185
   split, 187, 188
   state/federal fragmentation of, 33
   union relationship with, 186, 190, 191
   Whitlam dismissal and, 189
Australian Motor Enthusiasts Party, 214
Australian political system
   adhoc arrangements within, 31–3, 42–4
   bureaucracy in, 133 (see also Australian Public Service (APS))
   challenges facing, 13–18, 327–35
   citizens' groups in, see citizens' groups
   Constitution, see Constitution, Australian
   electoral systems in, see electoral system(s)
   executive branch, see executive branch
   features, 11, 121–2
   fiscal relations in, see fiscal relations, Commonwealth—state
   history, 7–11
   leadership in, see leadership, political; prime ministers

Australian political system (*cont.*)
  levels of government in, 24–6
  origin, *see* Federation, Australian
  parliament in, *see* Parliament, Commonwealth; parliaments, Australian (subnational); Westminster system
  political institutions fragmented by, 33–4
  power in, *see* executive power
  public service and, *see* Australian Public Service (APS)
  reforms within, 39–47
  relevancy of, 336–7
  representation in, *see* representation
  scale, 26
  study of, 11–12
  views on, 28, 44
Australian Public Service (APS)
  2018–19 review of, 150
  challenges facing, 147–50
  defined, 135
  digital technology in, 149–50
  employment, 136
  growth of, 137
  history, 135, 137
  Indigenous Australians and, 145–6
  ministerial leadership of, 86–7, 112
  policy work, 143, 148, 150–1
  politicisation of, 140–2
  portfolios, 136–7
  reflections on, 150–1
  reforms to, 137–41
  role of, 83, 133
  size, cost and efficiency, 147–8
  values, 133
  women in, 139
Australian Security Intelligence Organisation (ASIO), 101, 239
Australian Sports Party, 214
authority, 240

balance of power, 212
Bali bombing (2002), 13
Bandt, Adam, 64, 219, 228
Barton, Edmund, 9, 60
behaviouralists, 176
Bennelong Society, 331
Bernstein, Carl, 273
Besser, Linton, 285
bicameralism, 11, 55
Bill of Rights, 114–15
bills (legislative), 58, 67–70
  see also legislation
Bjelke-Petersen, Joh, 119
Black Lives Matter (BLM), 274, 319
Blair, Tony, 279
Bolt, Andrew, 17

Bonner, Neville, 57
branch stacking, 191
Brexit campaign, 288
British North America Act 1867, 108
Broadcasting (Ownership and Control) Act 1987, 281
Broadcasting Legislation Amendment (Broadcasting Reform) Bill 2017, 281
Brown, Bob, 213, 220, 221, 222
budgets, 147–8
bureaucracy
  Australian government, 133 (*see also* Australian Public Service (APS))
  criticisms of, 134, 137
  defined, 132
  necessity of, 132
  as organisational model, 134
  origin, 132
  reforms to, 137–9
Burke, Edmund, 168, 262
Burns, James McGregor, 242
business associations, 304

Cabinet
  assembling, 82, 88–9
  confidentiality in, 92–3
  decline of, 95
  defined, 81
  disunity in, 95–8
  'first minister' in, 111
  legitimacy of, 80
  prime ministerial relationship with, 89, 90, 91, 95, 96–8
  role of, 80, 82, 91, 111
  shadow, 82
  see also ministry
cadre party (type), 203
Canadian political system, 108, 161
Canavan, Matt, 46
cartel party (type), 203–4
Cash, Michaelia, 99
catch-all party (type), 188, 203
central agencies, 139
Centrelink, 149
certification schemes, 307
Channel Nine, 284
Channel Seven, 284
Channel Ten, 283, 284
chaos paradigm (media), 276–7
Chifley Government, 116
Children Overboard Scandal (2001), 93, 270
Chile, economic reforms in, 328
Chipp, Don, 218
Chomsky, Noam, 277
Christian Democratic parties, 205
Churchill, Winston, 237

citizens' groups
   Australian Hotels Association, 310
   benefits of, 308–9
   categorising, 303–5
   challenges for, 316–20
   concerns about, 309
   consumer activism by, 307
   documentary material by, 306–7
   elements, 302
   examples of, 299–305
   features, 303
   fragmentation of, 33
   funding, 317–18
   GetUp!, 310–11
   government engagement of, 311–16
   media coverage attracted by, 305–6
   representativeness of, 316–17
   strategies employed by, 305–8
   terms for, 302
   traditional advocacy by, 307–8
civil disobedience, 305–6
civil society, defined, 302
civil society organisations, 299–300, 314
Clark, Andrew Inglis, 167
classical liberalism, 27
climate change, 15–16, 248, 289, 312, 332
Closing the Gap (health policy), 314
coalition
   defined, 11
   history, 168–70
   LPA and National Party, 33–4, 192, 215, 216
Coalition of Peaks, 302, 314
codes (textual analysis), 271
coercive federalism, 43
Coles, Arthur, 227
collaboration, media, 284–5
collaborative federalism, 43
collaborative governance, 299, 313–15
collective ministerial responsibility, 92–3
colonies, Australian, 7–9, 54–5, 193
committees (Senate), 61, 65–6, 69–70
Commonwealth Electoral Act 1918, 161, 226
Commonwealth Franchise Act 1902, 55, 160, 161
Commonwealth Government
   bureaucracy in, *see* Australian Public Service (APS)
   COAG and, *see* Council of Australian Governments (COAG)
   constitutional powers, 29–30, 124–5
   cooperative federalism and, 31–3
   electoral system in, 163–6
   Federation reform and, 330
   formation of, 63–4
   High Court and power of, 116–17, 122, 123–4
   pandemic role of, 337
   Parliament, *see* Parliament, Commonwealth
   policy responsibilities, 329–30
   relevancy of, 336–7
   states' fiscal relationship with, 13–14, 28, 34–8, 40, 116
Commonwealth Grants Commission (1933), 32, 37–8
Commonwealth of Australia Constitution Act 1900, 9, 108
Commonwealth Public Service, 135
   see also Australian Public Service (APS)
Communist Party Dissolution Bill, 195
compulsory voting, 163
concurrent powers (Commonwealth/states), 29, 30, 34
confederal system of government, 7
confidence/no confidence motion, 63
confidentiality, Cabinet, 92–3
conformer groups (policy interests), 304
Connor, Rex, 189
Conran Review, 42
conscience vote, 69
Constitution, Australian
   amending, 46–7, 113, 115, 124–6, 313, 330
   components, 113–16, 117–18
   consitutionalism and, 109–12, 119, 121–2
   cooperative federalism and, 31
   coordinate federalism in, 29–30
   Executive in Council in, 117–18
   gendered representation in, 57
   High Court and. *see* High Court of Australia
   history, 9, 27, 28–9, 108
   literalist interpretation of, 119–21
   on marriage, 30
   on Parliament, 72, 125
   political parties absent from, 174
   powers in, 25, 29–30, 80
   public money allocation in, 116
   rights in, 16, 114–15
   Section 13, 114
   Section 15, 125
   Section 24, 72
   Section 44, 53–4, 111
   Section 51, 29, 30, 113, 123–4, 125
   Section 53, 120
   Section 57, 111, 114, 118
   Section 64, 109, 111, 118
   Section 71, 122
   Section 83, 111
   Section 92, 113
   Section 96, 32, 36, 116
   Section 101, 31
   Section 102, 113
   Section 109, 29, 30, 122
   Section 128, 46, 115, 124, 330
   structure, 9
   symbolic nature of, 125–6
   taxation in, 29, 34
   water resources in, 15

Constitution, United States, 272
Constitution Act 1855, 55
constitutional conventions, 109–12, 119, 121–2
constitutional crisis (1975), *see* Whitlam Government, dismissal of
constitutional government, 11
constitutional monarchy, 11, 81–2, 159, 238
constitutionalism, 110–12, 119, 121–2
constitutionality, 272
constitutions, role of, 108–9
consultants, external political, 148
consumer activism, 307
content (news media), 265
control paradigm (media), 277–8, 283
conventions, constitutional, 109–12, 119, 121–2
'Coombs Commission', 138
cooperative federalism, 31–3, 42–4
coordinate federalism, 29–30, 42
core executive, 83
Council of Australian Governments (COAG), 31, 39–40, 43, 46, 314
Country Party, 215–16
    see also National Party of Australia (NPA)
Court Government, 95
COVID-19 pandemic, 14, 40, 242, 336, 337
Cowan, Edith, 75
Credlin, Peta, 95, 96
Crook, Tony, 64, 217
crossbench, defined, 59
    see also independents; minor parties

data analytics, 286
data journalism, 285
data retention laws, 149, 332
Deakin, Alfred, 9, 29, 60, 116, 193
Debord, Guy, 269
decision-making, devolution of, 26–7
deductible gift recipient (DGR) status, 317–18
delegated legislation, 70
deliberative processes, 202
democracy
    Athenian form, 237
    challenges facing Australian, 327–35
    defined, 236, 271
    digital technologies' role in, 267–8, 276–7, 286
    leadership and, 236–40
    liberal, 10, 201, 236–40, 272
    media's role in, 271–7
    political parties' impact on, 174–6
Democratic Labor Party (DLP), 188, 212, 215
demonstrations, public, 305, 318–19
demos, defined, 236
Department of Foreign Affairs and Trade, 312
Department of Social Services, 312
departments, staffing levels in, 136
digital government, 149–50

digital technologies
    APS and, 149–50
    media and, *see* technologies, digital (media)
Disability Employment Framework, 312
diversity, in political leadership, 57, 75, 206, 252–5, 335
division of powers, 24
Dixon, Sir Owen, 239
documentary material, 306–7
Don Dale Youth Detention Centre, 273
donations, political, 87, 308, 317
Downer, Alexander, 249
Dropulich, Wayne, 214
Dutton, Peter, 96, 101

echo chamber effect, 268–9
economic inequality, 334
economic management, 137
economic policies, of political parties, 189–90, 196–7, 216
economic rationalism, 137, 189–90
economic reforms, international, 328, 329
economy, Australian, 14
education, special purpose payments and, 36–7
e-government, 149–50
elections, Australian
    1946–2019 results, 169
    2010 federal, 63–4, 175
    2016 federal, 73, 310–11
    2019 federal, 201, 265, 311
    about, 159
    citizens' groups and cycles of, 308
    conducting, 15
    history, 168–70
    timetables, 164
    vote-counting methods, 165, 166–7
    see also voting
elections, democratic, 159
elections, US Presidential, 278
electoral boundaries, 73
electoral challenges, in Australia, 14–15
electoral system(s)
    first-past-the-post, 167, 201
    Hare–Clark system, 167
    history and evolution, 74
    for houses of parliament, 56–7
    internet's impact on, 175–6
    joint committee on, 66
    across jurisdictions, 162–7
    parties related to, 199, 201–2
    political impacts of, 62–4, 74
    preferential, *see* preferential voting
    proportional, *see* proportional representation
    proportional preferential, 166
    representation in, 14, 168–70, 334–5
    see also voting

electronic voting, 175–6
elite party (type), 203
encoding/decoding model of communication, 271
The End of Certainty (Kelly), 10
engagement, citizen, *see* participation, citizen
Engineers case (1920), 114
environmental challenges, in Australia, 15–16
environmental groups, funding for, 317–18
Ettridge, David, 225
Euthanasia Laws Act 1997, 26
evaluation models, of citizen engagement, 315–16
Evans, Gareth, 66
Evatt, Herbert, 16
everyday makers (political actors), 179
exclusive powers (Commonwealth), 29
executive branch
    administrative executive, 81 (*see also* Australian Public Service (APS))
    committees' relationship with, 66
    core executive, 83
    growing powers of, 238–40
    instability in, 80
    leadership roles in, 238–40
    parliamentary relationship with, 61–2, 70, 99, 238–9
    political executive, 80–2, 84–7, 98–101, 111 (*see also* Cabinet; prime ministers)
    responsible government and, 83, 86, 98–101
executive dominance, of Parliament, 99
executive federalism, 43
Executive in Council, 117–18
executive power
    accountability of, 98–101
    centralisation and, 43–4
    defined, 80, 81, 84
    functions, 84–7
    growth of, 238–40
    legitimacy of, 80
    in the political executive, 81–2
executive presidents, 90
expert citizens (political actors), 179

Facebook, 268, 278, 287
factions/factionalism, 191–2
Fadden, Arthur, 194
Fairfax Media, 87, 96, 280, 281, 283
fake news, 262, 270, 287–9
Family First Party, 226
federal elections, *see* elections, Australian
Federal Executive Council (FEC), 81
federal government, *see* Commonwealth Government
Federal Parliament, *see* Parliament, Commonwealth
federalism
    Australia's version, *see* Australian political system
    coercive, 43
    collaborative, 43
    common features, 26–7
    cooperative, 31–3
    coordinate, 29–30, 42
    defined, 11, 24
    division of powers in, 24
    executive, 43
    international context, 26–7
    pragmatic, 31, 40, 43
    rationales for adopting, 27
    responsible government and, 99–100
    Westminster system mixed with, 29, 108
Federation, Australian
    defined, 24
    drivers of, 113
    evolution, 28, 31–3, 42–4
    history, 9–11, 27–9, 108
    policies central to, 10
    reform of, 39–47, 330
    see also Constitution, Australian
federation, defined, 7, 24
Femocrats, 139
filter bubbles, 268
financial assistance grants, 32, 37–8
fires, 16
First Nations peoples, *see* Indigenous Australians
first-past-the-post voting, 167, 201
fiscal challenges, in Australia, 13–14
fiscal relations, Commonwealth—state
    COVID-19 pandemic and, 40
    establishment of, 34
    imbalance in, 13–14, 28, 34–8, 40, 43, 116
    proposed reform of, 45, 46
    specific purpose payments, 36–7
Fitzgibbon, Joel, 93
forums, public, 312
Four Corners (TV program), 273
Fourth Estate (media), 262, 272
franchise, 55, 160–2
Fraser, Malcolm, 60, 82, 90, 118, 119, 121
Fraser Government, 145, 196
free-market ideology, 328–9
free speech, 17, 332
free vote, 69
Freedom House, 282
'front' parties, 214
frontbench, defined, 59
funds
    allocation of public, 111, 116
    citizens' groups, 317–18

Gaetjens, Phil, 140
Gallipoli, 16
Garrett, Peter, 94

gatekeeper, 277
GetUp!, 310–11
Gillard, Julia
   2010 federal election and, 63–4
   challenges faced by, 253
   climate change assembly by, 312
   on gender discrimination, 254–5
   leadership spills and, 98, 190
   leadership style, 90, 190
   'misogyny speech', 266
Gillard Government, 63–4, 175, 202, 227, 228
glass ceiling, 254
global financial crisis (2008), 12, 14, 336
globalisation, 333–4, 336–7
goods and services tax (GST), 36
governance
   collaborative, 299, 313–15
   defined, 132, 144–5
   government transition to, 144–6, 328–9
   implications, 146
   Indigenous systems of, 7
government
   Commonwealth, *see* Commonwealth Government
   confederal systems of, 7
   Court, 95
   digital, 149–50
   federal system, *see* federalism
   governance and, 144–6, 328–9
   levels (Australia), 24–6
   local, 25, 65, 133
   subnational, *see* states, Australian; territories, Australian
   unitary systems, 7, 26, 27, 120
Governor-General
   defined, 81
   executive powers, 70, 81–2, 118, 159, 238
   reserve powers, 59–60, 82, 118–22, 238
grants, financial assistance, 32, 34, 36–8
Greens (WA), 220, 221
Greens, The
   Australian Democrats and, 219
   internal politics, 222–3
   Labor agreement with, 228
   major parties and, 213
   organisation, 221–2
   origins, 219, 220–1
   political influence of, 175, 219, 223
   support base, 190, 220
group voting tickets, 167, 213, 214

Habermas, Jürgen, 265–6
Haines, Janine, 218
Hall, Stuart, 271
Hansard, 69
Hanson, Pauline, 224–5
   see also One Nation Party
Hare, Sir Thomas, 167
Hare–Clark system (voting), 167
Harradine, Brian, 227
Hawke, Bob, 89, 90, 138
Hawke Government, 141, 145, 148, 174, 189–90, 196
Henry, Ken, 150–1
Herman, Edward, 277
Hewson, John, 196, 249
High Court of Australia
   as 'activist', 123
   Aid/Watch Incorporated v Commissioner of Taxation [2010], 317
   appointments to, 62, 122–3
   Australian Communist Party v Commonwealth (1951), 239
   as 'conservative', 123
   Engineers Case (1920), 114
   'free speech' case, 17
   judicial review and, 116–17, 122–4
   Mabo Land-rights case (1987), 123
   media role as recognised by, 272
   on citizens' groups funding, 317
   Palmer v The State Of Western Australia [2021], 113
   Parliament dual citizenship case, 54
   R v Brislan (1935), 116
   significance of, 122–4
   Smethurst v Commissioner of Police [2020], 272
   Tasmanian Dam case (1983), 123–4
   Uniform Tax cases, 34, 116
   voting rights cases, 161
High Court of Australia Act 1979, 123
Hockey, Joe, 87
Home Insulation Program (HIP), 94
Hope, John (Earl of Hopetoun), 9, 60
'Hopetoun Blunder', 9, 60
horizontal fiscal imbalance, 37–8
Horne, Donald, 12
House of Assemblies, 56
House of Commons (UK), 112
House of Lords (UK), 111, 112
House of Representatives
   committees in, 65–6, 69–70
   constitutional powers, 112, 113, 119
   election timetable for, 164
   electoral system for, 56, 63, 164, 199, 201
   minor parties in, 212, 214
   seats in, 72, 164
   Speaker's role in, 58
   tenure within, 114
   women in, 75
house of review, 111
Howard, John
   asylum seekers and, 93
   Cabinet and, 89, 90

conservative messaging by, 191, 196–7
crisis management by, 85
on federalism, 28
leadership turnover and, 249
on ministerial responsibility, 93
Howard Government
　APS under, 142
　ATSIC dissolution under, 247
　citizens' groups defunding under, 317
　cultural conservatism of, 196–7
　on federalism, 44, 45
　goods and services tax and, 36
　on marriage, 30
　securitisation under, 100–1
Huggins, Jackie, 314
Hughes, Billy, 187–8
human rights, 114
Human Rights Law Centre, 319
'hung' parliament, 175

ideal party types, 202
identity, Australian, 16
immunisation (concept), 200
imperial benevolence policy, 10
independents, 212, 227–8, 247
Indigenous Australians
　Andrew Bolt court case and, 17
　APS and, 145–6
　colonial bureaucracy and, 135
　governance systems, 7
　justice system experience of, 320
　non-Indigenous population and, 12
　organisations representing, 302
　parliamentary representation of, 57, 88, 253, 335
　political leadership of, 246–7
　political participation of, 301–2, 314–15
　political recognition and representation, 17–18, 125, 313, 330–1, 335
　population percentage of, 17
　structural disadvantage affecting, 301
　voting rights of, 55, 161
individual ministerial responsibility, 93–4, 112
industry protection policy, 10
inequality, economic, 334
information and communication technologies (ICT), 268
insider groups, 303
institutions, political, 2, 246–7
interest groups, defined, 299
　see also citizens' groups
Intergovernmental Agreement on Federal Financial Relations (2008), 36
International Association for Public Participation, 315–16
International Consortium of Investigative Journalists (ICIJ), 276

internet
　activism using, 319–20
　as digital public sphere, 267–8, 276–7, 286
　crime on, 149
　freedom, in Australia, 289
　media landscape changed by, 279
　voting and, 175–6
investigative journalism, 273–5, 276, 283, 284–5

Jeremy Corbyn, 329
joint committees, 66
journalism
　audience participation in, 286
　challenges for, 286–9
　data reporting in, 285
　ethics in, 262
　funding, 286–7
　global collaborative, 276
　investigative, 273–5, 276, 283, 284–5
　opportunities for, 284–6
　public trust in, 287–9
　see also media
judicial review, 116–17
judiciary, 62, 115
　see also High Court of Australia
Judiciary Act 1903, 122

Katter, Bob, 228
Keating, Paul, 56, 90, 189, 196
Keating Government, 174, 189–90, 196
Kelly, Paul, 10
Kennedy, David, 57
Kernot, Cheryl, 218
Kerr, Sir John, 60, 82, 118–22, 189
Keynesian economic management, 137

Labor Party, *see* Australian Labor Party (ALP)
labour movement, 186
ladder of citizen participation model (evaluation), 315
Latham, Mark, 225
lawfare, 307
leaders
　challenges facing, 247–8
　charismatic, 240
　traits of, 241
　transactional, 241, 242
　transformational, 241, 248
leadership, political
　arenas of, 245–7
　authority and, 240
　challenges associated with, 247–8
　defined, 236
　democracy and, 236–40
　diversity in, *see* diversity, in political leadership

leadership, political (*cont.*)
   personalisation theory, 176, 243
   policy reform success and, 151
   political executive and, 84–7, 238–40, 241–5
   presidentialisation theory, 90–1, 243–4
   prime minsters' approaches to, 89–90
   theoretical models, 90–1, 176, 240–5
   turnover in, 248–51
Lees, Meg, 218
legislation
   anti-protest, 318–19
   anti-terrorist, 331–2
   data retention, 149, 332
   delegated, 70
   High Court's role in, 122–4
   media-related, 264, 281, 282–3
   parliamentary role in, 25–6, 29–30, 65–6, 247
   passing, process for, 58, 67–70
   political executive's role in, 85–6
   political parties' influences on, 174
   Westminster conventions and, 111
   WorkChoices, 197
Legislative Assemblies, 55, 56–7, 75, 166
Legislative Councils, 55, 56–7, 58
liberal democracy, 10, 201, 236–40, 272
liberal democratic theory of media, 271–2
Liberal Movement, 212
Liberal–National Party (LNP), 33, 64
Liberal Party of Australia (LPA)
   Cabinet assembly by, 88
   classification of, 202
   comparative perspective on, 205
   contemporary challenges for, 197–9
   donations to, 87, 308
   federalism approach by, 43, 44, 45
   formation and beginning of, 194–5
   history, 168–70, 192–7
   ideological divisions in, 193, 196–7, 198–9
   leadership in, 192, 197, 248, 249–50, 251
   National Party's coalition with, 33–4, 192, 215, 216
   origins, 185
   policy aggregation role of, 178
   quota opposition by, 75, 254
   securitisation and, 331
   state/federal fragmentation of, 33–4
liberalism, classical, 27
line agencies, 139
Lippmann, Walter, 277
Loan Council (1923), 31
'loans affair', 189
lobbyists, 308
local government, 25, 65, 133
Lyne, William, 9, 60
Lyons, Dame Enid, 75

Mabo Land-rights case (1987), 123
majoritarianism, 11
Manthorpe, Michael, 289
market-based governance, 328–9
Marriage Act (Cth), 30
marriage equality, 30, 199, 313
mass party (type), 203
McEwan, John, 216
McGowan, Cath, 227
McKenzie, Bridget, 94
McMahon, William, 90
McManus, Sally, 305
media, 264–5
   challenges for, 262, 286–9
   changing landscape of, 262
   chaos paradigm, 276–7
   citizens' groups use of, 305–6
   collaboration in, 284–5
   defined, 263–4
   democratic functions, 271–7
   digital technology and, 267–8, 276–7, 284–9
   as Fourth Estate, 262, 272
   freedom of, 262
   funding of, 272
   journalism, *see* journalism
   liberal democratic theory of, 271–2
   media effects theory, 270
   'media sphere' approach to, 264–5
   opportunities for, 284–6
   ownership, 262, 277
   personalised politics and, 243
   political economy theory, 277–8, 283
   propaganda model, 277
   public spheres and, 265–9
   public trust in, 287–9
   reception theory, 271
   socially responsible model, 272
   suspicion of, 269
   theories of, 269–72
   uses and gratifications model, 270
   volatility in landscape of, 262
   watchdogs, 282–3
media, Australian
   Cabinet leaks to, 93, 96–7
   challenges for, 286–9
   changing landscape of, 278–84
   collaboration in, 285
   digital influence on, 278–9, 286–9
   economic landscape of, 283–4
   as Fourth Estate, 272
   laws, 264, 281–3
   media freedom, 282–3
   moral panics and, 270
   new entrants, 284

opportunities in, 285–6
ownership, 280–2, 283
public funding of, 272
public spheres and, 267
public trust in, 288
media effects theory, 270
Meldrum-Hanna, Caro, 273
members of parliament (MPs), 59
Members of Parliament (Staff) Act 1984, 148
Menzies, Robert, 28, 74, 89, 194–5, 216, 249
metadata, 149, 289
'micro' parties, 178, 213
ministerial councils, 31, 42
ministry
    accountability in, 59–60, 86–7, 91–4, 99, 100, 111, 112
    advisers to, 98–9, 148
    choosing, 63, 82, 88–9
    'first minister', 111
    see also Cabinet
minor parties
    defined, 212
    'front' parties', 214
    in the House of Representatives, 212
    increase in, 213–14
    influence of, 212–13, 215, 247
    key players, 215–26
    'micro' parties, 178, 213
    perceptions of, 213
    proliferation of, 174, 175
    registration process, 226
    right-of-centre insurgent, 225–6
    in the Senate, 212, 228, 333
    see also specific parties
minority governments, 175, 202, 212, 227, 228
monarchy, constitutional, 11, 81–2, 159, 238
money, public, *see* funds
Montesquieu, Charles de Secondat, baron de, 61, 239
moral panics, 270
Morrison, Scott, 90, 140, 192, 198, 242
Morrison Government, 39, 46, 88, 147
Muir, Ricky, 213
Murdoch-controlled press, 273
Murray–Darling Basin, 15, 314
Murray–Darling Basin Authority (MDBA), 31

National Aboriginal Conference, 302
National Aboriginal Consultative Committee, 302
National Cabinet
    creation of, 39, 41, 46, 330
    defined, 32
    executive federalism and, 43
    format, 41
    on ministerial councils, 42

National Compact (policy framework), 314
National Congress of Australia's First Peoples (The Congress), 302, 314
National Federation Reform Council, 41
national identity challenges, in Australia, 16
National Indigenous Council, 247
National Party of Australia (NPA)
    challenges facing, 216
    impact of, 215
    leadership turnover in, 250
    Liberal Party's coalition with, 33–4, 192, 215, 216
    origin and ideology, 215–17
    support base, 217
nation-states, 3
native advertising, 287
New Public Management reforms, 132, 137–9, 144
New South Wales
    anti-protest laws in, 318
    collaborative governance in, 314
    colonial legislatures of, 55
    electoral systems in, 57, 163, 166
    Legislative Councils in, 56
    population and seats in, 72
New Zealand, 33, 204–5
news, defined, 263–4
News Corp, 280, 281, 283
news media, *see* media
newspapers, 279, 280–1, 286–7
NIMBYism, 317
Nixon, Richard, 273
normative, defined, 266
North Sydney Forum, 87
Northcote-Trevelyan Report (1854), 133
Northern Territory, 25–6, 46, 56, 57, 72, 163, 166
Nuclear Disarmament Party (NDP), 219, 220

Oakeshott, Rob, 227, 228
One Nation Party, 178, 217, 224–5
one vote, one value, 161
online activity, *see* internet; social media
Operation Fortitude (2015), 239
opinion, public, 248, 265, 277
opposition, defined, 59
Organ, Michael, 219, 220
Our Public Service, Our Future (report), 150
outsider groups, 303

'Pacific solution', 101
Palmer, Clive, 113
Palmer United Party (PUP), 213
Palmer v The State Of Western Australia [2021], 113
Panama Papers (2016), 276
Paradise Papers (2017), 276
Parkes, Sir Henry, 28, 108

Parliament, Commonwealth
   chain of responsibility in, 59–60
   challenges facing, 70–1
   constitutional powers, 29–30
   diversity in, 57, 75, 206, 252–5, 335
   election methods, 57
   eligibility, 53–4
   executive's relationship with, 61–2, 99, 238–9
   functions, 62–6
   houses of, 56
   'hung' parliament, 175
   Indigenous representation in, 57, 88, 253
   judiciary and, 62
   legislative role of, 26, 29–30, 65–6, 247
   operation of, 58
   partial separation of powers and, 61–2
   political parties in, 174–6
   population and seats in, 72
   procedural reforms, 125
   representation in, 14
   seating arrangements, 58–9
   term duration in, 125
   women in, 57, 75, 252
   see also Governor-General; House of Representatives; Senate
Parliamentary Inquiry into the Register of Environmental Organisations, 317–18
'parliamentary responsibility', 120–1
parliamentary systems, 11, 53, 55, 63, 238–40, 244
   see also Westminster system
parliaments, Australian (subnational)
   chain of responsibility in, 59–60
   challenges facing, 70–1
   diversity in, 57, 75, 252–5, 335
   election methods, 57
   executive's relationship with, 61–2
   functions, 62–6
   historical evolution, 55
   houses of, 56
   Indigenous representation in, 57, 253
   judiciary and, 62
   legislative powers, 25–6, 29–30
   legislative role of, 65–6
   operation of, 58
   partial separation of powers and, 61–2
   political parties in, 174–6
   seating arrangements, 58–9
   structure of, 56
   variations between, 71–2
   women in, 75, 252
Parliament's Standing Orders, 66
participation, citizen, 299–305, 311–20, 334–5
   see also citizens' groups
participation, democratic, 272

parties, political
   affirmative action in, 253–4
   Australian Labor Party, *see* Australian Labor Party (ALP)
   campaigning by, 178
   cartel party thesis and, 203–4
   challenges for, 190–2, 197–9
   classification of, 202–3
   comparative perspectives on, 204–6
   definitions, 171–2
   democracy and, 174–6
   distrust of, 170–1
   dominance of major, 74, 186
   donations to, 87, 308
   electoral stability and, 168–70
   electoral systems and, 62–4, 199, 201–2
   evolution of, 171, 202
   history, 11, 168–70, 174, 185–90, 192–7
   ideal-types, 202
   leadership in, 176, 251
   Liberal Party, *see* Liberal Party of Australia (LPA)
   minor, *see* minor parties
   organisation of, 33–4, 88–9
   parliamentary cohesion of, 205
   as policy aggregators, 178–9
   registration process, 226
   role and functions of, 74–5, 172–3
   state relationship with, 172
   theorising, 201
   voter relationship with, 176–8, 199–200, 213
partisanship, decline of, 200
partitocracy, 172
party identification (concept), 200
party system, defined, 186
   see also parties, political
paywall, 287
Peacock, Andrew, 249
Pearson, Noel, 246
personalisation theory, 176, 243
petitions, online, 319
Pharmaceutical Benefits Act 1944, 116
Playford, Tom, 249
plebiscites, 313
plurality voting, *see* first-past-the-post voting
policy, public
   citizens' groups and, 304, 311–16
   defined, 132, 142–3
   Federation and, 10
   making, *see* policymaking
   parliamentary role in, 65–6
   political leadership's impact on, 151
   public service role in, 143, 148, 150–1
   study of, 142
policy aggregators, defined, 178
policy cycle, 143, 196

policymaking
  as governance, 145
  models, 143
  political executive's role in, 65–6, 85–6
  process, 67, 143
  reflections on, 150–1
political actors, 3, 179
political advisers, 98–9, 148
political economy theory (media), 277–8, 283
political executive
  accountability of, 98–101
  chain of responsibility in, 86
  defined, 80–1
  leadership functions of, 84–7
  powers of, 81–2
  as symbol of national unity, 84
  see also Cabinet; prime ministers
political institutions, 2, 246–7
political parties, *see* parties, political
politics
  'arena' view of, 3
  Australian, *see* Australian political system
  definitions, 2–6
  historical shaping of, 2
  inevitability of, 4–5
  primacy of, 5
  'social process' view of, 4
polls, opinion, 248, 313
populism, 178, 224, 335
Port Arthur massacre (1996), 85
post-materialism, 177–8, 220
power, political, 2, 3–5
  see also executive power
powers, separation/division of, 24, 61–2, 239
pragmatic federalism, 31, 40, 43
preferential voting, 162, 164, 166, 199, 201, 214
Premiers' Conferences, 31
President (upper houses), 58
presidential systems, 85, 90, 244
presidentialisation theory, 80, 90–1, 95, 96–8, 243–4
prime ministers
  Cabinet's relationship with, 89, 90, 91, 95, 96–8
  challenges facing, 247–8
  COAG and, 40
  crisis leadership role of, 85
  defined, 81
  deposing of, 80, 89, 97, 98, 248–51
  election called by, 164
  leadership role, 82, 89–90, 238–40, 241–5
  legitimacy of, 80
  political centralisation around, 80, 90–1, 95, 96–8, 244
  responsibility of, 59, 118
priming theory (media), 270
prisoners, voting rights of, 161–2

private interest groups, 304
private members' bills, 69
privatisation, of government assets, 328, 333
production (news media), 264–5
promotional groups, 303
  see also citizens' groups
propaganda model (media), 277
proportional preferential voting, 166
proportional representation
  in councils, 56, 57
  defined, 162
  Hare–Clark system, 167
  minor parties and, 214
  potential political impacts of, 202
  in Senate, 56, 57, 166, 199, 201
ProPublica (online news), 284
public administration, *see* governance
public choice theory, 137
public forums, 312
public interest groups, 304
  see also citizens' groups
public participation spectrum (evaluation), 315–16
public policy, *see* policy, public
public sector, 135, 137–8
public servants, 83, 112
  see also administrative executive
public service, *see* Australian Public Service (APS); bureaucracy
Public Service Act 1999, 133, 135, 146
public sphere(s)
  defined, 262
  digital global, 267–8, 276–7, 286
  Habermasian concept of, 265–7
  multiple, 266–7

Queen of England, 159, 238
Queensland
  electoral system in, 57, 163, 166
  Legislative Council and, 56
  Liberal–National coalition in, 33
  population and seats in, 72
  surveys in, 313

R v Brislan (1935), 116
Racial Discrimination Act 1975, 17
radical groups (policy interests), 304
rational choice, in a democracy, 272
reception theory (media), 271
Redfern Statement (2016), 314
referendum elections, 313
Reform Act of 1832 (UK), 74
Reform of the Federation White Paper (Abbott government), 46
reformer groups (policy interests), 304
regional variation, in Australia, 12
Register of Environmental Organisations, 317–18

Reid, Elizabeth, 139
Reid, George, 9, 193
Reid, Scott, 115
reimbursement grants, 34
Reith, Peter, 93
Reporters Without Borders (RSF), 282, 283
representation
    citizens' groups and, 316–17
    electoral, 14, 168–70, 334–5
    Indigenous Australians, 17–18, 313, 330–1, 335
residual powers (states), 30
responsible government (Westminster system), 59–60, 83, 86, 91–4, 98–101
revenue
    2019–20 taxation, 13
    news media, 279, 286–7
    state/Commonwealth, 35, 116
Rhiannon, Lee, 222
right populism, 224
Rights of the Terminally Ill Act 1995, 26
Robert, Stuart, 93
'Robodebt' scandal, 149
Royal Assent, 58, 70
Royal Commission into Australian Government Administration ('Coombs Commission'), 138
Rudd, Kevin
    2010 leadership spill and, 63, 98, 190
    Cabinet and, 88, 90, 95, 97–8
    climate change and, 248
    leadership change reforms by, 191
    media diversity bid by, 282
Rudd Government
    APS under, 142
    'community cabinets' under, 312
    consultant use during, 148
    Home Insulation Program under, 94
    National Compact under, 314
    reforms under, 39, 46
    The Congress under, 314

Safeguarding Democracy (report), 319
same-sex marriage, 30, 199, 313
schools, special purpose payments and, 36–7
scrutineers, 165
scrutiny mechanisms, 99
Second Uniform Tax case (1957), 34
secret ballot voting, 163
sectional groups, 304
securitisation, 100, 101
select committees, 66
Senate
    committees in, 61, 65–6, 69–70
    constitutional powers, 111–12, 113, 120, 122
    election timetable for, 164
    electoral system for, 56, 57, 166, 199, 201
    executive accountability and, 99, 100
    political parties' role in, 174, 212, 214
    President's role in, 58
    seats in, 72, 164
    tenure within, 114
    views on, 56
Senate Select Committee on the Reform of the Australian Federation, 45
Senior Executive Service (SES), 140–1
separation of powers, 61–2, 123, 239
September 11 attacks, 101
shadow Cabinet, 82
Shooters Fishers and Farmers Party (SFF), 175, 217
Shorten, Bill, 191, 251
Single Member Plurality electoral system, *see* first-past-the-post voting
Single Transferable Vote system, *see* proportional representation
Skinner, Karen, 319
slacktivism, 299, 319–20
social cleavages, 167, 177
social media
    activism using, 319–20
    audience interaction through, 286
    campaigning using, 178
    as digital public sphere, 267–8
    echo chambers and, 268–9
    filter bubbles and, 268
    influence of, 278
    media landscape changed by, 279
    news impacted by, 262
social wage, 190
socialisation (concept), 177, 200
socially responsible model (media), 272
South Australia, 57, 72, 163, 166, 167
Sovereign, role of, 59, 159, 238
sovereignty, 3, 17–18, 24, 336
Speaker (parliamentary), 58
specific powers (Commonwealth), 29
specific purpose payments, 36–7
stakeholder groups, 312–13
standing committees, 66
State, the (political entity), 3
state paternalism policy, 10
states, Australian
    bureaucracy in, 133
    COAG and, *see* Council of Australian Governments (COAG)
    Commonwealth's fiscal relationship with, 13–14, 28, 34–8, 40, 116
    constitutional powers, 25, 29–30, 124–5
    cooperative federalism and, 31–3
    creation of new, 46
    electoral systems in, 163, 166–7

Federation reform and, 330
free trade between, 31, 113, 116
High Court and power of, 116–17, 122, 123–4
pandemic role of, 337
parliaments, *see* parliaments, Australian (subnational)
policy responsibilities, 329–30
population and seats in, 71–2, 164
revenue, 35
rights of, 43, 44, 45
safeguards for, 29
water resources controlled by, 15
Stott-Despoja, Natasha, 218
structural disadvantage, 301
submissions, written and oral (policy), 311–12
Sunrise Project, 317
supply bills, 118–19, 120–1
surveys, government, 313

Tampa, M.V. (ship), 100
Tangney, Dorothy, 75
tariffs, 116, 193, 216, 333
Tasmania
    anti-protest laws in, 318
    colonial legislatures of, 55
    electoral systems in, 163, 166
    forest peace process in, 314
    founding of, 55
    legislative election methods, 57
    population and seats in, 72, 164
Tasmanian Dam case (1983), 123–4
tax deductible donations, 317–18
taxation
    as concurrent power, 29, 34
    fiscal imbalance and, 13–14, 34, 116
    goods and services tax, 36
    Uniform Tax cases, 34, 116
    see also tariffs
technologies, digital (media)
    Australian media influenced by, 278–9
    challenges arising from, 286–9
    global public sphere and, 267–8, 276–7, 286
    liberating nature of, 276
    opportunities arising from, 284–6
    surveillance and, 289
    see also social media
technologies, digital (public service), 149–50
tendencies (factional), 191
territories, Australian
    bureaucracy in, 133
    constitutional powers, 25–6, 30
    electoral systems in, 163, 166–7
    parliaments, *see* parliaments, Australian (subnational)
    population and seats in, 71–2, 164
terrorism, 13, 101, 331–2

tied grants, 36–7
Torres Strait Islander people, *see* Indigenous Australians
Towards Responsible Government (report), 147
Trad, Jackie, 141
trade, 31, 113, 116, 193, 333
trade unions, *see* unions, trade
transactional leadership, 241, 242
transformational leadership, 241, 248
Trans–Pacific Partnership, 13
Trump, Donald, 288
Tungutalum, Hyacinth, 57
Turnbull, Malcolm
    fiscal imbalance and, 46
    leadership challenges for, 247
    leadership spills and, 97, 192, 197
    marriage equality and, 199
    as parliamentary performer, 90
Turnbull Government, 18, 150, 312
Twitter, 268, 278
two-party-preferred vote, 165

UK Parliament Act 1911, 111
UK political system
    2019 General Election, 201
    Brexit campaign, 288
    constitutionalism in, 110
    electoral system in, 167
    political parties, 204, 205, 251, 329
    representation in, 74
    Speaker's role in, 58
    as unitary, 120
    voting rights in, 160, 161
Uluru Statement (2017), 18, 330
Uniform Tax cases, 34, 116
Uniform Taxation Act 1942, 34
unions, trade, 33, 186, 190, 191, 300–1, 304
unitary systems of government, 7, 26, 27, 120
United Australia Party (UAP), 193–5
United Nations Universal Declaration of Human Rights, 114
United Tasmania Group (UTG), 220
US Constitution, 272
US political system
    2016 Presidential election, 278
    electoral system in, 167
    political parties in, 205
    separation of powers in, 61
    voting rights in, 160
    Watergate scandal, 273
uses and gratifications model (media), 270

vaccination rollout (national), 242
Vallentine, Jo, 220
vertical fiscal imbalance, 35–6, 40, 43, 45, 46

Vicki Lee Roach v Electoral Commissioner and Commonwealth of Australia [2007], 161
Victoria
   colonial legislatures of, 55
   electoral systems in, 57, 163, 166, 167
   electorates/MPs in, 57
   founding of, 55
   population and seats in, 72
voters
   anti-politics sentiment of, 335
   behaviour and perceptions of, 176–9, 200, 249
   broad groups of, 179
   party relationship with, 176–9, 199–200, 213
voting
   compulsory, 163
   electronic, 15
   internet and, 175–6
   secret ballot, 163
   whips and parliamentary, 67–9
   see also elections, Australian; electoral system(s)
voting age, 160
voting rights, 55, 160–2

wage arbitration policy, 10
war crimes, 273
Washington Post, 273
'Washminster' system, 108
watchdogs, media, 282–3
water resources, 15
Watergate scandal, 273
Watson, Chris, 9
Weber, Max, 134, 240, 242
welfare state, 134
Western Australia
   electoral systems in, 57, 163, 166, 167
   electorates/MPs in, 57
   founding of, 55
   party rivalry in, 33
   population and seats in, 72
Western Sydney Airport, 312
Westminster system
   Cabinet appointments in, 82
   constitutionalism and conventions of, 109–12, 118, 119, 121–2
   defined, 58
   executive leadership, 243
   federalism mixed with, 29, 108
   political parties in, 63, 174–6
   responsible government, *see* responsible government (Westminster system)
Westphalia, Peace of, 3
whips, legislative process and, 67–9
White, Richard (justice), 87
White Australia policy, 10
Whitlam, Gough, 188
Whitlam Government
   APS under, 138, 139, 140
   dismissal of, 59, 60, 82, 118–22, 189, 238
   Indigenous 'self-determination' policy under, 145
   political advisers in, 148
wildfires, 16
Wilkie, Andrew, 227, 228
Willacy, Mark, 273
Wilson, Alex, 227
Windsor, Tony, 227, 228
Womanhood Suffrage League of NSW, 160
women
   in the APS, 139
   in Parliament, 57, 75, 335
   political leadership and, 252–5
   voting rights of, 55, 160–1
Wood, Robert, 220
Woodward, Bob, 273
WorkChoices legislation, 197
workforce structure, changes to, 14
Workplaces (Protection from Protesters) Act 2014, 318
Wyatt, Ken, 88

Xenophon, Nick, 227

young people, voting rights of, 162
YouTube, 278